Understanding
dante

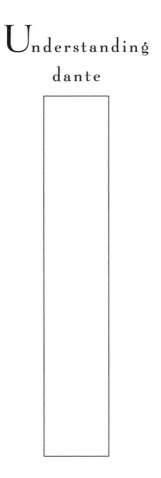

The William and Katherine Devers
Series in Dante Studies

Theodore J. Cachey, Jr., and Christian Moevs, editors
Simone Marchesi, associate editor
Ilaria Marchesi, assistant editor

VOLUME 5
Dante and the Grammar of the Nursing Body
Gary P. Cestaro

VOLUME 4
The Fiore *and the* Detto d'Amore: *A Late 13th-Century Italian Translation of
the* Roman de la Rose, *attributable to Dante*
Translated, with introduction and notes, by Santa Casciani
and Christopher Kleinhenz

VOLUME 3
The Design in the Wax: The Structure of the Divine Comedy *and Its Meaning*
Marc Cogan

VOLUME 2
The Fiore *in Context: Dante, France, Tuscany*
edited by Zygmunt G. Barański and Patrick Boyde

VOLUME I
Dante Now: Current Trends in Dante Studies
edited by Theodore J. Cachey, Jr.

Understanding dante

john a. scott

university of notre dame press
notre dame, indiana

Manufactured in the United States of America

Library of Congress Cataloging-in-Publication Data

Scott, John A. (John Alfred), 1932–
    Understanding Dante / John A. Scott.
        p.   cm. — (The William and Katherine Devers series in Dante studies)
    Includes bibliographical references and index.
    ISBN 0-268-04450-3 (cloth : alk. paper)
    ISBN 0-268-04451-1 (pbk. : alk. paper)
    1. Dante Alighieri, 1265–1321—Criticism and interpretation.   I. Title.   II. Series.

PQ4390.S464   2003
851'.1—dc21

2003050728

∞ *This book was printed on acid free paper.*

In loving memory of

Charles Till Davis and Vittorio Russo

*Their friendship and work inspire me to try to bridge the gap
between American and Italian scholarship on Dante*

Contents

About the

William and Katherine Devers
Series in Dante Studies

The William and Katherine Devers Program in Dante Studies at the University of Notre Dame supports rare book acquisitions in the university's John A. Zahm Dante collections, funds an annual visiting professorship in Dante studies, and supports electronic and print publication of scholarly research in the field. In collaboration with the Medieval Institute at the university, the Devers program has initiated a series dedicated to the publication of the most significant current scholarship in the field of Dante Studies.

In keeping with the spirit that inspired the creation of the Devers program, the series takes Dante as a focal point that draws together the many disciplines and lines of inquiry that constitute a cultural tradition without fixed boundaries. Accordingly, the series hopes to illuminate Dante's position at the center of contemporary critical debates in the humanities by reflecting both the highest quality of scholarly achievement and the greatest diversity of critical perspectives.

The series publishes works on Dante from a wide variety of disciplinary viewpoints and in diverse scholarly genres, including critical studies, commentaries, editions, translations, and conference proceedings of exceptional importance. The series is supervised by an international advisory board composed of distinguished Dante scholars and is published regularly by the University of Notre Dame Press. The Dolphin and Anchor device that appears on publications of the Devers series was used by the great humanist, grammarian, editor, and typographer Aldus Manutius (1449–1515), in whose 1502 edition of Dante (second issue) and all subsequent editions it appeared. The device illustrates the ancient proverb Festina lente, *"Hurry up slowly."*

DANTE

AL · DVS

Advisory Board

Albert Russell Ascoli, Berkeley

Zygmunt G. Barański, Cambridge

Teodolinda Barolini, Columbia

Piero Boitani, Rome

Patrick Boyde, Cambridge

Alison Cornish, Michigan

Robert Hollander, Princeton

Christopher Kleinhenz, Wisconsin

Giuseppe Mazzotta, Yale

Lino Pertile, Harvard

Michelangelo Picone, Zurich

John A. Scott, Western Australia

Preface

vagliami 'l lungo studio e 'l grande amore
che m'ha fatto cercar lo tuo volume.
—*Inf.* 1.83–84

After over fifty years of studying Dante and forty of teaching and writing about the poet in leading universities in the United States, Canada, England, and Australia, I have done my best to provide readers with a close analysis of his writings. I have omitted discussion of works, such as *Il Fiore,* that are not universally judged to be the result of Dante's genius.

My book is characterized by extensive quotations from each work, based on a study of the Italian texts. The translations are my own, as far as possible. I have tried to bridge a gap that often exists between Dante studies in English-speaking countries and the great tradition of Dante scholarship in the poet's homeland. Nowhere is this more evident than in chapter 10, which gives readers a detailed account of the poet of the *Comedy* and reveals some of the inevitable drawbacks to reading Dante in translation.

Information about Dante's life and times can be found in chapter 11 ("Dante and His Contemporary World"). A "Chronology, 1215–1321," gives dates of special significance to the poet's life and works. Further information about the poet may be sought in the recent biography by Stephen Bemrose, *A New Life of Dante* (Exeter: University of Exeter Press, 2002).

My book examines Dante's works roughly in the order of their composition: *Vita Nova* (chapter 1); *De vulgari eloquentia* (chapter 2); the lyric poetry (chapter 3); *Convivio* (chapter 4); *Monarchia* (chapter 5); the *Comedy* (chapters 6–10); the Latin epistles, *Questio de aqua et terra,* and eclogues (chapter 12). At the end of chapters 1–5, which treat Dante's so-called minor works, a short bibliography lists the most useful editions and translations of the works, as well as modern studies of special significance.

Preceding the first chapter, I have included, in addition to the chronology mentioned above, several sections that will be useful to readers. Many electronic resources exist for the study of Dante's career, works, and the transmission of his texts; I have listed the most generally useful of these tools in the section

"Electronic Resources." The editions I used in preparing the book are listed in "Editions of Dante's Works"; abbreviations used in the text and notes appear in "Abbreviations." A glossary of the main terms used in analyzing Dante's poetry appears as an appendix to the book, after the end of chapter 12 and before the endnotes.

Throughout the book, Dante's biblical quotations and allusions are cited according to the Vulgate, St. Jerome's Latin translation of the Hebrew Bible, known by Dante in several versions. The Vulgate's numbering of the Psalms differs from that found in the Hebrew Bible and familiar to most modern readers. Psalm 9 in the Vulgate combines Psalms 9 and 10 of the Hebrew Bible (Psalm 9.22 in the Vulgate is the beginning of Psalm 10 according to the Hebrew numbering); from Psalm 10 to Psalm 146, the number of each psalm is one lower in the Vulgate than in the Hebrew Bible. Psalms 146 and 147 in the Vulgate are the single Psalm 147 in the Hebrew Bible. In both the Vulgate and the Hebrew Bible, Psalms 148–50 are the same.

I should like to take the opportunity to mention two works not otherwise cited in this volume that must be commended:

Dante. Edited by Amilcare A. Iannucci. Toronto: University of Toronto Press, 1997.
> Essays by most of the leading Dante scholars in North America, with a guest appearance from Zygmunt G. Barański, who writes on "Dante and Medieval Poetics."

Dante poeta cristiano. Florence: Edizioni Polistampa, 2001.
> Essays by many eminent Italian Dante scholars and one of the leading Dante scholars in England: Piero Boitani, Patrick Boyde, Maria Grazia Ciardi Dupré Dal Poggetto, Anna Maria Chiavacci Leonardi, Francesco Mazzoni, and Carlo Ossola.

I wish to acknowledge the immense debt I owe to Martin Friedman. Many moons ago, in Berkeley, he asked me to recommend a study of Dante the poet. I did my best, and then confessed that I had long cherished the idea of writing such a study as part of a book on Dante's oeuvre. Over the years, Martin Friedman has acted as my Ideal Reader: his critique of everything I sent him has been the whetstone that has honed my endeavors. I wish to thank him for all he has done to make *Understanding Dante* a more effective study than it would otherwise have been. Support has also come from the Vice-Chancellery of the University of Western Australia. Over the years, Lino Pertile and my colleagues have helped me with their friendship and encouragement. I have been fortunate to be able to count on the friendship and impeccable scholarship of my close colleague, Lorenzo Polizzotto. I thank Theodore J. Cachey, Jr., and his advisors for agreeing to publish this volume in the William and Katherine Devers Series in Dante Studies. I thank Nancy Berliner for her professional artistry. The courtesy and generosity of everyone with whom I have come into contact at the University of Notre Dame Press have been deeply appreciated: I owe a very special debt to Jeannette Morgenroth, as well as to Ilaria and Simone Marchesi, who have done so much to bring this project to its conclusion, including the Herculean task of compiling the indexes. My heartfelt thanks go to all concerned.

☐ Like all contemporary works on Dante, the present volume is grounded in the work of generations, even centuries, of Dante scholarship. As a medieval writer put it, if we "moderns" can (on occasion) see farther than our predecessors, this is due to the fact that we are like dwarves standing on giants' shoulders.

My fervent hope is that this book will instill in others the burning desire I still feel to discover more about a poet who has enthralled so many readers in so many countries. As Eugenio Montale claimed (in the 1965 celebrations of the seven-hundredth anniversary of Dante's birth): "The *Commedia* is and will remain the last miracle of world poetry." If you cannot explain a miracle, is *Understanding Dante* an impossible task? I leave it to my readers to judge. And I take heart from Montale's assertion (in the same essay, *Dante ieri e oggi*): "The farther his world recedes from us, the greater is our desire to know him and to make him known."

Electronic Resources

A number of websites on the Internet offer a wide range of scholarly materials for students of Dante. All of Dante's works are available on the web, for example, at the Princeton and Columbia sites listed below.

Biblioteca della Letteratura Italiana

http://www.letteraturaitaliana.net

This site, the online version of the publisher Einaudi's ten-CD set, Punta Einaudi, offers a large number of Italian texts that can be downloaded and read with Acrobat Reader. For example, the poems of Guittone d'Arezzo, Guido Guinizzelli, Guido Cavalcanti, Cino da Pistoia, Petrarch, as well as Dante's *Rime* and other writings, are all accessible in reliable editions. The site includes 342 works by 205 authors, as well as bibliographies, dictionaries, commentaries, and chronological tables.

Biblioteca Italiana Telematica

http://www.cibit.humnet.unipi.it/

Dante Online

http://www.danteonline.it

This is the site of the Società Dantesca Italiana.

Dante Society of America

www.dantesociety.org

This site provides bibliographies, the possibility of consulting journals such as *L'Alighieri, Lectura Dantis, Letture Classensi, Deutsches Dante Jahrbuch,* and *Studi Danteschi.* It also publishes online the *Electronic Bulletin* of the Dante Society of America. Links are available to connect with Thomas Aquinas, *Summa Theologica;* the Latin Library; Medieval Literary Resources. A link is also available to the Mediasoft annotated *Divina Commedia* (in Italian).

Dartmouth Dante Project

This site may be reached directly via Telnet:

telnetlibrary.dartmouth.edu

At the prompt, type "connect dante"

This site is a treasury of commentaries on the *Comedy* from the fourteenth to the twentieth centuries (fifty-nine are already available), set up by Robert Hollander of Princeton University.

Digital Dante

http://www.dante.ilt.columbia.edu/library/index.html
This site includes Dante illustrations by such artists as Botticelli, Doré, and Salvador Dalí. Net resources: Dante studies; Medieval studies; The Classics; Italy Resources.

Princeton Dante Project

http://www.princeton.edu/dante/
This site should become a favorite. Among many valuable services, it offers online consultation of Paget Toynbee's *A Dictionary of Proper Names and Notable Matters in the Works of Dante,* revised by Charles S. Singleton (Oxford: Clarendon Press, 1968).

The William and Katherine Devers Program in Dante Studies

http://www.dante.nd.edu/
The site of the William and Katherine Devers Program in Dante Studies at the University of Notre Dame includes information about the university's Zahm Dante collection, one of the most important historical Dante collections in North America, as well as the Ambrosiana Microfilm Collection, the Ambrosiana Drawing Project, and the university's Medieval Institute library. The site participates in ItalNet, an international consortium making literary and scholarly resources in Italian studies available online. The Devers program's exhibition, *Renaissance Dante in Print,* accessible through the ItalNet links, provides much interesting information about Renaissance prints of Dante's works, as well as many fine digital reproductions of the prints themselves.

Editions of Dante's Works

The text of Dante's writings is cited throughout this book according to the editions listed below. I have also included information about translations of the *Comedy* that are under way and works that should be consulted along with the editions I have used. Other editions and translations for each work are included in the reading list at the end of the chapter in which the work is discussed.

The *Comedy*
La Commedia secondo l'antica vulgata. Edited by Giorgio Petrocchi. 4 vols. Florence: Le Lettere, 1994.

> Two excellent translations of the *Comedy,* with facing Italian text, are under way:
> — *Inferno* (2000); *Purgatorio* (2003). Translated by Robert and Jean Hollander, with an introduction and notes by Robert Hollander. New York: Doubleday, 2000 and 2003.
> — *The Divine Comedy of Dante Alighieri.* Vol. 1, *Inferno* (1996); vol. 2, *Purgatorio* (2003). Edited and translated by Robert M. Durling, with an introduction and notes by Ronald L. Martinez and Robert M. Durling. New York: Oxford University Press, 1996 and 2003.

Convivio
Convivio. Edited by Franca Brambilla Ageno. 3 vols. Florence: Le Lettere, 1995.

> Although the text of the *Convivio* is cited according to Franca Brambilla Ageno's edition, published by the Società Dantesca Italiana (Edizione Nazionale), Cesare Vasoli's detailed commentary remains invaluable:
> — *Convivio.* Edited by Cesare Vasoli and Domenico De Robertis. In Dante Alighieri, *Opere minori,* vol. 1, part 2. Milan and Naples: Ricciardi, 1988.

De vulgari eloquentia
De vulgari eloquentia. Edited by Pier Vincenzo Mengaldo. In Dante Alighieri, *Opere minori,* vol. 2, 3–237. Milan and Naples: Ricciardi, 1979.

Eclogues
Egloghe. Edited by Enzo Cecchini. In Dante Alighieri, *Opere minori,* vol. 2, 647–89. Milan and Naples: Ricciardi, 1979.

Latin Epistles
Epistole. Edited by Arsenio Furgoni and Giorgio Brugnoli. In Dante Alighieri, *Opere minori,* vol. 2, 507–643. Milan and Naples: Ricciardi, 1979.

Monarchia
Monarchia. Edited and translated by Prue Shaw. Cambridge: Cambridge University Press, 1995.

> I have followed the numbering of the chapters in Shaw's edition of *Monarchia;* however, the translation and commentary by Richard Kay should also be consulted:
> — *Dante's "Monarchia."* Translated, with a commentary, by Richard Kay. Studies and Texts, vol. 131. Toronto: Pontifical Institute of Mediaeval Studies, 1998.

Questio de aqua et terra
Questio de aqua et terra. Edited by Francesco Mazzoni. In Dante Alighieri, *Opere minori,* vol. 2, 693–880. Milan and Naples: Ricciardi, 1979.

Rime
Rime. Edited by Gianfranco Contini. In Dante Alighieri, *Opere minori,* vol. 1, part 1, 251–552. Milan and Naples: Ricciardi, 1984.

> Domenico De Robertis's edition of Dante's *Rime,* prepared for the Società Dantesca Italiana (Edizione Nazionale) reached me when this book was already in press (see chapter 3).

Vita Nova
Vita Nuova. Edited by Domenico De Robertis. In Dante Alighieri, *Opere minori,* vol. 1, part 1, 3–247. Milan and Naples: Ricciardi, 1984.

Works with controversial attributions to Dante

Il fiore and Il detto d'amore
Two works are attributed to Dante in some sources, but the attributions are controversial: *Il fiore* and *Il detto d'amore.* A fine edition with facing translation is available in

> — *"The Fiore" and the "Detto d'Amore": A Late 13th-Century Italian Translation of the "Roman de la Rose," Attributable to Dante.* Translated, with

an introduction and notes, by Santa Casciani and Christopher Klein-henz. William and Katherine Devers Series in Dante Studies, edited by Theodore J. Cachey, Jr., and Christian Moevs, vol. 4. Notre Dame, Ind.: University of Notre Dame Press, 2000.

For further information about these works, see also

— *The "Fiore" in Context: Dante, France, Tuscany.* Edited by Zygmunt G. Barański and Patrick Boyde. William and Katherine Devers Series in Dante Studies, edited by Theodore J. Cachey, Jr., and Christian Moevs, vol. 2. Notre Dame, Ind.: University of Notre Dame Press, 1997.

Abbreviations

Aen.	Vergil, *Aeneid.*
G. Boccaccio, *Trattatello*	*Trattatello in laude di Dante.* Edited by P. G. Ricci. In *Tutte le opere di Giovanni Boccaccio,* vol. 3, edited by Vittore Branca. Milan: Mondadori, 1974.
Brunetto Latini, *Tesoretto*	*Il Tesoretto.* In *Poeti del Duecento,* vol. 2, tomo 1, edited by Gianfranco Contini, 175–277. Milan-Naples: Ricciardi, 1960.
Brunetto Latini, *Tresor*	*Li livres dou Tresor.* Edited by F. J. Carmody. Berkeley: University of California Press, 1948.
Compagni, *Cronica*	Dino Compagni, *Cronica: Introduzione e note di Gino Luzzatto.* Turin: Einaudi, 1968.
Conv.	Dante, *Convivio.*
DCD	Augustine, *De civitate Dei (City of God).*
DVE	Dante, *De vulgari eloquentia.*
Ecl.	Dante, *Eclogues.*
ED	*Enciclopedia Dantesca.* 6 vols. Rome: Istituto della Enciclopedia Italiana, 1970–78.
Ep.	Dante, *Epistole.*
Inf.	Dante, *Inferno.*
Met.	Ovid, *Metamorphoses.*
Mon.	Dante, *Monarchia.*
OED	*Oxford English Dictionary.*
Par.	Dante, *Paradiso.*
Phars.	Lucan, *Pharsalia* or *De bello civili.*
PL	*Patrologia Latina.* Edited by J.-P. Migne. Paris: Garnier, 1878– .
Purg.	Dante, *Purgatorio.*

RVF	Petrarch, *Rerum vulgarium fragmenta (Canzoniere)*.
S. Th.	Thomas Aquinas, *Summa Theologica*. Translated by the Fathers of the English Dominican Province. http://www.newadvent.org/summa/
	Also available on CD-ROM from Harmony Media Inc., P.O. Box 138, Gervais, Oregon 97026.
Theb.	Statius, *Thebaid*.
Villani	Giovanni Villani, *Nuova cronica*. Edited by Giuseppe Porta. 3 vols. Parma: Ugo Guanda, 1990.
VN	Dante, *Vita Nova*.

Chronology, 1215–1321

Information about Dante's life can be found in chapter 11, "Dante and His Contemporary World." The most recent scholarly biography of Dante is by Stephen Bemrose: *A New Life of Dante* (Exeter: University of Exeter Press, 2002). For historical background, readers may wish to consult John Larner, *Italy in the Age of Dante and Petrarch 1216–1380* (London: Longman, 1980).

1215   Easter Sunday: Murder of Buondelmonte de' Buondelmonti (*Inf.* 28.103–11). Leading Florentines split into "Guelfs" (officially, supporters of the papacy) and "Ghibellines" (officially, supporters of the Holy Roman emperor).

1244   Loss of Jerusalem by the Christians.

1248   Emperor Frederick II and a Ghibelline force (led by the Uberti) drive the Guelfs out of Florence (*Inf.* 10.48).

1250   December 13: Death of Frederick II. Guelfs allowed to return to Florence (*Inf.* 10.49). Government of the Primo Popolo.

1252   Gold florin, the dollar of the Middle Ages, first minted in Florence. Dante berates Pope John XXII in *Par.* 18.130–36 for his avarice and "devotion" to John the Baptist, Florence's patron, whose image appeared on the florin. In *Inf.* 16.73–75, the poet condemns Florence's immense wealth and economic expansion, as he does again in *Par.* 15, where he evokes Florence's simplicity and frugality during his great-great-grandfather's era.

1258   Ghibellines expelled after conspiracy to break up the popular government, which was essentially Guelf.

1260   September 4: Crushing defeat of the Florentine Guelfs at the battle of Montaperti (*Inf.* 10.85–93). The Guelfs seek refuge in Lucca. Virtually the whole of Tuscany under Ghibelline control.

1265   May/June: Birth of Dante Alighieri in Florence. According to the Julian calendar, the sun was in the constellation of the Gemini from May 15 to June 14 (*Par.* 22.112–20).

1266   February 26: King Manfred (*Purg.* 3.103–43) defeated and slain at Benevento by Charles of Anjou, brother of Louis IX of France. Uprising in Florence against the Ghibellines.
       November: Prominent Ghibellines are expelled from Florence. Charles of Anjou is offered the lordship of the Commune for the next ten years.

1274	Death of St. Thomas Aquinas (*Par.* 10–13) and of St. Bonaventure (*Par.* 12).
1277	January 9: Marriage contract between Dante Alighieri and Gemma Donati.
1278	Partial pacification of the two factions by Cardinal Latino; however, the government remains in Guelf control.
1281/1283?	Death of Dante's father, Alighiero II (born c. 1220).
1282	Sicilian Vespers (*Par.* 8.67–75). The uprising against Angevin rule in Sicily that eventually led to the expulsion of the French from the island, which then came under the rule of Aragon.
1289	June 11. Ghibellines from Arezzo defeated at the battle of Campaldino (*Inf.* 22.1–5). Dante takes part in this military action, as well as in the siege and retaking of the fortress of Caprona on August 16 (cf. *Inf.* 21.94–96).
1290	June 8: Death of Beatrice.
1291	Fall of Acre, the last Christian stronghold in the Holy Land (*Inf.* 27.89).
1293/1294?	Dante writes *Vita Nova*.
1294	Election and abdication of Pope Celestine V (cf. *Inf.* 3.59–60), followed by the accession of Boniface VIII (cf. *Inf.* 19.52–57).
1295	Dante, now thirty years old, enters the Florentine political arena.
1300	February 16: First Jubilee (Holy Year) proclaimed by Boniface VIII with the bull *Antiquorum habet fida relatio* (*Inf.* 18.28–33; *Purg.* 2.98–99).
	May 1: Florence, totally Guelf for many years, now splits into two camps: the White Guelfs, led by the Cerchi *(nouveaux riches),* and the Black Guelfs, led by the tyrannical aristocrat Corso Donati, who had been exiled in 1299. Dante is associated with the Whites and their attempts to safeguard Florence's autonomy from the political scheming of Pope Boniface VIII. The Blacks include prominent papal bankers.
	June 15–August 14: Dante elected one of the six priors who govern Florence (for a period of two months). Fifteen leading Blacks and Whites (among the Whites, Dante's friend, the poet Guido Cavalcanti) are banished by the priors.
1301	November 1: Charles of Valois enters Florence with the pope's backing, ostensibly to pacify the feuding parties (*Purg.* 20.70–78). However, Charles's support of the Blacks leads to the expulsion of the Whites and the lifelong exile of Dante, who (on March 10, 1302) is sentenced to death at the stake, should he fall into the hands of the Florentine Commune.

1303	October 11: Death of Boniface VIII.
1303–6?	Dante writes *Convivio*.
1304–5?	Dante writes *De vulgari eloquentia*.
1304	July 20: Defeat of the exiled Whites and Ghibellines at La Lastra. Dante breaks away from his fellow exiles (cf. *Par.* 17.61–69).
1305	June 5: Election of Pope Clement V (*Inf.* 19.79–87; *Par.* 30.142–48).
1307?–21	Dante composes *Comedy*.
1309	Pope Clement V takes up residence in Avignon.
1313	The emperor Henry VII attempts to pacify northern and central Italy. Florence is at the heart of Guelf resistance. Dante denounces the "most wicked Florentines" in a Latin epistle (*Ep.* 7). He condemns Clement V for both simony and political treachery (*Par.* 30.133–48). August 24: Death of Henry VII.
1314	April 20: Death of Clement V. Dante writes a Latin epistle to the Italian cardinals (*Ep.* 11), urging them to elect an Italian pope and thus help to end the shameful exile of the papacy in Avignon and restore it to its providential seat in Rome. Eventually (in 1316), another Frenchman, Jacques Duèse from Cahors (*Par.* 27.58–60), will be elected pope as John XXII.
1312–18	Dante's second stay in Verona, as a guest of Cangrande della Scala.
1315	Florence, under severe threat from the Ghibelline leader Uguccione della Faggiuola, offers exiles the possibility of returning to the city, upon payment of a reduced fine and after a form of public penance. Dante refuses to accept any kind of "dishonor" (*Ep.* 12). On October 15 Robert of Anjou's vicar in Tuscany condemns Dante and his sons to death by beheading.
1317?	Dante writes *Monarchia*.
1319–21	Dante writes two Latin eclogues to Giovanni del Virgilio, professor of Latin poetry at the University of Bologna.
1320	January 20: Dante delivers a public lecture, *Questio de aqua et terra,* in Verona.
1321	Dante in Ravenna as the guest of Guido Novello da Polenta, nephew of Francesca da Rimini (*Inf.* 5.82–142). August–September: Dante sent as ambassador from Ravenna to Venice. The poet dies of malarial fever in Ravenna during the night of September 13–14.

Illustrations

Diagrams (engravings) from *Dante con l'espositione di M. Bernardino Daniello da Lucca* (Venice: Pietro da Fino, 1568). Reproduced from the original held by the Department of Special Collections of the University of Notre Dame.

Dante's *New Life*

Vita Nova

Since the beginning of civilized society, discovering life and love afresh has been the privilege of youth. No work declares this more forcibly than Dante's *Vita Nova* or *New Life*.[1] Composed c. 1294, the work consists of thirty-one of his early poems, accompanied by a prose narrative which affirms that they were inspired by his love for Beatrice, a Florentine woman who had died in her twenty-fifth year, in 1290. The title *Vita Nova* refers to Dante's youth (*Purg.* 30.115), while at the same time proclaiming a new life instilled by God's grace and love, which had inspired a new kind of love poetry.[2] Dante offers up his song of praise to his beloved as he maps out the stages in his gradual understanding of the true nature of love and the way this understanding had renewed his art. As later in the *Comedy,* the author's memory dictates the substance of the story (in prose), creating an essential distinction between Dante the narrator and Dante the protagonist.[3]

The opening sentence introduces the image of the Book of Memory, establishing both the tone and content of this slim volume. This image inspires the rubric—in Latin, as was common in medieval books—*Incipit Vita Nova* (Here begins a New Life).[4] In later years, the *Comedy* will represent the uttermost test of the poet's memory when Dante will attempt to express the totality of human experience. For the present, however, whole areas of reality are excluded from *Vita Nova*. Instead, it presents a unique world of youthful love and poetic vision.

Beatrice

Beatrice is at the center of the work's universe. We are told that she first appeared to Dante when both were in their ninth year (*VN* 2.1–2), she

1

slightly younger, having been born in 1266. Already at the very beginning of his "little book" *(libello)* the author tells us that Beatrice now enjoys the glory of Paradise by describing her as "the glorious lady of my mind" *(gloriosa donna de la mia mente)*—where the epithet *gloriosa* signifies that Beatrice enjoys the beatific vision in heaven, and *donna* retains its semantic connotations implying the *domina* of feudal society, accompanied by the allegiance and homage paid by the vassal to his lord or lady. The sentence goes on to reveal that her name was truly Beatrice, although many who called her by this name did not realize its significance. Two points are made here: Dante's belief that names should reveal the true essence of things (13.4), and his intention of discarding one of the basic conventions of courtly love. This convention required secrecy and discretion: the troubadour did not disclose the lady's identity, which remained hidden under a false name or *senhal*. Dante the narrator, however, claims that his beloved was aptly named *Beatrice,* in that she was for him a bringer of beatitude (and even at fifty or more years of age, he would still delight in the very syllables that made up her name, as we see in *Par.* 7.13–15). Although found in only two poems included in *Vita Nova* (both written after Beatrice's death),[5] her name constellates the prose commentary and is an essential element in her "beatification."

In *Vita Nova,* Love proclaims his entry into Dante's universe and Beatrice's epiphany with a solemn Latin formula whose biblical echoes underscore the role this young Florentine girl was destined to play throughout the poet's life, telling him: "Your beatitude has now appeared" (2.5:*Apparuit iam beatitudo vestra*). From this time on, Dante tells us, his soul was "wedded" to Love, so that, while still a boy, he frequently sought out that "young angel." Indeed, Dante tells us that, in Homer's words, Beatrice "did not seem to be the child of mortal man but of a god," a quotation that Dante—who knew no Greek (in *Iliad* 24.258, the phrase refers to Hector)—copied from a Latin treatise by St. Albert the Great and which we realize in retrospect is in fact the first step in setting up an analogy or parallel between Beatrice and Christ (cf. Matt. 27.54 and Mark 15.39: "Truly this man was the son of God!").

The prose "commentary" to the poems selected

Here, in the first few lines of the work, we catch a glimpse of the cultural world of *Vita Nova,* a world inspired by a truly human love grafted onto feelings of profound religious awe. Even at this early stage in his career, Dante was an original writer, constantly experimenting with and modifying traditional forms, modes, and subjects. The form of *Vita Nova*—a prose commentary written with the express purpose of "opening up" the messages contained in the poems and of setting them in their proper context (cf. Luke 24.32)—owes very little to the prose *razos* that briefly illustrated the lives and works of the trou-badours. *Vita Nova* is closer in spirit to the *prosimetrum,* or mixture of prose and verse, employed by Boethius in his *Consolation of Philosophy,* a work Dante tells us he read in an attempt to comfort himself after Beatrice's death (*Conv.* 2.12.2). Conferring a unique importance on Dante's early work, the prose commentary of *Vita Nova* is the first great example of Italian prose, forged by Dante into an instrument capable of expressing dramatic emotional experience—such as the flush of romantic love (11.1), its sublimation (18), a nightmarish, apocalyptic vision of the death of his beloved (23), and the certainty of her beatitude in heaven (42)—as well as an instrument capable of rivaling Latin in the analysis of problems concerning poetic technique (25) and semantics (40.6–7).

Unlike the miscellaneous collections of poems found in contemporary manuscripts, *Vita Nova* offers for the first time in Western literature a collection of poems selected (and commented on) by the poet himself. Dante thereby seeks to guarantee the authenticity of his poems, while at the same time (and even more significantly) he imposes his own interpretation of them on his read-ers.[6] The author's prose commentary creates its own historical perspective not only for the poems but also for the author's personal experience, on which the commentary strives to confer a unity that points from afar to the achievement of the poet's later years. The commentary reveals for the first time Dante's need to stop at certain moments in his career and take stock of what had gone before, to dissect the past before changing course, to analyze his artistic creations and relate them to an inner reality. Above all, *Vita Nova* shows us the ideal harmony between art and life that Dante strove to achieve. The work represents the first great step toward the narrative supremacy of the *Comedy* and that poem's unique synthesis of personal experience and universal significance.

Beatrice's revelations

Beatrice's second of nine "apparitions" occurs nine years after the first.[7] Instead of being clothed in red (2.3), the color of love and nobility, she now appears dressed in white (3.1), the color of angelic purity. At the end of the second chapter, Dante had declared his intention of omitting "many things" that would strike some readers as too fanciful when describing what he had known and felt at such an early age, in order to concentrate on what he found under the "leading paragraphs" in his Book of Memory. Dante now experiences what seems to be a totality of beatitude through Beatrice's greeting, which takes place at the ninth hour of the day (3:00 P.M.). Not only the word "beatitude" (3.1) but also the phrase "the lady of the greeting" (3.4) is replete with religious connota-tions, since the latter in Dante's Italian *(la donna de la salute)* means both the lady of the greeting and the lady "giving" beatitude or salvation.[8] In modern Italian, "greeting" would of course be *saluto,* but *salute* (deriving from Latin *salus, salutis*) is the normal form in *Vita Nova,* where its double meaning is stressed (e.g., 11.4: "it is clear that in her greetings *[ne le sue salute]* lay my beatitude *[la mia beatitudine]*")—a usage that led to its exclusion, together with the equally equivocal term "beatitude," by the censors of the Counter-Reformation from the first printed edition of *Vita Nova* (1576).[9]

First sonnet

The first poem, *A ciascun'alma presa e gentil core* (*VN* 3.10–12), supposedly written by Dante at the age of eighteen, describes a vision of Love holding Beatrice in his arms and feeding her with the poet's heart.[10] The narrator-commentator tells us that he had sent this sonnet to "many who were famous poets *[trovatori]* at that time" (3.9), inviting them to interpret the vision. The tradition of such discussions (*tensons,* in Provençal) began with a contest between troubadours (*trovatori* is a hapax in *Vita Nova*). Italian poets continued to exchange views on the nature and origin of love in their native medium, the sonnet, whose fourteen lines proved capacious enough for the clichés so often displayed. This tradition proved to be a boon for a fledgling like Dante. It enabled him to make contact with established writers and to make himself known at an early age. He tells us that he received many responses, including a sonnet from "the one I call the first among my friends" (3.14), the celebrated Florentine poet and aristocrat Guido Cavalcanti. Recognition by Cavalcanti, well known for his intellectual powers and his haughty manner (Boccaccio, *Decameron* 8.9), was a striking accolade for the young poet, and Cavalcanti's influence soon made its presence felt in Dante's poetry.

For the time being, however, Dante's first attempts at writing verse followed the older manner of Guittone d'Arezzo and the Sicilian-Tuscan school, with its frequently clumsy rhetoric and trite repetition of the lover's hopes and fears. Guido's reply (*per le rime,* using the same rhymes as in Dante's sonnet), *Vedeste, al mio parere, onne valore,* characteristically associates Dante's dream with death (l. 10), although Cavalcanti imagines that Love had saved Beatrice by making her feed on her lover's heart. Significantly for the young apprentice, Cavalcanti's reply greeted him as a member of that small band of "Love's faithful" who experience "all the nobility and all the joy and all the good man can know" (ll. 1–2). This flattering welcome was in utter contrast to the reply received from Dante da Maiano, who advised his "rather dim friend" to rid himself of such visions by giving his balls "a good wash."[11]

That Dante should have felt a close affinity with Cavalcanti, the Florentine magnate to whom he dedicated his *Vita Nova* and who encouraged him to write in the vernacular (*VN* 30.3), is hardly surprising. Nevertheless, while a number of Dante's poems (13–16) express a doleful Cavalcantian sense of the sufferings imposed by love, they contain little or nothing of the elder poet's tragic vision of love as a truly destructive, invincible force. On the contrary, at the very beginning of this work dedicated to Guido, Dante asserts that *his* love never ruled his being "without the faithful counsel of reason" (2.9)—a profoundly polemical statement in view of Cavalcanti's oft-repeated concept of love as a totally irrational force, and one that is soon reinforced in *Vita Nova* 4.2, where Love is said to command him "according to the counsel of reason."

Nothing outside the prose commentary links the first poem with Beatrice. The theme of eating someone's heart can be found elsewhere in medieval literature; the heart was seen as love's mansion and the physiological center of the human being. In the prose commentary, Love's first words to the dreaming Dante are *Ego dominus tuus* (I am your Lord), echoing the Vulgate's solemn pronouncement *Ego sum Dominus Deus tuus* (Ex. 20.2: "I am the Lord thy God"), and the eating of the lover's heart is made to signify that Dante's whole life was destined to be consumed by his love for Beatrice. However, the third chapter ends with the declaration that the vision's true meaning was not grasped by anyone at the time, although "now it is obvious to the most simple"—thus offering what is perhaps the most striking evidence of the two chronological planes in *Vita Nova,* the present act of narration on the one hand and past experience on the other.[12] The first poem is transformed by the prose commentary into a prophecy of Beatrice's premature death, especially given the critical detail that Love appeared to set off toward heaven with Beatrice still in his arms (3.7), a departure that sparked such overwhelming anguish in Dante that his dream was shattered. In the poem, however, the last six lines or sestet are constructed in such a manner that the first and last words describe the change in Love's state, from "happy" to "weeping," but with no hint of a celestial ascent. In the commentary, the final observation that no one understood the vision at the time can be seen to echo the fact that none of the disciples had understood Christ's prophecies of his death but that after his death and ascent to heaven they remembered and then understood what had been written about him (John 12.16). A first tessera has been provided for the Beatrice-Christ mosaic that will be developed later in Dante's "little book."

"Screen" ladies

No mention of Beatrice's name is found in the poem, which merely refers to *Madonna,* "wrapped in a cloth." In the commentary (3.4)—but not in the poem—this cloth is said to have the color of blood. As mentioned, such reticence was very much part of the courtly love tradition, which predominates in the first section of *Vita Nova*. Faithful to the code of secrecy, Dante outwits the curiosity of the envious (4.1: the hostile *lauzengiers,* a staple element in the game of courtly love), first of all by refusing to reveal the identity of the lady for whom he is visibly wasting away, then by choosing another lady as a "screen for the truth" (5.3). This decoy was found by chance one day in a church, described as "a place where words in praise of the Queen of Glory" were heard (5.1). Such periphrasis is typical of Dante's first narrative, in which no place or person is ever mentioned by name (apart from Beatrice and Cavalcanti's lady, Giovanna, in chapter 24), and even the word "church" or "Mary" seems to have struck its author as too concrete and precise. The Florentine setting, as evoked in *Vita Nova,* is never described in any realistic detail, since realism would limit the significance of the narrative. Dante's work, however, was an attempt to transcend reality, not to escape from it. *Vita Nova* offers us a young poet's effort to extract universal significance from an intensely personal experience—in a way far removed from the later realism of his *Comedy.*

In church, then, as Dante was riveted by Beatrice's beauty he became aware that another woman was seated in his direct line of vision. This woman and many onlookers thought that Dante was gazing at her; and they imagined that they had discovered Dante's secret. The poet rejoiced that his secret was safe; he decided to use this "noble lady" as a screen for his true love. For some years, Dante made use of this screen lady, writing a number of poetic trifles *(cosette per rima)* addressed to her—poems he omits from his present selection, except for those that appear "to be in praise of Beatrice" (5.4), the theme that will eventually be seen to have a revolutionary impact on Dante's art (18.9). We certainly cannot know the truth of the matter: how far Dante was being sincere and how far he was trying to justify any poetic involvement with other women. It is, however, misleading to judge Dante's intentions by what may or may not have taken place. What the author of *Vita Nova* was bent on revealing was the underlying pattern or essential meaning of his life, the vital thread that bound together all contingency and experience, however diverse, into the Book of Love (cf. *Par.* 33.85–93).

The end of the first section

The first screen lady left Florence and was replaced by another (chapters 7–9). Thus ends the first section of *Vita Nova,* marked by a crisis in Dante's relationship with Beatrice and a notable change in his poetic style. In this first section, Dante chose to include some five poems of the seventeen or so that remained from his years of apprenticeship (c. 1283–87). We find a "double sonnet"—*O voi che per la via d'Amor passate* (7.3–6)—with twenty verses instead of the usual fourteen, a form probably invented by Guittone d'Arezzo and rejected by both Cavalcanti and Cino da Pistoia. We know of only three double sonnets written by Dante, a second one appearing as a lament on the death of a young woman in *Vita Nova* 8.8–11. Dante also mentions a *sirventes* (now lost), which he had written in praise of the sixty most beautiful women "in the city where my lady was placed by the Almighty" (6.2). Both the form and the style of these early poems are archaic: for example, we find the use of *rima equivoca* (the same word—e.g., *parte*—made to rhyme with itself, though with a different meaning) and the term *servir[e]*, emblematic of the service offered to the lady according to the rules of courtly love, in *Cavalcando l'altr'ier* (9.9–12), a sonnet which nevertheless displays a new narrative power and economy of means. It is a graceful, light-hearted announcement of the poet's new "love" for the second screen lady, in total contrast with the two poems written on the death of a young lady (8.4–6, 8–11), although the poet himself tells us that it was composed only "some days" after the latter (9.1–8). All in all, this sonnet is proof of Dante's early technical proficiency as well as his ability to turn his hand to occasional poetry.

Before leaving the first section, we must emphasize that *Vita Nova* is not simply a prelude to Dante's masterpiece: the youthful *libello* needs to be approached and understood on its own terms. Dante was surely right to declare that certain elements in his youthful work were glimpsed "as if in a dream" (*Conv.* 2.12.4); and the *Comedy* itself presupposes a conversion in Dante's spiritual outlook. The clearest evidence that such a radical change was necessary is, I believe, to be found in the poem written as a lament for the departure of the first screen lady, *O voi che per la via d'Amor passate*. As the commentary tells us (7.7), the first three lines of the double sonnet are a literal translation of the Lamentations of Jeremiah (1.12), with the addition of the words *d'Amor*, the way of profane love: "O all ye that pass by the way, wait, and see if there be any sorrow like unto my sorrow." This sacred text, a part of the liturgy for Holy Week, traditionally evoked Christ's sufferings as the Man of Sorrows.[13] It would be difficult to find an example in all of Dante's writings that comes closer to blasphemy than this application of a well-known reference to Christ's Passion not just to a profane love but to what the author himself declared was a lie, a subterfuge invented in order to keep the truth hidden from the multitude.

Beatrice denies her greeting

Chapters 10 and 11 form a bridge between the first and second sections of *Vita Nova*. In chapter 10, Beatrice, shocked by the gossip surrounding

Dante's relationship with his second screen lady, refuses to greet him. The way this message is conveyed makes use of hyperbole borrowed from litanies to the Virgin Mary: Beatrice is hailed as the "destroyer of all vices and queen of virtues," and in her greeting lies all her lover's beatitude (10.2). Dante now writes a *ballata* in defense of his conduct, *Ballata, i' voi che tu ritrovi Amore* (12.10–15), which amounts to a variation on the Provençal *escondig,* a poem of exculpation that displays a pronounced archaic flavor and is the only example of this poetic form in *Vita Nova.* However, before giving the text of this poem, the poet is led by the denial of Beatrice's greeting to make a digression which is one of the great moments of early Italian prose, describing the miraculous effects of his lady's greeting:

> whenever she appeared . . . I had no more enemies; instead, I was overcome by a flame of charity which made me forgive all who had offended me; and if anyone had asked me anything at all, my only reply would have been simply, "Love." . . . It is therefore obvious that my blessedness lay in her greeting, which often overwhelmed my powers. (*VN* 11.1)

The next chapter attempts to describe Dante's despair at Beatrice's refusal to greet him. "Like a young child in tears after being beaten" (12.2), the poet falls asleep and has another vision of Love, who tells him that it is high time to put aside all decoys. In reply to the poet's question why he is weeping, Love tells him (again in Latin): "I am like the center of the circle, to which the parts of the circumference are all related in like manner; you, however, are not" (12.4). Dante, incapable of grasping Love's message, is told—and, for the first time, Love speaks in the vernacular—*Non dimandare più che utile ti sia* (Do not ask more than is right for you [cf. Romans 12.3]): the lover's understanding may still grow, but that will take time. The image of the circle was a traditional image of perfection; and it returns at the end of the *Comedy* in the shape of a wheel to denote newfound perfection and total compliance with God's will and his supreme love (*Par.* 33.115–20; 144). Here by contrast it conveys Dante's imperfect state as a lover, his lack of symmetry. His life is devoid of harmony: he does not observe the correct relationship or *proportio* between the various points on the circumference and the center of all things. Love's words also imply that love is at the center of all life, while Love's tears (12.4) suggest a foreknowledge of Beatrice's premature death, something not yet revealed to Dante. The lover must be prepared for the heaviest blow by first overcoming his present weakness and imperfections. All this information, given (or hinted at) in the elaborate prose commentary, is absent from the highly conventional *Ballata, i' voi che tu ritrovi Amore,* which may well strike the reader as an anticlimax.

The second section

The second section, comprising chapters 12–16, illustrates a feature that will be an essential element in the *Comedy:* Dante's ability to portray himself as he was at different stages in his life. Here, we must recall the basic distinction between the author-narrator and Dante the character in the narration. In this second section, Dante the protagonist suffers from his youthful understanding of love, a suffering expressed most naturally in a Cavalcantian poetic mode that illustrates the struggle waged between the lover's eyes, his heart and his soul, his vital spirits and his sighs of frustrated desire, which all appear as independent actors in love's drama. Nevertheless, Guido's insistence on the destructive effects of love (born, in his view, under the influence of Mars), from which stemmed the tragic grandeur of his poetic vision, remained utterly alien to Dante and undoubtedly led to Guido's downgrading in *De vulgari eloquentia* 2.2.8, which declares Cino da Pistoia to be the Italian love poet *par excellence* (see chapter 2).

The earliest evidence of Cavalcanti's influence can be found in the sonnet *Tutti li miei penser parlan d'Amore* (13.8–9). The age-old debate on the good and bad effects of love is given a new twist by the portrayal of a psychological conflict between four contradictory thoughts that tear at the poet's mind and lead him far from Love's equipoise at the center of the circle of being: "one makes me desire its [Love's] power, another argues its madness, another brings me sweetness through hope, another often makes me weep" (ll. 3–6). Dante's presence at a wedding is the next occasion for suffering. The sight of Beatrice destroys the poet's vital spirits. The change in his physical appearance is so great that ladies present begin to mock him, and a friend has to lead Dante away, so that his vital spirits may be "resurrected" and allow him to return from "that point in life beyond which one cannot go with the intention of returning" (14.8). The sonnet *Con l'altre donne mia vista gabbate,* in which the poet seeks to obtain compassion and understanding from Beatrice, is based on similar scenes in Provençal poetry, where the lover is subjected to mockery. At the same time, the poem's Cavalcantian elements highlighting the poet's tormented state and the deprivation of blessedness represent an advance on its predecessors. As in the other sonnets of this section, the syntax is more straightforward, the stock similes and antitheses of early love poetry are clearly rejected, and non-Tuscan forms are now generally eliminated. With *Ciò che m'incontra, ne la mente more* (15.4–6) and its accusation in line 12 that Beatrice's "mockery" slays Dante *(che 'l vostro gabbo ancide),* these are in fact the only poems directly addressed to Beatrice in the entire work.

The core discovery

The watershed is reached in chapters 17–19, the heart of Dante's *libello.* Cavalcanti's manner, although an improvement on Dante's earlier style, proved too narrow for the younger poet's restless genius: it obviously entailed imitation and did not offer that "new and nobler" subject matter which Dante had to discover for himself (17.1). Concentration on the lover's sufferings inevitably led to an egotism alien to the spirit of Dante's youthful work, creating an artistic impasse, a silence that could be broken only by the discovery of a new type of song that would justify the title *Vita Nova,* with its biblical echoes—e.g., Psalm 39.4; Augustine, *Enarrationes in Psalmos* 95.2; Judith 16.2, 15—and promise of a life utterly renewed by love. That discovery is shown to have been the result not of art but of an intuition forced from the lover's lips, when his love for Beatrice was finally uncovered and his behavior ridiculed by one of her companions. In a chapter memorable for its use of dramatic dialogue, the woman asks Dante to state the purpose of his love—which must surely be most strange and wonderful (*novissimo:* 18.3), since he is physically unable to endure being in Beatrice's presence. Dante responds to her irony by declaring that, whereas he had formerly sought happiness in his lady's greeting, now Love "has placed all my beatitude in *that which cannot be taken away from me*" (18.4; my emphasis), where we find words with a clear echo of Christ's reference to Mary's choice of the "better part" in Luke 10.42. Dante goes on to assert that his beatitude now lies "in those words that praise my lady" (18.6), but his persistent questioner points to the inconsistency between this declaration and what he had in fact written. The question acts as a catalyst. The poet is himself struck by this discrepancy; he wonders why he has avoided such a joyful theme and he decides henceforth to write only poetry in praise of Beatrice.

The immediate result is silence: the poet is struck by the magnitude of his task and fears that it lies well beyond his powers. However, when out walking one day by "a stream of clearest water," he is overcome by the urge to write poetry and the words of his first great canzone, *Donne ch'avete intelletto d'amore* (Ladies who have an understanding of love), spring to his lips in such a way that his tongue seemed to move "almost of its own accord." It would be difficult to exaggerate the importance of this poem in the economy of *Vita Nova* or, indeed, in Dante's poetry as a whole. The canzone was still at the center of his thoughts when in the *Comedy* Dante wished to mark the gap that separated him from his predecessors. In *Purgatorio* 24, he makes Bonagiunta da Lucca their spokesperson in recognizing that they had been incapable of discovering the "sweet new style" *(dolce stil novo)*. These three words have been lifted out of context and used to describe a "school" of poets comprising Guinizzelli, Cavalcanti,

Dante, Cino, and others. In context, however (*Purg.* 24.55–57), Bonagiunta's words refer to Dante's work and its fundamental inspiration as first exemplified in *Donne ch'avete.* The hallmark of this new poetry is its total fidelity to the dictates of Love (ll. 52–54), in a formula reminiscent of a passage in an *Epistola ad Severinum de caritate* by an otherwise unknown Brother Ivo:

> How, then, can a man speak of love who does not know love, who does not feel the power of love? A great deal can be learned from books concerning other subjects: this, however, is *either totally inside* [the writer] or not at all, because it does not communicate the secrets of its *sweetness* from without . . . the only person who can speak worthily of it is the one who arranges his words according to the inner dictates of his heart.[14]

Accordingly, Dante claims to be Love's scribe, the first to have "produced the new rhymes *beginning* 'Donne ch'avete intelletto d'amore'" (*Purg.* 24.50–51; my emphasis). The poem's stylistic qualities made it one of Dante's favorites (*DVE* 2.8.8 and 2.12.3).

In *Vita Nova,* however, it is above all the theme developed in *Donne ch'avete*—the totally new conception of love that inspired it—that causes it to be singled out as the great turning point in Dante's development as a love poet. The canzone's stanzas of fourteen lines reveal its affinity with the sonnet form, although the broad sweep and power of its vision cannot be found in any of Dante's sonnets. The opening line, invoking "Ladies, who have a [true] understanding of love," is charged with a potency that will become a characteristic feature of the poet's mature style. Here, the direct address to his chosen audience creates a sense of urgency concerning the poem's message and anticipates some memorable openings in the *Comedy*'s cantos (e.g., *Inf.* 19.1–6, *Par.* 27.1–9), as well as the famous invocations to its readers (e.g., *Purg.* 17.1–12, *Par.* 2.1–6). This—the first canzone in *Vita Nova*—contains a dramatic dialogue between the blessed and God in the second stanza, after an exordium that takes up the whole of the first stanza. The main theme—praise of Beatrice through a description of the effects her beauty and purity have on others—occupies the third and fourth stanzas. No longer a matter of the lady and her faithful lover, love's universe is here conceived as encompassing the whole of humankind. The poet as an individual exists only in order to attest to the miraculous effects of the beloved's presence: a living miracle, Beatrice destroys all evil thoughts; she brings nobility and salvation to others; and as nature's masterpiece, she is the very touchstone of beauty.

Beatrice's role, as described in *Donne ch'avete,* reflects the Christian Neoplatonic view of the human being as the midpoint of creation, a vital link between heaven and earth, between pure intellect and brute matter, uniquely capable of reconciling the needs of both.[15] Beatrice's death is hinted at in the opening of the poem's third and central stanza, where death is alluded to three times (in ll. 29, 34, and 36). Death is therefore at the poem's center. Indeed, in this poem Dante makes his first attempt to convey a vision of the whole universe—Beatrice/the damned/the saved; God/hell/heaven—in a poetic construct whose second stanza presents a veritable microcosm ranging from all the angels and saints (ll. 15–21) and God himself (ll. 22–27) to the living and the dead; and whose diction encompasses heaven, earth, and hell while ending on a note of celestial return.

In the canzone's third stanza, the poet declares his intention of describing Beatrice's power over others (l. 30). She mediates the return of souls to God through the midpoint of the poem (ll. 35–36), where the poet-lover asserts that those gazing on Beatrice who have evil or base hearts are either ennobled (and thus begin a journey of return to their Creator) or "they must die." The central scene is thus a miniature Last Judgment in Beatrice's universe, with the final lines of the third stanza proclaiming her salvific power over all who have spoken with her: "God has given her an even greater grace that anyone who has spoken to her cannot come to an evil end" (che non pò mal finir chi l'ha parlato).

The fourth stanza, which exalts the beauty and purity inhabiting Beatrice's mortal being, proclaims her condition as a miracle (l. 46: cosa nova—where the key word nova signifies "wonderful," "preternatural") and her identification with Love (l. 55). The prose commentary focuses surprisingly on the mouth (bocca) as the "goal" of Dante's desires—surprisingly, because this physical term is normally excluded from Dante's youthful poetry (cf., however, Inf. 5.136). Dante has boldly taken the religious icon of the Veronica (the veil on which Christ's face had been miraculously imprinted—see Par. 31.103–8) as a parallel for his vision of Beatrice's overwhelming beauty in its reflection of the divine Love that created the universe: "you see Love painted in her face, where no one can gaze for long at her" (ll. 55–56; cf. 40.1).[16]

Praise of the beloved, her beauty and virtue can be found in Dante's predecessors (e.g., in Guinizzelli's Io voglio del ver la mia donna laudare). However, that praise had never been accompanied by such depth of feeling or poetic power. This was truly Dante's own discovery, a new "poetry of praise," born of his innermost self and of the miracle that was Beatrice. Only the intensity and idealism of religious experience could provide an adequate touchstone for this outpouring of love and praise. The canzone is partly inspired by the Song of Songs, but the circumstances of Dante's initial inspiration are also reminiscent of one of the seven Penitential Psalms, in which the psalmist begs God to grant once more the joy of his saving power, with the famous supplication: "O Lord, open thou my lips; and my mouth shall show forth thy praise" (Ps. 50.17). So the poet's tongue now breaks forth in spontaneous praise of Beatrice (19.2). Although no direct biblical quotation is discernible in *Donne ch'avete*, we can grasp neither the poem's significance nor the message of *Vita Nova* as a whole unless we take into account the Pauline doctrine of the birth of the New Man as a result of baptism into the New Life of the spirit (Eph. 4.24). Similarly, Dante's baptism by Love—his newly acquired understanding of the true nature of love *(intelletto d'amore)*—transforms his whole being and leads him to offer up a new song of praise. Of divine origin (Ps. 39.4) and inspired by that Love which "moves the sun and the other stars" (*Par.* 33.145), this song is the supreme proof and direct result of the New Life that has taken possession of the poet's soul.

What is totally new is the fact that Dante's song is dedicated to praising Beatrice's miraculous qualities without any hope of external reward. Not only his predecessors but Dante himself had formerly hoped that devotion would earn a tangible reward, in his case, Beatrice's greeting. Now, however, Beatrice's lover imitates the highest form of Christian devotion in freely offering up praise of her beauty and goodness. So St. Augustine had written of the spontaneous love and praise of God: "What is 'gratuitous'? Himself for His own sake, not for any other reason" (*Enarrationes in Psalmos* 53). And, in classical antiquity—in a work Dante read soon after Beatrice's death (see *Conv.* 2.12.3)—Cicero had declared: "To love is nothing but to cherish the one you love . . . seeking no reward" (*De amicitia* 27.100).[17]

Sweet new style

Two words are inextricably linked with Dante's great love poetry: "sweet" (*dolce: Purg.* 24.57, 26.99, and 112) and "new" (*novo: Purg.* 24.57). As we have noted, the latter's semantic range included the connotations "unique," "wonderful," "miraculous." The renewal of the poet's inspiration is evident, not only in the content of the poems inspired by his new conception of love but also in their sweetness of language. This, in its turn, is based on an inner harmony, resulting from a musicality created by words selected for their *dolcezza,* or sweetness of sound. Some ten years later, the poet will provide us with specific examples of word forms designated as "urbane and combed" *(urbana pexa),* proclaiming them to be an essential ingredient in the sweet style of the most elevated lyric. Such words "leave a certain sweetness in the mouth, as do *amore, donna, disio, vertute, donare, letitia, salute, securtate, defesa*" (*DVE* 2.7.5). This list is in fact emblematic of the vocabulary used in *Donne ch'avete*—indeed, of the *Vita Nova* poems in general, where the two most frequently used substantives are *donna* (with fifty-six occurrences) and *amore* (fifty-four), the most common adjective is *gentile* (twenty-five occurrences), and virtually half of the 676 rhyme words (49 percent) conform to the poet's ideal of *dolcezza* (Boyde 1971, 91 ff.).

The author of *Vita Nova* thus shows himself faithful to the idea that love should combine chastity and sweetness: remaining chaste through the rule of reason, love is at the same time sweet in its expression—and, in *Convivio* 4, Dante was to contrast the sweet style of his love poetry *(Le dolci rime d'amor)* with the "harsh and subtle" verse (l. 14) required to discuss philosophical truths.

Love and the noble heart

Dante tells us that after the success enjoyed by *Donne ch'avete,* a friend asked him to define the nature and origin of love (cf. Cavalcanti's great poem *Donna me prega).* Taking from Guinizzelli the idea of the interdependence of love and the noble heart, Dante develops it with commendable philosophical rigor in *Amore e 'l cor gentil sono una cosa (VN* 20.3–5), describing the awakening of love in Aristotelian terms as the development from potentiality to act. The force or catalyst necessary for this development is the woman's beauty allied with her virtue, or, in the case of the woman who loves, a man's personal worth. Clearly not directly connected with the praise of Beatrice, this sonnet serves instead as a useful springboard to Dante's main theme. For, in the next sonnet *(Ne li occhi porta la mia donna Amore),* the poet uses this basic Aristotelian idea to illustrate the miraculous power of Beatrice's influence. Other women awaken love's potential through their beauty and virtue, but Beatrice's power achieves a philosophical impossibility, effects a miracle: the creation of love *ex nihilo,* even "where it does not exist potentially"—at least, according to the prose commentary (21.1).[18]

The death of Folco Portinari

Death is a recurrent motif in the second part of *Vita Nova,* which opens with the demise of Beatrice's father. Folco Portinari, who founded the hospital of Santa Maria Nuova in 1288, died on the last day of 1289. His last years covered a golden period in Florentine history; indeed, Giovanni Villani (8.89) highlighted the year 1283—the year when Dante at the age of eighteen met Beatrice again—as a joyous time of festivity and magnificence, made possible by a lull in the civic strife otherwise so typical of thirteenth-century Florence. In the 1290s, that struggle was to begin again in earnest. In many ways, Folco Portinari embodied the spirit of this peaceful interlude, which helped to set the tone of Dante's encounters with Beatrice as reflected in *Vita Nova.*[19] Dante tells us (22.3) that, at her father's death, many women shared Beatrice's sorrow; and, overhearing their report of her anguish, the poet was so saddened that the onlookers immediately noticed the change in his appearance. Still bound by the laws of "courtesy," Dante decided to express his feelings in two sonnets: in the first, he asks the women whether they have seen Beatrice and how she is feeling; in the second, he imagines their reply and their comments regarding his transformation by grief. The poems are scarcely of great interest in themselves, although we may note that the second sonnet would seem to have been written before the first, while Dante assures us that the circumstances offered "a worthy subject for poetry." The circumstances were, of course, the death of a father and a daughter's anguish and sorrow. In his commentary (22.2), Dante stresses the fact that there can be no closer "friendship" than that which exists "between a good father and a good child," where the masculine form *figliuolo* may possibly evoke a biblical echo (Luke 10.22). On the other hand, one of the most problematical aspects of Dante's personality is his total silence regarding his own father and their relationship.[20]

Premonition of Beatrice's death

A few days after the death of Beatrice's father, Dante was struck down by illness. On the ninth day, the thought of his own frailty led him to grasp the inevitability of Beatrice's death. This insight gave rise to a nightmarish vision in which disheveled women appeared to the delirious poet, telling him that he too would die, followed by other strange and horrible faces crying out, "You are dead" (*VN* 23.4). Having lost all sense of reality, he sees women weeping in the streets; the sun grows dark and the very stars seem to be shedding tears as birds fall from the sky and the earth quakes (cf. Matt. 24.29 and 51). A friend then appears and announces that Beatrice is dead. Through his tears, the poet looks up to heaven and catches sight of a multitude of angels "returning upwards," chanting *Hosanna in excelsis,* and preceded by a small white cloud. Convinced of the reality of his vision, he sees Beatrice's body with a white veil over her head and a beatific expression on her face that speaks to him of his beloved's union with God and makes him call upon "sweetest Death" to come to him. His delirium and constant weeping so alarm bystanders that in their attempt to console him, they interrupt his "vision" as he is about to exclaim: "O Beatrice, blessed are you!" (23.13). Ever faithful to the convention of secrecy, the poet hastens to add that, although he had already uttered the two words "O Beatrice," his voice was so shaken by sobbing that no one was able to understand what he had said.

When he had recovered from his illness, Dante set out to depict this vision in the second canzone included in *Vita Nova: Donna pietosa e di novella etate* (A lady pitiful and young). Manuscript evidence and the exceptional degree to which the verse reflects details given in the prose account make it likely that this poem was written specially for *Vita Nova* (De Robertis 1961, 154–55). If so, after reading the prose introduction, the poem comes as something of a disappointment. For example, the third line describes the poet as "often calling on Death." In the prose, on the other hand, Dante's invocation to "sweetest Death" comes as a powerful climax at the end of his delirious vision of Beatrice's dead body, whereas the frequency implied in the verse actually lessens the impact of the lover's despair. Similarly, the slight bathos of line 62 ("and if they [the angels] had said anything else, I would tell you"), despite the structural parallel with line 28, detracts from the description of Beatrice's ascent to heaven and the chant of the angels; readers hardly need to be persuaded in this way of the fidelity of Dante's reporting. The words "Hosanna in the highest" (Mark 11.10) marked Christ's triumphal entry into Jerusalem; here, they imply Beatrice's ascent to the heavenly Jerusalem.

On the other hand, we need only compare *Donna pietosa* with an earlier poem about death, *Morte villana* (8.8–11), to see how far the poet's art has progressed. The later work has a structural strength capable of bearing the full weight of Dante's vision. The dramatic prologue in the first stanza catches the reader's interest with the scene in a Florentine house where the apparent protagonist—the "lady pitiful and young" of the first verse—is sent off-stage by her companions, who try to comfort the sick man in brief passages of direct speech (ll. 11, 12, 22, and 26), whose dramatic effect Dante had learned from Cavalcanti. The first stanza is brought to an end on a note of suspense with the utterance of "my lady's name" (l. 14). Already in the action described, we have a foretaste of the *Comedy*'s narrative style, and the whole scene is characteristic of Dante's genius for dramatization. The poetic climax is reached in the fourth stanza, with the vision of "many fearful things" (l. 43: *cose dubitose molte*): signs of universal mourning traditionally associated with Christ's death and the end of the world. Thus, the sun is veiled and the earth quakes, as when the Redeemer died (Matt. 27.45, 51, and Apoc. 6.12–14 speak of similar portents). The fifth stanza brings the drama to its fulfillment by describing Beatrice's assumption to heaven, accompanied by a multitude of angels chanting "Hosanna" (Luke 2.13–15). Her transfiguration speaks of her reunion with God, so that the poet's cry—"Blessed is he who sees you, fair soul!"—echoes Ecclesiasticus 48.11 ("Blessed are those who have seen you"). The whole poem is an original synthesis of personal feeling and experience, intertwined with sacred motifs.

Beatrice's earthly apotheosis

Clearly, the poet is treating Beatrice's *imagined* death as an event bearing portents of universal significance associated with the death of Christ the Savior. Readers tempted to dismiss all this as poetic license must, however, come to terms with the next chapter, in which Beatrice's identification with Love is finally complete (24.5). She appears once more to Dante, preceded by Cavalcanti's lady, Giovanna, who was also known as Primavera (Spring). Dante tells us that both these names pointed to Beatrice's mission: like the spring season, Giovanna was to "come first *[prima verrà]* on the day when Beatrice will show herself after her faithful lover's prophetic vision" (24.4), even as John the Baptist had prepared the way for Christ, "the true light" (Isa. 40.3, John 1.23). Thus, at the very center of *Vita Nova*, Beatrice is preceded by Joan *(Giovanna)*, just as Christ was preceded by St. John the Baptist *(quello Giovanni*, the patron saint of Florence). The superiority of Dante's beloved over Cavalcanti's is manifest. Moreover, like Christ's death, Beatrice's demise is accompanied—in a vision—by signs of universal sorrow and destruction; like Christ, Beatrice is Love (*VN* 24.5). And her actual death leaves Florence in a state of desolation comparable to that of the Holy City of Jerusalem after its destruction (28.1; cf. Lam. 1.1–2): "How doth the city sit solitary, that was full of people! She that was mistress of the nations is now become as a widow!"

In order to understand the poet's intentions in setting up such astounding parallels between Beatrice and Christ, we must set aside any idea of blasphemy and realize that for a devout Christian it was possible to construct such comparisons, basing them on the principle of analogy. This analogy of proportion *(analogia entis)* could suggest similarities of action between Christ and a creature that made the creature a *speculum Christi* (mirror of Christ).[21] God created humanity in his own image: consequently, men and women may act as mirrors by reflecting their Creator. Like parallel lines, however, the two levels remain utterly distinct, separated by a space that remains constant and incalculable. Thus, on the restricted stage of *Vita Nova* we observe a drama enacted that is reminiscent of the Christian drama played out in the cosmos. In fulfilling this analogous role, Beatrice is the medium through which Dante reaches a degree of blessedness. She is physically removed from him by death but still able to point the way to salvation, as Christ does for the whole of humanity. In her goodness and beauty Dante glimpses the imprint of divine Love. Beatrice's death—described in *Donna pietosa* and thus bisecting the thirty-one poems of *Vita Nova*—is the central event in Dante's "little book," even as Christ's death on Calvary was the central event in the history of the world. No other poet had ever carried the praise of his beloved beyond her death; no other writer had dared to draw such an analogy. Dante was—and remains—unique.[22]

Personification allegory and vernacular love poetry

Beatrice's death is never described in its historical reality for reasons that Dante has placed beyond the reach of our mundane curiosity (28.2). Before this self-imposed silence, however, Dante offers us a digression (25) that is the joy of literary historians, and then three sonnets that mark the zenith of his art in praise of the living Beatrice.

The sonnet *Io mi senti' svegliar* (24.7–9) speaks of personified love as though it were a bodily substance endowed with understanding. The scribe of *Vita Nova* 25.1 hastens to clarify that "Love cannot in itself exist as a substance, but it is an accident in a substance." This Aristotelian terminology may indicate that Dante had already begun his apprenticeship as a philosopher, although the basic points mentioned at the beginning of chapter 25 would have been familiar to many educated laymen. Moreover, the sonnet had spoken of love as moving from place to place, whereas only a body is capable of locomotion, according to Aristotle (already referred to simply as "the Philosopher" in 25.2); the poem had also attributed to love the peculiarly human faculties of laughter and speech. This initial disquisition leads to a fascinating aside, when Dante tells his readers that they must realize that "in ancient times there were no love poems in the vernacular," but love poems were written by "certain poets in the Latin language" (25.3). He then claims that it is only in the past 150 years that the first vernacular poets appeared, adding the significant observation that "rhyming in the vernacular is the equivalent of writing verses in Latin" (25.4). The chronological sequence in Dante's account (Latin → vernacular) will mislead the reader who has not read *De vulgari eloquentia*. There we learn that for Dante, Latin was not (as it is for us) the root of the Romance languages: it was an artificial language, created at some unknown date in accordance with the fixed rules of grammar, in order to overcome the post-Babel deficiencies of the vernaculars or "natural" languages, their constant mutability in both space and time (for a fuller discussion of Dante's views on Latin and language in general, see chapter 2).

Dante tells us that what brought about this literary revolution—the decision to write love poetry in the vernacular—was the need for the female recipient to understand the words addressed to her: "And this is against those who write poetry in the vernacular on subjects other than love, since this type of poetry was originally conceived for writing about love" (*VN* 25.6). Such a restricted view of the range of vernacular poetry is utterly opposed to Dante's later theory and practice (cf. *DVE* 2.2.5–8) and was at least partly inspired by his rejection of the achievements of his predecessor, Guittone d'Arezzo (c. 1230–c. 1294; cf. *Purg.* 26.121–26). After coming under the spell of Guittone's rhetorical power and extravagance during the early years of his apprenticeship, Dante had turned away from this model, despite the passionate involvement with moral and political issues that Dante came to share with Guittone.[23] For the poet of *Vita Nova*, however, love was the only subject appropriate to vernacular poetry, where certain rhetorical figures (such as the personification of love) could be adapted from Latin poetry—"though not without cause, which may then be revealed in prose," precisely as the author of *Vita Nova* set out to do for his own love lyrics. Such is Dante's embryonic attempt to discuss the use of personification allegory in poetry, with an appeal to the authority of Latin poets.

At the time when he wrote *Vita Nova,* however, Dante's knowledge of classical antiquity was rudimentary. The quotations from Vergil, Lucan, Horace, and Ovid in 25.9 betray no evidence of familiarity with classical texts: they are passages that could be found in many medieval anthologies, and they appeared as isolated quotations in manuals. Nothing in *Vita Nova* suggests the direct contact and assimilation of the great writers of Roman antiquity that fired the poet in later years and led him to acknowledge his immense debt to Vergil, whom he chose as his guide through both hell and purgatory.[24]

Praise of Beatrice

With the great sonnet *Tanto gentile e tanto onesta pare* we return to praise of the living Beatrice.[25] This sonnet is in fact the quintessence of Dante's "sweet new style," with its fourteen lines of exquisite music conveying the magic of the lover's wonder and adoration. Beatrice "appears" as a miracle on earth: the verb *parere* (to appear), used no less than three times, expresses the physical manifestation of a superior spiritual reality. The effect of the word may be measured by its use in line 7, where earlier versions of the sonnet (before its inclusion in *Vita Nova* 26) offer the reading "I believe that she is something come down from heaven to earth, to make miracles known."[26] Instead, in *Vita Nova,* Dante changed the subjective *credo che sia* (I believe that she is) to the emphatic *e par che sia* (and she appears as), so that poetic hyperbole is replaced by impersonal reality, the disclosure of a spiritual phenomenon—a virtual epiphany—of which the poet is the objective witness and reporter. Beatrice is still "my lady" (l. 2), but the core of the poem's message is the universality of her influence, which is reinforced by the elimination of the earlier egocentricity in the description of the effects of her beauty and actions on her lover. Now, her beauty strikes the heart—not merely of the poet but of all who look at her (note the impersonal *chi la mira*—in a way that cannot be understood by anyone who has not experienced its sweetness. This sonnet creates an impression of absolute joy and serenity absent from earlier poems. Accordingly, traces of Cavalcanti's influence present in the first versions of *Tanto gentile* were eliminated in the version given in *Vita Nova*: e.g., Beatrice's beauty *wounded (fier [ferisce])* the eyes of those who beheld Beatrice's beauty, whereas now the eyes are the medium that allows the heart to experience such "sweetness" (l. 10: *che dà per li occhi una dolcezza al core*). Even the return to an earlier poetic technique—the repetition of *mostrare/ Mostrasi* in lines 8–9, which links the octave and sestet in a manner reminiscent of Provençal *coblas capfinidas*—is inspired by the same goal: the poet's intention to act as the recorder of objective evidence, proof of a superior reality revealed by this living miracle. The repetition thus appears to provide incontrovertible evidence of the poet's bold claim that Beatrice is "a thing come down from heaven to earth to show a miracle" *(una cosa venuta / da cielo in terra a miracol mostrare. / Mostrasi sí piacente).* The last six verses build up to a fourteenth line that is uniquely *a maiore* in stressing the last word of all, *Sospira* (Sigh), and creating a moment of magical silence. The result is a song of praise for a mortal woman that takes its place among the summits of the European love lyric.

As in chapter 14, Dante judges that this poem's meaning is so obvious that he does not divide it up into its various parts, those prose "divisions" of *Vita Nova* that reflect the Scholastic method of Aquinas's commentaries.[27] In the following sonnet on the theme of Beatrice's perfection, *Vede perfettamente onne salute* (*VN* 26.10–13), the poet proclaims that his lady's qualities are so pre-eminent that they bring praise not just to herself but to all women who come into her presence (l. 11, cf. Luke 1.48). With these two sonnets the public proclamation of Beatrice's perfection is complete, and Dante's major theme is virtually exhausted. The poet of *Tanto gentile* surely could not scale greater heights along the same path: rebirth of his love poetry was possible only through the death of the beloved.

The unfinished poem and Beatrice's death

For the present, Dante tells us that he wished to make up for the fact that he had not spoken of Beatrice's effects on himself: "and, thinking that I would not be able to narrate this in the short space of a sonnet, I began to write a canzone" (*VN* 27.2)—a surprising statement, when one considers that the poet's message is in fact summed up in its first four lines and is then fully developed in the fourteen verses required for the sonnet form. The canzone's composition, Dante tells us, was dramatically interrupted by Beatrice's death—so that we have only this first stanza, which is nevertheless a unique amalgam of the principal phases in Dante's love poetry, since it combines elements of the poet's dolorous Cavalcantian phase with those typical of the praise style *(stilo de la loda).* Love, which has held the poet in its thrall for so long, has been conclusively transformed from a harsh, painful experience into the sweetness he now feels in his heart (ll. 3–4: "just as he [Love] was harsh to me at first, so now he is gentle in my heart"). Such is the final tribute paid to Beatrice's influence during her lifetime on earth. These lines are also a clear rebuttal of Cavalcanti's pessimistic conception of love and its effects as described in Guido's sonnet, *Voi che per li occhi mi passaste 'l core.* Dante in fact condemns his "first friend" by using the same words (such as the emblematic *forte* of l. 3, associated with death in Cavalcanti) and the same rhyme scheme in the quatrains *(-ore, -ia);* whereas Cavalcanti's vital spirits are vanquished (l. 6: *che' deboletti spiriti van via*), Dante's only seem to flee (l. 6: *che li spiriti par che fuggan via*) but are in fact resuscitated by Love's power and Beatrice's salvific influence (ll. 9–14).[28]

Although the presence of a *settenario* or seven-syllable line (l. 11) would be virtually inadmissible in a sonnet, *Sí lungiamente m'ha tenuto Amore* has many affinities with the sonnet's typical structure of octave + sestet (two quatrains plus two tercets). Whether or not *Sí lungiamente* was originally conceived as a sonnet, however, its presentation in *Vita Nova* as an isolated stanza from an incomplete canzone creates a dramatic circumstance for the announcement of Beatrice's death. This is emphasized by the absence of any reference to "divisions" in his poem (references which are placed after the poems written during Beatrice's lifetime but which will precede those written after her death). The poem's last line is thus followed by the solemn declaration from the Lamentations of Jeremiah *(Quomodo sedet sola civitas),* which raises up the bereft city of Florence to a status in some way comparable to that of the Holy City. The unfinished poem—interrupted by God's calling Beatrice to heavenly glory—therefore comes to represent a life broken off so prematurely. The rest of the story must be written elsewhere: in heaven, and on earth by the poet left abandoned and disconsolate. We are thus offered a mutilated poem followed by a verse from the liturgy of Holy Week, followed by silence.[29]

Why should a description of the circumstances surrounding Beatrice's actual death be excluded from *Vita Nova* (28.2)? Perhaps because Dante relates only those events witnessed by him. But there are at least three other possible reasons the author gives us. First, death was not part of his New Life but only a temporary obstacle, soon overcome by the lover's fidelity to that same new life. Second, even if writing about these circumstances had formed part of the author's "present intention," the subject itself would have been far beyond his powers. And third, even if he were capable of writing about the subject adequately, he would be obliged to praise himself, "which is blameworthy above all things" (28.2; cf. *Conv.* 1.2.2–12). It is idle for us to indulge in speculation, since Dante gives us no other clues.

Beatrice and the number nine

What Dante does give us, instead, is a disquisition on the role played by the number nine in Beatrice's life and death: a quintessential detail, but one held back until chapter 29 (with a strategy found again in the *Comedy:* e.g., in *Inf.* 11.76–90, Virgil's explanation of the moral order of the infernal circles already visited). If Beatrice had been mere allegory, a figment of Dante's imagination (as some have maintained), the author of *Vita Nova* would surely have made her die on the ninth day of the ninth month, September. As it is, however, she died on June 8 in the year 1290. Proving that her death in fact occurred "in the first hour of the ninth day . . . in the ninth month of the year" (*VN* 29.1) therefore requires considerable ingenuity on Dante's part, leading him to refer to three calendars—Arabic, Syrian, and Christian. The celebrated ninth-century Arab astronomer Alfraganus (*Conv.* 2.5.16 and 13.11) provided the poet with the necessary loopholes for time and date, since for Arabs the day begins after sunset. Thus, the evening of June 8 was also "the first hour of the ninth day," while June corresponded to the ninth month *(Hazirân)* of the Syrian calendar! The year, furthermore, is one in which the perfect number ten had come round nine times in a century of the Christian calendar. These mental gymnastics may make the modern reader smile, but we must understand that they were inspired by a deep-rooted belief in an essential design woven into the universe by its Creator. As Augustine wrote in his treatise on free will (*De libero arbitrio* 2.16): "Divine wisdom is seen in the numbers impressed on all things."[30]

The prevalence of the number nine in the course of Beatrice's life, Dante explains, is partly due to the belief "according to Ptolemy and according to Christian truth" that there are nine moving heavens, which were all in perfect harmony at the moment of Beatrice's conception (29.2; cf. *Conv.* 4.21.7–10). A more subtle reason, however, is that "this number was herself, by analogy," for the root of nine is three, even as the root of all miracles is the triune Godhead, so that "this lady was accompanied by this number nine to signify that she was a nine, that is to say a miracle whose root . . . is solely the miraculous Trinity." Then he adds, modestly: "Perhaps a more subtle person would find a more subtle reason in this; but this is the one I see and the one I prefer" (29.4).

At this point, we may recall that (after a brief introductory section) the *libello* itself opens with the key word "Nine" (2.1). Dante first met Beatrice in his ninth year, and nine years elapsed before she first greeted him, making it possible for him to reach "the limits of beatitude" (3.2). Moreover, her greeting took place at the ninth hour of the day, while his first vision came "during the first of the last nine hours of the night" (3.8); the second vision, announcing Beatrice's death, comes at the ninth hour (12.9); and the third vision, when the veil is finally lifted, strikes the poet on the ninth day of his illness (23.2). The number nine itself appears exactly nine times in Dante's "little book" dedicated to the greater glory of Beatrice. Beatrice appears to Dante nine times in *Vita Nova*—with a final vision of her in heavenly glory (41.10–13) producing the perfect number ten.

Gorni (1990, 39) points out that a "more subtle reason" linking Beatrice with the number nine lies in the Latin form of her name, BEATRIX, in which the final letters IX represent the Beatrician number.[31] Another reason may be found in the fact that nine orders of angels move the heavens: Beatrice therefore reflects angelic as well as celestial perfection (as Dante hints in 29.2).

We may go on to discover (or imagine) that *Vita Nova* as a whole is structured so that its thirty-one poems are grouped around a trinity of canzoni framed by the perfect number ten, in the chiastic series 10 + I + 4 + I + 4 + I + 10, where the roman numerals indicate the full-length canzoni at *Vita Nova* 19.4–14, 23.17–28, and 31.8–17. (The work also contains a canzone fragment at 27.3–5 and one canzone consisting of only two stanzas at 33.5–8.) Alternative structures can be posited based on the number nine: 1 + 9 + 1 + 9 + 1 + 9 + 1, where the number nine appears three times (Singleton 1958, 79); or the sequence (1 + 9) + I + (1 + 3) + II + (3 + 1) + III + (9 + 1), a variant of the first grouping given above (Musa 1962, vii–xxii).[32]

With regard to the perfection of Beatrice's number, we must take into account the fact that the number nine was linked with the dates of the siege and capture of Jerusalem (4 Kings 25.1–3; Jer. 52.4–6). Worse still, the ninth hour was the moment when Christ died upon the cross.[33] Nevertheless, Dante went out of his way to emphasize the positive symbolism of the number, as we have seen.

Far from being merely arbitrary or quaint adornments, such structural details reflect the poet's belief in the harmony that governed the universe. A belief in the symbolic force of numbers stretches back through classical antiquity to Pythagoras, who—as Dante tells us in *Convivio* 2.13.18—"considered everything to be a number." In Christian times, the same message had been proclaimed by such writers as Augustine, Isidore of Seville, and the Victorines. In Dante's own century, the principle was reiterated in the biographies of Franciscan saints. The lives of God's elect were seen to reveal a providential plan governing the whole universe, even as the proportions of certain medieval churches reflected the divine order in creation: "Like Saints Francis, Clare, and Margaret, she [Beatrice] is both real creature and miracle; indeed, in her humanity she can be understood as the reflection of the eternal figure of Christ" (Branca 1988, 130). The lives of those *specula Christi* were likewise hallmarked: "nine years before being offered to God, three years of incipient grace, nine in the perfect state. In this way the lives of Margaret, Clare, and others are patterned" (ibid., 135). Indeed, two of these Franciscan saints belonged to the group of noble ladies who accompany Beatrice in *Vita Nova:* Umiliana de' Cerchi and Giuliana Falconieri, the latter a relative of Folco Portinari's daughter.

In his *Vita Nova*, Dante constructed his own legend of the Holy Beatrix, bringer of blessedness and a pointer to heaven. In this, he takes care (as did St. Augustine in his *Retractationes*) to impose an inner logic and existential coherence on his writings, pruning them of all inconsistencies. Hence, for example, his decision to omit poems addressed to Violetta (*Rime* LVIII: 23) or Lisetta (CXVII: 58); but he also excludes the only poem *(Lo doloroso amor)* written during Beatrice's lifetime that bears her name—paradoxically, as a bringer of torment and even death to her lover, who exclaims: "Through her I die, whose name is Beatrice" (LXVIII: 25, l. 14: *Per quella moro c'ha nome Beatrice*). Such transient episodes and feelings could have no place in the providential design and master plan of Dante's Book of Memory.

Dante's sorrow

Overwhelmed by Beatrice's death, Dante tells us (*VN* 30.1) that he wrote an epistle to the priors of Florence, describing the city's widowed condition and beginning with the verse from the Lamentations of Jeremiah: "I say this so that no one should be surprised if I quoted it above, almost as an introduction to the new subject matter that follows." Since the epistle was written in Latin, it was omitted from *Vita Nova,* a work intended from the start to be "entirely in the vernacular" (30.3). Nevertheless, Dante was careful to record the epistle's existence as the first example of his prophetic voice and thereby to express the need he was to feel ever more forcefully to move beyond Cavalcanti's limited personal horizon by inserting both his deepest emotions and his art in either a civic or a universal context.

After the poet's eyes had wept "for some time" (31.1), he decided to express his sorrow in a solemn canzone, *Li occhi dolenti per pietà del core* (My eyes that grieve for my heart's anguish), in some ways the fulfillment of the first canzone, *Donne ch'avete intelletto d'amore.* There are a number of structural parallels between the two poems. For example, in the first stanza of each, the fourth line states the poet's avowed purpose of expressing his feelings in similar terms: in order to "unburden my mind" *(Donne ch'avete)* and to "unburden my grief" *(Li occhi dolenti).* Indeed, the audience is the same: both poems are written exclusively for ladies "of noble heart" who understand the meaning of true love. The second stanzas of both poems portray a scene in heaven and describe Beatrice's being as reaching up to Paradise itself. In lines 15–21 of *Donne ch'avete,* the whole court of heaven entreated God that Beatrice might be added to their number. In lines 21–26 of *Li occhi dolenti*—with telling hyperbole and supreme theological inconsistency—the poet relates that God so marveled at the light of Beatrice's humility on earth that he decided to call such perfection to himself. In the third stanza of each poem, the poet describes the effects of Beatrice's presence on earth *(Donne ch'avete)* and then her absence *(Li occhi dolenti)* on both base and noble hearts. The third and fourth stanzas of *Li occhi dolenti* return from the universal to the particular by describing the poet's own anguished state. *Donne ch'avete* is a hymn of praise inspired by Beatrice's qualities. *Li occhi dolenti* is about Beatrice only insofar as it describes her new state in heaven and its effects on others, although it is the first poem to mention her name in its full, significant form (ll. 15 and 55). *Li occhi dolenti* includes lines of typically Dantean directness (ll. 27–28: "because He saw that this wretched life was not worthy of so noble a thing"), as well as an anticipation of *Paradiso* (l. 16: "in the kingdom where the angels have peace"). Finally, this, the fourth canzone in *Vita Nova*, shows us in the structure of its stanzas (where the tenth line of each is a *settenario*) that the poet was now moving away from basic similarities with the sonnet form, which had reappeared so strikingly in the single stanza of *Sí lungiamente.*

Next, we are told, the poet wrote a sonnet, at her brother's request, lamenting Beatrice's death. This undistinguished poem is a step backward, with the commentary (32.2) plunging us once more into the world of subterfuge and screen ladies, after the far more direct and personal style of *Li occhi dolenti.* Recognizing that it was *povero* (poor) and *nudo* (bare), the poet decided to add a "canzone" of only two stanzas to his gift, one stanza as if spoken by her brother and the other by himself, although Dante tells us that this difference may be apparent only to a "subtle" observer (33.2). In fact, there is a considerable change from the Cavalcantian mode of the sonnet to the "sweet new style" of the canzone, in which Beatrice's greeting is extended to the angels, who "marvel" at the light of love issuing from her greatly augmented spiritual beauty and which lights up the whole of heaven (33.8).

Anniversary poem

The next chapter provides evidence of the extent to which the poetry of *Vita Nova* is at times linked to specific occasions and events. It is clear that a number of Dante's poems had to be "recycled" in order to reflect their author's present purpose, his need to reveal the essential pattern that underlay the contingencies of his youthful experiences and to highlight the various stages in the history of his exclusive devotion to Beatrice. Here (34.1), we are told that the occasion for the poem selected was the first anniversary of Beatrice's death, when the thought of her led her disconsolate lover to "draw an angel on some wooden boards"—an act witnessed by some of his fellow Florentines and which may be taken as proof of the poet's skill as a draftsman.

The chapter is even more remarkable in that it has preserved a page from Dante's poetic notebook, in the form of two versions of the first quatrain of a sonnet written in June 1291. The first opening is the more successful with its straightforward syntax, whereas the second introduces—unexpectedly, at this point in the poet's development—the Sicilian forms *eo facia* (I was doing), as well as the "you" (*vi:* l. 4) who are led by the noble lady's perfection to come to see what the poet is doing; the statement to this "you," whose referent is unidentified in the sonnet, is so dependent on the prose commentary for clarification as to seem almost devoid of poetic autonomy. The first version is not found in the manuscript tradition before its inclusion in *Vita Nova*.[34] The essential difference between the two beginnings lies in their account of Beatrice's *valore,* her true worth. In the second version, her worth is merely a magnet exciting the curiosity of Dante's audience (ll. 3–4), whereas in the first, it is the essential reason why she has achieved glory in heaven. In other words, the first version confirms the "prophecy" of *Donne ch'avete* and the assertions contained in *Li occhi dolenti* and *Quantunque volte, lasso!* (33.8) that Beatrice is in heavenly glory: it embodies a vision far beyond the ken of Dante's predecessors. With this "first beginning," surely devised specially for its narrative function in *Vita Nova,* the sonnet marks a fitting conclusion to chapters 28–33 and to the year following Beatrice's death. Beatrice, who had been placed by God Almighty in Florence for her faithful lover's joy and edification (*VN* 6.2), has now been removed by God and placed in "the heaven of humility, where Mary is" (34.7).

A "noble lady" *(donna gentile)*

A new narrative phase opens with the announcement that some time after this anniversary, Dante found himself in a place full of memories that overwhelmed him. Looking up, he saw "a noble and very beautiful young woman who gazed at me with such compassion" that she seemed the very embodiment of pity (*VN* 35.2). Her compassion increased his sorrow to such an extent that he was moved to tears and had to leave the scene. The depth of feeling produced in the speaker by this first encounter is revealed in its last two lines, which proclaim that the lady is accompanied by that same Love which makes Dante weep (35.8). The attraction grows, leading the poet to hope that he will find relief in tears; but his eyes "are incapable of weeping in [her] presence" (36.5)—the first suggestion that the lady's power may overcome his sorrow. The point of crisis is reached and expressed through an inner conflict portrayed in the sonnet *L'amaro lagrimar che voi faceste* (37.6–8), in which Dante's heart rebukes his eyes for their fickleness. The next poem, *Gentil pensero che parla di vui* (38.8–10), tells us that his heart consents to entertain a "noble thought" *(gentil pensero),* which—the prose explains—was "noble in so far as it spoke of a noble lady; for the rest, it was most base" (38.4).

The vision of this noble lady caused Dante's heart to waver. A new vision, however, appears to him "almost at the ninth hour" (39.1): a striking vision of "this glorious Beatrice" dressed in red (the color of charity), as she had first appeared to the poet—and seemingly as young. Her redemptive work must begin all over again. The thought of her and of his love for her makes her errant lover repent of the way he has allowed his heart to be taken up by another, "for some days against the constancy of reason," so that he now rids himself "of this evil desire" and his every thought turns once more to Beatrice (39.2).[35]

Eastertide, 1292

After this "tribulation" (40.1)—the biblical connotations are highly significant[36]—Dante recalls seeing some pilgrims pass through Florence. The time was most probably Holy Week of 1292. Seeing the pilgrims lost in thought, Dante was struck by the fact that they were thinking of other things, perhaps of distant family and friends, so that they were evidently unaware of the great loss sustained by "the sorrowful city" (40.4). The poet decides to make his next sonnet address the pilgrims directly "as if I had spoken to them" (40.5)—an exhortation to his audience to share his innermost feelings. In an interesting aside Dante tells us that in contemporary usage a distinction was made between the broad meaning of the term "pilgrim," indicating "anyone who is far away from home" (as in the sonnet), and its narrower sense, applied only to those who undertake a pilgrimage to the shrine of St. James at Santiago de Compostela. This digression prefigures the future author of the *Convivio* with his encyclopedic learning and fine lexical distinctions, as he goes on to specify that those who journey overseas to the Holy Land are properly called "palmers" because of the palms they bring back as a reminder of their successful voyage, whereas those who simply journey to Rome are called *romei* (literally, "Romeos"; cf. Shakespeare's *Romeo and Juliet,* act 1, scene 5).

A visionary ending

Oltre la spera, the last poem of all, contains the *raison d'être* of the entire work, exalting as it does Beatrice in glory and the new power given to the poet's love—a "new understanding" (41.10) that stretches beyond the bounds of the physical universe and reaches as far as the Empyrean Heaven of pure light, the very mind of God, where Beatrice now enjoys the beatific vision. But *Vita Nova* is not the *Comedy.* Dante makes the journey only in the form of a sigh (emblematic of the whole atmosphere of his sweet new style), then his "pilgrim" spirit returns to earth with words that speak of Beatrice but are otherwise beyond her lover's comprehension. The apparent logical contradiction in the tercets led the Sienese poet Cecco Angiolieri to attack Dante in *Dante Alaghier, Cecco, tu' serv' amico* (Dante Alighieri, Cecco, your servant and friend) for claiming on the one hand that the words expressed were too difficult for him to comprehend, while, on the other, the poet assured his audience of "dear ladies" that he could understand his "sigh" well enough (*VN* 41.13). Cecco, who never lost an opportunity of parodying the subtle refinements of the sweet new style, delighted in pointing out that on this occasion Dante was hoist with his own petard. No doubt as a result of this barb, Dante goes to great lengths to explain his precise meaning in the prose commentary written expressly for *Vita Nova*. He fortifies his defense with a reference to Aristotle's *Metaphysics* (probably via St. Thomas's commentary), where the full weight of the Philosopher's authority is brought into play in an attempt to crush such gadflies as Cecco (41.6). What the poet cannot understand is Beatrice's new condition, which cannot be apprehended by the earthbound intellect any more than the sun can be beheld by human eyes. What he does grasp is Beatrice's name, which often recurs in his thought; hence, the word *'ntendo* in the sonnet's last line has both its primary meaning, "I understand," and its secondary sense, "I hear."

The audience is still essentially the same as the one chosen by Dante for the proclamation of his sweet new style in *Donne ch'avete intelletto d'amore*. One word is repeated from the previous sonnet: the term "pilgrim," here used to describe the "spirit" of the poet's thought, which journeys to heaven "like a pilgrim away from his native land" (41.5). Both in his description of this thought as a pilgrim in heaven and in the commentary explaining his use of the term, the poet must have been struck by the contrast thus created with the traditional Christian image of humanity's life on earth as a pilgrimage. Not only does his commentary paradoxically imply that heaven is a foreign land, but Dante's words "away from his native land *[patria]*" seem to contradict the basic theological concept of heaven as humanity's true home, indicated by the word *patria* in the Christian vocabulary (cf. *Purg.* 13.94–96). It is, however, possible to discover in "pilgrim" a key word creating an essential link between the poetic fantasy described in *Oltre la spera* and the "wonderful vision" announced in the brief final section (42.1).[37] From this perspective, the sonnet looks forward to what is possibly the germ of the *Comedy*, with its stupendous portrayal of Dante's pilgrimage through the other world. At the same time, the description of Love weeping in lines 3–4 makes us cast one last backward glance at the first vision of all, narrated in chapter 3, in which Love's tears had anticipated the calamity of Beatrice's death.

The narrative of this youthful love breaks off with this last vision, which makes Dante "decide not to write any more about this blessed soul" until he is capable of doing so "more worthily": "And in order to achieve this end I strive with all my might, as she well knows. So that if it please Him by whom all things live that my life continue for some years, I hope to write about her that which was never written about any other woman" (42.2; cf. Vergil *Eclogue* 4.53–54). Nothing could be more tantalizing. Even the phrase *io studio,* apart from its obvious meaning of "I strive," may well allude to the study of philosophy undertaken by Dante at about this time. What is certain is that he had not yet grasped the poetic form of the *Comedy* as we know it. Beyond that, there is only conjecture. Nevertheless, it seems likely that the germ of his great epic vision had been implanted in the poet's imagination. Paradise had been glimpsed; hell was yet to be experienced.

Conclusion

All too often, Dante's "little book" has been regarded as a dress rehearsal for the *Comedy,* his poetic masterpiece. The differences, however, are at least as important as the similarities. To appreciate the stylistic gap separating the two works, we need only recall the stark realism of some of the episodes in *Inferno* and the use of crude language even in *Paradiso* (e.g., *Par.* 17.129, 27.25–26). Nothing could be further removed from the style of *Vita Nova,* which epitomizes Dante's purist phase as a stylist. Here, his vocabulary is far more restricted and refined than that of his predecessors, and the rarefied atmosphere of the whole work can be indicated by the fact that, of the 229 nouns in its poems, no fewer than 150 are abstract. Moreover, only 6 are proper nouns, whereas in the *Comedy* 1,615 proper nouns will appear. Even more significant is the fact that only six similes occur in the poems of *Vita Nova,* whereas Dante's masterpiece glories in a host of similes and other rhetorical figures (Boyde 1971).

Another essential difference emerges from a consideration of the religious component, one of the obvious links between the two works. We have seen how carefully Dante built up the analogy between Beatrice and Christ, especially in chapters 23–24. The language describing Beatrice's first appearance is reminiscent of that used in the Gospels to proclaim Christ's birth; and to evoke Beatrice's death the writer borrows elements from the liturgy of Holy Week. On the other hand, we have also noted that the author of *Vita Nova* had recourse to such theological impossibilities as the attribution of wonderment to God (31.10)—a use of hyperbole quite inconceivable in the *Comedy.* The inquisitorial censors of 1576 were to some extent right to be troubled by Dante's use of religious elements in *Vita Nova,* a work in which he did not hesitate to use the language of Mariolatry when describing Beatrice as "the destroyer of all vices and the queen of all virtues" (10.2). As early as chapter 3, the writer plays on the semantic possibilities inherent in the word *salute* to insist that, for him, Beatrice is truly the *Beatrix,* the bringer of salvation (with echoes of biblical passages where Christ is designated as *salus nostra,* "our salvation"). At this stage, Dante employs straightforward metaphors; and—as we have seen—hyperbole is yet another of his devices, justified by the license accorded to poets (25.7). Both the narrator and the poet are guilty of theological audacity: the former when he goes so far as to refer to Beatrice as his "beatitude" when she is sitting in church (5.1), and the latter when he exploits a sacred text in *O voi che per la via d'Amor passate* (7.3).

Among Dante's writings in the vernacular only *Vita Nova* and the *Comedy* are based upon a fusion of human and divine love. The three essential stages in Dante's experience of love, as illustrated in *Vita Nova*—"outside" the poet's being (his lady's greeting); within him (praise of his lady); and above him (Beatrice in heavenly glory)—correspond to the three stages in the soul's ascent to God as posited by St. Bonaventure, the Franciscan theologian: *extra nos, intra nos, supra nos* (Singleton 1958, 105–7). On the other hand, *Vita Nova* does not truly describe a "journey of the mind to God" (it is not an *Itinerarium mentis in Deum,* to use Bonaventure's much-quoted title). Beatrice remains the terminus of the poet's love and praise. The woman he had first seen in a street in Florence is the sole inspirer of a work described by Dante himself as "fervent and impassioned" (*Conv.* 1.1.16), in which the original meaning of poetic texts—even one expressing the destructive torments of love (16.7–10)—is transformed through the unifying prism of the prose commentary into praise of the beloved. The bereaved lover's thoughts journey up to heaven—but they seek Beatrice, not God. The lover learns that his blessedness cannot be found in the woman's appearance or her greeting, but only in praise of his beloved. No other poet had ever declared his beloved to be one of the blessed in heaven. Yet, he never goes beyond this stage. The author of *Vita Nova* failed to see that beatitude can never be found in a creature[38]—a truth the poet of the *Comedy* was to illustrate so vividly at the end of his *Paradiso,* when Beatrice herself gives way to St. Bernard and the pilgrim's whole being is seized with the need to experience the beatific vision of God. Even though the religious atmosphere of Dante's youthful work is impregnated with Franciscan lore and motifs, its God is still "the Lord of courtesy" (*VN* 42.3).

Recent scholarship has explored the ways in which Dante's *libello* is a response "to the crisis of finitude which Beatrice's death revealed as the human condition as such. It is fair to say that, for the rest of his career, Dante continued to respond to this crisis in one form or another" (Harrison 1993, 43). Readers have learned to distinguish ever more clearly between the author/narrator and actor in both *Vita Nova* and the *Comedy.* For the first time in the jungle of medieval manuscript anthologies, an author gathered together the *disiecta membra* of poems he had written over some fifteen years: in so doing and in imposing an existential pattern on those poems, he conferred a New Life upon them and revealed to Love's faithful followers that "Beatrice's actions, occurring in time and space, have a figural dimension; her being, existing beyond such boundaries, an analogical one" (Hollander 2001, 39). *Vita Nova* is not, as has been claimed, primarily a treatise on the art of poetry.[39] It deals with problems regarding vernacular poetry in general and Dante's early poetry in particular, but its core subject is love. Love and poetry were of course inseparable for Dante. Especially through the medium of its prose commentary, *Vita Nova* gave new meaning and significance to both by imposing artistic unity on the multiformity of human experience, an accomplishment Dante was to achieve above all in his *Comedy*.

Texts and translations

Vita Nuova. Edited by Domenico De Robertis, with an introduction and extensive notes. This is the standard text of *Vita Nova*. In Dante Alighieri, *Opere minori,* vol. 1, part 1, 3–247. Milan and Naples: Ricciardi, 1984.

Vita Nuova. Italian text with facing English. Translated by Dino S. Cervigni and Edward Vasta. Notre Dame, Ind.: University of Notre Dame Press, 1995.

Other readings

Boyde, Patrick. *Dante's Style in His Lyric Poetry.* Cambridge: Cambridge University Press, 1971.

De Robertis, Domenico. *Il libro della "Vita Nuova."* Florence: Sansoni, 1961.

Gorni, Guglielmo. *"Vita nuova di Dante Alighieri."* In *Letteratura italiana: Le opere,* vol. 1 *(Dalle origini al Cinquecento),* edited by A. Asor Rosa, 153–86. Turin: Einaudi, 1992.

———, ed. Dante Alighieri, *Vita Nova.* Turin: Einaudi, 1996.

Harrison, Robert Pogue. "Approaching the *Vita nuova.*" In *The Cambridge Companion to Dante,* edited by Rachel Jacoff, 34–44. Cambridge: Cambridge University Press, 1993.

Hollander, Robert. *Dante: A Life in Works,* 12–40. New Haven: Yale University Press, 2001.

Mazzoni, Francesco. "Il 'trascendentale' dimenticato." In *Omaggio a Beatrice (1290–1990),* edited by Rudy Abardo, 93–132. Florence: Le Lettere, 1997.

Mazzotta, Giuseppe. "The Language of Poetry in the *Vita nuova.*" *Rivista di studi italiani* 1 (1983): 3–14.

Moleta, Vincent, ed. *"La gloriosa donna de la mente": A Commentary on the "Vita Nova."* Florence: Olschki, 1994.

Picone, Michelangelo. *"Vita Nuova" e tradizione romanza.* Padua: Liviana, 1979.

Santagata, Marco. *Amate e amanti. Figure della lirica amorosa fra Dante e Petrarca.* Bologna: Il Mulino, 1999.

Singleton, Charles S. *An Essay on the "Vita Nuova."* 1949. Reprint, Cambridge: Harvard University Press, 1958.

Valency, Maurice. *In Praise of Love.* New York: Macmillan, 1961.

Language and the craft of literature

De vulgari eloquentia

> Le poète se consacre . . . à définir et à construire un langage dans le langage.
>
> —Paul Valéry, *Variété: Situation de Baudelaire*

The title *Eloquence in the Vernacular* is tantalizing. Unfortunately, this Latin treatise, written by the greatest poet of the European Middle Ages, was left unfinished. In *Convivio* 1.5.10, after commenting on the mutability of vernacular languages as opposed to the essential stability of Latin, Dante states his intention of writing a book "on vernacular eloquence." This remark, together with the mention in *De vulgari* 1.12.5 of Marquis Giovanni of Monferrato as still alive, suggests that the work was composed c. 1304–5. Possibly drafted in Bologna during the first years of Dante's exile, the unfinished treatise is symptomatic of a strikingly analytical, reflective phase in the poet's career.

Like his *Convivio, De vulgari eloquentia* represents a critical summing-up of Dante's poetic performance, offering virtually no hint of the poetic development to come that was to give birth to the *Comedy*. Both works were intended to rescue the exile's reputation from the unjust accusations leveled against him in Florence and to prove to his fellow Italians how wise and knowledgeable he had become. A world of encyclopedic learning separates these works from the early *Vita Nova*. Their complementary nature may also be seen in the fact that

De vulgari eloquentia was intended (at least in part) to illustrate Dante's masterly technique in the field of lyric poetry, while *Convivio* set out to justify the subject matter of his great canzoni. Form is paramount in the one, content in the other. Both works are instrumental in fashioning the exile's political thought. The Latin treatise is concerned with the creation of an "illustrious" vernacular in Italy, such as the one found in the works of poets at the imperial court of Frederick II at Palermo; in the fourth book of *Convivio,* the necessity of a *universal* "Roman" empire captures the writer's imagination for the first time. Neither work was brought to completion.

The first book of *De vulgari eloquentia* (which was intended to comprise four books) is complete, but the second breaks off at the fourteenth chapter, in midsentence. In book 1, which deals with certain linguistic phenomena, Dante declares that he will examine all levels of style and language, from the most exalted down to that "of a single family." How far he had worked out the details of such a comprehensive analysis, we cannot say. Book 2 deals with the noblest poetic style. Book 3 would probably have extended this analysis to prose—and it is regrettable that we shall never know what this would have revealed about Dante's prose, at a time when the author of *Convivio* was engaged in creating a new literary language by composing the first *great work* of Italian prose. Book 4, as the writer assures us on four occasions, would have dealt with the comic style, the intermediate level in the medieval canon. For our understanding of Dante's ideas about literary composition and his own technique, the loss is incalculable.

The work opens with the grand flourish found later at the beginning of *Monarchia* and *Paradiso,* for Dante was never bashful about asserting his originality. "No one before us," he asserts, has written about eloquence in the vernacular, although its use is so essential to everyone, including even women and children, who strive to attain it "as far as nature allows." Of all Dante's works *De vulgari eloquentia* is the one in which he has the least recourse to "authorities," although a number of manuals had appeared on the "correct" way to write poetry (e.g., Raimon Vidal's *Razos de trobar,* c. 1200),[1] and Brunetto Latini had composed his *Rettorica,* an unfinished translation of and commentary on Cicero's *De inventione.* Now, inspired by God's Word "breathing down from heaven," Dante sets out to enlighten all those who "wander about like blind persons through the public squares," offering them the fruits of his own learning but also adding the wisdom of others to produce "the sweetest hydromel" (*DVE* 1.1.1). The future author of the *Comedy* already manifests his desire in both *Convivio* and *De vulgari eloquentia* to enlighten the greatest possible number of persons, without distinction of class or sex—including (in *Convivio*) all those hitherto abandoned or ignored by the elitist Latin culture of the age. It is therefore ironic that this work on vernacular eloquence was in fact written in Latin. However, since its author wished to have his credentials accepted in learned circles, he was clearly obliged to make a linguistic choice utterly at variance with the democratic flourish of his opening sentence.

The vernacular versus Latin (grammar)

There follows the equally paradoxical assertion that the vernacular tongue is nobler than Latin, since the vernacular is common to all peoples and because it was the first language used by humankind. It is, moreover, the product of nature (God's child) rather than of human skill. Dante defines vernacular languages as those "we acquire without any rules by imitating our nurse" (1.1.2). However, this communality must be paid for in terms of fragmentation (and the future author of the *Comedy* was only too aware of the heavy price paid). As a remedy, there exists "another, secondary language, which the Romans called 'grammar.' This secondary language is also possessed by the Greeks and others, but not by everyone; and few succeed in mastering it, for it requires assiduous study over a long period" (1.1.3).

The opposition grammar/vernacular was to persist for a long time to come in Western Europe, and "grammar" as a synonym for Latin gave its name to the grammar schools established in sixteenth-century England. In *De vulgari eloquentia,* however, the matter is more complex, for Dante conceives of grammar primarily as a remedy invented by human ingenuity to combat the fatal flaw in language after Babel, its mutability in both space and time: "This was what inspired the inventors of the art of grammar, which is nothing but a certain identity of speech, unchanged by either time or place" (1.9.11). Freed from individual caprice, this secondary language is invariable; it therefore makes it possible for future generations and even those who speak a different tongue to gain access to "the opinions and exploits of the ancients, as well as those who are different from ourselves because they live in different places" (1.9.11).

The vernacular's greater nobility derives from the fact that it was the natural, Edenic language, God's gift to the human race. This idea, however, contradicts Dante's argument in *Convivio* 1.5.14, where he justifies his decision to write a commentary in the vernacular on his Italian poems precisely on the grounds of Latin's greater nobility and the incongruity that would have resulted if it had been made to "serve" the vernacular. In that same chapter the author refers to his intention of writing a book on vernacular eloquence. It therefore seems likely that *De vulgari eloquentia* was begun after this section of *Convivio* was written and that it represents a further development in Dante's approach to resolving the dilemma: Italian or Latin?[2]

The choice was a difficult one. On the one hand, Latin was the universal language of the educated elite in Western and Central Europe (and few outside of that elite could read at all). Its audience was in some ways comparable to that of present-day English, transcending national boundaries. By no stretch of the imagination could it be described as a dead language. Indeed, Latin enjoyed an unparalleled literary tradition and international presence as the language of law and philosophy, church and state. All these factors must have been present in Dante's mind when, in the first book of *Convivio,* he asserted the greater nobility of Latin. Its ability to express the finest nuances of thought and feeling and its efficiency as an intellectual tool are subsumed in the affirmation of its greater beauty and power, for Latin follows art while the vernacular follows usage (*Conv.* 1.5.14). It is in fact surprising to note how long it took before a grammatical norm was established for the vernacular. In the case of Italian, it was not until the fifteenth century that a set of grammatical rules was compiled, and not until the sixteenth century that this example was multiplied and the codification of Italian vernaculars systematically attempted.

The terms "grammar" and "Latin" become interchangeable in Dante's text. As we shall see, in Dante's view, Latin was never the natural language of the Romans; it was not for him (as it is for us) the root of the Romance languages. And, if the superiority of Latin (as affirmed in *Convivio* 1) is based on its unchanging nature and especially its adherence to the rules of art, in *De vulgari eloquentia* it is precisely this artificiality that is emphasized and downgraded. In *Convivio,* the vernacular was seen as following the vagaries of usage. In *De vulgari,* on the other hand, the vernacular is hailed as the product of nature, itself God's child, whereas art—by definition, the imitation of *nature*—is at one further remove from the Creator. Another paradox involving *De vulgari eloquentia* lies in the fact that it is, despite differences, faithful to the overall spirit of *Convivio,* and in particular to the theory of nobility as the perfection of a natural gift, expounded in the fourth book. Dante's passionate belief in the potential glories of the Italian language, which had inspired his decision to write a vernacular treatise on philosophy (hitherto the monopoly of Latin, Greek, and Arabic), is now allied to a theoretical vindication of its nobler origin—although, as we have noted, the effective cultural superiority of Latin culture obliged Dante to write this treatise on vernacular eloquence in Latin. Ironically, while the treatise composed in the vernacular asserts the superiority of Latin, the one written in Latin proclaims the superiority of the vernacular.

Dante and the *Modistae*

On the assumption that *De vulgari eloquentia* was composed in Bologna, Maria Corti (1992) has pointed out the significance of the presence in that city of scholars such as Gentile da Cingoli, who were influenced by the new conception of grammar propounded by the *Modistae*.[3] The latter derived their name from the expression *modi significandi,* indicating a grammatical category used by them to account for linguistic phenomena. For the *Modistae,* grammar dealt with universals, elements common to all languages. The latter differ in the way they express such universals: to a large extent, grammar is thus seen as the linguistic potential or faculty possessed by the human race, which is then actualized in various ways through the "accidents" of the signifying *vox,* or word in any given language. Dante seems to have been stimulated by one or two aspects of the new approach to speculative grammar, but (as so often) he used them selectively. For example, the "inventors of the art of grammar" (*DVE* 1.9.11: *inventores gramatice facultatis*) are—in theory, at least—to be distinguished from the "makers of grammar" (1.10.1: *gramatice positores*). The "inventors" (philosophers, for the *Modistae*) discovered Grammar as a remedy to combat linguistic mutability, whereas the "makers" set about creating and formulating the constituent elements of the various grammatical languages (Latin, Greek, Hebrew). Despite this common ground, it is important to bear in mind the difference between the *Modistae*'s conception of speculative grammar as a scientific framework present in *all* languages and Dante's view of grammar as essentially restricted to a limited number of languages regulated by art.[4]

To conclude the first chapter of his scientific treatise on vernacular eloquence, Dante gives three reasons for the vernacular's greater nobility over not only Latin but all grammatical languages. It was the language first used by human beings; it is the one used throughout the inhabitable globe; and—most importantly—"it is natural to us, while the other [grammar] is rather the product of art" (1.1.4). Indeed, Dante's assertion here that the vernacular "is used throughout the world, although split into diverse pronunciations and word-forms" makes the vernacular—*not* his "Grammar"—the equivalent of the universal grammar posited by the *Modistae*.

Language, the hallmark of the human race

In typical medieval fashion, Dante proceeds to give us a brief history of language, starting with universals and descending to the particular. Language is proper to humans alone among all creatures: animals produce only sounds, while angels communicate directly without need of a "physical" language. Human beings alone need a "rational, sensory sign" (1.3.2): signs based on the senses, insofar as they are made up of sounds; rational, because of the meaning they are made to convey. Chapter 4 sets out to determine to whom language was first given; what was the first utterance made by a human being, to whom, where, and when it was addressed; finally, which language was used. Regarding the first question, sexism leads Dante to reject even the evidence of Holy Scripture, according to which "a woman spoke before anyone else," when Eve answered the devil's question, as reported in Genesis 3.1–3. He argues: "Although we find in Scripture that the woman spoke first, it is nevertheless more reasonable to suppose that it was the man who spoke first; and it is unseemly to think that such a noble human act did not proceed from a man rather than from a woman" (1.4.3). Both Adam's words at the sight of Eve and his naming of the animals (Gen. 2.19–23) are ignored by Dante, for whom language evidently meant dialogue and communication. As Barański has pointed out, the first nine chapters of this work, dealing with the vicissitudes of language from the creation of Adam to the tragedy of Babel, illustrate the fundamental link that existed for Dante between the Bible and God's gift of verbal communication by means of a rational sign. Moreover, in these opening chapters: "All that is left of the Biblical account are a few bare bones: the creation of Adam, the temptation by the serpent, and the failure of Babel" (Barański 1989b, 113).

Dante asserts that Adam's first cry must have been *El,* his word for God— but in which language? This question leads Dante to reflect on the parochialism that leads people to esteem their native tongue and birthplace above all others. Dante, exiled and condemned to death by his beloved Florence, proclaims his own conviction, free from all sentimental prejudice:

> But I, who have the world as my native land just as the fish have the sea, although I drank of the River Arno before I cut my teeth and I love Florence so dearly that for love of her I suffer an unjust exile, I base my judgment on reason rather than on feeling. And although for my own pleasure and the satisfaction of my senses there exists no better place on earth than Florence, after reading and rereading the writings of both the poets and other authors . . . I am of the firm opinion that there are nobler and more delightful lands and cities than Tuscany and Florence, of which I am both a native and a citizen, and that many nations and peoples use a language more agreeable and serviceable than the one used by Italians. (*DVE* 1.6.3)

After this moving digression, Dante states that a certain form of language *(certam formam locutionis)* "was created by God together with the first soul . . . and precisely this would be used in their language by all speakers [nowadays], if it had not been dispersed through human presumption" (1.6.4). The Aristotelian term *forma* designates the "medium" that actualizes potency. God created in Adam the faculty of giving utterance to a language in which signs and things were essentially connected through this gift, which included the capacity to construct the necessary lexis *(vocabulorum constructionem)* and syntax *(constructionis prolationem)*. Thus, Adam was able to "form" the language of grace, Hebrew *(hebraicum idyoma),* which the lips of the first speaker "made" or enunciated *(quod primi loquentis labia fabricarunt).*[5] This was the language used by Adam and all his descendants until the building of the Tower of Babel. After God punished its builders by sowing confusion among them, Adam's language was retained by the Hebrews, so that Christ might use the language "not of confusion, but of grace" (1.6.6), a belief in accordance with, for example, Augustine's *De civitate Dei* 16.11 and Rhabanus Maurus's *Commentary on Genesis* 2.11. All other languages after Babel are composed of arbitrary signs *(ad placitum:* 1.3.3, 1.9.6).

Adam's pronouncements in *Paradiso* 26 expressly contradict this section of *De vulgari eloquentia* on two essential points. Hebrew was *not* the original language "created" by Adam (which had in fact become extinct before Babel: *Par.* 26.124–26). Indeed, Dante warrants special mention in any history of linguistics for the fact that in that same canto (ll. 127–32) he makes Adam insist on the essential mutability inherent in *all* languages. This view of language as constantly changing from the very beginning of the human race, even before Babel ("Confusion"), was a truly revolutionary idea, expressed in the "sacred poem" and utterly opposed to the earlier thesis that Adam's language, Hebrew, remained unchanged after Babel in order that it might serve Christ in his work as Redeemer. The supreme proof of linguistic change is found in the name for God, which was *El (DVE* 1.4.4). According to authorities such as St. Jerome and Isidore of Seville, *El* was the primary name for God in Hebrew. However, in *Paradiso* 26.133–38, Adam asserts that in his original language God's name was *I* (signifying unity and perfection), but that it was later replaced by the Hebraic *El.*

Babel and its aftermath

It would be difficult to exaggerate the importance of Babel in Dante's view of history. He calls it a third rebellion, brought about by humanity's insatiable pride, after those that had led to the expulsion from Eden and the Flood. The tempter, this time, was Nimrod, "a mighty hunter before the Lord" (Gen. 10.9). Augustine had understood this biblical passage to refer to a giant, and the legend that Nimrod the giant had supervised the building of the Tower of Babel was current throughout the Middle Ages. Taking his cue perhaps from Genesis 11.8, Dante adds a picturesque and profoundly significant detail: namely, that a different (and mutually unintelligible) language was given as a punishment to each craft or profession (architects, stonecutters, bricklayers, et al.) according to a divinely inspired ratio—the greater the skill, the more barbaric the idiom (1.7.7). Here, we find for the first time in Dante's writings the principle of *contrapasso*, namely, that the punishment should reflect the nature and gravity of the sin, a concept that became one of the criteria for Dante's ordering of punishment in hell and purification in purgatory (cf. *Inf.* 28.142). As a medieval Florentine, the idea that groups of workers or guilds received mutually incomprehensible languages would have struck Dante as leading to the ultimate collapse of the polis. In the *Comedy*, Nimrod is assigned to the pit of hell (*Inf.* 31.43–81). As the instigator of linguistic confusion (Babel), he is utterly isolated from the other giants and sinners by his inability to comprehend any "rational" language and by his gibberish, which is "the parodic image of the Psalms" and the antithesis of Pentecost (Hollander 1992b). What was to become another characteristic feature of the *Comedy* is foreshadowed in the author's invocation or "appeal" to his readers: "See, reader *[Ecce, lector]*, how humankind . . . rose up for the third time to provoke the lashes through its foolish pride and presumption" (*DVE* 1.7.3).

Dante's predilection for the number three is evident in the next chapter, when he states that the men and women who came westward to Europe brought with them "a threefold idiom" (1.8.2): one language, which gave rise to those developed by three different peoples, with the Germanic in the north, the Greeks on the eastern borders, and those in the south who subsequently developed three separate languages, each characterized by the word for *yes*: "some say *oc*, some say *oïl*, and others say *sí*" (1.8.5). The common origin of these languages (which was *not* Latin, according to Dante) is attested by the fact that they use the same words for many things: for example, "God," "sky," "love." Clearly, those who say *oïl* are the French, those who say *sí* are Italians, and those who use *oc* for the affirmative are called Spaniards (cf. 2.12.3), although the area where this language is spoken is broadly identified as "the western part of southern Europe, beginning at the Genoese border" (1.8.6). Although Brunetto Latini had been to Spain, Dante seems to have had no real knowledge of Spanish; his conflation of Spanish and Provençal may possibly have been due to the fact that, in medieval times, at the University of Bologna Spanish students were classified as members of the "Provençal *natio.*" It is worth noting that, if Dante had believed Latin to be the common ancestor of his tripartite family of "Romance" languages, it would have been logical for him to name it at this point. Instead, conscious that he is sailing across uncharted waters, he tackles the problem of how this single language became fragmented. Anonymity thus remains the hallmark of the source of the "Romance" languages (1.9.2).

The mutability of language: "Grammar" as an artificial remedy

Dante is bent on emphasizing the mutability of all "natural" languages, an inevitable consequence of the unstable nature of human beings (cf. Dante's surprising admission in *Par.* 5.98–99). This obsession with linguistic change is one of the most striking features of Dante's artistic makeup. Both space and time create immense difficulties for the writer striving to communicate with other members of the human race. While linguistic variety is a self-evident fact, Dante is exceptional in pointing out the inevitability of diachronic linguistic change. In fact, time is perhaps the greater enemy, for "if the ancient citizens of Pavia were now brought back to life, they would speak a language unlike, or completely different from, the one spoken by its modern inhabitants" (1.9.7; cf. *Conv.* 1.5.9).[6] This chapter brings to a close the history of language from its original, prelapsarian unity to its contemporary state of diversity, fragmentation, and constant change.

Since it is safer to proceed along known paths, Dante states that he will deal with what he calls "our own language" (1.9.1): the tongues of Italy, France, and Spain. He reasserts their common origin. This time, the evidence adduced is the key word *amor* (love) as found in poems by Giraut de Bornelh (Provençal), Thibaut IV of Champagne (French), and Guido Guinizzelli (Italian). Dante wonders why the three contemporary languages of *oc, oïl,* and *sí* are internally fragmented. For example, in the Italian peninsula, the speech of Padua in the east differs from that of Pisa, its western counterpart, while even neighboring cities (such as Milan and Verona, Rome and Florence) and people with the same origins (the inhabitants of Naples and Gaeta, or of Ravenna and Faenza) have different dialects—"and, what is even more amazing, so do even those who live in the same city, such as the Bolognese who reside in Borgo San Felice and the Bolognese who live in Strada Maggiore" (1.9.5). The cause, he decides, lies in the fact that human beings are "most unstable and changeable animals"; hence their language, like their customs and manners, gradually but inexorably changes in both space and time. This insistence on the varieties of language found within a single region or city prepares the way for Dante's assertion that it was precisely in order to counteract the effects of natural linguistic change and fragmentation that Grammar was invented: "this grammar is nothing but a certain form of language which is identical and unchanged in different times and places" (1.9.11).

If we bear in mind Dante's intention to focus on "our language" (and—it is important to stress—his conviction that Latin was not the source but rather the *product* of the Romance group of languages), we may not be surprised by the fact that the legislators for Latin *(gramatice positores)* chose "*sic* as the adverb of affirmation" is deemed by him to confer "a certain pre-eminence on the Italians, who say *sí*" (1.10.1). French can boast that "because it is the easiest and most pleasing vernacular tongue [cf. Brunetto Latini's *Tresor* 1.7], whatever has been translated into or composed in vernacular prose belongs to it," while the *langue d'oc,* or Provençal, can claim that "eloquent users of the vernacular first used it for poetry as the sweetest and most perfect language." Nevertheless, Dante asserts the superiority of Italian on two counts: those who have written the sweetest and most subtle poems in the vernacular—such as Cino da Pistoia and "his friend" (Dante himself)—are its intimate friends and ministers; furthermore, "they seem to keep most closely to Grammar, which is shared by all, a point which, if considered rationally, is seen to be a most weighty argument" (1.10.2). He defers any further comparative assessment at this point, turning instead to an examination of the Italian vernacular.

The regional languages of Italy

As the first known Italian dialectologist, Dante correctly observes that dialects in Italy are divided into two groups. Looking southward from the vantage point of the Alps, Italy is divided into its right (western) and left (eastern) sides by the backbone of the Apennines, which acts as a watershed (cf. Lucan *Pharsalia* 2.396–410). With remarkable scientific rigor for his times (and perforce limited to personal experience), he goes on to identify fourteen major dialect regions, although he points out that if an exhaustive survey were made (including differences apparent in the speech of the same town, as he had noted in Bologna), "we should find that in this tiny corner of the world the varieties of speech not only add up to one thousand but even exceed this figure" (1.10.7).

After reaching the perfect number with chapter 10, in the next nine chapters Dante sets out to "hunt" for Italy's most "illustrious" vernacular (whose existence is taken for granted). According to medieval Christian thinkers, unity was supremely desirable, since it reflected the structure of the universe and its Creator. Thus, both practical and theoretical reasons inspired Dante in his search for one sovereign vernacular language throughout the length and breadth of Italy.

He begins by eliminating various pretenders to the title (chapters 11–15). Rome comes first, since the Romans claim precedence in all things; their speech, however, is nothing but a base jargon and the ugliest of all the Italian dialects, "which is hardly surprising, since it reflects the depravity of their customs and manners that makes them stink worse than all the others" (1.11.2). Dante's experience of the comic style is now brought into play as proof of their *tristilo-quium:* "they say, *Messure, quinto dici?* [Sir, what are you saying?]," where we note the Romans' use of the familiar "tu" form even with persons of rank (cf. *Par.* 16.10–11).

After this caricature of Roman speech, the other dialects get short shrift: every trick of the writer's trade is used to parody both the written and the spoken languages of the various regions. Dante's prejudices as a citizen of Florence help him to dismiss out of hand the speech of "the mountains and the countryside." The Sardinians are not even Italians, for "they alone seem to be without any dialect of their own, since they imitate Latin *[gramaticam . . . imitantes]* as apes do men" (1.11.7). On the other hand, the arrogance of the Tuscans incites Dante to lash out at their presumption, and the Florentines are placed first among the Tuscans, to be chastised for using such forms as *manicare* for *mangiare* (to eat) and *introcque* (meanwhile)—although these condemned words will appear in the *Comedy*'s omnivorous text (*Inf.* 33.60 and 20.130). In spite of these failings, some Tuscans have indeed demonstrated "their knowledge of the excellent vernacular: namely, Guido [Cavalcanti], Lapo, and another [Dante himself], all Florentines, and Cino of Pistoia" (1.13.4).

Of all the contenders, Sicilians have a greater claim than any other, "both because whatever poetry is written by Italians is called Sicilian and because many masters who are natives of Sicily have composed weighty poems" (1.12.2). Two points must be made: on the one hand, all early Italian poetry could be referred to as "Sicilian" (e.g., in Jofré de Foixà's *Regles de trobar*); on the other, Dante evidently read the works of the Sicilian poets in Tuscanized versions (which undoubtedly influenced his linguistic and aesthetic judgment of those poems). He asserts that Sicily's artistic renown survives as a terrible reproach to the present-day rulers of Italy, who are the very opposite of "those illustrious heroes, Frederick Caesar and his well-born son Manfred, who displayed the nobility and righteousness of their souls, and—as long as Fortune allowed—they pursued human values, disdaining all that is bestial" (1.12.4—cf. Ulysses' stirring call to his crew in *Inf.* 26.118–20; Frederick was to be placed among the heretics in hell [*Inf.* 10.119]; Manfred, in purgatory [*Purg.* 3.103–45]). Because of this supreme example, whatever was produced by "the noblest Italian spirits first saw the light at the court of these sovereigns"; and, since Sicily was the center of royal power, "whatever our predecessors wrote in the vulgar tongue was called 'Sicilian,' a name we accept and which our successors will be unable to change." All this is in utter contrast to the evil example set by Italy's present rulers, who only encourage murderers, hypocrites, and all "the followers of avarice" (1.12.5). Chapters 11–12 can assist us in charting the development of Dante's political thought. His praise of Frederick II—and, more especially, of his "well-born" son Manfred (in the face of Guelph insistence on the latter's bastardy)—is a pointer to a truly Ghibelline phase in the early years of his exile from Florence, which was soon to be tempered by his discovery of the essential role played by the empire of Rome in God's providential plan, a vision first apparent in *Convivio* 4.4–5 (c. 1306–7).

Dante reserves a surprising accolade for the speech of the inhabitants of Bologna, based on what he refers to as its "praiseworthy sweetness." Nevertheless, it must not be mistaken for the illustrious vernacular—this truth may be seen in the poems of Guido Guinizzelli and other Bolognese poets, who, as "illustrious masters and good judges of the vernacular," chose words "very different" from those used in their birthplace (1.15.6). In this same passage, the reference to poets as *doctores illustres* (illustrious masters) is a foreshadowing of the role assigned to Virgil in the *Comedy*. From the time when he began to write his moral canzoni, Dante's promotion of the didactic function of poetry appears as one of the important examples of *littérature engagée*—of which his *De vulgari eloquentia* is the first manifesto.

The illustrious vernacular

Having scoured the Italian peninsula, Sicily, and Sardinia, and having rejected all regional and local candidates, Dante is still unable to track down the elusive "panther" he has been hunting. According to medieval bestiaries, the panther was friendly to other animals; its fragrant breath drew beasts to its lair. The image of the panther is fitting, for the illustrious vernacular draws all noble spirits toward it, while its "fragrance is in every town, although it abides in none" (1.16.1). The author's Aristotelian training encourages him to seek a common measure, that unity to which all else can be referred. He argues that, despite the lack of political unity in the Italian peninsula, the Italians are "weighed and measured" by certain "habits, customs, and speech" (1.16.3). The linguistic norm for the multitude of Italy's regional dialects is in fact a vernacular that belongs to no single region but is distinguished by its "illustrious, cardinal, aulic, and curial" qualities (1.16.6). It is illustrious because its light raises men up to honor and glory, as well as to its own elevated position above the jungle of dialects: witness "the canzoni of Cino da Pistoia and his friend" (1.17.3). The champions of this illustrious vernacular surpass kings and nobles in renown; and Dante closes the chapter on a personal note, claiming that the sufferings of his own exile are cast in the shade by the sweetness afforded by such glory.

The illustrious vernacular is "cardinal," for *cardo* signifies a hinge on which all else revolves; aulic because, if imperial authority existed in contemporary Italy, this would be the language used in the imperial entourage or palace; truly courtly, for this vernacular reflects the usage of the noblest courts as well as the ideal of justice emanating from the courts of law. The absence of the imperial court from Italy is a tragic fact (cf. *Purg.* 6.97–117). Nevertheless, Dante argues that its members exist and only await their leader: "It is therefore untrue to say that the Italians lack a court," for an ideal court does in fact exist, "although it is scattered throughout the body" of the nation, yet united "by the gracious light of reason" (1.18.5). Book 1 ends with the proud assertion that such is in fact the supreme Italian language *(latium vulgare),* used "by all the illustrious masters who have written vernacular poetry in Italy," from Sicily, Apulia, Tuscany, Romagna, and the Marches (1.19.1). In book 2, Dante will set out to define who is worthy of using such language, its manner, subject, and audience.

Book 2

The long introduction is over. Originality was the hallmark of the first book, for which Dante had few guidelines, if any. What we have of book 2 is chiefly concerned with practical questions of poetic technique, based on the principle of *convenientia,* that the style must match the subject matter. If we turn to medieval manuals of rhetoric and poetics, we find that they deal primarily with figures of speech and other ornamentation.[7] One of the remarkable things about *De vulgari eloquentia* is that it ignores such details: its author evidently took them for granted and felt that he had more important matters to discuss and far more to offer his readers. Once again, no models fitted his interests. In the absence of models, Dante sets out to establish an authoritative tradition of his own by illustrating and analyzing the great examples identified by him in the field of the Romance lyric, while at the same time urging his readers to study the Latin tradition—all this, not encased in a system of abstract rules, but inspired by the practice of the greatest writers (an innovation of revolutionary importance, not unlike that of studying anatomy by dissection). In doing this, Dante turns most frequently to Provençal and Italian poets, only rarely to the French, and he has nothing to say about the first great flowering of troubadour poetry from Guilhem IX (1071–1127) to Bernard de Ventadorn (c. 1150–95).

Book 2 opens with the claim that the illustrious Italian vernacular may be used for both prose and for verse. In the first book of his *Convivio,* Dante had just announced that the accoutrements of poetry may constitute an obstacle for the expression of philosophical and moral truths (*Conv.* 1.10.12). In *De vulgari* 2.1.1, he nevertheless follows tradition in claiming "a certain primacy" for verse as a model for prose writers in the vernacular. In noting this apparent contradiction, we should bear in mind that it would have been impossible for Dante to find examples of illustrious Italian prose comparable to the best vernacular lyric poems.

Who may use the illustrious vernacular, and for which subjects?

At first, it might seem that all who write poetry should use the most illustrious language. This is not the case, however, and even the greatest poets should not use it in all circumstances. Dante demonstrates his originality as both artist and rhetorician by rejecting the typically medieval conception of beauty as consisting largely in complexity and ornamentation. Instead, he insists on the fundamental concept of compatibility *(convenientia):* "embellishment is the addition of something appropriate" (2.1.9).[8] Consequently, not every poet should use the illustrious vernacular, which must be accepted as the monopoly of those who excel in "both knowledge and talent," whereas most vernacular versifiers do not possess either of these essential qualities (2.1.8).

Likewise, the noblest language must only be used for the noblest themes. In order to identify these, Dante reminds us that human beings are made up of three parts: the vegetable part seeks what is useful, the animal what is pleasurable, and the rational what is good. This gives us a triad of noble themes: survival and well-being *(salus);* love *(venus);* virtue *(virtus).* By ignoring Guittone d'Arezzo's poetry (e.g., his great canzone lamenting the defeat of the Florentine Guelphs at the battle of Montaperti, *Ahi lasso, or è stagion de doler tanto*), Dante is able to claim that no Italian has yet written about war and well-being. Instead, the example he offers is that of the troubadour Bertran de Born (later condemned to hell by Dante—*Inferno* 28.133–42—for fomenting discord between Henry of England and his son, as well as for his abuse of his poetic gifts in inciting others to constant hostility and warfare). Most unexpectedly, the Italian cited for his achievement in the field of love poetry *(venus)* is Cino da Pistoia (c. 1270–c. 1336), whereas Dante reserves for himself the title of the Italian "poet of rectitude" *(virtus),* quoting the canzone written in the first years of his exile, *Doglia mi reca ne lo core ardire,* as the outstanding example in this category. Arnaut Daniel *(L'aura amara)* is singled out as the foremost Provençal singer of love; the troubadour Giraut de Bornelh *(Per solaz reveilar),* his contemporary, is hailed as the singer of rectitude.[9]

The canzone as poetic vehicle for the illustrious vernacular

Next, Dante announces that the noblest—and thus the only suitable—poetic form for the illustrious vernacular is the ode, or canzone. Following the hierarchy reflected in medieval collections of poems, Dante ranks the sonnet below *ballate* and the latter below canzoni in dignity and excellence. He points out that *ballate* need the cooperation of dancers "for whom they are composed," whereas canzoni fulfill the poet's purpose "on their own" (2.3.5)—a judgment that sanctions the divorce between poetry and music that had already occurred in thirteenth-century Italian verse, although the theoretical link was maintained. The supremacy of the canzone is proved by the fact that "although whatever is written in verse is a canzone [song]," the word itself signifies only this particular form of poem. Dante's belief that names reveal the true essence of things (*VN* 13.4) underlies this claim that the canzone is the supreme form in vernacular poetry. Canzoni bring greater fame to their authors and they are preserved more carefully than any other type of poem. Finally, proof of their pre-eminence is the fact that only canzoni cover every aspect of the art of poetry (2.3.8). Hence, the greatest works of the greatest poets are all in this form (not surprisingly, we may reflect, as the *ballata* and the sonnet were both recent Italian inventions, whereas canzoni had been composed for some two hundred years). We must also remember that everything we read in this section of *De vulgari eloquentia* was composed by a poet who proclaimed himself to be, above all else, the poet of morality and rectitude; sonnets, with their fourteen lines, could not offer the necessary scope for Dante's role as *cantor rectitudinis*.[10]

The canzone

From chapter 4 on, Dante is concerned with the form of the canzone and its constituent elements. First, Dante justifies his use of the term "poets" to describe not only the great Latin poets but also those who write in the vernacular, by stating that poetry is "nothing but a poetic creation [*fictio*] fashioned by rhetoric and music" (2.4.2). This brief definition has given rise to much controversy, chiefly concerned with the interpretation of *fictio*.[11] Poetry is a product of the creative imagination, which uses the powers of both rhetoric and music in order to lead men and women toward a higher reality or truth that can be perceived through poetry's essentially metaphorical techniques (the *modus transumptivus* of *Ep.* 13.9.27). Despite the formal divorce between poetry and music mentioned above, for Dante music was an essential ingredient, since it was an *ars* or intellectual discipline that reflected the order governing the entire universe *(musica mundana),* which should also regulate human nature *(musica humana).* In troubadour poetry, the text and its musical accompaniment were usually crafted for each other by the poet, although in practice a considerable degree of autonomy was allowed. In Italy, which had no secular musical tradition comparable to that of France, the relationship became less intimate, although the link is still stressed in Dante's treatise, where "music" refers to both the intonation and the accompaniment of poems by a professional musician (cf. *Purg.* 2.106–17), as well as to the general harmony created by word sounds and verse rhythms, which can have such a profound effect on the human soul (*Conv.* 2.13.24).[12] Poetry's final purpose is thus achieved with the help of rhetoric and music, the latter implying a rational ordering of sensuous effects and the creation of harmony reflecting that of the cosmos and of divine truth.

Dante then singles out the essential difference between the great poets of antiquity and the majority of those who write in the vernacular. The former obeyed the rules of art, whereas vernacular poetry has been written "according to chance"; hence, "the more closely we imitate the former, the better we shall know how to write poetry" (2.4.3). Readers of *Inferno* will doubtless think of the extraordinary tribute paid to Vergil in *Inferno* 1.79–87, when Dante claims that it was owing to his immense love and long study of Vergil's poetry that he had acquired "the beautiful style that has brought me honor." For a modern reader, it is difficult to grasp how Dante could find such a close parallel between widely different poetic techniques: the ancient tradition based on vowel quantity, on the one hand, and, on the other, poetry composed in the vernacular, with its syllabic stress and rhymes, influenced, moreover, by a tradition of Courtly Love unknown to the ancient world. It is surely obvious that what Dante meant by study and imitation was something far removed from the servile copying that moderns who prize originality above all else tend to associate with the word "imitation." Instead, the study of the great writers of the past must encourage individuals to achieve their full potential.

The noblest style

Poets must also take into consideration the limitations imposed by their own powers and the subject matter chosen. They will then select the most apt of three styles: "tragic," "comic," or "elegiac." Only the most elevated is worthy of the canzone, the illustrious vernacular, and its noble themes: the tragic style, as opposed to the inferior comic style and, the lowest style of all, the elegiac.[13] To grasp the significance of this triad, we must remember that tragedy and comedy as dramatic genres had died out with pagan antiquity, and that they were not to be reborn until the Renaissance. As used in *De vulgari eloquentia* (but cf. *Ep.* 13.10.29–31), the terms "tragic" and "comic" have little to do with a poem's subject matter. Instead, they indicate different steps in a stylistic hierarchy. If the subject requires the tragic style, then the illustrious vernacular must be chosen; consequently, the canzone is the form to be used. On the other hand, if the comic style is required, then the median style must be used in some places and, in others, the humble style. Dante states his intention of clarifying various essential stylistic criteria in book 4, which would have shed more light on what he meant by the comic style (2.4.6)—if only he had completed his treatise and thus saved us endless conjecture and polemics.

As it is, *De vulgari eloquentia* is a fragmentary work devoted exclusively (but not exhaustively) to the noblest, tragic style; it lacks the sections intended for an analysis of its humbler partners in the stylistic scale. What we have is both frustrating and fascinating. In what remains of book 2, Dante concentrates on the canzone and its concomitant "tragic" style that must serve the noble triad of "well-being, love, and virtue." The formal recipe contains the following ingredients: "magnificence of poetic line, elevated constructions, and verbal excellence" (2.4.7). Dante treats each of these in turn, in chapters 5 to 7. Before embarking on this task, however, he underscores the need for intellectual rigor, allied to technical and cultural expertise—those qualities possessed by great poets.

Dante now scrutinizes the merits of the various measures in vernacular verse, noting that its practitioners have used lines that vary from three to eleven syllables in length. Supremacy is accorded to the hendecasyllable on account of its ideal duration and its ability to accommodate complex structures and themes. Claiming that the greatest poets have all recognized this truth, Dante cites the opening line of a *canso* by Giraut de Bornelh *(Ara ausirez encabalitz cantarz),* explaining that this verse, while appearing to have only ten syllables, is in fact a hendecasyllable by virtue of its two final consonants, which count as a separate syllable, even as apocopation counts for two syllables, producing the form *bonté* from Latin *bonitatem* (cf. Italian *bontade > bontà*) in the opening line of a poem by Thibaut IV (count of Champagne and Brie, who became king of Navarre in 1234), *De fin amor si vient sen et bonté* (2.5.4). The hendecasyllable is more obviously illustrated in the works of Italian poets, including Guido Guinizzelli's famous love manifesto *Al cor gentil re[m]pa[i]ra sempre amore,* and Dante's own *Amor, che movi tua vertú da cielo.*[14] Verses with an even number of syllables are rejected out of hand because of their "uncouth" nature. This preference for odd numbers is typical of the Pythagorean-Christian tradition, according to which the even numbers from 2 to 8 needed the number 1 (symbolizing Form, the Godhead, and Cosmic Unity) in order to achieve the special significance found in 3 (the Trinity), 9 (its square—cf. *VN* 29.3), 5 (half of the perfect number 10, which closes the circle), and 7 (the gifts of the Holy Spirit, the churches in Asia Minor, the planets in the heavens). It must therefore have been with delight that Dante read in his beloved pagan poet the statement that "the divinity rejoices in an odd number" (Vergil *Eclogues* 8.75; cf. *DVE* 1.16.5).

Chapter 6 deals with the type of construction best suited to the noblest style. Four levels of sentence construction are illustrated. The simplest is shown in the statement "Peter greatly loves Dame Bertha." The next up the scale, "used by pedantic scholars and teachers," is—surprisingly—an example reflecting the writer's personal tragedy: "More than anyone, I am moved to pity for all those who, languishing in exile, can revisit their fatherland only in a dream." The third uses mordant irony in its praise of the marquis of Este's "judgment" and the "magnificence that make him loved by all" (cf. the condemnation of this same tyrant in *Inf.* 12.111–12, *Purg.* 5.77–78, 20.79–81). In the fourth example, the monopoly of "illustrious authors," Dante displays the complex ornamentations of the Latin style most admired in thirteenth-century Italy: "After the majority of your flowers *[florum]* had been wrenched from your breast, o Florence *[Florentia]*, in vain did the second Totila journey to Sicily *[Trinacriam]*" (2.6.4).[15] Once again, Dante's involvement in Florentine politics inspires him to illustrate this supreme level of sentence construction with a scathing reference to Charles of Valois as a second Totila, leader of the Ostrogoths and destroyer of the flourishing City of Flowers *(Florentia)*.

After this singular example of Latin prose, Dante clinches his point by citing poems by no fewer than six troubadours and five Italian poets, including his own *Amor che ne la mente mi ragiona*.[16] An interesting comment follows this impressive list: "Do not be surprised, reader, if I have called to mind so many authors, for I cannot indicate that construction which I call supreme *except by examples of this sort*" (2.6.7; my emphasis). As already indicated, this approach is typical of Dante's method in *De vulgari eloquentia:* instead of imitating the medieval manuals of poetics with their endless catalogues of tropes, Dante draws upon the living body of poetry, urging his readers to learn from concrete examples that his personal judgment selects for their edification. That this is an eminently personal selection is evidenced by the fact that nine (always a significant Dantean number) of the poet's own canzoni are cited for their excellence in *De vulgari eloquentia*. Next among the eighteen other poets whose works are cited come Giraut de Bornelh and Guido Guinizzelli (with four poems each). Dante also claims that much may be learned about this supreme type of construction by studying the greatest classical poets (Vergil, Ovid, Statius, and Lucan), together with the chief exponents of Latin prose (Livy, Pliny, Frontinus, Orosius, and "many others"). The list of prose writers contains some strange bedfellows: in its stark technicality, Frontinus's style is diametrically opposed to ornate thirteenth-century Latin prose, as taught in Italian schools and practiced in chancelleries. The omissions are even more startling; for example, Seneca, Boethius, and Cicero—especially the last two, in view of *Convivio* 2.12.2–3, where Dante tells us that he had begun to read them soon after Beatrice's death in 1290, as well as *Convivio* 2.15.1, where they are hailed as masters of rhetoric.

The appeal to Latin models is certainly unexpected. It may be regarded as further evidence of Dante's alienation from Guido Cavalcanti, the "first friend," for whom he had composed his *Vita Nova* in the vernacular (*VN* 30.3). Now, the future poet of the *Comedy,* who was to engage in constant discourse with his Latin forerunners, derides those who are foolish enough to place their trust "only in their native wit" (*DVE* 2.4.11). Instead, the art of poetry requires three things: intellectual depth, technical skill, and constant study. In his *Aeneid* (6.129–31), Vergil called the happy few who possess these qualities "the children of God," raised up to heaven by their ardent virtue and power. Hence, Dante thunders, let those who are mere geese desist from "trying to emulate the star-seeking eagle *[astripetam aquilam]*." *Astripetam* is almost certainly Dante's own creation—and it may well serve as an apt description of the poet of the *Comedy,* especially when conjoined with God's bird, the eagle (*Par.* 6.4), the only creature capable of looking straight into the sun (*Par.* 20.31–32), a symbol of the divine in creation (*Conv.* 3.12.7).

Lexis

Dante next (*DVE* 2.7) tackles the choice of words appropriate to the canzone's noble style, classifying them primarily on the basis of their phonic qualities as "childish," "feminine," "manly," "sylvan," and "urban" (urbane). This last group is further divided into those that appear (in terms typical of the Florentine wool trade) "well-combed and smooth," on the one hand, and "shaggy and unkempt," on the other. "Smooth" and "unkempt" words are to be avoided, leaving the "well-combed" and "shaggy": these represent the golden mean and "are those I call sublime" (2.7.2). Happily, Dante goes on to define what he means by these terms.

Urbane words that are "well-combed" must have three or "virtually three" syllables. They must not contain an aspirate; they must not have an "acute or circumflex accent" (truncated or abbreviated forms), a *z* or an *x,* "double liquids" *(ll, rr),* or a liquid placed immediately after a mute (e.g., *pr*). Instead, urbane words—such as *amore* (love), *donna* (lady), *disio* (desire), *virtute* (virtue), *donare* (to give), *letitia* (happiness), *salute* (health), *securtate* (safety), *defesa* (defense)—"leave a certain sweetness in the speaker's mouth" (2.7.5). The nine examples given may be grouped under the three themes that belong to the illustrious vernacular: love, virtue, and "arms" or well-being—with *letitia* included, despite the earlier banishing of the *z* (dental + s) sound, perhaps on semantic grounds but probably because of the tendency to pronounce *t* + *yod* as a palatalized *c* (cf. *patrici* [=*patrizi*] in *Par.* 32.116).

"Shaggy" urbane words are either necessary or ornamental. Examples of necessary words are the affirmative *sí* (yes), negative *no* (no), personal pronouns such as *me* (me), and the five vowels, as well as interjections "and many others." Ornamental words possess a certain roughness of accent, double letters, or liquids, as we find in *impossibilità* (impossibility), *speranza* (hope) and other words ending in *-anza* used in the early Italian lyric, *terra* (earth). The cunning juxtaposition of ornamental and well-combed words produces a synergistic harmony, similar to the variety Dante will seek in the rhyme scheme (2.7.6; cf. 2.13.13).

The structure of the canzone

Having dealt with the stylistic elements, Dante now specifies that the term *canzone* (song) signifies the poetic text and not its musical accompaniment or performance. The supreme form of the vernacular lyric is defined as "the ordering together of equal stanzas, without a refrain [or *ritornello*, characteristic of the *ballata*], dealing with a single subject in the tragic style, as I showed when I wrote *Donne che [sic] avete intelletto d'amore*" (2.8.8; cf. *VN* 19, *DVE* 2.12.3, and *Purg.* 24.51). The canzone's fundamental component is the "stanza," so-called because it is truly a *stanza* (room), a microcosm embodying the art of the whole poem. The canzone's artistic effect depends on three things: its melodic division, the arrangement of its various parts, and the number of syllables and lines of verse. All these components, once established in the first stanza, cannot be altered.

The remainder of the treatise as we have it deals with these factors, including a brief consideration of rhyme. Unfortunately, however, Dante decided to postpone a detailed discussion of rhymes in the projected fourth book of his treatise. As for the last part of book 2, in chapter 10 he deals briefly with the musical setting and its influence on the form of the stanza. It is possible, he writes, to find one continuous melody used throughout the poem, as in thirteen of the eighteen extant poems of Arnaut Daniel and in Dante's *Al poco giorno* (a *sestina*, based on Arnaut's *Lo ferm voler*). Most canzoni, however, incorporate *diesis*, a musical term Dante uses to indicate the transition from one melody to another: "there can be no *diesis*, as I use the term, unless a melody is repeated before or after the *diesis*, or both" (2.10.4). If a melody is repeated before the *diesis*, the stanza's divisions are called *pedes* (feet); after the *diesis*, the divisions are called *versus* (verses). If there is no repetition in the first section, it is known as the *frons* (forehead); if the second section is unitary, it is called the *sirma* or *cauda* (tail). Repetitions were, in fact, more common in the Italian canzone, probably because its stanzas tended to be longer and less numerous than those of the Provençal *canso*, where frequent repetition of brief melodic sections had to be avoided. All this, Dante reminds us, only goes to show how much variety and freedom of choice are given to those who write canzoni (2.10.5).

Dante's terminology is so foreign to the modern reader that at least two examples must be given to illustrate his theory and practice:

Section	Portion	*Voi che 'ntendendo*	Repetition	Rhyme
first section	first *pes* (ll. 1–3)	Voi che 'ntendendo il terzo ciel movete,		A
		udite il ragionar ch'è nel mio core,		B
		ch'io nol so dire altrui, sí mi par novo.	/	C
	second *pes* (ll. 4–6)	El ciel che segue lo vostro valore,		B
		gentili creature che voi sete,		A
	concatenatio (ll. 6–7)	mi tragge ne lo stato ov'io mi trovo.	//	C
second section	*sirma* (ll. 7–13)	Onde 'l parlar de la vita ch'io provo		C
		par che si drizzi degnamente a vui:		D
		però vi priego che lo mi 'ntendiate.		E
		Io vi dirò del cor la novitate,		E
		come l'anima trista piange in lui,		D
		e come un spirto contra lei favella,		F
		che vien pe' raggi de la vostra stella.		F

Section	Portion	*Amor che movi tua vertú da cielo*	Repetition	Rhyme
first section	first *pes* (ll. 1–4)	Amor che movi tua vertú da cielo		A
		come 'l sol lo splendore,		b
		che là s'apprende piú lo suo valore		B
		dove piú nobiltà suo raggio trova;	/	C
	second *pes* (ll. 5–8)	e come el fuga oscuritate e gelo,		A
		cosí, alto segnore,		b
		tu cacci la viltate altrui del core,		B
	concatenatio (ll. 8–9)	né ira contra te fa lunga prova:	//	C
second section	*sirma* (ll. 9–15)	da te conven che ciascun ben si mova		C
		per lo qual si travaglia il mondo tutto;		D
		sanza te è distrutto		d
		quanto avemo in potenzia di ben fare,		E
		pintura in tenebrosa parte,		F
		che non si può mostrare		e
		dar diletto di color né d'arte.		F

Like *Donne ch'avete intelletto d'amore*, the canzone *Amor che movi tua vertú da cielo* (obviously another of Dante's favorite lyrics) is cited twice in his *De vulgari eloquentia*. On the first occasion (2.5.4), this prayer to Love is quoted in order to demonstrate that the illustrious poets in the Provençal, French, and Italian traditions have chosen to begin their canzoni with a hendecasyllabic line. The second time Dante mentions *Amor che movi tua vertú da cielo* is to point out that in this canzone the *pedes* outnumber the *sirma* by eight lines to seven, whereas his *Donna pietosa e di novella etate* (*VN* 23) contains a *sirma* composed of eight lines, thus outnumbering the six lines of the *pedes* (*DVE* 2.11.7–8).[17]

A surprising omission from Dante's complex list is the stanza with an equal number of lines and syllables in both *frons* and *sirma*. A number of examples of this type of balanced structure are to be found in the works of the troubadours (including Folquet de Marseille's *Tan m'abellis l'amoros pensamen,* already cited as an example of the noblest style in *DVE* 2.6.6) and Italian poets (e.g., Guinizzelli's *Madonna, il fino amor ched eo vi porto* and Cino da Pistoia's *Quando potrò io dir: Dolce mio Dio*). We may note that in Dante's canzoni, there is an overall tendency for the second part to be longer than the first. Furthermore, in spite of the structural variety found in his canzoni, Dante shows a decided predilection for the tripartite scheme offered by *Amor che movi tua vertú da cielo,* with a first half divided into two *pedes,* followed by an undivided *sirma,* a structure that was to become the norm with Petrarch.

As we have seen, Dante proclaims the hendecasyllable to be the noblest line of verse, used by the greatest vernacular poets in their illustrious canzoni, although a combination of lines with seven and eleven syllables can be used to produce artistic excellence, provided the hendecasyllable remains dominant. Surprisingly, however, in the very next chapter Dante's list of examples illustrating the supreme degree of stylistic construction opens with Giraut de Bornelh's *Si per mos Sobretos non fos* (2.6.6)—a *canso* that does not contain a single line with eleven syllables.[18] Such an anomaly is a striking reminder that Dante never revised this work. Further evidence of this is provided by the fact that in general the second book is written in language that abandons the polished medieval Latin prose of book 1.

The twelfth chapter reiterates the superiority of the hendecasyllable, the true hallmark of the tragic style, and provides examples of its unalloyed use: Cavalcanti's *Donna me prega, perch'eo voglio dire* and Dante's own *Donne ch'avete intelletto d'amore*. Guinizzelli's *Di fermo sofferire* (now lost) is quoted, with other heptasyllabic opening lines, to clinch the point that such lines dilute the tragic style by introducing a certain "elegiac" element (2.12.6). The trisyllabic line is excluded from the tragic style—unless the three syllables form part of a hendecasyllable with *rimalmezzo,* as in Cavalcanti's *Donna me prega* and in Dante's

Poscia ch'Amor del tutto m'ha lasciato (a unique example among his numerous canzoni).

The last complete chapter (2.13) discusses a few rhyme patterns. First, we have the phenomenon known to the troubadours as *coblas dissolutas,* consisting of a stanza without internal rhyme (the rhymes, or rather the rhyme words, being repeated in the other stanzas according to a fixed pattern). Examples given are Arnaut Daniel's *Se·m fos Amor de joi donar* and Dante's *sestina, Al poco giorno.* The opposite phenomenon is found in stanzas built on a single rhyme, for which no example is given. As far as "mixed" rhymes are concerned, poets enjoy the greatest freedom in their choice of rhymes, and this is the feature on which they concentrate, in order to achieve "the sweetness" of overall harmony in their composition (2.13.4). At this point, an otherwise unknown Gotto of Mantua is mentioned, who recited to Dante a number of "good canzoni" he had written, all with a "key line" (2.13.5), that is to say, a line that rhymes with no other in its stanza but then is repeated or made to rhyme in the other stanzas (an effect not uncommon in troubadour poems with their *coblas unissonans,* and one which is also found in a few early Italian lyrics). Most poets, however, do not leave lines unrhymed in the stanza, although they may use different rhymes before and after the *diesis.* When the latter is the case, Dante strongly recommends the custom of making the first line of the second section rhyme with the last of the first, thus creating a "beautiful linking together *(concatenatio pulcra)* of the whole stanza"; *concatenatio* links the end of the first section and the beginning of the *sirma* in both *Voi che 'ntendendo* and *Amor che movi tua vertú da cielo* (see above). Freedom of choice is allowed for the arrangement of rhymes within the *frons* and *sirma,* although a rhyming couplet at the close produces "a most beautiful effect," in that the repeated rhyme brings the canzone to a harmonious conclusion "as the lines glide away into silence" (2.13.8). This was in fact one of Dante's favorite effects, employed in no fewer than sixteen of his canzoni.

Three dangers are to be noted and avoided. The first is excessive use of the same rhyme. Poets writing in the tragic style should also reject the gratuitous use of equivocal rhymes: homonyms and their derivatives, a feature prominent in the poetry of Guittone and his followers but one which always detracts from the poem's effect. Finally, "harsh rhymes" must be banished, "unless they are mingled with gentle-sounding ones, for a mixture of gentle and harsh rhymes adds splendor to the tragic style" (2.13.13). Dante now declares that he has completed the section on the arrangement of the different parts of the canzone (2.13.14). And the treatise itself comes to an abrupt end after a few lines of the fourteenth chapter, in which the question of the number of lines and syllables to be used in a stanza is broached.

Place of composition

As already mentioned, it is highly probable that Dante wrote at least part of *De vulgari eloquentia* in Bologna. His presence in one of the great centers of learning is made likely by a number of circumstances. First, the academic tradition at Bologna's famous university would have made the choice of Latin well-nigh obligatory, even for a treatise on eloquence in the vernacular. Despite the precedents of Brunetto Latini's *Rettorica* and his *Tresor*, Latin was still considered to be the only language suitable for technical subjects: Giles of Rome (Egidio Colonna, c. 1246–1316, in his *De regimine principum* 2.2.7) even maintained that Latin had been invented by philosophers who found vernacular tongues inadequate for expressing the subtleties and complexities of their subject. The fact that Dante decided to break with this tradition in *Convivio,* his philosophical "encyclopedia," and yet apparently interrupted the composition of that work in Italian in order to use Latin in his discussion of vernacular eloquence, only strengthens the likelihood that his choice of language may have been determined by the prestige enjoyed by Latin in academic circles at Bologna. As he makes clear in *Convivio* 1.3.3–5, he was only too conscious of the fact that many misinterpreted his exile and poverty. Moreover, as a self-educated writer, Dante needed all the respectability that an elegant composition in Latin could bring him. He could ill afford to arouse the ingrained prejudices of academics.

The Bolognese tradition boasted such masters of grammar and rhetoric as Boncompagno da Signa (c. 1165–c. 1240) and Guido Fava (c. 1190–c. 1243); the latter, in particular, must have influenced the composition of *De vulgari eloquentia.* For his part, Dante had his own highly original mind and experience, and he was well acquainted with the Latin classics of literary criticism, including Horace's *Ars poetica* and the treatise *Rhetorica ad Herennium,* used by Cicero in his *De inventione.* Dante's work makes frequent references to the writings of the "Sicilian" poets. Their influence was especially strong in Bologna, partly as the result of King Enzo's long imprisonment there (1249–72), when his royal presence and poetic activity helped to keep the Sicilian tradition alive with Guinizzelli (eventually, a Ghibelline exile) and other Bolognese poets. The works of the troubadours were likewise well known in Bologna. It seems very likely that *De vulgari eloquentia* was begun in a place where the exiled poet had access to the writings of a wide range of authors; and the contempt expressed for contemporary rulers in *De vulgari* 1.12.5 makes it unlikely that Dante composed the work while staying at a princely court. Moreover, the lack of specific references to troubadour poetry in the last section (*DVE* 2.7–14), together with the fact that the poem by Giraut de Bornelh cited in *De vulgari* 2.6.6 does not contain a single hendecasyllable, make it tempting to speculate that Dante may by then have left Bologna and thus found himself deprived of manuscript sources.

We must also note the preponderant role played by Cino da Pistoia on the Italian poetic scene, as it is portrayed in *De vulgari eloquentia*. Cino—not mentioned in *Vita Nova*—now replaces Guido Cavalcanti as Dante's "friend." He and Dante alone are quoted in *De vulgari* 1.10.4 as masters of the illustrious vernacular; they—and only they—are cited again in 1.17.3, as exponents of the tragic style, while Cino is acclaimed as the Italian "Poet of Love" in 2.2.9. It is surely significant that Cino was living in Bologna as a fellow exile from 1303 until c. 1306. Another striking feature of Dante's Latin treatise is the detailed knowledge it displays of Bolognese speech and its variations in different parts of the city (1.9.4), as well as the honor paid to it when it is singled out as the finest municipal tongue in Italy, with mention of some of its obscure poets, in 1.15.5–6. Such knowledge is clear evidence of personal experience and would support the conjecture that Dante moved from Verona to Bologna after the death of Bartolomeo della Scala in March 1304.

The work in general

As it stands, *De vulgari eloquentia* is to a large extent a critical summing-up of Dante's poetic career, carried out just before he embarked on the *Comedy*. The treatise is thus typical of the poet's method, whereby theoretical justification always followed poetic practice and marked the end of a phase in his artistic development (as in *Vita Nova* and *Convivio*). In the sections on the illustrious vernacular and its noble "tragic" style, the work illustrates a highly selective, purist moment in the writer's career, at a time when Dante saw himself above all as the poet of ethics and righteousness (2.2.8). Nevertheless, the experience acquired by the poet of love is basic to the whole work. Two canzoni found in *Vita Nova* are cited as examples of the noblest style. As we have seen, *Donne ch'avete intelletto d'amore* is very much at the center of Dante's critical exposition, exemplifying the art of the canzone in *De vulgari* 2.8.8, with its "sweet new style" (*Purg.* 24.49–57) offering a perfect example of the ideal harmony so prized in the Latin treatise. Indeed, of the nine words commended for their "sweetness" in 2.7.5, no fewer than six are found in this poem. Its seventy rhyme words all respect the criteria formulated in this section, and the poem's structure conforms to Dante's strict formula for the canzone form. On the other hand, the tentative, unrevised character of *De vulgari eloquentia* is once again evident in the fact that Dante's allegorical and doctrinal poems do not always measure up to those same criteria: for example, in *De vulgari* 2.12.5 Dante recommends a maximum of five *settenari* to a stanza, whereas *Doglia mi reca* (cited as an example of the tragic style in 2.2.8) has no fewer than nine of these lines in each stanza. When the canzone was written, *Doglia mi reca* was of course intended to show Dante to be the supreme Italian poet of righteousness: its subject matter was therefore all-important at that juncture, overriding every other consideration, including his adherence to the strict rules later elaborated in this treatise.[19]

Critical fortunes

De vulgari eloquentia played a notable role in the notorious "Questione della lingua," the problem of analyzing and defining what constituted standard Italian in a country that was to be politically united only in 1861. Giangiorgio Trissino (1478–1550) was responsible for the work's rediscovery at a time when Italian humanists were beginning their search for an acceptable literary language. He introduced it in debates at the Orti Oricellari in Florence in 1513, and in 1529 he published his own highly tendentious translation into Italian. Reactions were topical and impassioned. Dante's arguments in the first book were seized upon in an attempt to prove that he had been a pioneer of the "courtly language" solution, according to which standard literary Italian was to be based on a highly selective choice of "aristocratic" word-forms taken from various dialects. This linguistic cocktail was rejected by proponents of a radical "Florentine" solution, best reflected in Machiavelli's stimulating *Dialogo sulla lingua* (c. 1514), in which the author berates Dante for betraying his mother tongue, which had served him so well in the *Comedy*. It was likewise opposed to the Golden Age thesis advanced by Pietro Bembo (1470–1547) and other leading humanists, according to which standard literary Italian must be based on a fastidious imitation of fourteenth-century Tuscan authors (especially Petrarch for poetry and Boccaccio for prose).

The first edition of *De vulgari eloquentia,* published in Paris in 1577 by Iacopo Corbinelli, was launched as a counterattack against the linguistic pretensions of the Florentine colony in France. The work continued to provide occasional anti–Florentine/Tuscan ammunition until the nineteenth century, when (in 1868) Alessandro Manzoni declared that Dante's treatise was a work on poetic eloquence and had nothing to do with the problem of the Italian national language. Since then, the work has been left to scholars, who have engaged in endless debate on what Dante meant by his "illustrious vernacular."

De vulgari eloquentia as Dante left it contradicts both Trissino's view that it favored a linguistic hotch-potch and Manzoni's negation that the illustrious vernacular was in any way concerned with language outside the literary domain. The statements in *De vulgari* 1.18.2–3 regarding the illustrious vernacular's home at court and the assertion that "all those who attend royal courts always speak in the illustrious vernacular" are proof both that the illustrious vernacular would have been used in discussions at court concerning grave matters of state and human affairs, and that the author did not wish to limit himself exclusively to literary eloquence. Manzoni's radical attack on the traditional view was, however, a salutary reminder that Dante's primary intention was to discuss "the theory of eloquence in the vernacular" (1.19.2). Far from being an agglomeration of dialectal fragments, Dante's illustrious vernacular is a metaphysical entity that is seen to exist as the highest common denominator of the languages of Italy. It is a linguistic unity that may be reached by all noble souls aided by study and discretion, provided they are willing and able to discard the dross of their local language. In so doing, they will help to restore some of the pristine purity of language, lost at Babel.

Conclusion

Nevertheless, the illustrious vernacular is not cut off from Italy's regional dialects. Here we begin to see the importance of Dante's experiences as an exile, the broadening of his political and intellectual horizons, his growing realization of the need to overcome municipal chauvinism in the Italian peninsula. As we have seen in the praise lavished on Frederick II and Manfred, the political thread present in virtually all the works composed after 1302 is found for the first time in *De vulgari eloquentia*'s maze of technical debate and exposition. The exiled Florentine poet displays his awareness of the connection between Italy's lack of political unity and its linguistic fragmentation. His yearning for unity, which inspires his ideal of a noble language worthy of an ideal Italian national courtly center, is not simply the result of his apprenticeship in Aristotelian philosophy. Nor is the exile's plea for a unifying court in accord with the centrifugal traditions of the Florentine Commune.

For the first time, Dante is able to elaborate a theoretical formulation for his belief in the exalted mission of great poets. Custodians of the national spirit, they are seen as true teachers *(doctores)* in the three major fields of human activity *(salus, venus, virtus),* even as they restore and transmit spiritual harmony through the eloquence of their writings. Dante's *De vulgari eloquentia* is the first manifesto of literature no longer regarded as mere technique but rather seen as a profound expression of spiritual and national unity. At the same time, the work changes the traditional picture of Dante's approach to poetry. In the past, Dante has too often been portrayed as the rough genius, so filled with the message he wished to impart to a corrupt world that he had little time for the niceties of poetic form. This essentially Romantic view found an obvious antithesis in

Petrarch's carefully polished, exquisitely harmonious verses. With Vico and then the Romantics, Dante's stock soared as an example of genius untrammeled by petty artistic convention. The reality we glimpse through his Latin treatise on vernacular eloquence is quite different. It shows us a poet whose ear was as keenly musical as Petrarch's, though far wider in range, a writer who devoted at least as much care and attention to detail and questions of form as any of his successors in Italian poetry.[20] We also find a theorist who concentrated on the stanza as a unit rather than on the individual line of verse. In other words, we already catch sight of the poet able to conceive and dominate the immense mass of the *Comedy's* one hundred cantos.

The scope of *De vulgari eloquentia* is clearly far narrower than that of the *Comedy*. The treatise's insistence on the supremacy of the canzone and the noblest style is obviously at odds with Dante's deployment of the comic style in his Christian epic. Other differences spring to mind: the return of Cavalcanti in the *Comedy* (*Inf.* 10.58–72; *Purg.* 11.97–98), after his eclipse in *De vulgari* by Cino da Pistoia (who in his turn is excluded from Dante's masterpiece); the significant contrast already mentioned between the theory of Adam's name for God and the immutability of his original language down to the time of Christ (*Par.* 26.133–38). Further, Giraut de Bornelh is acclaimed in *De vulgari* 2.2.8 as Dante's opposite number, the "singer of righteousness" in Provençal, while Arnaut Daniel receives no outstanding accolade—a far cry from the famous passage in *Purgatorio* 26.115–26, in which the leading exponent of *trobar clus* is hailed as the greatest writer in the vernacular, against the claims made for Giraut by his supporters. Above all, in the Latin work, the canzone is prized as the supreme achievement of poetry in the vernacular—with little or no anticipation of the "sacred poem to which both Heaven and earth have set their hand" (*Par.* 25.1–2). And yet, despite these and other differences, *De vulgari eloquentia* prepares the way for Dante's masterwork by rejecting the limited horizon for vernacular poetry posited by the author of *Vita Nova*, who restricted its scope to the subject of love for a woman (*VN* 25.6), and—with his trinity of *salus, venus, virtus*—the Poet of Righteousness of *De vulgari eloquentia* may be seen as the forerunner of the Poet of Divine Justice who was to become God's scribe in what he would choose to call his *Comedy*.

Texts and translations

De vulgari eloquentia. Edited by Pier Vincenzo Mengaldo. In Dante Alighieri, *Opere minori*, vol. 2, 3–237. Milan and Naples: Ricciardi, 1979. The standard text, with Italian translation and notes.

De vulgari eloquentia. Edited by Aristide Marigo, with notes, commentary, and Italian translation. In *Opere di Dante,* vol. 6, 3d ed., edited by Pier Giorgio Ricci. Florence: Le Monnier, 1968. This edition is still a mine of information.

De vulgari eloquentia. Edited and translated by Steven Botterill. Cambridge: Cambridge University Press, 1996a. English translation.

"De Vulgari Eloquentia": Dante's Book of Exile. Translated by Marianne Shapiro. Lincoln: University of Nebraska Press, 1990. English translation, with copious notes and additional material.

Other readings

Ascoli, Albert R. *"Neminem ante nos:* History and Authority in the *De vulgari eloquentia." Annali d'italianistica* 8 (1990): 186–231.

———. "The Unfinished Author: Dante's Rhetoric of Authority in *Convivio* and *De vulgari eloquentia."* In *The Cambridge Companion to Dante,* edited by Rachel Jacoff, 45–66. Cambridge: Cambridge University Press, 1993.

Barański, Zygmunt G. "Dante's Biblical Linguistics." *Lectura Dantis [Virginiana]* 5 (1989b): 105–43.

Botterill, Steven. Introduction to his edition and translation (see above).

Corti, Maria. *"De vulgari eloquentia* di Dante Alighieri" (with bibliography). In *Letteratura italiana: Le Opere,* edited by Alberto Asor Rosa, 1:187–209. Turin: Einaudi, 1992.

Eco, Umberto. *The Search for a Perfect Language,* 34–52. London: Fontana, 1997.

Grayson, Cecil. *"Nobilior est vulgaris:* Latin and Vernacular in Dante's Thought." In *Centenary Essays on Dante by Members of the Oxford Dante Society,* 54–76. Oxford: Clarendon Press, 1965.

Mengaldo, Pier Vincenzo. "Dante come critico." *La parola del testo* 1(1) (1997): 36–54.

Scaglione, Aldo. "Dante and the Ars Grammatica." In *The "Divine Comedy" and the Encyclopedia of Arts and Sciences,* edited by G. Di Scipio and A. Scaglione, 27–41. Amsterdam: John Benjamins, 1988.

Dante's lyric poetry

Rime

Eighty and more lyrics (including thirty-one glossed by their author in *Vita Nova* and three in *Convivio*) are regarded as authentic by modern editors of Dante's *Rime*.[1] Two-thirds are sonnets (fifty-nine, of which twenty-five were placed in *Vita Nova*). Although these lyrics were never gathered together by their author into a sequential *Canzoniere* similar to Petrarch's, they contain well over 2,500 lines of verse, composed over a period of twenty-five to thirty years, beginning in 1283, when Dante was eighteen years old. They reveal a constant need for experimentation and renewal, a practice accompanied by "una serietà terribile" (Contini 1976, 6) that characterized the whole of his poetic career.

The thematic range of Dante's poetry until c. 1293–94 was limited to the subject of love, since (as we saw in chapter 1) the author of *Vita Nova* criticized vernacular poets who—like Guittone d'Arezzo—wrote on other themes. Very soon after writing this work, however, Dante began the study of philosophy in earnest and composed a poem on the true nature of nobility (LXXXII: 69).[2] In this canzone, he declares his intention of abandoning for the moment the sweet love poetry *(Le dolci rime d'amor)* he had cultivated in order to discuss the touchstone of nobility "in harsh and subtle rhymes" (l. 14: *con rima aspr' e sottile*). This momentous change of direction and manner was accompanied by the poet's entry (1295) into the Florentine political arena, which had been dominated by legislation passed in January 1293 that deprived magnates of their political rights. Although the magnates were not all of noble families, their social standing in the Commune fueled hostility against them, while their wealth and influence encouraged many to attack the feudal concept of nobility as a quality inherited and rooted in wealth.

Dante utterly rejects both links: riches are in fact base (*vili*, the opposite of *nobili*), and a good-for-nothing of noble ancestry is *vilissimo* because he has clearly failed to follow the good example offered him by his forebears. In a line that for its vigor anticipates the *Comedy*, Dante dismisses him as one who "is dead yet walks on earth!" (l. 40: *è morto e va per terra!*). As we saw in chapter 2, some ten or so years after finishing *Vita Nova* and as a result of writing this poem on true nobility and other poems connected with ethical problems, Dante claimed in *De vulgari eloquentia* that the noblest vernacular style must in fact deal with three major themes—feats of arms, love, and virtue—citing his own achievement as a poet not of love but of righteousness *(DVE* 2.2.8–9: *cantor rectitudinis).* This general development, accompanied by the broadening of his moral and intellectual horizons, points the way to the *Comedy,* which nevertheless remains a radical departure from all the poems that preceded it.

Early influences

Beginning his artistic apprenticeship at about the age of eighteen, the young Dante was at first influenced by the powerful figure of Guittone d'Arezzo. Guittone had forced his Tuscan vernacular to perform dazzling feats of rhetorical virtuosity with varying degrees of success in his lyrics, and he had preceded Dante in opening up the scope of the vernacular lyric to include moral, political, and religious themes. Guittone's style was characterized by, among other things, an excessive use of hyperbole, binomials (both synonymous, "I pray and request," and heteronymous, "I hear and see"), *rime equivoche* (homophones with different meanings), oxymora (e.g., "living death"), and antitheses. Dante quickly reacted against this powerful influence, and from *Vita Nova* to the *Comedy* his attacks on Guittone and his followers were filled with scorn tinged with acrimony (e.g., *DVE* 1.13.1, 2.6.8; *Purg.* 26.124–26).

The clearest evidence of Guittone's early influence is found in the exchange of sonnets between Dante and his namesake, Dante da Maiano (XXXIX–XLVII: 1–5). Dante da Maiano displays the most obvious features of Guittone's style: *rime equivoche;* compound rhymes (XLIV: 3a.2–8: *parla – par l'à – par là – parla*); rare, difficult rhymes (XLII: 2a.2–7: *gioco – coco – moco – voco*); repetition (ll. 3–11: *saver – sacciate – saver – saggia – saggio – saver – saggio*). Alighieri—then probably seventeen or eighteen years of age—is more restrained, although in *Lasso, lo dol che più mi dole e serra* (XLV: 4) he accepts the challenge of structuring a reply based on the rhyme sound *-omo* (used by his interlocutor in XLIV: 3a), with the result that a hornets' nest of *rime equivoche* virtually destroys the meaning of the sonnet's second quatrain.

Guittone's influence soon gave way to that of Guido Cavalcanti, to whom Dante dedicated his *Vita Nova* when he was twenty-eight or twenty-nine years old. In the intervening decade, the younger Florentine poet had abandoned the artifices of Guittone's style for the musical harmonies and some of the philosophical subtleties displayed in much of Cavalcanti's verse.[3] Even Cavalcanti's view of love as a negative force left its mark on some of the lyrics included in *Vita Nova* (especially in chapters 14–16), although from the outset Dante rejected the older poet's conception of love as an irrational, destructive experience through his revolutionary claim that his love for Beatrice had *always* been governed by the faculty of reason (*VN* 2.9). Indeed, after the ecstatic praise of Beatrice in *Tanto gentile* and *Vede perfettamente* (*VN* 26), Cavalcanti's conception of love is utterly rejected in lines 3–4 of *Sí lungiamente m'ha tenuto Amore* (*VN* 27.3–5): "as *harsh* as he [Love] was formerly to me, so now he is equally *sweet* in my heart" (my emphasis).[4]

Dante's first lyrics are typical of the poetic fashions cultivated by those who learned the art of writing verse chiefly from their Provençal and southern Italian predecessors. A Sicilian poet, Giacomo da Lentini, invented that most popular of forms, the sonnet, with its "narrow room" of fourteen lines. He and his fellow poets passed on an eclectic vocabulary made up of "Italian," Sicilian, Provençal, and French elements. Examples of non-Tuscan forms abound in Dante's early poems. For example, the canzone *La dispietata mente, che pur mira* (L: 13.29) has the southern imperative *sacciate* ("know"; Tuscan *sappiate*). In *Piangete, amanti, poi che piange Amore* (VI: 11, a sonnet later included in *VN* 8.4–6), we read Gallicisms such as *orranza* ("honor"; Tuscan *onore*), *sovente* ("often"; Tuscan *spesso*), and *plorare* ("to weep"; Tuscan *piangere*). *Plorare* may also be regarded as a Provençalism and thus joins a copious list that contains forms such as *parvente,* found in the first sonnet included in *Vita Nova* and derived from the Provençal *parven* ("opinion"; Tuscan *parere*). In a "double sonnet"—a form probably invented by Guittone and soon rejected by Dante—*Se Lippo amico se' tu che mi leggi* (XLVIII: 8), we find the Gallicism *m'appello* (Tuscan *mi chiamo*), the Sicilianism *esta* ("this"; Tuscan *questa*), and the Provençal *druda* ("lover"; Tuscan *amante*), without pejorative connotations, which will return in its masculine form to describe St. Dominic many years later in *Paradiso* 12.55.

As may be deduced from this last example, Dante rejected the use of non-Tuscan forms in the twenty years from roughly 1288 to 1308, only to readmit some of them as part of the *Comedy*'s polyphony. The same may be said of the so-called *rima siciliana,* which gave early Italian poets the freedom to compose "imperfect" rhymes of the type *nome – come – lume* (*Inf.* 10.65–69),[5] and in this early lyric the parallel *rima aretina [guittoniana]: scritto – metto* (ll. 4–5). The poetic license afforded by the *rima siciliana* arose from a misunderstanding occasioned by the versions of Sicilian poems given in manuscripts that were Tuscanized by scribes and thus offered imperfect rhymes such as *sentire – sospiri* (whereas the original Sicilian rhymes had been faultless: *sentiri – sospiri*).

The labored syntax of the first poem inserted in *Vita Nova* (3.10–12)—the sonnet *A ciascun'alma presa e gentil core* (1: 6), which Dante claims to have written at the age of eighteen—is evident in the first quatrain, with its main clause delayed until line 4. The two gerunds (ll. 9 and 11: *tenendo*, "holding"; *dormendo*, "sleeping"), the first referring to Love, the second to *madonna*, although acceptable in early Italian, are examples of a tendency generally avoided by the mature poet (modern Italian would require an adjectival clause or participle: *che teneva, la quale dormiva* or *addormentata*). Indeed, Patrick Boyde (1971, 174) maps the frequency of the use of the gerund in the *Vita Nova* poems as on average one in thirteen lines, a figure that drops to one in fifty-two lines in the later poems, in harmony with a general tendency to prefer more complex syntactical structures.

Another early poem, on the other hand, displays masterful syntax, as well as a delightful comic touch: the sonnet *Non mi poriano già mai fare ammenda* (LI: 14), written either in or before 1287. The poet declares that his eyes will never be able to make amends for their concentration on the Garisenda tower in Bologna, with their consequent failure to notice a celebrated beauty who passed by in the street below.[6] The vein of comic hyperbole continues with the vow that the poet will never make peace with his eyes; on the contrary, he intends to kill the guilty pair, "those dolts"—unless, of course, he decides to change his mind. The fledgling poet shows considerable technical skill in the use of enjambment in the first quatrain and (more unusually) in lines 11–12, where the adjective *dolenti* is separated from the noun it qualifies by the structural break between the sonnet's first and second tercets: *onde dolenti // son li miei spirti per lo lor fallire* ("so that my spirits are downcast because of their fault").

A charming youthful composition is the sonnet *Guido, i' vorrei che tu e Lapo [Lippo] ed io* (LII: 15), a wish fulfillment addressed to Dante's "first friend," Guido Cavalcanti (who replied with *S'io fosse quelli che d'Amor fu degno*), and probably to Lippo Pasci de' Bardi, a minor poet. The sonnet expresses the wish that the three men and their ladies might be taken by magic and placed in a boat, to live in total harmony "and talk there forever of love" (l. 12: *e quivi ragionar sempre d'amore*). The "good wizard" (l. 11) called upon to accomplish this feat is almost certainly Merlin, while Dante's female companion "who is at the number thirty" (l. 10) is most probably one of the "screen ladies" chosen to conceal the poet's love for Beatrice, since the latter's name (as he tells us in *VN* 6.2) insisted on occupying the ninth place in the list of the sixty most beautiful Florentine women contained in a *serventese* (now lost). *Guido, i' vorrei* bears some of the linguistic hallmarks of Cavalcanti's mellifluous style, which Dante adopted and developed to the limits of its expressive range.

The sonnet *Sonar bracchetti, e cacciatori aizzare* (LXI: 16), with its energetic opening (note the double consonants *-cch-, -cci-, -zz-*), offers a distant anticipation of powerful overtures—*attacchi,* as they are called in Italian—found in the *Comedy* (e.g., *Inf.* 19, *Purg.* 16, *Par.* 11). This sonnet is fairly unusual because the syntactical break occurs after the sixth line, not the eighth, and the break is emphasized by the adversative *Ed io* (But I). The first six lines conjure up a miniature Paolo Uccello in their evocation of the pleasures of the hunt—but for a man *not* enslaved by love. The extended conceit takes up the next six lines, in which the poet-persona is reproached for his lack of gallantry in abandoning beautiful ladies for sport and such rough amusements—reproached not by love, but by one of his own thoughts. This witty and original piece is brought to a close by a couplet in which Love is duly personified, and the "Cavalcantian" Provençalism *pesanza* (sadness, grief) makes its only appearance in Dante's writings: "Then, afraid that Love may overhear, / I am ashamed, and therefore weighed down with grief" *(Allor, temendo non che senta Amore, / prendo vergogna, onde mi ven pesanza).*

The canzone *Lo doloroso amor che mi conduce* (LXVIII: 25) is unique for the way it obsessively equates love for Beatrice with the poet's own death, especially in the first stanza: "The sorrowful love that leads me to my death . . . my life . . . sighs and says: 'I am dying on account of her whose name is Beatrice.'" The Beatrix of *Vita Nova*—whose name illustrates the role she plays in leading Dante toward blessedness and salvation—here inspires a love full of grief and suffering, even as her beauty leads her lover to death. Further, judged by the poet's standard practice, the canzone is technically deficient or archaic as an artifact: for example, we find an imperfect rhyme (ll. 23–26: *morto – scorto – ricolto*) and a Sicilian rhyme (ll. 44–46: *discigli – quigli*); two lines in each stanza are left unrhymed (called *espars,* in Provençal poetry: ll. 8, 11, 22, 25, 36, 39, 43, 45). Even more surprising than these structural anomalies is the claim made in the third stanza that the poet's soul, even if damned by God, will not feel the torments of hell, for it will be utterly absorbed in contemplating the image of Beatrice's beauty. The *envoi* asks death to find out why the light of Beatrice's eyes has been removed and whether it has been received by another; if so, "take away my illusion and I shall end my life with far less pain."

It is hardly surprising that this poem, with its insistence that love for Beatrice leads to death, was excluded from the celebration of Dante's *New Life*. We recall that in *Vita Nova* 10.2, Beatrice denies Dante her greeting. There, however, the consequences are quite different from those described in *Lo doloroso amor.* The author describes the miraculous effects of Beatrice's greeting, which fills him with so much love *(caritade)* that he forgives all his enemies (*VN* 11.1; cf. Matt. 5.44) while his vital spirits are overcome by a life-threatening ecstasy; since this has been denied him, he decides to place all his blessedness not in Beatrice's bodily presence but in the praise of her whole being (*VN* 18.8–9). Clearly, *Lo doloroso amor* is opposed to the spirit that inspired Dante's *Vita Nova*. In that *libello* the author lost no time in proclaiming that *his* love was always governed by reason—unlike that of his "first friend," Guido Cavalcanti, who not only wrote a parody of the kind of devotion and hyperbole inspired by Beatrice in his sonnet *Guata, Manetto, quella scrignutuzza,* but also proclaimed love to be a totally irrational and destructive force in his great canzone *Donna me prega.*

Unlike Cavalcanti, whose *ballate* represent one-fifth of his poetic output, Dante made scant use of this form, perhaps because of the *ballata's* characteristic refrain *(ripresa)* and its links with extemporary song and dance, whereas the canzone generally possessed its own specific musical accompaniment. Another reason may have been Dante's predilection for technical difficulties and challenges. The *ballata,* less noble than the canzone because of its simpler form (*DVE* 2.3.4–6), opens with a *ripresa* that announces the theme of the whole composition.[7] That Dante wrote only one *ballata* for Beatrice (*VN* 12.10–15) clearly indicates his lack of enthusiasm for this form.

Two *ballate* were probably composed for "screen ladies" (LVI: 21 and LXVIII: 65). The first is remarkable because it is the only poem with lines of nine syllables in Dante's oeuvre, as well as for its display of *rime tronche (farà – vedrà – verrà – canterà).* We may also note the Sicilian rhyme *sospire – disire,* and the Provençalism *umíle* in line 7, with its stress on the penultimate syllable (cf. XX: 40.71, and especially XVIII: 36.1, rhyming with *simíle,* where avoidance of the *rima sdrucciola* has obliged the poet to modify the normal Italian proparoxytone).[8]

Another two ballads (*ballate mezzane:* LXXXVII: 64 and LXXXVIII: 65) insist on the lady's youth but otherwise praise her being, as do the poems written for Beatrice (LXXXVII: 64.19: "a young angel *[angioletta]* who has appeared here") and those conceived for Lady Philosophy. Both could be interpreted allegorically to describe Dante's involvement with philosophy. In *I' mi son pargoletta bella e nova,* however, the diminutive *pargoletta* (young woman, or girl)[9] evokes for many readers one of Beatrice's reproaches *(Purg.* 31.59–60: *o pargoletta / o altra novità con sí breve uso),* when *Beata Beatrix* accuses her lover of having failed to learn the lesson afforded by her death: the need to recognize the vanity and transience of all earthly things. The structure of *I' mi son pargoletta bella e nova* is typical of Dante's *ballate mezzane,* with its *ripresa* of three hendecasyllables (YZZ) and stanzas of seven hendecasyllables (AB; AB; BZZ). A *ballata* made up solely of hendecasyllables as in this poem (and in LXXXVIII: 65, *Perché ti vedi giovinetta e bella*) was highly unusual and is further proof of Dante's preference for this most capacious and noblest of poetic lines.

Our last example of Dante's early verse, the sonnet *Com più vi fere Amor co' suoi vincastri* (LXII: 7), is memorable as the poet's first attempt to use harsh rhyme sounds or *rime aspre (vincastri – l'incastri – impiastri – lastri)*. Further, a bold enjambment unites the sonnet's octave and sestet (ll. 8–9): *Dunque, ormai lastri // vostro cor lo cammin per seguitare* (Therefore, may your heart now pave the way to follow).[10] The form *lastri* (for *lastrichi,* from *lastricare,* "to pave") is almost certainly one of Dante's first neologisms or verbal creations, a prominent characteristic of the poet's language in the *Comedy,* especially in *Paradiso.* As Contini (1946, 66) noted, this sonnet is probably the first fruit of Dante's encounter with the poetry of Arnaut Daniel, the *miglior fabbro* or better craftsman ("wordsmith") encountered on the highest terrace of Mount Purgatory (*Purg.* 26.117, 140–48), who was renowned for his difficult verse *(trobar clus)*. With their harsh rhymes and use of metaphor, the two quatrains of *Com più vi fere Amor co' suoi vincastri* are strong evidence of Arnaut's influence, set off against the conventional poetic language of the tercets.

The mature poet's "purist" phase

Dante's reaction against the older style of poetry typified by Guittone's works is best understood through an analysis of the poems selected by the younger poet for his *Vita Nova.* The climax of that work is reached with the discovery that the lover's happiness consists solely in the disinterested praise of his lady's beauty and goodness and their effects on others, followed by his need to overcome the loss sustained with Beatrice's death. In *Purgatorio* 24.49–62, Bonagiunta da Lucca is made to identify the beginnings of the "new poetry" *(le nove rime)* with the canzone that Dante placed at the ideological center of *Vita Nova: Donne ch'avete intelletto d'amore* (*VN* 19.4–14).[11] Dante the pilgrim replies (with a formula borrowed from a letter on *caritas,* the love of God, by an otherwise unknown Brother Ivo) that the excellence and originality of his poetry are the result of the fidelity with which he sets out the dictates of love in his poetry.[12]

In *Vita Nova* 19.2, Dante tells us that the opening verse of *Donne ch'avete,* which calls upon an ideal audience of noble ladies who understand the nature of true love, came to him spontaneously and remained in his mind "with great joy" for some days before he began to compose the rest of the canzone, with its four stanzas and *envoi,* each of fourteen lines. *Donne ch'avete* is one of the few canzoni by Dante to have a greater number of lines in the subdivisions *(pedes)* of the first part of each stanza than in the *versus* of the second part.[13] Thus, we find a sonnetlike structure of $(4 + 4) + (3 + 3)$, with the rhyme scheme ABBC / ABBC // CDD / CEE.[14] Unlike the sonnet's quatrain, however, here each *pes* contains three (not two) rhymes, so that the fourth line is independent of the first: ABBC (not ABBA). In addition, the third rhyme of the *pedes* recurs in the first line of each *volta*, which share only that one rhyme (CDD / CEE)—a pattern not found in any of Dante's sonnets.

The mastery and sweep of the syntax in *Donne ch'avete* are paralleled by the skillful exploitation of the stanza unit. The first stanza is given over entirely to the *proemio* apologizing for the poet's inability to deal adequately with Beatrice's worth; the second describes the heavenly hosts begging God to bring them Beatrice, the only thing lacking in paradise; the third describes Beatrice's miraculous effects on bystanders; and the final stanza exalts her as nature's masterpiece, the medium through which divine beauty may be glimpsed on earth, even as her face reflects the image of Divine Love. The *envoi* (ll. 57–70) dispatches this poem of praise to Beatrice, with the help of ladies and men of courteous, noble disposition.[15] The proem or preamble of the first stanza (see *VN* 19.15) and the *envoi* of the fifth stanza thus flank three central stanzas that convey the poem's message; the poem has an ideal Dantean scheme of $1 + 3 + 1$.

In the canzone described by Dante as his *trattato* (*VN* 20.2: treatise), whose structural and syntactic unity prefigures the formal mastery of the *Comedy,* we find all the characteristics of what may be called his purist phase, utterly devoid both of the rhetorical excesses so dear to Guittone and of the variegated verbal forms and textures that make up the polyphony of his *Comedy.* The harmonious sweetness, *dolcezza,* of Dante's "new style" (*Purg.* 24.57; cf. *Purg.* 26.112: *Li dolci detti,* "sweet sayings") is everywhere in evidence. Gallicisms and Provençalisms are virtually eliminated; there are no "difficult," rare, or harsh rhymes. No display of technical virtuosity is allowed to impede the flow of the poetic message. And of the nine words chosen for their "sweetness" in *De vulgari* 2.7.5, six are found in *Donne ch'avete: amore* (love) and *donna* (lady), with seven and eight occurrences, respectively; *disiata* (l. 29: desired), *vertute* (l. 38: virtue, power), *dona* (l. 39: gives), and *salute* (l. 39: good, happiness).

As opposed to the *Comedy*'s lexical richness (with almost 7,500 items), the *Vita Nova* poems contain only 229 nouns, 121 adjectives, and 244 verbs.[16] Moreover, common, familiar verbs contrast with the relatively sophisticated 24 most frequent—and overwhelmingly abstract—nouns. The indispensable *donna* heads the list with 56 occurrences, closely followed by *amore* and *core*, with 54 and 48 occurrences, respectively. Beatrice's name appears but seldom in poems included in *Vita Nova:* once, before mention of her death, it appears only in its familiar form, *Bice* (*VN* 24.8); afterwards, Beatrice is named (significantly enough) three times (*VN* 31.10, 31.14, and 41.13). Indeed, proper nouns are nine times less frequent in *Vita Nova* than in Dante's epic.

Such a contrast is symptomatic of the author's contrasting aims in the two works. In *Vita Nova,* everyday, concrete reality and its contingencies had to be sublimated and given a universal, transcendental meaning, whereas in the *Comedy* the pilgrim-narrator's visionary *iter* needed to be anchored as far as possible in sensory reality and transmitted in terms of mundane experience. Emblematic of the poet's wish to spiritualize Beatrice and the love she inspired in him is the fact that the word *bocca* (mouth) is always avoided in the *Vita Nova* poems (see *VN* 19.20); the later Dante introduced the literary idealization of the lady's parted lips suggested by her "desired smile" *(disïato riso)* in order to emphasize more powerfully Paolo's lustful kissing of Francesca's mouth *(Inf.* 5.136: *la bocca mi basciò tutto tremante).*

One of the most striking characteristics of Dante's career is the fact that at various stages he clearly felt the need to take stock of decisive periods in his career as a writer and to set out a balance sheet in such works as *Vita Nova, De vulgari eloquentia,* and *Convivio.* Indeed, each of these works gives little or no hint of what was to be the next step in its author's development as an artist. Only the celebrated finale of *Vita Nova,* with its declaration of intent—"to say about her [Beatrice] what has never been said of any other woman" *(VN* 42.2)— seems to look in the direction of the *Comedy.* For many years to come, Beatrice's lover devoted much time and energy to the study and praise of philosophy, to politics, and to enlarging the narrow horizon of his early literary output. In *Vita Nova* 25.6, Dante had programmatically confined vernacular poetry's compass to the single subject of love. However, in the 1290s, his passionate involvement with philosophy, followed by his entry onto the political scene, led to a preoccupation with ethics and a commitment as a writer that were to receive their theoretical justification in his *De vulgari eloquentia.*

Poetry and philosophy

As far as poetic technique is concerned, the first two poems chosen by the author of *Convivio* to illustrate his love of philosophy still exhibit the characteristics of the *dolci rime d'amor.* The poems are virtually indistinguishable from the love lyrics written for Beatrice, as Dante himself implies when he tells us in *Convivio* 2.12.8 that his audience would not have been prepared to accept a poem in praise of philosophy written in the vernacular.

Voi che 'ntendendo il terzo ciel movete (LXXIX: 59)

In the canzone *Voi che 'ntendendo il terzo ciel movete* (LXXIX: 59), Dante for the first time turned to allegory, creating a clear divide between the text's literal meaning and what he claimed was his real, intentional message. This is seen in the *envoi*, which begins: "My poem, I think there will be only a few who will truly understand your meaning *[tua ragione]*, because you express it in such a complex and difficult way. So, if you happen to come across persons who do not seem to have grasped it fully, I beseech you to take heart, my young darling, and tell them: 'Consider at least how beautiful I am!'" (ll. 53–61). Some ten years later, Dante was to call attention to this technical innovation.

This sophisticated use of the traditional *tornata* or *envoi* is but one of the ways Dante contrives to demonstrate his originality in handling long-established forms (the *tornada* was a common feature of the Provençal *canso,* while only six extant Sicilian *canzoni* contain one). In *Convivio* 2.11.2–9, he explains that a canzone's *envoi* was generally called a *tornata* (return), because the troubadours who first adopted this convention did so in order to return to the musical accompaniment. Including a *tornata* was not his usual practice, but when he did compose one, he intended to add something to the poem's message. This is the intention of the *tornata*'s warning in *Voi che 'ntendendo* that only a few will understand the poem's true meaning, but every reader must at least appreciate the poem's formal beauty.

The warning that the poem's true meaning will be understood by only the happy few is evidence that *Voi che 'ntendendo* was originally conceived with both a literal and a hidden, allegorical meaning—as Dante maintains in *Convivio* 2. Another clue pointing to the likelihood that *Voi che 'ntendendo* was originally conceived as a love poem addressed to philosophy may be found in the description of the Lady as "wise and courteous in her *greatness*" (l. 47: *ne la sua* grandezza; my emphasis). The term *grandezza* is not applied to any woman praised in the traditional love lyric. In the *Comedy, grande* (great) always denotes either material size or power, or authority, or majesty; the only woman to merit this epithet is Mary, Queen of Heaven (in *Par.* 33.13).

Apart from its allegorical dimension, this canzone shuns most of the rhetorical effects displayed in the medieval *ornatus* (tropes, antitheses, and other adornments). The language is typical of Dante's *poesia de la loda* (praise style), with one or two Cavalcantian echoes in the description of the tumult that threatens the lover's soul (ll. 26, 39–45).

Amor che ne la mente mi ragiona (LXXXI: 61)

Like Dante's earlier hymn of praise to Beatrice, *Donne ch'avete intelletto d'amore,* the second canzone written in praise of philosophy—*Amor che ne la mente mi ragiona* (LXXXI: 61)—is a poem of five stanzas. The prevalence of hendecasyllables in *Amor che ne la mente* is underscored by the presence of a *settenario* or heptasyllabic verse in the twelfth line of each stanza (cf. *DVE* 2.12.4–6). The *pedes* of both canzoni have the scheme ABBC / ABBC (with four lines to each *pes,* rather than the more usual three). However, *Amor che ne la mente* is more typical of Dante's practice in that its *sirma* exceeds the *frons* in length: C, DEeDFDF, GG (*DVE* 2.11.3; uppercase letters indicate hendecasyllables, and lowercase, the *settenario*).[17] As in this poem, with its stanzas of eighteen lines (8 + 10), Dante's later canzoni tend to avoid the fourteen-line (sonnet-length) stanza found in *Donne ch'avete* and early canzoni, thereby demonstrating the poet's mastery of increasingly complex syntactic and structural units.

Furthermore, as in *Voi che 'ntendendo,* a tornata is added to *Amor che ne la mente* in order to anticipate a possible misunderstanding on the reader's part: in this case, the fact that Dante's paean to his Lady (philosophy) seems to contradict what he had said about her in a sister poem, the *ballata, Voi che savete ragionar d'Amore* (LXXX: 60). There, the poet had complained of "a disdainful lady" (l. 3), "harsh in her beauty" (l. 23), who had made him quake (l. 28), whereas in *Amor che ne la mente* the lady is praised for her great humility, and "the joys of Paradise" (ll. 55–57) are found in her eyes and her smile. The apparent contradiction is resolved in lines that are unusual both for the way they create a dialogue with a sister poem and for their use of imagery, an uncommon feature in Dante's "purist" phase: "You know that the sky is always shining and clear and never darkens in itself; but at times for many reasons our eyes say that a star is dim. So, when it [the *ballata*] calls her [the Lady] proud, it does not consider her according to the truth, but only according to the way she appeared to it: for my soul was afraid, and still is afraid, so that everything I see seems harsh to me whenever she looks at me" (ll. 77–86).

A noteworthy feature of *Amor che ne la mente mi ragiona* is the poet's striking emphasis of the limitations of the human intellect, its inability to comprehend fully the transcendental truths of philosophy—all the more impossible, given that Dante's Lady Philosophy is a poetic amalgam of philosophy and divine wisdom (see ll. 1–4, 11, 16, 28–29, 43–44, 59–60; cf. Prov. 8 and Wisd. 8–9). A recurring theme of *Paradiso* is foreshadowed in lines 16–18, when the poet tells us that if his attempt to praise her is defective, the fault must be attributed to our "weak intellect / and our speech that does not possess the power to portray everything that Love says." Since Lady Philosophy's beauties transcend our understanding, the poet must be satisfied with what little he can say about them.

At the same time, her "miraculous" operations bolster our (Christian) faith, and it was for this purpose that she was ordained by God (ll. 53–54: *onde la nostra fede è aiutata: / però fu tal da etterno ordinata*)—a surprising elevation of the traditional Scholastic view of philosophy as *ancilla theologiae,* the handmaiden of theology. Even more unorthodox is the statement that Philosophy destroys "innate vices that debase human beings" (l. 67), a quasi-sacramental power usually attributed to divine grace but here posited for Philosophy by Dante's predilection for ethics.

Le dolci rime d'amor ch'i' solia (LXXXII: 69) and *Poscia ch'Amor del tutto m'ha lasciato* (LXXXIII: 70)

The poet's commitment to ethics finds its clearest expression in *Le dolci rime d'amor ch'i' solia* (LXXXII: 69), written in or soon after 1295. Here, for the first time, we discover the poet assuming the mantle of the "singer of righteousness" (*DVE* 2.2.8). At the age of thirty, and after his (late) entry into Florentine politics, Dante changed course as radically as any poet has ever done, now jettisoning allegory in order to deliver a clear moral message in an impassioned attempt to enlighten the broadest possible audience on the true nature of nobility. The theme was highly topical in Florence, where the flowering of a mercantile society had encouraged the questioning of traditional, feudal ideas. Hostility to the idea of hereditary nobility had in fact found practical expression in Giano della Bella's *Ordinamenti di giustizia,* passed in 1293, which deprived Florentine citizens classified as *magnati* of all political rights. Two years later, the *Ordinamenti* were modified to allow members of the minor nobility (including Dante) to take part in the political life of the Commune and to be eligible for political office by enrolling as members of a guild.

In *Le dolci rime d'amor ch'i' solia,* Dante no longer addresses the small band of Love's faithful followers (as in *Vita Nova*). Instead, his purpose is similar to what inspired the *Comedy:* to rid society of pernicious error and set it on the path leading to virtue and happiness. Until now, Dante's poetic career had concentrated on a narrow field of human experience. Henceforth, it would expand both thematically and technically until it was to give birth to the "sacred poem to which both heaven and earth have lent a hand" (*Par.* 25.1–2).

The poet declares at the very beginning of *Le dolci rime d'amor ch'i' solia* that he must for the moment abandon the "sweet style" he had cultivated when writing about love, in order to expound the true essence of nobility and refute the idea that nobility depends on wealth. True to the principle of *convenientia* that lay at the heart of medieval rhetoric, he will need to employ "harsh and subtle verse" (ll. 10–14: *rima aspr' e sottile*). This emphasis on the *asperitas* (harshness) of his new style, as opposed to the sweet harmonies of his love lyrics, accompanies the revolution in subject matter. Until now, Dante had expressed even his nascent passion for philosophy according to the themes and vocabulary of love poetry. Here, he suddenly takes up Tuscan vernacular poetry at the point to which Guittone had led it. The elaborate twenty-line stanzas of Dante's canzone have no other parallel than those of such poems as Guittone's *O dolce terra aretina.* Especially noteworthy in *Le dolci rime d'amor ch'i' solia* is the resonance of the adjacent rhymes in lines 10–17 of each stanza: in the first stanza, *stile – amore – valore – gentile –* sottile *– vile – gentilezza –* ricchezza (roman type indicates the shorter *settenari* or heptasyllabic lines, which augment the echoing of phonic effects).

As Dante explains in *Convivio* 4.1.10, allegory would have been a mere hindrance in this "necessary remedy" for a society that exalted the wicked and needed to be brought back quickly to good health. In prescribing this remedy, the poet does not hesitate (ll. 85–87) to quote the definition of virtue found in Aristotle's *Ethics:* "a habit of choosing that lies solely in the mean." Nobility is indissolubly linked to the moral virtues, but these are not the monopoly of no-bility. God alone confers nobility on the soul of an individual who will display the various virtues necessary in the various stages of life on earth. In the first line of the *envoi,* this poetic sermon is well characterized as the poet's *Contra-li-erranti* (l. 141: Against those who are in error), echoing the title of one of Aquinas's major works, his *Summa Contra Gentiles.*

A companion piece is *Poscia ch'Amor del tutto m'ha lasciato* (LXXXIII: 70) whose first line tells us that Love took pity on the poet's sufferings by departing from him. Dante's love for philosophy had encountered serious problems (cf. *Conv.* 4.1.8). He therefore sets out once again to refute error, this time con-cerning the nature of *leggiadria* (Provençal *leujaria*), a quality of urbane social intercourse (Fenzi 1997). Men who are "base and boorish" (l. 10) boast that they possess *leggiadria,* which in its true form makes its possessor "worthy of the im-perial mantle" (ll. 13–14). Dante goes on to ridicule those who think they can be *leggiadri* by ostentatiously dissipating their wealth; others constantly laugh and give themselves airs in an attempt to persuade others of their quick wit and intelligence. The final stanza lists positive effects of *leggiadria:* those who prac-tice it are generous givers, they are slow to anger, pleasant and charming in conversation, immune from vanity. After this list of qualities comes the final punch line (l. 133): "Those who live all do the opposite" (*Color che vivon fanno tutti contra*). As a result, there is no *envoi,* since virtually no worthy audience exists for Dante's poem (in l. 69, the poet tells us that he does not know whom to address)—his is the voice of one crying in the wilderness. Our moralist-poet takes pains to specify that *leggiadria* is not a "pure virtue," since it is unbefitting to those who should most practice virtue while dedicating themselves to the re-ligious life or to the acquisition of wisdom. The quality is instead required of the true gentleman (ll. 77–83). In spite of this prohibition, many years later Dante was to endow the Archangel Gabriel with this same quality, and in the highest degree (*Par.* 32.109), no doubt because of the way Gabriel pays court to and serves the Queen of Heaven.

Compared to Dante's other poems, *Poscia ch'Amor del tutto m'ha lasciato* has a number of unusual features. It is the only poem in which Dante used the pentasyllabic *quinario* (here, the eighth line in each stanza); and it is alone in using a *settenario* (instead of a hendecasyllable) for the first line of the *sirma*, which in Dante is usually made to rhyme (as here) with the last line of the *frons*, thus creating a "beautiful concatenation" (*DVE* 2.13.7) between the two parts of the canzone.[18] The poem is unusual (along with *Amor, che movi tua vertú da cielo*, XC: 67) in not ending each stanza with a rhyming couplet, a usage recommended in *De vulgari* 2.13.8. *Poscia ch'Amor* is exceptional in its use of a feature favored by Guittone: internal rhyme, with a trisyllable in the third and ninth lines of each stanza, "which answers the rhyme of the preceding line like an echo" (*DVE* 2.12.8). This pattern creates an unusually high percentage of *rime baciate:*

> Poscia ch'Amor del tutto m'ha *lasciato*,
> non per mio *grato*,
> ché *stato* non avea tanto *gioioso*,
> ma però che *pietoso*
> fu tanto del meo core
> che non sofferse d'ascoltar suo pianto;
> i' canterò cosí *disamorato*
> contra 'l *peccato*,
> ch'è *nato* in noi, di chiamare a *ritroso*
> tal ch'è vile e *noioso*.
>   (*Poscia ch'Amor del tutto m'ha lasciato*,
>   ll. 1–10; my emphasis)

The lexis likewise looks back to earlier practice, with frequent use of Provençal forms and Gallicisms, such as *messione* (l. 26: expenditure), *fallenza* (l. 32: fault), *genti coraggi* (l. 38: noble hearts), *donneare* (l. 52: to pay court to a lady), *blasmare* (l. 78: blamed), and *prenze* (l. 114: prince). *Poscia ch'Amor del tutto m'ha lasciato* would most probably have been glossed in *Convivio*, had Dante completed the encyclopedic work.

The *petrose* poems (C–CIII: 77–80)

Dante's involvement in the political life of Florence (1295–1301) presumably distracted the poet's attention from both the study of philosophy and his poetic craft. Indeed, in the sonnet *I' vegno 'l giorno a te 'nfinite volte*, Guido Cavalcanti reproached Dante for his "base life" (l. 9: *la vil tua vita*), for deserting the happy few and consorting with the common herd or *annoiosa gente* (l. 6). Nevertheless, this crucial period of civic and political involvement saw a radical change in Dante's art: his *rime petrose* (C–CIII: 77–80). In 1882 Vittorio Imbriani gave this name to the four poems— *Io son venuto al punto de la rota, Al poco giorno e al gran cerchio d'ombra, Amor, tu vedi ben che questa donna,* and *Così nel mio parlar voglio esser aspro*—after the woman of stone, *p[i]etra,* who figures prominently in them.

Most scholars accept the traditional dating of 1296 for all the *petrose.* The dating is based on an astronomical reference in the opening stanza of *Io son venuto,* understood as citing a conjunction of planets that occurred in 1296 (see below). There is no manuscript evidence for the dating and no concrete evidence that they were conceived as a series. In a transcription of fifteen of Dante's lyrics, Boccaccio allocated a central position (7–9) to three of the poems we have already examined, whereas he placed *Così nel mio parlar voglio esser aspro* at the very beginning of his selection. This sequence suggests, perhaps, that Boccaccio thought of *Così nel mio parlar* as having an even earlier date than the others he included and that he did not consider it one of a set (since he included only one of the four works we call the *petrose* poems). With a poet in constant search of self-renewal, it is not impossible to imagine that as early as 1296—two or three years after writing *Vita Nova*—Dante achieved the unparalleled stylistic revolution of his *petrose.*

Luciano Rossi (1995), however, takes lines 7–8 of *Io son venuto* to refer to the moon (cf. Boccaccio, *Teseida* 5.29)—not to Saturn—and suggests a post-exilic dating of December 1304. The links between what we call the *petrose* and the *Comedy* make this hypothesis an attractive one in any ideal map of Dante's poetic career. If the astronomical clue to the dating may be shifted to 1304, then the innovations correspond to a period preceding the *Comedy* but contemporaneous with the writing of *Convivio* I and *De vulgari eloquentia.*

Both 1296 and 1304 are not without problems for dating the *petrose.* If we posit the earlier date, we have to believe that a mere two or three years after finishing *Vita Nova,* Dante's style underwent such a radical change that, whereas the 676 lines of verse in *Vita Nova* contain 150 abstract nouns out of a total of 229, in *Così nel mio parlar* we find the 29 abstract nouns outnumbered by 48 concrete ones, many of which would have been inconceivable in the *libello* devoted to Beatrice. A similar argument applies to the later date, since *Così nel mio parlar* is a canzone and, as such, the poem should display only the highest, "tragic," style (*DVE* 2.4.5–6), but instead it deploys many words that are specifically excluded from the noblest style.

Io son venuto al punto de la rota (C: 77)

The first of the *petrose,* the canzone *Io son venuto al punto de la rota* (C: 77) opens with the first astronomical reference in Dante's oeuvre—a feature destined to play an important role in the *Comedy*.[19] The reference allows us to pinpoint the "fictional" date of the canzone as 24 December 1296. The conjunction of planets described in lines 3–9 occurred only twice in the poet's lifetime: at his birth in 1265 and again in 1296, when it was profoundly threatening to someone born under the sign of Gemini (l. 3: *il geminato cielo*).

The reference tells us that the beneficent influences of the sun and Venus (ll. 1–6) are at their weakest, while Saturn (coldest of the planets) rules over the night sky in winter, a symbol of both death and destruction. Thus, in the first stanza we learn that, although it is winter (Venus, the planet of love—and spring—is far removed from the earth) and the poet-persona finds himself at the lowest point of Fortune's wheel, thoughts of love never abandon him. As Durling and Martinez point out (1990, 83): "Inversion is a major idea governing the entire poem."

The rhyming couplet, with *rima equivoca,* at the end of each stanza hammers home the recurrent motifs (see table 3.1).

TABLE 3.1

Rhyme words in the couplet at the end of each stanza,
Io son venuto al punto de la rota

Line numbers	Rhyme words	Translation
12 and 13	*petra*	stone
25 and 26	*donna*	lady
38 and 39	*tempo*	time
51 and 52	*sempre*	always
64 and 65	*dolce*	sweet (used ironically)
71 and 72	*marmo*	marble

As in the first stanza of the poem, each stanza is structured according to the norm—with *pedes* in the first section (ll. 1–3 and 4–6) and an undivided second section or *sirma* (ll. 7–13). A syntactical break or opposition is created, however, by the *settenario* of the fourth line of the *sirma* (l. 10). This highly unusual feature has the effect of prolonging the initial statement beyond the *pedes* and phrasing it over nine lines. Each opposition is marked by the conjunction *e* (the adversative "and yet"), which is found in Latin—*odi et amo,* "I hate *and yet* I love"—and the Romance languages:

Io sono venuto al punto de la rota   *frons:*   *pes*
che l'orizzonte, quando il sol si corca,

ci partorisce il geminato cielo,
e la stella d'amor ci sta remota   *pes*
per lo raggio lucente che la 'nforca
sí di traverso che le si fa velo;
e quel pianeta che conforta il gelo   *sirma*
si mostra tutto a noi per lo grand'arco
nel qual ciascun di sette fa poca ombra:
e però *non disgombra*   [*settenario,* with conjunction, *e*]
un sol penser d'amore, ond'io son carco,
la mente mia, ch'è piú dura che *petra*   [*rima equivoca* in couplet at end]
in tener forte imagine di *petra.*
     (*Io son venuto al punto de la rota,*
       ll. 1–13; my emphasis)

––––––

I have come to the point on the wheel where the horizon, once the sun has set, gives birth to the twinned heaven for us, and the star of love is distanced from us by the shining ray that straddles her like a veil; and the planet that intensifies the cold shows itself to us in its entirety along the great arc in which each of the seven [planets] casts hardly any shadow: *and yet* my mind does not rid itself of even one of the thoughts of love that weigh me down, my mind harder than any *stone* in holding on tightly to an image of *stone.*

The first and second stanzas describe the winter solstice, yet the poet cannot free himself of even one of the thoughts of love that have "petrified" his mind. The third tells us that the birds have migrated or are silent, and every animal is released from love and desire; despite the changes of seasons in nature, the poet's love and "sweet thoughts" remain unchanged. The fourth continues to elaborate the topos of the contrast between the cosmos and the poet's inner world: the grass is dead, trees have lost their leaves, no flower has been spared by the cold; yet Love does not remove the cruel thorn from the poet's heart, so that he knows that he will always *(sempre)* suffer it, even if he were to live forever *(sempre)*. After the heavenly spheres, then the animals, then plants, stanza five descends to the lowest, most basic elements: the earth is covered by a hard, enameled surface, and "dead water" turns into glass because of the pressure of the intense cold; yet the poet's strife (l. 62: *la mia guerra*) continues, for if suffering is sweet, then death must be sweet above all else. In the *envoi,* the poet-lover asks: If love is found only in him and nowhere else in this frozen season that envelops the whole of nature, what will become of him in springtime, "when love pours down on the earth from all the heavens"? He will surely be petrified into lifeless stone *(marmo)*, if this young girl *(pargoletta)* retains her heart of stone *(marmo)*.

The technical virtuosity that is such an outstanding feature of the *petrose* is evident in this canzone. We have noted the structural intricacies of the stanzas, the elaboration of the contrast between the warmth and vigor of the persona's passion on the one hand, and the cold and dead season in nature on the other. We also find the direct influence of Provençal poetry coming to the fore (already glimpsed in *Com più vi fere Amor co' suoi vincastri*), with the same complex artistry as found in the poetry of Arnaut Daniel, the leading exponent of hermetic poetry, *trobar clus*.[20]

It usually goes unnoticed that, although *Io son venuto* is always grouped together with the *rime petrose,* only in the other three poems is the lady herself designated as *petra,* "rock." Here, the last verse tells us that she may retain a heart of marble, but it is her lover whose mind is "harder than any stone in holding on tightly to an image of stone" (ll. 12–13). This hermetic couplet may well contain a covert allusion to two classical myths and thus open up a new treasure trove for the poet who was to make such abundant use of classical mythology in the *Comedy.* If we evoke the scene where the Furies call upon Medusa in *Inferno* 9.52 (*"Vegna Medusa: sì 'l farem di smalto"),* then the lover's petrified mind in *Io son venuto* must surely evoke the myth of Medusa, who turned to stone all who looked on her (indeed, we find the word *smalto* in l. 59, a hapax in Dante's lyrics). The other myth is the one about the sculptor Pygmalion (Ovid, *Metamorphoses* 10.243–97), whose prayer was answered that his statue of an ideal woman might come to life. The marble mentioned twice in Dante's concluding lines (71–72) reinforces the idea of a statue hidden in his mind, "harder than stone" in preserving an image carved in it (ll. 11–12: *più dura che petra / in tener forte imagine di petra).*

The problem of the lady's identity is insoluble and unimportant. Beatrice *may* refer to the young girl *(pargoletta)* of *Io son venuto* in her reproaches in the *Comedy (Purg.* 31.59: *pargoletta)*—or to others implied by the diminutive (an unusual linguistic feature in Dante's lyrics). However, the overriding impression made by this group of so-called *petrose* is that Dante is stretching out for artistic, technical self-renewal in virtuoso fashion. It is the artist, not the lover, who is put to the test in this struggle with language and poetic creation. And it is Dante's emergence as a lord of language that fascinates us in these poems.

Al poco giorno e al gran cerchio d'ombra (ci: 78)

The *sestina,* the most complex of the verse forms used by the troubadours, was probably invented by Arnaut Daniel, whose *Se·m fos Amor de joi donar* is cited by Dante in *De vulgari* 2.13.2 as the model for *Al poco giorno e al gran cerchio d'ombra* (ci: 78).[21] As its name implies, the *sestina* is made up of six six-line stanzas. The last word of the preceding stanza appears as the last word in the first line of the next stanza. Traditional rhymes are replaced by what we shall still refer to as *rhyme words* (in the sense of the word at the end of each line of verse, or *mot tornat*). The six rhyme words that appear at the end of each line of the first stanza are subjected to a shifting order of *retrogradatio cruciata* through all six stanzas. This series of permutations—in which the rhyme words are transferred from one stanza to the next by both retrograde and crosswise motion—provides a poetic counterpoint in which all possible combinations of the rhyme words are realized and each rhyme word appears in all possible positions within the stanza, until the first rhyme word closes the sixth stanza (see table 3.2).

TABLE 3.2
Permutations of rhyme word sequence in stanzas of
the *sestina, Al poco giorno e al gran cerchio d'ombra*

Stanza	Rhyme word permutations					
1	A	B	C	D	E	F
2	F	A	E	B	D	C
3	C	F	D	A	B	E
4	E	C	B	F	A	D
5	D	E	A	C	F	B
6	B	D	F	E	C	A

The *sestina* ends with an *envoi* of three lines, in which all six rhyme words make their final appearance.[22] The technical challenge posed by this form was also taken up by, among others, Petrarch (who wrote eight *sestine* and one double *sestina* of twelve stanzas), Alberti (who produced five), and Sannazzaro; by Pontus de Tyard and the Comte de Gramont in France; by Opitz and Gryphius in Germany; as well as by Sir Philip Sydney, Algernon Charles Swinburne, Ezra Pound, T. S. Eliot, Elisabeth Bishop, and W. H. Auden (see, e.g., Auden's "Paysage Moralisé").

While words placed in the rhyming position are often privileged by their position at the end of the line and the phonic echo of one or more syllables, in a *sestina* each rhyme word recurs obsessively no fewer than seven times, creating a far greater impact than can be attributed merely to the number of its occurrences. The six key words in Dante's *sestina* are these:

ombra	(shade, shadow)
colli	(hills)
erba	(grass)
verde	(green)

petra   (stone, rock)
donna   (lady)[23]

Al poco giorno e al gran cerchio d'ombra reiterates the theme of *Io son venuto:* although it is winter, the season of persistent shadows, white hills, and dead grass, the poet-persona persists in his love. Now, however, the object of the persona's desire is described as "the hard stone *[petra]* which speaks and has senses as though it were a woman *[donna]*" (l. 6). The second stanza declares that the young woman's icy coldness remains as unmoved as stone *(petra)* even in spring, the season of love and change. Stanza three proclaims that wearing a grassy garland in her golden hair, she makes her lover oblivious of every other woman; love has locked him between *piccioli colli* (small hills, i.e., her breasts) more tightly than cement locks stone *(petra)*. In stanza four, her beauty has greater power than any gem *(petra),* and though the lover has fled over hill and dale in an attempt to escape, he can find no shadow to protect him from her light. Stanza five tells us that the lover once saw her clothed in green (the color of youth and hope) and so beautiful that she would have made even a rock *(petra)* experience the love he feels for her mere shadow; he therefore desires to be with her—but with her as deeply in love as any woman ever was—in a fair field and protected by high hills. The last stanza confesses the impossibility of such a hope, using the topos of *impossibilia:* rivers will have to flow uphill before this green wood will be set on fire with love for the poet-persona. Impossibility is emphasized by the separation of *s'infiammi* in line 33 from its object *di me* in line 34, followed by the only strong caesura in the poem. He would subject himself to any trial—be buried alive, like Merlin for love of Vivien; eat grass like Tristan, maddened by love (Picone 1995)—if only he could be rewarded by the sight of where her clothes cast a shadow *(ombra,* the rhyme word of line 1 that has now come full circle).

The first two verses of the *envoi* display the key words at the end of each hemistich, whereas the last line of the poem has the two remaining key words in the second hemistich:

> Quandunque i *colli* fanno piú nera *ombra,*
> sotto un bel *verde* la giovane *donna*
> la fa sparer, com'uom *petra* sott'*erba.*
>> (*Al poco giorno e al gran cerchio d'ombra,*
>>   ll. 37–39; my emphasis)

Even in winter, when the *hills* cast their darkest and longest *shadow,* the fine dress of *green* worn by the young *woman* eclipses the shadow, making it disappear just as one can hide a *stone* beneath the green *grass.*

The *envoi*'s simile is clear enough at a literal level, especially when we recall the hermetic qualities of imagery in *trobar clus.*[24] Durling and Martinez (1990,

114–17) identify the *petra* with the heliotrope, a variety of chalcedony that was thought to be capable of obscuring the sun and making its bearer invisible: "Dressed in green, the stony lady embodies the conjunction named in the lapidaries. . . . [Her] development moves thus: hardness and opacity (stone); hardness and translucence (snow); opacity and power (lodestone); transparency and power (gem); active light (sun)." For Picone (1995, 107), however, the woman appears as an enchantress (cf. Merlin's Vivien) and there ensues an imagined passionate embrace in the grass of the meadow where the woman of stone and her lover had first met. Such is the power of hermetic poetry.

Amor, tu vedi ben che questa donna (CII: 79)

Amor, tu vedi ben che questa donna (CII: 79) is traditionally categorized as a *doppia sestina*, "double *sestina*." However, unlike Petrarch's *doppia sestina* (*Rime sparse* 332, "Mia benigna fortuna e 'l viver lieto"), which has twelve stanzas of six lines and goes through the permutations of *retrogradatio cruciata* twice, *Amor, tu vedi ben che questa donna* has only five stanzas; each stanza, however, consists of twelve verses, twice the number of lines of a *sestina* stanza. Dante's poem also follows the *sestina* model in using a single set of rhyme words, repeated throughout the poem. The first stanza sets the pattern (see table 3.3).

TABLE 3.3
Stanza structure, rhyme words, and rhyme word patterns,
Amor, tu vedi ben che questa donna, first stanza

Stanza structure (section: division)		Rhyme words (line numbers below)			Rhyme word pattern
frons:	*pes*	donna	tempo	donna /	A B A /
		I	2	3	
	pes	donna	luce	donna :	A C A :
		4	5	6	
sirma:	*versus*	donna	*freddo*	*freddo* /	A D D /
		7	8	9	
	versus	donna	*petra*	*petra*	A E E
		10	11	12	

The permutations in the five stanzas of *Amor, tu vedi ben* are, however, simpler than in the usual *sestina* form. The pattern of rhyme words in the first stanza means that the first rhyme word *(donna)* occurs five times, while the second (l. 2: *tempo*) and third (l. 5: *luce*) remain without echo until the following stanzas; the fourth and fifth occur twice (*freddo* in ll. 8 and 9; *petra* in ll. 11 and 12). As in the *sestina,* the last rhyme word *(petra)* becomes the first (hence, the dominant) rhyme word in the second stanza—and so on, until each word has dominated one stanza of the poem. The dominant rhyme word in each stanza occurs in the second line of the next stanza but then is absent for some fourteen lines. The rhyme words in the six-line *envoi* form a simple retrogression of those in the last stanza *(donna – petra – freddo – freddo – luce – tempo),* with the central rhyme word (which had been rhyme C in the last stanza) repeated.

As may be seen from the pattern indicated in table 3.3, the stanzas are structured like those of a canzone, with a *frons* and a *sirma* (the latter with two *versus*); the *frons* is also divided into two sections *(pedes)* of three lines each, but the second and fifth lines are not rhymed within the *frons. Amor, tu vedi ben* is one of only two canzoni by Dante in which both major sections of the stanza are subdivided (the other is *Donne ch'avete intelletto d'amore*), and the *petrose* poem is unique in Dante's oeuvre in having *pedes* and *versus* of equal length. The result is that four rhyme words are repeated thirteen times, and one—*freddo*—no fewer than fourteen times (owing to its repetition in the *envoi,* ll. 63 and 64).

Freddo also dominates the central stanza of the poem, where "the macrocosmic-microcosmic parallelism is made explicit" between the lady's coldness and the dominance of cold over the sublunar realm of the world in winter (Durling and Martinez 1990, 146). This same stanza also offers the longest of the (relatively rare) similes in Dante's lyrics: the simile covers some twelve lines (25–36), in which the scientific phenomenon whereby water is transformed by intense cold into "crystal stone" *(cristallina petra)* is used to "explain" the fact that the woman's cold expression freezes the poet-persona's blood and his hot desire is changed into the cold element of his tears. So, too, analogies with the poet's art surface in this stanza and in the *envoi:* "And just as the water becomes permanently crystal, the poem takes on its form permanently" (Durling and Martinez 1990, 147).

Whereas in *Al poco giorno e al gran cerchio d'ombra* the rhyme words retain their primary meaning, in *Amor, tu vedi ben che questa donna* the demands of the exceptional rhyme scheme oblige the poet to have recourse to *rime equivoche* (homophones, with different meanings). In this canzone-*sestina, luce* is used both as a noun (l. 37: "light"; ll. 39 and 42: "eyes/look"; ll. 43 and 46: "daytime") and as a verb (ll. 40 and 65: "shines"). *Freddo* (cold) is both a noun (ll. 25, 27, 30) and an adjective (ll. 28, 31, 34). In *De vulgari* 2.13.13, Dante warns of the dangers of excessive repetition of the same rhyme, the use of *rime equivoche* ("which always seems to detract something from their meaning"), and the presence of too many harsh-sounding rhymes *(rithimorum asperitas)*. Apart from the fact that all three are characteristics of Arnaut Daniel's *trobar clus*—and Arnaut is hailed as Dante's foremost predecessor in *Purgatorio* 26.115–20—scholars have not perhaps accorded sufficient importance to the exception Dante makes in this same passage (Rossi 1995, 71–72): frequent repetition of the same rhyme may be justified if the poet intends to achieve "something new and previously unattempted in art," like a knight who insists on marking the historic moment of his dubbing by some special token *(prerogativa)*.

This is just what Dante tells us he attempted with *Amor, tu vedi ben che questa donna (DVE* 2.13.13), as the *envoi* itself makes clear: "I dare to create for this cold object the novelty *[la novità]* that shines through your structure, something never conceived at any time *[che non fu mai pensata in alcun tempo]"* (ll. 64–66). Here, instead of appearing as gratuitous elements (as so often in Guittone's poetry), the repeated rhymes, *rime equivoche,* and harsh rhymes are an integral part of the poem's structure.

Così nel mio parlar voglio esser aspro (CIII: 80)

Readers of *Così nel mio parlar voglio esser aspro* (CIII: 80)[25] must be struck by the unusually frank and impelling eroticism in this poem—which may well have earned Dante one of Beatrice's accusations in Eden, where, as already mentioned, she berates her lover for having allowed himself to be ensnared by "a young girl *[pargoletta]* / or other new (young) thing *[novità]* of such brief duration" *(Purg.* 31.59–60). Dante tells us that he was so overcome by a feeling of guilt that he fainted—for the third time in the *Comedy.* The metaphorical use of the verb *mordere* (to bite) in *Purgatorio* 31.88 (*Tanta riconoscenza il cor mi* morse) may conceivably be linked to the passion inspired by the *bella petra* celebrated in *Così nel mio parlar,* whose second stanza compares passion to a merciless file rasping away at the lover's life, *gnawing* through his heart layer by layer (l. 25: *sí di rodermi il core a scorza a scorza*), while the third stanza speaks of death *eating away* "with Love's teeth" at the poet's vital senses (ll. 31–32: *la morte, che ogni senso / co li denti d'Amor già mi* manduca). As in the *Comedy,* metaphors are now abundant.

Così nel mio parlar is structured as a regular canzone, with six stanzas of thirteen lines: ten hendecasyllables and three *settenari* (ten, the perfect number, and three evoking the Trinity), according to the pattern: ABbC / ABbC // CDdEE.[26] In terms of number of stanzas, number of lines per stanza, number of syllables per line, and the use of five rhyming couplets in thirteen lines, this structure was to become the most popular in the Italian lyric tradition. In *Così nel mio parlar,* however, the *frons* is longer than the *sirma,* which is fairly unusual in Dante (see note 13), and, with only five lines, this *sirma* is the shortest in his canzoni.

A unique feature of *Così nel mio parlar* among Dante's lyrics is that, from the sixth line down, only rhyming couplets *(rime baciate)* are found, according to the scheme BbC // CDdEE; this imparts a dancelike metrical movement of repetition, and the lightness mitigates the *asperitas* or harshness of much of the lexis. Of the eighty-three rhyme words, forty-four may be judged harsh *(aspre)*, but thirty-two conform to Dante's standards of sweet harmony *(dolcezza*, ending in a vowel – consonant – vowel),[27] a ratio in keeping with the poet's desire to maintain a combination of *asperitas* and *lenitas* (*DVE* 2.13.13). The *envoi* is typical of this mixture, with one *rim dissolut (donna)*, two "sweet" rhyme words *(invola – gola)*, and two "harsh" ones *(saetta – vendetta)*, with their double consonants, as well as the semantic harshness of the final word in the poem, *vendetta*.

The highest concentration of *rime aspre* occurs in the fifth stanza, which opens with the poet-persona's sudden revolt against all the laws of *fin' amors*, his vindictive desire to see Love split open the heart of a woman who is now nothing but a murderous assassin and thief (l. 58). She should be made to howl with desire "in the hot gorge" (l. 60: *nel caldo borro*). The rhymes create a synergetic effect of violent impulse and erotic desire: *mezzo – squatra [squartare*, "to quarter, to cut to pieces," with metathesis] *– atra – corro – rezzo – latra – latra – borro – soccorro*. The rhyme sequence *squatra – atra – latra* (found only in this canzone) reappears in the *Comedy* at *Inferno* 6.14–18 *(latra – atra – isquatra)*, where (in inverted order) it is used to indicate Cerberus's bestiality and violence.[28] It will come as no surprise to find that the word *borro* is a hapax in Dante's writings, signifying an abyss, gorge, or gully, and metaphorically—with the epithet *caldo* (hot)—the woman's vagina.

We find a relatively large number of *rime ricche (petra – impetra; arretra – faretra; induca – manduca; perverso – riverso – verso; corro – soccorro)*, with one *rima equivoca* at lines 58 and 59—*latra* (Latinism and noun, "thief") – *latra* (the verb *latrare*, "to bark furiously or howl"). Many of the rhyme words are formally excluded from the supreme style of the illustrious vernacular in *De vulgari* 2.7.5: for example, consonant groups of double liquids *(quelli – capelli; squille – mille – faville; corro – borro – soccorro)*; or a mute surd followed by a liquid *(petra – impetra – arretra – faretra; scopra – opra; squatra – atra – latra)*; and, of course, the emblematic opening rhymes of *aspro – diaspro*, with their central grouping of three consonants *(-spr-)*. The first rhyme word of the *envoi* identifies the "beautiful stone" *(bella petra)* as a woman *(donna)* and provides the only rhyme word that remains isolated in the poem *(rim dissolut)*.

With regard to scansion, the meaning of the text of *Così nel mio parlar* is supported with words having special rhythmic effects, as well as with enjambment, alliteration and repetition, and binomials:

- An exceptionally high number of verses with two adjacent stressed syllables create a subtle caesura between the hemistichs, for example:

l. 32:   *co li denti d'Amor / già mi manduca*
          with the teeth of love [it] is already devouring me

l. 53:   *Cosí vedess'io lui / fender per mezzo*
          Would that I could see him split [her heart] down the middle
          (with repetition of the initial *Cosí* of the poem's opening line)

l. 61:   *ché tosto griderei: / Io vi soccorro*
          for promptly I would cry: "I will help you"

- A strong *rallentando* effect, produced by the adjacent consonants *r* and *p,* underscores the imagined postorgasmic "peace":

  l. 78:   *e poi le renderei / con amor pace*
            and then I would give her, with love, peace

- Enjambment is another major feature, as in

  ll. 53–54: *Cosí vedess'io lui fender per mezzo*
              lo core
              Would that I could see him split down the middle
              her heart
              [Would I could see him split her heart in two]

The climactic fifth stanza offers a dramatic sequence of enjambments, for the lines just quoted are followed by

ll. 55–56: *poi non mi sarebbe atra*
            la morte
            then I would not find death black

Another emphatic enjambment links these verses—

ll. 59–60: *Omè, perché non latra*
            per me, com'io per lei . . .
            Alas, why does she not howl
            for me, as I do for her . . . ?

—where the impetus of the *settenario* seeks fulfillment in the hendeca-syllable at line 60.
The *sirma* offers only one example of enjambment:

ll. 62–63: *sí come quelli*
            che

- But there is a strong pause in the concluding verse:

  l. 65:   *metterei mano, e piacere'le allora*
            I would put my hand, and then I would find favor with her

- The finality of love's gnawing away at the lover's heart is underscored by alliteration and repetition *(reduplicatio)*:

  l. 25:   *sí di rodermi il core a scorza a scorza*

- Excluded from Dante's purist phase, binomials return:

  l. 67:   *scudiscio e ferza*
            whip and lash
  l. 69:   *vespero e squille*
            vespers and the evening bell

Metaphors abound. The woman is stone or rock, her hair is a whip and lash, her sexual organs are a "hot pit," while death "eats" away the lover's heart and life with Love's "teeth." The lover's desire is a "file" that rasps his life away. The image of a ship suggests the metaphor in line 20, where the "weight" of his unrequited love makes him "sink."

The diction shows the mature lyric poet moving away from Sicilian and Guittonian-Tuscan models. We may note, *inter alia,* the absence of the Sicilian conditional in *-ia (potrebbe,* l. 21; *farei,* l. 71); the choice of *bellezza* (l. 56) rather than the traditional *beltà / biltà;* the Florentine form *ignuda* (l. 8). More importantly, Dante's poetic vocabulary expands enormously: some sixty words appear here for the first time in an Italian lyric (e.g., *lima,* "file"; *manducare,* "to eat"; *sferzare,* "to whip"; *spezzare,* "to shatter"), including some that will not appear in the *Comedy,* such as *borro* (abyss), *bruca* (gnaws at), *increspa* (curls), and *scherano* (cutthroat).

Pointing in the direction of the *Comedy,* we have the Ovidian themes highlighted by Rossi (1995): the transformation of Atlas's bones into stones (Ovid, *Metamorphoses* 4.660); Medusa (*Met.* 5.217); and Niobe's fate (*Met.* 6.303–12). The "peace" attained in sexual union is celebrated in Ovid's *Ars amatoria* 413 and 459–60. Especially significant is the theme of the lover's tearing at the woman's tresses and the fact that the man's assault makes her turn pale like marble (Ovid, *Amores* 1.7.51–52; cf. 2.5.45–46).

In the *frons* of the sixth stanza of Dante's canzone, the poet imagines the joy of seizing the woman's fair tresses that have become a whip and lash for him, then snatching and pulling at them without "pity or courtesy," like a bear (a symbol of lust in medieval bestiaries) playing with his victim, "and though Love whips me with them, I would take my revenge more than a thousand times" (ll. 72–73).[29] The verbal violence and *asperitas* of the fifth stanza is followed by the sadistic desire for revenge in the final stanza, which nevertheless ends (l. 78) with the frustrated lover's dream of mutual appeasement.

Readers of *Inferno* will recall the dramatic scene in the pit of hell when the pilgrim violently seizes and twists the hair of Bocca degli Abati, the Florentine traitor, making him "howl" in the ice of Cocytus—where the verb *latrare,* which makes its first appearance in *Cosí nel mio parlar,* returns twice (*Inf.* 32.105 and 108; cf. *rezzo,* in l. 57 of *Cosí nel mio parlar* and in *Inf.* 32.75). And, in *Inferno* 32.127, another of this canzone's verbal innovations, *manduca* (l. 32)—the emphatic, Latinate form for "to eat, to devour"—returns to describe Ugolino's bestial gnawing at the skull of his neighbor in the ice. Even more noteworthy is the fact that the first line of this great canzone, *Cosí nel mio parlar voglio esser aspro,* clearly anticipates the famous opening of canto 32, in which the poet of the *Comedy* expresses his yearning for rhymes sufficiently harsh and grating to describe the evil pit of the universe—

> S'io avessi le rime aspre e chiocce,
> come si converrebbe al tristo buco
> sovra 'l qual pontan tutte l'altre rocce,

—an optative that prepares the way for the stupendous sequence of rhymes, *Osterlicchi – Tambernicchi – cricchi* (*Inf.* 32.26, 28, and 30), inconceivable in Duecento poetry before Dante's *petrose.*

We shall perhaps never know for certain when the *petrose* lyrics were written, but in any account of Dante's poetic apprenticeship they must be seen as anticipating some of the *Comedy*'s salient features. These include such a *tour de force* of adjusting sound to sense as the *rime aspre* that constellate Statius's discourse in *Purgatorio* 25, which would be unimaginable without the *petrose* (Russo 1971, 152–53). As Durling and Martinez put it (1990, 199): "The *petrose* are the first of Dante's works to explore the extent to which the speaker's predicament and the poet's art are instances of the cooperation of the whole of creation in the destiny of a single individual."

Tre donne intorno al cor mi son venute (CIV: 81)

One of the few certainties in charting Dante's poetic career is the fact that the canzone *Tre donne intorno al cor mi son venute* (CIV: 81) was written after he had been exiled and condemned to death by the Florentine republic. The canzone's theme is justice, likewise exiled and held in contempt, and Dante would almost certainly have written a commentary on this poem in the fourteenth treatise of his *Convivio,* in which he had planned to analyze this supremely human virtue (*Conv.* 4.27.11), as well as discuss the reasons why allegory was first used by "wise men" (*Conv.* 2.1.4).

The canzone consists of 107 verses: five stanzas of eighteen lines (of which twelve are *rime baciate*), followed by two *envois.* The *frons* has two *pedes* of four verses—two hendecasyllables and two *settenari* (AbbC / AbbC, an unusual pattern in Dante's verse); the *sirma* has ten lines, with three *settenari* and a final rhyming couplet (CDdEeFEfGG).[30] A unique element is the double *envoi* (a third has been conjectured).[31] The first *envoi* of *Tre donne,* with ten lines, echoes the rhyme scheme of the *sirma;* the second, of seven lines, has only one *settenario* (AXaBBCC).

Transcendental, eternal justice—*ius divinum et naturale*—is portrayed as a woman (Astraea, the sister of Venus, goddess of love), whose daughter and granddaughter (both conceived by parthenogenesis, hence unmediated) are human justice *[ius gentium]* and law *[lex humana].* Although it is no longer necessary to excuse or justify the use of allegory, readers would do well to remember that in Latin and the Romance languages, abstract qualities and virtues are overwhelmingly feminine in gender, and statues portraying La Giustizia as a woman would have been familiar to many of Dante's contemporaries. Be that as it may, even in the nineteenth century, when allegory was written off as a major handicap in poetry, Francesco De Sanctis, in his *Saggio critico sul Petrarca,* hailed this canzone as the finest allegorical poem ever written: such is the power of the allegorical element in *Tre donne.*

The opening stanza sets the scene with details taken over from traditional love poetry: three ladies have surrounded the poet-persona's heart, which they cannot "enter," for it is already occupied by Love, who governs the persona's whole life and being. The opposition created at the very beginning of the poem (ll. 2–3) between *fore* (outside) and *dentro* (within) is emblematic of the poet's own situation, exiled from Florence and all that he most cherishes (*Tre donne,* ll. 81–84, and *Par.* 17.55–57). After its semantic devaluation as an object of obsessive erotic desire in the *rime petrose,* the word *donna* now returns with its full etymological force as the feminine form of *dominus* (lord). In spite of their great beauty and power, the three ladies appear sorrowful and dismayed, miserably clothed, and abandoned by all, a state underscored by the epithet *solette* (l. 16); this word is not only a hapax in Dante's lyrics but also is one of the few diminutives used by him outside of the *Comedy,* where *soletta* will be used to describe, *inter alia,* the solitary figure of Matelda in the Earthly Paradise (*Purg.* 28.40).

We also notice the frequent use of binomials. In the first stanza, *dolente e sbigottita* (l. 9: sorrowing and dismayed) is followed in the next line by *discacciata e stanca* (driven away and weary); then in l. 15, in contrast to the golden age when the ladies were cherished, they now meet with nothing but hostility and indifference (l. 15: *or sono a tutti in ira ed in non cale*).

The use of binomials, excluded from Dante's purist phase, finds its lexical parallel in the use of a Gallicism (l. 23: *oraggio,* "shower"); a Provençal form (l. 29: *fello,* "angry"); and even the use of a Sicilian form (l. 83: *miso,* for Tuscan *messo,* "put, set") following closely upon the Sicilian *àve* (l. 83: *che m'àve* [Latin *habet,* "has"] *in foco miso,* "that has set me on fire"), which returns in the emphatic rhyming position in *Ma questo foco m'àve* (l. 85). Such a variety of lexical forms, unthinkable when Dante wrote his *Vita Nova,* is a modest adumbration of the *Comedy's* verbal riches.

Love—*caritas,* far removed from the *eros* of the *petrose*—is cultivated only by a few, as we learn in l. 31, where *vivanda* (food) looks forward to Dante's Banquet. In *Convivio* I the word *vivanda* occurs nine times and is associated with divine wisdom, the "bread" of angels (*Conv.* 1.1.7). Love tells the three exiled ladies to take heart as he seizes both his arrows (l. 59): according to tradition, one inspires hatred (here, of evil and corruption), the other inflames hearts with love of the virtues "born of our blood [who] go begging" (l. 64). Humanity, influenced by malignant stars, should weep over the state of the world, for love and the three forms of justice are eternal—and a time shall come when people will once again cultivate love of justice.

The last stanza introduces a change of mood, accompanied by a flurry of figurative language. After the ladies' "divine speech" (l. 73), we are brought back to the parallel between such exalted exiles and Dante's own banishment, so that—with a moral energy rarely found outside the *Comedy*—he regards his own exile as an honor (l. 76: *l'essilio che m'è dato, onor mi tegno*), for it is surely praiseworthy to fall with the good (l. 80: *cader co' buoni è pur di lode degno*). Reinforcing the *sententiae,* antitheses and personification, we find no fewer than thirteen tropes in thirteen verses (ll. 77–90; see Boyde 1971, 149).

One of these tropes describes how the contemporary world "turns the white flowers into dark" (ll. 78–79: *il mondo versi / i bianchi fiori in persi*). Commentators are at pains to explain that "the white flowers" must not be interpreted as a reference to the White Guelf exiles. Certainly, the primary meaning is the corruption of the good (the same image is found, e.g., in Panuccio del Bagno's *Lasso di far più verso,* ll. 5–6). Yet it is hardly possible to suppose that Dante could have used the contrast between white and black without associating it with his own condemnation as a White Guelf, which blackened his character for many who were so quick to believe the charges laid against him (*Par.* 17.52–53). In the second *envoi* the "white feathers" and "black hounds" (ll. 101–2) clearly refer to the White and Black parties, which the poem (addressed for the third time in l. 102) is enjoined to seek out and accompany. The poet is now ready to "hunt with the black hounds," although they still refuse to grant him peace, for they do not recognize his moral integrity (l. 105, with a possible echo of Christ's words in Luke 23.34, "Father, forgive them for they know not what they do"). Nevertheless, to forgive is fine victory in war *(ché 'l perdonare è bel vincer di guerra),* a saying originating in Seneca, with perhaps a Vergilian reminiscence (*Aeneid* 6.853).

The first *envoi* (ll. 91–100) had pursued a different allegorical mode. The poet tells his canzone to keep her nudity modestly covered; her outward beauty will suffice for the crowd (cf. the final verse of *Voi che 'ntendendo:* "Consider at least how beautiful I am"). If, however, the canzone can find a true lover of virtue, then she should disclose her "flower" and make all loving hearts desire it (ll. 96–100). This metaphor was traditionally associated with the lady's "rose," the erotic goal sought by the lover (cf. *Il Fiore*). Here, of course, it is linked to the *dolce pome* (sweet fruit), the allegorical message hidden from the corrupt mass.

The admission of a certain degree of guilt and repentance on Dante's part (ll. 88–90, 106–7) is in accord with evidence provided by Villani and Leonardo Bruni that, after the failure of the White exiles to return to Florence by force in 1304, the poet attempted to find a means of reconciliation with the victorious Blacks. It was, of course, a transient mood; and it cannot be understood to mean that Dante confessed to the charges laid against him by the Black faction. The proud claim that he remained in undeserved exile *(exul inmeritus)* is heard for the first time, possibly in that same year (*Ep.* 2.1.3), and was to be reiterated in 1310 and 1311 (*Ep.* 5.1, 6.1, 7.1), as well as throughout the *Comedy*.

The dating of the *Comedy* as initiated in 1306–7 (see chapter 6) certainly accords with the fact that, in *Tre donne,* the origin of the Nile is taken to be one of the four rivers of the Earthly Paradise (ll. 46–51: Gihon—see Gen. 2.10–14); this makes it unlikely that when he wrote the canzone (c. 1304), Dante had already imagined Eden to be located on the summit of Mount Purgatory and at the antipodes to Jerusalem. Perhaps too much has been made of the allusion to malignant astral influences (l. 68, where corrupt humankind is said to have "fallen under the rays of such a heaven"); nevertheless, it is certainly true that the author of the *Comedy* went to great pains to refute any idea of astral determinism by placing at the very center of the poem his belief in free will and the fact that the human soul, "which the heavens have not in their power," is ultimately free to choose what is just (*Purg.* 16.67–105). Nevertheless, *Tre donne* does contain lines that look forward to Dante's masterpiece: those already cited (76 and 80)—"the exile given me, I count an honor . . . to fall with the good still merits praise"—are worthy of the author of the *Comedy*'s unbowed spirit. The pathos of "Do you not feel pity for my (tearful) eyes?" (l. 44) anticipates Ugolino's anguished cry, "And if you do not weep, what *will* make you weep?" (*Inf.* 33.42). The phrase *l'ossa e la polpa* (l. 86: bones and flesh) returns as *d'ossa e di polpe* (*Inf.* 27.73) to indicate Guido da Montefeltro's mortal body (cf. *Purg.* 32.123).

The most striking characteristic of the canzone's structure, which links *Tre donne* with the *Comedy,* is the fact that the ninety verses of the five stanzas, followed by the first *envoi* of ten verses, create a unit with the perfect number one hundred. But the affinity goes deeper: both works convey an urgent moral message to a world that has gone utterly astray, and, already in *Tre donne,* Dante's condition is raised to a universal level through the parallel between his personal fate and the banishment of all forms of justice from a corrupt world. The same universality will be projected through the pilgrim's finding himself lost in the dark wood at the beginning of the *Comedy,* where he is both Dante and Everyman (although the journey, the quest, will be his alone). In *Tre donne,* Dante is already the indefatigable "preacher of justice" (*Ep.* 12.3.7) whose voice will resound throughout his sacred poem.

Sonnets exchanged with Cino (XCIV–XCVII, CX–CXV: 84a–88a)

As already mentioned, the sonnet is a major form of lyric poetry introduced or "invented" most probably by the Sicilian poet Giacomo da Lentini in the first half of the thirteenth century, and the form came to have unparalleled success in many European languages (often greater than the esteem it enjoyed in its homeland). The earliest sonnets that survive have two quatrains with alternating rhymes (ABAB / ABAB) and two tercets with various rhyme schemes based on combinations of either three rhymes (CDE) or two (CD); all the lines are hendecasyllabic.[32] For the most part, Cavalcanti, Dante, and Cino chose the innovatory scheme ABBA / ABBA *(rime incrociate)* for the quatrains, which was to be preferred by Petrarch and his followers (no fewer than 303 of Petrarch's 317 sonnets follow this pattern). In spite of its exclusive use of the supreme meter (*DVE* 2.5.8: *superbissimum carmen*) and the fact that Dante wrote at least 59 sonnets (or 291, if *Il Fiore* is his work, as has been claimed), he nevertheless judged the sonnet to be inferior in dignity to the canzone (*DVE* 2.3.5).

Cino (Guittoncino de' Sigibuldi) of Pistoia was born c. 1270 and died in 1336/37. It is therefore highly unlikely that (as has sometimes been asserted) he was one of the poets who penned replies to Dante's sonnet *A ciascun'alma presa e gentil core,* composed in 1283 (*VN* 3.10–12). However, after Beatrice's death (June 1290), Cino addressed a poem of condolence to Dante—*Avegna ched el m'aggia piú per tempo*—based on the metrical structure of Dante's canzone *Donna pietosa e di novella etate,* with its premonition of Beatrice's demise.[33]

In *De vulgari* 1.10.2, the superiority of the illustrious vernacular of Italy to the *langue d'oïl* and *langue d'oc* is attested by the fact that writers such as "Cino da Pistoia and his friend [Dante himself]" have used it to compose "sweeter and more subtle vernacular poetry." Indeed, cited as a supreme stylist in his canzoni (*DVE* 1.17.3) and as a master of the hendecasyllable—the noblest line of verse (*DVE* 2.5.4)—Cino is acclaimed as the "Italian" love poet par excellence, while Dante reserves for himself the title of "singer of righteousness" (*DVE* 2.2.8). Robert Hollander has claimed that the practitioners of the "sweet new style" celebrated by Bonagiunta in *Purgatorio* 24.55–62 were none other than Dante and Cino (Hollander 1992a), although no direct mention of Cino is made in the *Comedy*.

An exchange of sonnets between Cino and Dante (XCIV–XCVII, CX–CXV: 84a–88a) possibly took place before Dante's exile (in Foster and Boyde's numbering, Cino's sonnets in the series are designated with an *a* following the arabic numeral). The period of fairly intense poetic correspondence between the two men took place, however, during the years 1303–6, when Cino was also in exile, from his native Pistoia. This dating is borne out by the praise of Cino's achievement as a vernacular poet in Dante's *De vulgari eloquentia,* most likely composed in 1304–5.

All ten sonnets they exchanged have quatrains with *rime incrociate* (ABBA/ABBA), and the tercets of every response adhere to the pattern chosen for the sonnet that elicited it. Eight of the poems are about love.

In what is judged to be the first of the series (XCIV: 84a), Cino falls under the spell of a "noble lady" *(donna gentile),* who promises to beatify his heart (l. 4: *ella sarà del meo cor bëatrice*). Dante, whose exclusive devotion to his own Beatrice need hardly be emphasized, uses the same rhymes in his reply (XCV: 84), although he avoids such trite combinations as Cino's *dice – disdice* and *sguardo – dardo.* Instead, Dante introduces *rimas caras,* difficult rhymes, such as *elice* (l. 4: a Latinism from *elicio, elicere,* "to draw out"), and words hitherto excluded from his lyrics, such as *gagliardo* (cf., however, *Il Fiore* 61.11), *lombardo,* and *bugiardo.* Likewise, in *Io sono stato con Amore insieme* (CXI: 86), we find unusual rhyme words such as *palestra – balestra.* In *Degno fa voi trovare ogni tesoro* (CXIII: 87), the unusual rhyme *disvicina* occurs, as well as *foro – poro* and the Provençal term *croia* (l. 11: harsh, unhappy—used metaphorically), already found in Giacomo da Lentini and Guittone, but which was to return so forcefully in *Inferno* 30.102 (with the meaning, "hard").[34] As we read in Foster and Boyde (1967, 2:313): "Nowhere else [in Dante's lyrics] do the metaphors succeed each other so densely; nowhere does Dante draw his imagery from so many sources." In these sonnets, Dante derives his imagery from classical mythology, botany, the hunt (XCV: 84), archery, mineralogy, and medicine (CXIII: 87).

In *Degno fa voi trovare ogni tesoro* (CXIII: 87), and especially in *Io mi credea del tutto esser partito* (CXIV: 88), Dante reproaches Cino for his fickle heart. In *Io mi credea,* Dante uses the rhyming position to make a play on Cino's name, which turns up in the same position (l. 6: *un-cino*), by reproaching Cino for allowing himself to be caught on every hook (*Cino – uncino*), where the *rima ricca* between Cino's name and the word for "hook"—*uncino*—gives an ironic twist to the belief that names reveal the true nature of persons and things (cf. *VN* 13.4). On the other hand, in reply to Cino's question in *Dante, quando per caso s'abbandona* (CX: 86a), whether it is permissible to change the object of one's love, as Cino's experience would suggest, Dante asserts—in *Io sono stato con Amore in-*

sieme (CXI: 86)—that his whole experience of love since his ninth year (when he first met Beatrice) proves that the human will is never free within love's jurisdiction (ll. 9–10: *nel cerchio de la sua palestra / liber arbitrio già mai non fu franco*). Coming from an author who had placed so much emphasis on the fact that his love for Beatrice had always been controlled by reason (*VN* 2.9, for example), this astonishing confession is followed by the equally surprising statement that a new love may well replace one that is "weary" (l. 14: *stanco*). Dante also sent Cino an accompanying letter (*Ep.* 3), written in Latin and addressed by "the Florentine unjustly exiled" to "the exile from Pistoia," in which he appealed not only to experience but also to the authority of Ovid (*Met.* 4.1–35, 192–208, 389–415) in order to prove that "the appetitive faculty, which is the seat of love, is a faculty of sense" and that, once the first passion is exhausted, it is ready to turn to a new object of desire. Cecco d'Ascoli (Francesco Stabili, 1269–1327), who never missed an opportunity to criticize Dante, cited this sonnet and attacked its premise while professing the belief that only death can put an end to pure love (*L'Acerba* 3.1.1971–82).

Such sentiments probably also inspired at least in part the reproaches leveled at Dante by Beatrice (*Purg.* 30.115–38 and 31.22–63). Expressed during the period when both Cino and Dante were in exile, the idea that the will is never free in Love's arena was later rejected in the most forceful manner possible at the very center of the *Comedy*. And only a few years after writing *Io sono stato* and *Epistle* 3, the poet of the *Comedy* placed the belief in Love's omnipotence in the mouth of the damned sinner, Francesca da Rimini (*Inf.* 5.103). That belief is utterly refuted by Virgil, the pilgrim's guide (who—as the historical Vergil—had asserted in *Eclogues* 10.69 that Love conquers all!), in his discourse on love in *Purgatorio* 18. For, although love is the motive force behind all good and all evil (*Purg.* 17.91–105), human beings are endowed with free will, the power to choose between the love of good and the love of evil (*Purg.* 18.70–75). Such statements contradict what Dante had written to Cino in *Io sono stato con Amore insieme,* and they are clearly the result of a moral crisis and conversion that must have occurred sometime during the period 1306–8 and which led to Dante's writing a poem that shows men and women how they merit eternal damnation or salvation according to the way they respond to love. In fact, the poet's recantation of the idea that the human will is powerless against sensual love is far better documented than the assumption, so dear to many Dante scholars, that the author of the *Comedy* turned away from the love of wisdom and philosophy that had inspired his *Convivio.* The *Comedy* corrects a number of points made in the earlier work; nevertheless, philosophy itself continued to be highly valued on its own ground (*Par.* 10.133–38 and 26.25–30).

As Dante tells Cino in *Io mi credea,* the Florentine poet thought that he had abandoned the love lyrics of earlier years (l. 2: *queste nostre rime,* "these poems of ours"), since his ship (a metaphor for his poetic powers, as in *Par.* 2.3) must now steer a different course in deeper waters (ll. 3–4). While this metaphor may point in the direction of the *Comedy,* such a declaration of intent is typical of the new mission Dante had assumed as "the singer of righteousness" (*DVE* 2.2.8). And it is in this role that he exhorts Cino to correct his fickle heart "with virtue, so that your deeds may accord with your sweet words" (ll. 13–14)—where the expression *dolci detti* signifies the poetry of love as practiced by Guido Guiniz-zelli (*Purg.* 26.112), Cino, and Dante himself in his earlier lyrics.

*A*mor, da che convien pur ch'io mi doglia (cxvi: 89)

The canzone *Amor, da che convien pur ch'io mi doglia* (cxvi: 89) is also known as Dante's "mountain song," because of the invocation *O montanina mia canzon* (l. 76). It was probably composed c. 1307, while the exiled poet was stay-ing in the Casentino valley, surrounded by mountains, in the upper reaches of the river Arno (ll. 61–63).[35] The poem was apparently sent to Marquis Moroello Malaspina, accompanied by a letter (*Ep.* 4). The hospitality offered to the poet by Franceschino Malaspina and Dante's celebration of the family's good name and liberality are recorded in *Purgatorio* 8.112–39.

In the letter—as in the sonnet to Cino *Io sono stato*—the poet's will is utterly subject to Love's imperious commands. Here, he goes on to state that not only has Love slain *(occidit)* his virtuous resolve to abstain from thoughts and songs about women, but Love has also put an end to his assiduous meditations on things both celestial and earthly *(tam celestia quam terrestria).* A beautiful woman, who appeared "like a flash of lightning from above," has transformed him into Love's slave. The affinity with the situation described in *Io sono stato* is also found in the text of *Amor, da che convien,* where lines 26–27 of the canzone echo the sonnet's fifth and sixth verses (my emphasis):

Chi *ragione* o virtú contra gli sprieme	Quale argomento di *ragion* aVrena
fa come que' che 'n *la tempesta* sona	ove tanta *tempesta* in me si gira?
(*Io sono stato,* ll. 5–6)	(*Amor, da che convien,* ll. 26–27)

———

Anyone who urges reason or virtue	What rational argument can hold [me]
against him [Love] acts like one who	back when such a tempest whirls
cries out in a tempest.	within me?

As critics have noted, what may well be Dante's last canzone, *Amor, da che convien* bears little trace of the innovative elements found in his *petrose* or the poems composed during his exile. The poem is based on fifteen-line stanzas, shorter than any used in his late canzoni (*Tre donne* has stanzas of eighteen lines, while those of *Doglia mi reca* comprise twenty-one lines each). Stylistically, there is nothing remarkable about the structure of this canzone. Exceptional alliteration, however, begins in line 42, with V*ie via ve*drai (Soon enough you will see)—with an *accelerando* emphasized by syntactic doubling, whereby *vie via* is pronounced *vie vvia*—and is prolonged into the next line, with *Allor mi volgo per veder* (Then, I turn round to see).

The emphasis is never on the object of the persona's feelings (as it is so strikingly in the *petrose*); instead, it focuses on his inner suffering and mental state, brought about by his "rash soul" (l. 19: *anima folle*), which is well illustrated by the imagery of lines 37–40: "I know well enough that snow melts in the sun, but I cannot do anything about it: I am like a man in another's power who goes on his own two feet to the place where he is killed."[36] Paola Allegretti (2001), who has recently shown the influence of both Guittone and Ovid in this canzone, draws attention to the fact that in Dante's poem the city has been transformed into an alpine region, while the mountains have become the "savage" setting for love. As in a sonnet addressed to Cino (*Perch'io non trovo chi meco ragioni*, XCVI: 85), in the canzone's last stanza Dante complains that he is in a place empty of *donne* and *genti accorte* who understand the true nature of love (ll. 67–68). The *envoi* (ll. 76–84) speaks of the steadfast cruelty shown him by Florence, "devoid of love and stripped of compassion." The poet admonishes his canzone to tell his native city that he can "no longer make war on her," but that, even if Florence were to soften her attitude, he would no longer be free to return—an extraordinary, hyperbolical assertion of Love's power.

Had Dante already begun work on the *Comedy,* as his assiduous meditations in *Amor, da che convien* on things both celestial and earthly might lead us to suppose? We shall perhaps never know. The feelings expressed in the canzone, however, are essentially alien to the *Comedy.* This contrast is underscored by the use of the same rhyme pattern *(terra – serra – guerra)* that appears in the canzone's *envoi*—where the pattern is connected with Love's having rendered the poet incapable of returning to Florence—in the canto proclaiming the theological virtue of hope and the exiled poet's longing to return to his native city:

> Se mai continga che 'l poema sacro
> al quale ha posto mano e cielo e *terra,*
> sí che m'ha fatto per molti anni macro,
>   vinca la crudeltà che fuor mi *serra*
> del bello ovile ov' io dormi' agnello,
> nimico ai lupi che li danno *guerra;*
>   con altra voce omai, con altro vello

ritornerò poeta, e in sul fonte
del mio battesmo prenderò 'l cappello.

(*Par.* 25.1–9)

———

If it comes [and may it come] to pass that the sacred poem to which both
heaven and earth have lent a hand—so that it has withered me over
the years—should overcome the cruelty that bars me from the beautiful
fold where I slept as a lamb, an enemy of the wolves that make war on it;
then, with another voice, with another fleece I shall return as poet and
receive the laurel wreath at my baptismal font.

Amor, da che convien shows us for a last time Dante as the poet of earthly love,
rather than as the singer of righteousness.

Doglia mi reca ne lo core ardire (CVI: 83)

The canzone *Doglia mi reca ne lo core ardire* (CVI: 83) is cited by Dante
in *De vulgari* 2.2.8 as evidence of his claim to be Italy's "singer of righteousness,"
chiefly concerned with *directio voluntatis,* the supremacy of reason over desire
and the will. The stress on the first syllable of the initial word, *Dòglia*—unusual
here, as in *Dònne ch'avete intelletto d'amore*—signals the nervous energy main-
tained throughout the poem, which has the longest stanzas (twenty-one lines) of
any of Dante's canzoni.[37] The stanzas are also unique in having nine *settenari,*
which produce six *rime baciate* (rhyming couplets) and one rhyming triplet in
twenty-one verses. The *frons* has two *pedes* of five verses (with rhymes B and C
inverted): ABbCd / ACcBd. The *sirma* consists of eleven verses: DeeFfGHhhGG
(note the sequence *Hhh* in ll. 17–19 of each stanza, followed by the final rhym-
ing couplet). One detailed analysis of this milestone in the poet's development
demonstrates the unique place occupied by *Doglia mi reca* "among Dante's 'prepa-
rations' for the *Comedy*" (Boyde 1971, 331). Another critical analysis of the poem
shows that "Dante has here tapped into a well-spring of his poetic identity. . . .
[The] comparison of the lover to the miser lays the foundation for the moral
edifice of the *Commedia* . . . based on the notion of desire or love as the motive
force for *all* our actions" (Barolini 1993, 31–32).

Our brief overview can only highlight some of the rhetorical devices used
by the poet to persuade his immediate audience of *donne* (l. 3) that they must
banish love from the world and sacrifice their beauty, since men are corrupt.
This latter judgment is reinforced by repetition: "Omo *da sé vertú fatto ha lon-*

tana: / omo *no, mala bestia ch'*om *somiglia"* (ll. 22–23: Men have alienated them-selves from virtue: no, not men, [but] evil beasts in the likeness of men). From the second to the fifth stanzas, the repetition of the word for "slave" *(servo, serva),* usually in combination with its antonym *(signore, segnore,* "lord"), likewise ham-mers home the moral message that men are thralls to avarice (see table 3.4). Rhetorical questions abound (see table 3.5: note the syncopated sequence of rhetorical questions at ll. 90–94).

TABLE 3.4
Repetition of *servo, serva* and *signore, segnore* in *Doglia mi reca ne lo core ardire*

Line	*servo, serva* and *signore, segnore*	Comments
25	*voler cadere in* servo *di* signore	Line 26 extends the comparison chiastically to *di vita in morte* (from life to death)
43–44	Servo *non di* signor, *ma di* vil servo *si fa di chi da cotal* serva *si scosta*	
48	*questo* servo signor	oxymoron
64–65	*Chi è* servo *è come quello ch'è seguace ratto a* segnore	
98	segnore *a cui* servo *sormonta*	a lord enthralled by a slave

TABLE 3.5
Rhetorical questions in *Doglia mi reca ne lo core ardire*

Line	Rhetorical question	Translation
18	*Lasso, a che dicer vegno?*	Alas, what am I obliged to say?
75–76	*dimmi, che hai tu fatto, cieco avaro disfatto?*	tell me, what have you done, blind miser vanquished [by death]?
90–94	*Morte, che fai? che fai, fera Fortuna,*	Death, what are you doing? what are you doing, cruel Fortune?
	che non solvete quel che non si spende?	why don't you disperse what is unspent?
	se 'l fate, a cui si rende?	If you were to do so, to whom should it go?
	Non so	I don't know
123	*Volete udir se piaga?*	Do you want to hear how it offends?

The prophetic voice that cries out with such force in the *Comedy* is here prominent for the first time, conscious of the poet's mission to attack humanity's corruption with *parole quasi contra tutta gente* (l. 4: words against virtually everyone). Greed, we are admonished in a memorable line, can never be satisfied: *Corre l'avaro, ma più fugge pace* (l. 69: The miser runs, but peace runs even faster). Even more powerful and redolent of the *Comedy*'s poetic concision is the imprecation "Cursed be the bread wasted on you, which is not wasted on a dog!" for a dog is useful to his master (ll. 80–81: *Maladetto lo tuo perduto pane, / che non si perde al cane*). Avarice (the she-wolf of *Purg.* 20.10–12) is denounced as spiritual and ethical blindness (ll. 48–52) that enslaves our reason (ll. 95–98). And the imagery of falconry developed through lines 106–13 will be found again on the terrace of avarice in *Purgatorio* 19.61–67, when the pilgrim, exhorted to turn his gaze toward the heavenly *logoro* (lure), compares himself to the hawk that obeys the falconer's call. Here, instead, virtue as the falconer fails to entice the hawk representing the miser (ll. 112–13): "she throws the morsel toward him, so great is her concern for him; yet he does not [even] open his wings." As Boyde (1971, 151–52) remarks: "One feels for the first time that extensive sections were actually *conceived* in figurative language. . . . This is a development of the utmost importance. . . . It means that *metaphor is no longer a trope*" but in fact shapes the argument "at a poetic and not a logical level."

Doglia mi reca would probably have served Dante's purpose, if he had written the last book of *Convivio,* whose theme was to be the virtue of liberality (cf. *Conv.* 1.8.18). If so, the poem would have illustrated the terrible consequences of its opposite, the capital vice of avarice (*Purg.* 20.8: the evil that has invaded the entire world), with a relatively brief account of the happiness and nobility conferred by Virtue, God's servant, on humanity during its "short journey" on earth (*per lo corto viaggio,* ll. 27–42).

*S*e vedi li occhi miei di pianger vaghi (CV: 82)

The chronology of Dante's poems cannot be charted with certainty. The sonnet *Se vedi li occhi miei di pianger vaghi* (CV: 82: If you see my eyes wanting to weep) was possibly the last lyric he composed, since it most probably refers to events that took place in 1311 or 1312. In lines 6–7 it implores God to castigate the "one who murders Justice and then seeks refuge with the great tyrant," casting "such a chill of fear in the hearts of your faithful" (ll. 9–10). This is almost certainly a reference to Clement V's betrayal of Henry VII's imperial mission, the pope's removal of the papal court to Avignon, and his supposed subservience to Philip the Fair, king of France (cf. *Purg.* 32.142–60). If so, the sonnet must have been written once the pope's treachery had come out into the open (cf. *Par.* 30.142–48)—in other words, no earlier than 1311, when demands made by Clement in a letter addressed to Henry "show the Pontiff's absolute refusal to support Henry's program for imperial restoration in Italy" (Bowsky 1960, 108). The likelihood that Dante interrupted work on the *Comedy* in order to write a sonnet castigating Clement's opposition to Henry is increased by the fact that the poet also composed no fewer than three Latin epistles (*Ep.* 5–7) dating from 1310–11, on the political drama then unfolding.

To accuse Clement of murdering Justice would accord well with the poet's conception of justice. As we have seen in the canzone *Tre donne,* Dante portrayed justice as a triple emanation from God. In *Monarchia,* Dante asserted the belief that "the world is ordered in the best possible way when justice is at its most powerful" (1.11.1) and that "whatever God wills in human society must be judged to be pure and true right *[ius]*" (2.2.6), while the emperor is the one person capable of guarding and administering his ideal justice (1.13.7). To find happiness on earth and eternal beatitude in heaven, humanity must be guided by the emperor in temporal affairs and by the pope in spiritual matters. At the mathematical center of the *Comedy,* in its fiftieth canto (*Purg.* 16.97–114), papal and ecclesiastical interference in the emperor's sphere of temporal jurisdiction is denounced as the cause for the corrupt state of the world in 1300. The same diagnosis is repeated toward the end of the poem, when Beatrice describes the catastrophic effects of greed (*cupidigia,* the she-wolf and greatest obstacle to justice) and tells the pilgrim that in order to discover the cause of such universal corruption he need only "think that there is no one who governs on earth" (*Par.* 27.140). In the temporal sphere, those who reject the emperor's divinely ordained authority follow the terrible example set by the kings of France, who constitute "the evil tree that casts its shadow over the whole Christian earth" (*Purg.* 20.43–44), thus eclipsing the just rays of the imperial sun (*Purg.* 16.106–8). As set out in *Se vedi li occhi miei,* the prayer to God to strike down the one who murders Justice and to restore Justice—"for without her there is no peace on earth" (l. 14)—is entirely in keeping with the poet's mature political thought.

Se vedi li occhi miei has the distinction of being the only lyric by Dante to deal exclusively with a political theme. The sonnet is also the only one of Dante's poems to have been subjected to a thoroughgoing structuralist analysis (Jakobson and Valesio 1966). This analysis ignores the strong enjambment between the tercets, caused by the invocation to the "fire of love, light of heaven," which begins in line 11. From the point of view of poetic syntax, the two chief divisions do not correspond to the formal one between quatrains and tercets, since the second section (l. 11) is introduced by an emphatically adversative *Ma* (But) and continues through to the end of line 14. Nevertheless, for Jakobson and Valesio, the first quatrain expresses the poet's anguish and his prayer to God, and the second, the desire that the guilty one be punished; the first tercet evokes the fear that has gripped and silenced the faithful, while the second implores God to resuscitate Justice and ends with a vision of peace on earth. The authors also note that "the masculine *mondo* . . . , filled with infernal poison, is opposed to the feminine *terra* . . . , longing for peace" (Jakobson and Valesio 1966, 21). Moreover, "the correspondences between the borderlines in each pair of adjacent strophes are strengthened by the use of morphologic or syntactic units which do not occur in the other lines of the sonnet: *passato prossimo* between both internal strophes [ll. 8–9: *ch'elli* ha già sparto . . . *e* messo ha di paura], second-person subjunctive between initial strophes [ll. 4–5: *svaghi . . . paghi*], and appositions between both final strophes" (Jakobson and Valesio 1966, 25). The poem's urgent moral message means that "all three supreme topics of poetic art [*DVE* 2.2.7] . . . are in fact treated in this poem: *virtus* [virtue], *salus* [well-being] and 'the fire of love' (*amoris accensio*)" (Jakobson and Valesio 1966, 20).

Conclusion: Themes, influences, and forms

At the beginning of his career as a lyric poet, Dante wrote exclusively about love. Guittone's influence was quickly replaced by that of Cavalcanti. The latter's negative view of love as a destructive force is apparent in some of Dante's early lyrics (e.g., *Lo doloroso amor che mi conduce*), even in one or two included in *Vita Nova* (*VN* 16.7–10: *Spesse fiate vegnonmi a la mente*). Cavalcanti's stylistic "purity" was to have a more lasting influence. For Dante's conception of love, however, which is inexorably linked with the "noble heart" (*VN* 20.3–5: *Amore e 'l cor gentil sono una cosa*), the poet was indebted to his Bolognese predecessor, Guido Guinizzelli (d. 1276), whom Dante placed among those purifying their tendency to lust in Purgatory while hailing him as "master" in the field of love poetry (*Purg.* 26.97–99). But we may regard as Dante's original contribution the discovery that love could (and should) be gratuitous, seeking no reward outside praise of the beloved (*VN* 19.4–14: *Donne ch'avete intelletto d'amore*) and seen as capable of overcoming even death (*VN* 41.10–13: *Oltre la spera che più larga gira*).

The study of philosophy, probably begun in the last four or five months of 1293, as well as involvement in Florentine political life, opened up new horizons for Dante's poetry. At first, his passion for philosophy (the "love of wisdom") was expressed according to the "sweet rhymes" of conventional love lyrics. This was followed by a stylistic revolution, first visible in the poet's rejection of allegory and his search for "harsh and subtle" verses in *Le dolci rime d'amor ch'i' solia* (LXXXII: 69). Stylistic experimentation continued throughout the second half of the 1290s, especially in the *rime petrose*. Exile brought about further expansion of Dante's poetic vocabulary and deepened his ethical concerns. As we have noted both here and in the previous chapter, the themes of his lyric poetry came to include not only love but also security, well-being, and righteousness.

This amplification of themes had in fact already been pioneered by Guittone d'Arezzo (who died in 1294, in the same year as Brunetto Latini, Dante's other "teacher"). Guittone's powerful personality had influenced a whole generation of Tuscan poets, as well as the Bolognese Guido Guinizzelli. With canzoni, *laudi,* and other lyrics on moral, religious, and political themes, Guittone was a masterly innovator in Duecento poetry. It is hardly surprising, therefore, that Dante fell under his spell at the very beginning of his career (as we have seen in his exchange of sonnets with Dante da Maiano, XXXIX–XLVII: 1a–5).

The rejection of Dante's first poetic "father" came quickly enough, however, and continued throughout his lifetime—in his pronouncements, at least.[38] As we have had occasion to remark, when—in *Vita Nova* 25—Dante inveighs against those who write vernacular poetry on any theme except love, his target is evidently Guittone. A dozen years or so later, in *De vulgari* 1.13.1, the Aretine heads the list of Tuscan poets who have never rid themselves of their plebeian municipal tongue and who have failed to scale the heights of the illustrious vernacular (*DVE* 2.6.8), the only stylistic register suitable for the noblest form, the canzone. Guittone and his followers had not understood that poetry requires a profound understanding of the relationship between form and subject matter, that it cannot be achieved without a strict training of native wit, assiduous study and practice of the art, as well as the constant acquisition of knowledge (*DVE* 2.4.10). In *Purgatorio* 26.121–26, Dante would again decry those who praised Guittone for his poetic achievements, "until the truth obliterated" his fame thanks to the writings of more than one poet—including Guido Cavalcanti, Cino da Pistoia, and, of course, Dante himself (cf. *Purg.* 11.97–99).

Nevertheless, Guittone had shown the way, and his influence never completely faded; in Dante's later lyrics (and even in the *Comedy*), the poet borrowed discreetly from his predecessor. In *Così nel mio parlar* and the later canzoni, we find once again the binomials and antitheses that had been virtually eliminated from the poems selected for *Vita Nova* once the poet had discovered his new theme, the gratuitous praise of his beloved (*VN* 18.6–9). The binomials and antitheses return, together with other rhetorical devices used *ad nauseam* by Guittone, in Dante's later lyrics. As Boyde (1971, 321) remarks with regard to *Doglia mia reca:* "In large part," Dante's rhetorical devices "were derived from Guittone d'Arezzo—that is, from the very poet whose language and style seem to have been found intolerable by the young Dante and the mature Dante alike." As always, Dante took whatever he needed as grist to his mill.

As regards his choice of poetic forms, Dante judged the sonnet inferior not only to the canzone but also to the *ballata* in the stylistic hierarchy established in *De vulgari* 2.3.5. Although he composed unforgettable sonnets (one thinks immediately of *VN* 26.5–7: *Tanto gentile*), Dante appears to have felt constrained by the sonnet's fourteen lines, which afforded a narrow compass for his inspiration as a lyric poet (cf. *VN* 27.2). Nevertheless, what Gorni calls the "sacralità dell'incipit" is evident in the opening of even such a minor composition as *Piangete, amanti, poi che piange Amore* (*VN* 8.4–6: Weep, lovers, since Love is weeping).[39] Toward the beginning of his career, Dante composed three *sonetti doppi / rinterzati* (double sonnets), for example, *Vita Nova* 7.3–6, *O voi che per la via d'Amor passate,* which is described as a "sonnet" in the prose commentary (7.7), although as a double sonnet the poem extends over twenty lines (with a *settenario* introduced in ll. 2, 5, 8, 11, 15, and 19; cf. *VN* 8.8–11 and XLVIII: 8). Dante wrote at least one sonnet without any clear division between octave and sestet *(VN* 14.11–12: *Con l'altre donne mia vista gabbate);* nevertheless, he did not make any formal innovations in the genre.

As far as the structure of the canzone is concerned, Dante's insistence on its essential link with the *superbissimum carmen* of the hendecasyllable is in part a reaction against earlier practice. Guittone, for example, had written four canzoni composed entirely of *settenari* (e.g., *Tuttor, s'eo veglio o dormo,* with its seventy-two verses). The number of stanzas in Dante's twenty-one canzoni varies greatly, from a single stanza among his early compositions (XXIV: 46; XLIX: 9; LVII: 22) to as many as seven stanzas (LXXII: 69; LXXXIII: 70; CVI: 83), with five stanzas in no fewer than eight canzoni.[40] The length of each stanza is augmented in the later poems, accompanied by an increase in the deployment of *settenari: Poscia ch'Amor* has stanzas of nineteen lines, of which seven are *settenari* (and another two are pentasyllabic); *Le dolci rime,* stanzas of twenty lines, including seven *settenari; Tre donne,* stanzas of eighteen lines, of which seven are *settenari;* and the longest, *Doglia mi reca,* deploys stanzas of twenty-one lines, of which nine are *settenari.*[41] Only Guittone's canzoni display such formal variety, with stanzas of from fourteen to as many as twenty-seven lines. The verbal link between *canto* and *canzone* (both from *cantare,* "to sing") is paralleled by the fact that *Poscia ch'Amor* (133 lines) and *Doglia mi reca* (158 lines) foreshadow the length of the *Comedy*'s cantos, which vary from 115 lines (*Inf.* 6) to 160 (*Purg.* 32).

Whether or not the exchange of scurrilous sonnets with Forese Donati is authentic, the range and diversity of Dante's lyric poetry are quite extraordinary. In fact, it is possible to claim that no other major poet has displayed such a desire and capacity for repeated self-renewal. As the great nineteenth-century critic Francesco De Sanctis wrote of Dante's *rime:* "Neither before nor since has a lyrical universe been imagined so vast in scope and so deep in conception, so coherent in all its parts . . . [and] so personal" (De Sanctis 1964, 1.69).

Texts and translations

Dante's Lyric Poetry. Edited, translated, and annotated by Kenelm Foster and Patrick Boyde. 2 vols. (vol. 1, edition and translation; vol. 2, commentary). Oxford: Clarendon Press, 1967.

Rime. Edited by Michele Barbi. Società Dantesca Italiana. Florence: Le Monnier, 1960. Until De Robertis's recent edition, this was the most widely used edition for the numbering of the *rime.*

Rime. Edited by Gianfranco Contini. In Dante Alighieri, *Opere minori,* vol. 1, part 1, 251–552. Milan and Naples: Ricciardi, 1984. Until De Robertis's recent edition, this was the standard text of the *rime.*

Rime. Edited by Domenico De Robertis. Vol. 3, *Testi.* Florence: Le Lettere, 2002.

Other readings

Barolini, Teodolinda. "Dante and the Lyric Past." In *The Cambridge Companion to Dante,* edited by Rachel Jacoff, 14–33. Cambridge: Cambridge University Press, 1993.

Boyde, Patrick. *Dante's Style in His Lyric Poetry.* Cambridge: Cambridge University Press, 1971.

Durling, Robert M., and Ronald L. Martinez. *Time and the Crystal: Studies in Dante's "Rime Petrose."* Berkeley: University of California Press, 1990.

Gorni, Guglielmo. *Il nodo della lingua e il verbo d'Amore: Studi su Dante e altri duecentisti,* 187–215. Florence: Leo S. Olschki, 1981.

———. *Metrica e analisi letteraria,* 15–93 and 207–42. Bologna: Il Mulino, 1993.

Picone, Michelangelo, ed. *Letture classensi* 24 (1995), special issue: *Le "Rime" di Dante.*

four

Dante's Banquet of knowledge

Convivio

From internal evidence, we learn that Dante began to compose his *Convivio* or "banquet" of knowledge in the first years of his exile (c. 1303). This encyclopedic enterprise was intended to bolster his reputation by revealing the riches of medieval philosophy to a broad audience of men and women ignorant of Latin. The complete work was to have comprised some fifteen books (of which only four were written) and to offer extended commentaries to fourteen of Dante's own canzoni. The author's purpose was to provide those involved in practical affairs with the "scraps" of knowledge he had succeeded in collecting from "that table at which the bread of angels is eaten" (*Conv.* 1.1.7). Those scraps of wisdom and knowledge would be sufficient to satisfy the hunger of thousands (*Conv.* 1.12.12).

Two main obstacles prevent a large body of noble souls—"princes, barons, knights, and many other noble persons, not only men but women also"—from acquiring precious knowledge: their family and civic duties do not allow them "leisure for speculation," and/or they live far away from libraries and centers of learning (*Conv.* 1.1.4). By making essential knowledge accessible to such persons, Dante will allow them to overcome many handicaps and assist in ridding society of pernicious error and false judgments that create "the worst possible confusion in the world" (*Conv.* 4.1.7). In all this, we already hear the voice of the author of the *Comedy,* determined to set humanity on the right path in a world that has gone terribly astray.

Aristotle

"As the Philosopher says . . . all men naturally desire to know." This opening sentence reveals the driving force behind Dante's *Convivio* and places it firmly under the aegis of Aristotle, who is the Philosopher *par excellence,* "most worthy of faith and obedience" and "the master and guide of human reason" (*Conv.* 4.6.7–8). The modern reader is likely to take for granted the triumph of Aristotelian philosophy in medieval Western Europe and to discount such quotations and praise as mere lip service paid to "medieval orthodoxy." Nothing, in fact, could be further from the truth. Aristotle's writings had remained virtually unknown in the Latin West until the late twelfth century. Before this, whenever contacts were established with pagan philosophy, the mainstream of Christian thought had been influenced by Neoplatonism, which proved to be far more pliable to Christian attitudes and dogma. Aristotle's works were preserved by Arab and Jewish scholars, and eventually translated into Latin (from the Arabic or the original Greek, which had become incomprehensible to scholars in the West). These translations constituted the first rigorously scientific system to challenge the Christian view of the world; inevitably, they aroused both immense enthusiasm and great opposition. In 1210 and again in 1215, they were banned at the Sorbonne—the intellectual powerhouse of Latin Christendom—although they made their entry into its Faculty of Arts in 1255. The writings of Aristotle's Arabic commentators added further dangerous material and helped to provoke the bishop of Paris's condemnations proclaimed in 1270 and 1277. The struggle was eventually resolved by the Church's acceptance of Thomas Aquinas's heroic attempt to iron out the differences between "natural" Aristotelian philosophy and religious dogma. But the struggle was by no means over when Dante wrote his *Convivio*.

Another essential point is that Aristotle was not yet regarded as an authority of such prestige and scope that an appeal to his views on logic, metaphysics, natural sciences, politics, or poetics could be used to smother original thought, as was occasionally to happen in later centuries. For Dante, Aristotle had brought the essential science of ethics to perfection (*Conv.* 4.6.15). We must also remember that Dante's enthusiasm for the Greek philosopher was that of a largely self-taught man, someone who had just discovered the intense satisfaction and delights of intellectual speculation, in an age when such activity could strike an intelligent layman as an immensely exciting adventure. Above all, in order to try to understand Dante's intellectual position, we must realize that the Florentine poet and politician was no professional philosopher. His arguments and attitudes are those of a passionate amateur, who borrowed freely from a variety of sources.[1]

Philosophy

Similarly, the assertion that "all men naturally desire to know" was no cliché for Dante. All his later works were fired by this fundamental belief in the thirst for knowledge that is the distinguishing mark of human beings (cf. *Purg.* 21.1–3, *Mon.* 1.3–4). Dante therefore sets out to break down the elitist barrier of Scholastic philosophy, which was expounded in Latin as the only language fit for such study. Scorning professional scholars who study only for monetary gain, he invites all men and women of good will to share the meal he has prepared for his Banquet, in the conviction that "knowledge is the ultimate perfection of our soul, in which lies our ultimate happiness" (*Conv.* 1.1.1). This passionate belief also inspired the great doctrinal cantos of the *Comedy*. Here, it kindles the neophyte's ardor, urging him on in his self-appointed task. The author of *Convivio* was determined to break the monopoly of clerics and to open up the treasures of philosophy, in order to distribute its wealth for the good of society at large. But it was not his purpose to produce another *Tresor,* like that of his predecessor Brunetto Latini. This work, well known to Dante, was composed (just before the poet's birth) with encyclopedic intent and a desire to avoid all personal touches. Nothing could be further from Dante's own approach, which reflects every aspects of the writer: his experience of love, of politics, learning, art, and human nature. Everything he offers his readers in *Convivio* is rooted in his personal vision of society and the human condition.

Dante's passionate defense of Italian

After his exordium, Dante vindicates his purpose and authority in chapters 2–4, and then defends his choice of the vernacular language, Italian, in the last nine chapters of book 1. First, he apologizes for the autobiographical element (so much a feature of his vernacular trilogy: *Vita Nova, Convivio, Comedy*). The laws of rhetoric do not allow writers to speak about themselves, except for two compelling reasons. The first is the need to avoid great peril or infamy, which inspired Boethius (c. 470–c. 525) to defend his reputation in his *Consolation of Philosophy,* after he had been accused of treason and imprisoned by Theodoric, king of the Ostrogoths. The second justification occurs when others may derive great benefit from an account of one's own experiences (as with Augustine's celebrated *Confessions*). Dante is therefore inspired both by the desire to instruct others and by his need to rebut the accusation that he had "pursued so great a passion" (*Conv.* 1.2.16; cf. 3.1.11) as that described in the poems written for a Noble Lady *(donna gentile).* He will now explain their true, allegorical meaning, and show that they had been inspired not by passion but by virtue. Like Boethius, Dante struggled against the infamy of exile. On March 10, 1302, he had been condemned to death—supposedly for corruption while holding political office—by the government "of the most beautiful and most famous daughter of Rome," Florence, where "I desire with all my heart to rest my weary soul and end the time granted to me." Since then, Dante tells us, he has been forced to wander as "a pilgrim, almost a beggar, displaying fortune's wound against my will" (*Conv.* 1.3.4). Adrift like a ship without sail or rudder, blown hither and thither by the wind of poverty, Dante is only too conscious of the fact that his public image has been debased and his works devalued in the eyes of the multitude, who judge by appearances since they "live according to the senses and not according to reason" (*Conv.* 1.4.3). Thus traduced and humiliated by his unjust exile, Dante sets out to adorn his Banquet of Knowledge with a loftier, weightier style "so that it may acquire greater authority" (*Conv.* 1.4.13).

It is this experience of exile that underlies not only the ethical bent of the treatise but also the decision to write in Italian. In his wanderings in the Italian peninsula, Dante became aware of the immense potential of the Italian dialects, provided that they could be "regulated" by art and molded into a literary language, modeled in part on Latin. As we have seen in chapter 3, this conviction inspired the composition of his treatise *De vulgari eloquentia,* with its assertion of the vernacular's greater intrinsic nobility. It also led Dante to forge his own linguistic tools in *Convivio.* Having emulated the great Latin poets in his Italian poems, he now sets out to compete with the writers of Latin prose in their special preserve. The vernacular of *Vita Nova* is here made to embrace the whole range of intellectual and political interests occasioned by his study of philosophy and his exile. Dante has discovered the linguistic path that will eventually lead to the *Comedy.*

Defending his decision to write in Italian, Dante points out that a commentary is meant to serve the text. Because the text of his poems was in the vernacular, a commentary in Latin would not have been a servant but instead "sovereign, through nobility, efficacy and beauty" (*Conv.* 1.5.7). Latin is seen as a more efficient intellectual tool; it achieves greater beauty "because the vernacular follows usage, and Latin follows art" (*Conv.* 1.5.14). It is art that confers immunity from the changes that constantly plague vernacular languages. The great advantage enjoyed by Latin is its static form, governed and preserved by grammar, whereas "in the past fifty years many words have disappeared, have been born, and have changed" in the languages of Italy (*Conv.* 1.5.9). This painful awareness of linguistic change, expressed in both *De vulgari eloquentia* and *Convivio* is still present in the *Comedy.* It is also latent in Dante's use of the term "grammar" as a synonym for Latin in *Convivio,* for the vernacular "is fashioned at will and changes," remaining at the mercy of unstable human nature (*Conv.* 1.5.8).

Among other arguments marshaled against the use of a Latin commentary, Dante points out that it would have gone over the heads of many otherwise able to appreciate the Italian poems—while, paradoxically, expounding the latter's true meaning to many "such as Germans and English and others" who would have understood the Latin commentary but would have been incapable of enjoying the "beauty" of the Italian poems (*Conv.* 1.7.13). Although in *Convivio* Dante is chiefly concerned with the message his poems was intended to convey, as an artist he can never forget their aesthetic qualities. In fact, to the discomfiture of generations of translators of his *Comedy,* Dante declares that to translate poetry is an impossible task, since it inevitably destroys "all its sweetness and harmony." This is why "the verses of the Psalms are without sweetness of music and harmony, because they were translated from Hebrew into Greek and from Greek into Latin, and in the first translation all their sweetness disappeared" (1.7.14–15).

As we have noted, Dante's audience is the multitude of men and women who, through their involvement in practical affairs, have "abandoned literature to those who have prostituted it"—namely, scholars who study merely for monetary gain and social advancement (*Conv.* 1.9.3–5).[2] Dante's democratic purpose must not be obscured by the list already quoted, which begins with "princes, barons, [and] knights." Surprisingly enough for a work devoted to philosophy, its intended audience includes not only men but also women ("of whom there are many"), noble souls handicapped by their ignorance of Latin. We should not, of course, expect to find, in Dante's age and situation, a democrat in the modern sense. It is nevertheless to his eternal credit that, as one of the first lay "intellectuals," he did so much to reject the closed shop of medieval learning and helped to initiate the process of civilizing European society at all levels.[3]

Dante's spirited message rises to heights of passionate eloquence in the greatest hymn of praise ever written in honor of the Italian language. Freed even from the trappings of poetry, its beauty and power shall shine forth in its ability to reveal the "most profound and most original concepts," virtually as effectively as Latin itself (*Conv.* 1.10.12). Dante goes on to denounce those evil Italians who praise the vernacular of other nations and despise their own. They are swayed by five "detestable causes" (*Conv.* 1.11.1): blindness of judgment; bad faith, which leads a bad workman to blame his tools; a desire to be admired for exotic tastes; envy; and pusillanimity, which makes people undervalue what belongs to them. Such are the wretches who have no care for "this precious language"—whose only blemish is that "it is found in the harlot mouths of those adulterers" (*Conv.* 1.11.21). For his own part, Dante lists the many benefits Italian has given him: life itself, because of the bond it created between his parents; "moreover, this vernacular of mine led me to the world of knowledge, which is ultimate perfection" (*Conv.* 1.13.4–5). As we have seen, in *Convivio* 1.10, Dante claims that two of Latin's chief qualities, its beauty and efficacy, shall in fact distinguish the vernacular of Dante's present work. An element of stability, too, will be given to the vernacular. The writer's pride in his ability to wield and honor his native language is paramount.

The "bread" necessary for the Banquet has been purified. It is now time to begin serving it to the multitude. Like the Gospel's miraculous loaves, Dante's bread will satisfy the hunger of thousands. His Italian, the basis for a new culture, will be "a new light, a new sun, that shall rise when the old sun sets and shed its light on those who live in darkness and in the shadows" (*Conv.* 1.13.12). Deploying a prophetic tone and biblical language, Dante forecasts the eventual triumph of vernacular culture in the modern world. Centuries before Machiavelli and Galileo, Dante Alighieri must be accorded a place of honor among those who fought to break the stranglehold of Latin over Western European culture.

Book 2 (allegory and cosmology)

Allegory

After this long introduction, book 2 opens with a canzone probably written some ten years earlier: *Voi che 'ntendendo il terzo ciel movete*. The first lines of the commentary tell us that Dante's exposition will be both literal and allegorical, since "writings [the tantalizing term *le scritture*] can be understood and must therefore be expounded chiefly according to four senses" (*Conv.* 2.1.2). First, we have the literal meaning. Then comes the allegorical sense, which reveals "a truth hidden beneath a beautiful lie"—as when Ovid speaks of Orpheus taming the wild beasts and moving the trees and stones with his lyre, "which signifies that the wise man, with the instrument of his voice, can make cruel hearts tender and humble, and sway according to his will those whose lives are empty of knowledge and art: for those who are quite devoid of rational life are virtually like stones" (*Conv.* 2.1.3). We note in passing that the reason why this hidden, allegorical meaning was first used was to have been discussed in the fourteenth book of *Convivio*. Third is the moral or tropological sense, which may be found in the Gospels' accounts of the Transfiguration, when they tell us that Christ took with him only three of the twelve apostles: "from which the moral may be deduced that we should have few companions in whatever is most secret" (*Conv.* 2.1.5)—an intriguing example of medieval allegorical exegesis! The fourth sense is the anagogical, which points to "heavenly things of eternal glory" (*Conv.* 2.1.6), as may be seen in Psalm 113 [114]. This psalm narrates the story of Exodus, a historical fact which also points to the sanctification and the liberation of the soul from sin (cf. *Purg.* 2.43–48 and *Ep.* 13.7.21–22). Dante insists on the need for a thorough understanding of the literal sense before the others can be approached. He will therefore explain the literal sense of his poems before going on to discuss their allegorical meaning, their "hidden truth" (*Conv.* 2.1.15), while touching upon other senses, should the need arise.

Many modern scholars claim that in *Convivio* Dante asserted a fundamental distinction between the two types of allegory familiar to medieval exegetes: the allegory of the theologians, as exemplified in Scripture, which was based on a literal sense regarded as historically true; and the "allegory of poets," whereby a truth was superimposed on a literal sense that was a beautiful fiction or lie.

If, however, we turn to what Dante in fact wrote, we find that at this point the text of *Convivio* is riddled with omissions and scribal errors. This means that in 2.1.3, editors have had to supply their own conjectural readings in order to fill the obvious gap between two phrases found in the manuscript tradition: "The one is called literal . . . and this is the one which is hidden beneath the cloak of these fables, and is a truth hidden beneath a beautiful lie." In the extant text, there is no referent specified for "these fables." Scholars suggest that the term "these fables" indicates that all poetry consists of mere lies (as Aquinas and others maintained). However, there is nothing in Dante's text, as we have it, that justifies this supposition. The example given (Orpheus) may well point to specific "fables," such as those contained in the most widely read of pagan texts, Ovid's *Metamorphoses*. On the other hand, the fable or myth of Orpheus's descent to the underworld was also capable of receiving a Christological interpretation, whereby his descent to the underworld was regarded as a prefiguration of Christ's harrowing of hell.[4] It is in fact after referring to Orpheus's powers and their allegorical meaning that Dante makes his controversial aside (*Conv.* 2.1.4): "Truly, the theologians understand this allegorical sense in a different way from the poets; but since it is my intention to follow the poets' way, I shall understand the allegorical sense in the way it is used by poets." The terms "understand" (literally, "take": *prendono*) and "used" (*usato*) also point to another essential difference: the theologians' task *uses* allegory in order to interpret a given text, Holy Scripture, whereas poets *structure* their texts allegorically.

Instead of assuming that, at the time of writing *Convivio,* Dante judged all poetry to be nothing but a "beautiful lie," we should in fact take into account the following points. *Convivio* was written partly in order to rescue his reputation from the "infamy" of having betrayed Beatrice's memory by loving another woman (*Conv.* 1.2.15–16). In other words, the author's intention is to play

down or devalue the literal sense of the love poems selected (Voi che 'nten-
dendo and Amor che ne la mente mi ragiona), in order to claim that when the text
refers to love and feminine charms its true meaning lies elsewhere. We must
also realize that Dante never in fact uses the term "allegory of the theologians":
this phrase does not exist in his writings. Nor does he indicate in the slightest
way that he is concerned with a literal sense as understood by the theologians. It
must also be remembered that even the text of the Bible was not always taken
to be historically or literally true: for example, the erotic Song of Songs must
not be taken literally; instead, it was to be understood as "a truth hidden be-
neath a beautiful lie," signifying the human soul's longing for God. As so often
in his Convivio, Dante is here displaying his erudition by pointing out that theo-
logians always use the term "allegory" as referring to Christ and the Church.
Augustine of Dacia put it in a nutshell: allegory teaches you what you must be-
lieve (quid credas allegoria). For the theologians, allegory was concerned with the
Christian faith.

Any blanket devaluation of poetry as a mere lie is unthinkable for the au-
thor of the poems written in praise of Beatrice and then set in the elaborate
framework of Vita Nova. What is more, even in Convivio, allegory is jettisoned
in the poem chosen for the fourth book, Le dolci rime, whose subject—the true
nature of nobility—was of such universal import that "it was not right to speak
under any rhetorical figure . . . therefore, no allegory needs to be revealed,
but only the literal meaning discussed" (Conv. 4.1.10–11). Clearly, the author of
Convivio did not believe that the literal sense of the text of his canzone on no-
bility was a beautiful lie concealing a profound truth; it was instead judged ca-
pable of "bringing people back on to the right path regarding the proper under-
standing of true nobility" (Conv. 4.1.9). Even Ovid, the pagan mythographer, is
quoted as a reliable historical witness, together with Lucan "and other poets," in
this same work (Conv. 3.3.7–9), and Vergil's Aeneid is treated as a reliable his-
torical source (Conv. 4.26.9). Where his first two poems were concerned,
however, Dante was bent on minimizing their literal text/message in order to
reveal their hidden, "true meaning . . . which no one can discover if I do not ex-
plain it" (Conv. 1.2.17; cf. 2.12.1 and 15.2).

All this in no way undermines the claims made by Dante in his Comedy.
The vexed question of how much Dante expects of his readers in his epic has
been examined, most recently and convincingly, by Hollander (2001, 94–104).
Convivio, with its astonishing claim that secular writings may be structured and
expounded according to the four senses traditionally—and exclusively (Aquinas,
Quodlibetales 7.6.16)—reserved for the interpretation of the Bible, represents an
intermediate stage between the rudimentary discussion of allegory and figures
of speech in Vita Nova 25 and Dante's complex use of allegory in the Comedy.
There, in a unique amalgam that combines fabulous mythological figures such

as the Minotaur and Pluto with the most sacred personages of Christian history, we find what may truly be called Dante's figural allegory, something he made utterly his own.

The literal sense of *Voi che 'ntendendo*

Chapters 2–11 are concerned with glossing the literal sense of *Voi che 'nten-dendo*. We are told that the noble lady mentioned at the end of *Vita Nova* first appeared to Dante "accompanied by Love," when the planet Venus had accomplished two full revolutions after Beatrice's death in June 1290 (*Conv.* 2.2.1). According to Dante's astronomical lore, this brings us to a date near the end of August 1293—and to the first contradiction with the account given in *Vita Nova,* to which Dante himself refers us. In that earlier work (*VN* 35.1), we read that the Noble Lady *(donna gentile)* appeared to the grieving lover "some time after" the first anniversary of Beatrice's death (June 8, 1291). Even more disturbing is the fact that the account given in *Convivio* insists that a long struggle was waged in Dante's mind between the memory of Beatrice and his love for this Noble Lady, whereas *Vita Nova* speaks of the poet's sorrow and repentance after being tempted by the latter "*for some days* against the constancy of reason*" (*VN* 39.2; emphasis mine). *Convivio* celebrates Dante's enduring love for the Noble Lady; *Vita Nova,* on the other hand (composed some ten years previously), had spoken of his definitive return to Beatrice. Nowhere in the later work does Dante attempt to iron out the discrepancies between the two accounts. This has led some scholars to suppose that there existed a first version of *Vita Nova* which agreed with what we read in *Convivio,* because it ended with the episode of the Noble Lady (chapters 35–38), and that the present ending, celebrating the triumph of his love for Beatrice, was added after Dante had abandoned his *Convivio* (c. 1308) in an attempt to prepare the way for Beatrice's victorious return in the *Comedy.*[5] There is, however, not a shred of hard evidence to support this idea. We are therefore left with the contradictions (but also with the possibility that Dante *might* have decided to remove the discrepancies by changing the account given in *Vita Nova,* if he had ever finished *Convivio*). On the other hand, Peter Dronke (1997a, 16) puts forward the fascinating suggestion that perhaps "for some brief time near their beginning, Dante's philosophical studies . . . were not purely disinterested—and that he then came to recognize that some element . . . had been leading him towards philosophically false positions." This would explain the apparent contradictions in Dante's writings concerning the *donna gentile.*

As things stand, however, we must also take into account the fact that, in *Vita Nova* 35.4, 37.5, 39.7, Dante insists that the meaning of the sonnets describing this interlude is plain enough and without need of further explanation.

If the object of Dante's attraction was indeed Lady Philosophy, as we are told in *Convivio* 2.12.9 and 2.15.12, the author-commentator of *Vita Nova* could only with a degree of subterfuge assure readers that his sonnets' true meaning was obvious from their texts. The identification of the Noble Lady with Lady Philosophy is even more difficult to square with the description of his thought of her, which was noble only "in so far as it spoke of a noble lady; for the rest, it was most base" (*VN* 38.4): surely the strangest and most illogical way of describing what was later purported to be desire for true knowledge and wisdom—a description which then culminates in the identification of this desire as the "adversary of reason" (39.1). As Dronke remarks (1997a, 20), Dante "expected much both of his immediate and his future readers . . . At least part of his artistic originality lay in his refusal to harmonize."

What little evidence we have points to late 1293 and 1294 as the period when both poems were written that were later glossed in *Convivio* as exalting Dante's love of philosophy. Both in fact presuppose the present ending of *Vita Nova* with its vision of Beatrice in glory and the sonnet *Oltre la spera* (*VN* 41.10–13). We recall that Beatrice's lover had already been charged with inconstancy by his beloved (*VN* 12.6). After her death, for the author of *Convivio* to have laid himself open to a similar accusation would have been utterly incompatible with the dignity and authority Dante sought to acquire, especially given his lowly state in exile. It would therefore seem likely that the episode of the Noble Lady as recounted in *Vita Nova* was inspired by Dante's infatuation with a real woman (cf. *Purg.* 31.49–60), whereas *Amor che ne la mente* and *Voi che 'ntendendo* (especially the latter's *envoi*, ll. 53–61) were written to celebrate his newfound love for philosophy.

Astronomy and angels

In the third chapter of book 2, Dante explains that the third "heaven" is that of Venus. This leads to a long astronomical digression. Aristotle had stated that the heavens were eight in number. The truth, discovered by Ptolemy, is that there are nine heavens, ascending from the earth in the following order (which was retained in Dante's *Paradiso*): Moon, Mercury, Venus, Sun, Mars, Jupiter, Saturn, the Fixed Stars, and the Primum Mobile. The ninth, invisible heaven answered the need to explain motion in Aristotelian physics. According to the Greek philosopher, physical motion cannot be explained solely in terms of physical principles; it must depend on some immaterial cause, in order to break through the vicious circle of mover and object moved. This immaterial cause—the unmoved mover—is, in Christian terms, God, whose power of attraction over the Primum Mobile is so strong that the latter is propelled by the swiftest motion, since motion, when not due to a physical cause, is the result of unsatisfied long-ing. The Primum Mobile is motivated by its intense desire to be united with God, while it transmits motion to the rest of the universe. Finally, outside both space and time is found the tenth heaven or Empyrean, "posited by Catho-lics" (*Conv.* 2.3.8), the abode of God and the blessed souls, "according to the teaching of Holy Church, which cannot lie; and Aristotle seems to indicate this to those who understand him correctly" (*Conv.* 2.3.10). Possessing all that can possibly be desired, the Empyrean is a place of perfect peace, hence motion-less, situated in the very mind of God and encompassing the entire universe (*Conv.* 2.3.11).

The moving spheres are propelled by "substances separate from matter, namely Intelligences, commonly called Angels" (*Conv.* 2.4.2). Medieval angel-ology is hardly likely to make the modern reader's pulse beat faster. As we shall see, however, this apparently unrewarding subject holds an important clue for an understanding of Dante's philosophical (and idiosyncratic) outlook in *Convivio*. According to the Scholastic method, Dante first examines various con-tradictory opinions regarding these angelic propellers. Aristotle and others limited the number of angelic intelligences to the number of celestial move-ments; others, like Plato, extended their number to include all the different spe-cies of things. Plato called them Ideas, while the gentiles called them gods and goddesses, adored their images, and built temples in their honor (*Conv.* 2.4.6). Dante's syncretism is nowhere more in evidence than in this highly personal as-similation of the pagan deities of classical antiquity into Christian angelology (with lasting results, for no Olympian is found in *Inferno* and the same belief underpins Beatrice's discourse in *Par.* 4.58–63). Nevertheless, the pagans were defective in both their reasoning and knowledge (*Conv.* 2.4.8)—a significant statement, when we realize that this is the first reference to the limitations of human reason (an important theme that does to a certain extent temper the ra-tional optimism so evident in this work).

Everyone—"philosopher, Gentile, Jew, and Christian"—agrees that angels enjoy a state of blessedness. Moreover, "since human nature here on earth has not just one beatitude, but two, the one belonging to the life of practical affairs, the other to the life of contemplation, it would be irrational (for we see that they [angels] possess the beatitude of the active life in guiding the world) if they did not also possess the beatitude of contemplation, which is more excellent and more divine" (*Conv.* 2.4.9–10). This flatly contradicts Dante's basic premise that, since their intellect "is one and perpetual," angels can enjoy only one or the other type of beatitude, so that there must be a majority of angels who engage only in contemplation (*Conv.* 2.4.11–12). Dante further muddies the waters by agreeing that the contemplative life is the only one fit for the angelic nature.

Nevertheless, in 2.4.13, he contradicts his basic principle by wanting some angels "to contemplate *and* to move; he has thus fallen into a remarkable confusion" (Bemrose 1983, 86).

All this is clear evidence of the unsatisfactory state of *Convivio* and its manuscript tradition as we have it (Ageno 1995). Here, however, rather than a scribal error, it would seem that the confusion is due to the probability that Dante never revised his text. Of even greater interest is the fact that, whereas the distinction between the active life and the life of contemplation may strike us as a medieval commonplace (ultimately derived from Aristotle's *Ethics* 10.7–8), its application to angelic activity is neither Aristotelian nor Scholastic but very much Dante's own. His argument, based on the fact that human nature *on earth* is capable of two types of happiness, is not merely a glaring case of anthropomorphism. It is in fact typical of Dante's approach in *Convivio,* which tends to divide human activities into separate compartments. Unlike St. Thomas (*Contra Gentiles* 3.80.11), who stated that the angelic movers belonged to the order of the Virtues, Dante claims that each heaven is moved by a different category of angels, from the Seraphim downward (*Conv.* 2.5.6–13; the concept remains in *Par.* 28.64–129, although the correspondences between angels and the heavens they move are modified). Here, the hierarchy of nine angelic orders is split from top to bottom between, on the one hand, those angels who enjoy pure contemplation, and, on the other, those angelic intelligences who move the various spheres of the universe *(Voi che 'ntendendo)*. A similar dichotomy is noticeable in the fact that humanity's active life is considered solely with reference to the moral virtues; the intellectual virtues are the province of the contemplative life (*Conv.* 4.2.16–18). In this way, the theological virtues are ignored. This is surely a paradoxical situation for a Christian thinker—even for one concerned above all with ethics. The author of *Convivio* did not distinguish clearly between the Aristotelian conception of contemplation as an intellectual activity and the Christian emphasis on mystical contemplation and prayer. As a result, Dante reached what was virtually a theoretical impasse, which he circumvented by rehabilitating the life of action in this, a work written expressly for men and women wholly engaged in practical affairs.

In true Platonic vein, Dante ends his fourth chapter by stressing once more the limitations of the human intellect, since it is in part closed like the eyes of a bat "while the soul is bound and imprisoned by our body's organs" (*Conv.* 2.4.17; cf. 3.7.5)—a Neoplatonic view, contrary to Aquinas's conception of human beings as an essential amalgam of soul and body (*S. Th.* 1.76.4, 1.75.7.3). Limitations inherent in the human condition on earth are further emphasized in the next chapter, which speaks of the effects of Christ's revelation of things that would otherwise have remained hidden to humankind. We also learn that approximately one-tenth of the angels rebelled against God, thus creating a gap which humanity was destined to fill (*Conv.* 2.5.12).

Beatrice and the soul's immortality

Commenting on the struggle waged between his attraction to Lady Philosophy and the memory of Beatrice, Dante warns us that he will now mention Beatrice for the last time in this work. The thought of his beloved in heavenly glory sparks off a brief but important digression on the immortality of the human soul. It strikes the reader because of the deep emotional charge behind it and the dramatic implications it may well hold. Dante inveighs against the belief that there is no life after death: "the most foolish, the basest, and the most pernicious" of bestialities (*Conv.* 2.8.8). He insists that all writers agree that there is some immortal part in us: philosophers, pagan poets, the religions of the "Jews, Saracens, Tartars and whoever lives according to reason" (*Conv.* 2.8.9). If all were mistaken, including all those who have sacrificed this life for a better life to come, it would signify "that the most perfect animal, man, was the most imperfect—which is impossible—and that the part which is humanity's greatest perfection, reason, was the cause of this greatest flaw" (*Conv.* 2.8.11). Moreover, frequent proof of our immortality is to be found in "the divinations of our dreams," when the truth revealed must be derived from an immortal source and, consequently, transmitted to a similarly immortal element in our being (*Conv.* 2.8.13). It is interesting to note that Roger Bacon tells us that belief in the prophetic power of dreams was one of the "Aristotelian" errors condemned at the University of Paris in 1210. The idea seems to have been gradually discarded by professional philosophers, and it is not found among the ten syllogisms employed by Aquinas to prove the soul's immortality. Dante, however, accepted it through Cicero and Albert the Great from a long Neoplatonic tradition, but also from personal experience, which included Beatrice's appearance to him in dreams recorded in *Vita Nova* and alluded to in *Purgatorio* 30.133–35.

But it is not only the thought of Beatrice's fate that may have stirred Dante to make his impassioned declaration of faith: "and I thus believe, thus affirm and am thus certain of passing over to another, better life after this one, where that lady lives in glory of whom my soul was enamored" (*Conv.* 2.8.16). He was no doubt also moved by the memory of Guido Cavalcanti, his "first friend," who had died in August 1300. As his great canzone *Donna me prega* demonstrates, Guido subscribed to the Averroist belief that the intellect was granted to human beings only for their lifespan on earth and that after death the individual was destroyed. And it was with tragic compassion that the poet of the *Comedy* was to hint at his friend's possible damnation among "those who make the soul die with the body" (*Inf.* 10.13–15, 52–72). *Vita Nova* and a number of his early lyrics show how profoundly Dante was influenced by Cavalcanti's poetry. Whether or not he was ever tempted to follow his friend in rejecting the doctrine of personal immortality, it was a subject that evidently touched him to the quick, involving as it did the eternal destiny of both Beatrice and Guido, the two leading actors in Dante's youthful drama. Guido and Dante had both exalted intellectual activity on earth, sharing the belief that man is only truly alive when he "uses his reason, which is the life specific to him and the activity of his noblest part" (*Conv.* 2.7.4). For the author of *Convivio,* to believe that this noblest part abandoned the individual at death was a terrible betrayal of humanity's highest destiny—a betrayal, moreover, capable of degrading otherwise noble beings to the level of the beasts through the worst "bestiality" of all (*Conv.* 2.8.8).

An aside in the tenth chapter shows us that the future poet of the *Comedy* is already conscious of the danger of social standing and historical importance in exemplars of vices and virtues (cf. *Par.* 17.136–42): "How much wisdom and virtue remain hidden, because they lack this light [of reason]! And how much folly and how many vices are revealed because of this light! It would be better for the wretched, crazy, foolish and vicious great ones of this world to be of lowly condition, for they would not be so infamous then either in this world or after their death" (*Conv.* 2.10.9–10). In the last part of his commentary on the literal meaning of *Voi che 'ntendendo,* Dante turns to his poem's *envoi* and glosses its last verse (l. 61: "Consider at least how beautiful I am!"), establishing a theoretical distinction between his poem's formal beauty and the excellence of its content: "for goodness lies in the message, and beauty is in the choice and arrangement of the words; both provide pleasure, although goodness is the more pleasurable" (*Conv.* 2.11.4).

The *Consolation of Philosophy*

The last four chapters of book 2 are concerned with expounding the "true," allegorical meaning of Dante's canzone. He returns to the watershed event—Beatrice's death—that had left him distraught. Soon, he had turned to the writings of others who had likewise sought comfort for great distress: he began to read Boethius's *Consolation of Philosophy* (surprisingly described in 2.12.2 as "not known to many"), as well as Cicero's treatise on friendship *(De amicitia).* At first, Dante found the meaning of these ancient texts difficult to grasp, but "at last, I did so, as much as my knowledge of Latin and a little of my intellect made possible"—his intellect, which had already made him dimly aware of certain philosophical truths "as if in a dream, as may be seen in *Vita Nova*" (2.12.4).

Seeking consolation, Beatrice's unhappy lover found even greater rewards, as a whole world of knowledge gradually disclosed its treasures. Dante began to imagine Philosophy in the form of a noble lady (as Boethius had done at the beginning of his *Consolation*)—an association of ideas facilitated by the feminine gender of the term in both Latin *(philosophia)* and Italian *(filosofia)*.

Dante began to seek out Philosophy where she was truly to be found, "in the schools of the religious and in the disputations of philosophers" (*Conv.* 2.12.7). Although there was as yet no university in Florence, the two great teaching orders were well represented in the city: the Franciscans at Santa Croce, the Dominicans at Santa Maria Novella. By the end of the thirteenth century, the new Aristotelianism had met with considerable opposition from Franciscan theologians, so that the emphasis at Santa Croce remained on biblical exegesis and a detailed study of the first of the great medieval *Summae*, Peter Lombard's *Sentences* (cf. *Par.* 10.106–8). The Dominicans, on the other hand, were totally committed to the teaching of Christian Aristotelianism. It is therefore likely that Dante (who may well have been introduced to Aristotle's *Ethics* by Brunetto Latini) became acquainted with Aquinas's commentary on this celebrated work through the teachings of the Dominican Remigio de' Girolami. Remigio may also have influenced Dante's interpretation of Roman history, while his fervent desire for civic peace and exaltation of the common good would seem to have left their mark on the author of the *Comedy* and *Monarchia*.[6] It is also likely that Dante attended lectures at Santa Maria Novella, where the lectors organized disputations once a week. The term "disputation" was a technical one in medieval schools. It implied a debate, carried out before an audience of scholars, between the *opponentes,* who opened with a series of objections to a given doctrine, and the *respondentes,* who replied to each objection in turn. The debate was brought to a close by the *magister,* who gave the definitive exposition, acting as a kind of intellectual referee.

After some thirty months of study, the love of philosophy so gripped Dante's mind that it began to banish all other interests. To celebrate this new love, he composed *Voi che 'ntendendo,* in which he chose to express his involvement with philosophy "under the figure of other things" (*Conv.* 2.12.8). Dante tells us that he chose this allegorical method for two reasons: vernacular poetry was deemed unworthy of dealing with such an exalted subject, and his audience would not have believed him if he had merely declared his passion for philosophy in a literal way. In *Vita Nova* 25.6, written perhaps only one year before *Voi che 'ntendendo,* Dante had claimed that poetry in the vernacular must deal exclusively with the subject of love. His Florentine audience was obviously conditioned by the same prejudice, and only too ready to think that Dante had fallen in love with another woman.

The universe of knowledge and the pre-eminence of ethics

Expounding the allegorical meaning hidden in the canzone, Dante tells us that the third "heaven" mentioned in the third line also signifies the third "science" (cf. Latin *scientia,* "knowledge"), for each branch of knowledge is compared to one of the ten heavens (including the Empyrean) in an analogy that would have struck many of his contemporaries as old-fashioned. Dante, however, bravely sets out his reasons. Grammar is associated with the moon, rhetoric with the third heaven, Venus, to whose angelic movers Dante addresses his poem. The most interesting parallels are the final ones, when Dante is left with four sciences but only three heavens. The traditional order of the seven liberal arts given in 2.3.8 had produced one or two surprising results (dialectic = Mercury, geometry = Jupiter), but it had naturally corresponded to the first seven heavens. Now, however, Dante had to decide where to place physics, ethics, metaphysics, and theology, while taking into account the fact that placing them implied a hierarchy or scale of nobility. The order of the heavens also indicated greater or lesser proximity to God; hence, it was immediately apparent that theology must be placed at the top, with metaphysics in second place. Theology is thus an open-and-shut case: it is automatically assigned to the highest heaven of all, the Empyrean (in itself a theological "discovery").

The shock comes when we find that Dante reverses the expected order by attributing ethics to the ninth heaven (Primum Mobile) and by placing metaphysics beside physics, equating them both with the firmament or eighth heaven of the Fixed Stars (*Conv.* 2.13.8). Dante sets out his reasons for this highly unusual arrangement. Like the Milky Way, a multitude of fixed stars that "produce that white mass we call the galaxy" but are so small that they cannot be perceived from the earth, so metaphysics is concerned with "primal substances" which we cannot see or understand except through their effects (*Conv.* 2.14.7–8). Ethics or moral philosophy, on the other hand, is as necessary to life on earth as is the movement engendered by the Primum Mobile: if the latter did not move, "the order of the whole universe would be destroyed, and the movement [of the other heavens] would be in vain. Likewise, if moral philosophy were to cease, the other sciences would be hidden for some time, and happiness would be neither created nor experienced . . ." (*Conv.* 2.14.17–18). As Étienne Gilson pointed out, "The thesis which Dante here maintains is quite extraordinary for the Middle Ages" (1948, 105).

Lastly, the Empyrean, outside of space and time, is likened to the science of theology, "which is full of perfect peace" (*Conv.* 2.14.19)—a truly astonishing observation for a medieval Christian so cognizant of theological controversy (cf. *Par.* 29.88–117). Moreover, in a highly personal interpretation of a passage from the Song of Songs (6.7–8), Dante equates theology *not* with one of the sixty queens but with the perfect dove, thereby asserting its uniqueness but also effectively separating it from the other sciences, which were traditionally regarded as its handmaidens and thus subservient to theology.

By placing ethics above metaphysics, Dante parted company with both Aristotle and Aquinas. For his illustrious predecessors, metaphysics was the supreme science. For Dante, however, it had one great drawback: its tendency to isolate its practitioners from society and the needs of everyday life. Metaphysics was also concerned with a relatively small number of problems concerning God, the angelic intelligences, "prime" or formless matter (*Conv.* 3.8.15), all of which offered little scope for individual speculation. It could not be compared in utility to the discovery of a whole new social and intellectual perspective found principally in Aristotle's *Ethics,* a work that revolutionized the conception of society and political life in thirteenth-century Western Europe.[7] Nor must we forget that the author of *Convivio* was writing in exile, suffering from poverty and his exclusion from the political life of his beloved Florence. The *Epistle to Cangrande* places the *Comedy* under the aegis of ethics (*Ep.* 13.16.40): Dante's ordering of the sciences does the same for *Convivio*.

Homage is paid to theology, the highest and the purest of all sciences. Nevertheless, since its perfection depends on revelation and Christ's teachings, Dante will be content with the relative imperfection within his grasp. Whereas for Aquinas philosophy must remain subservient to the supreme science of divinity, for Dante its very existence "helps" the Christian faith (*Conv.* 3.7.16)—there is no hint of subordination or even of active collaboration between the two, such as we find in St. Thomas. Characteristically, the author of *Convivio* concentrates on the moral virtues, because they are subject to the human will and therefore the most human (*Conv.* 4.17.2). In general, Dante separates the human from the divine far more clearly than Aquinas; and in *Convivio* he pushes the distinction virtually as far as it will go within the bounds of Christian orthodoxy. In Dante's scheme of things, *relative* inferiority does not necessarily imply total subjection. We find this typically Dantean idea at the root of his analysis of the ideal relationship between the empire and the papacy (*Comedy,* the "two suns" of *Purg.* 16.107; *Mon.* 3), between philosophy and theology *(Convivio, Comedy, Monarchia),* and here—at the origin of such later developments—between ethics and theology.

The theme of the third book is announced in the last chapter. It will be the nobility of Lady Philosophy, full of sweetness, virtue, and knowledge. Her eyes are the philosophical proofs she offers, which confer blessedness on those who love her and "salvation from the death brought about by ignorance and vice" (*Conv.* 2.15.4). These extravagant claims are accompanied by the use of terms reminiscent of the mystics' passionate exaltation of the soul's longing for God, and they culminate in the assertion that philosophy is truly "the most beautiful and most virtuous daughter of the emperor of the universe, to whom Pythagoras gave the name Philosophy," so that, in his exposition of *Voi che 'ntendendo*, the word "love . . . always signifies the study" of philosophy (*Conv.* 2.15.12 and 10).

Book 3: A hymn of love to philosophical wisdom

All the resources of Dante's love poetry—combined with his eloquent prose commentary (inspired by the Sapiential books of the Vulgate and the Song of Songs)—are exploited to the full in the task of celebrating Philosophy's beauty and perfection throughout book 3. In his extensive commentary to his canzone *Amor che ne la mente mi ragiona* (written expressly to rebut the charge of inconstancy in love: 3.1.11), we immediately sense how passionately Dante experienced the joys of intellectual activity and the thrill of discovering philosophical truths, a passion that made him pass many nights immersed in fervent study while others slept and which even damaged his eyesight (*Conv.* 3.1.3, 9.15). His enthusiasm was difficult to contain. It overstepped the bounds of orthodoxy, when it caused him to claim that philosophy is a miracle in some ways more effective than Christ's miracles or those of the saints—"which are the principal foundation of our faith"—for these may be doubted by skeptics, whereas philosophy "is a visibly miraculous thing that can be experienced daily by the eyes of men, and she makes other miracles credible: hence, it is obvious that this lady with her wonderful countenance helps our faith" (*Conv.* 3.7.16). Indeed, throughout this section of his *Convivio* or Banquet of Wisdom, Dante's philosophical ardor is such that it seems akin to the ecstasy of contemplation described by Richard of St. Victor in his *Benjamin Major* (1.4): "the free penetration into the manifestations of wisdom by a mind suspended in wonder." And as Dronke remarks (1997a, 34), Dante "now claims for the Donna Gentile precisely that status of incarnate divine miracle, blessed in her effects, which he had claimed for Beatrice in the *Vita Nova*." Indeed, philosophy even possesses a miraculous ability to destroy vices that are innate, since "her beauty has the power to renew nature in those who gaze on her; which is a miraculous thing" (*Conv.* 3.8.20).

Philosophers are lovers of wisdom (*Conv.* 3.11.5). No one can be called a true philosopher who loves wisdom and knowledge "for utilitarian reasons as do lawyers, doctors and almost all churchmen, who do not study in order to become wise but to acquire money and rank" (*Conv.* 3.11.10). Philosophy leads to the perfection of humanity's noblest part, the intellect, conferring a beatitude which, however, differs from that enjoyed in paradise in that the latter "is perpetual, which this one cannot be for anyone" (*Conv.* 3.8.5). Here is the crux of the matter: despite later modifications, Dante sees the difference between earthly and heavenly beatitudes largely in terms of time and eternity, rather than in the interplay between nature and grace.[8] In fact, grace is virtually absent from *Convivio*'s depiction of life on earth.

On the other hand, Dante does make a clear-cut distinction between the human and the divine, although he regards the human being as a "divine animal" (*Conv.* 3.2.14) and he wholeheartedly accepts Aristotle's evaluation of philosophical speculation as a "divine" activity (*Ethics* 10.7). It is in the last chapter of book 3 that Dante most resolutely faces up to the problems posed by this optimistic view of the human condition. After reasserting his claim that in the possession of wisdom humanity sees all its desires fulfilled as human beings, he concedes that it may be difficult for some to accept this claim, since wisdom (now synonymous with philosophy) cannot "perfectly reveal certain things" to humankind *in via* (*Conv.* 3.15.7). Together with Christian doctrine, Augustine's celebrated statement at the very beginning of his *Confessions* (1.1) evidently reverberated throughout Dante's being: "You [God] made us for yourself and our heart is always restless until it finds peace in You" (cf. *Par.* 30.100–102). Dante now attempts to overcome this difficulty inherent in the human condition by stating that natural desire is always commensurate with a creature's capacity, "hence man's desire is limited in this life to the knowledge attainable here, and it does not go beyond this point except by error, which is outside nature's intention" (*Conv.* 3.15.9). Even angels cannot know everything. Hence, "since it is not given to our nature to know God and certain things in their essence, such knowledge is not naturally desired by us" (*Conv.* 3.15.10). It was only with great difficulty that a medieval Christian could make such a claim. Aquinas, for example, did not hesitate to affirm that the contemplation of things divine is "the activity most proper to man and the most delightful" (*S. Th.* 2.1.3.5). Aquinas denied that the desire for knowledge could be quenched in this life; and, momentarily casting Aristotle aside, he returned to the mainstream of Christian thought (e.g., *Contra Gentiles* 3.48) by refusing to accept the idea of a natural goal for humanity on earth that was not utterly subordinate to its supernatural destiny. However, no less an authority than Albert the Great, Aquinas's teacher, claimed that "although things divine are not perfectly conjoined to us in their own mode, they are nonetheless perfectly conjoined to us according to the measure of our disposition . . ." (Dronke 1997a, 45).

The influence of Albert the Great's writings on Dante's thought has been well illustrated by such scholars as Bruno Nardi, Maria Corti, and Cesare Vasoli. Not only does the Dominican theologian point the way for what we may term Dante's "philosophical optimism," but Albert (c. 1200–1280) also included a significant number of Neoplatonic elements in his fundamentally Aristotelian but eclectic teachings—elements that were clearly congenial to Dante's outlook.

Dante's Neoplatonism is evident in such passages as *Conv.* 3.6.4–6 and 3.7.2–7, which are based on a view of the created universe seen as multiplicity proceeding downward from the supreme unity existing in the First Mind of God and gradually becoming embroiled or imprisoned in matter and contingency—a vision that also inspired passages in the *Comedy* (e.g., *Par.* 13.52–78).

An even more significant aspect of Dante's philosophical eclecticism is the fusion of biblical Wisdom, together with the Bride of the Song of Songs, with the Platonic-Aristotelian figure of Lady Philosophy, so that she is now hailed as "bride of the Emperor of heaven . . . and not only bride, but sister and beloved daughter!" (*Conv.* 3.12.14). Philosophy is truly "a loving exercise of wisdom, which is found supremely in God . . . and is united to Him in perfect and true manner, as if by eternal marriage" (*Conv.* 3.12.12–13). Dante implies the consummation of this virtual marriage when, in 3.15.16, he glosses line 72 of the canzone—"She was the thought of Him who set the universe in motion"—by a direct quotation from Proverbs 8.27–30: "When God prepared the heavens I was present . . . when He laid the foundations of the earth, I too was with Him, setting everything in order and rejoicing every day." This heady intellectual eroticism prepares the way for the celebration of Beatrice's beauty in such passages as *Paradiso* 18.8–21, 27.104–5, and 30.19–33. Indeed, the transformation of the silent Beatrice of *Vita Nova* into the *Comedy's* loquacious spokesperson for Divine Wisdom is anticipated by Dante's portrayal of Lady Philosophy in *Convivio* 3. As will be seen later, in spite of the Christian taboo which forbade women to act as teachers of theology (1 Cor. 14.34–36), in the *Comedy* Beatrice is made to act not only as Dante's teacher throughout his heavenly ascent, but she even corrects churchmen on points of theology (*Par.* 29.70–126)—a revolutionary overturning of the gender roles made possible not only by the poet's vision of Beatrice Portinari in glory but also by his exaltation of God's "most beautiful and most virtuous daughter" in *Convivio* 3.[9]

Dante's orthodoxy

Such passionate enthusiasm for philosophy has led a number of scholars to assert that *Convivio* represents a stage in Dante's career when he became so besotted with his philosophical studies that subsequently he felt it necessary to repent of such a passion in his sacred poem. This hypothesis is not based on any solid internal evidence. As far as the latter is concerned, we may focus on two essential passages, both taken from the third book (which marks the zenith of his love and praise of Lady Philosophy). The first is proof that—unlike his Ulysses (*Inf.* 26.85–142)—the author of *Convivio* did not go beyond the bounds set by God, since he took care to translate and cite Ecclesiasticus 3.22 as a warning against sinful curiosity: "You shall not ask for things too high for you, nor seek out things too difficult for you; but consider those things that God has commanded you and do not be curious about His other works" (*Conv.* 3.8.2; see also St. Paul's exhortation cited in 4.13.9: "Do not strive to know more than is fitting . . ."). The second passage is the Platonic assertion of man's intellectual limitations in the last chapter of book 3, where Dante writes: "to a certain extent these things blind our intellect, in that they affirm that certain things exist which our intellect cannot gaze upon, namely, God, eternity and primal matter"—things whose existence we accept wholeheartedly as an act of faith (*Conv.* 3.15.6). Far from evoking an infatuation leading to a Ulyssean "mad flight" (*Inf.* 26.125), Dante tells us that his Lady's manner changed, so that her harsh disdain eventually caused him to moderate and even restrict his studies to a branch of ethics (*Conv.* 4.1.8–9). Deeply enamored of philosophy as he was, the man who asserted that the human soul "naturally desires and wants to be united with God in order to strengthen its own being" (*Conv.* 3.2.7) was no crypto-heretic or radical Aristotelian.[10]

The controversial problem that brought Dante to a metaphysical halt—"whether the prime matter of the elements was known by God" (*se la prima materia de li elementi era da Dio intesa*: 4.1.8)—was a Scholastic conundrum.[11] Various points must be borne in mind. First of all, the word *intesa* could mean either "understood" or "intended, created"—as is evident from *Paradiso* 27.114, where God alone is said to comprehend *(intende)* the Empyrean in a permanent act of creation. Second, in Aristotelian terms, prime matter is not "something": as sheer potentiality, it is always undetermined being, by definition unknowable. How, then, is it possible to square prime matter's incomprehensibility with God's omniscience? And if the idea of primal matter could not be in God's mind, how could he have created it? These philosophical problems proved too great for Dante; wisely, he turned away from them. There is no indication that his difficulties were heretical—as they would most definitely have been, if they had been concerned with the (Aristotelian) eternity of matter or its creation at any remove. Indeed, if Dante had wished to signify the temptation of heretical belief, the logic of his allegory would have obliged him to indicate a moment of succumbing to temptation; and not, as he depicted himself, temporarily *repulsed* by his Lady's harsh behavior. What the beginning of *Convivio* 4 does reflect is his state of mental confusion and his inability to find a way out of a philosophical impasse. Later, in *Monarchia* 1.3.8, Dante would resolve the issue by declaring that it is impossible to divorce the potentiality of matter from its realization, while in the *Comedy* he would convey both the distinction between matter and form *and* their simultaneous creation by the image of three arrows shot from a three-stringed bow with the speed of light (*Par.* 29.22–36). Many years before, however, the fledgling philosopher had been stymied by an apparently insuperable problem.

Since the issue is vital to a proper understanding of Dante's thought, we must now turn to the *Comedy,* to examine the possibility that its author went on to reject philosophy. There, we find that the poet—whose intellectual outlook was conditioned at an optimistic moment in the history of Christian philosophy, when revelation and rational enquiry were judged compatible by such Christian stalwarts as Albert and Aquinas—did not hesitate to place that radical Aristotelian and Aquinas's opponent, Siger of Brabant, among the blessed in heaven (*Par.* 10.133–38). Of even greater significance is Virgil's role in the poem: just as the emperor, aided by the teachings of philosophy, must guide humankind to the happiness signified by the Earthly Paradise (*Mon.* 3.16.7–10), so Virgil guides Dante to this very same goal. A key episode in this connection is the one set on the shores of Mount Purgatory (*Purg.* 2.112–23), in which Cato rebukes Dante, Virgil, and others for listening to the sweet tones of *Amor che ne la mente mi ragiona,* Dante's own canzone, intoned by Casella and which had been chosen for commentary in *Convivio* 3. For some scholars, Cato's rebuke (ll. 121–23) is aimed not at simple negligence but at the love of philosophy that had inspired the hymn of praise penned by Dante years before in *Convivio* 3.[12] To interpret the episode, we need to ask ourselves a simple question: Could Dante have expected contemporary readers of *Purgatorio* to know that *Amor che ne la mente* was really a love poem addressed to Lady Philosophy, rather than a straightforward love poem as its citation in *Purgatorio* 2 implies? The answer must be firmly in the negative, for the unfinished *Convivio* remained unread by and virtually unknown to Dante's contemporaries.[13] Thus, the opposition intended is between the pilgrims' negligence, brought about by the power of music and the appeal of what would have been for Casella and the disembodied souls a song about human love, on the one hand, and their urgent need to proceed on the path toward purification and God, on the other—as exemplified by the chanting of Psalm 113, which signifies the liberation of the soul from sin (*Conv.* 2.1.7).[14]

There is in fact not one piece of compelling evidence that Dante, both philosopher and poet (who described himself as philosophy's friend in *Epistole* 12.3.6 and who wrote *Monarchia* and the *Questio de aqua et terra,* as well as *Paradiso* in the last decade of his life), ever renounced philosophy as a means of arriving at the truth necessary to humanity on earth. Indeed, in the eighth heaven, Dante goes so far as to claim that his love of God had been inspired not only by revelation *but also by proofs provided by philosophy* (the *filosofici argomenti* of *Par.* 26.25; see also, 46–48). Instead of positing a rejection of philosophy in the *Comedy,* we ought rather to regard the universal hierarchy and the problem of causality sketched out in the third book of *Convivio* as the philosophical embryo that developed into an essential part of the *Comedy*'s intellectual infrastructure.[15] Our conclusions must also take into account the fact that, because of insurmountable difficulties posed by certain metaphysical questions, Dante turned his full attention to the study of an ethical problem highly relevant to contemporary society: the nature of true nobility. Philosophy thus remained for Dante "a loving use of wisdom, which exists above all in God" (*Conv.* 3.12.12), but also one that could—and did—provide humanity with eminently practical answers concerning essential problems posed by society on earth.

Book 4: Philosophy, society, and politics

The fourth book—whose ostensible subject is the definition of nobility—provides us *inter alia* with the matrix of Dante's political thought, the result of his discovery regarding Rome's imperial destiny. This section of *Convivio* (as long as the other three parts combined) was written about 1306 as a commentary to the canzone *Le dolci rime d'amor ch'i' solia* (LXXXII: 69). Presumably, it was completed just before Dante embarked on the *Comedy*. Dante tells us that his study of philosophy made him love those who seek the truth and hate the followers of error and falsehood. One error above all others was most pernicious not only to the individual but to society as a whole: the idea that nobility consists in "ancient wealth and fine behavior" (*Conv.* 4.3.6), a fallacy responsible for a state of dire confusion in the world. Since, however, he attributes this definition of nobility to Frederick II, Dante sets out to reassure his readers that the rebuttal of this philosophical error in no way impugns the emperor's authority in its proper sphere. The way he does this leads to a quite extraordinary digression, covering two whole chapters (*Conv.* 4.4–5). Dante, a citizen of Guelf Florence, for the first time clearly upholds the imperial thesis while further proclaiming his belief that God had populated pagan, republican Rome "with citizens not human but divine" (*Conv.* 4.5.12), granting them divine assistance at crucial moments in their history, in order that Rome might unite the world in the universal peace necessary for the coming of its Savior.

Rome and her universal empire

This political conversion is paralleled by the rediscovery of the true message of Vergil's *Aeneid,* with its paean to Rome and its imperial destiny. In *Inferno* 20.113–14, we are told that Dante was well acquainted with every line of Vergil's poem—an unusual feat in an age when the classics were chiefly known through quotations and extracts found in anthologies. The first evidence we have of a detailed and comprehensive knowledge of Vergil's great epic appears at *Convivio* 4.26.9, where Dante refers for the first time to the sixth book of the *Aeneid,* with its description of Aeneas's descent to the underworld and the foretelling of Rome's mission to unite the world.[16] Vergil, now acclaimed as "our greatest poet" (*Conv.* 4.26.8), is quoted as God's mouthpiece in 4.4.11, when *Aeneid* 1.278–79 is translated as proof that Divine Providence had chosen the Roman people to rule the world without limit of place or time: "to them have I given empire without end." This—Vergil's authentic historical and political message—had been ignored for a thousand years or more; and this is surely at least one of the reasons why his shade first appears to Dante in the *Comedy* as "someone who seemed weak through long silence" (*Inf.* 1.63).

In *Convivio* 4.4.1, Dante declares that the empire is rooted in the needs of society, which is organized with one end in view, a life of happiness. Since, as Aristotle declared, "man is by nature a social animal," individuals are incapable of fulfilling this collective purpose without guidance from the emperor, who is at the apex of the civil hierarchy and thus immune from greed. From this summit, he administers justice and secures peace for states, families, and individuals.[17] The need for unity—that *reductio ad unum* so characteristic of medieval thought—is asserted (*Conv.* 4.4.5–6), although Dante quickly passes on to illustrate the legitimacy of the Roman claim to supreme temporal power. Opponents (such as the Guelf extremists, who could claim the support of no less an authority than St. Augustine) claimed that Roman power was based on force alone; but force was only the instrument, "hence, not force, but reason—and divine reason at that—was the first cause of the Roman Empire" (*Conv.* 4.4.12).

The fifth chapter sets out to document the teleological process whereby God willed and brought into being the empire of Rome. That empire was decreed by God as the means of establishing the unity and peaceful state of the world necessary at the time of Christ's Incarnation. Similarly, Dante manipulates traditional chronology in order to prove that the origins of this historical process (both secular and divine) were laid *simultaneously* by Divine Providence through the birth of David, Christ's ancestor, in Israel, on the one hand, and the "birth" of Rome, on the other, when Aeneas made his epic journey from Troy to Italy (*Conv.* 4.5.4–6). Rome is thus placed firmly at the center of universal history, with the Romans viewed as another chosen people. And it is important to notice that the whole of this fifth chapter is truly a hymn of praise to the Eternal City and its *pagan* past, a hymn hardly relevant to the digression concerning the emperor's authority. Dante's newfound belief in the need for a supreme universal authority in the secular sphere, complementary to the pope's spiritual authority, takes on a radically new dimension, thanks to his discovery of the essential role played by Rome in God's blueprint for the world. As we have just seen, this discovery was made through Vergil's *Aeneid,* in which the Guelf exile found an impassioned justification of Rome's imperial mission. Thus, beginning with a reaffirmation of Frederick II's imperial authority, Dante's justi-

fication of the empire turns into a glorification of Rome, the city's name re-
peated obsessively in the fifth chapter, which exalts the citizens of her pagan
past as "divine, in whom not human but divine love inspired their love for her"
(*Conv.* 4.5.12). All who refuse to accept this providential design are condemned
for speaking "against our faith" in denying "what God has thus providentially
ordained!" (*Conv.* 4.5.9). This divine inspiration motivated Fabricius, Curius,
Mucius, Regulus, and—above all—Cato (cf. *Purg.* 1–2). God, we are told, acted
through these agents in preparing the way for and then setting up the Roman
Empire, while intervening at crucial moments in the history of pagan Rome
to save her from the Albans, the Gauls, the Carthaginians, and lastly from her
own son, Catiline—in a lengthy rhetorical sequence punctuated by the fourfold
repetition of the question "And was not the hand of God present?" (*Conv.*
4.5.18–19).[18] The apotheosis of Rome ends with the statement that even the
stones of the city's walls are "worthy of reverence" and the very soil on which
Rome stands is more worthy than is commonly proclaimed or realized by men
(*Conv.* 4.5.20).[19] By the time he came to write *Convivio* 4, the various pieces in
Dante's jigsaw of universal history had fallen into place. Its grand design was
to remain unaltered through the *Comedy* and *Monarchia,* to the poet's death
in 1321.

The digression continues in the sixth chapter. After the supreme political
authority, the supreme philosophical authority must be identified. Dante there-
fore sets out to prove that Aristotle is the philosopher "most worthy of trust
and obedience" (*Conv.* 4.6.6). Once again, the unifying principle is invoked: all
human activity on earth is directed toward a single end, namely the life for
which human beings are ordained insofar as they are human. With this end con-
stantly in view and with his quasi-divine intellect, Aristotle brought the science
of morality to its final perfection (*Conv.* 4.6.16). Hence, as the "master and guide
of human reason" (*Conv.* 4.6.8), he is the supreme authority in the sphere proper
to philosophy. This division of humankind's natural or secular activities into
two spheres under two mutually autonomous authorities is typical of Dante's
method. The two are complementary: the emperor is to be guided in his task by
philosophical truths, for government without the aid of philosophy "is dan-
gerous" and philosophy deprived of the emperor's authority has no practical
effect, whereas when the two are united, they are "most useful and most pow-
erful" (*Conv.* 4.6.17). The perfection of this union is exalted in the Bible (Wisd.
6.23); its antithesis is now found in the rulers of Italy, apostrophized as "ene-
mies of God" (*Conv.* 4.6.20). But the cause of Italy's woes is not merely the
wicked incompetence of its rulers; it is to be found above all in the absence of
an emperor who, endowed with the bridle of Roman law, must guide humanity
on earth and restrain its will even as a good horseman controls his steed (*Conv.*
4.9.10).

The nature of nobility

Following the Scholastic method of philosophical analysis, Dante exposes contemporary fallacies about his stated theme, nobility. To be condemned above all is the foolish individual who claims that he is noble because his father or grandfather was truly worthy, "although he himself is worth nothing" (*Conv.* 4.7.2). In fact, he is even more to blame, for his life and actions ought to have followed the glorious example set by his predecessors. In order to drive his point home, Dante invents a parable of two people lost in the snow. The first finds the right way, without any help; the second loses his way and falls into thorn bushes and ruins. Which of the two is to be judged worthy? This is the first of a number of poetic images in book 4 that point the way to the *Comedy's* superabundance of imagery (cf. 4.7.3, where error is pictured as an all-devouring weed in a field that must be cleared by the author, as well as the image cited above of the human will as a horse and the emperor as its rider, which will reappear in *Purg.* 6.88–93).

Dante not only rejected the feudal concept of nobility, he was also opposed to the world of nascent capitalism with its lust for wealth. He now devotes three chapters (*Conv.* 4.11–13) to proving that riches, far from being indispensable to nobility, are essentially base. There is no justice in the way they are distributed; their promise of contentment is utterly false; and their evil allurements have been denounced by David, Solomon, Cicero, Horace, Seneca, Juvenal, and "every other writer and poet" (*Conv.* 4.12.8). The desire for riches destroys not only individuals but also cities and whole regions. It leads men to commit every possible crime and even to desire the death of a father, so that both canon and civil law have as their chief aim the need to protect humanity from the effects of greed, which only increases with the possession of wealth (*Conv.* 4.12.9). Dante deals with the objection that knowledge, too, must be base, since like wealth it instills a desire that never ceases to expand and can never be wholly satisfied. He quickly goes on to proclaim the perfection of knowledge, although once more he has to wrestle with its relative imperfection on earth, owing to the limitations of human nature. In the acquisition of knowledge, an individual moves from one step to the next. In this progression, each step is mastered, thus achieving ever "greater perfection," whereas a desire for riches is based on a constant frustration devoid of all perfection (*Conv.* 4.13.2). Furthermore, it is wrong to claim that the natural desire for knowledge cannot ultimately be gratified, for it can in fact be wholly satisfied, provided it remains within its natural limits, as Averroës (1126–98) and Aristotle imply and St. Paul makes clear (Rom. 12.3). Indeed, the right measure of knowledge is analogous to the just use of wealth. In the fourteenth chapter Dante attacks the static nature of feudal society with its illusion that time can help to confer nobility through the possession of "ancient wealth" (*Conv.* 4.14.1). In the next chapter he adduces humanity's descent from Adam, to prove that individuals must be capable of becoming noble through personal worth, whether or not they belong to the nobility. In typical fashion, Dante goes out of his way to show that it is universally believed that humanity had a single ancestor—even by such disparate authorities as Aristotle, the Christian faith, "which cannot err," Plato, Ovid, and "the religion and ancient belief of the Gentiles" (*Conv.* 4.15.5).

Second part of book 4

With the second half of book 4, we arrive at the *pars construens* or positive part of Dante's exposition. First, he defines the term "nobility" as indicating in common usage the perfection of a thing's nature, as when people speak of a noble horse or a noble stone because they have realized their full potential as horses or stones (*Conv.* 4.16.4). In order to discover the hallmark of nobility in human beings, we must examine its effects, "which are the moral and intellectual virtues" (*Conv.* 4.16.10). The practical bent of Dante's interests in *Convivio* 4 leads him to put to one side the intellectual virtues in order to concentrate on the moral virtues. In fact, he asserts that the latter are the most truly human of all virtues, "because in all respects they lie within our power" (*Conv.* 4.17.2). The underlying distinction between the active life and the life of contemplation leads to the most stringent separation of these two spheres of human activity with their respective virtues. Dante is careful to remind his readers of the superior happiness afforded by contemplation (*Conv.* 4.17.9); and everything in his recent experience—his exile and his passionate involvement with philosophy—leads him to echo Aristotle's praise of this intellectual activity.

On the other hand, what Dante takes away from the active life by affirming its relative inferiority, he generally restores in practice. A fascinating example of this vindication of the active life is the liberty Dante takes with the traditional interpretation of Christ's words to Martha. In Luke 10.42, Christ tells Martha, as she busies herself "with many things," that her sister Mary has chosen "the best part of all" by neglecting practical cares and giving her undivided attention to the words of her Savior. This episode was commonly interpreted as signifying the relative merits of the lives of action and of contemplation. Dante, however, applies not to Mary but to Martha (the active life) Christ's words "However, one thing is necessary" *(Porro unum est necessarium),* and he proceeds to apply them to Martha's actions (*Conv.* 4.17.10). In the Gospel text, "one thing" is clearly opposed to the multitude of Martha's cares, whereas the shift in Dante's translation of the Vulgate's *porro* (however) to "*certainly,* one thing is necessary" transforms the radical opposition implied by Christ's words into an acknowledgment of the utility of the active life. This interpretation is very much Dante's own: in harmony with *Convivio*'s revaluation of the active life, it flatly contradicts the pronouncements of such authorities as Augustine, Gregory the Great, Bede, and Anselm.

Nobility, however, is not merely a question of possessing moral and intellectual virtues; it is the overall perfection of human nature. Such perfection makes human beings hardly lower than the angels (Ps. 8.6–7). It is given not to families but to individuals, when God finds the soul "ready and disposed to receive this divine act" (*Conv.* 4.20.7). Dante sets out to demonstrate how this union is accomplished, first by rational inquiry and then by following the revealed truths of theology. As far as philosophy is concerned, the opinions of Plato, Pythagoras, and others are discarded in favor of Aristotle's judgment. Yet, even while offering a scientific description of human conception, Dante cannot refrain from expressing his wonder at the miraculous fusion of body and soul and at the mysteries of God's ways (*Conv.* 4.21.6). He returns to his task by explaining that the creation of the embryo is effected by the sperm (the female ovum was judged to be essentially passive). This active element varies in its elemental composition, its generative virtue, and it is subject to certain celestial influences at the moment of conception. Then, divine intervention adds the intellectual principle: the "rational" soul, whose purity depends on the greater or lesser perfection of the embryo.

This explanation is at variance with the teachings of both Averroës and Aquinas, but it follows the doctrine expounded by Albert the Great in his *On the Nature and Origin of the Soul*. As already stated (*Conv.* 3.2.11–14), the basis of all life is found in the vegetative soul; animals also possess a sensitive soul, while humans add a third essential element, the rational soul.[20] The problem for orthodox Christians lay in safeguarding the unity of the tripartite human soul against radical Aristotelians (who believed in the separateness of the rational soul from the vegetative-sensitive compound), and the obvious misconception that three separate souls exist in humans. Dante was to return to this problem in *Purgatorio* 25.37–75, one of the peaks of his philosophical poetry and a passage that completes the views set forth in *Convivio* 4.[21] Whereas the vegetative and sensitive souls are both produced by the formative power of the male seed—a process induced by the power of the heavens (thereby providing a scientific basis for a qualified belief in astrological influences)—the miraculous transformation of an animal embryo into a human being is an act performed directly by God and thus untouched by astral determinism. In both texts (*Conv.* 4.21.5 and *Purg.* 25.65) Dante refers to the infusion of the "possible intellect" by God. It was this cognitive faculty that made impossible any form of individual immortality, according to Averroës (*Inf.* 4.144), for the possible intellect was "loaned" to the individual and remained distinct, united with the human body only until death severed all links. For Dante, however, the possible intellect is totally united with

the individual through its absorption of the active elements present in the vege-
tative-sensitive compound, which transforms the whole into "one single soul"
(*Purg.* 25.67–75).

Nobility is a divine gift made to the individual capable of receiving this
"seed of happiness" (*Conv.* 4.21.8). So much seems clear to Dante from his study
of natural science. As far as theology is concerned, Dante tells us that God simi-
larly endows the soul with the gifts of the Holy Spirit in accordance with the
individual's receptivity (*Conv.* 4.21.11). That he should have developed such
an idiosyncratic theology, which omits all reference to the Christian sacrament
of baptism, shows how deeply Dante was conditioned by his attempt to turn
professional philosopher.

Differences between book 4 and books 1–3

We must now assess some fundamental differences between the fourth and the
first three books of *Convivio*. The differences between the two sections (the first
three books and book 4) are striking and indicative of a different approach that
prepares the way for Dante's poetic masterpiece (Corti 1983, 123–45).[22] Sympto-
matic of this change of perspective is Dante's idiosyncratic interpretation of the
visit by the three Marys to Christ's empty tomb in the twenty-second chapter
of the fourth book. He tells us that the three women may be taken to represent
the "three sects of the active life, namely Epicureans, Stoics, and Peripatetics,
who go to the sepulcher, that is, this world, which is the home of corruptible
things, and seek the Savior, that is happiness *(la beatitudine),* and do not find it
there" (*Conv.* 4.22.15). The angel's words to the women tell us what our no-
bility in fact teaches us: that "whoever looks for happiness in the active life" will
not find it there; instead, happiness will go before us "in Galilee, that is to say
in speculation" (*Conv.* 4.22.16). Dante points out that the Bible says that Christ
and beatitude will *precede* us, not that they will be with us, since "in our con-
templation God always lies ahead of us, and here we can never reach Him, who
is our supreme beatitude" (*Conv.* 4.22.17). This is quite different from the as-
tounding claim made near the end of the third book, when Dante asserts that
the *theological virtues* make it possible for men to "rise up to philosophize in that
heavenly Athens, toward which the Stoics, the Peripatetics, and the Epicure-
ans hasten together in common accord and by the light of eternal truth" (*Conv.*
3.14.14–15). The radical optimism of "a philosophical utopia—a heaven of rea-
son, rather than of theology's saints and angels" (Dronke 1997a, 35), so char-
acteristic of the third book, is now tempered by a vein of orthodox skepticism
concerning the powers of human reason unaided by grace. This shift in outlook
is reflected in the sources quoted by Dante. For the first time, in the fourth
book religious sources are quoted more frequently than Aristotle (whereas in the

second book quotations from Aristotle were three times, and in the third book more than twice, as numerous as quotations from religious authorities).

Returning to the twenty-second chapter of the fourth book, we find further evidence of this important shift. Whereas in book 3, humanity's desire for knowledge was limited to the kind of knowledge attainable on earth and could therefore be wholly satisfied (*Conv.* 3.15.9), now in 4.22.13 the life of speculation cannot be practiced to perfection on earth, since it will be fully realized only in the vision of God, "the supreme object of our understanding." Aristotle's optimism is replaced by the Christian concept of the limitations of life on earth, expressed in terms Aquinas might have used. Similarly, in the third book, the active life is linked to the moral virtues and offers a secondary happiness, while the life of the intellect provides the greatest possible happiness through the perfection of human reason (*Conv.* 3.15.4). In book 4, however, Dante has added a verbal marker of prime importance—the little word *quasi*—so that we now read that human happiness can be found "virtually imperfect *(quasi imperfetta)* in the active life, in other words in the practice of the moral virtues, and then almost perfect *(perfetta quasi)* in the practice of the intellectual virtues." Both ways, however, are intended to lead to "supreme happiness, which cannot be had here on earth" (*Conv.* 4.22.18). Another important factor is the addition of the cardinal virtues as necessary for the proper ordering of the active life (*Conv.* 4.22.11). However, the greatest switch from Aristotelian to Christian ethics occurs in the surprising metamorphosis of magnanimity from the Aristotelian virtue connected with honor and fame (*Conv.* 4.17.5) to its Christianized form, whereby it becomes a synonym of the cardinal virtue of fortitude, which had led Aeneas to go down "into hell in search of the soul of his father Anchises and face up to so many dangers" (*Conv.* 4.26.7–9). Together, all these elements contribute to the process that transformed the optimistic Christian humanist of the third book of *Convivio* into the Christian world-judge of the *Comedy*.

The four ages of man

We must now return to the twenty-third chapter, where, in characteristic fashion, Dante follows up his theoretical exposition of the origins of nobility with an eminently practical application. For this, he divides human life into four ages: adolescence (which lasts until our twenty-fifth year); youth (twenty-five to forty-five); old age, from forty-five to seventy; and an occasional bonus of some ten or eleven years constituting extreme old age *(senio)*. Dante's love of symmetry is obvious in the way he divides up the biblical span of seventy years with twenty years spreading out in both directions from the midway point of thirty-five, flanked by two periods of twenty-five years, in the sequence 25–35–45–70 (35 − 10 = 25; 35 + 10 = 45; 45 + 25 = 70). He also mentions that Plato lived to be eighty-one years old, on account of his natural perfection, adding that Christ would no doubt have lived to this age, if he had not been crucified—another homage paid to the number nine (of which eighty-one is the square), which had accompanied Beatrice throughout her life on earth (*VN* 29.2).

All this may seem rather quaint. More important is the fact that, for Dante, nobility expresses itself in different ways during the various phases of human life. We also find some significant changes to a number of basic Aristotelian concepts already introduced. For example, the list of the eleven moral virtues given in 4.17.4–6 is taken from Aristotle, because "where Aristotle's divine opinion has spoken, I feel that every other opinion should be discarded" (*Conv.* 4.17.3). However, when Dante comes to discuss these same moral virtues as the effects of nobility, he gives a different list, very much his own and which he elaborates through the rest of the fourth book. Aristotle's list presupposes a static view of the human personality in a fully developed, adult being. Instead, Dante's conception of nobility goes hand in hand with the biological development of human beings and traces an evolutionary progression toward the higher virtues.[23] Thus, adolescence is seen as the time when human beings concentrate on their physical development, so that its virtues include obedience and bodily grace (*Conv.* 4.24.11). In old age humans must cultivate the supreme virtues of prudence and justice, so that, if they reach their physical peak at the age of thirty-five, it is only in old age that human beings attain their moral peak.

Equally significant is the fact that Dante places his virtues in an active social context. The most striking example is that of justice, the most lovable and most "human" of all the virtues (*Conv.* 1.12.9), now defined in Aristotelian terms as the virtue that makes us "love and practice righteousness in all things" (*Conv.* 4.17.6). This blanket definition acquires its civic status in 4.27.10, when we are told that a man must be just in his old age "so that his judgments and his authority may be a light and a law to others."[24] Equally important is the fact that Aristotle had excluded prudence from his list of moral virtues, because he considered it to be an intellectual virtue. In signaling prudence as the prime virtue of old age, Dante restores the rational element to virtuous action. The cardinal virtue of prudence is in fact indispensable as a guide to action, since it gives true counsel and ensures success "in human affairs and activities" (*Conv.* 4.27.6); and it is the one thing Solomon asked for when God offered to give him anything requested (3 Kings 3.9–10; *Par.* 13.94–108).

We thus witness the gradual development of the human being's personality from the preoccupation with physical development in adolescence to altruism in old age, when the elderly "must open out like a rose which can no longer stay closed but must cast its perfume abroad" (*Conv.* 4.27.4). The divorce brought about by the rigid separation of the active life and its moral virtues from the contemplative life with its intellectual virtues is now quietly annulled in Dante's evolutionary view of nobility, whose last stages are governed by the alliance of prudence with justice. The moral virtues have been intellectualized and the individual's role in society is brought to the fore.

Such harmony is of prime importance. Nevertheless, it leaves out a whole area of human experience that was to be of paramount importance to the author of the *Comedy*: the area concerned with religious belief and practices, which is only hinted at in Dante's description of extreme old age. No particular virtues are assigned to this exceptional stage, although we read that it befits the noble soul at this point "to return to God" and to "bless the voyage" accomplished during its sojourn on earth (*Conv.* 4.28.2). Death must be a "haven"; and, in preparing for it, the sails of earthly concerns and activities must be lowered in order that the haven may be reached in safety and peace. Here we find the first mention of the human being's relationship with God. Until now, life on earth has been viewed as an essentially autonomous process, with duties imposed by participation in a social community. Only now is the religious dimension of life addressed. This fact alone must make us realize how very different *Convivio*'s perspective is from the all-embracing view that inspired Dante's *Comedy*.

Equally startling is the way in which this new dimension is illustrated. The soul's return to God is exemplified by Lucan's account of a pagan marriage and divorce. Marcia's return as Hortensius's widow to Cato, her first husband, is interpreted allegorically as showing that "the noble soul at the beginning of extreme old age returns to God. And what earthly man was more worthy to signify God than Cato? None, surely" (*Conv.* 4.28.15). Cato reappears in the *Comedy* as the guardian of purgatory; and it is clear how profoundly Dante was impressed by the praise of Cato found in ancient writers. It is nevertheless well-nigh incomprehensible that a pagan suicide (who was also Caesar's implacable enemy) should be chosen to signify God at the end of *Convivio* 4. Possible reasons why Dante chose Cato as guardian of his purgatory are examined in chapter 9, especially the Christological accretions to his pagan life. For the time being, we may simply note that line 123 of *Le dolci rime* ("from the moment she weds with the body") implies that Marcia's marriage to Cato required Cato to represent *the human body* in this strangest of all allegories. Subsequently, full of admiration for the Stoic hero (cf. *Conv.* 4.5.16), Dante must have shifted his allegorical aim to focus on the soul's final return to God (*Le dolci rime*, l. 137). Hence, his attempt to justify this immense conceptual leap: "what earthly man was more worthy to signify God than Cato? None, surely." But nothing should dull our amazement at this particular *tour de force*, whereby we find the greatest poet of the Christian faith illustrating humanity's relationship with its Creator through the example of a pagan divorce and remarriage!

After the shock of this allegorical interpretation and intrusion (in *Conv.* 4.1.10–11, Dante had declared that he rejected the use of allegory in *Le dolci rime* in order to make its message more effective as a necessary remedy for a social ill), the fourth book is brought to an end. *Convivio* is thus left interrupted, with less than one-third of the projected book written—and with a final reminder that individuals cannot be ennobled by their families. The essential link between nobility and philosophy is also proclaimed: "for they love each other so greatly that nobility always asks for her, and philosophy does not cast her sweetest gaze elsewhere" (*Conv.* 4.30.6).

Conclusion

The imposing fragment known as *Convivio* must be regarded as vital evidence of an important stage in Dante's development as both a writer and a thinker, in which we find a number of significant elements pointing in the direction of Dante's masterpiece. Four of its most striking features—boundless confidence in the Italian language (book 1); appropriation of biblical allegory for secular writings (book 2); faith in the ultimate compatibility of philosophical inquiry and revealed dogma (book 3); the belief that the Roman Empire had been chosen by God to unite the whole of humanity (book 4)—all bear witness to the work's importance in Dante's career as both writer and thinker. From a stylistic point of view, it would be difficult to imagine the *Comedy* without the experience of the earlier work (whose prose was a necessary stage in and testing ground for Dante's development as a writer).[25] It was during this "unpoetic" phase in Dante's development—the period from 1303 to 1308, which saw the production of both *De vulgari eloquentia* and *Convivio*—that the future poet of the *Comedy* mastered the art of expressing the most complex subtleties of human thought. What had hitherto appeared as the monopoly of an intellectual elite—especially ethics or "morality . . . the beauty of philosophy" (*Conv.* 3.15.11)—was for the first time effectively transmitted through the "natural" medium of the vernacular and thus made accessible to a new class of reader. The audience for which Dante was to write his *Comedy* had already appeared on the writer's horizon.

Similes (scarce in Dante's early writings) are more frequent in *Convivio*—a development that anticipates one of the glories of his poetic masterpiece. Especially noteworthy is the prevalence of similes and metaphors in the final chapters of the last book. We may take as our example:

the noble soul in its last age . . . returns to God, as to *that port* from which it left when it first entered *the sea* of this life . . . *the path* . . . straight and true, untroubled by *violent storms* [cf. *Inf.* 26.136–42] . . . a natural death is for us like *reaching port after a long journey*, and coming to rest . . . like a *goodsailor* . . . so we must lower *the sails* of our earthly activities [cf. *Inf.* 27.79–81] . . . like a *mature apple* [cf. *Par.* 26.91–92] . . . And *like someone* arriving after a long journey, before entering *the gates of his native city*, is greeted by the citizens, so the noble soul is greeted . . . by *the citizens of eternal life* . . . and it feels that it has left behind *the inn* and returned *home* [cf. *Inf.* 15.54], that it has left behind *the journey* and returned to *its city* [cf. *Purg.* 16.96 and *Par.* 30.130], that it has *left the deep and returned to port*. (*Conv.* 4.28.1–7; my emphasis)

This dense cluster of images is followed by an address to the reader of a kind that will be such a striking feature of the *Comedy*'s prophetic voice: "O you wretched and base souls who rush to this port under full sail, and where you ought to find rest . . . you wreck yourselves at the very place to which you have been journeying for so long!" (*Conv.* 4.28.7; cf. 3.5.22; 3.15.17; 4.6.19–20; 4.27.13–14).

Another feature common to both works is their structural symmetry, based on the principle that "we say that something is beautiful, when all its parts are in due accord" (*Conv.* 1.5.13), as well as the importance of numerology in medieval art. Instead of the trinitarian number that is at the basis of the *Comedy*, the number 15 (3 × 5) is the architectural unit of books 2, 3, and 4 (Simonelli 1970, 2:193). In book 4, with its thirty chapters, the first fifteen refute common errors concerning nobility while the next fifteen expound the author's thesis. Dante's sense of balance and proportion—what he was to call the "bridle of art" in *Purgatorio* 33.141—is already in evidence, especially in the fourth book.

All this is but a signpost pointing in the direction of what we know was the inevitable outcome. In his *Comedy*, Dante would contradict a number of assertions made in *Convivio*. For example, Guido da Montefeltro and Bertran de Born are both damned (*Inf.* 27–28), instead of praised (Guido for his tardy conversion and Bertran for his liberality: *Conv.* 4.28.8 and 4.11.14). In *Paradiso* 2.61–148, Beatrice is made to refute the Averroistic hypothesis concerning the cause of the spots visible on the moon, replacing a physical explanation by a metaphysical one, indicating the degree of beatitude enjoyed by the angels who impart its motion to the moon. Another retraction is found in *Paradiso* 28.121–35 (cf. *Par.* 8.34–37), when the angelic hierarchy described in *Convivio* 2.5.6 (cf. Brunetto Latini, *Tresor* 1.12) is rearranged according to the sequence first found in a sixth-century text, *The Celestial Hierarchy*, attributed to Dionysius the Areopagite. As Hollander observes (2001, 90), "The later poem at times tackles the task of clearing the record of errors in *Convivio*. And it is clear that some of these are not trivial."

It appears that until the very last moment Dante intended to finish his massive enterprise: as late as *Convivio* 4.26.8, he looks forward to book 7, while, in 4.27.11, justice is for the second time selected to be the theme of book 14. What caused him to break it off, in all likelihood we shall never know. The election of Henry of Luxembourg as emperor on November 27, 1308, soon brought a sense of new urgency to Dante's political message. For this message, the synchronization of pagan and religious history in the persons of Aeneas (ancestor of Rome) and David (ancestor of Christ) is of the utmost significance (*Conv.* 4.5.6), since—as we have seen—it shows that Dante felt he had traced the twin paths that led to the establishment of God's providential design, with its "two suns" established to guide humanity to happiness on earth and to beatitude in heaven (*Purg.* 16.106–8).

Two essential things were still lacking: a belief in the supremacy of poetry as vehicle for the communication of a universal message, as well as the religious dimension and vision that together were to fashion the *Comedy*'s universe. Poetry, with its "ornaments," is here seen as a distraction for the reader (*Conv.* 1.10.12). In his *Vita Nova*, Dante had already set his hand to writing a prose commentary to certain of his poems, but these remained the core element of that *libello*. Instead, in *Convivio*, the poems chosen are little more than a pretext for a dazzling display of erudition and dialectic. The moment of Dante's conversion to poetry as the supreme medium for the expression of the totality of human experience and knowledge remains hidden; but it is evident that in writing *Convivio* he had not yet found his vocation as *poeta-theologus*.[26] As far as that vocation is concerned, we have seen that the author of *Convivio* was convinced that philosophy helped the Christian faith (*Conv.* 3.7.16), that Holy Church could not utter falsehood (*Conv.* 2.3.10), and that its doctrines commanded supreme authority (*Conv.* 4.15.9). Nevertheless, these principles had to be fused by the white heat of its author's religious and poetic convictions in order to create the explosion that gave birth to Dante's sacred poem, his *Comedy*.

Texts and translations

Convivio. Edited by Franca Brambilla Ageno. 3 vols. Florence: Le Lettere, 1995.

Convivio. Edited by Cesare Vasoli. In Dante Alighieri, *Opere minori*, vol. 1, part 2. Milan and Naples: Ricciardi, 1988. Although the text of the *Convivio* is cited according to Franca Brambilla Ageno's edition, published by the Società Dantesca Italiana (Edizione Nazionale), Cesare Vasoli's detailed commentary remains invaluable.

Other readings

Ascoli, Albert R. "The Unfinished Author: Dante's Rhetoric of Authority in *Convivio* and *De vulgari eloquentia*." In *The Cambridge Companion to Dante,* edited by Rachel Jacoff, 45–66. Cambridge: Cambridge University Press, 1993.

Corti, Maria. *La felicità mentale: Nuove prospettive per Cavalcanti e Dante,* 38–155. Turin: Einaudi, 1983.

Dronke, Peter. *Dante's Second Love: The Originality and the Contexts of the "Convivio."* Leeds: Maney and Sons, 1997a.

Foster, Kenelm. "Religion and Philosophy in Dante." In *The Mind of Dante,* edited by U. Limentani, 47–78. Cambridge: Cambridge University Press, 1965.

Gilson, Étienne. "Philosophy in the *Banquet*." In *Dante the Philosopher,* translated by David Moore, 83–161. London: Sheed and Ward, 1948.

Hollander, Robert. "Dante's Deployment of *Convivio* in the *Comedy*." *Electronic Bulletin of the Dante Society of America,* October 7, 1996; with Lino Pertile's response of October 8.

Lansing, Richard. "*Convivio*." In *The Dante Encyclopedia,* edited by R. Lansing, 224–32. New York: Garland, 2000.

Scott, John A. "The Unfinished *Convivio* as a Pathway to the *Comedy*." *Dante Studies* 113 (1995a): 31–56.

Simonelli, Maria. "*Convivio*." In *Enciclopedia Dantesca,* 2:193–204. Rome: Istituto della Enciclopedia Italiana, 1970.

Took, John F. *Dante: Lyric Poet and Philosopher: An Introduction to the Minor Works,* 81–122. Oxford: Clarendon Press, 1990.

Vasoli, Cesare. Introduction and commentary to *Convivio*. In Dante Alighieri, *Opere minori,* vol. 1, part 2, xi–lxxxix + 885. Naples: Ricciardi, 1988. See also his "Dante scienziato e filosofo." In *"Per correr miglior acque . . . ": Bilanci e prospettive degli studi danteschi alle soglie del nuovo millennio. Atti del Convegno di Verona-Ravenna, 25–29 ottobre 1999,* vol. 1, 71–91. Rome: Salerno Editrice, 2001.

Dante's vision of world empire and peace

Monarchia

A fascinating document, *Monarchia* shows us Dante passionately involved in one of the great ideological struggles of history, with some ideas already out of date (as political ideologies often are at the height of a conflict of power), but wielding his pen with as much expressive force and efficacy as in some of the outstanding passages of the *Comedy*. In this treatise, written in Latin, the author's self-confidence is greater than in *Convivio*: he does not hesitate to cross swords with the great twelfth-century theologian Peter Lombard (*Mon.* 3.7.6) or to take on the most eminent churchmen and scholars of his day in attacking their interpretations of Christ's message. The work also demonstrates the same kind of philosophical expertise and formal unity that characterize the *Comedy*.

Date of composition

The dating of *Monarchia* is a much-debated issue. The opening of the second book ("The kings of the earth . . . the princes have gathered together against their Lord and against his Christ") indicates a moment of opposition to the emperor's authority. For some scholars, this points to the critical stage in Henry VII's Italian campaign (1311–13), when Dante's beloved city, Florence, and Robert of Anjou did their utmost to destroy imperial power and authority in Italy. Others, however, argue from the treatise's lack of resentment against the pope that it was composed before Clement V betrayed "lofty Henry"

(*Par.* 30.137–44)—a betrayal that surfaced most clearly at the time of Henry's coronation (June 29, 1312), although it was already evident in papal policy of the previous year. If we accept as genuine the reference in *Monarchia* 1.12.6 to the fifth canto of *Paradiso* (and the manuscript evidence is in favor of its authenticity),[1] then we must suppose that *Monarchia* was the product of the papal-imperial conflict, perhaps drafted earlier but given its definitive form no earlier than 1314 (when Dante had probably begun work on *Paradiso*) and most likely as late as 1317–18. This dating is profoundly significant, since it implies that Dante's theoretical political tract is in fact complementary to the message delivered in his *Comedy* to a corrupt world.[2]

Purpose of the work

Like all the works composed during Dante's exile, *Monarchia* was intended to edify his contemporaries and influence their conduct: "the present subject is not directed primarily toward theoretical speculation but toward action" (*Mon.* 1.2.6).[3] It shares with the *Comedy* the intention to sway not only fellow Italians, but the whole of humankind and posterity as well. This aim is paralleled by a static view of human nature that sees humanity's needs as eternal and unchanging. Such a view is typical of the medieval outlook; it is at the opposite pole from, say, that of Machiavelli (1469–1527), which was to emphasize the importance of adapting theory to differing circumstances, since one solution, however desirable, cannot be applied indiscriminately to all situations. Instead, Dante, with his firm belief in an omnipotent creator, believed that God took an active interest in what he had created. Moreover, since God could not will two contradictory things, the basic problem was to discover what he willed. Once this is known, the answer must remain constant, and it will indicate the path that can lead humanity to happiness and salvation. The only way to set about it, Dante tells us in *Monarchia* 1.2.4, is to start from first principles.

The subject of *Monarchia* is world government, a topic Dante judged to be of the greatest importance to humanity, although it offered no immediate financial reward. Its author's method will reveal the essential truth "about temporal monarchy" (*Mon.* 1.1.5). Whereas contemporary tracts concentrated on points of law and trite *exempla,* Dante conducts his inquiry on a philosophical plane, using Aristotelian syllogistic reasoning, while making due reference to the Bible and especially to Christ's own words. First comes the definition: "temporal monarchy, commonly referred to as the empire, is the rule of one individual over all other authorities" (*Mon.* 1.2.2). Dante then has to qualify this statement by adding that the monarch's or emperor's authority extends "in and over those things that are measured by time," thus making the traditional distinction between the temporal realm and the spiritual, the latter subject only to eternity.

Dante addresses three fundamental questions in *Monarchia,* each the topic of a book of the treatise:

Book 1. Is such authority necessary for the well-being of the world?
Book 2. Did the Roman people rightfully assume that universal authority?
Book 3. Does the emperor's authority stem directly from God, or is it dependent on God's vicar or minister, the pope?

The first book therefore concentrates on political theory; the second, on history; the third, on the relationship between the universal secular authority and the papacy.

Book 1: Is the empire necessary?

As already mentioned, a basic tenet of *a priori* reasoning is the need to begin one's investigation by creating essential guidelines in the shape of first principles. Dante therefore sets out to discover how to reach humanity's universal goal as established by nature. In so doing, Dante shifts his view of this universal goal from the generic one of happiness (as stated in *Conv.* 4.4.1) to a specific and highly controversial one: namely, the need "to actualize at all times the full potential of the possible intellect" (*Mon.* 1.4.1). The previous chapter asserts that the distinctive characteristic of human beings is their "ability to understand by means of the possible intellect" (*Mon.* 1.3.6), a faculty that is unique to men and women, since only humankind possesses both a body and a mind. Animals lack the capacity to reason, while in angels intellect and being coincide, so that their intellects are constantly operating to their full capacity. The human intellect, on the other hand, exists as a potential faculty that functions only intermittently.

In order to glimpse the explosive charge of Dante's statement, we must briefly glance at one of the salient features of Aristotelian thought. In his *De anima* (3.5), Aristotle distinguished between man's "possible" intellect with its immense potential and the "agent" or "active" intellect, which acts upon intelligible notions in the same way that light brings out the potentiality of color.[4] Radical Aristotelians in the Middle Ages accepted the idea put forward by the great Arab philosopher Averroës (*Conv.* 4.13.8; *Inf.* 4.144) that the intellect was one and eternal—and that a single allocation was given to human beings only for their lifetime, thus denying the immortality of the individual soul. It is in fact this latter view that distinguishes the heretics placed in the sixth circle of

Dante's hell (*Inf.* 10.13–15), while in *Purgatorio* 25.61–66 the poet specifically refers to Averroës' error in positing a divorce between the human soul and the possible intellect.

Here, however, in the opening chapters of *Monarchia*, Dante seizes upon two aspects of Averroistic thought—the epistemological importance of the Aristotelian concept of a possible intellect and the unity of humankind—to prove his main thesis that the world must be united under one ruler. Intellectual unity would be one of the beneficial consequences of such political unity, enabling men and women to achieve their maximum potential of intellectual activity. As usual, Dante was not slow to exploit any concept that could add grist to his ideological mill. In this case, however, any reference (such as that in 1.3.9) to the work by Averroës in which "the Commentator" asserted the unity of the possible intellect was likely to be misunderstood. It did indeed spark off violent condemnation by Guido Vernani, a Dominican who wrote a refutation of *Monarchia* in 1329 and seized upon the statements in chapter 4 of book 1 as proof that Dante had taught that "there is one single intellect in all men, which opinion . . . is a grave error invented and broadcast by that Averroës cited by him."[5] That it was possible to be truly eclectic within the bounds of orthodoxy is shown by the fact that St. Albert the Great (c. 1200–1280) held views similar to Dante's. In his commentary on Aristotle's *De anima* (3.2.13), Aquinas's teacher speaks of the universal nature of the intellect and tells us that all speculative intellects are one insofar as they are speculative intellects, "but many according to their appurtenance to various individuals," adding that Averroës says much the same thing, "although he differs slightly from us as far as the abstraction of the intellect is concerned." That single word "slightly" speaks volumes. Although the future saint wrote a specific rebuttal of Averroës' doctrine of the unity of the intellect, he was nevertheless prepared to play down the essential differences between himself and the great Arab commentator when it suited him. And it is Albert—not Aquinas—that Dante followed in his detailed account of the origin of the human soul and its possible intellect in *Purgatorio* 25.

It is therefore necessary to refute Vernani's accusations. Dante's assertion that humanity must realize the total capacity of the possible intellect must not be taken to imply that this intellect is a separate substance. If, for example, the words "human soul" were substituted for "possible intellect" in the phrase "always to actualize the full power of the possible intellect," we should hardly suppose that Dante believed in a single soul separate from humanity. We may also note that Dante precedes his mention of Averroës by the fundamental axiom that potentiality cannot exist in a void. As always, in our analysis of complex philosophical problems, we must never forget that Dante was not a professional philosopher. As already mentioned, his purpose in *Monarchia* (as in the *Comedy:* cf. *Ep.* 13.16.40–41) was not so much speculation as action (*Mon.* 1.2.6). He was determined to establish the rightful authority of the universal empire willed by God, and he took from the philosophical and historical culture of his times whatever seemed likely to develop and strengthen his argument. For Dante, the possible intellect was primarily identified with the essential act of acquiring knowledge. For Averroës, the unity of the possible intellect was a scientific fact; for Dante, the intellectual unity of the human race was a goal to be attained through the establishment of a universal community on earth. Whereas for Averroës a small elite of philosophers could best carry out the task of realizing the possible intellect's potential, nothing less than the totality of humankind could achieve Dante's goal. Hence, the assertion that "the activity proper to *humanity considered as a whole* is constantly to actualize the full potential of its possible intellect, primarily through thought and secondarily through action as an extension of thought" (*Mon.* 1.4.1; my emphasis). In good Aristotelian terms, thought or speculation is an activity "which is almost divine" (*Mon.* 1.4.2)—to which Dante adds the Christian rider "Thou hast made him [man] a little lower than the angels" (Ps. 8.6).[6]

Human society's need for peace

This universal goal can be reached only when the world is at peace, for even as the individual needs peace and quietude in order to acquire wisdom and prudence, so the human race needs a state of peace in order to carry out its divinely appointed task of intellection. This grandiose vision may have been inspired at least in part by a Dominican lector at Santa Maria Novella in Florence, Remigio de' Girolami (d. 1319), who described humanity's dual aim to achieve temporal and spiritual peace in his *De bono pacis*.[7] Dante may well have transferred the theologian's concept of *pax spiritualis* to a practical plane, making the peace of the spirit directly dependent on the peace of this world. Be that as it may, as a result of Dante's intense idealism, his vision of a political utopia was fashioned by various elements, such as his reading of Vergil's "imperialist" poetry and the latter's forecast of the "universal peace" that for the medieval Christian heralded Christ's birth (*Purg.* 22.71–73); as well as his study of Aristotelian philosophy and his personal interpretation of the Church's vision of a universal community, transported from the realm of faith to the secular sphere of human reason.

As already mentioned, one of the cardinal advances in the culture of Western Europe was the rediscovery of Aristotle's *Politics* and his other writings whereby the recognition of men's and women's need for mutual help as "political" or social animals led to a greatly strengthened affirmation of their secular needs and organization (cf. *Par.* 8.115–17). Dante magnifies this basic need for human beings to live in a community far beyond Aristotle's vision of a Greek city-state and even beyond contemporary concepts of empire to proclaim the universality of his world empire. First, he combines the Greek philosopher's axiom that a group united in its purpose must be ruled by one leader (Aristotle, *Politics* 1.5) with the Christian view of a God who made man in his image and likeness (Gen. 1.26). One God rules the heavens: humanity must therefore strive to mirror the divine by being truly united; so, too, one ruler must govern the human race and the things of this earth. The whole of this section of *Monarchia* (*Mon.* 1.5–9) is fired by the conviction that unity is best and that multiplicity must be brought back to unity whenever possible (cf. 1.15.3: "to sin is nothing but to spurn unity and move towards plurality"). Hence, "humanity is in its ideal state when it is governed by one ruler (as by a single source of motion) and by one law (as by a single movement)" (*Mon.* 1.9.2). Chapter 10 expresses the need for a supreme tribunal to which local rulers may appeal in order to settle their differences.

Structure of book 1

The plan of book 1 is now evident. Its first three chapters are devoted to an introduction and to humanity's goal on earth; the fourth discusses the benefits of universal peace; chapters 5–9 stress the importance of political unity worldwide; 10–13 deal with justice and its antithesis; 14–15 return to the essential theme of unity; and 16 provides the conclusion, with the theme of unity reiterated and capped by a quotation from Psalm 132.1: "Behold how good and how joyful it is for brethren to live together in unity." Unlike *Convivio* and *De vulgari eloquentia*, *Monarchia* is a completed work, whose precise symmetry and arrangement of detail reflect the mind that produced the crystalline structure of the *Comedy*. We note the way the opening and closing chapters of each book, with their rhythmic prose patterned on the *cursus* of medieval Latin and their abundance of scriptural allusions, create a frame of reference for the exposition of the three main themes: that world empire is a necessity; that this empire was given by God to the Roman people for all time; and that the emperor's authority derives directly from God.

With the restoration of a chapter division at 3.10.18 (suppressed by Ricci in his 1965 edition but restored by Shaw),[8] books 1 and 3 both contain sixteen chapters, with a central book of eleven chapters, making a total of forty-three (4 + 3 = 7) chapters in the work. *Monarchia* is in fact based on the numbers three and seven: three recalling the Holy Trinity, and seven the number of Creation, with holiness (the seven gifts of the Holy Spirit), the three theological and four cardinal virtues, knowledge (the seven liberal arts), and universality. Dante's method of investigation is moreover based on syllogistic reasoning, which conforms to the Christian principle of three-in-one: three terms, three propositions, with one conclusion—just as the whole work is made up of three propositions set forth in its three books. *Vita Nova*'s number nine is also in evidence, with nine quotations from Vergil's *Aeneid* concerning Aeneas's triple nobility, nine heroes of ancient Rome cited in book 2, and nine hierocratic arguments in book 3. As we have already noted in chapter 1, God was said to have placed number as a governing factor in creation (Wisd. 11.21), and medieval artists used numbers to reflect that reality and give symbolic weight and depth to their works.

Justice and the empire

For the author of the *Comedy,* the idea of justice is indissolubly linked with the concept of the empire and the emperor's primary role as the custodian and dispenser of the Law (*Par.* 18–20).[9] Chapter 11 of *Monarchia*'s first book is fundamental in this regard, with its axiomatic opening: "the world is ordered in the best possible way when justice is at its most powerful." To clinch his point, Dante quotes Vergil's famous line "Now the Virgin returns, Saturn's reign returns" (*Eclogues* 4.6), explaining that the Virgin stands for justice and Saturn's reign signifies humanity's Golden Age. This is a good illustration of the elasticity of allegorical interpretations, for in *Purgatorio* 22.66–81 Dante makes this Vergilian line refer to the birth of Christ, of whom Vergil had been the unconscious prophet—while in *Epistole* 7.1.6, this same line is applied to Henry VII, whose coming to Italy was regarded as heralding the advent of a new age of justice for that troubled land.

Here, in *Monarchia* 1.11.11, Dante goes on to cite Aristotle to prove that it is greed that most directly threatens justice: "When greed has been utterly eliminated, nothing remains opposed to justice." In this short phrase, Dante gives us the very kernel of his political thought. Greed or *cupiditas* is the most universal and the most destructive sin of all. It is figured in the she-wolf of the *Comedy* (*Inf.* 1.49–60; *Purg.* 20.7–15), and when it returns toward the end of the poem it is shown to be the root cause of the universal tragedy played out on earth (*Par.* 27.121–41; 30.139–41). Specifically opposed to the remedial guidance offered by the emperor, it leads humanity to destruction and popes to hell. Freed from greed, the human race would inevitably accept God's moral order by practicing and enjoying the benefits of justice. The proponents of peace, justice, and charity must therefore unite to combat the forces of greed. The emperor is most exempt from this vice. Since his jurisdiction extends everywhere and everything belongs to him, he should (and must) rise above the allurements of greed (hence the condemnation of "German Albert" and his father as victims of greed in *Purg.* 6.97–117). As the ultimate custodian of justice, the emperor offers the best guarantee of humanity's essential freedom, which—Dante insists—is based on free will. Here, at *Monarchia* 1.12.6, in declaring that freedom of the will is God's greatest gift to human nature, Dante refers to *Paradiso* 5.19–24: *sicut in paradiso*

"Comedie" iam dixi (as I have already said in the *Paradiso* of the *Comedy*), using the emphatic *dixi*, "I have said," instead of the authorial "we." This cross-reference places the text of *Monarchia* as we now have it in the final stage (post-1314) of Dante's career. Scholars, like Bruno Nardi, who imagine an opposition between *Monarchia* and the *Comedy* are forced to reject this reference as spurious in order to allow for an earlier dating of the Latin treatise. Yet the evidence offered by the manuscript tradition of *Monarchia* is clear, and no good reason has been adduced to explain why this cross-reference should have been invented and added by another hand (or by Dante at a later date).

Through free will, then, "we enjoy happiness as men here on earth, and happiness as gods in the next world" (*Mon.* 1.12.6). Chapter 14 specifies that the emperor's universal authority does not mean that he must interfere in every regional or municipal matter. Justice is absolute, but "law is a rule to govern life" (*Mon.* 1.14.5: *est enim lex regula directiva vite*). Governments must therefore accept the fundamental principles of justice upheld by the emperor and apply them in various appropriate ways, just as the practical intellect receives universal truths from the speculative intellect and then applies theoretical principles to the particular problem at hand.

The concluding chapter of the first book clinches the whole argument by an appeal to history, which shows that never since the Fall "was there peace throughout the world except under the emperor Augustus, when a perfect monarchy existed" and humanity "was happy in the calm of universal peace, as is attested by all historians, famous poets," St. Luke, and St. Paul (*Mon.* 1.16.1–2). That happy state was "first rent by the talon of greed" when Constantine mistakenly divided up the empire. This, the first of three references to Constantine's "Donation" (*Mon.* 1.16.3; 2.11.8; 3.10), comments on the disastrous consequences of the emperor's supposed gift of Rome and the western half of the empire to Pope Sylvester and to the latter's successors in gratitude for his cure from leprosy.[10] Humanity is now shipwrecked by the multiplicity of its desires, which obscure the single goal of happiness attainable through justice, even as both its intellects (theoretical and practical) are sick and unmindful of the Holy Spirit's exhortation to live united in brotherhood. History and bitter experience thus fully support the theoretical proposition that the empire, one and immutable, is necessary for the well-being of the world.

B ook 2

The second book opens with a biblical quotation: "Why have the nations raged . . . ? The kings of the earth have arisen, and the princes have gathered together against the Lord and against his Anointed [*Christus eius:* Ps.

2.1–3]." This is followed by one of the most precious autobiographical fragments Dante has left us. He tells us that he himself had once been amazed at the way in which the Roman people had been elevated to world dominion, "because, looking at the matter in an entirely superficial way, I thought they had gained their supremacy not by right but simply by force of arms" *(Mon.* 2.1.2: *illum [romanum populum] nullo iure sed armorum tantummodo violentia obtinuisse arbitrabar).* This opinion corresponded to the radical Guelf view, and it was naturally espoused by the young Dante, who grew up in the Guelf commune of Florence. Presumably just after his exile (and certainly before he came to write *Convivio* 4.4–5), when Dante finally penetrated "to the heart of the matter," his amazement was replaced by "a kind of scornful derision" for those who shared that view, since he was led "by the most compelling signs" to understand that it was in fact God's Providence that had guided the Roman people to their triumph *(Mon.* 2.1.3). Derision and scorn must, however, give way to charity, which requires Dante to "break the chains of ignorance" and "pour forth the light of correction" *(Mon.* 2.1.5). It is this, he assures us, that leads him to reiterate the psalmist's words within the space of a few lines and to cry out "in defense of that glorious people and of the emperor . . . 'Why have the nations raged . . . against their Lord and against his Christ?'" *(Mon.* 2.1.4).[11] This exceptional repetition of a biblical text underscores the writer's passionate commitment to his cause.

Rome acquired empire in conformity with God's will

The purpose of the second book is to show that the Roman people acquired universal empire by right *(de iure).* Throughout *Monarchia* Dante opposes the views of the hierocrats and Guelf extremists; but here, his unnamed adversary is none other than St. Augustine. In the fourteenth book of his *De civitate Dei,* Augustine had emphasized the opposition between God's ideal city and the cities and kingdoms of this earth, which, without justice, are nothing but "great robberies" *(magna latrocinia:* 4.4) rooted in sin and acquired by violence. In exemplary opposition, Dante insists that right exists in God and is willed by Him. The basic principle underlying book 2 is therefore "what God wills in human society must be held to be true and pure right" *(Mon.* 2.2.6). In order to discover God's will we must search for "clear signs *[ex manifestis signis]"* *(Mon.* 2.2.7)—a belief that lies at the root of medieval symbolism (cf. Rom. 1.20) and that also nourishes Dante's teleological view of history *(Par.* 6).[12]

Vergil's role

Just as Dante composed book 1 under the aegis of "the Philosopher" (Aristotle), so Dante's chief authority in book 2 is Vergil, "the Poet." For example, in chapter 3, "our divine poet Vergil" (*Mon.* 2.3.6) is made to testify to the supreme nobility of Aeneas, "the father of the Roman people," and to the fact that the latter were "the noblest under the heavens" (*Mon.* 2.3.17). The way this claim is backed up is of interest on two counts. The first is the fact that Dante no longer attributes to Frederick II the definition of nobility as consisting in virtue and ancient wealth, as he had done in *Le dolci rime* and *Convivio* 4.3.6. He now assigns it correctly to Aristotle (*Politics* 4.8). Whereas much of the fourth book of *Convivio* was devoted to refuting the idea that nobility was linked to inherited wealth, now that the formula is ascribed to Aristotle and—necessarily accompanied by virtue—it is accepted for Dante's present purpose. It would be naïve to imagine that Dante recanted his former opinion in deference to Aristotle. He could simply have omitted the quotation. Why, then, did he include it? Not, surely, to signal a change of heart or the acceptance of the idea of inherited nobility as a feudal monopoly. Instead, the most likely reason is that it served his specific aim of establishing the unique nobility of the Roman people, derived through both Aeneas's own virtue and that of his ancestors. Indeed, Dante goes on to show that each of the three regions of the world (Asia, Africa, and Europe) "made him noble, both through his ancestors and through his wives" (*Mon.* 2.3.10). Aeneas was thus ennobled by marriage: his first wife, Creusa, daughter of King Priam of Troy, was from Asia; his second "wife," Dido, was queen of Carthage, in Africa; and his third, Lavinia, "mother of the Albans and the Romans . . . was from Italy, the noblest region of Europe" (*Mon.* 2.3.16–17).[13]

The apparent contradiction between *Convivio* 4 and this third chapter of book 2 of *Monarchia* is here attenuated by Dante's (mis)quotation of Juvenal, whereby the latter is made to declare (through Dante's crucial addition of the word *animi,* "of mind," 2.3.4) that "nobility of mind [*nobilitas animi*] is the sole and only virtue." On the other hand, the difficulties of reconciling the two points of view have led some scholars to suppose that Dante had not read the fourth book of Aristotle's *Politics* when he wrote *Convivio.* We cannot even be sure that Dante read Aristotle's text (in Latin translation) rather than a commentary on the *Politics.* Whatever the truth of the matter, however, Dante's decision to quote Aristotle's definition of nobility (without explanation or any attempt to reconcile the fundamental contradiction) is yet another indication that *Convivio* was not only abandoned by its author but that he took it for granted that his readers would not have seen that unpublished text.

Miracles and Roman heroes

The fourth chapter lists the miracles God performed "so that the Roman empire might achieve supremacy" (*Mon.* 2.4.5), including the occasion when Rome was saved by a goose "never seen before" that roused the defenders of the Capitol when at night the Gauls tried to take this last stronghold by stealth (*Mon.* 2.4.7–8). Guido Vernani (in 1329, the first critic of *Monarchia*)[14] thought it hardly necessary to point out that such supernatural events, if they really happened, must have been the work of witchcraft, while this same story had struck St. Augustine as yet another example of the Romans' superstitious credulity (*DCD* 2.22 and 3.8). However, already in *Convivio* 4.5.17–20, Dante had singled out such events in Roman history as proof that God had intervened on behalf of that "holy, dutiful and glorious people"—as the Romans are designated in the following chapter, which exalts their spirit of self-sacrifice and their repression of greed as more worthy than is commonly proclaimed or established, while Cicero's republican idealism (*De officiis* 2.8.26–27) is offered as evidence that "the senate was a haven and a refuge for kings, peoples, and nations," so that Roman rule "deserved to be called protection rather than domination of the world" (*Mon.* 2.5.7).[15]

Dante's selection of Roman heroes—here, as in *Convivio* 4.5.13–17—is in part based on St. Augustine's longer list (*DCD* 5.18), but it is made with a very different purpose in mind. Augustine attributed their exploits to the overweening pride and ambition that devoured the Roman spirit. If pagan pride had achieved so much, then surely Christian virtue, inspired by charity, must scale even greater heights. Dante, however, implicitly rejects this accusation of pride when he attributes all those heroic deeds to an overwhelming desire to serve and augment "the public good with toil, with poverty, with exile, with the loss of their children, the loss of their limbs, even with the sacrifice of their lives" (*Mon.* 2.5.8). His Roman heroes are the same as those celebrated as the "instruments" of "Divine Providence" in *Convivio* 4.5: Cincinnatus, Fabritius, Camillus, Brutus, Mucius Scaevola, the Decii, and—above all—Cato, who "in order to kindle the love of freedom in the world . . . chose to die a free man rather than remain alive without freedom" (*Mon.* 2.5.9–16).[16]

After this, the central and longest chapter in book 2, Dante asserts that "the Roman people were destined to rule by nature" (*Mon.* 2.6.11). Nature required a world leader for humanity: Rome was the place; her citizens the people chosen. The truth of this fundamental assertion is attested by recourse to Vergil, whose authority in Dante's view seems close to that of a sacred text. He quotes the passage from the great imperialist book of the *Aeneid* (6.847–853), in which Anchises tells Aeneas that other nations shall excel in the arts and sciences but that the task of the Roman people will be to rule over the nations: "Your arts shall be: to impose a lasting peace, to spare the conquered and to subdue the proud."

God's will is now adduced to explain Rome's success. This is revealed to human beings either through the proper use of reason or by faith. In passing (*Mon.* 2.7.4), Dante unhesitatingly asserts that "a man who has never heard of Christ and is therefore without faith cannot be saved, however perfectly he has been endowed with and practiced the moral and intellectual virtues. Human reason on its own cannot see the justice of this, although aided by faith it can"—a problem that had troubled Dante on many an occasion (as the Eagle declares in *Par.* 19.67–78) and one that forms the backdrop to the amazing vision of the souls of Ripheus and Trajan, apparently pagan souls miraculously redeemed in the Heaven of Justice (*Par.* 20.44–72). Far from being antithetical, these two works of Dante's later years, *Monarchia* and *Paradiso,* are in fact complementary, although their vantage points are necessarily different.

For modern readers, the weakest chapters in the whole work are no doubt chapters 8 and 9, based on the belief that God is always on the side of the victor—or, as Dante puts it by quoting an unidentified saying, "Let Peter bless the one to whom God grants victory" (*Mon.* 2.8.1). Thus, it was in accordance with the divine will that the Romans won the race for world dominion against all competition. Dante claims that Alexander the Great, who came closest to winning the prize, is reported by Livy as having "collapsed in Egypt before receiving a reply [to his ultimatum] from the Romans, virtually in the middle of the race" (*Mon.* 2.8.8; far from reporting such an event, Livy in fact maintains that most probably the Romans had never heard of Alexander). Even shakier is Dante's axiom that "whatever is acquired through trial by combat is acquired by right" (*Mon.* 2.9.1), a relic of the feudal worldview and the tradition of invoking God's judgment in such trials. This custom had already been strongly criticized by theologians as an exaltation of the strong against the weak (e.g., Aquinas, *S. Th.* 2.2.95.8.3). To bolster this conviction, however, Dante goes so far as to alter the whole import of Christ's words (Matt. 18.20: "where two or three are gathered together in my name, I am there among them") in his bold claim that God is present in such confrontations, "since he himself promised us as much in the Gospel" (*Mon.* 2.9.5). Thus, God is seen to have ensured victory for Aeneas against Turnus, for the Horatii against the Curiatii, for the whole of the Roman people against the Sabines and the Samnites, for Scipio against Hannibal. Once again, Scripture is pressed into service: "A Roman could truly have said what the Apostle told Timothy [2 Tim. 4.8]: 'There is laid up for me a crown of righteousness'; 'laid up,' that is, in God's eternal providence" (*Mon.* 2.9.19).

Christ and the empire

Chapter 10 opens with the observation that so far Dante's arguments have been grounded chiefly in rational principles. Now, proofs will be sought in principles of the Christian faith. Indeed, Christ himself is offered as the supreme proof that the Roman Empire was willed by God, since he chose to be born and enrolled as a member of the human race through an edict emanating from Roman imperial authority (cf. Luke 2.1–7). Moreover, "if the Roman Empire was not lawful [de iure], Adam's sin was not punished in Christ" (Mon. 2.11.1). In order to savor and appreciate Dante's quixotic reasoning, it is necessary to recall one of the legalistic aspects of medieval theology, according to which a penalty imposed by an unlawful judge was not a punishment but an injury. Thus, Christ's passion would not have been a punishment for original sin if it had not been ordered by an appropriate judge, who had to have "jurisdiction over the whole of humankind, since it was the whole of humankind that had to be punished in Christ" (Mon. 2.11.5). It is clear that Tiberius Caesar would not have had such jurisdiction if the Roman Empire had not been founded on right. Hence, the empire's authority had to be both universal and willed by God. Although it struck the Dominican Guido Vernani as the height of madness and impiety in its claim that the punishment for original sin was subject to any earthly authority, such is also the legalistic basis for Justinian's discourse in Paradiso 6.82–90.

This claim concludes the argument of the second book, so that while book 1 ended with a reference to Christ's birth in the fullness of time, book 2 ends with the boast that it is now clear that Christ sanctioned the empire "both at the beginning and at the end of his earthly campaign" (Mon. 2.11.7). This is followed by a lament addressed to Italy: "O happy people, o how glorious Ausonia, if only the man [Constantine] who weakened your empire had never been born, or if he had never been led astray by his own pious intentions!" (cf. Par. 20.55–60).

Book 3

Like the second book, book 3 opens with a quotation from Scripture. Here, the passage quoted (Dan. 6.22) is redolent of the Comedy's prophetic tone, revealing Dante as the intrepid champion of truth and justice: "He [God] shut the lions' mouths and they did not harm me, for I was found just in his sight." In a manner that looks forward to Cacciaguida's exhortation in Paradiso 17.124–35, Dante puts on "the breast-plate of faith" (1 Thess. 5.8) and, fired with the divine inspiration that had filled Isaiah, he now enters the arena "to cast out the wicked and the liar from the ring" (Mon. 3.1.3). As promised, he will now confront one of the great problems of his time—the relationship between the empire and the papacy—and determine whether the emperor's authority derives immediately from God or whether it is transmitted to him through the pope.

In the period following the collapse of the Roman Empire in Western Europe, the bishop of Rome had been subject (at least, in theory) to the political authority of the emperor in Constantinople. With the rise of the Holy Roman Empire, emperors in the West had even deposed popes. However, a new age of hierocratic claims dawned with the election of Hildebrand as Pope Gregory VII in 1073. Gregory did not hesitate to affirm that the pope alone could use the imperial insignia and that the supreme pontiff had the authority to depose emperors. In Dante's time, Boniface VIII not only proclaimed that the temporal power was subject to the pope's spiritual authority, but he also asserted the papal right to transfer control of the empire *(translatio imperii)* from the Romans to the Franks or—if he deemed it necessary—to any other people. These papal claims were anathema to Dante, who decided to refute them in the third book of his treatise on empire.

The second and third chapters are crucial to this aim in that they set out the principle that will guide Dante's investigation and identify his opponents. This basic principle is that "what is contrary to nature's intention goes against God's will" *(Mon.* 3.2.2). His opponents (who deny that the emperor's authority stems directly from God) are divided into three groups. The first includes certain pastors and the spiritual head of Christ's Church, whose authority is clearly limited by the statement that to him must be given "not whatever is due to Christ but whatever is due to Peter" *(Mon.* 3.3.7)—a clear rebuttal of the claims of popes to a fullness of power *(plenitudo potestatis)* by virtue of their assumption of the title *vicarius Christi.*[17] Such opponents are led astray by their zeal for the Church. By contrast, the stubborn greed devouring the second group makes them sons of the devil (John 8.44) and leads them to deny the sacred principles on which the empire was founded, although they proclaim their filial loyalty to Christ's Church.

The third group is made up of those "who are called 'decretalists' and who are utterly ignorant of both theology and philosophy" *(Mon.* 3.3.9). Dante professes due respect for the decretals, a collection of papal decrees or epistles first compiled by Gratian c. 1140 in an attempt to settle various legal points governing the practical affairs of the clergy. Gratian's *Decretum* was augmented by Gregory IX in 1234; a sixth book was added by Boniface VIII in 1298, and further additions were made by Clement V in 1314. Dante placed Gratian in heaven for his great enterprise *(Par.* 10.103–5). The "decretalists" or ecclesiastical lawyers who interpret the decretals are quite another matter, however, for they are led by greed to exploit and pervert canon law, which was in fact set up in order to combat human greed *(Conv.* 4.12.9). As puppets of greed, the decretalists neglect to study the Gospels and the writings of the Church Fathers. It is therefore useless to engage in discussion with opponents whose bad faith is motivated by greed. While showing proper devotion toward Christ, the Church, and "the shepherd," Dante will argue his case only with the first group—those who are led by "some zealous concern for Mother Church," although "they are ignorant of the truth we are seeking" (*Mon.* 3.3.18).

Structure of book 3

The plan of the third book and the method adopted are now visible. Book 3 is based in part on the model of the *Quaestio* in Scholastic debates: its author sets out to beat the theologians at their own game. Their rules made it essential to proceed to the refutation of errors after the introduction (chapters 1–3) and to examine the evidence supporting his view (chapters 13–16). Dante elects to debate nine of his opponents' chief arguments. In this choice, he displays a deep familiarity with his opponents' claims that the dependence of the empire on the Church may be proved by reference to Holy Scripture and historical precedent. He therefore selects—and demolishes—six arguments based on Scripture: three from the Old Testament (chapters 4–6) and three from the New Testament (chapters 7–9), followed by three arguments based on history and reason (chapters 10–12).

Sun and moon analogy

The first weapon to be demolished in the papal arsenal is the argument that the creation of the sun and moon provides a confirmation that the magnitude and splendor of the spiritual power was intended to outshine the feeble light cast by the moon over temporal affairs. Throughout the thirteenth century, the sun-and-moon parallel was used to emphasize both the greater dignity of the papacy and the complementary nature of the two supreme powers on earth. Especially by Boniface and the extreme hierocrats, this traditional imagery was twisted to prove the empire's total subordination to the papacy: the decretalist Hostiensis had argued (c. 1250) that even as Ptolemy stated that the sun is 7,644.5 times larger than the moon, so "the sacerdotal dignity is seven thousand, six hundred and forty-four and a half times greater than the royal" (Tierney 1980, 156). However, in the decretalist's view, it was no longer even a question of relative dignity, for, like the moon, the empire was deprived of all light, hence of all independent authority, except that which it supposedly obtained from the papal sun.

In the *Comedy,* Dante countered these arguments by referring to the papacy and empire as "two suns" which light up two different but complementary paths, that of the world and that of God (*Purg.* 16.106–8). In this quite exceptional, literally absurd, unscientific image Dante harked back to the "two great lights" of Genesis 1.16 and did his utmost to avoid connotations of relative size and brilliance. What was admissible in a poem, however, would have been utterly out of place in the rational, Scholastic context of *Monarchia*. Dante therefore begins by pointing out that two fundamental mistakes may be made in any allegorical interpretation: the one, by attempting to impose an allegorical interpretation where none was intended by the author; the other, by interpreting the allegory in a way not intended by the author. Those who make such mistakes through ignorance "should be diligently corrected and then excused, just as one should excuse someone afraid of the lion in the clouds [thunder]" (*Mon.* 3.4.10). On the other hand, those who willfully distort the truth must be treated as tyrants who trample on and exploit constitutional laws, "for they sin not against Moses, not against Job, not against Matthew, not against Paul, but against the Holy Spirit who speaks through them" (*Mon.* 3.4.11). The formula *sun:moon = papacy:empire* is demolished by the fact that all government is "a remedy against the infirmity of sin" (*Mon.* 3.4.14)—a statement that may appear to contradict the belief that men and women are destined by nature to be members of a state or organized society (*Mon.* 1; *Par.* 8.115–17). Given that humanity had lost its state of innocence in Eden, Dante was able to reconcile the Aristotelian view of society as a necessary and (postlapsarian) "natural" state with the Christian idea that humankind had no need of government in its state of pristine innocence. This is in fact the message of *Purgatorio* 27.139–42, when Virgil "crowns and miters" Dante as they enter Eden: now, purged of all tendency to sin, the pilgrim no longer needs to be guided by either emperor (crown) or pope (miter); instead, he must be governed solely by his will, now "free, upright, and whole." Moreover, Dante goes on to argue, humanity had not yet appeared when the sun and moon were created on the fourth day, according to Genesis. To produce remedies against the consequences of sin would have been utterly superfluous at that stage: such a chronological error cannot be attributed to the Creator.

The second refutation is the gentler way, whereby the error is reflected upon and an essential correction made. Although the moon does not produce abundant light except for that which it receives from the sun, nevertheless its movement is independent and it is not without its own light, as may be observed during an eclipse. In order to function more effectively, however, the moon does receive some light from the sun, thus increasing its power. Similarly, secular government—which does not owe its authority to the spiritual power—can operate more successfully "through the light of grace that in heaven and on earth the blessing of the Supreme Pontiff infuses into it" (*Mon.* 3.4.20).

Biblical precedents

The selection and deposition of Saul by Samuel (1 Kings [Sam.] 10.1 and 15.23–28) was used as evidence by hierocrats to prove that temporal power could be bestowed and taken away by the Church (*Mon.* 3.6.1–2). Dante, however, denies that Samuel was acting as God's vicar; he was in fact sent by God as his legate or special messenger. As such, he was merely the tool and mouthpiece of his Lord—as are angels, through whom God accomplishes many things that may not be done by St. Peter or his successors. The latter are Christ's vicars and "no vicariate, human or divine, can be equivalent to the primary authority." Unlike Christ, for example, popes cannot contravene the laws of nature or create anything, nor can they validate baptism. A cardinal weapon in the papal armory is confronted in chapter 8: Christ's words to Peter, "And whatever thou shalt bind on earth shall be bound in heaven; and whatever thou shalt loose on earth shall be loosed in heaven" (Matt. 16.19). These words (cited by Boniface VIII in his bull *Unam sanctam* of 1302) were supposed to confer on the pope his "plenitude of power" *(plenitudo potestatis),* hence his capacity to ratify or annul any secular authority. Instead, Dante proves yet again his dialectical skills by contending that the term "whatever" is necessarily circumscribed by Peter's office, which is inherited by his successors. It would be absurd to suppose that a pope can annul a valid marriage or "absolve me even if I do not repent, which even God cannot do" (*Mon.* 3.8.7; cf. *Inf.* 27.112–29 regarding the latter impossibility, dramatically illustrated with tragic consequences for Guido da Montefeltro, when he is tricked by Boniface VIII's promise to grant him absolution, without due repentance for his sin).

Finally, Dante examines the Gospel passage perhaps most often quoted in support of the hierocratic case, from St. Bernard's moderate interpretation to the radical claims of thirteenth-century popes and decretalists: "Behold, here are two swords" (Luke 22.38), the words supposedly uttered by Peter. The hierocrats argued that the swords were entrusted to Peter alone and that they signified supreme spiritual and temporal power. Dante ripostes: "This must be flatly denied, both because that reply would have been contrary to Christ's intention and because Peter was in the habit of replying in haste, only considering things in a superficial manner" (*Mon.* 3.9.2). He goes on to argue that the phrase must be examined in context (and it is surprising how often this necessary step was omitted in medieval exegesis). Dante tells us that the words were spoken on the day of the Last Supper, at which time Christ foretold his Passion and departure. Whereas before he had sent his followers without scrip, purse, or sandals, "now, whoever has a scrip let him take it with him, and his purse also; and whoever has no sword must sell his cloak and buy one" (Luke 22.35–36). This, Dante argues, shows clearly what Christ meant. He did not intend two swords to be given to one man, but that there should be twelve swords, one for each apostle. His purpose was to warn them of the dangers they would have to face after his crucifixion. If Peter's meaning had been the one invented by the hierocrats, Christ would surely have rebuked him, as he did on other occasions when Peter spoke out of turn. Dante insists that, in evaluating the context, not only the circumstances but also the speaker's character must be taken into account. Peter's impetuosity is more than once illustrated in Scripture, at times to his credit, as when it led him to recognize Christ's divinity (Matt. 16.15–16). In fact, Peter's straightforwardness makes nonsense of the tortuous reasoning of Dante's adversaries. If, then, there is any allegorical meaning to be found in the episode of the two swords, it must refer to Christ's words "I have not come to bring peace, but a sword" (Matt. 10.34), while the two swords may also signify the words and actions necessary for the apostles to accomplish Christ's purpose. This ninth chapter shows Dante at his argumentative best, placing a biblical passage in its rightful context and taking into account a speaker's psychological makeup. The self-assurance he displays in taking on experts in biblical exegesis is a striking feature of Dante's personality. It is perhaps a pity that in this case he forgot to point out that the words under discussion were not in fact pronounced by Peter alone but by all the apostles.

Constantine's "Donation" and historical precedents

The Donation of Constantine, already referred to at the end of the first and second books, is confronted in chapter 10 of book 3. Although eminent jurists such as Gratian had their doubts about the validity of the supposed gift of the western half of the empire to the popes, no one in Dante's time possessed the necessary philological knowledge to demolish the document on linguistic and historical grounds (as was to happen with Lorenzo Valla's devastating critique in the fifteenth century). Dante had little choice but to accept the forgery as genuine. However, he argues that Constantine was not empowered to give away any part of the empire, nor was the Church entitled to receive such a gift. The emperor does not in any way own the empire, it is not his to give away, for "to divide the empire is contrary to the office delegated to the emperor" (*Mon.* 3.10.5). His duty is to ensure the unity of humankind under one supreme political authority. Indeed, to divide up and give away any part of the empire would be tantamount to rending Christ's seamless garment, which even Christ's murderers dared not divide (John 19.23–24). This reference sends us back to the close of book 1, where the arguments for the essential unity of the empire were formulated and where the same garment "rent by the talon of greed" (*Mon.* 1.16.3) already symbolizes humanity's political unity under the rule of the emperor. In *Unam sanctam* (1302), Boniface VIII had used the image of Christ's tunic to signify the indissoluble unity of his Church. Laymen like Dante had by now learned from their adversaries, and how to attack the hierocrats with their own weapons.

Aristotle proves that for a gift to be valid, two conditions are necessary: the donor must be entitled to make the gift, and the recipient to receive it (*Ethics* 4.1). Dante observes that the Church was quite unfit to receive temporal power, because of Christ's express prohibition against the provision of gold and silver (Matt. 10.9–10). The doctrine of evangelical poverty (the belief that the Church should practice the poverty attributed to Christ and his disciples in Scripture) was an explosive charge that led to the rebellion of the Waldensians in the twelfth century and ultimately to the Reformation and beyond. The most formidable inquisitor of the fourteenth century, Nicholas Eymerich, denounced the concept of evangelical poverty as the root cause of contemporary heresy. In Dante's last years, exaltation of the original Franciscan ideal came to be seen more and more as an attack on the papacy's pomp and luxurious way of life. Finally, in 1323—two years after Dante's death—Pope John XXII declared that it was heresy to claim that Christ and the apostles possessed nothing. The poet of the *Comedy* had sought a compromise (*Par.* 12.121–26), although he fiercely asserted the ideal of poverty rejected by Church leaders, after the "first rich father" had accepted Constantine's tragic gift (*Inf.* 19.117; *Purg.* 32.124–29).[18]

The eleventh chapter sets out to demolish the argument that Charlemagne's coronation by the pope in the year 800 signified that "all those who have been emperors of the Romans since that time are Defenders of the Church *[advocatus ecclesiae]* and must be called to this office by the Church" (*Mon.* 3.11.2 [Ricci 3.10.18]).[19] It is well-nigh impossible to suggest the connotations of the phrase *advocatus ecclesiae* in an English translation: the Latin implies that the pope could summon the emperor to his aid *(advocare)*. The title assumed special relevance during the summer of 1312, when Pope Clement declared that Rome did not in any way come under imperial authority: Henry VII, although emperor, must only visit the Holy City at the pope's specific summons and he must leave again as soon as the latter decided he should depart, whatever the circumstances. The emperor's office as Defender of the Church did not confer special rights so much as the obligation to carry out papal commands; the title itself was less an honor than the consequence of an oath of fealty. Dante's disillusionment with Clement's strategy and tactics may well have inspired this brief chapter and its rejection of such historical precedents on the grounds that "the usurpation of a right does not constitute a right" (*Mon.* 3.11.3 [3.10.20]). The pope could not confer the imperial office on Charlemagne (or on anyone else), just as the emperor Otto I was not entitled to depose Benedict V or to reinstate Pope Leo VIII.

After the arguments drawn from history, the appeal to reason must be heard (*Mon.* 3.12.1 [3.11.1]). According to Aristotle's *Metaphysics* (10.1), all things belonging to the same species are referred to one thing, which is their common measure (cf. *DVE* 1.16). We have already mentioned how powerful the quest for unity *(reductio ad unum)* was in medieval thought. This fundamental principle is—as the "title" implies—at the very heart of Boniface VIII's claims in *Unam sanctam*. The hierocrats argued that all men must be reduced to a single unit; and that, since the pope could not be subject to any worldly authority, it followed that the emperor, like all humankind, must be governed by the pope. Dante objects that it is one thing to be a man and another to be pope or emperor. As men, both "must be referred to the perfect man, who is the measure of all others" *(optimus homo: Mon.* 3.12.7 [3.11.7]).[20] As Gilson states, "Whenever Dante has to settle a conflict of authorities, his first care is to define the *genus* of the authorities in question"; here, the single term which is the measure of all men is "the pattern of the virtuous man as described in the final books of. . . [Aristotle's] *Ethica ad Nicomachum*" (1948, 188–89). As pope and emperor, the two cannot be referred to each other but to a common measure that exists above them "in which they find their unity" *(Mon.* 3.12.9).

Dante's solution

The positive section or *pars construens* begins with chapter 13. Its thesis is that the imperial authority derives directly from God. The Church cannot be the source of imperial authority, since the latter already exercised "all its authority, at a time when the Church either did not exist or did not exert any power" *(Mon.* 3.13.3). As already mentioned, Christ recognized the authority of the Roman Empire, as did St. Paul (Acts 25.10). Nowhere in the Bible is it possible to discover that any "involvement in or concern for temporal things was recommended for either the first or the later priesthood. On the contrary, I find that the first priests were expressly debarred from such involvement . . . as were the priests of the new dispensation in Christ's words to his disciples" *(Mon.* 3.14.4–5; *Purg.* 16.131–32). The core of Dante's argument rests on the axiom that the Church's essential "form" is "the life of Christ . . . for his life was the model and exemplar for the Church militant . . . and above all for the supreme pastor, whose task it is to feed the lambs and the sheep" *(Mon.* 3.15.3). Christ himself renounced all temporal government, when he stated to the representative of Rome's imperial authority, "My kingdom is not of this world" (John 18.36). Dante glosses: "As the model for the Church, he had no concern for this [earthly] kingdom" *(Mon.* 3.15.5–6).

Having established that the empire does not depend on the Church, in his final chapter Dante sets out to prove his claim that the emperor derives his authority directly from God. In support of this highly controversial view, he first reminds us that human beings are unique in that they are an amalgam of corruptible and incorruptible elements, body and soul. Man is therefore alone in having "two final goals, one of them his goal as a corruptible being, the other in so far as he is incorruptible" (*Mon.* 3.16.6). This idea is startling, to say the least, and utterly opposed to Aquinas's orthodoxy, which rigorously maintained the subjection of humanity's earthly goal to its one final, celestial goal.[21] Instead, Dante accepts St. Albert's vision of two beatitudes accessible to human beings. Dante goes on to explain that the two goals are: "happiness in this life, which consists in the exercise of our own powers and is figured in the earthly paradise; and the happiness of eternal life, which consists in enjoying the vision of God (to which our own powers are incapable of raising us, except with the help of God's light) and which is figured in the heavenly paradise" (*Mon.* 3.16.7). The ways of reaching these two goals are different (cf. *Purg.* 16.106–8). The first—earthly happiness—is attained "through the teachings of philosophy, provided that we follow them by practicing the moral and intellectual virtues; the second is achieved through spiritual teachings which transcend human reason, provided that we follow them by practicing the theological virtues, namely faith, hope, and charity" (*Mon.* 3.16.8).

These separate—but complementary—ways have been revealed to us: the one by human reason, the other by the Holy Spirit. We should note the relative degrees of the truths accessible to humanity *in via*. On the one hand, human reason has shown—through philosophers—*all* we need to know about our earthly goal and happiness. On the other, the Holy Spirit has revealed "through the prophets and sacred writers, through Jesus Christ the Son of God, coeternal with Him, and through his disciples" a necessary, but perforce limited, knowledge of supernatural truths (*Mon.* 3.16.9). Nevertheless, human greed would undermine all this, if humankind were not held to the right path like horses "by bit and bridle" (Ps. 31.9, whose opening words are sung by Matelda in *Purg.* 29.3). Once more, Dante compares humanity to a horse that must be guided and checked by the emperor, its rider (*Conv.* 4.9.10; *Purg.* 6.88–90). Here, however, it is a question not of one horseman alone, but of a "twofold directive power according to . . . [humanity's] twofold goal"—where we note once again the singular *duplicem finem* (*Mon.* 3.16.10). This twofold power is constituted on the one hand by the pope, who must lead men and women to eternal life in accordance with the truths of revelation, and on the other by the emperor, "who must guide the human race to temporal happiness in conformity with the teachings of philosophy." To be sure, the latter goal will remain unattainable if the tidal waves of greed are not calmed. This, then, is the goal for which the emperor should strive with all his might, "that in this little abode of mortals life may be lived in freedom and peace" (*Mon.* 3.16.11).[22] And in order that he may carry out his task effectively in this world, the emperor's authority as "guardian of this world" is established directly by him who can see the overall plan of the universe: "God alone chooses, he alone confirms" (*Mon.* 3.16.12–13). Indeed, the title of imperial "elector" is misleading, for those who elect the emperor are in fact merely "the heralds of divine providence" *(denuntiatores divine providentie).* When their choice is not unanimous—as happened after Henry VII's death, with the double election of Lewis of Bavaria and Frederick of Austria in October 1314—the electors' disunity is solely the result of the "fog of greed" *(nebula cupiditatis)* that blinds some of them to the truth of God's dispensation *(Mon.* 3.16.14).

In all this, Dante is bent on emphasizing the fact that God's choice has been made even before the election takes place, and that the emperor's authority cannot be modified in any way by ecclesiastical reaction. The coronation ceremony is only a solemn, public ratification of an individual *chosen and willed by God.* Dante has now fulfilled his threefold aim, having demonstrated that the empire is necessary for the well-being of the world; that it rests with the Roman people for all time; and that the emperor is chosen and appointed directly by God. Before closing, however, he takes care to warn his readers that the third truth should not be taken so strictly as to imply that "the Roman prince is not in some sense subject to the Roman Pontiff, since our temporal happiness is in some sense ordained for our eternal happiness. Caesar must therefore show that reverence towards Peter which a firstborn son owes to his father; so that, illuminated by the light of paternal grace, he may himself more effectively light up the world, over which he has been set by Him alone who governs all spiritual and temporal things" *(Mon.* 3.16.17–18). The phrase "in some sense/way" *(quodammodo),* used to describe the manner in which our temporal felicity is ordained for eternal beatitude, has caused rivers of ink to flow. One thing seems certain: it does not define the relationship between the temporal and spiritual spheres in any clear-cut way; moreover, Dante had no intention of offering a precise definition. On the other hand, it is no afterthought added merely to salvage appearances. It was in fact prepared for as early as the fourth chapter, in which Dante makes a similar codicil affirming the emperor's greater efficacy when aided by the light of the pope's benediction *(Mon.* 3.4.20, already cited; cf. *Ep.* 5.10.30). *Quodammodo* had been used by a number of writers since Huguccio of Pisa had first employed the term, at the end of the twelfth century, to deny the emperor's subordination to the papacy in temporal affairs. It was in fact part of the terminology currently used in this debate by moderate supporters on both sides, in order to reaffirm the superiority of the spiritual power in the universal scale of values, without sacrificing the empire's political autonomy.[23]

Dante could only end his political treatise with the reminder that the things of this world are in a certain sense ordained for humanity's eternal destiny. If he had begun with such a statement, his position would have been undermined from the very beginning. As it is, Dante's basic position is in fact mirrored in an anonymous tract, *Memoriale imperatori correctum,* written after Henry VII's coronation in 1312 and which claims that Henry's coronation oath to the pope did not constitute "a sacrament of subjection or vassalage . . . but one of reverence and humility."

The repetition of the singular "twofold goal" in *Monarchia*'s final chapter (*duplex finis*, 6; *duplicem finem*, 10) may perhaps be regarded as attenuating the heterodox assertion that human beings have two ultimate goals (*duo ultima*, 6). This twofold goal is in fact well illustrated in the context of Dante's poem. Not only does an Aristotelianized Virgil, the herald of the empire, lead the pilgrim to the Earthly Paradise, even as the emperor must lead humanity to its earthly felicity, symbolized by Eden; but Beatrice then takes over with her spiritual guidance and leads the pilgrim to the beatitude of the Heavenly Paradise. This diegetic sequentiality is brought into focus at the very center of the poem in the surprising image of the "two suns" (*due soli*) that must guide humanity along its two paths, the one set out on earth and the one that leads to God (*Purg.* 16.106–8). What must be synchronized on earth, with all the associated problems of autonomy and hierarchy, is thus demonstrated diachronically in the action of the *Comedy*. As the divine poem makes abundantly clear, Dante could not accept the confusion of political power with spiritual authority. Not only did he proclaim this message in the fiftieth canto—at the very center—of his Christian epic, but even in its final stages, Beatrice is made to repeat the same diagnosis from the heights of paradise: the corruption so prevalent in the contemporary world is due to the fact that there is no emperor to rule and guide humanity to its earthly goal (*Par.* 27.139–41).

Monarchia was exploited by the imperial propaganda of Lewis of Bavaria (d. 1347), especially at the time of his descent into Italy in 1328. It was condemned to the flames by Pope John XXII's legate in 1329. It remained a powerful weapon against papal policies in the temporal sphere. It had the honor of being translated into Italian by the great humanist scholar, Marsilio Ficino (1433–99). A more dubious distinction came its way when, in 1554, it was placed on one of the first versions of the Index of Prohibited Books. Some five years later, it appeared in print for the first time in the fiercely Protestant city of Basel. The first edition in Italy was published by Zatta, in Venice, in 1758. It was not until 1881 that the work was removed from the Index by Pope Leo XIII, eleven years after the annexation of Rome by the new Italian state. Its origin and fortunes reflect the tortuous relationship of church and state in the land that once saw the birth of St. Francis and until recently had a Bank of the Holy Spirit.

Texts and translations

Monarchia. Edited and translated by Prue Shaw. Cambridge: Cambridge University Press, 1995. This is an excellent edition and translation, with notes.

Monarchia. Edited by Bruno Nardi. In Dante Alighieri, *Opere minori,* vol. 2, 241–503. Milan and Naples: Ricciardi, 1979.

Dante's "Monarchia." Translated, with a commentary, by Richard Kay. Studies and Texts, vol. 131. Toronto: Pontifical Institute of Mediaeval Studies, 1998. This translation contains a detailed commentary.

Other readings

Cassell, Anthony K. "*Monarchia.*" In *The Dante Encyclopedia,* edited by Richard Lansing, 616–23. New York: Garland, 2000.

Davis, Charles Till. *Dante and the Idea of Rome.* Oxford: Oxford University Press, 1957.

Kay, Richard. "The Intended Readers of Dante's *Monarchia.*" *Dante Studies* 112 (1994): 19–31.

Took, John F. *Dante, Lyric Poet and Philosopher: An Introduction to the Minor Works,* 147–73. Oxford: Clarendon Press, 1990.

Vasoli, Cesare. "Filosofia e politica in Dante fra *Convivio* e *Monarchia.*" *Letture Classensi* 9–10 (1982): 11–37.

Vinay, Gustavo. *Interpretazione della "Monarchia" di Dante.* Florence: Le Monnier, 1962.

The *Comedy*, prolegomena

The prologue scene (*Inferno* 1–2)

No poem is more firmly set in both time and eternity. The fictional date for the journey through the otherworld described in Dante's *Comedy* is Eastertide 1300.[1] Easter is the time of both creation and renewal/resurrection. Christ's descent to hell showed that descent *(katabasis)* must precede ascent *(anabasis)*; so, the pilgrim's descent into hell begins on Good Friday and continues through Easter Saturday. At dawn, on Easter Sunday, the pilgrim arrives on the shores of the Mountain of Purgatory, where he spends three nights, before passing through the Earthly Paradise and rising up with Beatrice at high noon on Wednesday of Easter week, unimpeded by the weight of sin or the body (or temporal sequences), to the utmost limits of the universe and thence to a vision of the Godhead outside of space and time.

The poem's fictional chronology and date of composition

Such is the precise fictional chronology that underpins the narrative structure of the *Comedy* and helps the reader to grasp the way it unfolds over more than fourteen thousand lines of verse. Its author is ever mindful of the chronological limit imposed, with its requirement that all the souls encountered must have died before March 1300.[2] Any reference to an event that occurred after this date is set in the future: as, for example, when Beatrice points to the seat in paradise reserved for the soul of the emperor Henry VII "that *will be* august down below and *will come* to direct Italy before she is so disposed" (*Par.* 30.136–38; my emphasis). It is, however, clear that this "prophecy" was made after Henry's death in August 1313; in fact, this closing section of *Paradiso* was almost

167

certainly composed in Ravenna in the last year or two of the poet's life.[3] In *Inferno* 19.76–84, the simoniac pope Nicholas III forecasts that, after his death in 1303, Boniface VIII will not have to wait as long as he (some twenty years) for the next pope (Clement V) to arrive and propel him further down the infernal rock-shaft. Scholars are divided in their reactions to this, the only chronologically precise prophecy in the poem. Many believe that Dante only made predictions after the event; hence, they argue that the passage must have been inserted after Clement's death in April 1314, probably when the poet revised his *Inferno* (Petrocchi 1969, 89ff.). There is, however, no concrete evidence that Dante revised the first *cantica;* moreover, Clement's notorious ill health plagued him during the whole of his pontificate and may well have led the poet to predict that the pope would die before 1323.[4]

When did Dante begin work on the *Comedy?* The narrative formula in the opening line of *Inferno* 8, "To continue, I say" *(Io dico, seguitando),* has been seized upon by at least one modern scholar as proof of Boccaccio's statement that Dante wrote the first seven cantos before his exile (1302), that later they were found among his papers left behind in Florence and shown to the poet Dino Frescobaldi, who sent them to Marquis Moroello Malaspina, with whom Dante was then staying in the Lunigiana (c. 1306). Boccaccio himself expresses his doubts about the veracity of this account, as Ciacco's forecast in *Inferno* 6.64–72 of the political turmoils of 1301 and 1302, if composed before these events, would imply that Dante possessed the gift of prophecy.[5] No scholar of note now believes that the *Comedy* was begun before Dante's exile from Florence. The earliest date held with conviction is 1304;[6] however, the majority view is that the poet began work on his Christian epic in 1306/7. An earlier date would seem to be excluded for a number of reasons.

First of all, the views expressed in *De vulgari eloquentia* (c. 1304–5) on the craft of poetry proclaim the supremacy of the sublime or noblest style and the pre-eminence of the canzone as the supreme poetic form—views that are incompatible with the writing of a vernacular epic embracing every stylistic level from the most vulgar to the sublime. Moreover, in Dante's single-minded aim to exalt and favor the "illustrious vernacular" in *De vulgari eloquentia* he restricted its use to the "best subjects": namely, well-being, love, and virtue.[7] Nothing could be further from the poetics that gave birth to the all-encompassing polyphony of the *Comedy*, which includes words banned in the Latin tract: for example, *introcque* in *Inferno* 20.130, condemned as an example of Florentine jargon in *De vulgari* 1.13.2, together with the verb *manicare*—which nevertheless appears in Ugolino's tragic tale *(Inf.* 33.60); nor does the poet of *Paradiso* hesitate to place a word like *cloaca* (sewer) on the lips of the august St. Peter himself *(Par.* 27.25). Written at a time when Dante was inclined to favor prose over poetry as a medium for the transmission of philosophical ideas and knowledge *(Conv.*

1.10.12), *De vulgari eloquentia* looks backward in drawing up a balance sheet of Dante's poetic activity from its beginnings to the lyric poems written just after his exile (e.g., *Doglia mi reca*). The "comic" style is here defined as a mixture of styles (*DVE* 2.4.6), combining both the middle and lowest registers—but it cannot have recourse to the noblest style, whereas in the *Comedy* this will be used at times even in *Inferno* (e.g., *Inf.* 2.52–120).

Convivio was begun just before *De vulgari eloquentia* (*Conv.* 1.5.10) and appears to have been interrupted c. 1307. Although for a number of scholars *Convivio* represents a philosophical dead end antithetical to the *Comedy,* the work (and in particular its last book) displays a number of links with Dante's poem. The most obvious and generic one is the choice of Italian as opposed to Latin for the dissemination of philosophical truths to as wide an audience as possible—a choice condemned by Dante's younger contemporary, Giovanni del Virgilio, who told him to stop throwing pearls before swine.[8] As we noted in chapter 4, the poem's encyclopedic universe is made possible—in part, at least—by the author's experience of Italian prose in *Convivio,* which refined and expanded his native language into an artistic medium capable of expressing the most complex truths, a language destined to be what he called "a new light, a new sun, that shall rise when the old sun [Latin] sets and shed its light on those who live in darkness . . ."[9] No writer has ever penned a more passionate defense of the Italian language or shown greater faith in its possibilities. Similarly, perhaps no Christian writer of the Middle Ages was so convinced of the ultimate compatibility between the rational truths of philosophy and the revealed truths of religion. This conviction of the divinely inspired harmony between faith and reason gave rise to the exaltation of Lady Philosophy in *Convivio* 3 and was to be trumpeted from the heights of paradise (*Par.* 26.23–48). Dante not only placed the radical Aristotelian philosopher Siger of Brabant among the wise in paradise but he even went so far as to make Thomas Aquinas claim that his former adversary had taught *invidiosi veri,* "truths" that aroused both envy and hostility (*Par.* 10.138).[10]

We must also note the fact that *Convivio's* last book displays a new attitude toward the Roman Empire and its providential mission as depicted in Vergil's *Aeneid*. Vergil is now "our greatest poet" (*Conv.* 4.26.8).[11] In the *Comedy,* the pilgrim's guide in the first two realms of the afterlife faithfully accomplishes the task allotted to the emperor on earth—to lead humanity to the earthly happiness prefigured by the Earthly Paradise, "in conformity with the teachings of philosophy," according to *Monarchia* 3.16.10. In order to do this, however, the historical Vergil had to be transformed into the Aristotelianized Vergil of the *Comedy,* where he becomes the "sea of all wisdom" (*Inf.* 8.7), representing the union of philosophical teaching with imperial authority essential for perfect government (*Conv.* 4.6.18)—with the genius of Latin poetry added for good measure. Finally, the paucity of similes in Dante's early poetry is in stark contrast to their ever-increasing presence in the prose of *Convivio*, particularly in the final chapters, where a dense cluster of similes and metaphors is accompanied by an address to the reader of the kind that was to become such a striking feature of Dante's epic. In this same final section, Cato, the pagan suicide, makes his first appearance as a *figura* of the Godhead.[12]

All this is not to deny the many and profound differences between the two works. *Convivio* was abandoned by Dante—almost certainly in order to begin work on his great religious epic. Religion is low on the horizon of the prose work: there, the return to God is left to extreme old age. A number of opinions put forward in *Convivio* are overturned and corrected in the poem.[13] Just as fundamental is Dante's turning away from prose, his "conversion" to poetry as the supreme instrument for the expression of the totality of human experience and knowledge. The change is as radical as it is total, for the canzone *Le dolci rime d'amor,* chosen for commentary in *Convivio* 4, serves as little more than a springboard impelling both author and reader to concentrate on the virtually autonomous prose section of this last book. But in the *Comedy* Beatrice (absent from the prose work after *Conv.* 2.8.7–16) returns in glory to lead her repentant lover to the vision of metaphysical truths and God's ultimate reality. Dante now rejoices in his power to "put into verse" things that are difficult enough even to conceive or imagine (*Purg.* 29.42). Throughout the poem, he demonstrates poetry's ability to engage not only our rational faculty but every part of our complex nature and being. Casting off the limitations imposed by his philosophical quest in *Convivio,* Dante finally finds his vocation as a poet-theologian.[14] Clearly, in order for this to come about, it was necessary for his religious beliefs to fuse with the atoms of *Convivio*—indeed, with his whole experience of life—in order to create the poetic explosion that gave birth to the *Comedy.*

After abandoning work on *Convivio,* Dante most probably began to write his epic in or about 1308. *Inferno* contains frequent references to the first years of the poet's exile; the latest event specifically alluded to is the capture of Fra Dolcino in 1307 (*Inf.* 28.55–60), while in the same area of the poem (*Inf.* 26.7–12) the reference to Prato's hostility to Florence may have been inspired by events that occurred on April 6, 1309, when Prato rebelled against Florentine rule and expelled its Black Guelfs. The apparent contradiction between Manto's presence among the soothsayers (*Inf.* 20.52–56) and Statius's statement in *Purgatorio* 22.113 that Manto is among the pagans in limbo raises a doubt that cannot be lightly dismissed. No scholar seems willing to admit that Dante's powerful memory could be fallible, yet the reading still accepted in virtually all modern editions implies that the poet did not return to his text and iron out possible inconsistencies.[15] Whether or not this was the case, I judge the following "ideal" scheme for the composition of the poem to be the most likely: *Inferno,* 1307/8–10; *Purgatorio,* 1310–13/14; and *Paradiso,* 1315/16–21.[16]

The poem's title: Why "comedy"?

Dante referred to his poem both as his *Comedy* (*Inf.* 16.128, 21.2) and as the "sacred poem" (*Par.* 23.62, 25.1): the epithet "divine" was added to the title "comedy" for the Venetian edition of 1555—either because of its subject matter or in recognition of the "divine" poet's unique achievement, although the epithet is already associated with either *Paradiso* or the whole poem in Boccaccio's *Trattatello* (484: 185). The original title, *Commedia (Comedía),* has provoked a great deal of comment and bewilderment from the very beginning.[17] As we have noted, the term "comedy" appears twice in the poem and once in the controversial *Epistle to Cangrande* (13.10.28). The latter asserts that "comedy is a poetic narrative genre different from all others. It differs from tragedy in its subject matter, because tragedy at the beginning is admirable and peaceful, but at the end is foul and horrible . . . Instead, comedy begins with a difficult situation but its plot has a happy ending . . ."[18] Such apparent clichés concerning the subject matter have aroused the indignation of scholars who reject the epistle's authenticity. In particular, it is difficult to square its definition of tragedy with Virgil's reference to the *Aeneid* as his "high tragedy" in *Inferno* 20.113, since the Latin epic was left unfinished and certainly has no discernible "foul and horrible" end in view. Two scholars have, however, argued strongly that the definitions given in the epistle are in fact applicable to Dante's poem. In a stimulating study, Hollander has illustrated the tragic aspects of Dante's pagan guide, condemned for all eternity to limbo in hell, even though (according to *Purg.* 22.64–90) Vergil unconsciously prophesied Christ's coming—and posthumously converted Statius to Christianity.[19] And Giorgio Agamben has illustrated the way in which the *Comedy*'s title points at the deepest level to the sinner's justification through Christ. Thus, the hero of the *Aeneid,* in spite of his sense of piety and love of justice, is found in the tragic, first circle of hell (*Inf.* 4.122), whereas the *Comedy*'s pilgrim, although lost in the dark wood of sin and error, is nevertheless destined for eternal beatitude (*Purg.* 32.101–2). As Agamben pithily argues: "Christ's death delivers humanity from tragedy and makes comedy possible."[20]

However, most scholars have followed the fourteenth-century commentator Benvenuto da Imola in his statement (1887, 1.18–19) "I say that the author decided to call his book a Comedy because of its lowly, vernacular style," while Benvenuto was quick to point out that the poem contained tragedy and satire as well as comedy. To appreciate what was understood by the "comic" style, we must return to the second book of *De vulgari eloquentia,* in which Dante defined comedy in terms of a subject matter that required an appropriate style alternating between the median and the lowly registers.[21] Dante's own poetic production up to that time (c. 1305) had favored the "tragic" or noblest style of the illustrious vernacular (*DVE* 2.5.4, 2.6.6, 2.8.8). Its great drawback lay in the limitations imposed on the subject matter, which, in order to observe the fundamental principle of compatibility between style and content, was of necessity restricted to elevated themes and personages (*DVE* 2.2.5ff.). When Dante attempted to describe the whole gamut of human (and suprahuman) experience in his Christian epic, in such a way that "the word may not be different from the fact" (*Inf.* 32.12), he felt impelled to go far beyond the constraints of contemporary stylistic norms and genres. In order to describe the result, he chose two terms to describe his aims: "comedy" (more elastic and comprehensive than any other in the stylistic canon), and "sacred poem." As we have seen, the fact that the former is found only in *Inferno,* the latter in *Paradiso,* does *not* mean that each term is limited to its particular context. Instead, the two are intimately related and practically synonymous for the Christian poet, who based his style on that of the supreme exemplar, the Bible. In so doing, as Zygmunt Barański points out, "Dante brought together in a single work all the elements of the 'comic' which his culture recognized, but which it never actually conflated. It needed the poet's great syncretic imagination to reveal comedy's true potential."[22] The *Comedy*'s style was thus both humbler and more sublime than anything found in classical antiquity, although it was in Vergil that Dante had found inspiration for his "beautiful style" in his earlier poems, written in the "tragic" style (*Inf.* 1.86–87).[23] Instead, like Christ's own story, the *Comedy* plumbs the depths and scales the heights of humanity's thoughts and actions, while its stylistic range mirrors this totality.[24]

When educated Greeks and Romans, nurtured in the schools of classical rhetoric, ridiculed the "barbaric" style found in Scripture, apologists, such as St. Basil (c. 330–79) and St. Ambrose (c. 339–97), defended the simple, direct language found in the New Testament. Since the Christian message was intended to be understood and taken to heart by all men and women, it must of necessity be expressed in a language and style accessible to everyone. We must, however, be careful not to attribute such catholicity of intent to the author of the *Comedy,* as is frequently done in discussions concerning Dante's poem and its intended audience. All too often, this is implied when we are told merely that Dante wrote not in Latin but in Italian—a language "in which even simple women converse" (*Ep.* 13.10.31). However, the poet of the *Comedy* rejoices in expressing concepts that stretch the limits of our imagination and our intellect, as well as those of language. As he admits at the very beginning of the third *cantica,* his task in *Paradiso* is in a fundamental sense an impossible one, for words cannot signify what it means to transcend the human state. In order to drive the message home to the reader, the poet invents the verb *trasumanar* (to transhumanize). At the same time he declares that the words *(verba)* or "signifiers" of even the august language of philosophy, Latin, would be unequal to such a task: "Trasumanar significar *per verba /* non si poria" (*Par.* 1.70–71). Latinisms such as *trasumanar* are especially frequent in *Paradiso,* but they are only one of the difficulties encountered in the third *cantica,* difficulties so great that the poet warns his readers that anyone who has not acquired the necessary knowledge must give up at this point (*Par.* 2.1–16). The cliché that Dante wrote his encyclopedic poem for "everyman" is in fact negated by his statement that the third, final section may be attempted only by those "few who early on reached out with your necks for the bread of the angels" (ll. 10–11), in other words, by those who have already studied and acquired some knowledge of theology and heavenly or divine wisdom.

The Prologue: *Inferno* 1-2

The *Comedy* opens abruptly. Without rhetorical flourish or invocation, the narrator simply states "In the middle of the journey of our life, I came to myself in a dark wood, for the straight way was lost" (*Inf.* 1.1–3). Except for the "I" and the "dark wood," readers are not told *who* is lost or *where.* Yet contemporary readers must have known that this was a poem written by Dante Alighieri, and the controversial *Epistle to Cangrande* claims that it bore the title "Here begins the Comedy of Dante Alighieri, a Florentine by birth not by conduct" (*Ep.* 13.10.28). And we may be sure that contemporaries would have grasped the image of the dark wood as a metaphor reflecting the confusion of sin and error leading to perdition, especially at a time when vast tracts of medieval Europe were still covered by forests that inspired primordial fear—especially in town-dwellers such as the inhabitants of northern and central Italian communes.

The literal meaning of the first line is that Dante was in his thirty-fifth year when he suddenly realized that he had lost the true way. Born in 1265, Dante accepted the psalmist's reckoning that the natural lifespan for human beings is seventy years (Ps. 89.10), although life expectancy was far lower in reality and less than 5 percent of the population reached that canonical age. This divorce between theory and fact is a good example of the *a priori* approach favored by medieval *mentalités* that could dismiss earthly "reality" whenever it appeared to contradict "authority" (especially that of Holy Scripture). Dante Alighieri the individual was therefore approaching the highest point of this notional lifespan, since "the apex of the arc of our life is thirty-five" (*Conv.* 4.24.3) and he would be thirty-five years old in May/June 1300. That same year would also see Dante reach the summit of his political career, when he was elected one of the six priors governing Florence from June 15 to August 15.[25]

Such was at least in part the significance of the fictional date for Dante Alighieri, who is supposed to have claimed (in a letter now lost) that all his later troubles stemmed from his election to the highest political office in Florence.[26] However, the date chosen by the poet for his journey to the next world also held other, universal connotations. In *Inferno* 21.112–14, we are reminded that it took place exactly 1,266 years after Christ's crucifixion. That interval is intended to make readers aware of the Imitation of Christ that lies at the heart of Dante's pilgrimage. We may recall that the year 1266 had seen the birth of Beatrice, the being instrumental in making possible Dante's "lofty flight" to God (*Par.* 15.54) and the one whose descent to limbo saves the pilgrim in a way analogous to Christ's *descensus ad inferos*.[27] Christ, Dante stated (*Conv.* 4.23.10), had died in his thirty-fourth year; the pilgrim, who is thirty-four years old, must now begin his descent to hell, followed by resurrection or rebirth (through purgatory), and finally his ascension to heaven, in imitation of his Redeemer. Ignoring the vagaries of the calendar (in 1300, Good Friday actually fell on April 8), the poet chose the ideal date of March 25 for the start of his pilgrimage, because in universal history March 25 signified not only the creation of Adam but also the date of the Savior's Incarnation and of his Crucifixion.

Again, 1300 was a memorable landmark because it saw the great innovation of a Holy Year, which for the first time granted penitent pilgrims "the fullest pardon of all their sins," provided that they made a stated number of visits to the basilicas of the apostles Peter and Paul in Rome.[28] The parallel with the otherworldly pilgrimage undertaken by the Dante of the *Comedy* to "that Rome of which Christ is a Roman" (*Purg.* 32.102) is manifest. The year 1300 was regarded by many as the herald of a new age, a new century.[29] Certainly, in Florence, March 25 was the date signaling the beginning of the New Year.[30] Thus, the central events in universal history—the Incarnation, birth, and death of Christ—could all be recalled at the dawn of a new era. So, too, we come to perceive in the opening lines of the *Comedy* a surprising mixture of individual elements that are raised up to a plane of universal significance—for example, in the very first line, underscored by the linguistic markers *MI ritrovai/NOSTRA vita*. In other words, the poem offers readers a unique portrayal of autobiographical elements of generic and transcendental import: a combination which, encapsulated in the perfection of its literary form, has ensured the *Comedy's* appeal and relevance to readers of every possible background and belief over what will soon be some seven hundred years.

The poem's ternary structure

The first three lines of verse also form the first *terzina* or building block of the triune structure. *Terza rima* (as it is termed even in English) has been attempted by poets such as Byron and Shelley, but our language does not possess a sufficiently bountiful supply of words that chime to the same sound to make possible extensive use of *terza rima* in English poetry. It was devised by Dante, who employed its interlocking pattern in a potentially open-ended sequence such as the one evident in the first nine lines of *Inferno: a (vita) – b (oscura) – a (smarrita); b (dura) – c (forte) – b (paura); c (morte) – d (trovai) – c (scorte).* The pattern continues (d – e – d / e – f – e / f – g – f, and so on) to the end of each canto.[31] Since Dante employs the hendecasyllable, the "most splendid" line of Italian verse (*DVE* 2.5.3), each *terzina* consists of three lines containing eleven syllables: thirty-three syllables in all.

As we saw in chapter 1, already in *Vita Nova* 29.3 Dante had demonstrated that Beatrice was a miracle, denoted by the number nine and thus rooted in the number three, signifier of the Holy Trinity. Here, in "the sacred poem," the Christian poet based the entire structure of his work on the number three, thereby fashioning a work of art intended to imitate Nature, the child of God (*Inf.* 11.97–105). As St. Bonaventure wrote in his *Breviloquium* (2.12), "The created world is like a book in which the creative Trinity shines forth, is represented and read."[32] So, God's Book of Creation is reflected in Dante's poem, which highlights the trinitarian number in its three *cantiche,* with three subsections to each *cantica,* and its three guides (Virgil, Beatrice, and Bernard the intercessor). Furthermore, each *cantica* ends with the same word, *stelle* (stars), and each is composed of thirty-three cantos, a number corresponding to the years of the Redeemer's life on earth (plus one more in the case of hell, typifying its dysfunction and disharmony, but which nevertheless contributes to the total of one hundred, a number indicating perfection according to medieval symbolism).[33] Above all, as already indicated, the poem's very structure is based on the triune *terzina,* which "privileges the ending, the moment of closure and makes it coincide with the beginning. This logical reversal is theologically the movement of conversion, of death and resurrection . . . Christian history or Biblical allegory . . . move in the same way as *terza rima*" (Freccero 1986, 264–68). As we have had occasion to note, number symbolism played an essential role in medieval aesthetics, which harkened to the words Solomon addressed to the Creator: "you have arranged all things by measure and number and weight" (Wisd. 11.21).[34] In Dante's hands the *terzina,* the fundamental unit of this sacred poem, took on both the malleability and the discursive-narrative possibilities of prose.[35]

Allegory

The opening scene of the poem is notable for the presence of a traditional type of allegory whereby something is introduced merely as a signifier whose existence is entirely dependent on what is signified. The dark wood is not to be taken as an actual forest in which the pilgrim Dante found himself lost in 1300. It exists solely for the purpose of indicating the dangers of mortal sin and error, the loss of the path leading to salvation.[36] Likewise, the three beasts—the leopard (l. 32), lion (l. 45), and she-wolf (l. 49)—have no existence, except insofar as they indicate certain terrifying threats to the pilgrim's progress. They remain stereotypical fictional animals; no reader believes that the poet requires her or him to accept their existence outside of the scene portrayed and *for which they were invented* (on the basis of Jer. 5.6: "a lion from the forest has attacked them, a wolf from the desert has ravaged them, a leopard beleaguers their cities"). Having no independent existence of their own, the three beasts are merely allegorical signifiers, pointing to sins or categories of sins that have little or nothing to do with the real nature of leopards, lions, and wolves. Rather than the traditional term of "personification allegory" (e.g., Love in Ovid: cf. *VN* 25.9), it would perhaps be more fitting to describe this reduction of human behavior and states of mind to static, undeveloped images as *an allegory of reification.*[37] What we must understand above all is that for the most part Dante jettisoned this artificial method of narrative construction in the *Comedy,* replacing it with a revolutionary strategy that truly animates his story.[38] Inspired by the typological or figural interpretation of sacred history, the author of the *Comedy* chose to portray men and women who had possessed a real, historical earthly existence. Far from being mere abstractions or *exempla,* such as we frequently find in medieval literature, the characters encountered by the pilgrim throughout his journey do *not* exist solely in order to indicate certain categories of sin or virtue. Francesca da Rimini (*Inf.* 5), while condemned for her sin of lust, is no superficially attractive but fundamentally repulsive "siren," and the Emperor Justinian does not appear in paradise (*Par.* 6) simply as a personification of the Ideal Prince or Just Ruler. Like virtually all the souls with whom the pilgrim engages, Francesca and Justinian are integral parts of the poetic artifact, yet they retain the full weight and complexity of their humanity—a feature of the poem that for many readers confers a unique quality on Dante's *Comedy.*[39] Taking his cue from Hegel's *Lectures on Aesthetics,* Auerbach (1957, 167–68) explained that this unique quality is due to the fact that, as readers of the *Comedy* encountering its *dramatis personae,* "we behold an intensified image of the essence of their being, fixed for all eternity in gigantic dimensions, behold it in a purity and distinctness which could never for one moment have been possible during their lives upon earth."

The three beasts of canto 1

Regarding what we have termed "reification allegory," it is of course true that, in *Vita Nova* 25.10, Dante asserted that any poet worthy of the name must be able to divest his words of their allegorical cocoon in order to reveal their "true meaning." This is what he set out to do for two of his poems in the second and third books of *Convivio*, when he claimed that the Noble Lady *(donna gentile)* was in fact Lady Philosophy. However, the arbitrary nature of the linguistic sign is greatly magnified when readers have to depend solely on their wit, knowledge, and judgment for the deciphering of allegorical riddles—as centuries of Dante scholarship bear out. Regarding the enigma of the three beasts of canto 1, an important clue is surely the curse the poet-narrator hurls in *Purgatorio* 20.10–12 against the ancient she-wolf whose insatiable appetite finds more victims than "any other beast." Since this occurs on the terrace where the tendency to avarice is purged, the equation *she-wolf* = *avarice* seems evident at that point. Her appearance as the worst danger besetting humanity in the opening scene may, however, be taken to indicate the generic sin of greed, of which avarice was the most specific offshoot in the medieval canon. Greed, all-encompassing, all-threatening, the destroyer of justice, is the generic sin most opposed to justice and the root of all evil, according to St. Paul.[40] In the later Middle Ages, the sins of avarice and greed thus came to replace the emblematic feudal sin of pride, especially among the merchant classes of the Italian communes.

A clue to the identification of the leopard may be found in the springlike atmosphere surrounding its appearance, so that the hour of day (early morning) and the "sweet season" give the beleaguered wanderer cause to hope for deliverance (ll. 37–43): this may indicate lust as the typical sin of youth (or the sins of incontinence, or, according to a recent hypothesis, envy and partisan hatred). Later, at *Inferno* 16.106–8, we are told that the wanderer-turned-pilgrim has a cord about his waist, with which he had once "thought to capture the leopard with the spotted hide." There, we are caught up in a true *mise en abîme* before the yawning chasm of lower hell: the cord cast down by Virgil to "capture" Geryon, the symbol of fraud, is the one with which Dante had hoped to capture the leopard. Geryon is clearly identified as "that filthy image of fraud" (*Inf.* 17.7), a cardinal point that makes the interpretation of both cord and leopard yet more problematic. The cord would seem to symbolize either chastity/humility (the Franciscan girdle) or fraud itself (according to many, including fourteenth-century commentators). The latter possibility underlies the view that "the *lonza* . . . symbolizes the temptation of *malizia* . . . it signifies not the committed sin of fraud, but rather the test of man's potential for malice."[41] As Bruno Nardi points out, on the other hand, in Aristotle's *Ethics* (7.7 and 11) fraud and lust are linked on the grounds that the latter implies seduction—a point already made in the commentary by Dante's son, Pietro.[42] Similarly, Guido da Pisa interprets the cord as a sign of "fraudulent intention," since the goddess of love uses this cord to bind even the wise man. Nevertheless, he interprets the three beasts as symbolizing "lust, pride and avarice" (Guido 1974, 303). The lion would thus signify the sin of pride in what may be regarded as a typically schematic progress: lust (youth), pride (maturity), greed (old age): synchronically, on the other hand, the beasts represent the obstacles placed by the devil along the path of earthly existence (Mazzoni 1967, 100–101). Other scholars are equally convinced that the beasts reflect "the triple division of Hell into sins of disordered appetite (she-wolf), violence (lion), and fraud (leopard)" (Durling 1997, 86). Yet others interpret the sequential appearance of the beasts as signifying this same moral ordering of hell: leopard (incontinence), lion (violence), she-wolf (fraud).

It would surely be counterproductive to delve deeper into this allegorical maze. The reader will by now have had ample opportunity to appreciate the point already made: that this type of allegory illustrates the essentially ambiguous nature of the linguistic sign.

Virgil, the pilgrim's guide through both hell and purgatory

Help comes to the beleaguered Christian from an unexpected quarter, when he sees "someone who seemed weak from long silence" (*Inf.* 1.63). The shade introduces himself as the author of the *Aeneid,* not only the greatest Roman epic but the greatest poem known to Dante (who could not read Greek).[43] Why did Dante choose him as his first guide through the otherworld, and why is Virgil "weak from long silence" when he first appears to Dante in his mortal danger? The answers have been multifarious. Often, Virgil—whose identity as a pagan is highlighted in *Inferno* 1.72 and 125—is taken to be the representative of Reason or of what human reason can achieve on its own, without the aid of Grace; and this is certainly his role in *Purgatorio* 18.46–48, one that is further defined by contrast with Beatrice's, which is to deal with matters of faith. Moleta (1997, 37) has demonstrated the dialectic between the pilgrim's fear and the "humane, affective, all-embracing trust in reason" he acquires thanks to Virgil's "call to the whole man, governed by reason." Yet Dante's Virgil is far more than an allegorical figure representing Reason. He is master, sage, doctor/ teacher (terms used well over one hundred times in the *Comedy*), father-figure (there are no fewer than twelve occurrences of the term "father" applied to Virgil), and even mother-figure (*Inf.* 23.38). Just as important in Dante's lexicon, given his claim that great poets are God's beloved (*DVE* 2.4.10), is the fact that Virgil is the supreme *poeta,* the term used to designate him some twenty-one times, as well as once in a passage (*Par.* 25.8) to express the fervent hope that Dante himself will one day return to Florence, no longer a mere vernacular rhymester (*dicitore per rima*) but recognized and crowned as a true *poeta* in that same Florentine baptistery where he had become a member of Christ's body.[44] Again, all three occurrences of the term *saggio* in the poem refer to Virgil, as well as eight of the ten occurrences of *savio* (e.g., *Inf.* 7.3: "That noble sage, who knew all things").

After Auden's pronouncement that "poetry makes nothing happen" and the doctrines of art for art's sake and hermeticism, any insistence on the alliance between poetry, knowledge, and wisdom such as we find embodied in Dante's Virgil may be difficult for the modern reader to accept. Poetry in our contemporary world would seem to exist in a largely autonomous sphere, distinct from both science and wisdom. Nevertheless, the idea that poetry should instruct at the same time as giving pleasure has been one of the constants in Western culture, at least into the nineteenth century, and it is certainly an essential element in the dynamics that inspired Dante's poetry. The story of Francesca and Paolo shows the pitfalls of reading merely for pleasure (*Inf.* 5.127–28), as the lovers' tragic plight is highlighted in a poem written with the specific aim of "removing those living in this life from a state of wretchedness and leading them to a state of happiness . . . for the whole work was conceived not for speculation but for a practical purpose" (*Ep.* 13.15.39–16.40; *Purg.* 32.103–5; *Par.* 17.127–32, 27.64–66).

But after these preliminary considerations, we are still far from having answered the fundamental questions: Why is Virgil weak? In what way has he been silent? Why did Dante choose a pagan poet to guide and protect him through both hell and purgatory? If his guide was intended to be simply an embodiment of reason and all that it could attain without the help of revelation and grace, then the obvious choice for Dante would surely have been Aristotle, the greatest philosopher the world had ever seen, "the master of those who know" (*Inf.* 4.131). However, even Aristotle would have been an incongruous guide through that quintessentially Catholic realm, purgatory. In medieval times, guides to the Christian afterlife were always angels, monks, or holy men; the Latin poet Vergil, who lived before Christ (70–19 B.C.E.), would have struck Dante's contemporaries as a most unlikely and unexpected choice.[45] Admittedly, Vergil had acquired a reputation as a sage and (probably as late as the thirteenth century) as a magician; he was even believed by some (including Constantine the Great and St. Augustine) to have foretold Christ's birth in his *Fourth Eclogue*.[46] Dante the pilgrim praises Vergil's eloquence, and he surprisingly claims that Vergil was the sole model for "the pleasing style that has won me honor" (*Inf.* 1.79–87)— surprisingly, because (as we have seen), prior to the *Comedy*, Dante's style hardly seems to be derived from Vergil. In the *Comedy*, on the other hand, with its wealth of similes and its all-encompassing stylistic range, Dante may well have felt that he had transposed Vergil's poetic technique to vernacular poetry while placing it at the service of the revealed truths of Christianity—even as he now combined the characteristics of the so-called *rota Virgilii*, which comprised the humble style found in Vergil's *Bucolics*, the median style in his *Georgics*, and the sublime style in his Roman epic.

Dante's Virgil is weak through long silence, primarily because his "political" message has not been heeded. The Roman poet had sung of the eternal destiny of imperial Rome, its mission to dispense justice and to bring peace to the world in his great epic—now, for Dante, the bible of the empire (Nardi 1983, 301).[47] It was this message that had been ignored for so long, by both opponents and supporters of the medieval empire (*Par.* 6.97–111). This was in fact the lesson that Dante had gradually discovered beneath the allegorical incrustations deposited through the centuries on Vergil's poem, and which he had first proclaimed in his *Convivio* (c. 1306/7). God had chosen the Roman people to rule the globe for all time—a message driven home by a quotation from *Aeneid* 1.279, where Vergil is said to be speaking in God's name *(in persona di Dio parlando)*: "To them have I given empire without end" (*Conv.* 4.4.11). While the epithet *fioco* (weak; hoarse) may also indicate Virgil's blurred outline as a shade and his *lungo silenzio* may also point to his lack of faith, his weakness and long silence point to the fact that Vergil's voice—his message to humanity concerning the divine mission of the Roman Empire—had likewise been silent in that it had failed to reach the hearts and minds of countless generations.[48] Now, in 1300, when not only Dante the pilgrim but the whole world has lost the right way, when no emperor is in Rome to provide peace, justice, and good government for the world, Virgil's message is indeed weak and unheeded.

Here, we strike at the very heart of the *Comedy*'s fundamental allegory and the way it illustrates Dante's message given in the closing chapter of his *Monarchia*. Humanity has two goals, temporal happiness on earth and eternal happiness: the first symbolized by the Earthly Paradise, the second by the celestial paradise. God has provided two guides to lead men and women to these goals: "the supreme Pontiff, who must lead humanity to eternal life" in obedience to revelation, and "the emperor, who, in conformity with the teachings of philosophy, must lead humanity to temporal happiness" (*Mon.* 3.16.10). That this latter task must be achieved "according to the teachings of philosophy" *(secundum phy-*

losophica documenta) indicates the need for an Aristotelianized Virgil in addition to the "profound sense of the divine" and the proclamation of Rome's imperial, civilizing mission found in Vergil's work.[49] The *duplex finis* and the *duplex directivus* of the Latin treatise are in fact acted out in Dante's great Christian epic. Whereas a pagan guide through hell, with its moral order based largely on Aristotelian ethics, might be just conceivable, such a guide through the Christian realm of purgatory is quite unthinkable unless justified by a complementary role. That role reflects the emperor's mission on earth: to lead humankind to the temporal happiness prefigured in Eden. And that is exactly what Virgil does. In the *Comedy,* he leads Dante to the Earthly Paradise, where he leaves him precisely at the moment when Beatrice arrives to guide the pilgrim along the suprahuman journey to the eternal paradise outside of space and time. All in all, it is not inappropriate that a pagan Virgil should represent an initially pagan empire (although, as we shall see in the next chapter, "pagan" Virgil is granted some amazing insights into Christian belief).

Moreover, Virgil's words to Dante on their arrival in Eden—"I have drawn you here with wit and with art" (*Purg.* 27.130)—may be seen to allude to that alliance between philosophy and imperial authority so fervently espoused in the closing paragraph of *Convivio* 4.6, since "the latter without the former is dangerous, and the former without the latter is made weak . . . let the authority of philosophy be united with the imperial one in order to provide good and perfect government." Dante the pilgrim is then (*Purg.* 27.142) crowned and mitered by Virgil, pointing to the fact that both empire and papacy were instituted by God as remedies against sin; having reached a prelapsarian state, the pilgrim's will is wholly free and sound. As Dante emphasized in his *Monarchia* (3.13.3), the empire already possessed all its authority before Christ founded his Church.

Beatrice and Bernard

The corollary to this equation is not that, in *Paradiso,* Beatrice performs a task analogous to the pope's, for the latter's mission must obviously be carried out on earth.[50] Instead, for his guide in the extraterrestrial journey through the various heavens to the Empyrean, Dante makes another extraordinary choice: a Florentine woman not recognized as a candidate for beatification by the Church; one who—in an age obedient to the Pauline injunction (1 Cor. 14.34–35) that women must not teach but keep silent—lectures and corrects the pilgrim from the very beginning (*Par.* 2.49–148) and goes so far as to upbraid theologians and preachers for the nonsense they broadcast on earth (*Par.* 29.70–117). Once again, Dante's choice cannot be understood through allegorization: Beatrice does not represent dogma, theology, the Church, or revelation.

She is for Dante, as Mazzoni has written (1997a), the supreme example of the trinitarian analogy imprinted with greater or lesser clarity in every human creature, now shining forth as *speculum Dei,* in a state of union with God posited by the poet and thus acting as a divinely sent intermediary between the pilgrim and his Creator.[51] And, for the revelations of the three concluding cantos of the *Comedy,* Beatrice summons a third guide (*Par.* 31.65–66), this one—at last—an orthodox choice, a soul canonized in 1174 and thus proclaimed by the Church to be truly *in gloria* and united with God. He is none other than Bernard of Clairvaux (d. 1153), famous for his sacred eloquence, his warnings to the pope not to be embroiled in struggles over the things of this earth, his contemplative mysticism, and his devotion to the Virgin Mary (Botterill 1994a and 2001; Mazzoni 1997b).

Biblical and Vergilian elements and motifs

The following considerations, while concentrating on the first two cantos of the poem, aim to give some idea of the way in which Dante amalgamated biblical and Vergilian motifs and allusions in his *Comedy,* which he himself described as "the sacred poem to which both heaven and earth have lent a hand" (*Par.* 25.1–2). Moore (1896) identified in the *Comedy* some 255 specific references to the Bible; Hollander (1993b) lists some 364 certain or "almost certain" Vergilian citations. What we are concerned with is not the identification of source material but rather intertextuality, understood as the investigation of "the relationship between a text and the various languages or signifying practices of a culture and its relation to those texts which articulate for it the possibilities of that culture."[52]

Typical in the opening scene is the marriage or interweaving of biblical and Vergilian elements. The former were commonplace in medieval literature, when human actions tended to be seen as reflecting the two greatest moments in history: the Fall and the Redemption. In the *Comedy,* the abrupt opening echoes the biblical drama of King Hezekiah, the words of thanksgiving offered to God for his miraculous recovery from mortal danger (Isa. 38.10–20): "In the middle of my days I must go down to the gates of the underworld *[ad portas inferi]* . . . You will correct me and make me live . . . and you have saved my soul that it should not perish, you have thrown behind you all my sins . . . Save me, O Lord." By this strategy of biblical intertextuality, the poet presents himself at the beginning as a man threatened by spiritual death, crying out for help and forgiveness, and he even intimates that his *Comedy* will have a happy ending (cf. *Ep.* 13.10.29). At the same time, the phrase *cammin di nostra vita* (the journey of our life) and the pilgrim's condition remind us of St. Paul's warning that "while we are in the body, we walk away from God" (2 Cor. 5.6), with its antitype in the medieval view of this life as a pilgrimage, intended to be a return toward God, our heavenly home (*Conv.* 4.12.14–19).

Likewise, as we have noted, the three beasts that threaten and then stop the pilgrim's progress are found in Jeremiah 5.6: "A lion from the forest has attacked them, a wolf from the desert has ravaged them, a leopard beleaguers their cities." Their message is also found in Scripture: "Everything that is in the world is lust of the flesh *[concupiscentia carnis]*, lust of the eyes *[concupiscentia oculorum]*, and pride *[superbia vitae]*" (1 John 2.16). However, in *Aeneid* 1.323 Venus's imaginary sister is described by her as girt with a dappled lynx's hide *(maculosae tegimine lyncis),* a Vergilian detail that would appear to have transformed the biblical *pardus* or leopard into a lynx (or *felis pardina*), with its *pel macolato (Inf.* 1.33). So, Hollander (1969, 81–92) points to a web of Vergilian reminiscences in the prologue scene. The image of death by drowning (*Inf.* 1.22–27) recalls the fate of Aeneas and his companions battered by the storm at sea (*Aen.* 1.81–143). Like Dante the lost wanderer, Aeneas also tries to find the way to safety on high; three beasts make their appearance; the Trojan hero is saved by Venus's intervention (cf. Beatrice's intercession, inspired by love, in *Inf.* 2.58–72); Jupiter forecasts the advent of a great temporal leader (*Aen.* 1.286–96; cf. *Inf.* 1.100–111: Virgil's prophecy of the *veltro* or greyhound that shall save Italy and humanity by driving the she-wolf back to hell). Aeneas's words to Venus in *Aeneid* 1.384— "Myself, unknown and destitute, I wander through the Libyan desert"—offer a good analogy to Dante's general plight and his wandering through the desert landscape *(Inf.* 1.29: *per la piaggia diserta).* As Hollander observes, "Dante, like Goethe, is too great a poet not to imitate a great predecessor" (1969, 92).

The Vergilian vision of Rome's imperial destiny, which had long been lost, may help us to glimpse a further dimension in Dante's allegorical framework. The she-wolf is an age-old symbol for Rome: she had suckled its founder, Romulus. Like most phenomena, the wolf could be perceived both positively *(in bono)* and negatively *(in malo).* An ancient statue of a wolf stood in the Lateran Palace, in the very hall where the pope dispensed justice. Here, in *Inferno*, the wolf appears as an infernal caricature of Rome's mission to dispense justice to the world (*Aen.* 6.851–53). One of the characteristics of hell is to present the pilgrim with a terrifying vision of the good corrupted by the distorting mirror of evil: so, for example, Dante faints as he glimpses his love for Beatrice degraded into the incestuous relationship between Francesca and Paolo (*Inf.* 5.139–42). So, too, the Roman wolf is now transformed into its antithesis and comes to symbolize that voracious greed which destroys all justice (*Mon.* 1.11.11; *Purg.* 20.10–12). As we have noted, greed, *cupiditas,* had been singled out by St. Paul as the root of all evil: greed in its broadest sense, an inordinate desire for any temporal good and thus the root of all sin.[53] Virtually synonymous with avarice, its semantic field is as extensive as that of the Freudian libido. For example, it is the popes' mad desire for temporal power, their *libido dominandi,* and their practice of simony that have corrupted the world (*Inf.* 19.104–5). The image of the wolf then returns as a biblical motif in *Paradiso* 9.130–32, where we are told that it is money with its power over human *concupiscentia* that has led astray the whole Christian flock, "since it has turned the shepherd into a wolf" (cf. Acts 20.28–29), while no less an authority than St. Peter himself cries out from heaven that ravenous wolves, dressed as shepherds, have invaded God's church (*Par.* 27.55–57).

Archetypal images: Forest/desert/sea

After the downfall of the Roman Empire in Western Europe, immense tracts of land were overgrown with forests, which filled town-dwellers with fear—a primordial reaction, enhanced by the presence of robbers and outlaws who lay in wait for the traveler. Unlike the *contado,* the forest was regarded as "a space . . . unmarked by human action, hence inhabited by demons and evil."[54] It was part of "the fundamental opposition in the medieval system of values, between the city *(civitas),* the real and symbolic center of culture, and the forest, the geographical and mental embodiment of wilderness."[55] Dante's dark and savage wood in which he is lost was thus a forceful and immediately comprehensible image for contemporary readers. It would, however, have been only with hindsight that they perceived the pattern in the poem's narrative whereby the initial wood of sin may also be seen as an antitype of the "divine forest" of Eden (*Purg.* 28.2), found on the summit of Mount Purgatory. With hindsight, too, readers come to realize that the wanderer is afforded a glimpse of that goal at the very beginning: the hill with "its shoulders clothed already with the rays of the planet that leads us straight on every path" (*Inf.* 1.16–18), and the sun established as a symbol of that "spiritual and intelligible sun," the Godhead, according to *Convivio* 3.12.6–7.[56] Dante attempts to climb toward it, but he can only limp as his "halted foot was always the lower" (*Inf.* 1.30). The terrified pilgrim sees from afar the hill of salvation: his right foot, signifying the discernment *(intellectus)* of the good, is healed but his left foot is still impeded by the stain of original sin on his will *(affectus).*[57] As a consequence, his attempts to ascend are frustrated and then terminated by the appearance of the three beasts that prey on his vulnerability to sin. To reach the Edenic wood, the wanderer needs to do two things: he must become a pilgrim and follow a heaven-sent guide, and he must descend into hell before he can be purged of sin. He must also receive the necessary grace to begin the *askesis* that leads to purification of the wounds inflicted by sin. As St. Bernard had written, "Who dares climb the

mountain of the Lord? . . . Only the humble man can safely climb the moun-
tain"[58]—a truth illustrated by Virgil's girding the pilgrim's body with the reed
symbolizing humility in the opening canto of *Purgatorio* (1.94–95, 133–36).

The first image describing the wanderer's state is the simile by which he is
compared to a man who, having just escaped from drowning, looks back at the
dangers of the deep that had threatened to destroy him (*Inf.* 1.22–24). After a
brief rest, he continues along "that deserted slope," where the allusion to a spiri-
tual wasteland reflects the state of the sinner's heart: "the desert is the evil heart,
because it is not cultivated and . . . beasts inhabit it."[59] Like the forest, the desert
was traditionally antithetical to the city; and Dante was a true son of Florence,
the city he loved with all his being: for him, there was "no more agreeable place
on earth" (*DVE* 1.6.3). Florence is a landlocked city, moreover, without a sea-
faring tradition; so that Dante naturally regarded the sea as a hostile element—
nowhere more so than in the Ulysses episode, where the Greek hero and his
companions cross the "desert" waters of the Ocean and meet their tragic end in
a whirlwind that casts them down to hell, in sight of the purgatorial Mountain
(*Inf.* 26.124–42). In this intratextual web, we also note the image of Mount Ida,
once "happy with water and foliage," now "desolate" *(Inf.* 14.97–99: *diserta),* thus
symbolizing the corruption of the postlapsarian world.

Exodus

An intertextual dimension may now be added. A hostile sea and
a desert are of course found in the Bible. They evoke the central theme of
Exodus, chosen by the poet as the allegorical model for his own journey from
the infernal wood to the heavenly city. Beatrice, after the pregnant reference to
Dante's *alto volo* (as opposed to Ulysses' *folle volo*), speaks of the theological vir-
tue of hope as the great motive force behind the extraordinary grace that has
made it possible for Dante to abandon Egypt, the land of sin, and journey
to Jerusalem, to behold the heavenly goal and God himself (*Par.* 25.49–57). The
redemption of Israel from the bondage of Egypt and the journey through
the desert to the Promised Land were, for Dante and his contemporaries, actual
events in recorded history but also a pointer to—a *figura* of—"our redemp-
tion accomplished through Christ," as well as signifying "the conversion of the
sanctified soul from the bondage of this earthly corruption to the freedom
of everlasting glory" (*Ep.* 13.7.21; cf. *Conv.* 2.1.7).[60] To drive the point home, the
poet has the souls sing *In exitu Israël de Aegypto* (Ps. 113) as they arrive at the
shores of purgatory. Unlike the wanderer in the initial prologue scene, they will
be allowed to journey up the mountain and thence to union with God, without
visiting hell.

The message is clear. The scene on the shores of Mount Purgatory is a re-enactment and the figural fulfillment of the Exodus. Even as the waters of the Red Sea parted miraculously to enable the Hebrews to escape from slavery, so the angel and the souls entitled to purification and salvation glide miraculously (*Purg.* 2.31–33) over the perilous waters of the Ocean that had destroyed Ulysses and his companions, with the angel's wings in stark contrast to Ulysses' oars, which had propelled the foolhardy crew to its doom.[61] The poet, however, is bent on emphasizing the significance of the entire psalm, for he adds an unusual rider (ll. 47–48): "*In exitu Israël de Aegypto,* they were singing all together with one voice, with as much of that psalm as is written thereafter." He thus emphasizes the significance of the *whole* of Psalm 113,[62] which praises God for the way he had protected and watched over his chosen people, for the crossing of the River Jordan, whose waters were "turned back" *(conversus est retrorsum),* and for other miracles performed during the journey to the Promised Land. Particularly relevant to the situation of the new arrivals on the shores of Mount Purgatory are the last two verses (17–18): "Not the dead shall praise you, O Lord; nor all those who descend into hell. But we who live bless the Lord, from this time on and for evermore." The poet evidently wants his readers to be reminded of the entire text of the psalm, and thus be made aware of another aspect of the contrast between hell and purgatory. The "dead" and those who have gone down to hell cannot praise the Lord, an idea conflated in the invocation to the Muses at the opening of the second *cantica*: "But here let dead poetry rise up again, o holy muses" (*Purg.* 1.7–8).[63] The souls in hell, having "lost the good of the intellect" (*Inf.* 3.18), are the victims of the death brought about by vice and ignorance (*Conv.* 2.15.4), and they will be subject to the "second death" on the Day of Judgment (*Inf.* 1.117; Apoc. 20.14), whereas the souls destined for salvation are truly and forever alive (John 6.47) and therefore bless their Savior. Souls go down to hell with "ferocious laments," cursing God and their parents, whereas the souls destined for salvation make their way to purgatory while chanting songs of praise (*Purg.* 12.112–14).

The psalm's reference to the River Jordan may perhaps be taken as confirmation of the allusion to this river in the lines describing Dante's plight: "Do you not see the death that attacks him there, by the river in flood where the sea does not prevail?" (*Inf.* 2.107–8). Although the waters of the Jordan were traditionally regarded as a *figura* of baptism, in flood they formed yet another obstacle to Israel's entrance into the Promised Land, so that by the power of "the living God" they were miraculously dried up (Josh. 3.15–17, 4.7). Certainly, the concept of death threatening the wanderer also evokes the "Sea of solitude (which is now called Of the Dead)" into which the River Jordan flows (Josh. 3.16). Historically, the Red Sea, the desert, and the River Jordan were milestones in the journey from Egypt to the Promised Land. Moreover, given the polysemic nature of medieval allegory, the allusion to Jordan contained in the metaphor of *Inferno* 2.108 does not necessarily exclude other possibilities. The most likely one is that the swollen river (*fiumana*) indicates the mortal dangers that surround us in this life, especially the current of greed.[64] Unlike the Israelites of old, the wanderer cannot cross this river and enter into the promised land or climb the hill of salvation. Yet, at the same time, the *fiumana* points to another river, Lethe, in whose waters the pilgrim will undergo a re-enactment of baptismal purification (*Purg.* 31.91–105).[65]

Beatrice and grace

However summary our overview, one basic element of Christian theology must be broached. Dante studies in the second half of the twentieth century were greatly influenced by the writings of Charles Singleton. They proved invaluable in helping to counteract the aesthetic prejudices of Benedetto Croce and his followers prevalent in the first half of the last century. Nevertheless, one fundamental question needs to be re-examined: When does Dante receive the grace necessary to undertake his journey of regeneration and salvation?

In his pioneering study *Journey to Beatrice*, Charles Singleton insisted that the pilgrim's journey through both hell and purgatory, "the whole area of Virgil's guidance in the *Comedy*," was nothing but a preparation for grace (1967, 46). According to Singleton, when the pilgrim Dante is reunited with and then guided by Beatrice, he passes "out of a first conversion into a second, wherein the soul attains to that meritorious justice which is given with sanctifying grace and the infused virtues" (67). The justice first attained, under Virgil's guidance, is "a justice which is discernible by the natural light of reason and *without benefit of the light of sanctifying grace* . . . To journey with Virgil is to journey by that natural light which may not extend beyond such confines" (257–69; my emphasis).

As Mastrobuono (1990, 1–129) has demonstrated, Singleton failed to understand the theology of grace. There can be no "human justice" attained with Virgil, followed by "transhuman justice" reached with Beatrice. Instead, there are two facets of grace: "operating grace," which justifies the soul, and "cooperating grace," which—as its name implies—requires the cooperation of the individual's free will (*S.Th.* 1.2.111.2). Justification is the result of operating grace. Subsequently, cooperating grace (also known as "sanctifying grace") must be at work for the individual to earn the reward of eternal life and union with God. Hence, "there is no such thing as 'meritorious justice,' as Singleton maintains.

The justice of justification cannot be merited, whereas the justice of merit, which is the right to the reward of eternal life, is earned *after* one has been justified" (Mastrobuono 1990, 29; my emphasis).

This clarification is no mere theological nicety. It affects our whole understanding of the cause behind Dante's supernatural journey. Especially after Augustine's teachings on grace and their influence on medieval theology, the need for the pilgrim to have received the gift of grace *before* reaching Eden on the summit of Mount Purgatory—indeed, *before* undertaking the descent into hell under Virgil's guidance—would have been obvious to any of the poet's enlightened Christian contemporaries. So, Aquinas quoted his august predecessor, "he [Augustine] said that without grace men cannot do any good whatsoever" (*S. Th.* 1.2.109.4, resp.). In the pilgrim's case, God moves his heart, for any human soul "is naturally capable of grace . . . having been made in God's image, it is capable of receiving God by grace, as Augustine says" (*S. Th.* 1.2.113.10, resp.). Dante must first make an essential act of humility (*Inf.* 2.31–33): "But why should I go there? or who grants it? . . . neither I nor others believe me worthy of that." Virgil's account of the intercession undertaken by Mary, Lucia, and Beatrice then urges Dante to cooperate with the will of heaven and thus to overcome the sense of his own unworthiness, which would otherwise be transformed into the sin of pusillanimity.

If we turn to the early commentators, we discover that Ottimo, Benvenuto, Buti, and the poet's son Pietro all interpret Mary or the "noble lady" of *Inferno* 2.94 as in this context symbolizing *prevenient grace* or *operating grace* (i.e., grace antecedent to conversion). Even more relevant is the fact that, in his commentary on this passage, the poet's own son points to precisely that same distinction between "operating" and "cooperating" grace which Mastrobuono has reintroduced into Dante studies through an examination of Thomist doctrine. Mary and Lucia are thus regarded by Pietro Alighieri as representing operating grace and cooperating grace, respectively, *in this context*.[66] At the very end of the poem, Mary's role as described by Bernard is again equated to the gratuitous gift of grace in the very last canto of the poem (*Par.* 33.13–18): "Lady, you are so great and so powerful that if anyone wants grace and does not turn to you, his desire wants to fly without wings. Your benign nature will succor not only those who ask, but many times freely runs ahead of the asking."

The pilgrim's entire journey, not merely in *Paradiso* but from the end of *Inferno* 2 to his vision of God in *Paradiso* 33, is the result of the fivefold effects of grace as catalogued by Aquinas (*S. Th.* 1.2.111.3, resp.): (1) the soul is healed; (2) the soul desires the good; (3) the soul is given the means to practice that good; (4) it is enabled to persevere with the good; (5) it can reach the glory of the celestial paradise. Dante's journey under Virgil's guidance is *not* a preparation for grace. Instead, it is the result of his reception of and cooperation with grace, as outlined in the prologue scene. No one—least of all a pagan poet—could prepare the sinner for a gift that may be granted gratuitously and instantaneously by God alone. Singleton has therefore transferred "divine powers from God to Virgil" (Mastrobuono 1990, 75).

To discern the pattern of conversion in the prologue scene, we must note especially two moments.[67] The first, at the end of canto 1 (ll. 130–35), consists of Dante's acceptance of the plan for his salvation outlined to him by Virgil: "Poet, I beg you *by that God whom you did not know, so that I may flee this evil and worse,* that you lead me where you have now just said, so that I may see St. Peter's gate and those whom you tell me are so sorrowful" (my emphasis). The second, crucial moment occurs after Virgil's speech recounting the intercession of the three blessed ladies in *Inferno* 2, when Dante's failing powers and courage are revived, like flowers opening to the sun's rays after the night frost (ll. 127–32); he now answers "like a person freed." The she-wolf had driven the wanderer down to "where the sun *is silent*" (l. 60; my emphasis), a striking example of poetic synesthesia denoting the fact that God's voice does not reach the wanderer now lost. That God's grace returns to touch the sinner's heart and give him the necessary strength is thus indicated by what may at first reading seem to be an unremarkable poetic simile denoting renewed strength. Like the flowers warmed by the sun's rays, Dante's will returns to his "first purpose," as a result of operating grace. In other words, the pilgrim is now ready to cooperate in God's plan by undertaking the arduous journey through hell, purgatory, and paradise, as outlined by Virgil at the end of canto 1.[68]

That this journey is made possible, and is made possible *only*, by God's grace is emphasized at various stages. One of the most striking instances occurs just after the pilgrim has passed through the gates of Dis. Among the heretics, he finds Cavalcante de' Cavalcanti, the father of Guido, hailed as his "first friend" in *Vita Nova* 24.3, 25.10, 30.3. Recognizing Dante Alighieri, Cavalcante asks why, since his journey through hell is presumably due to intellectual prowess *(per altezza d'ingegno),* he is not accompanied by Guido. Dante replies: *Da me stesso non vegno* (I do not come on my own) and points to Virgil as the person leading him "perhaps to one your Guido held in disdain" (*Inf.* 10.55–64). The interpretation of these words is one of the most controversial points in Dante studies. The translation given of *cui* as "to one" chooses one of two possibilities: in Dante's text, the word *cui* could mean "whom" (direct object: Virgil or Beatrice, traditionally understood as the object of Guido's disdain); the preferred choice, however, takes *cui* to mean *ad eum quem / ad eam quem,* thus implying that Cavalcante imagines that Virgil is leading Dante to Beatrice or God, or even, as has recently been argued, the Virgin Mary.[69] What is certain is that Dante's reply to Cavalcante implies that his journey could not be undertaken through personal merit or intellectual powers. Commentators—for once—are virtually unanimous in interpreting the words *Da me stesso non vegno* as indicating the pilgrim's recognition of the need for divine help and grace in order to undertake his journey through the otherworld.[70]

Not surprisingly, direct references to the grace granted to Dante are absent from *Inferno.* In *Purgatorio,* however, they abound and clearly indicate the grace necessary to *undertake* the journey, long before the meeting with Beatrice in Eden. The first reference is found during Dante's meeting with Ugolino Visconti, when the latter calls out to Corrado Malaspina: "Up, Conrad! come and see what God has willed *through grace*" (*Purg.* 8.65–66; emphasis mine). This is reinforced by Visconti's address to Dante (ll. 67–69), in which he mentions the gratitude the pilgrim must feel toward God for having received such exceptional grace. Guido del Duca and Hugh Capet similarly recognize God's grace operating in the pilgrim (*Purg.* 14.79–80; 20.41–42). Dante himself ascribes his journey to the effects of grace in the central canto of the poem (*Purg.* 16.40–42); but the clearest proof is surely found in the words he addresses to the souls purging lust on the topmost terrace, just before his arrival in Eden and his reunion with Beatrice: "I am climbing up through here so as to be blind no more; there is a lady above who gains grace for me, as a result of which I bear my mortal body through your world" (*Purg.* 26.58–60).

Conclusion

In the effort to decipher Dante's message as set out in the *Comedy,* scholars are obliged to discover as much as possible about medieval literature, society, language, history, philosophy, and theology. It is clearly impossible for one person to be an expert in all these fields; and the pitfalls are many. This chapter has therefore attempted to offer a sample of the kind of analysis to which the whole poem must be subjected; the large number of essential references to the work of other scholars represents merely the tip of the collaborative iceberg. The ideal behind our critical enterprise is of course found in Dante's paradise:

> Diverse voci fanno dolci note;
> così diversi scanni in nostra vita
> rendon dolce armonia tra queste rote.
> (Par. 6.124–26)

———

Different voices make sweet notes: so different degrees in our life create a sweet harmony among these spheres.

seven

Dante's other world

Moral order

The moral order of *Inferno*

Inspired by a profound understanding of human nature, the poet delays all explanation of the ethical system underlying his *Inferno* until readers have accomplished almost one third of their infernal journey. At long last, in canto 11 (the number eleven implying sin, as it distances itself from the perfection of ten)—after the travelers have visited no fewer than six of the nine circles (and the pilgrim is as much in the dark as are readers of the poem)—Virgil delivers a lecture in which he uses the basic Aristotelian distinction between incontinence *(incontenenza)* and malice *(malizia)* to differentiate the sins punished in the first six circles from those found within the City of Dis. Clearly, the lower down the sin is placed, the graver and the more condemnable it is. And, as Virgil reminds his pupil *(Inf.* 11.79–84), the study of the seventh book of Aristotle's *Ethics* should have already taught him that incontinence denotes an inability to control one's passions, whereas sins of malice are committed through deliberate choice.[1] Thus, before reaching the walls of the City of Dis, the travelers pass through the circles of limbo or Lack of Faith, Lust, Gluttony, Avarice, and Anger. The fact that both avarice and its opposite, prodigality, are punished in the fourth circle illustrates another Aristotelian concept: that virtue is a golden mean between two extremes of vice—a truth reinforced in the very next circle, where the consequences of both anger and sloth *(accidia)* are punished.[2]

In lines 28–66, Virgil names many of the types of sin punished in Lower Hell. They are divided into sins of Violence *(Inf.* 12–17), Fraud *(Inf.* 18–30), and Treachery *(Inf.* 32–34). An outstanding omission in Virgil's catalogue is the sin of heresy, a sin of the intellect unknown to pagan antiquity.[3] Since the moral order of *Inferno* is based on Aristotle's ethics, many critics have been led to claim that Dante was unsure where to place heresy. It is, however, clear that the poet was primarily concerned with the effects of sin on society. He therefore placed the heretics at the entrance to the City of Dis to give a dramatic illustration of the fact that the effects of heresy were utterly divisive, setting brother against brother, citizen against citizen. It is no accident that, among the heretics, the leader of the Ghibelline party in Florence, Farinata degli Uberti, is forced to spend eternity next to one of the leaders of the opposing faction, Cavalcante de' Cavalcanti (*Inf.* 10.52–54)—thus anticipating the message of Florence's self-destruction through civil faction, hinted at in *Inferno* 13.143–50. Indeed, both faction and heresy destroy the community, for "every kingdom divided against itself shall perish, and every city or family divided against itself, shall fall" (Matt. 12.25). Unity and love are the hallmark of heaven, the City of God; division and hatred, that of hell, the Devil's City.[4]

The indissoluble link between Dante the Christian and Dante the citizen explains why the author of the *Comedy* chose to disagree with the redoubtable theologian Thomas Aquinas, by placing sins of violence in the seventh and sins of fraud in the eighth circles of his *Inferno*. St. Thomas (who plays an essential role in *Par.* 10–13) had declared that "other things being equal, it is a graver sin to harm someone openly, as by violence, than secretly" (Reade 1909, 350). Dante, on the other hand, places the fraudulent thieves in the seventh subdivision of the eighth circle (*Inf.* 24–25) but the violent highwaymen Rinieri da Corneto and Ranieri de' Pazzi in the first subdivision of the seventh circle (*Inf.* 12.135–38). For Aquinas, robbery was "a more grievous sin than theft" because of the "ignominy or injury to the person, and this outweighs the fraud or guile" implicit in theft (*S. Th.* 2.2.66.9, resp.). However, for the author of the *Comedy*, rather than injury to the individual, it is the community that is the chief victim: the overriding criterion is a political one that measures the harm inflicted on society and its members.[5] In *Paradiso* 8.115–17, Charles Martel's question whether it would be worse for man if he were not a citizen obtains (for once) an unequivocal reply from Dante the wayfarer that human beings are destined to live as members of a community. In fact, the same Latinism *cive* (citizen)—here, denoting humanity's role on earth—is also used to indicate humankind's eternal destiny as citizens of God's City in *Purgatorio* 32.101–2.

The poet highlights the rupture of social bonds brought about by fraud through two physical breaks in the infernal landscape. The first is encountered after the circle of Violence (*Inf.* 17); no paths lead down to the realm of Fraud in nether Hell, so that Dante and Virgil must be transported down there on Geryon's back. The second is the chasm with the pit of hell down below, where traitors are impaled in the ice of Cocytus—and which the travelers can reach only by being lifted down by the giant Antaeus, thus signifying the ultimate break-down of civil society.

Although *Inferno*'s moral scheme is Aristotelian in its overall divisions, the Greek philosopher did not tackle the question of whether sins of fraud are worse than sins of violence. On this issue, Dante found support for his visceral hatred of treachery in Cicero's *De officiis* 1.13.41, where he read: "While wrong *(iniuria)* may be committed, then, in two ways—either by force or by fraud—fraud seems to belong to the fox, force to the lion; both are most alien to man, but fraud is the more odious." Yet even though most commentators point to this source, they fail to note that while agreeing with Cicero that fraud is a worse category of sin than violence, Dante in fact ignores the animal imagery of the lion and the fox[6] and—far from presenting fraud as "most alien to man"—he stresses that, while in hell it is practiced by Satan and his followers, on earth fraud is a virtual mo-nopoly of humankind: *è de l'uom proprio male* (*Inf.* 11.25). Fraud is declared to be most hateful to God, because it implies misuse of the God-given intellect, the very faculty intended to distinguish human beings from beasts. Dante's condem-nation of treachery was in fact so absolute that it led him to illustrate the quasi-heretical idea that certain acts of treachery are so utterly evil that they cause a human soul to be sent down to the pit of hell even before death overtakes the body (thus negating the possibility of conversion [cf. *Purg.* 3.133–35]), which is then governed by a devil for the rest of its time on earth (*Inf.* 33.124–38). This dramatically highly effective but theologically perverse concept was echoed by Chaucer in *The Man of Law's Tale* (2.778–84) and censored by the Inquisition in Spain.[7] It may have been one of the reasons why the provincial chapter of the Dominican order banned Dante's works, in Florence, in 1335.[8]

The *Comedy*'s message (reiterated in *Monarchia*) is that humanity on earth must live at peace, in a universal community where justice reigns supreme and where the Christian code of behavior is respected by all. Fraud and, above all, treachery make this impossible by destroying the natural bonds of love and trust that underpin society. As Dante had written in *Convivio:*

> And those things which do not immediately display their defects are the more dangerous, because often we cannot be on our guard against them. This is what we find in a traitor: he puts on every appearance of being a friend and so earns our trust, but under the mask of friendship he conceals the fact that he is our enemy. (*Conv.* 4.12.3)

So, Charles de Valois entered Florence in 1301, under the guise of peacemaker sent by the pope. Using Judas's jousting "lance," however, he ripped open Flor-ence's guts (*Purg.* 20.73–75). This royal Judas thus paved the way for Dante's suf-ferings and lifelong exile from the city and everything he loved most.

As defined in *Inferno* 11.52–53, treachery is fraud employed to harm some-one who has reason to trust the traitor. It is, however, questionable whether all the sinners who would qualify as traitors are in fact punished in Cocytus. It may be argued that no figure in medieval society commanded more trust or obedi-ence than the pope. Yet, it is precisely the pope who is ultimately responsible for the treachery and corruption that have made the world evil in 1300, since the whole world has been led astray by the terrible example set by an evil shepherd (*Par.* 18.125–26). The solemn injunction the Redeemer had given no fewer than three times to the first, archetypal pope was "Feed my sheep" (John 21.15–17).[9] When Dante dares to condemn contemporary popes to hell, he accuses them of simony (the selling of holy things and ecclesiastical benefices) and places them in the third of the *Malebolge* (the subsections of the eighth circle, Fraud). The poet obliquely compares Nicholas III to a "perfidious assassin" (*Inf.* 19.50). As the false shepherd, he and other corrupt popes have ignored St. Peter's own ex-hortation to tend and feed God's flock "not for filthy lucre but of your own accord" (1 Pet. 5.2). Instead, they have turned God into a thing of gold and sil-ver and made gold and silver into their gods (*Inf.* 19.112).

We must therefore ask ourselves whether, after reading such an impassioned attack, it is still possible to believe that the sin of simony constitutes simple fraud, committed against those who have no particular reason to trust you, as its place-ment in the eighth circle apparently declares (*Inf.* 11.54). Should it not in fact rank as treachery, the betrayal of a sacred trust? We must also ponder its ordering in the third subsection of the eighth circle, for in the fifth *bolgia* we find those guilty of the lay equivalent of simony: namely, barratry (the selling of civil hon-ors and offices). We remember that Dante himself had been accused of this crime against the state. Can we really suppose that the poet of the *Comedy* judged the sale and corruption of temporal offices and privileges to be a graver sin than the sacrilegious bartering of sacred things, as his ordering would suggest? Dante's magical powers as a narrator may well lead us to forget that "for all its apparent objectivity, [the poem] is a representation . . . designed to promote the *illusion of objectivity*" (Barolini 1992, 15; my emphasis). The very punishment of the simo-niac popes—the fact that they are buried upside down (*Inf.* 19.46)—reflects the fact that they had inverted God's moral order by selling things of the Spirit for material gain. The infernal rock in which they are imprisoned is, as we shall see, an infernal caricature of the Rock of Faith, which remains as a perpetual indictment of St. Peter's unworthy successors whose avarice "corrupts the whole world, by trampling the good and raising up the wicked" (*Inf.* 19.104–5).

One possible explanation for the poet's choice of the third *bolgia* as the place where simony is punished is the significance of the number three as a pointer to the triune God (*VN* 29.3) and to the simoniacs' crime in selling the things of the Holy Spirit. Whether or not this be so, the fierce denunciation of Simon Magus

in the opening lines and the passionate condemnation contained in the apostro-
phe to the simoniac popes in lines 90–117 express an anger that is hardly war-
ranted by the sin's location, while it is in utter contrast to the "comic" episode of
the barrators in *Inferno* 21–22.[10] The emotional charge of this whole episode is
in fact unique in *Inferno,* as the pilgrim's use of the word *folle* indicates in *Inferno*
19.88: "I do not know if I was now too brazen [*folle,* literally 'mad']."[11] This ap-
parent inconsistency in the classification of the sin of simony (paralleled by the
location of the violent against God, the blasphemers, who are found *before* the
violent against nature) is a salutary reminder that the author of the *Comedy* was
a poet and not a theological computer.

The moral order of *Purgatorio*

Unlike its forerunners, Dante's purgatory is quite different from his
hell in many of its important features. First, it is utterly distinct, not only in its
location but also in the fact that light and beauty are (intermittently) present.
Second, the whole purpose of the purgative process is not to punish but to elimi-
nate the seven capital vices and the stains left by sin, in order that the human
soul may be reunited with its Creator. As Cogan (1999, 88) remarks succinctly,
"What is corrected in Purgatory are vices, not actions." Although the concept of
purgatory has been rejected by many Christians, its justification lies in the fact
that, at the moment of death, most human beings would appear to require some
form of purification before they are fit to enjoy the beatific vision and thus see
the Godhead "face to face" (1 Cor. 13.12). Purgatory also stressed the unity of
Christ's Church in its various forms: the Church Militant on earth; the Church
Suffering in purgatory; the Church Triumphant in paradise. As the Council of
Lyons proclaimed in 1274, the prayers of members of the Church on earth help
souls in purgatory, since the latter "are served by the suffrages of the living faith-
ful, to wit, the sacrifice of the mass, prayers, alms, and other works of piety that
the faithful customarily offer on behalf of others of the faithful according to the
institutions of the Church."[12]

So, the souls Dante meets in *Purgatorio* remind him constantly of their need
to be assisted by the prayers of the living: "for here we gain much from those
back there [on earth]" (*Purg.* 3.145). In fact, the souls are so insistent in their en-
treaties for help that the pilgrim turns to Virgil in apparent wonder, recalling *Ae-
neid* 6.376, where the Sibyl tells the wretched Palinurus to desist from hoping to
change through prayer what has been decreed by the gods. Virgil explains that
this was true when he had written his poem, at a time when pagan prayers were
invalid. Now, however, "justice's peak is not lowered because the fire of love ful-
fills in an instant what those who are stationed here must satisfy" (*Purg.* 6.37–39).

What must be satisfied is of course God's justice, which, in purgatory, is tempered by hope.[13]

In *Purgatorio* 16, the poem's central canto, the basic tenet of its moral system is affirmed against all those who believe in astral determinism or the omnipotence of human passion: God endows human beings with free will. Indeed, without this divine gift, "it would not be justice to have joy for good and mourning for evil" (*Purg.* 16.70–72). In other words, heaven and hell—the very stuff of Dante's Christian epic, the ultimate destiny of each human being—would be unjust. In the next canto (*Purg.* 17.91–139), Virgil asserts the fundamental principle that love is the source not only of all virtue but also of all sin. As Aquinas had affirmed (*S. Th.* 1.2.28.6, resp.): "Every agent, whatever it be, performs every action from love of some kind." Dante's poetic genius takes up this general law and applies it to the moral order of purgatory. As in *Inferno* (where Virgil explains the Aristotelian ordering of sins in hell only after the first six circles have been explored), so here the theoretical justification follows and illuminates the past experience of the encounters with souls on the first three terraces of the mountain. Whereas sins punished in hell are classified according to a tripartite Aristotelian-Ciceronian taxonomy (incontinence-violence-fraud), in purgatory the souls on their way to salvation are purged of their tendencies toward the seven capital vices—the first time that the latter are used as a taxonomy in descriptions of the other world.[14] It is no longer sin but the tendency toward and the habit of sin that must be eliminated before the soul can be reunited with God.[15] Just as the worst types of sin were punished in the pit of hell, so the logic of the purgatorial ascent requires that the worst vices (beginning with pride) be purified at the beginning, when the soul is farthest from God.

In *Purgatorio* 17.91–96 we learn that there are two types of love: the first is instinctive and placed by God in all his creatures (cf. *Par.* 1.109–20); the second requires human beings, who are endowed with reason and free will, to make a choice. The first is blameless; the second may err through being directed toward the wrong object or toward a good object but with defective or excessive energy. Thus, the first three terraces display souls guilty of directing their love against their neighbors (Pride-Envy-Anger),[16] while on the fourth terrace souls are purged of their insufficient love of God and the good (Sloth); on the last three terraces of the mountain, we find those who had loved secondary, transient goods to excess (Avarice-Gluttony-Lust).

According to tradition, the repentant souls in purgatory were purified by fire, in that this was "not only an essential, required accessory of purgatory but also, in many cases, its very embodiment."[17] Dante's originality is striking in this respect, since fire is found on only *one* of the mountain's seven terraces: the last, where the tendency to lust is eradicated. It is significant that the pilgrim has to pass through the wall of fire, both as an indication of a general law that human beings must be purged of lust before union with God becomes possible and as a reminder of the myth that, since the Fall, Eden is inaccessible and sealed off by fire.[18]

Another telling example of the poet's originality is his invention of ante-purgatory, a zone at the base of the mountain where various categories of sinners have to wait before they can venture into purgatory proper. All the souls vividly illustrate the Christian idea that it is only at the moment of death that the individual's fate is determined for all eternity. As Cogan (1999, 10) points out with admirable concision, "Virtue and vice, in Aristotelian terms, are fundamentally irrelevant to the question of salvation or damnation. Both virtue and vice depend on habit, but salvation and damnation do not."

The first example is a truly dramatic one. Near the base of the mountain are found those who had died under the ban of excommunication. This spiritual weapon, at times abused for political purposes, cannot prevent the human soul from turning to God and making due repentance *in articulo mortis,* as we learn from the lips of Manfred, Frederick II's illegitimate son, who, in 1259, had been subjected to the major form of excommunication and thus sentenced "with Judas the traitor into the fire and with the devil" (Morghen 1951, 329–30). Nevertheless, as Manfred tells us, not even this terrible anathema can prevent Eternal Love from rescuing the human soul from perdition "while hope has still any flower of green" (*Purg.* 3.133–35). Only God (and the *Comedy's* author) can know that Manfred is destined for heavenly beatitude, while his father is damned among the heretics (*Inf.* 10.119). Like the other souls found in antepurgatory, the excommunicate have to undergo a form of penal sentence: they are obliged to wait outside the gate of purgatory for a period thirty times greater than that of their exclusion from the life of the Church on earth. A similar punishment is meted out to those guilty of extreme negligence in various ways, but their waiting period is limited to the time they had spent on earth. Whereas the process of purification in purgatory proper is not a punishment but a purgation willingly undertaken by the souls (who are only too eager to cooperate with God's grace), in antepurgatory there is nothing the souls can do to help themselves—although their exile may be shortened by prayers offered up for them by the living (*Purg.* 3.142–45). While at first sight Belacqua seems still to be indulging in his habitual sin of sloth, he is in fact—ironically—quite right in stating that for him (and his companions in antepurgatory) it is pointless to strive to enter purgatory before the appointed time: *"andar in sù che porta? / ché non mi lascerebbe ire a' martíri / l'angel di Dio che siede in su la porta"* (*Purg.* 4.127–29; What is the use of climbing? for God's angel who is seated at the Gate [of Purgatory] would not let me proceed to the sufferings [inside]).

The "law" of *contrapasso* in hell and purgatory

Most Dante scholars identify the relationship whereby the suffering undergone (willingly, in purgatory) reflects the nature of the sin punished or purged as a *contrapasso* (but see the warning sounded in Armour 2000). The word itself—a hapax legomenon—is found in *Inferno* 28.142, when Bertran de Born, holding his severed head in his hand, exclaims: "Thus the *contrapasso* is observed in me." A famous troubadour, Bertran is placed by Dante among the sowers of discord for encouraging Prince Henry to rebel against his father, Henry II of England. His punishment thus reflects the vivid force of metaphor in the medieval universe by illustrating the fact that he had been guilty of high treason against the "head" of state as well as of severing the ties that bound him to the "head" of his family.[19] Dante's *contrapasso* (counter-suffering) was borrowed from Scholastic translations of Aristotle. It implied "equal suffering repaid for a previous action" (*S. Th.* 2.2.61.4, resp.), while harking back to the biblical "an eye for an eye, tooth for tooth, hand for hand, foot for foot, burn for burn, wound for wound, bruise for bruise" (Exod. 21.24–25), as well as the basic principle that "one is punished by the very things by which one sins" (Wisd. 11.16).[20]

Contrapasso in hell

Many of the examples of *contrapasso* in *Inferno* are simple and direct in their message: the lustful are tossed about in a tempest (as they had been by their passions), the gluttons wallow in mud and hail (reflecting their banquetings' inevitable outcome of excrement and urine), hypocrites are encased in cloaks of burnished gold that is really lead, the basest of all metals. Other examples are more complex. The heretics are buried in tombs (*Inferno* 9–10): those who had denied that there was life beyond the grave have for all eternity what they had foreseen as humanity's destiny—eternal encasement in a tomb. Moreover, their sepulchers are like furnaces, recalling the fire to which heretics were condemned on earth. The tombs are open for the present, but they will be sealed for all eternity after the Last Judgment, for the open tomb was an iconographic symbol of both the Resurrection and the Day of Judgment they had rejected. As we have seen, their divisive beliefs and acts are punished by the fact that enemies on earth are now "united" as neighbors in the infernal tomb.

In *Inferno* 19.13–30, the simoniac popes are buried upside-down in the floor of hell, with flames licking the soles of the latest recruit's feet, which protrude from a shaft in the rock. The *contrapasso* is here at its most complex. Instead of turning their desires heavenward, these corrupt churchmen had sold the things of the Holy Spirit (just as Simon Magus had attempted to buy them from St.

Peter: Acts 8.9–20): so, their heads are now pointing down toward Satan, imprisoned at the earth's center. Their feet are licked by flames, in an infernal parody of Pentecost, when the Holy Spirit descended in the shape of tongues "as though of fire" *(linguae tamquam ignis)* on the heads of the apostles (Acts 2.3–4). Everything here is turned upside-down: feet, instead of the noblest limb, the head; the infernal rock that imprisons them, instead of the Rock of Faith on which Christ founded his Church. Indeed, the whole scene reflects the fact that the lives and actions of these wretched churchmen had inverted God's moral order, which requires that the things of the Spirit be valued above all else.[21] The sinner selected, Nicholas Orsini, had been pope during Dante's boyhood, reigning from 1277 to 1280. Like all supreme pontiffs, Nicholas III had declared himself to be the "heir of St. Peter," thus establishing himself as St. Peter's direct successor "without intermediaries" (Ullmann 1975, 25). However, with supreme irony, he who had been St. Peter's successor is now damned as a follower of the *wrong* Simon—Simon Magus (Acts 8.9)—from whom the sin of simony took its name and whose name resounds as an ironic clarion call in the striking opening to the canto: *O Simon mago . . .* Christ's renaming of Simon was the most illustrious example of the belief that names should reflect the true nature and role of both persons and things (*VN* 13.4). Simon the fisherman's future role was emblazoned in the name "Peter" *(Petrus)* that Christ imposed on him with the words "You are rock *[Petrus]*, and upon this rock *[petram]* I will build my Church, and the gates of hell shall not prevail against it" (Matt. 16.18).

The Rock of Faith is thus indirectly evoked as a perpetual indictment of the first pope's corrupt successors, who are now encased upside-down in the infernal rock of the realm of Fraud. As Singleton (1965b) has shown, the apocryphal *Actus Petri cum Simone* relates that Simon Magus was cast down in midflight by God. This legend, together with bas-reliefs showing him hurtling down toward the earth and breaking his leg in the presence of Peter and Paul, may well have inspired the poet and led him to imagine the simoniac popes in that head-down position as an infernal parody of the apostolic succession. We may also be reminded of a vital element in Christian tradition, according to which St. Peter was granted his wish to be crucified upside-down.[22] This act of supreme humility—Peter's belief that he was unworthy to be crucified in the same position as Christ, the Founder of the Church—is parodied in the punishment of the evil popes who are now crucified in the bowels of the earth, from which had come the gold and silver they had adored.

Contrapasso in *Purgatorio*

Just as the moral order of *Purgatorio* is less complex than that of *Inferno,* so the relationship between the sufferings willingly undergone and the sin purged is apparently simpler—with an essential difference, that the sufferings in purgatory are undertaken by souls precisely in order to reform the vicious habits they had displayed while alive on earth.[23] The ex-proud are bent double under huge weights, in an attitude opposed to their "stiff necks" on earth (Exod. 32.9, 33.3; *Purg.* 11.52–54), an attitude that signals the crushing of their tendency to pride, the source of all sin and therefore ubiquitous in hell (Ecclus. 10.15). Omberto Aldobrandesco, Count of Santafiora, tells the pilgrim that it is because he did not practice humility among the living that he now has to bear the full weight of his former pride in order to eradicate the stains left by this vice in his soul while at the same time satisfying God's justice (*Purg.* 11.70–72). In an autobiographical aside (*Purg.* 13.136–38) Dante confesses that he can already feel the weight of the rock that will bear him down on the first purgatorial terrace as a result of his earthly pride—a unique moment of self-accusation. The envious, clothed in hair-cloth, leaning on and supporting each other, have their eyelids sewn up with wire, a reminder of the fact that in life the spectacle of both the misfortunes and the successes of others had caused them to sin through envy. However, the full extent of the purgatorial *contrapasso* is far wider in scope, and the pattern is in fact a complex one, first traced by De' Negri (1958). Each terrace offers examples of the virtue opposed to the sin being purged (with an episode taken from the life of the Virgin as the first illustration of this virtue), together with examples of the sin punished. The scheme reveals Dante's penchant for structural symmetry: examples of virtue / encounters with souls / examples of sin punished / angel citing an appropriate beatitude.[24]

The most complex of these patterns is found on the terrace of Pride (*Purg.* 10–12), where the examples are carved into marble at the base of the mountainside (so that the proud, bent double, can meditate on them). Humility is illustrated by the Annunciation, accompanied by episodes taken from the lives of King David and the Emperor Trajan (an unusual trio: the mother of Christ; an ancestor of Christ; and a Roman emperor—the latter, an unexpected exemplar for the supreme Christian virtue of humility). The souls of the proud recite a modified form of the prayer *Our Father,* illustrating both their charity in praying for souls on earth and the fact that souls in purgatory are incapable of being tempted to sin (*Purg.* 11.19–24): "Do not test our strength, so easily subdued, against the ancient adversary, but set it free from him [the devil] who so goads it [to evil]. This last prayer, dear Lord, we do not make for ourselves—for there is no need—but for those who have stayed behind [on earth]." There follows a series of thirteen examples of pride punished, in scenes the souls contemplate carved in the rock beneath their feet (*Purg.* 12.14–63). The first (ll. 25–27) displays Lucifer's precipitous fall from heaven, paralleled in the second scene by Briareus (ll. 28–30), struck down by Jove's thunderbolt for taking part in the giants' revolt against the gods. The pair provides a good example of Dante's syncretism; rather than rejecting Greco-Roman mythology as entirely false, he credits it with a kernel of truth (cf. *Conv.* 2.4.6–7). The sculpted examples continue, alternating between Old Testament history and classical mythology, for thirty-six verses or twelve ternary units, in which four groups of three *terzine* begin with the letters V then O then M (VOM = MAN), an acrostic repeated in lines 61–63, which portray proud Troy reduced to ashes. The first four *terzine* show humankind's rebellion against the divinity; the next four, human pride; the last group, the pride of tyrants. The symmetrical ordering, dear to medieval aesthetics, is overarched as in a musical phrase by the acrostic VOM, reminding the reader that humanity's original sin was one of pride, when Adam and Eve succumbed to the Tempter's promise, "You shall be like gods" (Gen. 3.5; *Par.* 26.115–17). At the end of the terrace, an angel pronounces the beatitude "Blessed are the poor in spirit" (*Purg.* 12.110; Matt. 5.3). The pilgrim suddenly realizes that one of the seven *P*s—(each *P* signifying *peccatum*, "sin") imprinted on his brow by the angel at the entrance and symbolizing the effects of the seven capital vices—has been removed. This pattern is repeated after the pilgrim has traversed the other six terraces, until finally in the Earthly Paradise, all memory of sin is removed by the waters of the River Lethe while memory of everything good is restored by the waters of Eunoè (*Purg.* 28.127–30; 33.91–96).

The moral order of *Paradiso*

The moral order of paradise is exemplified by the method invented to indicate the varying degrees of beatitude enjoyed by the souls in heaven. As Beatrice tells Dante in *Paradiso* 4.28–48, all the blessed are united with God in the Empyrean Heaven, outside the created universe. Nevertheless, true to the Scholastic axiom that there is nothing in the intellect that was not first present in the senses *(nihil in intellectu quod non fuerit prius in sensu)*, Dante avoids one of the weaknesses of modern theology, its attempt to approach God and spiritual matters mainly through abstractions. Instead, the poet resolutely asserts the need to make allowances for the limitations of the human intellect, which are catered to by Holy Scripture when it attributes "feet and hands to God but means something else" (ll. 44–45) or when angels are portrayed with human features, bodies, and wings. Hence, the blessed spirits will appear to the pilgrim as though they inhabited the various spheres, although all of them in fact "adorn the first sphere" (l. 34). In other words, the pilgrim and we, as readers, are informed that virtually the whole of what is described in most of *Paradiso* is pure allegory or an extended metaphor. What appears to the pilgrim and is narrated by the poet from canto 1 to canto 30 is not to be taken as literally true about paradise, whose reality must in every sense be sought at a higher level.

This ladder of vision, blessedness, and desire constitutes the dramatic nucleus of Dante's *Paradiso*, an ascent marked by a constant increase in light and beauty (especially in Beatrice's radiant splendor).[25] As so often, the poet seizes upon an aspect of medieval science in order to drive home his moral lesson. It was believed that the earth cast its shadow as far as the third "heaven," the planet Venus (*Par.* 9.118–19). Dante the narrator uses this aspect of the physical universe to underscore the lowest degrees of blessedness enjoyed by the souls who appear in the first three spheres and to indicate the fact that their merits on earth had been limited in various ways. The souls that appear to Dante in the lowest sphere, that of the moon, are those of two women, Piccarda Donati and the Empress Costanza, whose families span the three realms of the afterlife: Piccarda's brother Corso is destined for hell, where—as we have noted—Costanza's son, Frederick II, already resides among the heretics; Piccarda's other brother, Forese, is on the terrace of Gluttony in purgatory, while Costanza's grandson Manfred is in antepurgatory. Both women had entered convents and dedicated their virginity to God; both, however, had been forced to leave the cloister and marry—although Piccarda now asserts that Costanza in her heart had remained faithful to her vows (*Par.* 3.115–17). This leads Beatrice to explain that a distinction must be made between Costanza's absolute will and her relative will. Like most Christians—and unlike St. Lawrence and Mucius Scaevola (a pagan hero of ancient Rome!)—Costanza and Piccarda had been swayed by force and the machinations of evil men (*Par.* 4.73–114). While Costanza's absolute will remained faithful to God, her relative will was to some extent defective and gave in to threats of violence.

The moon was traditionally associated with mutation and instability.[26] The souls' relative moral imperfection is also reflected in the moon's appearance, the fact that spots appear on its bright surface. The whole light metaphysics of the *Comedy* is present *in nuce* in Beatrice's lecture (*Par.* 2.61–148), as she refutes Dante's previous "Averroistic" explanation of the reason why spots appear on the moon (*Conv.* 2.13.9), which had been based on a physical hypothesis about the planet's varying density.[27] Here, through Beatrice, the poet gives us a metaphysical explanation of Neoplatonic origin (cf. Aquinas, *De coelo* 2.16). In the heavens, the happiness of the angelic orders is united with the spheres they cause to move.[28] Hence, it is both the moon's distance from the highest heaven, the Primum Mobile, and the fact that its movers are the lowest order of angels that explain the spots on the moon's surface, since the radiance of all the heavenly spheres is a visible manifestation of "the happy nature from which it originates, [for] the mixed power shines through the body as happiness does through the pupil of a sparkling eye" (*Par.* 2.142–44).[29]

In similar fashion, the souls that appear to the pilgrim in Mercury (moved by archangels) accomplished great things on earth, but they did so primarily in order to acquire honor and fame; in desiring glory, they loved the true good with less intensity (*Par.* 6.115–17). The third heaven or sphere, Venus, at a mean distance of some 2 million miles from the earth, is moved by the Principalities (*Par.* 8.34, although Dante had attributed its motion to the Thrones in *Conv.* 2.5.13).[30] Venus is the obvious setting for those who had been famous lovers on earth—a motley crew that includes a member of the French Angevin dynasty, Charles Martel (whom the poet had met in Florence in 1294); Cunizza da Romano, the lover of the Italian troubadour Sordello, who ended her days in Florence, in the house of Cavalcante de' Cavalcanti; Folquet, another troubadour, who became bishop of Toulouse in 1205 and took part in the persecution of Albigensian heretics; and the Old Testament harlot Rahab, who—an ancestress of Christ (Matt. 1.5; James 2.25) and a prototype of Mary Magdalene— came to be regarded as a *figura* of the Church.[31] Cunizza stresses the fact that although it may be difficult for many on earth to understand the positive reality of Venus's influence, she rejoices in it, for, as Folquet explains, "We do not repent here, but we laugh, not for the guilt, which no longer comes to mind" but for God's providential design, the divine alchemy capable of turning the mud of human passion into spiritual gold (*Par.* 9.103–8). Another doubt regarding the moral order of paradise is resolved by Piccarda and then by Justinian: the former explains that the blessed souls who appear to the pilgrim in the lower spheres *cannot* desire a greater degree of beatitude, because they totally accept God's will (*Par.* 3.70–87); the latter asserts that part of the souls' beatitude springs from their awareness of the perfect equivalence between their deserts on earth and their reward in heaven (*Par.* 6.118–26). Significantly, the poet of the *Comedy* sides with St. Thomas (against the Franciscan primacy of love) in claiming that both for angels and for humans heavenly beatitude consists in *vision:* "From this it can be seen [*veder*] that beatitude is based on the act of see-ing [*vede*], not on the act of love, which then follows" (*Par.* 28.109–11).[32]

Like *Inferno* 9–10 and *Purgatorio* 10, the tenth canto of *Paradiso* marks an essential transition from one moral category to another. The narrative contrast could not be greater. From the fierce invective against the corruption of the Church on earth (*Par.* 9.127–42), where the she-wolf of greed has transformed the shepherd into a wolf, the poet invites his readers to contemplate the most profound mystery of the Christian faith, the belief in a triune God, and to admire the skill displayed by the Holy Trinity in the creation of the heavens with their perfect order and dual motion (*Par.* 10.1–21). Now, above the earth's shadow, the two space-travelers rise up through the spheres in which the pilgrim sees the souls of those who had cooperated fully with the influences of God's heavens. No trace of moral imperfection remains.

The fourth sphere, that of the Sun (moved by the Powers), reveals twenty-four spirits who had sought and practiced wisdom on earth and whose heavenly brilliance is even greater than the sun's (*Par.* 10.40–42)—a physical impossibility that emphasizes the supernatural order of these celestial regions. The souls' search for the truth on earth is now complemented by their achievement of harmony in paradise, a harmony visible in their symmetrical ordering into three circles—with two circles of twelve spirits named (reflecting the cosmic order manifest in the zodiac)—as well as in their heavenly chanting and their unified circular motion. St. Thomas not only praises the founder of the Franciscan Order, but he also introduces his terrestrial adversary, Siger of Brabant, as one who had taught "truths" that had earned him hatred and hostility on earth (*Par.* 11.40–117; 10.133–38). Similarly, St. Bonaventure praises St. Dominic and attributes to Joachim of Fiore the gift of prophecy he had denied him in life (*Par.* 12.46–141).[33] The Dominican's praise of Francis and the Franciscan's praise of Dominic constitute further examples of ideal heavenly harmony, as opposed to the discord on earth.

The souls of the wise naturally include those of theologians, such as Albert the Great (d. 1280), St. Thomas's teacher, whose influence on Dante was far-reaching.[34] They even include the only contemporary pope "canonized" by the poet, although no mention is made of his elevation to the papacy as John XXI (pope, 1276–77): he is merely "Peter of Spain, who shines down there in twelve books," those of his popular manual of logic or *Summulae logicales* (*Par.* 12.134–35). More surprising for the modern reader is the fact that the soul that shines brightest of all in the first circle—brighter than Aquinas himself (*Par.* 10.109)—is that of Solomon. St. Thomas hastens to assure the pilgrim that Solomon received from God "such deep wisdom. . . that, if truth be true, no second [man] ever rose to see so much" (ll. 112–14). In *Paradiso* 13.37–111, Aquinas explains to Dante in what way Solomon was unique. When God offered to give him whatever he requested, Solomon asked for "kingly prudence" (13.104). God therefore granted him a "wise and discerning mind," so that "no one like you has been before you and no one like you shall arise after you" (3 Kings 3.12). This explains Solomon's relative perfection as the exemplar of kingship, his supreme ability to govern his people by following the dictates of justice and wisdom. The moral superiority attributed to Solomon in the first circle of the wise is testimony both to Dante's belief in the sacred autonomy of the civil power and to his conviction that authorities are competent only if each remains in its proper sphere.[35]

The spectacle witnessed by the pilgrim in the fourth heaven is brought to a close by a hymn in praise of the Holy Trinity, repeated three times by the twenty-four spirits (*Par.* 14.28–33; cf. 13.25–27).[36] This is followed by the appearance of a third group of heavenly spirits and a reference to the Holy Spirit (Love), even as the opening reference to the Trinity (*Par.* 10.1–6) praised the order imposed on Creation by the Father, while the entire heaven of the wise is placed under the aegis of the Son, who is both "Supreme Wisdom" (*Inf.* 3.6) and the Sun of Justice, *Sol justitiae,* Christ's prophetic title (Mal. 4.2).

The fifth heaven—that of Mars, the pagan god of war and first patron of Florence (*Inf.* 13.143–45)—occupies a central position among the nine spheres or heavens of the created cosmos. Its moral significance is based on the cardinal virtue of fortitude, displayed by the angelic Virtues (who imitate the strength and fortitude of the Godhead), as well as by the warrior saints who appear in a great cross of brilliant lights, and lastly by the pilgrim himself. The latter receives from his great-great-grandfather Cacciaguida—who died c. 1147 wearing the sign of the cross during the Second Crusade—the news that he will be driven into exile and forced to leave behind everything he holds most dear (*Par.* 17.46–60), moreover that he must reveal to the world everything that has been disclosed to him, however unpleasant the consequences for others and even for himself (ll. 124–42). Here, at long last, the pilgrim receives the answer to the question he had posed at the very beginning (*Inf.* 2.13–36): Why should Dante Alighieri—neither Aeneas, the ancestor of Rome, nor St. Paul, apostle to the gentiles—undertake a journey through the other world? God's plan for him is now revealed. The message he must take back to a world gone astray will be bitter at first; nevertheless, it will provide vital moral nourishment when digested (*Par.* 17.127–32). Beatrice's command to write down what he has seen "for the good of the world that lives badly" (*Purg.* 32.103–5) is here reformulated in the most solemn manner by a blessed spirit able to read the decrees of Divine Providence (*Par.* 17.43–45). Unlike the ambiguous oracles of old, the Christian martyr Cacciaguida shows Dante how the pilgrim-author's epic *imitatio Christi* requires him to take up his cross and bear faithful witness to God's truth with supreme fortitude, even unto death (Schnapp 1986).

In the sixth sphere—that of Jupiter—the pilgrim encounters a multitude of spirits who had loved and practiced justice to the highest degree on earth. After forming the thirty-five letters of the divine command to earthly rulers and judges found in the opening of (Solomon's) Book of Wisdom, "Love justice, you who judge the earth," their brilliant lights fashion an eagle (*Par.* 6.4: "God's bird"). The eye and eyebrow of the eagle are composed of six lights *(lumi)* or spirits. Not surprisingly, perhaps, David—Christ's regal ancestor and author of the Book of Psalms—forms the pupil of the eagle's eye. As Beatrice observes (*Par.* 20.67–69), what is astonishing, however, is the fact that in this august company (David and Hezekiah; emperors Trajan and Constantine; with a solitary "modern" ruler, William II of Sicily) we find Ripheus, an obscure Trojan mentioned some three times in the second book of the *Aeneid.* In this salutary shock to his readers' expectations, our poet claims that a pagan renowned for his love of justice in Trojan antiquity (*Aen.* 2.426–27) had received baptism by desire and had practiced the three theological virtues in ancient Troy.[37] Vergil's pessimistic account of the way the pagan gods had allowed Ripheus, the greatest lover of justice among the Trojans, to be slaughtered is now corrected by Dante's boast that, however incredible it may appear to the world below, the Christian God so loves justice that he granted an eternal reward to Ripheus (cf. Acts 10.35: "in every nation, anyone who fears Him [God] and practices justice is acceptable to Him"). In its opposition to greed and its encouragement of the supreme virtue of charity, justice is the most "human" of virtues (*Conv.* 1.12.9). Equally noteworthy is its link with the empire, which is symbolized by the eagle in Justinian's discourse (*Par.* 6) and here in the symbiotic relationship Justice-empire, for justice is most effective when administered by the universal emperor (*Mon.* 1.11.8).

Now, Dante and his guide rise up to Saturn, the seventh sphere and highest of the "heavens," which acts as a bridge between earthly activity and the things of God and eternity. It is understandably the place where the pilgrim sees the souls of those who had dedicated their lives to contemplation, the highest form of human "activity" on earth. To mark the change, the "sweet symphony of paradise" is silent (*Par.* 21.58–59), not only because at this level it would overwhelm the pilgrim's senses but also because its silence evokes that of the cloisters, which once provided such a rich harvest for paradise, although nowadays virtually no one ascends to paradise (*Par.* 22.73–78).

The message of monastic corruption is broadcast by St. Benedict (d. 543), founder and creator of Western monasticism as a cenobitic institution governed by a Rule that reflected the Roman concern for order and stability, at a time when the emperor Justinian was accomplishing his "lofty work" of codifying Roman laws (*Par.* 6.10–24).[38] Benedict is in fact preceded in Dante's account by another Benedictine, St. Peter Damian, born in Ravenna (c. 1007) some three hundred years before the exiled poet wrote the final cantos of his *Paradiso* in that same city. A reluctant cardinal and a dedicated Church reformer before returning to the cloister where he lived out the last seven years of his life, Peter Damian upbraids the modern princes of the Church for their luxury and ostentation, which are utterly opposed to the example set by St. Peter and St. Paul (*Par.* 21.127–35).

To understand the tragic force of Dante's denunciation of the greed and corruption of the monastic orders, we must remember that the ideal expressed by St. Bernard and shared by so many in the Middle Ages had led to the belief that the monastic way of life gave its practitioners a head start in the race to salvation, so much so that they were known as "the religious" *(viri religiosi),* "in contrast to all other men whether secular or clerical."[39] However much men and women came to value an active life in this world, withdrawal from it for the sake of contemplating the things of heaven continued to exert its fascination as an ideal. Even Dante—the true son of a flourishing Italian commune, convinced as he was of the importance of being a "citizen" (*Par.* 8.115–17)—believed that the contemplative life was superior to the active life, as the exalted station of the contemplative spirits in the seventh heaven demonstrates. Already in *Convivio* 4.22.17, he had claimed that "contemplation is more replete with spiritual light than anything else existing down here on earth"—an estimate borne out by the fact that the pilgrim's eyes cannot behold Beatrice in her overwhelming beauty and splendor at this stage in his ascent (*Par.* 21.7–9).

As another of Benedict's spiritual sons, St. Bernard (chosen by Dante as his intercessor with the Virgin Queen of Heaven) wrote, "The contemplative life . . . consists in renouncing the world and in delighting in living for God alone" (Gardner 1972, 172). This ideal is vividly illustrated by the golden ladder that links Saturn with the Empyrean: it is the ladder seen in a dream by Jacob that reached up to heaven, with God's messengers descending and ascending (Gen. 28.12). St. Peter Damian described the ladder in one of his letters as a symbol of the Way of Contemplation, "the golden way that leads men back to their homeland *(ad patriam)*" (PL 145.248). Through it, humanity receives help from God in order to rise up to him spiritually and intellectually while on this earth, for "we descend by self-exaltation and ascend by humility."[40]

Beatrice's gaze is sufficient to impel Dante up the ladder to the Heaven of the Fixed Stars (Di Fonzo 1991), entering the eighth heavenly sphere in the constellation of the Gemini, under which the poet was born and to which he gives thanks for his intellectual and poetical powers (*Par.* 22.112–20).[41] This stage in the ascent completes Dante's presentation of the moral order of heaven (those who had made unstable vows; those who did what is right chiefly for honor and fame; the lovers; the wise; the warriors; the just; those who had given themselves up to a life of contemplation). However, as we have already noted, the scenes witnessed by the pilgrim during his ascent are a kind of phantasmagoria orchestrated especially for him (and, of course, his readers), in order to illustrate graphically a hierarchy of categories or groups. In fact, as Cogan (1999, 220–22) argues, "The degrees of blessedness revealed to Dante during his journey do not correspond to any human estimation of the relative value of actions of the sorts represented by the souls in the different spheres. . . . The value of any and of all actions . . . comes from their participation in a universe of action that in its totality and form reflects the divine nature."

A different kind of moral order is, however, observable in the *reality* of the celestial rose, once the pilgrim is finally able to contemplate "both the courts of heaven made manifest" (*Par.* 30.96). In the court of heaven as described in *Paradiso* 32, it is the individual's historic role and merit that reign supreme: Eve, the universal mother, is found directly below Mary, the mother of God; St. Peter (certainly no contemplative!) is seated next to Mary (Adam is nearest to her, on her left [*Par.* 32.118–26]), with the founders of three religious orders—Francis, Benedict, and Augustine—beneath John the Baptist (Florence's patron saint, seated next to St. Peter: ll. 31–35).[42] Schnapp (1991b, 214) points to the fascinating exception created by Beatrice, "who alone is seated in the same groupings of souls as a man," which "places her alongside Rachel, the symbol of the contemplative life, while at the same time identifying her with the authority of Christ and the Church, both vested in Peter."

The poet's personal evaluation of sins

Although as readers of the poem we are apt to be mesmerized by its author's skill in creating the illusion of an objective system of reward and punishment, we should not forget that the *Comedy* is grounded in Dante's psychological makeup and his vision of life, both clearly conditioned by his personal experience. As already noted, at its very beginning (*Inf.* 3), the pilgrim's journey into the afterlife takes him to a place of the poet's own invention: a state, neither heaven nor hell, in which, suspended for all eternity, he finds the cowards who refused to make a choice, and therefore mingle with the angels "who did not rebel, nor were they faithful to God, but were for themselves" (*Inf.* 3.38–39)— a conception of angelic neutrality quite opposed to Aquinas's angelology, but illustrative of the poet's contempt for a lack of *energeia* in all creatures. Life, for Dante, consisted above all in making an existential choice. Even more surprising than the location assigned to them is the *contrapasso* these sitters-on-the-fence are forced to endure, which surely strikes the reader as unpleasant as any invented for the damned souls in hell. Vainly running naked behind a banner, they are stung by insects and forced to shed their blood and tears, which they had carefully spared on earth but which are now devoured at their feet by loathsome worms (*Inf.* 3.52–69).

There follows an equally idiosyncratic presentation of the souls in limbo. Although it is the first circle of hell, Dante's limbo is quite extraordinary in a number of ways. In Latin theology, there were two categories: the *limbus patrum,* in which those who were destined for salvation but lived before Christ had to wait until the work of Redemption was fulfilled (as Virgil recounts in *Inf.* 4.52–63); and the *limbus infantium,* which received the souls of unbaptized infants. After Christ's harrowing of hell, only the latter continued to exist: a state of natural felicity deprived of the vision of God, hence without any form of beatitude.[43] Dante, however, virtually ignores the unbaptized infants, in order to concentrate on another category of unbaptized souls, the heroes and heroines of human thought and achievement. Indeed, his admiration for the "great spirits"

(*Inf.* 4.119) who did not know Christ led him to reject the Catholic tradition which denied the possibility that there could have been virtuous pagans not saved by God's grace. In that tradition, faith is essential if actions are to be pleasing to God, but those destined for salvation who lived and died before Christ (the prophets and virtuous Jews of the Old Testament) were saved by a special dispensation of grace. Early commentators on the poem are clearly embarrassed by the presence of adult pagans in limbo; and their embarrassment turns to near-panic when they come to the noble castle (*Inf.* 4.106ff.), with its seven walls and gates, shady lawns, and sunny open spaces where ancient philosophers and poets indulge in intellectual conversation. Although some of the details are controversial, it is clear that the extraordinary presence of light in the first circle of hell reflects the truth that had been glimpsed in part by the souls during their time on earth. This is in clear violation of the law ordaining the darkness of hell, the "blind world" as it is defined in that same canto (*Inf.* 4.13). An even greater shock to the orthodox is the presence here of the two most influential Arab philosophers, Avicenna and Averroës, notorious for their dangerous teachings based on Aristotelian doctrine, and Saladin, founder of the Ayubite dynasty, who recaptured Jerusalem from the crusaders in 1187.

Readers nowadays may be delighted to discover such "modern" broad-mindedness, although they would do well to venture cautiously down this track. The preferential treatment accorded to such pagans as Homer, Aristotle, Plato, Aeneas, and Julius Caesar, as well as to the followers of Islam mentioned above, is a direct result of two essential aspects of Dante's thought. The first is his fascination with magnanimity, the hallmark of the elite according to Aristotle's *Ethics* (Forti 1977; Scott 1977). The memory of these outstanding men and women still thrills the Christian poet (*Inf.* 4.119–20). The other is Dante's desire to exalt the founders of the empire and the wisdom of pagan antiquity on which its authority rested in the purely human sphere. The presence of Avicenna and Averroës reinforces the point that philosophy must be independent of theology, just as the empire must be independent of the papacy in temporal matters—a point made even more forcefully in *Paradiso* 10.133–38, where (as we have already mentioned) the poet places the radical Aristotelian philosopher Siger of Brabant among the saints who had cultivated wisdom on earth.

In this Christianized version of Vergil's Elysian Fields, Dante may appear to come dangerously close to the Pelagian heresy, which asserted that worthy pagans had been saved through their own efforts. Augustine had denounced this view as the height of folly, declaring that without God's gift of grace, it was impossible for human nature to avoid mortal sin and damnation; and St. Antonino (1389–1459), bishop of Florence, was to reject Dante's limbo as inconsistent with Catholic teaching. Nevertheless, while it is important to realize that Dante's Christian beliefs were not held blindly, and that on the question of limbo (as on one or two other points of doctrine) he enjoyed what may be called a certain "pre-Reformation license," it is just as important to remember that the *Comedy* as a whole demonstrates quite clearly that its author was a faithful upholder of the essentials of Christian dogma as interpreted in his times. As far as limbo and its privileged pagans are concerned, we must remember that Dante was a Christian poet for whom hell was a terrible reality; and the inhabitants of limbo *are in hell*. Despite the noble castle and their *locus amoenus,* the souls "without hope live in desire" (*Inf.* 4.42), as Virgil tells his charge. In other words, condemned to an eternity of frustration, they are deprived of that union with God for which, like all souls, they were created.[44] The tragedy of eternal damnation incurred by the virtuous heathen is one that continues to haunt the pilgrim right up to the Heaven of Justice, even as it—by his own admission—haunted the man Dante through so much of his lifetime (*Par.* 19.32–33, 67–90).

As Moore noted over a century ago (1899, 210), the attitudes and emotions evinced by the *Comedy*'s creator and protagonist do not always reflect the supposed gravity of the sin. This may be seen in various ways. The punishment devised for the gluttons (*Inf.* 6.7–12: they are immersed in a stinking quagmire and battered by "the eternal, cursed, cold, and heavy rain") is so reminiscent of feces and urine that it is described by the pilgrim as "the most disgusting" imaginable (*Inf.* 6.48). Even more surprising is the behavior of both Dante and Virgil in the circle of wrath, when, far from feeling any kind of compassion for a sinner (as with Francesca and Ciacco), the pilgrim spurns, with extraordinary anger, a sinner who identifies himself simply as "one who weeps" (*Inf.* 8.36), retorting: "With weeping and mourning, accursed spirit, now remain; for I recognize you, although you are filthy all over" (ll. 37–39). It is as though the pilgrim were infected with the sin punished in this circle: his reaction, like his language, is surprisingly extreme. Yet, after pushing the sinner back "with the other dogs," Virgil applauds this outburst of anger with a biblical echo, "Disdainful spirit, blessed is she that bore you!" (*Inf.* 8.44–45; cf. Luke 1.28, 48), and commends his desire to see the sinner "doused in this broth."

Critics have accused the poet of ferocity, vindictiveness, and implacable hatred, although it seems unlikely that the poet would wittingly have portrayed himself as nourishing these un-Christian sentiments. Instead, we must take into account the fact that the pilgrim has to learn that pity for the damned is an offense against God's justice (*Inf.* 20.27–30); and, much later in hell, he delights in tricking a traitor (*Inf.* 33.148–50). But at this point in the journey it would seem appropriate to recall that anger is viewed in contrary ways in the Christian tradition. Righteous anger is necessarily controlled by reason: Christ's anger at those who had turned the House of God into a den of thieves was not a vice but "zeal for the Lord's house," an action undertaken for justice's sake.[45] The sinner against whom Dante vents his anger is a fellow-Florentine, Filippo dei

Cavicciuli, a Black Guelf and a member of the insolent Adimari family (*Par.* 16.115–18; Boccaccio, *Decameron* 9.8), known as "Filippo Argenti" because of his ostentatious prodigality in shoeing his horse with silver. In his arrogance and insolent display of wealth, Filippo Argenti is judged to be symptomatic of the corruption that has overtaken contemporary Florence, as opposed to the frugality of the Florentines of earlier times when the city was "at peace, sober and modest" (*Par.* 15.99). It is the decadence of his native city, inspired by "pride, envy and avarice" (*Inf.* 6.74; 15.68), that kindles Dante's anger. Finally, we may note a moral crescendo as the expression of anger moves from Dante to Virgil (*Inf.* 8.121), and then to the righteous or divine anger displayed by the heavenly messenger who opens the gates of the Devil's City (*Inf.* 9.33, 76–99).

The opposite reaction is found in *Inferno* 16.7–90, where Dante (both author and protagonist) treats the homosexual Florentines who have sinned against Nature, God's daughter, "with greater respect than any other infernal figures except those in Limbo" (Hollander 1997). Virgil not only tells his charge that he must show respect and courtesy to these sinners, he even adds that, if it were not for the rain of fire that beats down on them, it would be more fitting for Dante to run to greet his fellow-citizens than to wait for them to come to him (*Inf.* 16.16–18). Two of these sinners, Iacopo Rusticucci and Tegghiaio Aldobrandi, had already been singled out by the pilgrim and praised for their good actions in *Inferno* 6.79–81 (although in asking Ciacco about their fate he had revealed his ignorance of God's judgment on these and other great Florentines). In canto 16, however, the pilgrim confronts that judgment when he encounters their spirits, yet he continues to feel reverence and even affection for them—so much so that he is tempted to embrace them (an action that, he feels sure, would have won Virgil's approval [*Inf.* 16.46–51]). Nowhere else in the *Comedy* do the poet, the pilgrim, and his guide so hate the sin and so love the sinner!

As a final observation on Dante's personal reaction to the sins so vividly portrayed in his *Comedy,* we should note the scorn heaped on usurers in *Inferno* 17.43–75, while bearing in mind the likelihood that the poet's father was a moneylender.[46] These sinners are ironically represented with their professional moneybags hanging from their necks, pouches which furnish an infernal parody of the nobility debased by usury, for on each is imprinted a bestial version of the coat of arms of the family to which they belonged. Nowhere else perhaps does the poet show such contempt as here, where Reginaldo degli Scrovegni, identified by a coat of arms bearing a pregnant blue sow, "twisted his mouth and stuck out his tongue, like an ox licking its snout" (*Inf.* 17.74–75). This grotesque scene anticipates the moment in purgatory when the pilgrim is clearly relieved to discover that Statius was not guilty of avarice, but of prodigality—a sin far more becoming to a poet (*Purg.* 22.19–42).[47]

Dante's other world

Topography and demography

A reader of the *Comedy* must be cognizant of the fact that Dante's epic stands at the pinnacle of a long tradition of visionary literature inspired by fundamental Christian beliefs. If we exclude the Bible, this tradition most probably began in the third century with the *Apocalypse of Paul,* originally written in Greek and translated into Latin c. 500; in its Latin versions it had a notable influence on medieval conceptions of the otherworld. In the twelfth century, a significant change occurred: the majority of accounts of the world beyond the grave became more complex, and they were no longer penned by clerics.[1] The eschatological vision of Western Christianity also underwent a momentous change from the one prevalent in the early Middle Ages: now, the primary focus was directed toward the Last Judgment with its concomitant fears, rather than to the idea of a heavenly Jerusalem, the ultimate destination for all believers in Christ, as depicted in the Apocalypse, or Book of Revelation. The most obvious indication of this shift is to be found in the representations of the Last Judgment on the tympana of many French cathedrals. In Italy, in the twelfth and thirteenth centuries we find this motif portrayed in mosaic in the cathedral at Torcello; and, in frescoes, in Santa Cecilia in Trastevere (Rome), Santa Maria Maggiore (Tuscania), Santa Maria in Piano (near Loreto Aprutino) and the church of Donnaregina (Naples), as well as at the cathedral in Ferrara. For our purpose, its most significant depiction is found in the powerful mosaics of the Florentine baptistery, Dante's "beautiful San Giovanni," where he first became a follower of Christ and to which he longed to return with his whole being (*Par.* 25.1–11). Indeed, during Dante's formative years, these mosaics were "the most notable works of modern art in Florence" (Wilkins 1983, 145). The Last Judgment was also portrayed in Sant' Apollinare Nuovo at Ravenna, the town that offered a refuge to the poet during the last years of his life. The effects of this major shift are evident in visionary literature: descriptions of paradise, predominant until the twelfth century, were now largely replaced by descriptions of the torments of hell and the sufferings of the damned souls.[2] As Jacques Le Goff relates, "The Franciscan preacher Berthold of Regensburg, in the thirteenth century, calculated the chances of damnation at 100,000 to 1, and the customary image used to convey the proportion of the elect and the damned is that of the small group of Noah and his companions as opposed to the great mass of humanity destroyed by the Flood" (1988, 325).

Interestingly enough, in the century that saw the birth of Dante Alighieri, no visions are recorded,[3] although in Italy, during the period 1275–1300, Bonvesin da Riva offered in the first section of his *Libro delle tre scritture* a description of "the twelve torments of hell" (l. 5), and in the third section he depicted the heavenly Jerusalem with its "twelve glories" or beatitudes (ll. 17–20). At about the same time, two poems written by Giacomino da Verona attempted to describe the sufferings of the damned in some 340 lines of verse *(De Babilonia infernali)*, which are counterbalanced by the largely sensual delights of paradise in the 280 verses of his *De Ierusalem coelesti*. A truly remarkable text is the *Libro della scala,* which was translated from the Arabic into Castilian c. 1260 at the court of Alfonso X of Castille, and then into Latin *(Liber scalae)* and Old French *(Livre de l'Eschiele Mahomet)*. It tells of Muhammad's journey through the other world, guided by the Archangel Gabriel. From Jerusalem, the Prophet ascends to heaven via the ladder that gives its name to the account; he sees two rivers originating in the Earthly Paradise (cf. *Purg.* 28.121–33); he visits the eight heavens; he then arrives at God's throne and is entrusted with the Koran. Muhammad also traverses the seven regions of hell, with their various torments, and after being instructed on the Last Judgment by Gabriel, Muhammad returns to Mecca where he attempts to convince his fellow citizens of the truth of his vision.[4] The *Liber scalae* is mentioned by Fazio degli Uberti in his *Dittamondo* (c. 1345). Even more pertinent is the fact that in the year 1260 Brunetto Latini–Dante's "mentor" (*Inf.* 15.82–87), who was to write his *Tesoretto* with Ovid as guide for his allegorical journey—was sent as Florentine ambassador to the court of Alfonso X. The question of the *Comedy*'s "sources," as well as its possible links with the *Liber scalae* and the eschatology of Islam, is one of the many that remain open in the field of Dante studies, although recent contributions by Cesare Segre (1984), Alison Morgan (1990), and Maria Corti (1995, 2001) have clarified many issues.

Topography of the *Comedy*

The topography of Dante's other world is both realistic and at times confusing. Unlike earlier visions, the *Comedy* clearly distinguishes between hell and purgatory, whereas the latter had traditionally been cast as a temporal annex to hell. According to Dante, however, hell extends downward from the central point in the Northern Hemisphere (Jerusalem) to the earth's center, whereas purgatory is situated at the antipodes to Jerusalem. Purgatory's huge mountain was most probably caused by Lucifer's fall after his rebellion (*Inf.* 34.121–26). As Lucifer-Satan hurtled down through space toward the nobler, Southern Hemisphere, the landmass retracted, shielded itself beneath the waters of the ocean, and re-emerged in the Northern Hemisphere. In order to avoid contact with God's adversary, the earth created a channel through which Lucifer descended until he became imprisoned in its core, while the mass thus displaced rose up in the Southern Hemisphere to create the mountain on which, according to the poet, both purgatory and Eden are situated. Dante's Mountain of Purgatory is thus over 3,200 miles high, according to medieval calculations of the distance from the earth's surface to its center (*Conv.* 2.6.10).[5]

Hell

The *Comedy*'s portrayal of hell as situated in the bowels of the earth is of course traditional. Associated with the sealed "abyss" or "bottomless pit" of Apocalypse 20.3, hell corresponded to the Hebrew Sheol (Ps. 15.10), the abode of the dead, conceived as a subterranean region enveloped in utter darkness. Christian hell was also a place of torment with fire and brimstone: "Individuals were judged according to their works . . . This is the second death. And anyone whose name was not found written in the book of life was thrown into this lake of fire" (Apoc. 20.13–15; cf. 21.8). Topographical details borrowed from classical antiquity were added by our poet, such as the quadripartite infernal river structure. Dante names the infernal waters according to the model found in Vergil's *Aeneid:* thus, we find Acheron (canto 3), Styx (canto 7), Phlegethon (canto 12), and Cocytus (cantos 32–34), while Vergil's Lethe, which ran through the Elysian Fields, is placed in the Earthly Paradise (*Purg.* 28–33), where it is twinned with a stream of the poet's invention, Eunoë (so-called for its "memory of the good," from the scraps of Greek accessible to Dante). On the other hand, in *Inferno* 14.112–38, Virgil maintains that the infernal rivers are in fact one channel, which changes names at different levels: "But the account of its source and direction of flow is not . . . even remotely scientific in character . . . it is quite deliberately allegorical and biblical" (Boyde 1981, 69). Other innovations include the addition to Christian hell of Phlegyas, the ferryman of Styx, and Charon, who transports the damned souls across Acheron. The latter's description in *Inferno* 3.82–111 so influenced Michelangelo that he introduced the mythological Charon into Christian iconography of the Last Judgment.

Diagram of Dante's Hell, *Dante con l'espositione di M. Bernardino Daniello da Lucca*
(Venice: Pietro da Fino, 1568). Reproduced from the original held by the
Department of Special Collections of the University Libraries of Notre Dame.

The terrain and trappings of Dante's *Inferno* are generally mapped out with great precision and a wealth of realistic detail not found in previous descriptions of hell. For example, when Dante steps inside Phlegyas's boat, it sinks lower in the water, indicating the bark's physical reaction to the weight of a living body (*Inf.* 8.25–27). Again, the foul air of hell makes it necessary for Dante and his guide, Virgil, to rest a while (*Inf.* 11.10–12), and the pilgrim's descent on helicopter-like Geryon is described with astonishing imaginative realism (*Inf.* 17.100–136). Even a reading of *Inferno* 13, with its infernal wood in whose "strange trees" the souls of those who had committed suicide are imprisoned, captivates readers to such an extent that they find the hellish scene on the whole more realistic and convincing than a not dissimilar episode in Boccaccio (*Decameron* 5.8), although this is set in a real forest just outside Ravenna. Indeed, as Barolini claims, Dante's narrative techniques in the *Comedy* are so powerful and bewitching that they bring about "our narrative credulity, our readerly incapacity to suspend our suspension of disbelief" (1992, 16).

As the pilgrim descends into lower hell, the descriptions become ever more precise. The ninth of the ten ditches of Malebolge is twenty-two miles, the tenth eleven miles in circumference (*Inf.* 29.8–10, 30.85–87). From this and other information given in the last eight cantos it is possible to extrapolate the diameters of all ten ditches, and Satan's height and that of the giants surrounding the pit of hell. Nevertheless, as Kleiner points out, Satan's height (2,500 feet) is such that the traitors dangling from his mouth are in fact "much too far away from the travelers to be identified or described" (1994, 43–55). Similarly, the distance separating the last ditch from Satan's huge bulk means that when the pilgrim tricks Frate Alberigo (*Inf.* 33.149–50), he should be only a few hundred yards from Satan. Hence, Kleiner concludes that, when Dante's measurements are examined closely, "they reveal a terrain *dis*ordered by number and measure," so that we, the readers, "are tricked (or enlightened) by the poet's spurious claims to mimetic precision in the very circles devoted to the punishment of fraud" (1994, 47–49).

As well as creating an overpowering impression of verisimilitude, the topography of Dante's hell serves to make readers aware of major ethical boundaries in the classification of the sins punished (as opposed to the chaotic and generic listings found in vision literature). The entrance to hell itself is marked by the kind of gateway that guarded access to medieval towns: above it, an inscription (*Inf.* 3.1–9) solemnly proclaims an eternity of suffering imposed by God's Justice, while the gateway guards nothing, since the entrance to hell is open to all who died in a state of mortal sin. The City of Dis, with its watchtowers or *meschite* (mosques) closely guarded by medieval demons (*Inf.* 8.70ff.), is a physical sign or signal to the reader that graver categories of sin will be found punished within the city (a signal soon reinforced by the detailed information provided by Virgil in *Inferno* 11.76–90). The next topographical and moral boundary is the steep cliff overhanging the pit of nether hell (*Inf.* 16–17). In its depths are punished the sins of fraud: as indicated in chapter 7, the topography convey the poet's fundamental message that fraud destroys the very fabric of society, making communication and trust impossible. Hence, there are no bridges, ladders, or stairs to connect upper with lower hell; and a similar device is used to underscore the terrible effects of treachery, the sin punished at the lowest level: only a monstrous being, a giant acting as an infernal crane (*Inf.* 31.112–45), makes it possible for Dante and Virgil to reach the ice of treachery and then Satan himself.

Purgatory

As already indicated, purgatory (if mentioned at all) was traditionally little more than an annex to hell, with the important distinction that its punishments were temporal and consequently they would cease either when a soul was purified, or at the end of time. In a fundamental study, Jacques Le Goff (1984, 337) counters the traditional view that Dante's location of purgatory on a mountain was entirely original. Instead, he claimed that of all the topographical imagery offered by previous descriptions of the other world, the poet chose "the one image that expresses Purgatory's true logic, that of the climb: a mountain."[6] The earliest account of purgatory in popular tradition, *St. Patrick's Purgatory* (c. 1180), placed it on a mountain in Connaught. Other instances show that there certainly existed purgatorial mountains before the *Comedy*. Morgan (1990, 158) has discovered a text by Étienne de Bourbon (c. 1260) that chose the Sicilian volcano Etna for the purgatorial site. However, she argues convincingly that Dante's mountain "has its origin not in any traditional iconography for purgatory, for there was none, but in the learned traditions of Eden and of Jerusalem" (1990, 160). The Garden of Eden is situated on the "holy mountain of the Lord" in Ezekiel 28.14, and a tradition going back to the fifth century underlay Walafrid Strabo's claim recorded in the twelfth-century *Glossa Ordinaria* that the Earthly Paradise was "in the midst of the Ocean . . . remote from our region, on a high site, reaching almost to the circle of the moon" (Morgan 1990, 160–61). It was probably this tradition, supported by Bede and Rhabanus Maurus, that led Dante to place purgatory on the slopes of the Mountain of Eden, which he situated in the ocean of the Southern Hemisphere at the antipodes to Jerusalem.[7]

Although the concept of some form of purification after death goes back at least as far as St. Augustine, purgatory was first authoritatively defined in a letter of 1254 by Pope Innocent IV, and it only received official recognition in Dante's own lifetime, at the Second Council of Lyons in 1274. However, in an attempt

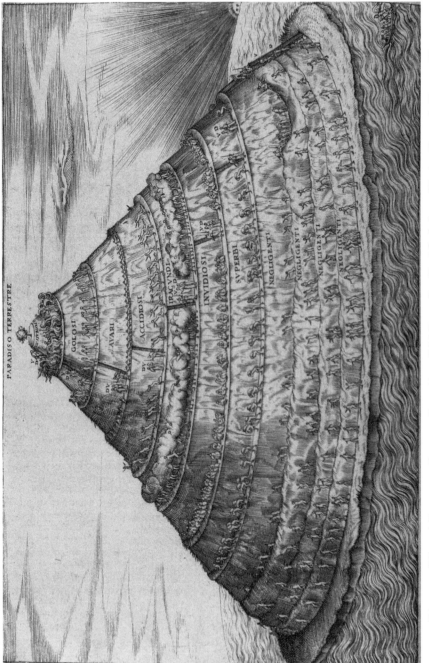

Diagram of Dante's Purgatory, *Dante con l'espositione di M. Bernardino Daniello da Lucca* (Venice: Pietro da Fino, 1568). Reproduced from the original held by the Department of Special Collections of the University Libraries of Notre Dame.

to resolve differences between Roman and Orthodox teachings, no mention was made of the actual location of purgatory. This omission certainly allowed Dante scope for his creative fantasy. The author of the *Comedy* was in fact the first to place purgatory next to the Earthly Paradise, thus creating a clear physical, geographical link between the two essential episodes in human history: the creation of humankind in Eden and its redemption through Christ's crucifixion at its antipodes, Golgotha, which made possible the purification of souls on the mountain with Eden at its summit, prior to their ascent to the heavenly paradise. Thus, the hour of Christ's death on the cross—the ninth hour—meant that it was three o'clock at night on the mountain of Purgatory, before the symbolic dawn of redemption.

In the undifferentiated visions of purgatory as an infernal annex, devils obviously had a role to play. In Dante's innovative purgatorial setting, however, angels replace the devils. Moreover, *Purgatorio* is original in its systematic approach to the purification of souls from their vices or tendencies to sin. In an extraordinary discourse extending over two cantos (*Purg.* 17–18), Virgil tackles a problem that was central to debates waged by medieval theologians, poets, and philosophers: the nature of love. Dante's Virgil here refutes the opinion that "love conquers all," held by the historical Vergil (*Eclogues* 10.69) and professed by such authorities as Ovid in antiquity and in the Middle Ages by Andrew the Chaplain and a host of protagonists in the literature of courtly love.[8] Instead, at the very center of the *Comedy*, the poet's belief in the supremacy of rational choice is asserted. In *Purgatorio*, Virgil stresses the fact that human beings are made for love (18.19) and that love is the root cause not only of all virtue but also of all sin (17.91–105). Love directed toward wrong objects, excessive love of secondary goods, inadequate love of the Supreme Good—in other words, the seven capital vices—all three forms of sinful love are purged or purified on the various terraces of the Mountain of Purgatory. This process of transformation is new in Dante, who "took what was popularly imagined as an upper chamber of hell and turned it into an extended passage to heaven" (Hawkins 1999, 254–55).

Before entering purgatory proper, however, the travelers pass through an area that is entirely Dante's invention. Just as hell is preceded by a vestibule (*Inf.* 3), which is the poet's original creation, so purgatory is preceded by an extensive region, known as antepurgatory.[9] The idea that certain categories of souls cannot immediately begin the process of purgation may possibly have its origin in a line of Vergil describing those who "put off atonement for sin until death's late hour" (*Aen.* 6.569). Certainly all the souls found in antepurgatory had been guilty, in various ways, of the sin of negligence. It is only in the tenth canto (cf. *Inf.* 9–10) that the travelers finally pass through the gate into purgatory proper. Once they begin their ascent, the climb becomes less and less toilsome as they make their way up, from terrace to terrace. Indeed, Virgil tells the pilgrim

(*Purg.* 4.88–94) that when the climb feels as easy as if he were a boat floating downstream, he will in fact have completed the process of purgation.

As indicated, an essential characteristic of purgatory is the fact that it is a temporal state, unlike hell and paradise. It will therefore cease at the Last Judgment, after which there will remain only the eternal states of separation from or union with God. The poet underscores this idea in two ways: by employing the temporal sequence of alternating day and night, and by describing the pilgrim's dreams on each of the three nights spent on the mountain. Since purgation is a cooperative process, requiring not only human will but also divine grace, darkness—the absence of God's light—signifies a moment of enforced stasis and sleep (*Purg.* 7.43–60). The pilgrim's three dreams (*Purg.* 9.13–33; 19.1–33; 27.94–114), each introduced by the phrase *Ne l'ora che* (At the hour when), all contain elements regarding matters of immediate and past concern, but they also in various ways point to his destination at the top of the mountain, the Earthly Paradise. The first dream emphasizes the divine aid that comes to him through the figure of an eagle (in the dream) and St. Lucy (in reality); the second, the dangers inherent in the love of secondary goods; the third, the joys of Eden.[10]

Paradise

The word "paradise" derives from an ancient Iranian word denoting a royal park. It passed into Hebrew with the meaning of "garden" and was used to signify the Garden of Eden or Earthly Paradise. By New Testament times the word had acquired three distinct meanings: a garden, the Earthly Paradise, and a celestial paradise, the resting place for the righteous dead. The idea of paradise as a garden with an eternal springtime (where no peasant would have to toil) is found in some popular descriptions of the world beyond the grave. However, the urban revival of the eleventh and twelfth centuries made the vision of "the holy city of Jerusalem," bejeweled and made of pure gold (Apoc. 21.10–25), particularly welcome as indicating heaven, especially in contrast to the cramped, malodorous reality of earthly towns and cities.[11] It was an image exploited in their preaching by the new mendicant orders, which were particularly influential, since "wherever there was a town there were friars; and without a town there were no friars" (Southern 1990, 286). For many, the grandeur of a celestial city came to replace the natural simplicity of Eden. The *Apocalypse of Paul,* in which the "urbanization of Paradise is pushed to the limit," was now seen to conflate the two elements, since the Garden and its four rivers are found within the walls of its heavenly City (Le Goff 1992, 266 n. 25). In a similar vein, Gherardesca (1210–69), a woman tertiary of the Camaldolese order, gave a detailed

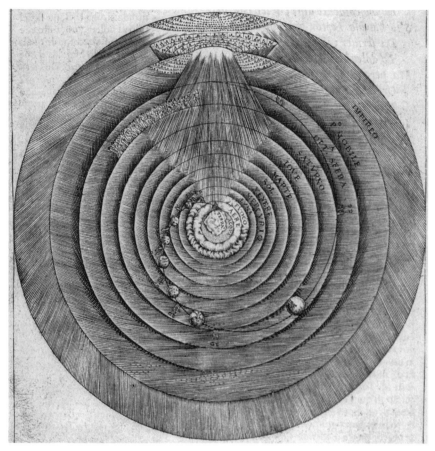

Diagram of Dante's Paradise, *Dante con l'espositione di M. Bernardino Daniello da Lucca* (Venice: Pietro da Fino, 1568). Reproduced from the original held by the Department of Special Collections of the University Libraries of Notre Dame.

description of heaven seen as a city-state with a vast parklike territory. This had an immediate and obvious appeal for a northern Italian audience, familiar with the city-state and its surrounding *contado:* "For them the city held the good life. There one could escape the oppression of hunger, cold, and darkness" (McDannell and Lang 1988, 76).

However, most theologians found such imagery far too terrestrial, in part because the ancient underworld's binary horizontal scheme (left → torment; right → happiness) had been replaced by Christianity's vertical opposition, with a subterranean hell opposed to a celestial paradise. In the thirteenth century, influenced by the rediscovery of Aristotle and Ptolemy, many accepted their theory that the earth, instead of being flat, was a fixed sphere situated at the center of the universe. This was the model used by Dante in his *Convivio, Comedy,* and *Questio de aqua et terra.* Each of the seven moving celestial bodies was set in its own sphere, with the "fixed" stars in an eighth, outer sphere. An absolute divide in the cosmos was marked by the sphere of fire. Fire, the lightest of all elements, was held to rise naturally toward its "home," a sphere located just below the orbit of the moon. The sublunary world was characterized by change and imperfection. However, everything in the moon and above was unchanging and motion was of the perfect kind, namely circular. Motion was imparted to the universe through the ninth heavenly sphere or Primum Mobile, while Aristotelian physics explained motion as the result of a force applied to what would otherwise be a stationary body. This led to the belief in an unmoved and unmoving Prime Mover, the source of all motion, which moved things through love (*Metaphysics* 12.7.1072b.3–4). The Primum Mobile was thus moved by its love for God and was held to communicate motion to the rest of the universe. This love of God is, as Dante puts it in the last line of his Christian epic, "the love that moves the sun and the other stars" (*Par.* 33.145).[12]

The belief that everything in the created universe had its proper place extended, of course, to human beings, who were seen as exiled on earth from their heavenly home or *patria.* As Beatrice explains to Dante in a grand cosmic sweep in *Paradiso* 2, every part of God's creation is endowed with an instinctual drive that impels it "through the great sea of being" toward its appointed goal (ll. 109–20).[13] Now that the pilgrim is freed of all impediment (the weight of sin, eliminated in purgatory) he *naturally* rises up in a providential return to his maker (ll. 136–41). The creature instinctively loves its Creator: it naturally desires to return to the source of all happiness (*Purg.* 16.85–90). Or, as Augustine wrote in his *Confessions* (13.9):

> In your gift we rest; there, we enjoy you. Our rest is our true place. Love lifts us up to that place . . . In your good pleasure lies our peace [cf. *Par.* 3.85]. Our body with its weight strives toward its proper place. Weight does not

tend downward only, but to its proper place. Fire rises up, a stone sinks down . . . Things out of their proper place are restless . . . My weight is my love: by this love am I borne wherever I am carried. By your gift, we are enkindled and borne aloft . . . your good fire enkindles us and propels us upward, to the peace of Jerusalem.

So, Dante rises up with Beatrice through the various heavenly spheres: Moon, Mercury, Venus, Sun, Mars, Jupiter, Saturn, the Fixed Stars, Primum Mobile, and—finally—the Empyrean, the true heaven. This heaven of "light and love" (*Par.* 27.112), unlike the Empyrean of the Schoolmen (for whom it was the outermost of the concentric heavenly spheres), is immaterial: it exists outside of both space and time. It is the "heaven of divine peace" (*Par.* 2.112), for it is the abode of God and the blessed, whose desire for union with their Creator is utterly satisfied (*Par.* 4.28–36). In a miraculous terzina (*Par.* 30.40–42), Dante describes the nature of the Empyrean Heaven, situated beyond the physical universe, as consisting of

> luce intellettüal, piena d'amore;
> amor di vero ben, pien di letizia;
> letizia che trascende ogne dolzore.

———

intellectual light, full of love; love of true good, full of joy; joy that transcends all sweetness. [Note the form *dolzore* (Italian *dolcezza*), redolent of the sweetness experienced by the lover in Provençal poetry.]

The poet uses every poetic means at his disposal to convey his message, weaving it around the key words—love *(amor),* light *(luce),* and happiness *(letizia)*—and, with a technique reminiscent of the troubadours' *coblas capfinidas,* placing *amor* and *letizia* at the end of a line and at the beginning of the next: *amore/amor; letizia/letizia.* This light is no physical phenomenon but the *lumen gloriae,* a celestial light that makes God visible to his creatures and thus fuels both the love and the beatitude of the blessed.

"The earth was still a formless void, and darkness covered the face of the abyss . . . Then God said, 'Let there be light'; and there was light. And God saw the light, that it was good" (Gen. 1.2–4). Light is the physical manifestation of beatitude in Dante's *Paradiso.* Hell, on the other hand, is a place devoid of all light (*Inf.* 5.28), although Aquinas insisted that there was nevertheless a modicum of light in hell, in order that the damned should perceive all the things that tormented them (*S. Th.* 3. *Suppl.* 97.4, resp.). In Dante's purgatory, light reveals the most beautiful colors and enhances natural phenomena found on earth. In *Paradiso* 28.16–39, God is first seen as a laser-point of blinding light, about which circle the nine angelic orders. Thus, Dante's ascent through the various physical heavens or spheres is accompanied by a constant increase in light, taxing to its utmost the imagination of the poet who declared at the very beginning that the intensity of light was such that it seemed as though God had placed a second sun in the heavens (*Par.* 1.61–63). The opening lines of *Paradiso* declare that God's *glory* or presence is manifest throughout the universe, which is more or less resplendent with beauty and light in its various parts, according to their receptivity. Indeed, for many familiar with the symphony of light and color found in Gothic cathedrals, light and beauty were synonymous, for, as Grosseteste opined, "light is beautiful in itself . . . its nature is simple and all things are like to it. Wherefore it is integrated in the highest degree and most harmoniously proportioned and equal to itself: for beauty is a harmony of proportions." St. Bonaventure went so far as to declare that "by their greater or lesser participation in light, bodies acquire the truth and dignity of their being."[14] Light, physical and metaphysical, is therefore a manifestation of goodness, joy, and beatitude; light is both an expression of divine beauty and its reflection in the universe.[15]

The poem's demography

Statistics regarding the population of Dante's three realms vary. However, we may note that there are nearly 600 named "characters" in the *Comedy* (far more than any comparable work apart from Ovid's *Metamorphoses*).[16] About 250 of these are from Dante's own times or the recent past, another 250 from the classical period, and about 80 from the Bible. Curtius quotes the great historian Robert Davidsohn's claim that of the 79 damned souls in *Inferno,* 32 were Florentines and 11 Tuscans. In *Purgatorio,* the pilgrim finds only 4 Florentines and once more 11 Tuscans, "in Paradise but two Florentines" (Curtius 1953, 366). Unfortunately for Davidsohn and Curtius, the last count is quickly disproved; there are at least four Florentines found among the blessed: Beatrice, Piccarda Donati, as well as Cacciaguida and his mother (*Par.* 16.35). These statistics point to one of the sublime paradoxes of Dante's poem: its universality—its message for the whole of humankind—grounded in the peculiar conditions prevailing in the Italian peninsula in the year 1300. So, in *Inferno* 32–33, the ice of nether hell appears to be populated by Tuscans. Only 2 non-Italians are identified: Mordred, condemned for treachery against his uncle (*Inf.* 32.61–62), King Arthur; and that arch-traitor of the Middle Ages, Ganelon (*Inf.* 32.122), Roland's stepfather.

Bergin (1970, 20–21) observes that the population is "less dense" as we ascend through the universe: he finds a total of 162 identifiable figures in *Inferno,* 77 in *Purgatorio,* and 72 in *Paradiso.* The decline is even more striking if we limit the count to characters who speak: 50 in *Inferno,* 38 in *Purgatorio,* and 23 in *Paradiso* (counting the synthetic eagle as six). Delmay (1986, vii–xix) gives a different count, a grand total of 364 personages (including 31 nonhuman figures, devils, angels, and others that cannot be identified), as follows:

Inferno: 64 (speaking) + 146 (silent) = 210
Purgatorio: 41 (speaking) + 25 (silent) = 66
Paradiso: 23 (speaking) + 65 (silent) = 88

The longest speaking part in *Inferno* is Ugolino's (*Inf.* 33: 72 lines), considerably shorter than Justinian's (the whole of *Par.* 6: 142 lines) and those of other celestials, such as St. Thomas (e.g., *Par.* 11: 121 lines), St. Bernard (*Par.* 32: 126 lines), and of course Beatrice, who speaks often in the first thirty cantos of *Paradiso.*

All these statistics are clearly of limited value, although they do give some idea of the wealth of the poet's imagination, and they also reflect the common belief that hell was far more densely populated than heaven. This point is underscored in two key places in the poem: on the first terrace of purgatory, where the angel laments that few souls now undertake the process of purification, although humanity is in fact created to fly up toward God (*Purg.* 12.94–96); and in the celestial rose of the blessed, where Beatrice points out that the seats of the elect are almost full (*Par.* 30.130–32).[17]

Classification of the poem's *dramatis personae*

The extraordinary range of characters presented in the *Comedy* is a prominent feature of Dante's poem, and one that clearly inspired both Giovanni Boccaccio in his *Decameron* and Honoré de Balzac, when the latter chose the title *La Comédie Humaine* for his novels depicting French society from 1799 to 1848.[18] However, no one can rival the medieval poet in his chronological range, which extends from the creation of Adam through the whole of history down to 1300 and beyond, with a cast of characters taken from the Bible, from the Greco-Roman classics, and from history. It must be stressed that while these labels are useful for modern readers, for Dante and his contemporaries biblical characters were regarded as historical figures, as were many of the fictional or mythological characters of classical literature. As well as obvious cases such as Vergil's Aeneas and Dido, it seems likely that for the author of the *Comedy* Orpheus possessed historical reality (*Inf.* 4.140); and Dante even claims that the struggle between Hercules and the giant Antaeus took place "in Africa, according to the written evidence" (*Conv.* 3.3.8).

The most exhaustive analysis of the inhabitants of the other world in both popular vision literature and Dante is that of Morgan (1990), from which the following information is largely taken. Only biblical figures such as patriarchs and prophets are found in the apocryphal accounts (such as the *Apocalypse of Baruch*), which usually place them in paradise. After St. Augustine (d. 430) and St. John Chrysostom (d. 407), hell figured more prominently as the destination not only for infidels but also for sinful, unrepentant believers. In the Carolingian era, accounts of the other world have a political emphasis, while even Church leaders are now condemned: "Walafrid describes Bishop Adalhelm suffering alongside Charlemagne" (Morgan 1990, 52). In the eleventh century, the spotlight shifts from well-known *exempla* to otherwise unknown individuals or collectivities. The visions recorded in the twelfth century (e.g., *Vision of Tundale*) offer for the first time a combination of all these elements as well as distinctive individual portraits.[19]

Contemporary figures

From Morgan's analysis, it is clear that Curtius was wrong in his assertion (frequently repeated by other scholars) that the poet's drawing upon characters from contemporary history constitutes "the most impressive and most fertile innovation which Dante's genius incorporated into the antique and medieval heritage" (Curtius 1953, 365). In fact, "the *Comedy* contains a lesser, not greater, proportion of contemporary characters than the visions" (Morgan 1990, 57). Where Dante is innovative is in his placement of popes in hell. Beside one "historical" pope (Anastasius II, 496–98, condemned as a heretic in *Inf.* 11.8–9), of the six popes who reigned during Dante's lifetime we find no fewer than three consigned to hell (Nicholas III, Boniface VIII, Clement V), with a fourth (Celestine V) condemned among the cowards rejected by both heaven and hell (*Inf.* 3.59–60).[20] Otherwise, contemporary society (1265–1300) provides emperors (Rudolph of Hapsburg, and Henry VII [d. 1313], for whom a seat is reserved in heaven); kings (eight, including Charles I of Anjou and Philip III of France); nobles (the largest category with well over fifty representatives, far more than in the visions); and churchmen, other than popes (ten, far fewer than in the visions); and commoners (over twenty), including a poet (Bonagiunta), musician (Casella), shoemaker (Asdente), philosopher (Siger), astrologer (Guido Bonatti), miniature-painter (Oderisi), forger (Mastro Adamo), and highwayman (Rinieri da Corneto).[21]

Biblical and classical figures

Of the forty-six biblical characters found in Dante's other world, forty-one are among the blessed in paradise, while five are consigned to hell (Nimrod, Potiphar's wife, Judas, Caiaphas, and Annas). Eighteen of these do not appear in extant previous visions of the other world. Dante departs from the tradition that biblical characters were to be found in the Earthly Paradise (awaiting Christ's Second Coming) by placing them in the Empyrean, where they enjoy the beatific vision.[22]

The inclusion of a large number of classical personages—some eighty-six in all—is (together with the damnation of popes) the most striking innovation in the *Comedy*.[23] When, rarely, mythological characters do appear in the preceding vision literature (e.g., Vulcan in the *Vision of Tundale,* c. 1250), they are ones who have been transformed into monsters by the popular imagination. In Dante's poem, the majority are found in limbo (a total of fifty-one souls, despite Augustine's authoritative condemnation of even the most illustrious pagan Romans); another thirty-one are in various circles of hell; Cato and Statius are in purgatory, destined for salvation; Trajan and Ripheus are found in paradise. Statistics, however, cannot give any idea of the extent of Dante's originality in placing a pagan suicide, Cato, as the guardian of that most Catholic realm, purgatory, and in choosing Vergil, a pagan poet, to be his guide through both hell and purgatory.[24]

Historical figures

With the proviso stated regarding the fluidity of what constituted history for Dante, we may now turn to the sixty-three historical personages mentioned in the *Comedy.* In previous visionary literature, historical figures were nearly always saints. In the *Comedy,* canonized saints are of course found in paradise (e.g., Lucy, Benedict, and Bernard), but they form an exiguous minority.[25] Instead, Dante's paradise is populated chiefly with historical figures, and part of the poem's originality consists in the large number of individuals drawn from the past: 21 percent of its population is made up of historical personages, as opposed to 7 percent in the visions. As one would expect, churchmen and theologians are well represented (including Archbishop Ruggieri degli Ubaldini among the traitors in hell and Pope Martin IV among the ex-gluttons in purgatory). A category without precedent, however, is composed of figures chosen from the medieval French *chansons de geste:* Ganelon, the traitor already mentioned, who is imprisoned in the ice of Antenora; Roland, Rainouart, William of Orange, alongside the celebrated leader of the First Crusade, Godefroy de Bouillon

(d. 1100), and other warrior spirits in the cross of the Heaven of Mars (*Par.* 18.43–48). Sovereigns had figured in previous visions (Charlemagne, King Ae-thilbealdus of Mercia, King Ludovic). Dante's political vision not only places Charlemagne in heaven and tyrants in hell (*Inf.* 12), but includes a large group of contemporary rulers among the negligent princes in antepurgatory (*Purg.* 7–8). The poet celebrates Justinian's achievements in *Paradiso* 6, exalts the just rulers in *Paradiso* 18–20, and grants pre-eminence to King Solomon in *Paradiso* 10.109–14 and 13.103–8. A unique category bears witness to a relatively new social phe-nomenon, the existence of a class of persons dedicated to intellectual pursuits but unconnected with the monasteries and without revenues from land, which appeared with the rapid development of urban life in the twelfth century.[26] Brunetto Latini, who taught the young Dante "how man makes himself eter-nal" (*Inf.* 15.82–87) and was the Florentine pioneer "in the development of early civic humanism" (Davis 1984, 176), is an outstanding representative of this new category.

A majority (59 percent) of the historical personages are in paradise; 30 per-cent are in hell. Dante was a far sterner judge of his contemporaries, however, of whom no less than 53 percent are condemned to hell and only 8 percent are in paradise (Morgan 1990, 60). The percentages will of course be different after the Last Judgment, once purgatory will have ceased to exist. Nevertheless, the imbalance will remain: ultimately 70 percent of the historical characters will dwell in paradise and 30 percent in hell; and, although 47 percent of characters from Dante's own times will be saved, 53 percent will be damned.

Useful and illuminating as it is, such an analysis cannot convey the manifold ways in which the poet invests so many members of his numerous cast with a concrete reality. The *Monk of Eynsham* (c. 1196) offers more characters (twenty-nine) than any other vision prior to the *Comedy*. Dante offers the reader some three hundred (see note 16), with twenty-four individuals named and presented in the Heaven of the Sun alone. But what makes his Christian epic unforget-table is its immense stylistic range, matching the polyphony of Dante's po-etic language. If ever it was true to say that language reveals the person, then we may claim that probably no other writer can rival Dante's ability to evoke a complex, lifelike personality with amazing verbal economy. The most cele-brated character in the *Comedy,* one that has inspired countless readers, musicians (Tchaikovsky, Zandonai), and artists (Ingres, Rodin), as well as other writers (Leigh Hunt, D'Annunzio), is found in the fifth canto of *Inferno,* often referred to as the canto of Francesca da Rimini. Yet, under the spell of the poet's dra-matic genius, few ponder the fact that Francesca occupies only the second half of the canto, or that Dante has given us not a mere sketch but an unforget-table, fully realized portrait of a noblewoman with a tragic flaw that seals her damnation in the space of fewer than two hundred words. Indeed, Francesca's whole being is encapsulated in three *terzine* (*Inf.* 5.100–108), each beginning with the word *Amor*. Even more concise and just as revealing is the first exchange between the pilgrim and Farinata degli Uberti, the great Ghibelline leader, damned among the heretics. Farinata's first question—"Who were your ancestors?" (*Inf.* 10.42)—already reveals his obsession with politics. Five words (*"Chi fuor li maggior tui?"*) tell us that Farinata, unlike his neighbor Cavalcante, is not interested in the astonishing fact that a living man is journeying through hell. The pilgrim's speech tells him that here is a fellow Florentine. He is not at all interested in Dante the individual. Instead, his sole concern is to place a political label on the stranger. And Farinata's supreme egotism is revealed in line 47, when he replies that Dante's family had been greatly hostile *"to me* and to my family and to my party" (my emphasis), ten words that sum up Farinata's whole *raison d'être:* self, clan, and political party. Vanni Fucci, the sacrilegious thief, is summed up in one obscene gesture (*Inf.* 25.1–3).

Never has Buffon's dictum been truer that the style reveals the person: *le style est l'homme même.* However, far from merely revealing Dante's own poetic personality, his protean style adapts itself to reveal the innermost recesses of the souls portrayed—and always with the utmost economy of means.

nine

Dante and classical antiquity

Major and startling innovations, such as the choice of the Latin poet Vergil as Dante's guide through both hell and purgatory and the inclusion in the *Comedy* of characters taken from classical antiquity, demonstrate the importance that ancient Roman literature, history, and mythology held for "the chief imagination of Christendom," as Yeats defined our poet.[1] We must, of course, remember that—although he hailed Aristotle (384–22 B.C.E.) as the philosopher par excellence, "the master of those who know," admired and honored by the *filosofica famiglia* in limbo (*Inf.* 4.131–33)—Dante, like so many in our contemporary world, could not read Greek, and, deprived of any direct acquaintance with Greek literature, he could only echo conventional tributes paid to Homer as the supreme poet the world had known (*Inf.* 4.94–96; *Purg.* 22.101–2). The following sections will examine Dante's relationship with major classical thinkers and writers.

Aristotle

After the closure of the philosophical schools at Athens by the emperor Justinian in the year 529, Greek thought was preserved in Byzantium and in the Arab world, especially by the Persian Avicenna (980–1037; *Inf.* 4.143) and the Andalusian Averroës (1126–98; *Inf.* 4.144), the latter acclaimed as "the commentator" for his attempts to salvage and explain "pure" Aristotelian doctrine. In fact, the rediscovery of Aristotelian thought, which evolved rapidly in the hundred years preceding Dante's birth, is one of the major landmarks in the intellectual history of Western Europe. Few thinkers have ranged so widely, influencing the study of logic, metaphysics (a term originating in the sequence of

Aristotle's writings), epistemology, physics, biology, meteorology, mathematics, psychology, rhetoric, dialectic, aesthetics, and politics. Above all, for Dante, Aristotle virtually invented ethics as a branch of philosophy while demonstrating the true nature of earthly happiness (*Mon.* 1.1.4).

By the time of Dante's birth in 1265, about fifty-five of the works ascribed to Aristotle had been translated into Latin. Some of the older translations were executed from Arabic texts; discrepancies and contradictions were gradually noted—as by Dante in *Convivio* 2.14.6–7, where he attributes these to errors made by the translators while accepting the version given in the *translatio nova* by William of Moerbeke (from the Greek, and used by Aquinas) as opposed to the reading in the *translatio vetus* by Gherardo da Cremona (from the Arabic, used by Albert the Great). For the first time, Christians were attempting to come to terms with a comprehensive philosophical system of pagan origin and to reconcile its naturalistic view of the universe with the Christian belief in Creation and its view of humanity's role on earth. The new university institutions played an essential role in this process of assimilation, with the University of Paris as its dynamic center. Although decrees prohibiting the reading of Aristotle's works were published in 1210 (Sens), 1215 (Paris), and 1231 (Gregory IX, *Parens scientiarum*), papal prohibitions lost their edge after Gregory's death in 1241. The new Dominican order—the first religious order to make study an essential part of its discipline—produced the two leading interpreters of Aristotelian thought: Albert the Great (d. 1280; *Par.* 10.98–99), whose stay in Paris (1240–48) marked a turning point in the history of Aristotelianism; and his brilliant pupil, Thomas Aquinas (d. 1274; *Par.* 10.82–138, 11.19–139, 13.31–142). Both influenced Dante profoundly: Albert, especially for his vindication of the validity of natural knowledge as distinct from revealed doctrine or supernatural wisdom.[2]

By 1265 Averroës's interpretation of Aristotle's *De anima* had won over some of the leading scholars in the faculty of arts at Paris (including Siger of Brabant, whom the poet introduces among the wise, in *Par.* 10.133–38). Averroës posited a single "potential" intellect, immortal, which was active in human beings during their lifetime but departed at their death: clearly, this was a heretical belief, since it denied the basic Christian doctrine of individual human immortality (*Conv.* 2.8.7–16; *Inf.* 10.13–15; *Purg.* 25.61–75). This belief also implied that the soul is not the substantial form of the human body. It was attacked most forcefully by Aquinas in 1270 *(De unitate intellectus contra Averroistas)* and officially condemned by the bishop of Paris in 1270 and again in 1277. The first thirteen years of Dante's life were thus a period of great ferment in the leading intellectual center of Christendom. In 1277, however, the condemnation in Paris of a hotchpotch of 219 propositions, including some put forward by Aquinas, meant that the golden age of Christian syncretism for which Albert and Thomas had worked so energetically was virtually over.[3]

In *Convivio* 2.12.2–4 Dante confessed that "some time after" Beatrice's death in 1290 his lack of philosophical training made it difficult for him to understand even Cicero's *De amicitia* and Boethius's *Consolation of Philosophy*. He therefore began the study of philosophy in earnest "where it was truly to be found, namely in the schools of the religious and the disputations of the philosophers" (*Conv.* 2.12.7), perhaps with the Franciscans at Santa Croce in Florence and almost certainly with the Dominicans at Santa Maria Novella, where weekly debates on philosophical and theological matters were open to laymen.[4] Dante probably also studied philosophy in Bologna, where committed Aristotelians such as Gentile da Cingoli were teaching in the prestigious lay university. He thus acquired an eclectic body of philosophical knowledge based on medieval interpretations of Aristotle, with significant Neoplatonic elements derived from such sources as Boethius, Pseudo-Dionysius, the *Liber de causis*, Avicenna, and Albert the Great.[5]

As we have seen, vindication of Aristotle as a teacher of ethics is to be found in the astonishing fact that the overall moral structure of Dante's Christian hell is grounded in Aristotle's threefold division of sinful behavior as set out in what Virgil, addressing Dante in *Inferno* 11.80, refers to as "your Ethics" (the work Aristotle dedicated to his son Nicomachus). In *Paradiso* itself, Aristotle is still hailed as "your master" (*Par.* 8.120: notice the plural "*maestro* vostro," echoing *Conv.* 4.23.8, *lo maestro della* nostra *vita*). Aristotle's inevitable limitations as a pagan thinker, solely dependent on the powers of human reason, are indicated in *Purgatorio* 3.34–36. Nevertheless, it was the Greek philosopher who had also demonstrated by philosophical reasoning the love of God felt by "the eternal beings." These philosophical proofs—together with the Bible and other religious authorities—reinforced Dante's love of the Christian God (*Par.* 26.25–48). Finally, and most significantly, it was Dante's passionate belief in the intellectual and political unity of humankind that led the poet of the *Comedy* to invent an Aristotelianized Virgil, whose task it was to lead the pilgrim to Eden—thereby illustrating the poet's conviction that it was the task of the Roman Empire and its emperor (heralded by Vergil in his *Aeneid*) to lead humanity to terrestrial beatitude ("figured in the earthly paradise") by following the teachings of (Aristotelian) philosophy and dispensing justice (cf. *Mon.* 3.16.7–8).

Vergil / Virgil

Dante's choice of Vergil as his Aristotelianized guide has been discussed in chapter 6.[6] It was from Vergil that Dante claimed to have derived the beautiful style that had brought him honor—especially through the use of the extended simile, which is virtually absent from his earlier poetry—although we realize that the Christian poet's stylistic register in his *Comedy* offers the broadest possible range, quite unlike the noble style sustained throughout Vergil's "high tragedy," as his great epic the *Aeneid* is described in *Inferno* 22.112–14.[7]

Virgil, the guide

Recent scholarship has rightly stressed Virgil's pagan limitations as displayed in Dante's poem.[8] We must never forget the obvious fact that the choice of a pagan poet to accompany a Christian through purgatory ran counter to all expectations in the medieval Christian universe. Poets were not infrequently condemned as liars; indeed, "whatever gold one might sift *ex sterco Vergilii,* excrement was still excrement . . . the practice of the literary art was, at least until Petrarch made it overwhelmingly glorious, . . . under continual attack from the secular and (especially) the regular clergy" (Hollander 1980, 49–50). How daring, then, to select as one's guide and teacher Vergil, a pagan seemingly hopelessly disqualified as a guide in all matters touching upon the Christian religion, above all in that quintessentially Catholic realm, purgatory!

Admittedly, Virgil acknowledges his ignorance of the Mountain (*Purg.* 2.61–63)—although, as we shall see, this "ignorance" is surprisingly qualified. Dante did not invent a previous journey through purgatory for his guide, as he did with the notorious Erichtho episode in order to justify Virgil's firsthand knowledge of hell (*Inf.* 9.22–27).[9] Nevertheless, this handicapped pagan continues to guide the pilgrim through this Christian realm, dispensing good counsel (*Purg.* 12.82–87) and even elucidating the moral order of purgatory, based on love as the root of all human actions, whether good or evil (*Purg.* 17.91–139). In this latter discourse, Virgil demonstrates a surprising knowledge of Christian doctrine for a pagan condemned to limbo.[10] He is granted an even more astonishing grasp of Christian theology when he correctly defines the mystery of the triune God in *Purgatorio* 3.36 as "one substance in three persons." He is also accorded the status of prophet in his forecast of the *veltro* that shall come to save humanity from the she-wolf of greed (*Inf.* 1.101–11).[11] Such inconsistencies are but part of the larger picture of Dante's complex portrayal of his beloved Virgil in the *Comedy,* where he is tragically doomed to be eternally separated from the God he helped to reveal to at least one other Latin poet, Statius (*Purg.* 22).

Clearly, Virgil's vision is myopic: it is limited to the mission with which he is entrusted by Beatrice, at the instigation of the Virgin Mary and St. Lucy (*Inf.* 2.97–114). He comes to save Dante from the savage wood and the three beasts, to lead him down through the pit of absolute evil and up the mountain of purification to the divine wood of Eden, where he crowns and miters the pilgrim (who is now "free" and "whole": *Purg.* 27.139–42) in a ritual that strikingly illustrates that humankind in Eden had no need of church or state, pope or emperor.[12] As a pagan, Virgil rightly confesses his limitations, as at *Purgatorio* 18.46–48, where he ends his definition of love with the caution that his explanation extends only as far as "reason can see"; for a superior understanding, Dante must await the coming of Beatrice, who will enlighten him on "matters of faith" (cf. *Purg.* 15.76–78). And, on reaching the Earthly Paradise, he tells his charge, "You have come to a place where I by myself can discern no further" (*Purg.* 27.128–29).

Virgil's failings are well illustrated. Whereas he commands obedience from the mythological guardians of the circles of incontinence, his first encounter with Christian devils at the gates of the City of Dis leads to a setback that leaves the pilgrim trembling with fear (*Inf.* 8.94–9.13). Virgil's impotent anger at the devils' resistance (8.121) before the entrance to the Devil's City must be compensated for by the rightful anger of heaven that overcomes all opposition (*Inf.* 9.33, 64–106).

Later, Virgil is deceived by the Malebranche—and taunted by a hypocrite for his gullibility (*Inf.* 23.142–44). As we have already noted, in *Inferno* 20 he is made to contradict or correct Vergil's tale concerning the foundation of Mantua. After being rebuked by Cato for loitering with the other spirits to listen to Casella's song (*Purg.* 2.112–33), Virgil resolves the pilgrim's doubts concerning the validity of *Aeneid* 6.376 by explaining that the souls in antepurgatory and purgatory rightly ask for help through the prayers of those on earth who are in a state of grace, although his poetic text was correct in stating that it was impossible for mortals to change the will of the gods, since "prayer was divorced from God" in the pagan world (*Purg.* 6.28–42). Here, the pilgrim's doubts are set to rest about the veracity of the Vergilian text with its apparent contradiction of Christian doctrine regarding the efficacy of prayer, while at the same time Dante stresses the tragedy of the human condition in pagan antiquity.

This dialectic of double-entry bookkeeping is hardly surprising where a pagan guide is concerned. Too much has perhaps been made of Virgil's pagan "blindness." Within purgatory proper—precisely where one would expect it to be at its most vulnerable—Virgil's limited competence is hardly ever questioned. It is Virgil who tells Dante to stop bending over to see the illustrations of pride punished (*Purg.* 12.76–77); it is he who finds the right ploy to make Dante walk through the wall of fire that still separates Beatrice and her lover (*Purg.* 27.35–54). It is Virgil who judges the pilgrim's will finally to be "free, upright, and whole," so that he may freely follow its promptings (*Purg.* 27.140–42). And, on no fewer than two occasions, Virgil is identified as the instrument of Dante's salvation, the one who saved him "from that life" signified by the dark wood (*Purg.* 23.118–20 and 30.51). As Robert Hollander (1991, 92–93) points out: "But Virgil must pay a fee to be included in Dante's poetic universe . . . Not only must he undergo eternal damnation and see his text mutilated as the Christian poet chooses, but the great pagan shade, now a Christian *après la lettre,* must consent with the vigor of a new convert." How far we choose to stress his inadequacies as a guide or oracle depends on our point of view.

It is surely necessary to bear in mind the driving force of Dante's narrative genius, which eschewed monotony. If the pilgrim's journey had been without obstacles, if he had been guided by an angel or by a saint (as in many twelfth-century visions), there would have been no *Comedy* as we know it, with its powerful sense of drama. As it is, Virgil's predicament introduces into the poem a sublime element of tragic pathos.

Virgil and the pilgrim

The relationship between the pagan guide and his Christian pupil is an evolving and highly dramatic one. At first, Virgil is the stern master (2.45 ff., 3.76 ff.). In *Inferno* 3.121, however, Virgil for the first time addresses Dante as *figliuol mio,* while Virgil himself is referred to as Dante's *dolce padre* at *Inferno* 8.110. Virgil's concern for his charge's welfare is compared to maternal love in *Inferno* 23.37–51, when he saves Dante from the Malebranche's clutches by clasping him to his breast "as his son, not as a companion." Finally, Virgil is hailed as *dolcissimo patre* (*Purg.* 30.50), the only person in the poem to be awarded this superlative, reminiscent of the *pater optime* used only once by Vergil, when Aeneas recounts the moment of pathos when he lost his own father, Anchises, "solace of every care and chance" (*Aen.* 3.708–11). The loss of his beloved Virgil causes Dante to weep, even as Augustine had shed tears over Dido's fate but "shed no tears for my own plight" (*Confessions* 1.13). Virgil is of course replaced by Beatrice, who upbraids Dante for his anguish caused by Virgil's sudden departure, warning him that he must save his tears for his own sins: "Dante, though Virgil depart, do not weep yet, do not weep yet, for you must weep for another sword" (*Purg.* 30.55–57). Here, the term "sword" itself recalls Augustine's foolish tears shed "for Dido, who surrendered her life to the sword," even as the pilgrim's own words "I know the signs of the ancient flame" (l. 48) are a literal translation of Dido's words as she feels love rekindled in her breast (*Aen.* 4.23: *adgnosco veteris vestigia flammae*). The intertextual web extends even further, to another of Vergil's works, the *Georgics,* to the tragic moment when Orpheus's severed head floating downstream calls out at the loss of his beloved: "Eurydice . . . ah, hapless Eurydice," while the riverbanks resound with the echo "Eurydice" (*Georgics* 4. 525–27). This repetition, which parallels Orpheus's lament (with the direct address *te, dulcis coniunx . . . te . . . te . . . te decedente canebat,* ll. 465–66), resounds with immense force and pathos in Dante's heartbroken cry:

> Ma Virgilio n'avea lasciati scemi
> di sé, Virgilio dolcissimo patre,
> Virgilio a cui per mia salute die'mi.
> > (*Purg.* 30.49–51)

———

But Virgil had left us bereft of himself, Virgil, sweetest father, Virgil to whom I had entrusted my salvation.

Readers cannot fail to be moved by the crescendo of feeling in "*Virgilio … Virgilio dolcissimo patre … Virgilio a cui per mia salute die'mi,*" whereby Virgil's thrice-repeated name is placed at the beginning of the last verse, which proclaims Virgil's providential mission to save Dante at the very moment of his return to hell. And the reiteration of Virgil's name is then paralleled by the threefold repetition of *piangere* in Beatrice's stern admonition that Dante (named here for the first and only time in the poem) has other, more urgent reasons to shed his tears:

> "Dante, perché Virgilio se ne vada,
> non *pianger* anco, non *piangere* ancora;
> ché *pianger* ti conven per altra spada."
> > (*Purg.* 30.55–57; my emphasis)

———

"Dante, although Virgil has departed, do not weep yet, do not weep yet; because you must weep for another sword."

Like Orpheus, Beatrice descends into the underworld to rescue Dante; unlike Orpheus, she is ultimately successful in her mission—thanks to Virgil, the pagan.

Vergilian echoes in the *Comedy*

As Virgil returns to everlasting, hopeless longing, his texts are exploited "with remarkable richness" by the Christian poet (Jacoff 1991a, 137). According to the latest count, Vergilian borrowings, quotations, and adaptations in the *Comedy* number almost four hundred. Their presence is initially overwhelming, with seventy possible Vergilian echoes in the first 707 lines of *Inferno* (Hollander 1993b, 248). Perhaps the most significant adaptation of a Vergilian text in the Christian epic is the use made of Vergil's *Fourth Eclogue* in *Purgatorio*

22.64–74, when Statius, the first-century author of the *Thebaid,* is made to ascribe to Vergil's influence not only his own worth as a poet but even his conversion to Christianity, after praising the *Aeneid* in lines containing a sequence of words placed in the emphatic rhyming position—*Purg.* 21.95, 97, 99: *fiamma–mamma–dramma*—that will be dramatically echoed in the passage describing Dante's severance from his beloved guide and companion, Virgil *(Purg.* 30.44, 46, 48: *mamma–dramma–fiamma).*

In *Purgatorio* 22.70–72, Statius explains that he had read Vergil's *Fourth Eclogue* as an unconscious prophecy of Christ's coming and the dawn of a new golden age, accompanied by Justice and a new "golden race"—an interpretation put forward by Lactantius, Constantine, Augustine, and Abelard, among others, especially of lines 5–10: "The great line of the centuries begins anew. Now the Virgin [Astraea or Justice] returns, the reign of Saturn returns; now a new generation descends from heaven on high . . . and a golden race springs up throughout the world!"[13] Furthermore, if Statius's conversion was due to Vergil's *Fourth Eclogue,* his very salvation from mortal sin was effected through his (profoundly personal) interpretation of two lines from the *Aeneid,* the poem to which he owed all his literary merit. As he tells Virgil, although he is purifying his soul on the same terrace as the avaricious Pope Adrian V, he was in fact guilty of the opposite excess, the sin of prodigality (cf. *Inf.* 7.40–45). However, after reading *Aeneid* 3.56–57, he repented of his sins.

The words Dante places in Statius's mouth are a notorious travesty of that Vergilian text, which had expressed horror at the treacherous murder of Priam's son Polydorus, committed by Polymnestor in order to seize the treasure Priam had placed in his safekeeping: "To what do you not drive the hearts of mortals, o accursed hunger of gold!" Dante, however, interprets this as "Why do you not *govern,* o sacred hunger of gold, the appetites of mortals?" (emphasis mine). In other words, *cogis* (you compel) and *sacra* (accursed) are given new meanings, utterly at variance with the Vergilian context. Scholars have argued endlessly about these contradictions. What should be evident is that Dante—who claimed to know the whole of the *Aeneid* by heart (*Inf.* 20.114)—could not possibly have misunderstood Vergil's condemnation of the murder committed, against the sacred laws of hospitality. Proof of this is the fact that "Polymnestor who killed Polydorus" is mentioned (*Purg.* 20.115) as one of the terrible examples of sins committed through avarice. Attempts to iron out the contradictions lead Sapegno and Petrocchi to adopt the reading "Per che" in *Purgatorio* 22.40 (with the unlikely meaning of "to what" or "through what devious channels," instead of the obvious "Perché?" = "Why?"), and to confer on the Italian *sacra* the meaning of "moderate." We should note that, despite Dante's polemical attitude toward riches, the idea of a "sacred" (i.e., moderate) hunger for gold fits in well with the idea of a golden age, while the early commentators had no difficulty in taking *sacra fame* as signifying virtue's golden mean (Shoaf 1978). Also relevant is the fact that, as the fourteenth-century commentator Francesco da Buti pointed out, authors in what we now term the Middle Ages would happily alter the meaning of quotations in order to suit their own purposes—not unlike Lewis Carroll's Humpty Dumpty's attitude toward semantics: "When I use a word . . . it means just what I choose it to mean—neither more nor less."[14] It is surely evident that Statius's readings of Vergil's text are highly personal ones, as he himself indicates in *Purgatorio* 22.38 with regard to *Aeneid* 3.56–57, if the word *intesi* (*quand' io intesi là dove tu chiame*) signifies "I understood / interpreted" the meaning of Vergil's passionate exclamation against the weaknesses of human nature (l. 39, *crucciato quasi a l'umana natura*). This use of the verb *intendere* with this meaning of "to understand [the deeper meaning]" is well attested in Dante's writings, and in this context it is also consonant with his understanding of poetic allegory as a hidden truth.[15]

The ways in which Vergil's text has been "corrected" in order to adapt and revise it in accordance with the *Comedy*'s Christian view of history and the human condition have been well analyzed by Hollander and Schnapp.[16] Schnapp, while recognizing the similarities between the meeting of Aeneas and his father, Anchises, in *Aeneid* 6 and that of Dante and his ancestor Cacciaguida at the center of *Paradiso*, emphasizes the need for "the missing master-signifier of the *Aeneid* and yet its secret protagonist, the cross of Christ"—so that, with the addition "of Christ's law of love . . . to the Anchisean representation of history, the contaminated elements fall away, and Vergil's text at last becomes complete" (Schnapp 1986, 27–28). Moreover, Cacciaguida's initial welcome *in Latin* to the pilgrim in *Paradiso* 15.28–30 (*"O sanguis meus . . . "* ["O blood of mine, o superabundance of God's grace, to whom—as to you—were the gates of heaven ever opened twice?"]) points to the heart of Dante's Christian rewriting of *Aeneid* 6 by fusing classical *pietas* and Christian piety, and replacing "the paralyzing riddles" of pagan antiquity with "the clear words and 'precise Latin' of Christian revelation" (Schnapp 1986, 149). As a result, in Dante's epic we find "a consistent identification of Virgil and his epic with conditions of hopelessness, incompletion, and loss, while the Christian poet and poem emerge as figures of hope, completion, and gain" (Schnapp 1991c, 155).

Virgil's tragic flaw

Clearly, Dante's invention of a Christian Statius, whose conversion and salvation were due not only to God's grace but also—and specifically—to messages found in Vergil's works, throws Virgil's plight into tragic relief. This is underscored by Statius's remark that Vergil had lit up the path for others (*Purg.*

22.67–69): "You did as one does who walks at night, carrying the light behind him yet does not help himself, but he enlightens those who follow." Here, with terrible irony, the Christian poet adds a further dimension to his beloved guide's tragic flaw: Virgil's lack of belief in the true God, whom he only glimpsed in hell (*Inf.* 4.53–54), so that he is condemned to hopeless frustration for all eternity "not for doing but for not doing" (*Purg.* 7.25). With even greater irony, the author of the *Comedy* included among God's elect one of the truly minor characters in the *Aeneid*, Ripheus, the eminently just Trojan, scarcely mentioned by Vergil (*Aen.* 2.339, 394, 426–28). Taking his cue from the latter verses, as well as a passage in Boethius (Scott 1989), Dante placed the pagan Ripheus in his paradise (*Par.* 20.67–72, 118–29) as evidence of his Christian God's love of justice and equity, as opposed to the callous indifference of Vergil's pagan gods *(dis aliter visum)*. So, the author of the *Aeneid* (*anima naturaliter Christiana* for Tertullian) is damned, while a lesser poet, Statius, and an otherwise unknown Trojan are saved!

At this point, we must surely come to realize that Virgil's greatness as a "living" character in the *Comedy* depends on his damnation. A happy ending, leaving Virgil forever in supernal bliss, would have reduced Dante's guide to the unidimensional figure of the traditionally omniscient angelic or saintly plenipotentiary.[17] Such an ending would also have impoverished the Christian poet's tragic vision of the glory that was pagan Rome, with its immense achievements starkly viewed against the finality of Christ's words (Mark 8.36): "For what will it profit a man to gain the whole world and yet lose his soul?" Dante's narrative genius understood the need for Virgil's brief moment of doubt and helplessness when faced with the spectacle of absolute evil before entering the Devil's City (*Inf.* 8–9), the need to make his pagan guide fallible at certain points in the action. On the other hand, as we have noted, Dante provides Virgil with knowledge of the Holy Trinity and of the charity displayed by the souls in heaven, as well as the unique topography of the Mountain of Purgatory (*Purg.* 4.88–96, 15.67–75, 17.127–39); he makes Virgil cite Genesis, in *Inferno* 11.106–8; and the pilgrim receives both hope and enlightenment from his pagan guide in Christian [ante]purgatory (*Purg.* 4.29–30), acknowledging him as his "teacher" (*dottore: Purg.* 18.2, 21.22, 24.143), and his "good master" *(il buon maestro)* even as late as *Purgatorio* 26.2.

But what is most surprising, as we have noted, is not the fact that the Christian poet pointed to deficiencies in his pagan guide, but that he should have dared to choose Virgil as his mentor through the Christian realm of purgatory. The only explanation for this totally unexpected role must lie in the fact that Vergil was for Dante above all the bard of the empire, who celebrated Rome's eternal destiny "in the first book of the *Aeneid*, when he says, speaking on God's behalf: 'To them—namely, the Romans—I set no limits either in space or time;

to them have I given empire without end'" (*Conv.* 4.4.11). It is worth repeating that, even as the emperor, assisted by the "teachings of philosophy" (*Mon.* 3.16.10–11), must lead humanity to the temporal happiness prefigured by the Earthly Paradise, so an Aristotelianized Virgil guides Dante to the Earthly Paradise situated on the summit of the Mountain of Purgatory. As Hawkins (1999, 209) has demonstrated, at the poem's center (*Purg.* 13–17), we also find "the bizarre phenomenon of an Augustinian Virgil" whose account of heavenly charity (*Purg.* 15.73–75) and his analysis of the ordering of love (*Purg.* 17.106–39) are in fact based on a passage from Augustine's *De civitate Dei* and *De doctrina christiana*—a debt all the more "outrageous" in that "Dante has given Augustine's description of the economy of heaven to the writer against whom Augustine more or less openly waxed polemical . . . a purveyor of pagan delusion."

Yet Virgil is also the historical Vergil, "honor and light" of other poets, to whose beloved *Aeneid* Dante devoted much study, and from whom he felt he had learned the art of great poetry (*Inf.* 1.82–87). However, that realism which reveals itself in memorable details also makes the poet face up to the consequences of his Christian faith and to portray with unerring dramatic skill the tragic limitations of ancient humanism with its blindness to the central event of universal history: Christ's redemption of humanity.[18] Yet when all is said and done, because Vergil's *Aeneid* was for Dante virtually the "bible of the empire" (Nardi 1983, 301), it had to be Virgil who rescued Dante from "that life" of corruption (*Purg.* 23.118–20); it had to be Virgil to whom Dante gave himself for his salvation (*Purg.* 30.51). Just as Dante's Virgil is now enhanced by possessing the virtues of the two great cultures of pagan antiquity—the Greek, which had taught the world philosophy and science, and the Roman, destined to govern the earth under the rule of law—even so, this purely human greatness is thrown into dramatic relief by the tragic pathos surrounding his damnation.

Ovid

Ovid's influence is second only to that of Dante's beloved Vergil, with some seventy-five passages from the *Comedy* listed by Moore (1896) as Ovidian citations or echoes—although the Oxford scholar was inclined to restrict Dante's knowledge of Ovid's writings to the *Metamorphoses* and the *Remedia amoris*.[19] If we accept a recent judgment that "no Roman poet can equal Ovid's impact upon western art and culture" (Hinds 1998, 512), it should come as no surprise to discover that Dante was fascinated by this gold mine of ancient mythology, as well as by the figure of the poet in exile.[20] As E. R. Curtius points out (1953, 18): "In the beginning of the *Metamorphoses,* the twelfth century found a cosmogony and cosmology which were in harmony with contemporary

Platonism. But the *Metamorphoses* were also a repertory of mythology as exciting as a romance. Who was Phaeton? Lycaon? Procne? Arachne? Ovid was the *Who's Who* for a thousand such questions." What is far more surprising is that the Christian poet Dante placed the one whom Chaucer in *The House of Fame* described as "Venus clerk, Ovyde" among the virtuous pagans in limbo—and that he continued to use Ovidian themes and images even to the end of his *Paradiso*. Without bowdlerizing Ovidian myth to the extent found in the (contemporaneous) *Ovide moralisé,* Dante omitted the scabrous details in the story of how Europa made herself a "sweet burden" (*Par.* 27.83–84) as well as Ganymede's ravishment to heaven, which is introduced as a parallel to the pilgrim's own experience of being carried aloft to the entrance of purgatory by St. Lucy (*Purg.* 9.19–60).

Indeed, the whole *Comedy* may be seen as a series of supernatural metamorphoses activated by God's justice.[21] In order to demonstrate the truth that divine justice inspires its earthly counterpart—justice dispensed by the emperor—in the Heaven of Justice (*Par.* 18.73–117) the final M (standing for MONARCHIA) of "DILIGITE IUSTITIAM QUI IUDICATIS TERRAM" (Love justice, you who rule the earth [Wisd. 1.1]) is metamorphosed by the divine artist into the head and neck of an imperial eagle. The Ovidian myth of Argus (*Met.* 1.622–723) is superseded by the vivifying metamorphosis of Christ on Mount Tabor (*Purg.* 32.64–81; Matt. 17.2).[22] Pier della Vigna's soul is divided from his body for all eternity and is imprisoned in a thorn bush, whose unnatural roots (*nove radici: Inf.* 13.73) testify to the metamorphosis *in malo* of Frederick II's logothete who had committed suicide,[23] while both *Purgatorio* and *Paradiso* illustrate the gradual metamorphosis of the human grub into an angelic butterfly, according to the striking image found in *Purgatorio* 10.124–26. The infernal metamorphoses of the thieves are explicitly intended to outdo both Ovid and Lucan (*Inf.* 25.94–102), for—as Dante points out—despite Ovid's virtuosity he had never imagined a transmutation whereby two forms (the Aristotelian term denoting the shaping of matter into its specific nature) were able to exchange their matter or bodily shapes. This boast is not so much "a temporary fall into a poetic of hubristic display" (Jacoff and Schnapp 1991, 10) as a proclamation of the superiority of the Christian poet's vision, aided by God's grace.[24] What had been revealed as through a glass darkly to the greatest poets of pagan antiquity is now made manifest to God's scribe in all its misery or glory. So, as Virgil, Dante, and Statius enter the Earthly Paradise, Virgil tells the pilgrim, "Those who in ancient times sang of the golden age and its happy state, perhaps, in their Parnassus, dreamed of this place. Here, humanity's root was innocent; here, perpetual spring and every fruit; this is the nectar mentioned by all."[25] The last three lines (*Purg.* 28.142–44) allude to essential ingredients in Ovid's description of the Saturnian golden age

(*Met.* 1.89–112: *sine lege fidem rectumque colebat . . . ver erat aeternum . . . iam flumina nectaris ibant*).

To return to the *Comedy* viewed as the Christian *Metamorphoses,* the opening lines of Ovid's poem (1–5) proclaim the poet's intention: "My mind is bent to tell of bodies changed into new forms. Ye gods, for you yourselves have wrought the changes, breathe on these my undertakings, and bring down my song in unbroken strains from the world's very beginning even unto the present time."[26] Might not these same words have been echoed or penned by the Christian poet who called on Apollo, Minerva, and the nine Muses to guide him—the new Jason (*Par.* 2.16–18, 33.94–96; cf. *Met.* 7.1 ff.)—in his heroic journey through uncharted waters? The Christian bard extends his scope from "the world's very beginning" to the end of the universe and of time itself, whilst Jason's quest for the Golden Fleece is itself transformed into the Christian's quest for union with God.[27]

In order to reach that goal, the pilgrim has to undergo a metamorphosis far beyond the human condition and beyond the scope of all language, however poetic, however powerful, since *Trasumanar significar* per verba / *non si poria* (*Par.* 1.70–71: It would be impossible to signify "transhumanization" in words). The Latin phrase *per verba* also points back to the greatest exponent of transformation, Ovid, already evoked in the comparison with Glaucus in the preceding lines (67–69; cf. *Met.* 13.898–968): "While gazing at her I underwent a change within as Glaucus did when he tasted the herb that made him a companion in the sea of the other gods," where the word for companion (*consorte,* literally "sharing the same fate") also evokes St. Peter's call to his fellow Christians to partake in the divine nature (2 Pet. 1.4: *divinae consortes naturae*). Yet the only *exemplum* Dante gives of this Christian metamorphosis is in fact the Ovidian myth (*Met.* 13.906–63) of the fisherman who was transformed into a pagan deity by eating miraculous sea grass. Just as the ultimate Christian *deificatio* of union with God cannot be adequately described *per verba*—not even through the language and poetic imagination of the ancient master of metamorphosis—so both the insanity and inhumanity of Athamas (responsible for the death of Ino and their two sons; *Met.* 4.512–30) and the overwhelming grief felt by Hecuba at the death of her children which caused her in her madness to "howl like a dog" (*Inf.* 30.20; cf. *Met.* 13.568–69) are declared to be less horrifying than the spectacles revealed by the depths of hell (*Inf.* 30.22 ff.).

Three Ovidian myths have a special relevance to Dante's own journey: those of the Argonauts, Phaëthon, and Icarus.[28] The originality of the poet's unique task is emphasized at the beginning of *Paradiso* (2.16–18), with a glancing reference to Jason and his companions, while at the very end of the poem (*Par.* 33.94–96) the ineffable experience of the beatific vision arouses in the pilgrim an amazement not unlike that experienced by the sea-god Neptune as he beheld for the first time the shadow of a ship, the *Argo*. Between the greatest human exploit of the ancient world and the divinely inspired audacity of the Christian poet, we find an interval of some twenty-five centuries, bisected by the central event of Christian history, the Incarnation. Ovid's tale of Phaëthon (*Met.* 2.19–328), who begged Apollo to prove his paternity by granting Phaëthon's wish to drive the chariot of the sun and who was then hurled to his death by Jupiter's thunderbolt in order to save the world from being incinerated, is evoked in *Inferno* 17.107–11, where Phaëthon is coupled with Icarus to describe the fear experienced by the pilgrim while on Geryon's back. The most significant reference, however, is the one contained in the opening of *Paradiso* 17, where Phaëthon is not named directly but cited as a warning to fathers not to grant a son's every request. Just as Phaëthon had gone to his mother, Clymene, to learn the truth about his father, so the pilgrim Dante now turns to Cacciaguida for knowledge about his fate. However, "Instead of the erring Phaeton . . . on his catastrophic *mala via*, Dante will prove to be a triumphant Christian charioteer, a Phaeton made good, a Phaeton who may rightfully lay claim to the heavens" (Schnapp 1991a, 219). The parallel myth of Icarus's disastrous flight too near the sun (*Met.* 8.223–35; *Inf.* 17.109–11) reinforces the opposition between, on the one hand, the hubris of both Icarus and foolhardy *magnanimus Phaëthon* (*Met.* 2.111) and, on the other, Dante's own ascent above the sun to beyond the outermost limits of the universe, made possible only by God's grace and "that compassionate lady who guided my feathered wings to such a lofty flight" (*Par.* 25.49–50).

In his *Convivio,* Dante had set up a surprising equation: pagan divinities = Plato's Ideas/Aristotle's Intelligences = the angelic movers of the heavenly bodies, although the ancients had not seen the truth "because of either defective reasoning or defective teaching" (*Conv.* 2.4.8). Not only did the Christian poet accept the fundamental reality of the pagan pantheon, but he used monstrous figures from mythology (with a sprinkling of Christian devils) to act as Lucifer's subalterns in hell. Dante never followed the medieval custom of turning Apollo, Mercury, and Vulcan into Satan's henchmen. Indeed, although St. Benedict speaks of the worship accorded to Apollo at Monte Cassino as part of the "evil cult that seduced the world" (*Par.* 22.45), "nowhere, not even in this passage of *Par.* XXII, does Dante suggest, as had so many Christian writers, that Apollo is . . . a demon" (Bemrose 1983, 135). In fact, at the very beginning of *Paradiso* (1.13–36), the poet implores "good Apollo"—that same Holy Spirit that had inspired the biblical scribes (*Mon.* 3.4.11; 2 Pet. 1.21)—"for this last labor to make me the vessel of your power," a phrase that combines in exemplary fashion a Vergilian echo *(Eclogues* 10.1: *Extremum hunc, Arethusa, mihi concede laborem)* with a Christian reference to St. Paul as God's vessel, chosen to broadcast his message to all the peoples of the earth (Acts 9.15; cf. *Inf.* 2.28). The poet then beseeches Apollo to enter into his breast "and inspire, as when you drew Marsyas forth from the sheath of his limbs" (*Par.* 1.19–21). The divine afflatus *(spira tue)* is the same inspiration that Dante claims for his poetry as God's scribe in *Purgatorio* 24.52–54:

> E io a lui: "I' mi son un che, quando
> Amor mi spira, noto, e a quel modo
> ch'e' ditta dentro vo significando."[29]

———

> And I to him: "I am one who, when Love inspires me, notes down and then I express what he dictates within me."

On the other hand, the reference to Marsyas is at first sight a puzzling one. In Ovid (*Met.* 6.382–400), we read of Marsyas, who took up the flute discarded by Athena and challenged Apollo, god of music and the arts, to a contest judged by the Muses. Apollo won, and—in one of the most sadistic punishments ever inflicted by a pagan deity on a mortal—Ovid describes how the god has Marsyas tied to a tree and flayed alive, so that as Marsyas "screams, his skin is stripped off the surface of his body, and he is all one wound: blood flows down on every side, the sinews lie bare . . . you could count the entrails as they palpitate, and the vitals showing clearly in his breast" (ll. 387–91). What is important here is the fact that "Apollo's cruel act is unusually described by the [Christian] poet . . . as the pulling off of Marsyas from his flesh . . . as if the god were lifting the mortal out of himself" (Chiarenza 1975, 136). Dante is of course addressing Apollo, not Marsyas. He is calling on the *Christian* God of poetry *(O buono Apollo)* to inspire him, to play the flute in his stead, to take over at this crucial stage in his journey: *spira tue*. To signify the effect of such divine inspiration, he has recourse once again to an Ovidian myth—but he alters it radically, so that it becomes an image of *transcending* mortality, for he tells us that Marsyas had been *pulled* out of his bodily flesh (and thus liberated from his earthly "prison" and its limitations). Rather than a terrible punishment or an image of death, the myth of Marsyas is here refashioned to point to the pilgrim's own transcending of his mortal state, an experience Dante encapsulated in the word he invented, *trasumanar*.

Another example of the Christianization (or correction) of Ovidian myth is found at the climactic moment when the pilgrim realizes that he will have to pass through a wall of fire in order to enter Eden and be reunited with Beatrice. Just as Pyramus and Thisbe had been separated by a wall between their houses in Babylon, so Virgil tells Dante, *"tra Bëatrice e te è questo muro"* (*Purg.* 27.36). However, whereas the sensual love of the Babylonian lovers led to a double suicide at the foot of a mulberry tree, whose fruit was metamorphosed from white to the color of blood (l. 39), Beatrice's lover will be shown the path to eternal life and bliss, once he has passed through the purifying fire and is reunited with the Beatrix he had lost. Moreover, understood through the lens of biblical exegesis, the mulberry tree "evokes the Cross . . . To receive the mulberry is to be inflamed not by sensual desire but by the blood of self-sacrifice, by death to the self in Christ. It is to kill the serpent of *concupiscentia* with a leaf from the sacred tree/cross, and to re-enter the Garden of eternal life" (Moevs 2000, 10).

Likewise, the tragic sacrifice of innocent Hippolytus, banished from Athens, and his subsequent reincarnation as the unrecognizable Virbius (*Met.* 15.497–546) could be understood by Christian interpreters as a *figura* of Christian resurrection. In the context of Cacciaguida's prophecy (*Par.* 17.37–99), this image of death and rebirth points to Dante's martyrdom of exile from Florence, as well as to his journey from hell to heaven and eternal life. As such, the image of Hippolytus is opposed to that of Phaëthon, evoked in the opening lines of the same canto, for "in a Christianized reading, one myth is the story of damnation, the other of salvation" (Chiarenza 1983, 145).

In Dante's program of syncretizing pagan beliefs and Christian dogma, Ovid is quoted in *Convivio* 4.15.8 as evidence that the human race is descended from a single individual (*Met.* 1.78): to believe otherwise is "quite false according to the philosopher [Aristotle], according to our Faith which cannot lie, according to the law and ancient belief of the Gentiles" (*Conv.* 4.15.5). In *Purgatorio* 25.22–24, another Ovidian myth is offered as a "realistic" explanation for the process whereby the disembodied souls of the penitent gluttons can experience hunger. The pilgrim is puzzled by the sight of spirits that had appeared on the sixth terrace of the mountain, as emaciated as the starving Jews during the siege of Jerusalem (*Purg.* 23.28–30). He asks Virgil how it is possible to waste away in purgatory, where there is no physical need for food. Before he hands the question over to Statius for a sustained, scientific answer, Virgil tells Dante (*Purg.* 25.22–24) that it will be enough for him to recall the fate of Meleager (as recounted by Ovid in *Met.* 8.451–525), whose body "was consumed when the firebrand was consumed," in order to understand that bodies can be affected by external causes—as the odor of fruit and of water torments the former gluttons (*Purg.* 23.34–36). Virgil's words to the pilgrim are clearly based on the assumption that what we refer to as "myth" possesses an ontological reality and thus the status of an authoritative *exemplum*. Indeed, the very structure of Dante's purgatory is based on *exempla* taken from the Bible, from history, and from myth: examples of pride punished (*Purg.* 12.25–63) include not only "historical" figures such as Saul, David, and Holofernes, but also—and placed on an equal, exemplary footing—Briareus and his fellow giants, Niobe, Arachne, and Alcmaeon, all taken from the Ovidian treasury. All in all, as J. H. Whitfield claims (1989, 18), "Dante is not only Ovid's finest customer, he is the chief celebrant of the fame, the dignity, the seriousness of Ovid. As a witness for the defence we shall hardly find his like in the whole of literature."[30]

Lucan

Virgil's presentation of the supreme poets of antiquity in *Inferno* 4.88–90 ends with *"l'ultimo Lucano."* Like his uncle Seneca, Lucan (39–65 C.E.) was born in Spain, but he studied at Rome and Athens. He was first encouraged by Nero, then disgraced and forced to commit suicide. His *Pharsalia* or *De bello civili* is the greatest Latin epic after the *Aeneid*. Its ten books deal with historical events during the fateful years 49–48 B.C.E., beginning with Caesar's crossing of the Rubicon and ending, unfinished, with Caesar in Alexandria. Its three protagonists are Caesar, Pompey, and Cato the Younger, "an impossibly virtuous specimen of the Stoic saint" (Anderson and Hardie 1998, 424). This anti-*Aeneid* offers a stark and deliberate contrast to Vergil's vision of Rome's imperial destiny, concentrating instead on the destruction of Roman liberty and its republican virtues. It is in fact only by an astonishing sleight of hand—his "subversive reading" of the *Pharsalia*—that Dante succeeded in marrying both Vergilian and Lucanian elements in his *Comedy*.[31] As a result, Lucan's epic is in many ways second in importance only to Vergil's "bible of the Empire" among Dante's classical models, for "whereas the *Aeneid* had celebrated Rome's providential origin, the *Pharsalia* had celebrated the equally providential culminating phase of the eagle's 'flight' exalted by Justinian in *Par.* 6.55–72" (Paratore 1968, 84).

Cato, guardian of purgatory

In *Convivio* 4.28.13–15, Cato's remarriage to Marcia as recounted by "that great poet Lucan" (in *Pharsalia* 2.326–73) is given an astonishing allegorical meaning, when Dante makes it signify the noble soul's return to God in old age. Even more surprising is the corollary: "And what earthly man was more worthy of signifying God than Cato? None, certainly." Equally unexpected for readers of *Inferno* 34, who have just found Brutus and Cassius crunched with Judas Iscariot in Lucifer's jaws as traitors to their rightful lord, is the presence in the very next canto (the first of the new *cantica*) of Cato (95–46 B.C.E.), Caesar's great opponent. Readers suddenly discover that Cato is the guardian of the seven terraces of Christian purgatory, despite his triple handicap as a pagan and a suicide implacably hostile to the first *de facto* emperor (*Conv.* 4.5.12).

Cato, the suicide

It is a fact sometimes overlooked by Dante scholars that no pagan is found among the suicides punished in the unnatural wood of *Inferno* 13. Cleopatra and Dido—perhaps the most famous female characters in antiquity to have committed suicide—are damned for their lust in the second circle of hell, while Lucretia is in limbo (*Inf.* 4.128) despite her condemnation by St. Augustine (*DCD* 1.19). Among Dante's contemporaries, both Nicholas Trivet and the Dominican Remigio de' Girolami regarded Cato's suicide as a positive act, although neither went so far as to describe it as an "ineffable sacrifice" (*Mon.* 2.5.15).[32] It is therefore not *in spite of* but *because of* his suicide, his virtual martyrdom as the guardian "of true freedom" (ibid.), that Cato is praised. While Cato's suicide is not mentioned in *Convivio,* it is celebrated in both *Monarchia* and the *Comedy,* where Dante's quest for spiritual freedom is likened to the freedom for which Cato "refused life" (*Purg.* 1.71–72).

Cato's opposition to Caesar

However convinced Dante was of the essential role played by the Roman Empire in God's blueprint for humanity, he could not close his eyes to the terrible price paid in the destruction of Republican Rome, so that—even in his first joyful announcement of that divine establishment (*Conv.* 4.5.12)—the time when Rome's greatness was exalted "not by human but by divine citizens" is paradoxically limited to the period stretching from "Brutus the first consul to Caesar the first supreme prince." Clearly, "Dante considered himself a continuer of the republican tradition even in his imperial aspirations" (Hollander and Rossi 1986, 60).

Cato's opposition to Julius Caesar must be understood in the light of the way both men are portrayed in Lucan's epic. Here, Caesar is clearly the villain, guilty of the heinous crime of disobeying the Roman Senate and launching a civil war. His bloodlust is highlighted: "Frantic for war . . . [h]e would rather burst a city gate than find it open to admit him; he would rather ravage the land with fire and sword than overrun it without protest from the husbandman. He scorns . . . to act like a peaceful citizen."[33] Caesar is described as both a tyrant (*Phars.* 10.342) and a traitor: like Dante's Ulysses, Lucan's Caesar does not hesitate to sway his audience with deceitful words and his oratorical skills (ibid., 9.1061–63). Such a judgment, coming from one of the greatest poets of imperial Rome, was not to be taken lightly, especially as treachery is the worst type of sin punished in Dante's hell. Finally, the antithesis set up by Lucan between Cato and Caesar could not be more striking than it appears in the latter's contempt for the law, exemplified by the words he is made to speak after he has crossed the Rubicon: "Here I leave peace behind me and *the laws which have already been violated*" (*Phars.* 1.225; emphasis mine). In radical contrast stands Lucan's Cato—who "worshipped justice and practiced uncompromising virtue" (*Phars.* 2.389)—true to Vergil's vision of Cato the lawgiver among the just souls of Elysium *(Aen.* 8.670: *secretosque pios, his dantem iura Catonem).* Like the exiled Dante who made a party for himself *(Par.* 17.68–69), "Cato alone established a definite party for the Republic . . . and there were left between them [Caesar and Pompey] but these two—the Republic and Cato" (Seneca, *Epistulae morales* 104.30–32).

In Lucan's opposition Caesar/Cato we may see foreshadowed the bipolarity of the empire, willed by God for the peace and happiness of the world, but obliged—like all earthly institutions—to work through the dialectic of secular history. In this regard, the reference to Caesar in *Inferno* 4.123 as "armed, with griffin eyes" warrants closer analysis than it has generally received. Caesar stands beside the Trojan hero Hector and Aeneas, father of Rome and her empire, a triad encapsulating Dante's view of the providential process whereby the Roman Empire was created in the fullness of time, so that it might sanction Christ's crucifixion and thus his redemption of fallen humanity *(Mon.* 2.11). As Fra Giordano told the Florentines in 1305, the griffin was "an animal . . . fierce beyond measure" (Armour 1989, 37). As a terrifying predator, it reflects the picture of Caesar found in Lucan's poem. In *Inferno* 4.123, the epithet "armed" is especially significant, in view of Caesar's decision to unleash a civil war by crossing the Rubicon with his armies in defiance of the Roman Senate. Even more meaningful is the phrase in which Caesar's *aspectus terribilis* is depicted: *con occhi grifagni* (with griffinlike eyes), implying the violence and aggression necessary for the establishment of the Roman Empire. However, with a typically Dantean verbal strategy, this striking detail also looks forward to the close of *Purgatorio,* where the griffin, now tamed under the Christian dispensation, symbolizes (according to a recent hypothesis) the emperor's essential role as the supreme custodian and dispenser of justice on earth.[34]

Augustine denounced Cato's suicide as a sign of weakness; as proof, the saint pointed out *(DCD* 1.33) that, if Cato had truly believed that it was impossible for a free man to live under Caesar's rule, he should have urged his son to join him in committing suicide. Dante may well have decided to turn Augustine's stricture on its head. The very fact that Cato exhorted his son to submit to the rule of Caesar as first emperor could be taken as proof that Cato had ultimately accepted the necessity of the empire in the divine plan.

Cato the pagan

For Cicero *(De finibus* 4.16), Cato was the "exemplar of all the virtues," a phrase echoed by Dante in *Convivio* 4.28.19 and highlighted by the splendor of the four cardinal virtues that illumine Cato's face in *Purgatorio* (1.37–39) "as if the sun had been before him." The sun is an image of divine grace throughout the poem (cf. Matt. 13.43). As a Christian reader, Dante was surely struck by possible parallels with Christ in Lucan's references to Cato as both scapegoat and redeemer. In book 2 (ll. 306–13) of the *Pharsalia*, Cato wishes that he could make atonement for "the crimes of all," while he expresses the fervent hope: "Let my blood redeem the nations, and my death pay the whole penalty" incurred by Rome. No less a figure than Pope St. Gelasius I (492–96) interpreted these words as referring to Christ's role as savior.[35]

How was the way prepared for the exaltation of Cato found in Dante's *Convivio, Monarchia,* and *Comedy*? All the thirteenth- and fourteenth-century commentaries written on the *Disticha Catonis,* a school text which "informed the thinking of mediaeval men" (Hazelton 1957, 173), claim that it deals with the four cardinal virtues. Almost two centuries before Dante, Peter Abelard (1079–1142) wrote his *Dialogus inter philosophum, Iudaeum et Christianum,* in which not only is Lucan's Cato seen as symbolizing justice, the greatest of the cardinal virtues, but his conduct is likened to that of God himself as ruler of the universe. From the end of the eleventh century, *Pharsalia* 2.380–83 were taken as proof that Cato possessed the four cardinal virtues (De Angelis 1997, 72–75).

Why, then, does Dante not claim that Cato also possessed the theological virtues, without which he could not be saved? The answer must surely be that the author of the *Comedy* was convinced—primarily through his reading of Lucan's epic—that Cato had been granted the gift of implicit faith. As Aquinas wrote:

> Many pagans received a revelation concerning Christ . . . If, however, some were saved without such a revelation, they were not saved without faith in the Savior; for, although they did not have explicit faith, *they nevertheless had implicit faith in divine providence,* believing God to be the liberator of humankind in ways He would choose according to His pleasure . . . (*S. Th.* 2.2.2.7, ad 3; my emphasis)

Unlike Trajan and Ripheus (*Par.* 20.106–29), whom Dante credits with explicit faith, Cato, he believed, possessed implicit faith. Certainly, the evidence found in Lucan's poem, underscored by the appellation "sanctus" (*Phars.* 9.555) and the description of Cato as "full of the God whom he bore hidden in his mind" (9.564), would have strengthened Dante's determination to offer Cato as a unique *exemplum* of implicit faith.

We can point only briefly to other Lucanian elements in the *Comedy*. Mention has already been made of both the "outdoing" of Lucan and Ovid in *Inferno* 25.94–102 and the Erichtho episode. According to *Inferno* 9.19–30, Dante's guide tells him that, shortly after his death, he (Virgil) had been "conjured" by the sorceress Erichtho and made to fetch a soul from Giudecca, the lowest section of hell. The ostensible reason for this invention is to reassure Dante, as we see from Virgil's words (l. 30): "I know the way well; so, take heart." Lucan's Erichtho (*Phars.* 6.507–830), who knew "the Stygian abodes and the mysteries of subterranean Dis" (l. 514), replaces Vergil's Sibyl, who had denied Aeneas access to Tartarus (*Aen.* 6.563), and, by ranging over the entire underworld, Erichtho provides Lucan's readers with "a quite literal, if disorderly *Inferno,*" while at the same time destabilizing Virgil's authority in Dante's poem (Schnapp 1997, 126). Other implications are that savage, Dracula-like Erichtho still holds sway in Christian hell and that prophecy by the dead in the *Comedy* represents "the revival by Dante of a classical, literary tradition" (Wilson 1997, 37), as the purpose of Erichtho's necromancy in Lucan is to foresee the future through a soul devoid of the gift of prophecy.[36] All in all, as Schnapp suggests (1997, 115), the *Pharsalia,* an epic without classical deities and dealing with "a nearly contemporaneous subject-matter," one moreover with comic interludes, came closest among the ancient epics to Dante's revolutionary *Comedy* and its rejection of the straitjacket imposed by the *genera dicendi.*[37]

Statius

If Lucan provides this kind of link between the great poets of antiquity and their modern emulator and rival, Dante's Statius (c. 45–c. 96 C.E.) offers an ideological bridge between pagan and Christian poetry (although—still according to Dante, *Purg.* 22.90—fear led him to remain a covert Christian convert).[38] Dante makes him a native of Toulouse (like the rhetorician Lucius Statius, born c. 58 C.E.), although Statius was in fact born in Naples. Publius Papinius Statius composed an epic, the *Thebaid,* about the fratricidal struggles between Oedipus's sons, as well as the unfinished *Achilleid.* The trio of poets who make their way up through Dante's terraces of gluttony and lust thus come to symbolize the trajectory of epic poetry: from pagan Vergil, through the crypto-Christian Statius, to the poet who proclaimed himself to be the scribe of the Christian God. On entering the Earthly Paradise, Vergil has to return to perpetual exile in limbo, while Dante and Statius continue their progress through Eden (*Purg.* 30–33).

As Wetherbee (1988, 80) claims, Statius's *Thebaid* highlights "the element of inhumanity in traditional religion," whose antithesis is set up in the poem with the altar of Clementia (*Theb.* 12.481 ff.): "an altar belonging to no god of power . . . none did she condemn or refuse their prayers . . . to no metal is the divine form entrusted, in hearts and minds does the goddess delight to dwell. The distressed are ever nigh her" (*Theb.* 12.481–95). Some thirteenth-century commentators in fact drew a parallel between this altar and the altar to the un-known God of Acts 17.23 ("What therefore you worship in ignorance, this I [Paul] proclaim to you").³⁹ Other crypto-Christian elements have been pointed out by C. S. Lewis (1957), particularly Statius's belief in the brotherhood of hu-manity, and his depiction of the "merciless" gods of pagan Olympus as little better than tyrants (*Theb.* 12.184). Jupiter, however, comes close to resembling the Christian idea of the Creator (3.218: *sator astrorum,* "creator of the stars"), his anger is soon abated, and he is sparing of human blood (7.199–200). Most importantly, perhaps, when Menoeceus accepts certain death for the sake of his native city, the poet's comment in *Thebaid* 10.629–30 "brings us . . . to some-thing like a doctrine of Grace."⁴⁰

No one can know for sure why Dante chose "his" Statius to refute the Averroistic doctrine of monopsychism and to expound the way in which the human soul is created by God and how it is that souls divested of the body can appear as shades with bodily passions (*Purg.* 25.37–108).⁴¹ What is abundantly clear, on the other hand, is the use Dante made of Statius's *Thebaid* in his *Inferno.* In the Middle Ages, its legendary history made Thebes a byword for cruelty, incest, treachery, murder, and fratricidal warfare. For Dante, it was hell on earth, and his denunciation of Pisa includes the damning description of it as a "new Thebes" (*Inf.* 33.89) for having condemned Ugolino's "innocent" chil-dren to starve to death. Indeed, the whole of lower hell is an enlarged mirror image of Thebes, as well as of Florence, another modern counterpart. In *Inferno* 32.10–11, the poet's invocation to the Muses who helped Amphion to build the walls of Thebes suggests that Dante is here constructing another and even more terrible Thebes—one where the cruelty of "Theban furies" is immeasurably surpassed (*Inf.* 30.1–27).

Capaneus

Theban material makes its first appearance in the third section of the seventh circle. Among the blasphemers, Capaneus is an unforgettable figure of mad pride and fatuous rebellion against the divinity he knew (*Inf.* 14.46–72). Virgil explains that Capaneus was one of the seven kings who attempted to storm Thebes, in order to place Polynices on the throne from which he had been excluded by his brother, Eteocles. From *Inferno* 26.52–54, we recall that the brothers' mutual hatred divided the fire on their funeral pyre (*Theb.* 12.429–32). Dante's Capaneus boasts that his indomitable spirit of rebellion is unbroken even in hell, and that Jove will never be able to feel that he has overcome his enemy with "happy vengeance" (*Inf.* 14.51–60). Virgil retorts—with unusual violence—

that Capaneus's untamed pride is in fact his greatest punishment. Turning to Dante, Virgil tells him that on earth Capaneus held—and he *still* appears to hold—"God in disdain" (*Inf.* 14.70), where Virgil's words give the lie to the idea that God is never mentioned in *Inferno*. The most deeply religious of ancient poets is thus made to give a theological commentary on Capaneus's sin. Its madness can best be punished through its own rage, of which Capaneus is in fact the only victim; and his condition in hell illustrates the axiom that a soul possesses for all eternity whatever it chooses at the moment of death.

It is remarkable that Dante should have selected a pagan as the only example of blasphemy in his Christian hell. This surprising choice should make us reflect on Dante's belief that all humanity must obey and fear God under whatever mask he may be known. Within the poem's economy, it places Capaneus in exemplary opposition to both Cato and Ripheus: Cato, who had affirmed the ubiquity of God's [Jove's] presence, and Ripheus, the greatest lover of justice in ancient Troy. Capaneus, the pagan king who despised both religion and justice (*Theb.* 3.602–3) and claimed that God was but a figment of human fears (3.615–17, 661), is condemned for all eternity for his blaspheming pride (cf. *Inf.* 25.13–15). Not only is he damned for his blasphemies but, as Hollander (1985, 24) has shown, Jove's conquest had been swift and absolute: "And here he is, lying supine in the flakes of fire, imagining Jove wearying poor Vulcan . . . with his supplicating cries for more bolts." Indeed, when Capaneus first challenged Jove on the walls of Thebes, the god "laughed at the madman" (*Theb.* 10.907–8); then a single thunderbolt, "hurled with all of Jove's might" (927), annihilated him. All that is left of Capaneus's huge bulk, now in hell, is vainglorious bombast and rage.

The *bolgia* in which soothsayers are punished is peopled with characters taken from or mentioned in the *Thebaid:* Amphiaraus, Tiresias, and Manto. Pluto's words to Amphiaraus, another of the seven kings, as the latter rides his chariot down to Hades (*Theb.* 8.84–85: "But what shall be thy doom . . . who rushest headlong . . . on a forbidden path?") are freely adapted by Dante in *Inferno* 20.31–36. They are now attributed to the Thebans, with the ironic "Why are you leaving the war?" (*Inf.* 20.34) inspired by Statius's commentary: "Now they [the Thebans] mock the witless augur's death" (*Theb.* 8.225–26). Statius's text continues: "And again they vie in praising their own Tiresias" (226–27). Tiresias, Manto's father and the most famous soothsayer of ancient times, is in fact Amphiaraus's neighbor in Dante's hell, although his empirically based judgment that women experience greater sexual pleasure than men (*Met.* 3.322–33) is omitted by the Christian poet. In spite of the epithet *lo* dolce *poeta* (the *sweet* poet: *Conv.* 4.25.6; my emphasis) describing Statius's poetic voice, what struck Dante first and foremost was the horrific element in the Latin poet's tragic tale of the accursed city of Thebes. In the depths of hell, Ugolino, gnawing at Archbishop Ruggieri's skull, "where the brain joins the nape" (*Inf.* 32.129), is compared to Tydeus, who, mortally wounded by Menalippus, nevertheless killed his enemy and had his severed head brought to him, whereupon Tydeus sank his teeth into his trophy, "befouled with the shattered brains' corruption and his jaws polluted with living blood—nor can his comrades wrest it from him" (*Theb.* 8.760–61).

Dante's choice of Statius as one of the two ancient poets who accompany Dante during the last part of his climb up the Mountain of Purgatory also reflects the Christian poet's political concerns: Vergil, as the herald of the Roman Empire; Statius, through his descriptions of the breakdown of justice and the horrors of civil, fratricidal war, as "the poet of civic harmony and political order, ideals central to the *Commedia*" (Kleinhenz 1988, 43). Statius's poem was yet another rich source of information concerning classical mythology. Ettore Paratore (1976b, 422) points out that Statius's speech in *Purgatorio* 25 constitutes "the triumph of the art of allusion." The reference in line 79 to Lachesis, one of the Fates, who spun out the wool representing the individual's allotted lifespan, cannot be derived from Vergil or Lucan; but her name is mentioned no fewer than three times in the *Thebaid*. The same derivation from Statius explains the presence in *Purgatorio* 21.27 of Clotho, the youngest of the Fates, and of Atropos, the bringer of death, in *Inferno* 33.126. Likewise, Clio, the muse of epic deeds and history, is named in *Purgatorio* 22.58 with reference to the *Thebaid,* where her name is mentioned twice, whereas it does not appear in the *Aeneid, Metamorphoses,* or *Pharsalia.*

Ulysses

We may well ask ourselves why the leading figures in *Inferno* who converse with the pilgrim—such as Francesca, Farinata, Brunetto, and Guido da Montefeltro—are all chosen from recent (Italian) history—with the sole exception of Ulysses. To find the answer, it will be necessary to examine in some detail Dante's encounter with Ulysses as recounted in *Inferno* 26 and identify its literary antecedents within a rich web of intertextual references.

Dante ignored the Homeric account of Ulysses' return to his native land. Instead, he made his Ulysses sail through the Straits of Gibraltar and on a southwesterly course, until he and his companions were destroyed by a whirlwind as they approached the Mountain of Purgatory.[42] Although Dante's Ulysses is punished, together with Diomedes, for three sins of fraud, the dramatic emphasis is placed on his final exploit and tragic end. Despite the pilgrim's instinctive fascination with the sin or sinners punished in the eighth *bolgia* (*Inf.* 26.19–24) and the poet-narrator's confession that he needs to control and check his intellect "more than is my custom" (l. 21),[43] it is hardly likely that Dante was afraid that he might be damned for Ulysses' sins as listed in lines 58–63: inventing the stratagem of the wooden horse that sealed Troy's fate, leading Achilles to his death by shaming him into taking part in the Trojan War, and the theft of a sacred statue. Instead, it is the ancient hero's perverse use of his great intellect and oratorical skill that is metaphorically encapsulated in his final voyage, which is first described in hell as a "mad flight" (*Inf.* 26.125) and finally as "the mad crossing of Ulysses" from the heights of the physical universe (*Par.* 27.82–83), where the attempted "flight" is rightly seen from heaven as a downward trajectory to damnation.

The contrast with Dante's own journey is clear and striking. Ulysses' voyage springs from a vain curiosity to explore unknown regions, and—far more significantly—it contravenes the natural limits imposed by the deity he knew and should have respected. As the hero himself tells us, Hercules placed his pillars or "warnings" at the straits "in order that man should not venture beyond" (*Inf.* 26.107–9). Dante the pilgrim, on the other hand, undertakes his perilous journey only after he has been assured that it enjoys the protection of "three blessed ladies" and is thus willed by God (*Inf.* 2.124–25). It is indeed a "lofty flight" for which Dante's wings are unerringly guided by Beatrice (*Par.* 15.53–54, 25.49–50).[44] As we have seen, the pilgrim's mythical antitypes are Icarus and Phaëthon. His predecessors are Aeneas and St. Paul, both historical figures for Dante. It is therefore as Aeneas's contemporary that Ulysses is chosen. The implications of such a choice offer a fascinating range of parallels and contrasts.

Ulysses/Aeneas

Ulysses is characterized by his wanderlust. After the fall of Troy, he spends some ten years wandering around the Mediterranean. So does Aeneas. The latter, however, does everything in his power to fulfill his destiny, as he emphatically declares in *Aeneid* 1.380: "I seek Italy, my country [*Italiam quaero patriam*] and a race sprung from Jove most high." Unlike Ulysses, the intrepid voyager, Aeneas contrasts his continuing quest with the rest granted to those Trojans who had already found asylum (*Aen.* 3.493–97): "Live happily, you whose destiny is already achieved; we are still summoned from fate to fate . . . No sea need you plough, no ever-retreating Ausonian fields need you seek." The Trojan hero's words may recall the weary voice of the Florentine exile for whom the sea was a hostile element, as he cried out: "From the time when the citizens of Rome's most beautiful and famous daughter, Florence, were pleased to cast me out of her sweet bosom . . . truly, I have been a ship without sail and without rudder, carried to various ports and river mouths and shores" (*Conv.* 1.3.4–5).

The reference to Aeneas in *Inferno* 26.93 as he who named Gaeta is crucial in that it reinforces the contrast between the Trojan hero and Ulysses, made vivid in the next lines, 94–99: "Not my fondness for my son, nor reverence for my old father, nor the love I owed Penelope, which should have made her happy, could overcome in me the ardor I felt to gain experience of the world and of human vices and merit." Translated as "reverence" or "pity," the Italian *pietà* (l. 94) nevertheless resounds with echoes of the Latin terms *pietas* and *pius*, the epithet most frequently associated with Aeneas, denoting his "salient virtue, the respect for duty and authority" (Tarrant 1997, 179). Creusa, Aeneas's wife, had died during the flight from Troy. Unlike Ulysses, who abandoned Penelope, Aeneas does everything in his power to find his wife: "I filled the streets [of the doomed city] with shouts and in my misery, with vain iteration, called Creüsa again and yet again" (*Aen.* 2.769–70). Creusa's ghost appears to him telling him that he must obey the will of the gods, must accept exile and wandering before he is destined to find happiness again in a new kingdom. In a gesture to be repeated with his father's shade (*Aen.* 6.700–701)—and, in the *Comedy*, between Dante and Casella (*Purg.* 2.79–81)—Aeneas attempts to embrace his wife's ghost and "thrice the image, vainly clasped, fled from my hands" (*Aen.* 2.793). Driven by his sense of duty and his love for his father and son, *pius* Aeneas carries Anchises on his shoulders and takes his son, Ascanius, by the hand, resolved to lead them to safety overseas. In total contrast, Ulysses sacrificed father, wife, and son to his curiosity and wanderlust.

Ulysses / Cato

Both Ulysses and Cato lead their men through a desert, the latter through the hostile sands of Libya, the former through the desert waters of the ocean. Before facing the perils of the African desert, Cato addresses his companions in words not unlike those used by Ulysses to persuade his men to undertake their "mad flight": "You who have chosen . . . to follow my standard to the death with head unbowed, prepare your minds for a high exploit of valor and for utmost hardship"; unlike Ulysses, Cato does not "intend to deceive any man, nor to draw the army on by concealing the danger" (*Phars.* 9.379–89).[45] Like the Greeks, the weary Romans see the familiar constellations disappear below the horizon, until they arrive at the temple of Ammon, representing the very limits of human knowledge and experience. Cato, "inspired by the god he bore hidden in his mind" (9.564), refuses to consult the oracle and he accepts the limits imposed by nature and heaven's will. Two lines in Lucan's text are of special relevance: "Did he [the Creator] choose these barren sands that a few might hear his voice? *Did he bury truth in the desert?*" (9.576–77; my emphasis). Dante's

Ulysses, on the other hand, urges his men to seek virtue and knowledge in the uninhabited ocean, a "world without people" (*Inf.* 26.116–20), appealing to their noblest aspirations, and reminding them that they were not "made to live like brutes," as their former mishaps with Circe had driven home. The utter absurdity of Ulysses' quest for virtue and knowledge in desert waters is fully revealed when we remember that, for Dante, men and women are meant above all to live in society, as members of a united community.[46]

Ulysses / Moses and Solomon

We may now discover further parallels and oppositions. As Hollander shows (1969, 124–26), on the shores of purgatory, "The figural presence that emanates from Cato is Moses." For our present purpose, we note that Moses led his people safely through a sea and across a desert to the Promised Land, whereas Ulysses led his men through the wastes of the ocean to their doom. In his folly, like the Alexander the Great of medieval legend, he attempted to go beyond the bounds of the inhabitable world and was struck down before he could reach the site of the Earthly Paradise.[47] Instead, for Dante—condemned to wandering in exile—it is "by sitting and being quiet that an individual grows perfect in prudence and in wisdom" (*Mon.* 1.4.2).

Ulysses is utterly lacking in prudence, the greatest of the cardinal virtues, an essential quality in a leader, one clearly possessed by Dante's Cato (*Purg.* 1.37–39), while the attributes of prudence and wisdom inevitably bring to mind Solomon, the greatest of kings. In an important episode in *Paradiso*, Solomon's light (the brightest among those who had loved wisdom on earth) is identified by St. Thomas as belonging to one whose wisdom was without equal. What distinguishes Solomon is the fact that, when God urged him to choose whatever gift he desired, Solomon asked for "a heart quick to learn, so that I may be able to judge your people, and discern between good and evil" (3 Kings 3.9). Dante's Thomas exalts Solomon for requesting—not things that are good in themselves and even essential in a different context (theological, philosophical, and scientific knowledge)—but "kingly prudence," the ability to govern his people justly and to lead them along the right path (*Par.* 13.94–108; *Conv.* 4.27.6). Since the greatest antagonist of justice is cupidity in all its manifestations, the ideal emperor will be free from greed, for his jurisdiction is bounded only by the ocean, *terminatur Occeano solum* (*Mon.* 1.11.11–12). Ulysses was also king of Ithaca; but, a prey to intellectual *cupiditas*, he abandoned the people he should have governed according to the dictates of love and justice, and set sail into the farthest reaches of the uninhabitable ocean, leading his small band of faithful followers to their doom.

Ulysses / Dante

The opposition between Ulysses' and Dante's journeys and the pilgrim's need to curb or bridle *(affrenare)* his intellect on reaching this *bolgia* have already been noted. The sin punished is a type of fraud, carried out by guile or cunning. What characterizes Ulysses and Guido, his neighbor in the eighth *bolgia,* is the fact that both lacked prudence in their actions on earth: they were incapable of foreseeing the consequences of their actions. Cunning or craftiness, *astutia,* is a sin carried out by guile *(dolus)* and opposed to the cardinal virtue of prudence. As Aquinas points out, "The execution of craftiness . . . is effected first and foremost by words, which hold the chief place among those signs whereby a man signifies something to another man . . . hence guile is ascribed chiefly to speech. Yet guile may happen also in deeds."[48] Ulysses, the enemy of the Trojan race that was "the noble seed" of the Roman people chosen by God to rule the world (*Inf.* 26.60), is denounced in the *Aeneid* (2.164) as "the inventor of crimes" and "lies" (*fandi fictor,* 9.602). The Greeks were notorious in Roman literature for their slyness, and Ulysses/Odysseus was celebrated for his exceptional intelligence as well as his "weaving of an endless web of lies and fancies" (M. Grant 1998, 78). It is therefore hardly surprising that recent studies have emphasized Dante's need to call into question the virtues of rhetoric (as vaunted, for example, by Brunetto Latini) and "the fundamental rupture between truth and a language which is caught in the world of contingency. In this sense, fraud is not simply the sin of Ulysses, but the very condition of discourse" (Mazzotta 1979, 82). As a lord of language, Dante was sent by his patron Guido Novello on an embassy to Venice in 1321. Most probably, he had already been one of the ambassadors dispatched by the Florentine Republic to Boniface VIII in 1300 and again in 1301. He had firsthand experience of the ways in which language can be used to deceive, trick, and injure others, including oneself.

Intellectual hubris is also clearly in evidence. Thus, Ulysses is "a lightning rod placed in the poem to attract and defuse the poet's consciousness of his presumption in anointing himself *scriba Dei*."[49] Conscious of his own worth, "sixth" among the greatest poets the world had ever seen (*Inf.* 4.102), prone to pride (*Purg.* 13.136–38), Dante was well aware of the pitfalls in his path—as he indicates by referring to the need to bridle his intellect and by holding fast to a rock to stop himself from falling into the eighth *bolgia* "without being pushed" (*Inf.* 26.43–45). Furthermore, even in *Convivio* (4.13.9), Dante insisted that we need to accept human limitations and (by quoting St. Paul, Rom. 12.3) that all things, even knowledge, must be pursued in moderation. Adam's and Eve's "going beyond the sign" (*Par.* 26.115–17) in eating from the archetypal tree of the knowledge of good and evil had destroyed humanity's natural perfection, even as Ulysses had violated the signs placed by Hercules, *ne plus ultra* (as stated in the corresponding canto of *Inferno* 26.106–9). The call to intellectual humility is part of the *Comedy*'s message in deed (*Purg.* 1.133–36), word, and thought—as in the call *State contenti, umana gente, al* quia (*Purg.* 3.34–37).

As a king, Ulysses should have loved and cultivated wisdom in order to rule his people justly (*Par.* 18.91–93). The poet who described himself as "a man preaching justice" (*Ep.* 12.3.7) condemned Ulysses for the ways in which he betrayed this, the most human and most lovable of all virtues (*Conv.* 1.12.9). For both Aristotle and Christian theologians, justice required that all persons be given their due: *suum cuique tribuere*. Ulysses admits that he did *not* give his wife the love that was due to her *(Inf.* 26.95–96: *'l debito amore / lo qual dovea Penelopè far lieta)*. Nor did his father, son, or subjects receive their due from the Greek hero. Forced into exile, Dante had to leave behind in Florence everything he loved most dearly (*Par.* 17.55–56); he saw his sons unjustly condemned to death as they grew to manhood; he longed with all his being to return to his beloved native city, "the beautiful fold" where he had slept as a lamb (*Par.* 25.5) and where he had drunk the waters of the River Arno before cutting his first teeth (*DVE* 1.6.3). Such a man, seized with nostalgia, could never admire the centrifugal Ulysses who sacrificed everything to his *folle volo* across the desert waters.

And yet, Dante also tells us that he had come near to damnation on account of his own *follia*—in sight of those same waters that never saw anyone sail over them who returned to tell the tale (*Purg.* 1.58–60, 130–32). Dante's complex response to sinners such as Francesca, Farinata, and Ugolino was grounded in the fact that as a man he had known the illusions of "courtly" love, political ambition, and a father's love for his children, though incapable of shielding them from the consequences of his own actions.[50]

The answer to our initial question about Ulysses is now evident (and it is reinforced by the appearance of an Italian contemporary, Guido da Montefeltro, in the next canto). Only a figure from the remote past of classical antiquity could provide such a complex web of allusions and parallels. That figure, Ulysses, ranged diachronically through the historical process that saw the destruction of Troy, the establishment of the universal empire of Rome, right down to the personal drama of Dante Alighieri, citizen of the Republic of Florence. The manifold oppositions noted—Ulysses/Aeneas, Ulysses/Cato, Ulysses/Moses, Ulysses/Solomon, Ulysses/Dante—tell us that as a man, Ulysses should not have ventured into the uninhabitable world; as an individual, he should have loved and cared for his father, wife, and son; as an old man, he should have returned to Ithaca and prepared himself for death (*Inf.* 27.79–81, *Conv.* 4.28.7); as a king, it was his duty to govern his people according to the supreme virtues of justice and prudence.

To conclude our discussion of Dante's relationship with classical antiquity, we must emphasize the fact that Dante was not a humanist. As we have seen, he was quite capable of exploiting classical texts in cavalier fashion, unlike the humanists who accorded those texts immense respect in their quest for authenticity. From their point of view, he chose to throw pearls before swine by writing about sublime subjects in the vernacular—as Giovanni del Virgilio was quick to complain (*Ecl.* 1.6–24). Nevertheless, for the Christian poet of the *Comedy,* the treasury of Aristotelian philosophy and Latin literature was a vital and ever-present resource. It is one of the ironies of history that the humanists' later attempts to restore the Latin language to the perfection it had reached in the writings of Vergil and Cicero in reality helped to turn it into a "dead" language, incapable of serving the needs of contemporary Christian humanity.

Instead, Dante's Ulysses stands as a perpetual reminder of the vitality of ancient myth in our Western culture. Like Dante's Virgil, his Ulysses is also a constant reminder of the tragedy of ancient, pagan civilization: even as Virgil is obliged to leave the Earthly Paradise as soon as his role as guide is complete, so Ulysses and his companions are doomed to die a terrible death by drowning as they arrive in sight of that same paradise. It is only after Christ's sacrifice that the ancient taboo may be—at least, metaphorically—lifted and the Christian pilgrim can enter and delight in an earthly paradise that symbolizes the state of happiness attainable in this life, *beatitudinem huius vite* (*Mon.* 3.16.7).

If now we wish to measure the distance that separates Dante from earlier ages, we need only recall that a student at Ravenna at the end of the tenth century, "on being accused of heretical beliefs, claimed to have been misled by demons in the guise of Vergil, Horace and Juvenal," or perchance listen to the voice of St. Peter Damian (whom Dante places in paradise) as he cries out, "I reject Plato . . . I set no store by Pythagoras. I renounce the works of Aristotle and Euclid . . . What use would I have . . . for the fantasies of poets who are in any case mad?"[51] Instead, Dante did not hesitate to evoke Vergil's Sibyl in the very last canto of his sacred poem (*Par.* 33.66); and, as Nardi reminds us, the greatest of all Christian poets was also the first to call upon the ancient Muses to inspire his poetry.[52]

The poet of the *Comedy*

Inevitable linguistic difficulties accompany any attempt made by a non-Italian reader to appreciate the poetry of the *Comedy*. Dante's dramatic genius, his use of imagery and symmetry, his religious, philosophical, and political ideology—all this may be savored in translation. But the poetic essence of his masterpiece, its quiddity, can only be discovered through the original Italian, since (as the author of the *Comedy* pointed out) poetry cannot be translated without loss of its "sweetness and harmony."[1] For Matthew Arnold, the line *E 'n la sua volontade è nostra pace* (*Par.* 3.85: And our peace is in His will) was one of the "touchstones" of poetry, couched as it is "in words which even those who know no Dante know" (Eliot 1965, 46). The prevalence of the rich, open sound of the Italian *a* combined with the semantic connotations of the divine Will and Peace/Beatitude create a synergetic combination of sound and meaning indicating the universal harmony of heavenly concord—expressed within the limitations but also with all the power of human language.[2] Likewise, although he insists that his heavenly "experience" is ineffable (*Par.* 1.70–72), Dante describes the *lumen gloriae* of paradise in unforgettable terms:

> luce intellettüal, piena d'amore;
> amor di vero ben, pien di letizia;
> letizia che trascende ogne dolzore.
> (*Par.* 30.40–42)[3]

Here, harmony is partly the result once again of the vowel "music," as well as the interplay of liquid and plosive consonants *(l, r, m, n; t, p, d, b)*. Moreover, we find a microcosmic example of the *Comedy's* formal symmetry in the repetition of key words, leading to a climax: *piena d'amore; amor . . . pien di letizia; LETIZIA che trascende ogne dolzore.* A reader familiar with Provençal poetry will understand that the Italian poet is using a technique similar to that of the *coblas capfinidas,* where the first word of a stanza echoes or repeats the last of its predecessor. So now this unit of three lines, Dante's *terzina,* is interlaced with and bound together by the essential concepts of heavenly love and bliss. At the same time, echoes of courtly love and its earthly joys are evoked by the word for "sweetness" chosen by the poet—a form unique in the *Comedy* and one directly reflecting the Provençal *doussor* (instead of the normal Italian *dolcezza*)—in order to drive home the concept of a bliss transcending all sensual happiness. Again, the repetition of the pause *(caesura)* after the sixth syllable in the first two lines finds its fulfillment in the uninterrupted flow of the third line, which sets its seal on the ascent from human joy to heavenly beatitude.

Yet, as any reader of *Inferno* soon realizes, the *Comedy's* linguistic texture is made up of an immense variety of sounds and rhythms, both sweet and harsh, majestic and demotic. The poet who longed to possess the "harsh and grating" verses *(rime aspre e chiocce)* necessary to describe the pit of hell and absolute evil (*Inf.* 32.1–12) was truly a lord of language, capable of deploying the entire gamut of expressivity in a unique amalgam of sound and meaning. Not only do we find such words as *cul* (arse) and *trulla* (farts) used in *Inferno* (21.139; 28.24), but from the heights of paradise Beatrice hurls the word *porci* (pigs) to describe ecclesiastical corruption on earth.[4] Dante's tonal range extends from the mellifluous evocation of Beatrice's eyes in *Inferno* 2.55 *(Lucevan li occhi suoi più che la stella)* to the lashing irony (emphasized by the force of the double consonants, owing to "syntactic doubling" in Italian) of the description of Florence as *tu [r]ricca, tu [c]con pace e [t]tu con senno!* (*Purg.* 6.137);[5] from the entrancing spectacle of the sun's rays seen dancing on the sea at dawn, after the gloom of *Inferno (Purg.* 1.117: *il tremolar de la marina)* to the shock registered at the horrors encountered in the "blind world" of hell, including the terrifying spectacle of a damned soul gnawing at his neighbor's skull *(Inf.* 33.77–78: *co' denti, / che furo a l'OSso, COME d'un CAN, FORTI.* (Words in upper case denote emphasis: here, the alliteration in *come . . . can* reinforces the plosive force of the monosyllabic *can,* which jolts the reader back to Ugolino's *bestial segno* [*Inf.* 32.133] after his tragic account of his children's death).

Versification

As mentioned in chapter 6, for his "sacred poem" Dante chose the "most splendid" line of Italian verse (*DVE* 2.5.3), the hendecasyllable. Each line of verse contains eleven syllables, with stressed syllables arranged in various patterns. To scan the hendecasyllable, certain conventions must be taken into account:

Synaloephe: the coalescence of two vowels, one at the end and the other at the beginning of two contiguous words—for example *selva oscura,* which scans as four syllables in *Inferno* 1.2: *sel-vaos-cu-ra.* This normally occurs, except when the second vowel bears the stress and the first vowel is an *a, e,* or *o* (e.g., *paùra*) or when the contiguous vowels are in the rhyming position.[6]

Elision: the suppression of a vowel. In the second and fourth *terzine* of *Inferno* 1, there are ten examples of elision: *Tant'è . . . ch'i' . . . ch'i' . . . v'ho . . . com' i' v'intrai . . . tant' era . . .* The absence of elision gives added force to the statement *qua dentro / è 'l secondo Federico (Inf.* 10.119; my emphasis). The second line in the poem scans *mi / ri / tro / vai / per / u / na / sel / vaos / cu / ra; l.* 8, *ma / per / trat / tar / del / ben / ch'i' / vi / tro / va / i.*

Synizesis (synaeresis): the contraction of two vowels into a single syllable. *Dio* (God) is always scanned as one syllable (except when followed by a vowel), "the greatest homage paid by Dante to the supreme One" (Fasani 1992, 59). The first-person pronoun *io* mostly counts as one syllable; however, diaeresis can occur.

Diaeresis: the separation of a diphthong into two vowels. This places a climactic stress on, for example, *ïo, che al divino dall'umano, / a l'etterno dal tempo era venuto,* in the context of *Paradiso* 31.31–40: if barbarians were astonished when they gaped at the glory that was Rome in all her greatness, how much more was *I* amazed when I arrived in Paradise![7]

The tenth syllable of the verse is always stressed, and in the (unusual) case of a line ending with a stressed syllable (which must end in a vowel) the hendecasyllable contains only ten syllables, since the *accento tronco* is taken to indicate apocope *(cittade > città, virtude > virtú)*: hence, there are only ten syllables in *Inferno* 32.62: *con / es / soun / col / po / per / la / man / d'Ar / tù.* In similar fashion, lines with *rime sdrucciole* (with the stress on the antepenultimate syllable) contain twelve syllables—*Inferno* 15.1: *O / ra / cen / por / ta / l'un / de' / du / ri / mar / gi / ni.* The sixth or fourth syllable generally bears the other main stress, as in *Inferno* 1.1–2: *Nel mezzo del camMIN di nostra VIta / mi ritroVAI per una selva osCUra.* In this first verse, the caesura created by the (slight) pause after the dominant stress divides the line into a rhythmic pattern of two unequal hemistiches termed *a maiore* (the longer preceding the shorter: 6 + 5), while the second verse is *a minore* (4 + 7). The *Comedy* has been declared a milestone in the history of Italian poetry because of the way in which the final vowel of a word bearing the stress on the penultimate syllable *(accento piano)* is eliminated— another example of apocope that occurs only within the line of verse and which affects *e* (but not when a feminine plural), *o, i* when they follow *m* (only in the case of the first person plural of verbs), *l*, *n*, and *r* (Fasani 1992, 28–33). So, the first line of the first canto is *Nel mezzo del* cammin *di nostra vita*, while the thirty-fifth line reads: *anzi 'mpediva tanto il mio* cammino.

Other patterns contribute to the richness and variety of the *Comedy*'s poetry. For example, the stress pattern [1/2]–4–7–10, which confers a special impetus to the verse. Charon's repeated blows are echoed in *Inferno* 3.111, with its *rallentando* on the three syllables of *s'adagia*: *BATte col REmo qualUNque s'aDAgia*. Capaneus's mad challenge to God is conveyed with the vigor of *e ME saETti con TUTta sua FORza* (*Inf.* 14.59), while the angel's speed in crossing the desert waters is implied by the rhythm of *ed el sen GÍ, come venne, veLOce* (*Purg.* 2.51). The diaeresis emphasizes Christ's obedience in *Paradiso.* 7.99: *con umilTAte obeDÏ/ENdo / poi;* and we may return to *Inferno* 33.78, quoted at the end of the previous section, in order to observe that an exceptional stress on the ninth syllable results in a hiatus (indicated by a comma in modern editions) that draws the reader's attention back to Ugolino's bestial act, after his tragic account: *che furo a L'OSso, come d'un CAN, FORti*. A similar stress (with only a slight hiatus between the ninth and tenth syllables) underscores the direction of humanity's instinctive flight toward its Creator in *Purgatorio* 12.95: *o gente uMAna, per volar SÚ NAta*. The line's first syllable may be stressed for special emphasis (*Inf.* 25.94, 97: *TACcia Lucano . . . TACcia di Cadmo . . . ;* 26.1: *GOdi, Fiorenza, poi che se' sí grande; Purg.* 6.85: *CERca, misera . . . ; Par.* 19.115, 118, 121—where the stress is reinforced by anaphora: *LÍ si vedrà . . . LÍ si vedrà . . . LÍ si vedrà . . .*), or for particular solemnity (*Par.* 33.1, 3, 13: *VERgine Madre . . . , TERmine fisso . . . , DONna, se' tanto grande . . .*), as well as when introducing (or completing) a simile, as in *Inferno* 25.79–82, *COme 'l ramarro . . . SÍ pareva . . . ,* and in *Paradiso* 23.25, *QUAle ne' plenilunïi sereni*. An unusual effect is achieved when the main stress is withheld until the seventh syllable *(Inferno* 10.33: *da la cintola in sú TUTto 'l vedrai).*[8] Quite exceptionally, caesura (with enjambment) follows immediately on caesura in order to break up the line and convey emotive shock:

> E lo spirito mio, / che già cotanto
> tempo era stato / ch'a la sua presenza
> non era // di stupor, / tremando, / affranto /
> sanza de li occhi aver piú conoscenza . . .
> (*Purg.* 30.34–37)[9]

The lexis of the *Comedy*

In 1963 it was possible to claim that more than half of Italian words in contemporary usage were already found in thirteenth-century Italian, with

no less than 15 percent owing their currency to Dante (De Mauro 1963, 173).[10]
The *Comedy's* success (followed by that of Petrarch's vernacular poems and Boc-
caccio's prose) was a determining factor in the "victory of Tuscan and the rele-
gation of every other Italian speech to the level of dialect" (Dionisotti 1967, 91).

The poet of the *Comedy* drew upon groups of consonants banished from
the "tragic" style in *De vulgari* 2.7.4–5, not only in order to describe the ugly re-
ality of evil and corruption but also for many of the elevated, doctrinal pas-
sages in the poem.[11] For example, Statius's discourse in *Purgatorio* 25 (especially
ll. 52–72) contains such forms as the double liquid consonant in *errante* (l. 63),
the combination —*ttr*— in *dottrina* (l. 64), technical terms such as *intelletto pos-
sibile* (l. 65), *organo* (l. 66), *l'articular del cerebro* (l. 69), and the phrase *e sappi che*
(l. 68), which echoes the *Et scias quod* of Scholastic discourse.[12] We may also
ponder the example of two words specifically banned from the noble style in *De
vulgari* 2.7.4, on account of both their connotations and their phonic character-
istics: the proparoxytonic *femmina* (clearly opposed to *donna* in *VN* 19.1) and the
all-too-"physical" consonant grouping of *corpo* ($k + rp$) replaced by *persona* in
the love lyrics and *Inferno* 5.101. In the *Comedy*, we find no fewer than nine oc-
currences of *femmina* in *Inferno* and *Purgatorio* (including one positive use in
Purg. 24.43; but see the scathing reference to Eve in *Purg.* 29.26), with none in
Paradiso. *Corpo* comes into its own, with some fifty-five occurrences (and is even
repeated in the line *ch'esser convien se corpo in corpo repe, Par.* 2.39), with a gradual
increase from seventeen occurrences in *Inferno* to eighteen in *Purgatorio* and
twenty in *Paradiso* (with no fewer than eight occurrences in *Par.* 2, where Dante
echoes the Pauline "whether in the body . . ." [2 Cor. 12.2] and then introduces
the word to refer to the heavenly bodies or spheres). The *Comedy* thus bears wit-
ness to both the broadening of the poet's style and the "redemption" of words
previously rejected on semantic and/or phonic grounds. In striking contrast to
the restricted vocabulary employed in *Vita Nova* and recommended in *De vulgari
eloquentia,* the poet of the *Comedy* has recourse to both contemporary regional
Italian and Latin, even introducing his own inventions, in order to fashion a style
that—like the Bible's—encompasses all facets of human experience, sublime
and vulgar, extraordinary and everyday. Clearly, Dante's choice of lexical forms
is prompted by his desire to use ones appropriate to the context, as, for example,
with the variants used for "old man": the infernal boatman Charon is described
as *un vecchio* (*Inf.* 3.83); Cato's majestic personality, on the other hand, is indicated
by the Gallicism *veglio* (*Purg.* 1.31; cf. *Inf.* 14.103); and finally, St. Bernard is ex-
alted by the Latinism *sene,* first in the emphatic, rhyming position and then
accompanied by the epithet *santo* (*Par.* 31.59, 94). Another example is the use of
speglio for "mirror" (found four times, always in the rhyming position) instead of
the normal *specchio,* with the Latinizing hapax *speculi* reserved for the angels that
reflect the light of the Godhead (*Par.* 29.144).

While it is possible to claim that "the *Comedy* as a whole is Dante's most Florentine work, both in its phonetic, morphological and syntactical structure and in its fundamental lexis" (Baldelli 1978, 93; 109), any reader of the Italian text should be aware of the diverse strands that make up the poem's linguistic web.

Latinisms

The use of Latinisms in the *Comedy* constitutes one of the major differences between Dante's lyrics and the "sacred poem." Given the prestige enjoyed by Latin as the language of learning and of the Church (cf. *Conv.* 1.5.7–14), it is hardly surprising to find almost five hundred Latinisms in Dante's Christian epic, with three times more of these forms in *Paradiso* than in either *Inferno* or *Purgatorio* (including Latin quotations and words adapted from Latin), although calculations vary, depending on the way in which the term is applied.[13]

We find Latin quotations taken from the Bible and from Church liturgy. The multitude of Latinisms in *Paradiso* is clearly a consequence of both the generally elevated style and the technical theological discourse. Terms from medieval Scholasticism are inserted: *necesse* (*Par.* 3.77; 13.98–99); *etsi* (*Par.* 3.89); *subsisto* (*Par.* 29.15). The term *iura* indicates the study of Roman law (*Par.* 11.4), and *si est dare primum motum esse* signifies the study of philosophy (*Par.* 13.100). The conjunction *ne* (= *nec*, lest) is employed after the Latinizing *veramente* (*verumtamen*, however) in *Veramente, ne forse tu t'arretri* (*Par.* 32.145). Three souls—Pope Adrian V (*Purg.* 19.99), St. Bonaventure (*Par.* 12.93), and most notably Cacciaguida (*Par.* 15.28–30)—use Latin terms in their discourse with the pilgrim. Justinian's panegyric to the Roman Empire in *Paradiso* 6 not surprisingly contains a number of Latinisms: proper names (*Pirro, Torquato, Quinzio, Deci, Fabi); substantives (*cirro*, plow, l. 46; *baiulo*, bailiff, l. 73); verbal forms (*labi*, you descend, l. 51); and *mirro*, Dante's own invention (I celebrate [with myrrh], l. 48). Similarly, in the first nine lines of *Paradiso* 24, Beatrice's solemn prayer to the three apostles contains the following Latinisms: *sodalizio, eletto, ciba, preliba, mensa, prescriba, rorate;* and, after the pregnant *civi* (l. 43), used to indicate the "citizens" of heaven, St. Peter's examination of Dante's faith incorporates such Scholastic terms as *querente* (l. 51), *sustanza/sustanze* (ll. 64, 69, 75), *quiditate* (l. 66), *silogizzar* (l. 77) and *silogismo* (l. 94). St. Bernard's prayer to the Virgin in the last canto of the poem features *grazia* (l. 14), *benignità* (l. 16), *misericordia* (l. 19), *magnificenza* (l. 20)—Latinisms made familiar as a result of their use in sermons and prayer— as well as *meridïana face* (l. 10), *infima lacuna* (l. 22), *nube* (l. 31). And, in the opening canto of *Paradiso*, the theme of ineffability (language's inability adequately to convey the pilgrim's supernatural experience of heaven, his *deificatio*) is declared in the phrase *Trasumanar significar* per verba / *non si poria* (*Par.* 1.70–71).[14]

As already noted, not even the noblest resources of the Latin Bible or of the Latin Fathers *(per verba)* are capable of signifying what is meant by the word the poet must now forge in order to indicate his going beyond the human condition, his *transhumanization*.

Dialects

At the opposite end of the medieval poet's stylistic scale we find words chosen from various dialects of the Italian peninsula, especially from the northern regions. So, we find a typically northern voicing of intervocalic consonants in *figo* for *fico* (*Inf.* 33.120), *lido* (*lito*, *Purg.* 17.12), and *sego* (*seco*, *Purg.* 17.58). According to Machiavelli's *Dialogo intorno alla nostra lingua*, the form *co* for *capo* (*Inf.* 20.76, 21.64; *Purg.* 3.128 [in both cases, *co del ponte*]; *Par.* 3.96) was found in "Lombardia" (i.e., northern Italy). *Vinegia* (Venice, *Par.* 19.141) evokes the Venetian ducat *(il conio di Vinegia)*, while *arzanà* is the Venetian form conjuring up the feverish activities of the maritime republic's celebrated arsenal in *Inferno* 21.7. In *Paradiso* 19.137, the northern lexeme *barba* (uncle) is used to refer scathingly to King James of Maiorca, whose foul deeds are denounced in line 136. *Scranna* (seat, *Par.* 19.79) and *sorco* (mouse, *Inf.* 22.58) are both from Romagna, and *scane* (*Inf.* 33.35, canine teeth) is probably of Genoese origin (Rohlfs 1990, 165). The northern form *orecchia* is found for the singular "ear," but the plural form is generally *orecchi* (seven occurrences), with the feminine plural *orecchie* appearing only once (*Inf.* 8.65). *Ora,* the Tuscan form for "now," is found within the line of verse (e.g., *Purg.* 20.120: *ora a maggiore e ora a minor passo*), whereas its northern synonym *adesso* appears only in rhyme (*Purg.* 18.106, 24.113). The pilgrim's speech is recognized as Florentine by a number of souls (e.g., *Inf.* 10.25–27), while Venedico Caccianemico's Bolognese origin is signaled by his use of *sipa* (*sí*, yes, *Inf.* 18.61). Fra Gomita twice uses the Sardinian form *donno* (lord; from the Latin *dominus*: *Inf.* 22.83 and 88); and, in *Purgatorio* 24.55, Bonagiunta reveals his birthplace to be Lucca by pronouncing *issa* for "now" (cf. *Inf.* 23.7). Its cognate *istra,* used by Virgil, illustrates the latter's anachronistic "Lombard" speech in *Inferno* 27.20–21. No southern dialectal forms are found (if we except the controversial *ghiorioso* in Pier della Vigna's speech, *Inf.* 13.62, for which see Sanguineti 2001, 68).

On the other hand, the esteem in which Dante held his "Sicilian" predecessors (*DVE* 1.12) explains the presence of "Sicilian" forms sanctioned by their writings. Thus, we find the present indicative *veggio, deggio, cheggio* (*vedo, devo, chiedo, Inf.* 15.116–20) and the subjunctive *aggi* ([*tu*] *abbia, Par.* 5.127) as well as *aggia* ([*egli*] *abbia, Purg.* 6.102).[15] Sicilian forms of the "imperfect" tense are also found: *avieno, potiensi* (*ave[v]ano, pote[v]ansi, Inf.* 9.39 and *Par.* 7.88). The conditional tense in *-ia* is likewise of Sicilian provenance: *poria* (*potrebbe, Inf.* 28.1; *Purg.* 17.63; *Par.* 1.71), *avria* (*avrebbe, Purg.* 23.33), as is the past participle *feruto* (*ferito, Inf.* 24.150, 25.105). The form *lo* for the masculine definite article was the only one found in southern Italian: it is retained as an alternative to *il,* with 448 occurrences in the *Comedy,* compared to 799 for *il:* for example, *Lo giorno se n'andava, e l'aere bruno* (*Inf.* 2.1). Virgil is described as *lo buon maestro* (*Inf.* 4.31 and 85, 7.115, 8.67, 19.43, 21.58, 29.100), *lo dolce padre* (*Inf.* 8.110), *lo verace duca* (*Inf.* 16.62), *lo più che padre* (*Purg.* 23.4), and *lo dolce padre mio* (*Purg.* 25.17, 27.52). We find one example of *il* used before a masculine noun beginning with *z: tu vedresti il Zodïaco rubecchio* (*Purg.* 4.64).[16]

Gallicisms and Provençalisms

The prestige enjoyed by troubadour poetry and French literature accounts for the presence in the *Comedy* of numerous words originally found in Old French and Provençal.[17] As we have seen, the Provençal form *dolzore* is chosen (but only once, in *Par.* 30.42) instead of the native *dolcezza,* to evoke the joys of *fin' amors* as celebrated in troubadour poetry. The most striking use of the Provençal language is of course the *tour de force* in *Purgatorio* 26.140–47, where Dante inserts no fewer than eight hendecasyllabic lines of the literary language used by Arnaut Daniel, the supreme craftsman or *miglior fabbro* (l. 117 of poetry in the vernacular): *Tan m'abellis vostre cortes deman . . . sovenha vos a temps de ma dolor!*[18]

Gallicisms extend from a word for such a basic action as eating, *mangiare* (*Inf.* 33.141; Italian *manducare, manicare*), to the term for the art of poetry: Virgil is made to refer to his own verse as *rima* (*Inf.* 13.48: *la mia rima*), a word derived from the Latin term *rhythmus,* rhythm (which was not restricted to rhyming verse). *Obliare* (*Purg.* 2.75, to forget); *roggio* (*Purg.* 3.16, red); *ostello* (*Par.* 17.70, hostel or haven); *saggio* (*Inf.* 1.89; *Purg.* 16.133, wise, sage); even Dante's infernal *bolge* come from Old French *bolge* (leather pouch or purse, Latin *bulga*). In the first canto, *abbandonai* (l. 12), *lonza* (l. 32), *gaetta,* and the construction *a la* (l. 42) are Gallicisms; *selvaggia* (ll. 5, 93), *veltro* (l. 101), and *noia* (l. 76) are of Provençal origin. In most cases, it is not possible to know which forms would have struck Dante as loanwords, since nearly all had received literary consecration in the writings of his "Sicilian" and Tuscan predecessors.

Obvious exceptions are such outright Gallicisms as *argento* meaning "money" (*Inf.* 32.115: *l'argento de' Franceschi; Par.* 17.84); *lo fiordaliso* (*Purg.* 20.86, fleur de lys) and *giuggia* (judges, in the same canto, l. 48); also, *vengiammo* (*Inf.* 9.54) and *villa* (town, *Inf.* 23.95; *Purg.* 15.97). On two occasions, the poet highlights the fact that he is using a Gallicism: *semplice* to mean "straightforward, honest" in *Purgatorio* 16.125–26 *(che mei si noma, / francescamente, il semplice Lombardo),* and the technical term *alluminare* (Italian *miniare*) for the art of illuminating manuscripts *(Purg.* 11.81, *quell'arte / ch'alluminar chiamata è in Parisi).*[19]

Neologisms

The poet's titanic struggle to describe his journey through the other world, while pushing the expressivity of language beyond its limits in an attempt to encompass the totality of human thought and experience, also gave rise to the need to create new words and forms. Although recent philological advances have considerably reduced the number of words previously thought to have been coined by Dante, about one hundred neologisms in the *Comedy* still testify to his linguistically creative genius.

The description of the "comic" scenes between the barrators and their tormentors yields *arruncigliare* and *acceffare* (*Inf.* 21.75, 22.35, 23.18: to seize with a grapnel *[ronciglio]* or with the snout *[ceffo]*); the result of the purgatorial experience is encapsulated in Dante's verb *dismalare*, to disevil *(Purg.* 13.3: *lo monte che salendo altrui dismala); imparadisare,* to imparadise, signifies Beatrice's opening up of the joys of heaven to Dante *(Par.* 28.3: *quella che 'mparadisa la mia mente).* Many of the neologisms are verbs (often reflexive) formed by parasynthesis (a combination of preposition and object), particularly with the prefix *-in: insemprare [in + sempre],* to convey the eternity of heavenly bliss *(se non colà dove gioir s'insempra, Par.* 10.148); *indiarsi [in + dio],* to indicate proximity to and conformity with the Godhead *(D'i Serafin colui che più s'india, Par.* 4.28); *indracarsi,* to pursue like a dragon *(L'oltracotata schiatta che s'indraca / dietro a chi fugge . . . , Par.* 16.115–16); *inurbarsi [in + Latin urbs],* meaning to migrate to the city *(quando rozzo e salvatico s'inurba, Purg.* 26.69); *adimare [ad + imo, Latin imus,* lowest], indicating the descent of a river *(Infra Sïestri e Chiaveri s'adima / una fiumana bella, Purg.* 19.100–101), and the pilgrim's glance earthward in *Adima / il viso e guarda come tu se' vòlto (Par.* 27.77–78). A striking trio of the poet's inventions is offered by the verse *s'io m'intuassi, come tu t'inmii (Par.* 9.81), preceded by *s'inluia* (l. 73). These three neologisms all indicate the blessed souls' capacity, derived from their union with God, to enter into and therefore to "read" another's mind: *in + tu/ me/lui.* The traditional iconographical association of the color blue with the Virgin's mantle, as well as the color of the cloudless sky *(Purg.* 1.13: the sweet color of an oriental sapphire) when the sun—symbol of God's grace—is at its most resplendent, would seem to have inspired both the description of Mary as *il bel zaffiro* (the beautiful sapphire) and the neologism *s'inzaffira (del quale il ciel più chiaro s'inzaffira:* with which the brightest heaven is ensapphired) in *Paradiso* 23.101–2.

Rhyme[20]

Statistical evidence provided by Robey shows how far Dante expanded his range of rhymes in his "sacred poem," while many of the forms found in the rhyming position are not found in other positions in the line of verse.[21] As the reader will have noticed, the poet's use of unusual, rare words is often necessitated or justified by the demands of the *Comedy*'s rhyme scheme (although a contemporary claimed that the poet was never distracted by these difficulties).[22] In fact, most of Dante's Latinisms and neologisms are found (chiefly in the rhyming position) in *Paradiso,* the *cantica* which contains an abundance of theological, philosophical, astronomical, and juridical terms, and where the poet consciously strives for ever greater eloquence to overcome the difficulties of making manifest even a slight shadow of his celestial experience (*Par.* 1.13–27). Ignazio Baldelli has also demonstrated that the opening and closing *terzine* of the cantos (in which the first rhyme-word is only echoed once; *aba; zyz*) account for fifty-eight rhymes used only once (*rime* hapax: Baldelli 1997, 34). Afribo's recent study (2002) offers a detailed analysis demonstrating the "monotonous" and "monochromatic" use of rhyme-forms in Italian lyric poetry of the thirteenth century, as opposed to the veritable "explosion" of new rhyme-sets in the *Comedy*.

Before proceeding to an overview of the *Comedy*'s rhymes, it is necessary to define the various categories:

Rime piane are accented on the penultimate syllable ("feminine rhymes") and make up the vast majority of rhymes.

Rime sdrucciole are accented on the antepenultimate syllable ("triple rhymes": *Inf.* 15.1–3, *màrgini – àrgini*).

Rime tronche are accented on the final syllable ("masculine rhymes": *Inf.* 20.74–78, *può–co–Po*).

Rime composte are made up of two or three words (*Inf.* 30.87, *non ci ha* [pronounced *nóncia*] rhymes with *oncia* and *sconcia;* in *Inf.* 28.123, the normal stress *Oh mè* is modified to *òme,* to rhyme with *come* and *chiome);* also, *rima derivativa,* whereby rhyming words have the same stem: *solvi–rivolvi–solvi* (*Inf.* 11.92–96).

Rime identiche: rhymes on the same word. Only three verbal forms in the poem (*per ammenda, Cristo, vidi)* are made to rhyme with themselves in units of threes (but cf. *Purg.* 33.10–12).[23] The most celebrated are the four units— *Paradiso* 12.71–75, 14.104–8, 19.104–8, 32.83–87—where the name of Christ is made to rhyme with itself, possibly in atonement for Dante's having used the Redeemer's name as a rhyme-word in the scandalous context of the sonnet *Bicci novel, figliuol di non so cui* (LXXVII: 74.11), as well as in the *Fiore* (if he was indeed the author), where *Gesocristo* is made to rhyme with *ipocristo* (104.9–11: "hypocrite," with an echo of "Antichrist"; Casciani and Kleinhenz 2000, 243 n. 2).

Rime equivoche: homographs, such as the noun *cerchi* (circles) and the verbal form *cerchi* (you search; *Purg.* 17.137–39). There are eighty-four instances of *rima equivoca* in the *Comedy* (but see the warning given in *DVE* 2.13.13 against *inutilis equivocatio,* since it detracts from the thought expressed).

Rime ricche: the initial consonants of the stressed syllables are identical. *Inferno* 1.39–41: *cagione – stagione.*

Rimas caras: Provençal terminology signifying "difficult" rhymes, which frequently occur in opening *terzine: Inferno* 11.13 *(ripa – stipa),* 15.1–3 *(margini – aduggia – argini); Purgatorio.* 20.1–3 *(pugna – spugna); Paradiso* 7.1–3 *(sabaòth – malacòth),* 13.1–3 *(cupe – rupe).*

Rhymes in the *Comedy*

The number of different rhymes in the *Comedy*'s 14,233 lines is 753. The number of rhymes used only once (i.e., in only three lines or in only two if at the beginning or the end of a canto) is 240: "Dante was an extraordinarily inventive rhymer—much more so than his later rivals in this respect, Pulci and Tasso."[24] The ten most common rhymes are *-ura* (153), *-io* (140), *-ente* (133), *-etto* (131), *-ia* (121), *-ai* (118), *-enti* (111), *-era* and *-ore* (both 108), *-one* (101). The fifty most common rhymes are found in just over 30 percent of the poem's lines (Robey 1997, 126). There is an increase from *Inferno* to *Paradiso* in the number of accented front vowels in rhyme-words *(e* and *i),* with a predominance of accented back vowels *(o* and *u)* in the rhyme-words of the first *cantica.* This would appear to support the traditional view that front vowels tend to express light and joy, while back vowels may evoke feelings associated with darkness and oppression.[25]

In the rhyming position, we find non-Tuscan forms such as the following: literary Sicilian *vui* (*Inf.* 5.95: "corrected" to *voi* by Petrocchi), *fora (sarei: Purg.* 26.25, but in seventeen occurrences within the line, *fora = sarebbe), este [è]* (*è: Par.* 24.141); Gallicized forms such as *dispitto* (*Inf.* 10.36), *sorpriso* (*Purg.* 1.97), *pareglio* (*pari: Par.* 26.107–8);[26] Provençal forms in *-aia* (*aia = abbia: Inf.* 21.60), *raia* (*raggia: Purg.* 16.142), and *ploia* (*pioggia: Par.* 14.27, 24.91); as well as forms belonging to northern Italian dialects, such as *palagio* (*palazzo: Inf.* 34.97), *ancoi* (*oggidi: Purg.* 13.52, 20.70, 33.96). The demands of the rhyme scheme justify the inclusion of non-Tuscan plurals such as *le membre* (rather than *le membra: Inf.* 29.51; *Purg.* 6.147), *le calcagne* (*Purg.* 12.21, 19.61), or the Emilian form *a mano stanca* (*a sinistra: Inf.* 19.41). Western Tuscany (Pisa, Lucca, Siena) provides—but again, only in the rhyming position—*fersa* (*ferza: Inf.* 25.79), *abbo* (*ho: Inf.* 32.5), *crese* (*credette: Purg.* 32.32), as well as *terminonno* (*terminarono: Par.* 28.105, the third person plural form of the past definite rejected by Dante in *DVE* 1.13.2). Northern *scintilla* (spark) is found only once (in the rhyming position: *Par.* 28.91), whereas Tuscan *favilla/faville* recur fifteen times. Rural Tuscan offers the difficult but splendid metaphor *paroffia* (parish: *Par.* 28.84), *brolo* (garden: whence "garland" in *Purg.* 29.147), *rubecchio* (reddish: *Purg.* 4.64), with four occurrences of various forms of *lassare* in rhymes (whereas *lasciare* and its derivatives are always used within the lines of verse). Interesting linguistic evidence is provided by Guido da Pisa (writing only a few years after Dante's death), who points out that the form *lici* (there: *Inf.* 14.84; *Purg.* 7.64) is peculiar to Florentine speech.[27] Florentine vernacular usage also supplies *allotta* for five rhymes (*allora* is used within the verse), as well as *introcque*, the only word capable of rhyming with *nocque* (*Inf.* 20.128–30).

In the *Comedy*, Dante eschews the use of such easy rhymes as would be provided by the infinitive form of the first conjugation. In the *Comedy*, there are twenty-nine examples of rhymes with the verbal infinitive ending *-are*, with only one example found in *Paradiso* (13.93: *dimandare*).[28] Adverbial endings in *-mente* are likewise rarely found in rhyme (and in decreasing numbers: six instances in *Inf.*, five in *Purg.*, only three in *Par.*; and note the striking dislocation of the adverbial suffix in *Par.* 24.16–17: *così quelle carole differente- / mente danzando . . .*).

The relatively frequent use of Latinisms in *Paradiso* has already been noted. In rhyme, we find retention of consonant groups with Latin *l*, instead of the vernacular outcome in *i* (four occurrences: *-emplo [Par.* 18.122–26, 28.53–57, *templo* vs. vernacular *tempio*, *essemplo* vs. *es[s]empio]*). The Latinate suffix *-abile* (vernacular *-evole*) is reponsible for one of only two clusters of *rime sdrucciole* in *Paradiso*: 26.125–29 (*incosummàbile–razionàbile–duràbile*). In *Paradiso* 6, among the massive presence of Latinate forms in Justinian's exaltation of the Roman Empire, we find that Latinisms make up the rhyme-words of nine successive tercets: *cuba–Iuba–tuba, latra–Cleopatra* [rather than the vernacular form *Cleopatràs* in *Inf.* 5.63]–*atra, colubro–rubro–delubro* (*Par.* 6.68–81). In this same canto, moreover, lines 44–51 offer the rhymes *Pirro–cirro–mirro* and *Fabi–[Aràbi]–labi*. Here once again we may note the use of proper nouns, which in the *Comedy* are nine times more frequent than in *Vita Nova*.[29]

At the opposite end of the stylistic scale, in the cantos describing the eighth and ninth *bolge* of hell, Dante creates unusual rhymes, in part through the use of "harsh" consonantal sounds.[30] *Inferno* 28 is unique in that it offers no fewer than three departures from the *Comedy*'s usual rhymes: a *rima sdrucciola* (ll. 80–84: *Cattòlica–Maiòlica–argòlica*), a *rima composta* (ll. 119–23: *come–chiome–Oh me*), and a *rima tronca* (ll. 32–36: *Alì–qui–così*). Toward the end of the next canto we find some striking examples of the *rime aspre e chiocce* that Dante will evoke at the beginning of *Inferno* 32: *Stricca–ricca–s'appicca; occhio–Capocchio–t'adocchio* (*Inf.* 29.125–36).[31] Then, in *Inferno* 32.26–30, the virtuoso poet produces the stupendous sequence *Osterlicchi–Tambernicchi–cricchi*, while for good measure he adds rhymes incorporating a double *z* (ll. 68–75: *Pazzi–cagnazzi–guazzi; riprezzo–mezzo–rezzo*)—a feature banned from the noble style in *De vulgari* 2.7.5— together with one of the three *rime tronche* (ll. 62–66: *Artú–piú–fú*) found in this section of hell (*Inf.* 28–32).[32] One of the outstanding characteristics of Dante's poetic practice in the *Comedy* is the exposure given to unusual forms (Latinisms, neologisms) by placing them in the rhyming position—a feature not found in *Vita Nova* or in the poetry of Cavalcanti and Cino, and one that would be shunned by that other master craftsman, Petrarch.[33]

To conclude our section on rhyme in the *Comedy*, we may notice the striking repetition of a rhyme-group to underline the opposition between Ulysses' hubris and the pilgrim's humility.[34] In *Inferno* 26.137–41, the Greek hero's "mad flight" is punished by a whirlwind that sinks his craft and sends him and his companions to their death in the depths of the ocean: *un turbo* nacque . . . *Tre volte il fé girar con tutte* l'acque . . . *e la prora ire in giú, com' altrui* piacque. At the close of *Purgatorio* 1 (130–36), the pilgrim and his guide observe the deserted shore of the ocean, *che mai non vide navicar sue* acque; Virgil then girds his charge with the reed symbolizing the supreme Christian virtue: humility, *Quivi mi cinse sí com' altrui* piacque—whereupon this Christian Golden Bough *si* rinacque, a verbal pointer to the process of spiritual rebirth the pilgrim will undergo in purgatory. Finally, it may not be irrelevant to note that in this poem describing Dante's vision of the other world we find no fewer than 129 forms of the verb *vedere* placed in the emphatic, rhyming position;[35] even more significant perhaps is the fact that, with forty-five occurrences (predominantly in *Paradiso*), various lexical forms based on *disio* and *disiare* make up the largest group of cognate rhyme-words in the poem.

Syntax and *terzina* unit (tercet)[36]

Dante's mastery of syntax, which respects all the exigencies of rhyme and meter, constitutes an outstanding literary achievement not seen in Europe since Roman antiquity. The paratactic nature of medieval narrative, with its disjunctive periodicity, is in marked contrast with the broad, spacious, flowing structure of, for example, the opening of *Purgatorio* 30:

> Quando il settentrïon del primo cielo,
> che né occaso mai seppe né orto
> né d'altra nebbia che di colpa velo,
>   e che faceva lí ciascuno accorto
> di suo dover, come 'l piú basso face
> qual temon gira per venire a porto,
>   fermo s'affisse: la gente verace,
> venuta prima tra 'l grifone ed esso,
> al carro volse sé come a sua pace;
>   e un di loro, quasi da ciel messo,

"Veni, sponsa, de Libano" cantando
gridò tre volte, e tutti li altri appresso.
                        (*Purg.* 30.1–12)

————

When the Seven Stars of the first heaven, which have never known either sunset or sunrise, nor veiled by any mist except that of sin, and which there made everyone aware of his duty, just as the Bear does for whoever steers to return to harbor, stopped still: the true band that had come first between the griffin and those stars turned toward the chariot as toward their peace; and one of them, like a messenger from heaven, chanted "Come, o bride, from Lebanon!" calling three times, and all the others followed. (The notorious difficulties of rendering Dante's text in translation are proof, if any were necessary, of the poet's mastery of Italian syntax.)

The caesura in line 7 (*Quando il settentrïon del primo cielo . . . fermo s'affisse: // la gente verace . . . al carro volse sé come a sua pace*) is striking in its unusual positioning and effect. This sentence, which stretches over some twelve lines, is yet further evidence that "in the whole poem only about one in thirty sentence endings fall[s] at the end of the first or second lines of the *terzina*," a syntactical phenomenon markedly less frequent in both *Purgatorio* and *Paradiso* (Robey 2000c, 809). One finds a corresponding increase in the number of sentences that encompass two or more *terzine,* rising from 290 in the first *cantica* to 432 in *Paradiso.*

A truly remarkable example of the poet's ability to express in verse (and without sacrificing syntactic clarity) things that are in themselves difficult to conceive (*Purg.* 29.42) is Solomon's answer to the question posed by Beatrice on the pilgrim's behalf: whether the light enveloping the blessed souls will remain the same for all eternity. It takes up no fewer than twenty-four verses (*Par.* 14.37–60), displaying syllogistic reasoning with a perfect mastery of both form and content, and encapsulated in lines 40–51 like some overarching musical phrase with its crescendo in the final *terzina:*

> . . . "Quanto fia lunga la festa
> di paradiso, tanto il nostro amore
> si raggerà dintorno cotal vesta.
>
> La sua chiarezza séguita l'ardore;
> l'ardor la visïone, e quella è tanta,
> quant' ha di grazia sovra suo valore.
>
> Come la carne glorïosa e santa

fia rivestita, la nostra persona
piú grata fia per esser tutta quanta;
         per che *s'accrescerà* ciò che ne dona
di gratüito lume il sommo bene,
lume ch'a lui veder ne condiziona;
         onde la visïon *crescer* convene,
crescer l'ardor che di quella s'accende,
crescer lo raggio che da esso vene."
                    (*Par.* 14.37–51; my emphasis)[37]

The last three lines reinforce the two basic principles of Dante's paradise: the fundamental idea that vision precedes love (cf. *Par.* 28.109–10),[38] and that celestial luminiscence is both an indication and a vehicle of beatitude.[39] Together with the preceding *terzina,* they also offer a complex example of chiasmus when juxtaposed with lines 40–42: brilliance–love–vision–grace/grace–vision–love–brilliance. These verbal pyrotechnics are complemented by the ensuing simile of fiery coal that remains visible at the center of the flames emanating from it; even so will the resurrected body, transfigured, outshine the souls' present brilliance—an original contribution to Christian doctrine but one which echoes the poet's insistence on the perfect totality of the human being (cf. *Inf.* 6.103–11). As Rachel Jacoff insists, "Although the soul's longing for the body is a theological topos, nowhere is it expressed with such unalloyed passion as in Dante" (Jacoff 2000, 132).

Enjambment

A study by G. Lisio (1902, 96) claimed that one-seventh of the *Comedy's* lines of verse do not correspond to the grammatical clause, with ever greater freedom displayed as the poem progresses. The poet increasingly makes the syntactical unit correspond to the *terzina:* exceptions to this general tendency decrease from 101 in *Inferno* to 63 in *Purgatorio,* and 44 (some of them quite startling) in *Paradiso* (Lisio 1902, 115). In the whole poem, only nineteen sentence-breaks occur in the middle of a line.[40] On the other hand, enjambment (the continuation of a clause beyond the line) is frequently used to great effect: one notable example is the division of the ejaculatory phrase *Ave, Maria,* which focuses the reader's attention on Mary's name in *Paradiso* 3.121–22: . . . *e poi cominciò* "Ave, / Maria" *cantando* . . . Indeed, whereas instances of enjambment are "usually fewer than fifteen per canto in *Inferno,* they rise to the thirties, forties, and fifties in *Paradiso* . . . The line is no longer a sufficient unit for Dante's thought here" (Ferrante 1993a, 159).[41]

In the first canto of the poem, enjambment is strikingly employed (ll. 39–40, 42–43) linking a group of three tercets, with a strong pause at the end of line 43 heightened by the unexpected adversative *ma* introducing a new hostile element:

> Temp' era dal principio del mattino,
> e 'l sol montava 'n sú con quelle stelle
> ch'eran con lui quando l'amor divino
>> mosse di prima quelle cose belle;
> sí ch'a bene sperar m'era cagione
> di quella fiera a la gaetta pelle
>> l'ora del tempo e la dolce stagione;
> *ma* non sí che paura non mi desse
> la vista che m'apparve d'un leone.
>> (*Inf.* 1.37–45; emphasis mine)

Enjambment separates the adjective from its substantive in *Inferno* 1.73–74 and gives it added emphasis: *Poeta fui, e cantai di quel giusto / figliuol d'Anchise che venne di Troia;* also, for example, in *Purgatorio* 7.101–2, *fu meglio assai che Vincislao suo figlio / barbuto, cui lussuria e ozio pasce.* In *Inferno* 30.18–19, the same phenomenon ignores the end of the tercet (l. 18), separating the noun from its complement: *in su la riva / del mar,* and in *Inferno* 20.4–5, the article from the noun: *per li / luoghi;* the preposition is divided from its object in, for example, *Purgatorio* 18.89–90: *dopo / le nostre spalle,* as are the verbal components in *Purgatorio* 9.22–23: *fuoro / abbandonati . . .* Enjambment is a truly striking feature of Bonconte's account of his death in *Purgatorio* 5.100–129: *e quivi / caddi, e rimase la mia carne sola . . . e quel d'inferno / gridava . . . ne l'aere si raccoglie / quell' umido vapor . . . Giunse quel mal voler che pur mal chiede / con lo 'ntelletto . . . coperse / di nebbia . . . venne / di lei . . . tanto veloce / si ruinò . . . e quel sospinse / ne l'Arno . . . la croce / ch'i' fe' di me . . .* This rapid, precipitous account of Bonconte's last moments on earth is set off by the perfect equipoise of Pia's steadfast request for the pilgrim's prayers (ll. 130–36).

Enjambment is also prominent whenever Beatrice discourses on the relationship between humankind and God, as in *Paradiso* 7.67–102:

> "Ciò che da lei sanza mezzo distilla
> non ha poi fine, perché non si move
> la sua imprenta quand' ella sigilla.
>> Ciò che da essa sanza mezzo piove
> libero è tutto, perché non soggiace
> a la virtute de le cose nove."
>> (ll. 67–72)

> "Ficca mo l'occhio per entro l'abisso
> de l'etterno consiglio, quanto puoi
> al mio parlar distrettamente fisso.
>
>   Non potea l'uomo ne' termini suoi
> mai sodisfar, per non potere ir giuso
> con umiltate obedïendo poi,
>
>   quanto disobediendo intese ir suso;
> e questa è la cagion per che l'uom fue
> da poter sodisfar per sé dischiuso."
>   (ll. 94–102)[42]

Diegetic enjambment is a striking feature of the narrative links between the final verse of *Inferno* 24 and the opening line of *Inferno* 25, but its most dramatic effect in the narrative occurs in the last two cantos of the poem. Readers, conditioned by the linking together of ninety-eight cantos, are taken utterly by surprise by the last line of *Paradiso* 32 ("And he began this sacred prayer:"), which—instead of rounding out the canto—propels them to the opening verse of the last canto ("Virgin Mother, daughter of your son"), without rest or pause of any kind.[43]

Syntax, alliteration, and chiasmus

Especially toward the end of the poem, Scholastic discourse and Dante's previous attempts at the articulation of complex thought in his *Convivio* influence the syntax, leading to such exploits as the twelve consecutive tercets of *Paradiso* 29.10–45, in which Beatrice explains the creation of the universe to the pilgrim. This tendency toward complexity may be indicated by the number of sentences that overlap the single *terzina* unit, which increases from 290 in *Inferno,* to 334 in *Purgatorio,* and to 432 in *Paradiso.* Similes are frequently arranged over two tercets (vehicle + tenor: *Inf.* 1.22–27), but in *Inferno* 26.25–42 two similes both take up nine lines, with each vehicle defined in two tercets (ll. 25–30, 34–39). The extended vehicle in the simile that sets the scene in *Inferno* 24.1–15 is interwoven with a series of four rhymes linked by assonance, *anno–anca–agna–accia,* and it includes two pairs of *rime equivoche* (*tempra–tempra, faccia–faccia:* a feature condemned in *DVE* 2.13.13), while its function as simile is only revealed in line 16, *Cosí mi fece sbigottir lo mastro* (So the master made me afraid). The opening simile of *Paradiso* 23 extends over no fewer than five tercets. The opening of *Inferno* 13 consists of three tercets, each beginning with anaphora (a sequence resounding with *Non*), with the second tercet describing the unnatural setting chosen for the punishment of the "unnatural" sin of self-destruction, which is underscored by the contrastive *ma* placed in the sixth syllable of each line:

> *non* fronda verde, / *ma* di color fosco;
> *non* rami schietti, / *ma* nodosi e 'nvolti;
> *non* pomi v'eran, / *ma* stecchi con tòsco.
>
> > (*Inf.* 13.4–6)

In similar fashion, Cacciaguida's discourse in *Paradiso* 15.100–111 illustrates the happy state of the Florence he had known, with four tercets each beginning with the emphatic *Non (Non avea catenella . . . Non faceva . . . Non avea case . . . Non era vinto),* reinforced through additional repetition at the beginning of lines 101, 105, and 107: *NON gonne contigiate . . . NON fuggien . . . NON v'era giunto . . .;* and, in lines 100 and 101, *NON corona . . . NON cintura.*

The circularity and unity of the Trinity is underscored by chiasmus:

> Quell' *uno e due e tre* che *sempre vive*
> e *regna sempre* in *tre e 'n due e 'n uno.*
>
> > (*Par.* 14.28–29; my emphasis)

And in *Paradiso* 20.94–99, we find a veritable "orgy" of alliteration (Baldelli 1973, 944):

> "*Regnum celorum v*iolenza pate
> da caldo amore e da *v*iva speranza,
> che *v*ince la di*v*ina *v*olontate:
> > non a guisa che *l'*omo a *l'*om sobranza,
> ma *v*ince lei perché *v*uole esser *v*inta,
> e, *v*inta, *v*ince con sua beninanza."[44]

Alliteration in the last line of *Inferno* 5, *e caddi come corpo morto cade,* combined with the "thud" of the double consonant in *caddi,* followed by assonance in *corpo morto* and the "swooning" effect of the full measure of the long *ah*-sound in *cade,* evokes the sound of a body suddenly falling to the ground. Rhythmic flow is evident, for example, in *che parton poi tra lor le peccatrici* (*Inf.* 14.80), but in the same canto at line 39 special emphasis is placed through alliteration on the redoubling of the pain: *sotto focile, a doppiar lo dolore.* Alliteration is prominent in the last two lines of *Paradiso* 5, at the beginning of line 138 and at the end of line 139: *e così chiusa chiusa mi rispuose / nel modo che 'l seguente canto canta.* Here, its effect is to close the rhythmic and phonic round of the canto as a poetic unit, while at the same time safeguarding the narrative's linear progression.

Reduplicatio and anaphora

As we have just seen, rhetorical embellishments are used to great effect. Anadiplosis or *reduplicatio* consists in beginning "a sentence, line or clause with the concluding, or any prominent, word of the one preceding" *(OED)*. Three examples follow: *Purgatorio* 27.92, *mi prese il sonno; il sonno che sovente;* the repetition of *vidi (Io vidi . . . e vidi . . . e vidi . . . io vidi . . .vid' io)* as a leitmotif of Cacciaguida's portrayal of an idyllic Florence *(Par.* 16.88–151); and the threefold repetition of Virgil's name (with its sentimental climax struck at the beginning of the third line) in:

> Ma Virgilio n'avea lasciati scemi
> di sé, Virgilio dolcissimo patre,
> *Virgilio* a cui per mia salute die'mi.
> > *(Purg.* 30.49–51; my emphasis)

The supreme example of what may be achieved by a combination of anadiplosis, alliteration, and assonance is the poet's final attempt to convey the mystery of the Trinity at the end of the poem:

> O luce etterna che *sola* in te *sidi,*
> *sola t'intendi, e* da *te intelletta*
> *e intendente te ami e arridi!*
> > *(Par.* 33.124–26)

Anaphora, another form of repetition whereby the same word is used to open a series of two or more verses or syntactical units, is found in the opening *terzina* of *Inferno* 3, which strikes the reader forcibly with its surprising mimesis of direct speech—and now emphasized by the use of upper case (as in some editions: e.g., Sapegno 1957, 30; Lanza 1996, 23): PER ME SI VA . . . PER ME SI VA . . . PER ME SI VA.[45] The most celebrated example is undoubtedly found in *Inferno* 5.100–106, where the key word *Amore* introduces each of the three *terzine* and the inevitability of love is emphasized by the internal repetition of the verbal forms in the central *terzina:* Amor, *ch'al cor gentil ratto s'apprende . . .* Amor, *ch'a nullo* amato amar *perdona . . .* Amor *condusse noi ad una morte* (my emphasis). We encounter the most extended use of anaphora in *Purgatorio* 12.25–63. The repetition of *Vedea* in the first four *terzine* describing examples of the proud punished, followed by the vocative *O* which opens the next four, and by *Mostrava* at the beginning of each of the last four, with the whole rounded off in the thirteenth *terzina* with its recapitulation of *Vedeva/o/mostrava:* all these elements contribute to the acrostic *VOM* (*uom:* man) thereby reminding us of the fact that the Fall was occasioned by the fundamental sin of pride. Similarly, the political corruption of European rulers is emphasized by the acrostic *LVE* (*lue:* pestilence), formed by three groups of three *terzine,* the first beginning with *Lí,* the second with *Vedrassi,* the third with *E (Par.* 19.115–41). Other notable examples are found at the end of the pilgrim's journey with its insistence on the vision granted him *(Par.* 30.128–31: *Mira . . . Vedi . . . vedi),* in Bernard's prayer to the Virgin *(Par.* 33.19–20: *In te misericordia, in te pietate, / in te magnificenza, in te s'aduna . . .),* and toward the middle of the poem, in the prophetic vision of Christ's passion played out once again at Anagni:

> *veggio* in Alagna intrar lo fiordaliso,
> e nel vicario suo Cristo esser catto.
>   *Veggiolo* un'altra volta esser deriso;
> *veggio* rinovellar l'aceto e 'l fiele,
> e tra vivi ladroni esser anciso.
>   *Veggio* il novo Pilato sí crudele . . .
>   *(Purg.* 20.86–91; my emphasis)

Imagery and figures of speech

As we have observed, the opening lines of *Inferno* 13 describe the unnatural wood of the suicides by means of a series of negatives *(neun sentiero . . . Non fronda verde . . . non rami schietti . . . non pomi . . . Non han sí aspri sterpi né sí folti)* that highlight the fact that self-destruction goes against the most basic instinct, that of self-preservation. As a result, the wood *(bosco,* l. 2) is both an infernal relative of the *selva selvaggia* in which the pilgrim had been lost and an objective correlative illustrating the suicides' condition. As part of the landscape, the wood is a striking example of the significance of the physical setting of Dante's other-world. Other instances of symbolic use of landscape in the first two *cantiche* might be cited, such as the abyss that divides upper hell from the lower levels where sins of fraud are punished, the ice of Cocytus, and the mountain of purgatory; however, for our present purpose, we shall concentrate on the images employed in Dante's metaphors and similes.

Metonymy and metaphor

We begin with a passage illustrating Dante's use of metonymy: the substitution of a word or phrase with which it is closely associated.[46] A *terzina* from Hugh Capet's speech on the terrace of avarice offers three examples of metonymy, one in each line:

> "ch'a la *corona vedova* promossa
> *la testa* di mio figlio fu, dal quale
> cominciar di costor *le sacrate ossa."*
>   *(Purg.* 20.58–60; my emphasis)

------

that, to the widowed crown the head of my son was elevated, [my son] from whom the consecrated bones of these [kings] began.

Here, the "widowed crown" signifies the "vacant throne" (itself another metonymy) of the monarchy; Hugh's son's "head" received the crown; it was Robert of course who was "promoted" or elevated to the kingship; and the "consecrated bones" are an example of a specific type of metonymy (synecdoche) pointing to the consecration of the Capetian kings in the cathedral at Reims. In lines 73–75 of the same canto (as noted in chapter 7), Hugh foresees that his descendant Charles of Valois will use "the lance with which Judas jousted" to "rip open Florence's belly" (*e solo con la lancia / con la qual giostrò Giuda, e quella ponta / sì ch'a Fiorenza fa scoppiar la pancia*). The first metaphor *(la lancia)* evokes jousting in medieval tournaments. Rules governing the joust were obviously based on a code of honor that excluded all forms of treachery. Here, however, we have a member of the royal house of France who shows himself to be a follower of the arch-traitor Judas Iscariot. The second metaphor *(la pancia)* has been brilliantly analyzed by Emilio Pasquini, who—noting that Florence is personified as a woman—traces the genesis of Florence's belly back to Mastro Adamo's deformed paunch (*l'epa croia* of *Inf.* 30.102) and its development through the stinking guts of the *femmina balba* (*Purg.* 19.32–33) that appears to the pilgrim in a dream just before his encounter with Hugh Capet. This leads to the "almost Shakespearean" image of Florence's guts spilling out and thus symbolizing the corruption of the commune destroyed by treachery.[47]

The absence of God and his Light are implied by the metaphor "blind prison"—used to describe hell itself (*Inf.* 10.58–59)—and (in a more complex way) by the sun's "silence" in *Inferno* 1.60, when the she-wolf pushes the pilgrim back to "where the sun is silent." (The same metaphor of the sun and its light as implying God and his voice/grace that can no longer reach the sinner's heart is behind the phrase *d'ogne luce muto* [*Inf.* 5.28], which does not merely imply that it is bereft of all light, but that light is "silent" [cf. Durling's translation, "where all light is silent"].) This example also points to the importance of the demands of the rhyme scheme (an element easily overlooked by readers of translations) in promoting the use of metaphorical language: here, *face–pace–TACE* (ll. 56–60; emphasis mine). In the example of metonymy discussed above, the *corona vedova* includes the metaphor of the widow, which we find used most compellingly in *Purgatorio* 1.25–27, when the Northern Hemisphere (where humanity must live since its expulsion from Eden) is described as *vedovo sito,* because it is deprived of the sight of the four stars symbolizing the infused cardinal virtues. In *Purgatorio* 6.113, Italy is "widowed" because she has been abandoned by the emperor. The image of the widowed city (like so many of Dante's metaphors) is taken from the Bible: *Quomodo sedet sola civitas plena populo! facta est quasi vidua domina gentium* (Lam. 1.1). The same biblical image described Florence's condition after

Beatrice's death in 1290 (*VN* 23.1), and—some two decades later (May–June 1314), in *Epistle* 11.1.1—it was used by Dante to portray the state of Rome, abandoned by the papacy installed at Avignon.

Another metaphor with a biblical flavor is that of the thirst for knowledge innate in human beings, found at the beginning of *Purgatorio* 21: "The natural thirst that is never quenched except by the water for whose grace the Samaritan woman begged" (*Purg.* 21.1–3; cf. John 4.6–15 and *Conv.* 1.1.9). Thirst is literal, never metaphorical, in *Inferno* (*Inf.* 30.56, 121, 126). On the other hand, it is found six times as a metaphor in *Purgatorio* and ten times in *Paradiso,* where it signifies the creature's instinctive urge to return to God and be reunited with him (*Par.* 2.19), as well as the pilgrim's burning desire to see the reality of heaven (*Par.* 30.74). As Lino Pertile points out, "Dante's Paradise . . . is hardly the kingdom of quiet and immobility we might have expected; indeed it is perennial motion, desire and ardor, hunger and thirst" (1993b, 155). This dynamic quality is in no small measure a consequence of the poet's use of metaphor.

The golden "ladder" that reaches up for the contemplative spirits from the heaven of Saturn to the Empyrean—another biblical image (Gen. 28.12)—is a visual metaphor for the souls' mystical ascent to God during their lives on earth (*Par.* 21.25–33). The "rose without thorns" of Christian iconography or the *rosa mystica* indicates Mary, while the saints are lilies in "the beautiful garden" or paradise in Beatrice's question to the pilgrim:

> "Perché la faccia mia sí t'innamora,
> che tu non ti rivolgi al bel giardino
> che sotto i raggi di Cristo s'infiora?
>   Quivi è la rosa in che 'l verbo divino
> carne si fece; quivi son li gigli
> al cui odor si prese il buon cammino."
> (*Par.* 23.70–75)

———

Why does my face so captivate you that you do not turn your gaze to the beautiful garden which blossoms beneath Christ's rays? There is the rose in which God's Word was made flesh; there are the lilies whose fragrance inspired [others] to follow the right path.

The role of metaphor in mystical writings is well known. It is therefore hardly surprising to find that St. Bernard's prayer to the Virgin is couched in a whole series of metaphors. The Virgin is the "fixed goal" decreed by Divine Providence for the redemption of humankind (*Par.* 33.3: *termine fisso d'etterno consiglio*). Love was "rekindled" in her womb, whereby this flower—the "white rose" (*Par.* 31.1) of God's elect in paradise—"blossomed" *(Par. 33.7–9: si raccese l'amore . . . cosí è germinato questo fiore).* For the blessed souls in heaven, Mary *is* a "noonday torch of love," as well as a constant "fountain of hope" for humanity on earth (ll. 10–12: *Qui . . . meridïana face . . . giuso . . . di speranza fontana vivace).* Anyone who wishes to obtain Grace without recourse to Mary's intercession entertains a desire which "would fly without wings" (ll. 13–15: *sua disïanza vuol volar sanz'ali).* The saint "burns" (l. 28) in order that the pilgrim who has voyaged from the "lowest hole" (l. 22) in the universe may have all the "clouds" (l. 31) removed from his mortal being so that the "supreme pleasure" (l. 33: God's beauty) may be revealed to him.

Especially significant is the wing metaphor. The supremely negative example of this image is created when the oars of Ulysses' craft are transformed into "wings" for the "mad flight" that leads him and his companions to destruction (*Inf.* 26.124–42). The positive connotations of the image are highlighted by Cacciaguida when he refers to Beatrice as "she / who gave you wings for the lofty flight" (*Par.* 15.53–54). John Freccero (1986, 17) cites Bernard Silvestris's gloss to the myth of Daedalus and his dedication of "the oarage of his wings *[alarum remigium],* that is, the exercise of his reason and intellect" to Apollo. For the Neoplatonists, such a flight represented the soul's return to God. Moreover, Dante's surname can be taken as a pointer to his mission. For the man who believed that one's name reveals one's essential nature, his family name Alighieri/Alaghieri could reveal "the skeleton of Virgil's neologism, *ala + gero* [*Aen.* 12.249]; and what is more, there was the bonus that it afforded special prominence to the essential feature *ala* [wing]" (Shankland 1975, 775). And Beatrice's pivotal role is again stressed in Dante's identification of her as "that compassionate one who guided my feathered wings on such a lofty flight" (*Par.* 25.49–50).

The poem's second line presents the reader with the archetypal image of the "savage wood" or forest, a metaphor for the sinful state in which the pilgrim Dante finds himself in the opening scene. There is an undeniable echo, a parallel with the Brunetto Latini of the *Tesoretto,* who also lost "the highway *[il gran cammino],*" and wandered lost in a strange wood *(una selva diversa),* from which he looked up at a mountain and saw a large number of beasts.[48] As Jacques Le Goff has demonstrated (1992, 58), in Western Europe of the Middle Ages the fundamental dualism was "between nature and culture, expressed in terms of the opposition between what was built, cultivated, and inhabited (city, castle, village) and what was essentially wild (the sea and the forest, western equivalents of the eastern desert)." Thus, Falsembiante in the *Fiore* boasts: "I no longer care for hermitages, or to live in deserts and in forests . . . I make my humble home in cities and in castles . . ." (Casciani and Kleinhenz 2000, 277). The forest/wood of popular imagination was a dangerous place, harboring ferocious animals and men: wolves, brigands, outlaws, and murderers. The city, on the other hand, was ideally portrayed, with its citizens living in concord and justice. When Dante re-calls his native city as it was in his youth, he uses the metaphor of the sheepfold *(bello ovile)* in which "lambs" live in security and well-being (*Par.* 25.5)—al-though like everything in the medieval universe, the city also had its semiotic counterpart *in malo,* in the terrestrial Babylon and in the Devil's City beyond the grave.[49] The literal story of the *Comedy* is thus a journeying from the dark wood, the vestibule of hell, through the City of Dis, followed by an ascent to the "divine forest" of Eden, and thence to the City of God or Paradise, "that Rome of which Christ is a Roman"; so that the court of heaven, first seen as a white rose, is finally identified by Beatrice as "our city" (*Par.* 30.130).

One of the most potent metaphors in the *Comedy* is that of the Book of Creation. Hugh of St. Victor wrote that the whole universe is like a book writ-ten by God's "finger."[50] This image comes to life in one of the last metaphors of the poem, when the poet claims that in the depths of God he saw "bound to-gether in one volume all the pages that are scattered throughout the universe":

> Nel suo profondo vidi che s'interna,
> legato con amore in un volume,
> ciò che per l'universo si squaderna.
> (*Par.* 33.85–87)

The poet invents the word *squadernare* on the basis of the precious *quaderno* in which contemporary merchants and governments kept their records (cf. *Purg.* 12.105). The prefix *-s* (as in *slegare,* to unbind; *sfiorire,* to wither; *sfasciare,* to shat-ter) conveys the idea that the book's pages or quires have been torn asunder and scattered throughout the universe.[51] Instead, in God's depths the poet (like St. Francis, the poet of *Laudes creaturarum*) can now see the essential unity of all cre-ation, the binding together by Love of all the multiple facets of God's work. The book image is especially striking if we recall that until (and well after) the in-vention of printing, a book was a truly precious object that could be possessed by only the happy few. Even more significant is the fact that in Dante's time most men and women were illiterate. They were well aware of their inability to interpret the "signs" on the page of a book or of a Bible glimpsed in a church, although they knew that a privileged minority was able to understand the mes-sage transmitted by those letters. Similarly, the signs placed by God in his cre-ation could not be read in their totality by most Christians: their message re-mained hidden.

Another powerful metaphor is found in *Purgatorio* 7.31–32, when Virgil ex-plains to Sordello that he is eternally relegated to limbo, together with "the in-nocent children / bitten by the teeth of death" *(dai denti morsi de la morte)* before the traces of original sin could be eliminated by baptism. The Lombard "tooth" *(il dente longobardo)* is said to have attacked Holy Church in *Paradiso* 6.94–95. But whereas the Bible employs this metaphor in the same way in Psalm 123 [124].6, "Blessed be the Lord, who has not delivered us as prey to their teeth" *(dentibus eorum),* there is nothing to prepare us for *Paradiso* 26.49–51, when St. John tells the pilgrim to tell the blessed spirits what other "ropes" *(corde)* pull him toward God in order to show "with how many teeth this love bites you" *(con quanti denti questo amor ti morde),* a metaphor that returns in Dante's reply that his love of God is the result of all possible "bites" (l. 55: *Tutti quei morsi . . .*).

Already in the fourth canto of *Paradiso* the poet underlines the need for figurative language when dealing with certain metaphysical truths beyond human comprehension, since human understanding has to be mediated through the senses.[52] At the very beginning of his *Summa Theologica* (1.1.9), Aquinas had likewise gone out of his way to declare that it was fitting *(conveniens)* for Scripture to portray "divine and spiritual things through material ones . . . it is moreover natural for man to arrive at understanding via things of the senses, since all our understanding originates from the senses. Hence it is proper *(convenienter)* that in Holy Scripture things of the spirit should be relayed to us under the images *(metaphoris)* of corporeal things." Aquinas's Latin *(conveniens . . . convenienter)* is virtually echoed in Dante's:

> Cosí parlar *conviensi* al vostro ingegno,
> però che solo da sensato apprende
> ciò che fa poscia d'intelletto degno.
> Per questo la Scrittura condescende
> a vostra facultate, e piedi e mano
> attribuisce a Dio e altro intende;
> e Santa Chiesa con aspetto umano
> Gabrïel e Michel vi rappresenta,
> e l'altro che Tobia rifece sano.
> (*Par.* 4.40–48; my emphasis)

This kind of language is necessary for your minds, since it is only from the senses that they can take what they then make worthy of intellection. It is for this reason that Scripture makes allowances for your faculties and attributes hands and feet to God, but means something else; and Holy Church portrays Gabriel and Michael with human features, as well as the other who cured Tobias.

Beatrice has in fact been at pains to explain to the pilgrim that everything he has seen so far in paradise (and everything he will see until he reaches the

Empyrean) is nothing but an extended metaphor, constructed precisely in order to give him a graphic portrayal of the different degrees of beatitude enjoyed by the blessed (ll. 28–39). "As 'place' the heavens are like so many movie-screens which serve as temporary projection centers for an essentially spaceless reality" (Brandeis 1960, 143). All the blessed are in fact united with God in the Empyrean heaven outside of space and time. It is therefore only in *Paradiso* 30 that the pilgrim sees what had appeared as flowers (the saints) and sparks (the angels) transformed into the reality of "both the courts of heaven" (ll. 94–96). Until that climactic moment, what he has observed is merely "shadowy prefaces of the truth" *(Par.* 30.78: *son di lor vero umbriferi prefazi).* The poet has coined the epithet *umbriferi* (from the Latin *umbrifer,* shade-bearing) and has applied it to the word *prefazio,* which occurs at only this point in the poem—with the connotation of the liturgical *praefatio* leading to the climax of the Mass. Similarly, God is first seen as an infinitesimally small point of intense light on which heaven and all creation depend *(Par.* 28.16–42); and the poet shares with his ideal reader the knowledge that a mathematical point has a spatial position but no magnitude or dimension *(Conv.* 2.13.27). At the moment of the Beatific Vision, Dante describes the Trinity as it appears to him in the shape of "three circles of three different colors but of equal circumference" *(Par.* 33.116–17), the circle symbolizing both perfection and infinity. Nevertheless, this metaphorical portrayal of the triune God is as inadequate as is all human language to convey the imprint left on the poet's mind of what he glimpses at the climax of his pilgrimage (ll. 121–23). As in all mystical experience, language—however powerful, however figurative—must ultimately be found wanting. This failure of metaphorical language is expressed by a simile that compares the pilgrim who attempts to fathom the mystery of the Incarnation and the hypostatic union in Christ to the geometrician who tries to measure the circle but lacks the formula needed to perform his task (ll. 133–38).

Simile

The abundance of both metaphor and simile in Dante's Christian epic is due in no small part to the poet's vision of a universe in which the various sections and fragments of God's Book of Creation were all interconnected.[53] With almost six hundred similes, the *Comedy* is light-years away from the poetic universe of Dante's early poems, where imagery is both traditional and sparse.[54] Only six similes are found in the poems selected by Dante for his *Vita Nova.* Such restraint was in accord with the theory and practice of medieval rhetoric. Both Geoffrey of Vinsauf and Matthew of Vendôme declared that the use of similes was obsolete. In his *Ars versificatoria* (4.3–5), written before 1175, Matthew ruled that similes should not be excluded altogether but used more sparingly than by the ancient poets, who indulged in a profusion of "poetic fancyings . . . this however is not permitted to contemporary versifiers" (Matthew of Vendôme 1981, 94). It is indeed astonishing to find that the epic similes that are such an essential ingredient in Vergil's *Aeneid* and Statius's *Thebaid* were in fact suppressed by their medieval adapters (Boyde 1971, 301).

But if we turn to the opening of *Paradiso* 13, we find an immensely complex simile that weaves its way through some twenty-four lines of verse, with three *terzine* urging the reader to imagine ("and keep the image in mind," l. 2) fifteen stars of the first magnitude visible in our night sky, then the seven members of the Great Bear, together with the two brightest from the Little Bear. While retaining a mental picture of these twenty-four brilliant stars, the reader must then imagine that they are divided into two constellations both similar in shape to Ariadne's Crown (ll. 13–15), concentric but revolving in opposite directions (ll. 13–18). Then, obedient to the threefold exhortation "Imagini" (ll. 1, 7, 10), the reader's imagination will have a pale shadow (*avrà quasi l'ombra,* l. 19) of the celestial reality observed by the pilgrim in the Heaven of the Sun. In other words, this injunction to the reader functions as a simile: what appears to Dante in the fourth heaven is *like* twenty-four of the stars visible to humanity on earth, *if* they were divided into two circles of twelve stars, one of which must be imagined to move in a clockwise, the other in a counterclockwise, direction. Here, we have the basic function of simile (indeed, of all imagery) in Dante's description of his journey through the other world: it is not for ornamentation as in the classical epics of Vergil, Lucan, and Statius. It is a direct appeal to readers to proceed from the known to the unknown, so that they may *imagine* what the poet claims to have seen. This primary need is foregrounded in *Purgatorio* 13.100–102 (my emphasis):

> Tra l'altre vidi un'ombra ch'aspettava
> in vista; *e se volesse alcun dir 'Come?',*
> lo mento a guisa d'orbo in sù levava.

———

> Among the others I saw a shade that looked as if it were waiting; *and if someone were to say "How so?"* it was raising its chin as the blind do.

So, in *Purgatorio* 8.28–29, the angels' clothes are green like the new leaves of early spring, while the damned souls of the eighth *bolgia* appear like a multitude of fireflies at dusk (*Inf.* 26.25–33). Yet, if it were simply a question of stirring the reader's imagination and setting the infernal scene, this latter simile would surely suffice. Instead, the poet offers a second comparison (ll. 34–42) by which the flames concealing the sinners are compared to the flame Elisha saw when

Elijah's chariot was taken up by a whirlwind to heaven. About one-tenth of the *Comedy*'s similes are derived from the Bible or mythology. In such cases, other elements beyond the pictorial, other connotations and allusions, are present. In this example, such elements are so important that Dante seems to have overlooked the simple fact that the comparison is hardly convincing as an aid to the reader's imagination: as Elisha could only *see* a flame (where previously he had seen Elijah), so the flames of the eighth *bolgia* move *(tal si move ciascuna)* and each conceals a sinner. The firefly simile is far more effective as an aid to conveying the pilgrim's vision of the eighth *bolgia*. However, the evocation of the biblical episode (4 Kings 2.11–14) not only raises the stylistic level (thus preparing the way for the Ulysses episode) but it also contains important foreshadowing of Dante's version of the Greek hero's story: "fire, whirlwind, horses/vehicle, the crossing of a body of water, and the question of seeing Elijah in the flames" (Durling and Martinez 1996, 408). Of paramount importance is the fact that "Elijah is the explicit antitype of Ulysses" (Mazzotta 1979, 91). The greatest of the Hebrew prophets, Elijah was "like fire" and his prophetic words "burned like a firebrand" (Ecclus. 48.1). He led his people toward righteousness and social justice. Instead, Ulysses, bereft of prudence (the greatest virtue in a leader) led his men to their doom with his cunning eloquence: "And the tongue is a fire . . . itself set on fire by hell" (James 3.6). Thus, whereas Elijah's eloquence burned like fire, now Ulysses himself burns in a tongue of flame.[55] Most forceful is the semiological opposition between the downward trajectory of Ulysses' craft and the upward flight or surging of the horses that draw Elijah's chariot heavenward (l. 36: *al cielo erti levorsi*).

Similes based on common or everyday experience often add a "realistic" note to Dante's narrative. Two of the most celebrated occur in *Inferno* 15.17–21, when a group of souls peer at Virgil and Dante "as in the evening people look at one another under the new moon; and they knit their brows as an old tailor does at the eye of his needle." In *Inferno* 22.25–28, the barrators, in their attempts to avoid total submersion in the pitch, are compared to bullfrogs in a ditch that keep only their snouts out of the water, while the rest of their bodies remains hidden. In *Inferno* 32.31–35, the same image of the frog (now croaking) with its snout above the water in summer is used to indicate the position of the souls who had betrayed their kin and who are buried up to their necks in the ice of Cocytus. This rapid sketch of the frog croaking while the countrywoman dreams of the harvest to come is in utter contrast to the plight of the denizens of Cocytus's frozen landscape. Nevertheless, both elements (the frog and the *villana*) "perform the true poetic action of the passage, silently affirming that in the lake of ice there are no comfortable creatures, no autumn, no harvest and no dream of fair futures" (Brandeis 1960, 137). Other imagery from the world of nature plays a straightforward role. In *Paradiso* 8.52–54, Charles Martel compares the effulgent light that conceals his spirit from Dante's gaze to "an animal swathed in its own silk" (cf. *Par.* 26.97–102). In *Purgatorio* 10.124–29, human beings on earth are metaphorical grubs destined to grow into angelic butterflies in their flight to God; all too often, however, they remain "like defective insects, like worms in whom full formation is lacking." In *Paradiso* 10.88–90, St. Thomas explains that the charity that inspires the blessed so conditions their behavior that, if they were to refuse to share "the wine from their flasks" with the pilgrim, they "would be no more free" than water is not to flow down to the sea.

Equally significant is the fact that, in *Paradiso* (the realm at the farthest remove from our everyday, terrestrial experiences) Dante does not hesitate to use conflicting images in order to "reflect the paradoxes that run through man's conception of the divine . . . Paradise is the realm of resolved paradoxes . . . God, of course, is the ultimate reconciliation of opposites." The moon "is like a cloud (*Par.* 2.31), a diamond (33), a pearl (34) and water (35). The mind cannot picture a substance which is solid, diaphanous, transparent and opaque at the same time . . . the Rose . . . is at once a flower of innumerable petals (30.117), an amphitheatre with its seats nearly filled (30.131), and a city (30.130) . . . God is both center and circumference, the core and the boundaries of the universe" (Ferrante 1983, 127–29).

Because Vergil was the outstanding poetic model for Dante (cf. *Inf.* 1.82–87), it is fascinating to see how the medieval Christian author adapts one of his borrowings. In *Aeneid* 6.309–12, Aeneas sees the throng of souls who rush toward Charon, the infernal ferryman: "thick as the leaves of the forest that fall down at the first frost of autumn, and thick as the birds that from the seething deep flock toward the shore . . . they stood, begging to be the first to be ferried across . . ." The images of autumnal leaves and birds are similarly used by Dante to evoke the damned souls ferried across the Acheron: "As in autumn the leaves detach themselves one after the other, until the branch sees all its raiment on the ground: so Adam's evil seed throw themselves from that shore one by one, when beckoned to, each like a falcon to its lure" (*Inf.* 3.112–17). The most obvious difference is the behavior of the souls: in Vergil, they rush forward in the hope of crossing the infernal river and stretch out their hands "in yearning for the farther shore" (*Aen.* 6.314); in Dante, the damned gnash their teeth as Charon tells them that he will lead them "to the eternal darkness, to heat and freezing" (ll. 86–87), even as he "beats with his oar" those who lag behind (l. 111). However, the adaptation and transformation of the Vergilian simile go far deeper. In the *Aeneid,* the images are evoked to stress the immense number of souls waiting to cross the Acheron; they have a cumulative effect. In the *Comedy,* they have been separated into two parts, each with its specific function. First, the leaves: it is not just their number (Vergil's *multa . . . folia*) but the inexorable baring of the branches and fluttering down of the leaves that struck Vergil's "disciple." The idea of the bare branch contemplating the ground strewn with its dead leaves is Dante's own, and it adds a note of pathos absent from Vergil's passage. The change from the Latin plural *(multa)* to the Italian "one after the other" *(l'una appresso de l'altra)* highlights the Christian concept of the individual soul's destiny. And Vergilian symmetry is discarded by Dante, who uses the leaves to indicate movement and fragility, while the image of the birds *(multae . . . aves)* is transformed by reference to the medieval art of falconry into a highly effective evocation of the souls' total obedience to Charon, whereby their "fear is turned into desire" (l. 126).

At other times, the simile (as in the case of Elijah) is heavily dependent on a cultural context. Some knowledge of medieval scientific, astronomical lore is needed to understand the transformation in St. Peter's appearance described in *Paradiso* 27.14–15: "such as Jove would become, if he and Mars / were birds and exchanged their plumage." In order to grasp the metamorphosis, readers must know that the planet Jupiter "appears white, almost silvery, among all the stars" *(Conv.* 2.13.25), whereas Mars is of a fiery reddish color. As St. Peter inveighs against the wretch on earth who has corrupted his burial place, his color changes from that of the pale planet/god of justice (Jupiter) into that of the ruddy planet/god of war and revolution (Mars); and, as a result, the whole of heaven turns red. Beatrice's appearance also changes: "and I believe that such an eclipse took place in Heaven when the Supreme Power suffered" *(Par.* 27.35–36). According to the Gospels (e.g., Luke 23.44–45), at the moment of Christ's death on the cross "darkness spread over the whole earth . . . and the sun was darkened." Both the allusion to the scene at Golgotha and the technical word *eclissi* (eclipse) suggest blackness, a sign of universal mourning. On the other hand, the simile's vehicle suggests the blush of shame for another's crimes *(Par.* 27.31–34): "And as a virtuous lady remains sure of herself, yet is abashed while listening to the account of another's fault, so did Beatrice change in appearance." It is therefore most likely that Dante here is evoking the universe's mourning for the death of the Redeemer (cf. *Vita Nova* 23.5 and ll. 49–53 of *Donna pietosa*) with a poetic license that sees the eclipse of the sun (symbol of God) in terms of the dark red (almost black) color of the last drops of the blood Christ shed for the redemption of the human race. The color of clouds lit up by a darkening sun and of a lady's blush add little to Dante's narration. However, the fact that the color which spreads over the whole of heaven *(tutto 'l ciel cosperso)* is due to the rays of the *sole avverso* (ll. 28–30) is not merely an Ovidian echo: "And red as the clouds which flush beneath the sun's slanting rays *[adversi solis]*" *(Met.* 3.183–84). The sun as a symbol of God's grace is surely latent in the term *lo sole avverso,* where the epithet may be taken to mean both "opposite" and "opposing": opposed to the corruption of God's vicar on earth (cf. *Inf.* 10.46–47). This may suggest the idea of the sun's eclipse—but an eclipse that is not a natural phenomenon. The image contained in "such an eclipse I believe occurred in heaven *('n ciel)*" employs the word *ciel* not merely in its physical meaning but in its religious connotation: "heaven." The image is also linked to a tragedy of universal significance; it is in fact apocalyptic in its reverberations. The eclipse at Christ's Passion is evoked in order to prepare the way for St. Peter's denunciation of his unworthy descendants who are nothing but rapacious wolves (*lupi rapaci*, l. 55) dressed as shepherds of Christ's flock—the flock which is also Christ's bride nourished by the *blood* of Peter and the first popes (ll. 40–45). Red is the symbolic background to this drama: red, the color of blood, shame, and anger. As Richard Lansing (1977) has argued: "Many of Dante's similes are extraordinarily suggestive of a full range of associations in which the visual often gives way to the conceptual."[56]

Similes may be contained in one line of verse, as at the end of the pilgrim's encounter with Francesca *(Inf.* 5.142: *e caddi come corpo morto cade),* "and I fell as a dead body falls" (preceded at the close of the previous canto—*Inf.* 4.136—by another typical medieval simile *per brevitatem*: *e caddi come l'uom che 'l sonno piglia;* and I fell like a man overcome by sleep).[57] They may even extend over eighteen lines, as in the example chosen from *Paradiso* 13, cited above. Thematic clusters are also in evidence. One is found in *Purgatorio* 28, where no fewer than three similes evoke classical myths. The first (ll. 49–51) compares the as-yet-unidentified Edenic figure of Matelda to Proserpina in her beauty and chastity. The erotic allusion to her abduction by Pluto is amplified in the next simile, which claims that the goddess of love, Venus, never shone so brightly—even when the goddess was most wounded by Cupid's dart in her love for Adonis (ll. 64–66). The third erotic image compares Dante's "hatred" of being separated from Matelda by Lethe to Leander's feelings for the Hellespont in stormy weather, when it prevented him from spending the night with his beloved Hero, priestess of Aphrodite (ll. 70–75). Not only are readers expected to understand the mythological allusions but they are also expected to discover the unifying thread linking the three similes: in the pilgrim's case, his ardent desire for a state of innocence, beauty, and justice, combined with regret for the loss of the Edenic state through original sin.

As the pilgrim hesitates to cross the wall of fire guarding the Earthly Paradise, the poet refers to another Ovidian myth. "As, at Thisbe's name, Pyramus opened his eyes at the point of death and gazed at her, when the mulberry became blood red" (*Purg.* 27.37–39), so Dante's reluctance to pass through the wall of fire is overcome by Virgil's spur when he points out that "this wall" is what separates Beatrice from her faithful lover (l. 36). Ovid tells the story of two young lovers in Babylon who were separated by a wall in *Metamorphoses* 4.55–166. Pyramus, mistakenly believing that Thisbe was dead, committed suicide, whereupon the mulberry's white fruits were changed forever to bright red.

As Freccero notes (1986, 176), "Anyone acquainted with the tradition of the *Ovidius moralizatus* would have known that the famous love story was interpreted . . . with Pyramus as Christ, who stained the tree with his blood." The second line of canto 27 does in fact refer to the shedding of Christ's blood—*là dove il suo fattor lo sangue sparse*—while the geographical references to the Ebro and Ganges rivers and Jerusalem-purgatory trace a cross on the earth's surface. Ovid's tree of death thus becomes a tree of life through Beatrice (Moevs 2000). The wall that separates the two ancient lovers is replaced by the wall of fire surrounding Eden since the Fall, now overcome by the living Dante thanks to Beatrice's name (truly, a "bringer of blessedness") and the anticipated beauty of her eyes (ll. 52–54). Once he is inside Eden, the Ovidian myth returns with regard to the pilgrim's inability to identify God's justice in the tree "twice despoiled." It is difficult to accept the traditional interpretation placed on the reference to Pyramus in Beatrice's rebuke to the pilgrim: "And if your vain thoughts had not been water of Elsa around your mind, and their delight a Pyramus at the mulberry, through so many circumstances alone you would have recognized in the prohibition the tree to be, in the moral sense, God's justice" (*Purg.* 33.67–72). Traditionally, the references to the "water of Elsa" (a river in Tuscany) and "Pyramus" have been taken to signify the petrifying or staining of Dante's intelligence, which had been indulging in "vain thoughts." However, we must analyze Beatrice's assertion more carefully. First, she states that *li pensier vani* have encrusted or petrified Dante's mind; next, that the attraction they exert on him is like *un Piramo a la gelsa*. What, we must ask ourselves, was Pyramus's condition "at the mulberry"? There, he mistakenly deciphered a sign (the bloodstained veil dropped by Thisbe). This error of interpretation led to his death; so, now, Dante's "vain thoughts," his inability to decipher the meaning of the pageant in Eden (and, in particular, the sign representing God's justice) might well have had equally fatal consequences for the pilgrim.[58]

The return of the same "vehicle" in different contexts may reveal a semiological progression from evil to good unfolding in the poem's imagery. This is so with the image of the falcon. On his first appearance, the devil Calcabrina is likened to a falcon angry because it has lost its prey (*Inf.* 22.130–32). Seven lines later the same image becomes a metaphor applied to the devil Alichino, where it signifies an aggressive bird of prey, a hawk armed with fierce talons (*Inf.* 22.139: *sparvier grifagno*). In the very different context of the Valley of the Negligent Rulers in antepurgatory, the two angels that guard the souls from the dangers posed by the serpent are described as "hawks of heaven" (*Purg.* 8.104: *astor celestïali*). So far, the emphasis has been on the bird's swiftness, strength, and aggressive nature, but a radical shift occurs in *Paradiso*. The first occurrence is problematical: in *Paradiso* 1.49–51, the simile of a reflected ray of light that "returns on high" is itself compared to a *pelegrin che tornar vuole,* where the word *pelegrin* has traditionally been understood to indicate the pilgrim who wishes to return home (even as Dante now longs to regain his heavenly *patria*). It is, however, possible to read *pelegrin* as referring to the "peregrine" falcon, trained to take off vertically from its owner's hand. This bird simile would follow on naturally from the comparison with the eagle's mythical ability to look steadfastly into the sun (in l. 61, the sun is a symbol of the Godhead). The peregrine's vertical flight would then allude to the speed and verticality of Beatrice's and Dante's ascent to God, whereas the pilgrim's desire to return home would convey the emotive force behind that ascent. It may be that the poet did not wish to choose one possible meaning of *pelegrin* to the exclusion of the other. Great poetry, like great music, contains (semantic) chords generating overtones and undertones in the receptive reader.[59] However that may be, there is no ambiguity in the falcon simile of *Paradiso* 19.34–39, which compares the symbolic eagle of the heaven of Jupiter to a falcon freed from its hood that expresses its joy by "applauding with its wings." Readers will already have encountered the falcon simile in *Purgatorio* 19.64–69 as well as the metaphor contained in the preceding lines (62–63), whereby God *(lo rege etterno)* is seen as the falconer who calls back his creatures with the "lure" *(al logoro)* of the celestial spheres. So, the simile in *Paradiso* 19 reinforces the idea that the human being is sent forth by God into this world to do his bidding and then return to him. The heavenly eagle is utterly subservient to the divine will, even as men and women should respond like trained falcons to God's call.

The voyage of the Argonauts

The *Comedy* is the story of a journey or extraordinary pilgrimage through the universe, first a descent to the pit of hell, then a climb up the Mountain of Purgatory, and finally an instantaneous ascent through the various spheres of the physical universe to God's dwelling place beyond space and time. In the last part, it is also a voyage through uncharted waters. We shall now examine how the two strands, *pilgrimage* and *voyage,* are brought together and fulfilled in the poem's final cantos.

Both at the beginning and at the end of *Paradiso* the myth of the Argonauts is evoked.[60] After warning the (theologically) unprepared reader to return to shore, Dante refers to the archetypal voyage across uncharted waters: "Those illustrious heroes who crossed to Colchis / were not as amazed as you will be / when they saw Jason become a ploughman" (*Par.* 2.16–18). In Ovid's version of the myth, it was not the crewmen of the first ship (the *Argo* + *nauta,* sailor) who were amazed when Jason ploughed the field sacred to Mars with the firebreathing bulls, but the natives of Colchis as they observed his apparently impossible feats (*Met.* 7.120). Here, however, Dante implies that his select band of readers must be transformed into Argonauts who will accompany the poet on his unique enterprise. From Statius (*Thebaid* 5.343–45), our poet would have learned that the Argo's crew included Orpheus (the first poet-theologian), as well as Castor and Pollux, *Oebalidae gemini* (ibid., ll. 437–40), whom Dante identified with the Gemini (*Purg.* 4.61), those "glorious stars" to which he owed his native wit and genius (*Par.* 22.112–14).[61] These profoundly significant details may help to explain why the myth of the Argonauts "brackets" the whole of the third *cantica*. To return to Jason's feat, we must recall that ploughing is a traditional metaphor for writing: so now, the Christian audience of *Paradiso* will be struck with wonder as they follow the poet's ship making its way across untraveled waters (*Par.* 2.7, *L'acqua ch'io prendo già mai non si corse;* cf. *Par.* 23.67–69) and observe his "plough" or pen as it describes the mysteries of paradise. Like Jason who had to overcome mortal dangers, so the poet of *Paradiso* has to face up to St. Paul's terrifying claim that he knew a man who "was caught up into Paradise *and heard mysteries no man is allowed to utter*" (2 Cor. 12.3–4; my emphasis).

In the poem's last canto, the narrator warns his readers that what he saw was greater than any language can convey and that his memory was defeated by *tanto oltraggio* (the mystic's *excessus mentis: Par.* 33.55–57). Then, in the poem's last mythological image, *letargo*—a Latinism introduced by Dante into Italian—appears together with the legend of the primordial sea voyage in an attempt to render Dante's oblivion and ecstasy:

> Un punto solo m'è maggior letargo
> che venticinque secoli a la 'mpresa
> che fé Nettuno ammirar l'ombra d'Argo.
> (*Par.* 33.94–96)

————

One point is the cause of greater oblivion in me than twenty-five centuries to the enterprise that made Neptune gaze in awe at Argo's shadow.

As Robert Hollander points out: "The Pilgrim is Jason, on the way to getting the Fleece; the Poet is Neptune, watching him do so" (1969, 230–31). While this distinction between the pilgrim and the poet undoubtedly bears these associations, we would also argue that Neptune necessarily points to the true Godhead.[62] We further note that the Christian Neptune is not angry, as in the classical myth; instead, he leads Dante's ship to its heavenly destination and allows it to return safely to earth, even as Jason's bark had sailed back to Greece with his prize. Lastly, we note that the arc of twenty-five centuries separating

Dante from the Argonauts is temporally bisected by the central event in human history, the Incarnation. This time span thus contains three momentous voyages: Jason's, and then God's own voyage down to earth and back to heaven, of which Dante's is the mirror image.[63]

Dante the prophet

In the Heaven of the Fixed Stars, Dante had expressed his fervent hope that the poem to which both heaven and earth have contributed might overcome the cruel sentence of exile that had excluded him from "the beautiful sheepfold where I slept as a lamb." He would then return as a poet "with a different voice now, with a different fleece" to receive the laurel wreath at the place where he had received the sacrament of baptism:

> Se mai continga che 'l poema sacro
> al quale ha posto mano e cielo e terra,
>   sí che m'ha fatto per molti anni macro,
> vinca la crudeltà che fuor mi serra
> del bello ovile ov' io dormi' agnello,
>   nimico ai lupi che li danno guerra;
>   con altra voce omai, con altro vello
> ritornerò poeta, e in sul fonte
> del mio battesmo prenderò 'l cappello.
>   (*Par.* 25.1–9)

The *Se . . . continga* in the first line is not so much a hypothetical clause (If it should come to pass . . .) as it is an introduction to what the exiled poet longs for with all his being, a burning desire that opens the canto dedicated to the theological virtue of Hope. Hence, the optative subjunctive (May it come to pass . . .) and the choice of that very same verbal form *(contingat)* found in Aeneas's prayer that he may be granted his wish to be reunited with his beloved father (*Aen.* 6.108–9). The essential link with the Argonaut expedition lies in the fact that this longed-for return in triumph to Dante's native city must perforce take place after he has reached his heavenly goal and returned to earth—with his own Golden Fleece. For the first time, Dante refers to himself as *poeta,* a word hitherto reserved for the greatest poets of antiquity (and, for those who delight in numerology, this is its twenty-fifth occurrence in the *Comedy,* found in the twenty-fifth canto of *Paradiso*): a true "poet," thanks to the *sacro poema* that will, on account of its heavenly inspiration, outshine the greatest poems of pagan antiquity. Dante will no longer be simply the poet of earthly love. His new voice will show him to be God's faithful scribe, as he had first claimed in his reply to the Tuscan rhymester Bonagiunta (*Purg.* 24.52–54): "And I to him: 'I am one who, when Love breathes within me *[Amor mi spira],* takes note, and whatever he dictates within I express *[vo significando].*'"[64]

Sarolli has argued that the reference to the new fleece in *Paradiso* 25.7 must be the fleece of a goat: "The Poet, here, metaphorically standing as a *typus caprae,* becomes therefore typologically *typus prophetae*" (1971, 405). I agree with his conclusion that the poet is highlighting his role as a prophet, but would point to the precise location indicated by the poet. It is to the Florentine Baptistery, his *bel San Giovanni* (*Inf.* 19.17), that Dante dreams of returning to be crowned and thus winning recognition as both poet and prophet in the place where he had become a member of Christ's Mystical Body, the Church. In *Purgatorio* 22.151–54, where St. John the Baptist is hailed as an antidote to gluttony, Dante speaks of the locusts and wild honey that were his only food in the desert. The poet sings the praises of Florence's patron saint by sending his readers back to Christ's words: "Amen, I tell you that there has not arisen among those born of women one greater than John the Baptist" (Matt. 11.11; Luke 7.28). Florence's patron saint was in fact the last of the prophets and the essential link between the Old and the New Covenants, regarded by some as the greatest of all prophets in that he had seen the true Messiah and had even recognized the miracle of the Incarnation while still in his mother's womb (Luke 1.44). His words "Behold the Lamb of God, behold the one who takes away the sin of the world" (John 1.29) were forever repeated in the climactic moment in the Mass, and were associated with his prophetic spirit in Christian iconography. Truly, Dante the exile must have regarded his poem as the voice of one crying in the wilderness (John 1.23; cf. *Par.* 17.133–35).[65] Lastly, and most significantly for our present purpose, John in the wilderness wore "his garment of camel's hair" (Matt. 3.4), clothing also associated with the prophet Elijah (4 Kings 1.8).[66] I would therefore argue that *altro vello* in *Paradiso* 25.7 implies that, like Jason's return with the Golden Fleece, Dante's homecoming will be accompanied by a "new fleece" representing his new poetic mission as God's scribe, whose prophetic role is symbolized in the camel's fleece worn by the patron of Florence—the prophet who had baptized Christ.

Paradiso 25 is of course the canto describing the pilgrim's "examination" in hope, and both Beatrice *and God* (the sun that illuminates the whole of paradise) stand guarantor for the fact that no other living soul possesses this virtue to a greater degree (ll. 52–57). It is precisely on account of his immense capacity for hope that Dante has been granted the privilege of seeing the Heavenly City ("to come from Egypt to Jerusalem") during his lifetime:

> "La Chiesa militante alcun figliuolo
>   non ha con piú speranza, com' è scritto

nel Sol che raggia tutto nostro stuolo:
  però li è conceduto che d'Egitto
vegna in Ierusalemme per vedere,
anzi che 'l militar li sia prescritto."

(Par. 25.52–57)

———

"The Church Militant has no child with greater hope, as it is written in the Sun Who irradiates all our host: therefore, it is granted to him to come from Egypt to Jerusalem in order to see [the heavenly City], before the end of his preordained struggle [on earth]."

Hope is in fact the supreme theological virtue necessary for prophets.[67]

Imagery in *Paradiso*

Finally, a series of three images connected with the goal of Dante's pilgrimage is introduced in *Paradiso* 31.31–40 with the allusion to the amazement experienced by the barbarians when they first beheld the glory that was Rome. How much more amazed then is Dante, our pilgrim who has left behind him Florence (the devil's corrupt city) in time and who has now arrived at the heavenly city in eternity, that Rome "of which Christ Himself is a Roman" (*Purg.* 32.102)! In lines 43–48, the poet compares himself directly to a pilgrim gazing in wonder at "the temple of his vow" and hoping to have the capacity to relate his experiences faithfully on his return. The motif returns a second time in lines 103–11, when Dante compares himself to one who has made a pilgrimage from a distant land to Rome in order to see the sacred Veronica with Christ's features portrayed on the *vera icon*. The progression from the first to the third image is one of zooming in to an ever-smaller space with more intense focus, as the poet guides us from the broad outline of the cityscape, to the church, and lastly to the sacred image.

Indeed, throughout *Paradiso*, "the simile is almost the sole means available for visual articulation of reality" (Lansing 1977, 154), for it is only through the created things seen and experienced in this world that on earth we may come to know something of the invisible nature and power of the Creator (Rom. 1.20: St. Paul's words are cited by Dante in both *Ep.* 5.8.23 and *Mon.* 2.2.8). The simile contained in *Paradiso* 10.139–48 is the first literary reference to the mechanical clock, which was invented "sometime between 1277 and 1300."[68] The spirits that appear in the fourth heaven move like the parts of a clock that summons the faithful to prayer while, like the clock's sweet chimes, they "render voice to voice" in perfect harmony. The phrase *tin tin sonando* (l. 143) is one of the most striking of the poet's onomatopoeic inventions (perhaps suggested by the *tinnitus* or "tinkling sound" of Vergil's *Georgics* 4.64). The image thus conveys both the precise motion and the harmonious sounds made by the heavenly chorus.[69] The wheel simile in the penultimate line of the poem plays a similar role:

> ma già volgeva il mio disio e 'l *velle,*
> sí come rota ch'igualmente è mossa,
> > l'amore che move il sole e l'altre stelle.
> > > (*Par.* 33.143–45)

———

> But already the love that moves the sun and the other stars propelled
> my desire and my will as a wheel turning evenly [is propelled].

Lino Pertile (1995b) submits these last three lines of the *Comedy* to detailed analysis. He concludes that two wheels are implied: the external "wheel" of the universe and the internal, metaphorical wheel of the pilgrim's soul, now synchronized with the movement of the entire universe and with its love and desire for God. He quotes Boethius: "O happy breed of men, If only the love whereby the heavens are ruled, Might rule your hearts" (*Consolation of Philosophy* 2.8.28–30). In *Monarchia* 1.9.2, in fact, Dante cites these same lines after affirming that "the whole of heaven is regulated in all its parts, motions, and movers by a single motion, namely that of the Primum Mobile, and by a single mover, who is God." The Primum Mobile as the ninth heaven and the first (most rapidly) moving part of Creation conveys motion to the rest of the universe—motion that is the result of Creation's love for and desire to be united with its Creator (*Conv.* 2.3.9; *Par.* 1.76–77), the unmoved mover (Aristotle, *Metaphysics* 12.7.1072b, 3; *Par.* 23.112–14). Yet, while two wheels may be implied by the simile, the movement of one wheel—*rota ch'igualmente è mossa*—is specified in the text. This singular unit underscores the total fusion of the pilgrim's desire and reason.[70] I would agree that *igualmente* (l. 144) signifies uniform circular motion. And the circle "has been universally accepted as the symbol of eternity and never-ending existence. As the monogram of God, it represents not only the perfection of God but the everlasting God . . ." (Ferguson 1961, 153; cf. *VN* 12.4).

Uniform circular movement was attributed to the heavenly spheres, but it was hardly a characteristic of turning wheels in Dante's world (not even in clocks, with their escape mechanism)—with one outstanding exception. André Pézard (1965, 1674) was surely right to see in the simile an image of the wheel that turns in perfect synchronization with the potter's hands. Nothing in the medieval poet's (or reader's) experience could rival the uniform motion imparted by a master craftsman to the potter's wheel. Anyone who has witnessed the creation of an artifact through the shaping of a turning mass of clay by human hands will grasp the point that this familiar image implies God as the supreme *artifex,* God who crafted the living Adam out of clay (Gen. 2.7). Thus, Dante's entire being is now propelled by and turns in unison with "the love that moves the sun and the other stars"—that desire for union with the Godhead which is the source of motion in the universe and the very *raison d'être* of what we now call the "Divine" *Comedy.*[71] As Augustine had addressed God at the beginning of his *Confessions* (1.1): "You have created us for Yourself *[ad te]* and our heart is always restless, until it comes to rest in You *[in te]*." The entire *Comedy* represents motion toward God *(ad te); and* it ends—as should all human longing—in God *(in te),* where, as God's scribe assures his readers, "every desire" *(ciascuna disïanza)* is "perfect, ripe, and whole" *(Par.* 22.64–65, *perfetta, matura e intera).*[72]

Appendix: The *Comedy* and the Bible

Any account of the *Comedy*'s poetry must at least touch upon the inspiration Dante drew from the Bible (see Moore 1896, 47–91; Kleinhenz 1986a, 1997; Barblan 1988; Esposito et al. 1996; Hawkins 1999, 2000). In this chapter, we have had several occasions for tracing his imagery to biblical sources, and, given that Dante's "reverence for the authority of Scripture is unbounded" (Moore 1896, 47), it seems appropriate to observe and illustrate, even briefly, the important role played by this essential influence upon the construction of the greatest Christian epic.

The Latin Vulgate Bible familiar to Dante was based on St. Jerome's translation, dating from the late fourth century. The thirteenth-century edition of the Vulgate prepared at the University of Paris (consisting of a single volume, and with chapter divisions) was widely used by members of the preaching orders and university students. Unlike modern Bibles, medieval Bibles generally presented the biblical text accompanied by a host of commentaries, of which the best known is the twelfth-century *Glossa Ordinaria.*

The *Comedy* contains more than 570 biblical citations and allusions, and a careful inventory of them suggests that Dante drew his inspiration chiefly from the Psalms, the Song of Songs, Isaiah, Jeremiah, the Gospels, Paul's Epistles, and the Apocalypse. While *Inferno* has the lowest number of direct scriptural citations, *Purgatorio* offers the highest number (thirty, with about another forty allusions)—reflecting humanity's need on earth to follow and obey God's Word.

Biblical citations

An outstanding example is found at the beginning of *Purgatorio:* "'*In exitu Israël de Aegypto,*' they all sang together with one voice, *together with all that is written in that psalm*" (2.46–48, my emphasis). No clearer signal could be sent by the poet to his readers to urge them to consult the entire text of Psalm 113 [114/115], with its hymn of joy for God's deliverance from the land of sin and bondage. As Singleton (1965a) insists, the theme of a voyage from error to salvation permeates the whole *Comedy.* Traditional exegesis—and Dante himself (*Ep.* 13.7.21; cf. *Conv.* 2.1.6–7)—offered four levels of interpretation of the psalm's opening verses. Historically, they signified the Exodus at the time of Moses; allegorically, our redemption through Christ; morally (tropologically), the soul's conversion from the wretchedness of sin to a state of grace; anagogically, the sanctified soul's liberation from the servitude of corruption to the freedom of eternal beatitude. The three "mystical" senses of Scripture all pointed to the soul's purgatorial journey or situation, its passage from Egypt to the Promised Land, its heavenly *patria,* God's city, traditionally referred to as the heavenly Jerusalem. Indeed, as we have noted in *Paradiso* 25.55–57 Beatrice speaks of Dante's pilgrimage from this world to paradise as his journey "from Egypt . . . to Jerusalem"—a quite extraordinary privilege for someone still in his mortal body. Although rarely mentioned by interpreters of the poem, the psalm's concluding verses (17–18)—signified by *Purgatorio* 2.48—are especially relevant to the situation of these souls in purgatory, saved from the jaws of spiritual death: "The dead shall not praise you, O Lord; nor shall all those who go down to Hell. But we who live will bless the Lord from this time on and evermore."

Five of the nine beatitudes proffered in the Sermon on the Mount (Matt. 5.3–11) incite the penitential souls on each of the terraces of the Mountain of Purgatory to practice a virtue antithetical to their sin. *Beati pauperes spiritu!* (*Purg.* 12.110: Blessed are the poor in spirit) is chanted on the terrace of pride. *Beati misericordes* (*Purg.* 15.38: Blessed are the merciful), the fifth beatitude, inspires the antidote to envy on the second terrace. *Beati mundo corde!* (*Purg.* 27.8: Blessed are the pure in heart) rings out on the last terrace, where the tendency to lust is eradicated. On the third terrace, the beatitude is expanded by the poet's gloss: "Blessed are the peacemakers who are without sinful anger!" (*Purg.* 17.68–69), based on the conventional distinction between sinful and righteous anger (cf. *S. Th.* 2.2.158). The most puzzling citation consists of just two Latin words in *Purgatorio* 19.50 (*Qui lugent:* who mourn), followed by an Italian paraphrase in lines 50–51, "declaring them to be blessed, / for their souls shall be possessed of consolation." These clues indicate the third beatitude (Matt. 5.5: "Blessed are those who mourn, for they shall be comforted"), which serves as a promise to those now expiating their addiction to the sin of sloth. These spirits "mourn" their former enslavement by a sin known as *acedia* or *tristitia,* a state of spiritual gloom and apathy that had led them to avoid pain and suffering on earth, even as it had prevented them from loving God with their whole heart.

A dense hub of biblical citations and allusions is found in the cantos devoted to the Earthly Paradise (*Purg.* 28–33). Particularly noteworthy is the opening of the last canto, immediately following the apocalyptic vision of the Church's tragic vicissitudes in *Purgatorio* 32. The seven virtues intone, *"Deus, venerunt gentes,"* the psalm (78) lamenting the destruction of Jerusalem and its holy Temple, calling on God to wreak vengeance on those guilty of defiling his sanctuary. Beatrice's anguish at the prostitution of Christ's Church is likened to Mary's at the foot of the Cross. Her face red with shame and prophetic anger, Beatrice stands up and proclaims Christ's words at the Last Supper, when he foretold his death and resurrection: "A little while, and you will no longer see me; and again a little while, and you will see me" (John 16.16). The repetition is underscored by the unusual phenomenon of identical rhymes in lines 10 and 12 *(videbitis me/videbitis me).* As Beatrice's words confirm in lines 34–35, the reference here is to the Body of Christ, his Church, which awaits a reformer to restore it to its pristine virtue and its true role on earth.

Modified citations of the Bible and liturgy

While a direct biblical citation introduces the final canto of *Purgatorio,* a striking example of a sacred text modified by one crucial word opens the final canto of *Inferno.* There (*Inf.* 34.1), with the addition of the word *inferni,* the initial verse of the great processional hymn *Vexilla regis prodeunt* by Venantius Fortunatus, in praise of the Cross and of Christ's redemption of humankind, is transformed into an infernal parody. The original text celebrates "the banners of the King [of Heaven, as they] go forth; resplendent is the mystery of the Cross, whereby in His flesh the Creator of flesh was hung on the gibbet." During Passiontide, the hymn was accompanied by the fervent prayer "Save me, o Lord, from the evil man." Here, in the pit of hell, Virgil (the pagan guide!) uses this mangled citation to draw Dante's attention to the immense lump of matter that is Satan, immobilized in the ice of Cocytus. Just as Dante's love for Beatrice is distorted in the infernal mirror illustrating Francesca's damnation thus causing the pilgrim to faint at the end of *Inferno* 5, so here the antithesis of the Holy Trinity is first glimpsed as a huge windmill, and then appears in grotesque form with three faces and six arms. Instead of the banners of the King of Heaven moving in stately procession *(prodeunt)* and leading humanity to salvation, those of the King of Hell crucified in the ice are fixed, serving only to propel an icy blast—a further grotesque detail parodying the spiration of the Love uniting God the Father to his Son. Instead of emphasizing the power of evil and Satan (as Milton was to do in *Paradise Lost*), Dante insists on their fundamental impotence. Our poet evidently agreed with Augustine, who declared: "I did not know that evil is nothing but the removal of good until finally no good remains" (*Confessions* 3.7).

A quite different effect is achieved by the greeting chanted by the multitude of angels in *Purgatorio* 30.19: *"Benedictus qui venis!"* (Blessed are you who come!). The soul that will appear is that of Beatrice, heralded by the word *sponsa* in line 11 (the bride, traditionally interpreted as the human soul wedded to Christ: Song of Songs 4.8) but *not* by the masculine *Benedictus,* which sends the reader back to the triumphal acclamation of Jesus on his entry into Jerusalem (Matt. 21.9): "Blessed is he that comes *[qui venit]* in the name of the Lord." In *venis* (you come, instead of *venit,* he comes), we have a clear pointer to the imminent arrival of Beatrice, who will descend from the Heavenly Jerusalem. Why, then, did the poet not modify still further this biblical text, in order to make it fit the feminine person of Beatrice *(Benedicta quae venis)*? As in the masculine image evoked by the *ammiraglio* simile found later in line 58, so here the masculine *Benedictus qui venis* should compel the reader to seek out the role now assumed by the young woman Dante had known and loved in Florence. Beatrice now appears as a *figura Christi,* for in the Earthly Paradise she prefigures the role of Christ the Judge at his Second Coming. As Christ will come to judge all humanity at the end of time (an event alluded to in ll. 13–15, as well as in the image of the rising sun, ll. 22–27), so Beatrice comes to judge Dante, once the procession (representing the history of the world from Genesis to the Apocalypse) has come to a halt (ll. 1–7). There is no suggestion that Beatrice *is* Christ or that her nature is divine; the gulf that divides the creature from the Creator remains absolute. Nevertheless, Beatrice and Christ may perform similar actions on different planes—which, like parallel lines, will never meet. In any figural relationship, both entities remain discrete (Auerbach 1959). Thus, by maintaining the Gospel's *benedictus,* and changing *venit* to *venis,* Dante jolts us into an awareness of Beatrice's role at this juncture, a role circumscribed by the action of the *Comedy.*

The Bible and Dante's prophetic mode

A host of biblical indicators confirm Dante's role as a prophet, as well as the chronological indicators: 1266, birth of Beatrice; 1290, death of Beatrice; 1300, Dante's conversion and journey to God; 1335, the year when the poet would have reached the canonical age of seventy and have been blessed by

God (cf. Dan. 12.11–12; Gorni 1990, 125–26; see also Nardi 1983, 265–326; Mineo 1968, 161–354; Morghen 1983, 109–57; Schnapp 1986; Gorni 1984, 1990). Like the prophets of old, the Florentine exile was not without honor save in his own country (Matt. 13.57); like Moses, Isaiah, Ezekiel, and others, Dante at first doubts his ability to carry out his prophetic mission (*Inf.* 2.10–35). Cacciaguida predicts that his great-grandson's message will leave a bitter taste in the mouths of many (*Par.* 17.117; cf. Jer. 31.30); nevertheless, he must not hesitate to disclose every detail of his vision (*Par.* 27.64–66). The poet of the *Comedy* clearly assumed the prophet's mantle at the same time as his new "voice" (*Par.* 25.89).

The nineteenth canto of *Inferno* signals a radical departure (and a new prophetic tone), with its dramatic opening violently condemning Simon Magus and his wretched followers.[73] Dante expected his readers to be familiar with the episode of Simon the Magician in Acts 8.9–24. When Simon offered Peter and John money for the gift of transmitting the Holy Spirit, Peter immediately rebuked him: "May you and your money be damned, because you thought you could acquire God's gift with money." According to the apocryphal *Acts of Peter and Paul,* Simon challenged the apostles to a flying contest; but when St. Peter made the sign of the cross, Simon fell headlong to the earth. This legend may have inspired the punishment devised for the simonist popes, who are upside-down in the rockshaft of hell (l. 46), reflecting the fact that they had inverted God's moral order, placing gold and silver above the gifts of the Spirit. Moreover, the flames licking the soles of their feet are an infernal parody of the way the Holy Spirit descended on the heads of the apostles as tongues of fire at Pentecost (Acts 2.3–4). And, from the very beginning, with its apostrophe "O Simon Magus," we are meant to grasp the fact that these sinners (and, in particular, the Petrine successors of the first pope) were followers of the *wrong* Simon. They are thus imprisoned in the rock of hell that is the antithesis of the rock on which Christ founded his Church, when he renamed Simon "Petrus" (Matt. 16.18) in the most celebrated example of the belief that names should reflect a person's essential nature and role on earth (*VN* 13.4). Their position is also a moral distortion of St. Peter's supreme act of humility, when he chose to be executed head down out of respect for his crucified God.

Obeying Cacciaguida's injunction, and like Nathan, the prophet who foretold God's punishment for David's sins (Sarolli 1971, 233–46), Dante does not hesitate to denounce the crimes of a trinity of corrupt popes: Nicholas III, Boniface VIII, and Clement V. In a cluster of biblical allusions, the poet (speaking through the damned Nicholas) tells us that Clement, a shepherd without respect for human or divine law, "will be another Jason, like the one we read of in Maccabees": according to 2 Maccabees 4.7–8, Jason purchased the high priesthood from the emperor Antiochus IV Epiphanes. Similarly, Bertrand de Got will promise to hand over to Philip the Fair the tithes raised in France over a period of five years, in exchange for his election as Clement V in June 1305 at the conclave held at Perugia (Villani 9.80).[74] For the first time in the poem, Dante the pilgrim speaks out directly in a violent diatribe that leads the author to comment, "I do not know whether I now became too rash" (l. 88). A similar chastisement of the princes of the Church gathered in conclave after Clement's death is found in *Epistle* 11, written in 1314, offering further proof that its author was fully aware of his audacity, although he proclaims himself to be the least of Christ's sheep, filled not by any lust for gold but by divine grace and holy zeal for the well-being of God's Church (*Ep.* 11.5.9; cf. 1 Cor. 15.9 and Ps. 68.10). In *Inferno* 19.90–93, the opening words of the pilgrim's invective refer to Christ's donation of the keys of the kingdom of heaven to the archetypal pope, after he had renamed Simon "Rock" (Matt. 16.19). For this priceless gift, Christ demanded no treasure but only that his disciples should follow him (Matt. 4.19). Again, Peter and the other apostles did not ask for gold or silver when they elected Matthias to take the place of Judas (Acts 1.13–26). The echo of Christ's injunction to his followers not to possess gold or silver or even money (Matt. 10.9) returns with even greater force in line 112, when the outraged pilgrim accuses the simonists of having turned God into a thing of gold and silver. In lines 106–11, the poet affirms that the author of the Apocalypse had foreseen their evildoing and corruption when he described the Great Whore fornicating with the kings. In spite of Apocalypse 17.1–14 and the explanations given in verses 9–14, Dante here interprets the seven heads and ten horns of Apocalypse 17.3–10 as signifying the seven gifts of the Holy Spirit and the Ten Commandments (cf., however, *Purg.* 32.142–53), which had nourished the Church hierarchy "for as long as virtue pleased her husband [the pope]." Now, these degenerate, idolatrous churchmen—and, in particular, the successors of St. Peter—have made gold and silver into their gods (Hos. 8.4).

Dante's prophetic role is yet again and most clearly proclaimed in Beatrice's command (*Purg.* 33.52–57): "Take note [the emphatic *TU nota*]; and just as these words are proffered by me, transmit them to those who live the life that is a race to death." We recall the Lord's injunction to his prophet Isaiah (Isa. 6.9): "Go, and say to this people." The pilgrim assures Beatrice that his mind bears the imprint of her words as wax receives that of a seal: so, having received the divine command "Take a great scroll and write on it," the prophet of old *sealed* his teaching among his disciples (*signa legem:* Isa. 8.16). Again, even as God told Jeremiah, "Gird then your loins and stand up, and tell them everything that I command you . . ." (Jer. 1.17), so Cacciaguida urges Dante to reveal the totality of his vision (*Par.* 17.127–29), despite the bitter taste it will leave in the mouths of sinners (cf. Apoc. 10.8–11).

The prince of the apostles will likewise tell the pilgrim not to conceal what he, Peter, does not hide (*Par.* 27.64–66). The corruption of the papacy in 1300 is denounced in language that was to shock the sense of decorum prevalent in the Renaissance (cf. note 4). How could a word like *cloaca* (sewer) come out of St. Peter's mouth (*Par.* 27.25)? The answer lies both in the analysis of Peter's fiery character and hasty speech (*Mon.* 3.9.9) and in the fact that Dante modeled his polyphonic style and lexis on the full range of scriptural language. Peter's outburst in *Paradiso* 27.19–27 is a good example of his impetuous nature (and of the poet's outrage at the corrupt example set):

> . . . "Se io mi trascoloro,
> non ti maravigliar, ché, dicend'io,
> vedrai trascolorar tutti costoro.
>
>   Quelli ch'usurpa in terra il luogo mio,
> il luogo mio, il luogo mio che vaca
> ne la presenza del Figliuol di Dio,
>
>   fatt' ha del cimitero mio cloaca
> del sangue e de la puzza; onde 'l perverso
> che cadde di qua sú, là giú si placa."

"If I change color, do not be surprised, for, as I speak, you will see all of them [the blessed] change color. He [Boniface VIII] who usurps on earth my place, my place, my place that is vacant in the presence of the Son of God, has turned my burial ground into a sewer of blood and stench; hence, the perverse one [Satan] who fell from up here, is content down there."

Such down-to-earth vulgar language as in the expression *a sewer of blood and stench* (cf. *la puzza del peccato, ché pute a Dio,* the stench of sin, which stinks to God, in a sermon delivered by Giordano da Pisa in 1306) ultimately derived from—and was sanctioned by—the Bible itself (e.g., Joel 2.20: "and its stink [*foetor*] shall rise up, and its stench [*putredo*] shall rise up . . .").

Sermo humilis

No one has written in more masterly fashion than Erich Auerbach on the revolution in literary genre and style brought about by Christianity. For the first time, "sublime" events of universal importance were recorded in the low, "humble" style *(sermo humilis).* As Auerbach points out (1965, 56): "Vulgarisms and realism are significant hallmarks of the Christian *sermo humilis . . .* because they are used in speaking of serious and profound matters, and because such 'low locutions' are transformed by their contact with the serious and the sublime." The *sermo humilis* of Christian writers implied "a direct human contact" between author and reader, "a note that was lacking in the sublime style of Roman antiquity" (ibid., 57) but which is a hallmark of the *Comedy,* especially in Dante's addresses to his readers (Russo 1970): for example, in urging them to search for the allegorical lesson in *Inferno* 9.61–63 or to lift up their gaze *with him* to the heavens (*Par.* 10.7).

As far as lexis is concerned, even the most vulgar words were retained in Christian literature. Consider, for example, "*manducare* and *eructare* (literally 'to gobble with much chewing' and 'to belch'). Time and again these words were ridiculed, but the congregations did not give them up" (Auerbach 1965, 58). Their use was justified by their presence in Scripture: for example, the forty-fourth Psalm opens with *Eructavit cor meum verbum bonum* (My heart belched forth a good word), and Christ's words at the institution of the Eucharist were translated as *Accipite, et manducate* (1 Cor. 11.24: Take and chew up). Whereas in *De vulgari* 1.13.2 the phrase *manichiamo, introcque* (meanwhile, let's eat) is condemned by Dante as an example of the Florentines' foul speech *(turpiloquium),* utterly unworthy of the "tragic" style, both *manducare* and *manicare* are found in the *Comedy,* in the tragic episode of Ugolino: "and just as bread is chewed *[si manduca]* out of hunger" (*Inf.* 32.127); "and they, thinking that I did it out of a desire to eat *[per voglia / di manicar]*" (*Inf.* 33.59–60). The presence of *introcque* in the last line of *Inferno* 20 could strike even Machiavelli's intensely Florentine spirit as "clumsy," and in the same passage of his *Dialogo intorno alla nostra lingua* he reproached his illustrious predecessor for introducing into his poem such a "filthy" word as *merda* (shit: *Inf.* 28.27), as well as Vanni Fucci's obscene gesture (*Inf.* 25.2).

Already one of Dante's contemporaries, the protohumanist Giovanni del Virgilio, took the poet to task for employing *the jargon of the marketplace (Ecl.* 1.18: *sermone forensi)* in treating grave matters. In his reply Dante clearly defended his use of *comica . . . verba (Ecl.* 2.52), words typical of the comic style, for which Giovanni had criticized him. Readers will note that Machiavelli's examples are taken from *Inferno,* where it would be possible to claim that the context justifies linguistic vulgarity. This is also the section of the poem in which Dante refers to it as his "comedy" (*Inf.* 21.2; cf. 16.128), some two lines after using *introcque* and nineteen lines after Virgil's reference to the *Aeneid* as his "high tragedy" (*Inf.* 20.113).[75] Yet, as we have seen, even in what is clearly the most exalted section of "the sacred poem" (*Par.* 23.62 and 25.1), the word "sewer" is placed in the august mouth of the archetypal Vicar of Christ. St. Bernard's prayer to the Virgin, on the other hand (*Par.* 33.1–39), combines and transcends the resources of both classical and Christian rhetoric (Auerbach 1949). In the Middle Ages, the idea of a *rota Virgilii* (Vergil's wheel) was commonly accepted to show that the greatest Latin poet had used the low style in his *Bucolics,* the intermediate style in his *Georgics,* and the weighty or sublime style in his *Aeneid.* As St. Augustine had pointed out (*On Christian Doctrine* 4.20), the Bible provided examples of all three stylistic levels. In his "sacred poem," Dante imitated God's way of writing in his synergetic fusion of a vast range of styles in order to express not only the fullness of human experience but even what lies "beyond the utmost bound of human thought."

Dante and his contemporary world

Godi, Fiorenza, poi che se' sí grande
che per mare e per terra batti l'ali,
e per lo 'nferno tuo nome si spande!

(Inf. 26.1–3)

───────

Rejoice, Florence, for you are so great you beat your wings over sea
and land, and your name is broadcast throughout hell!

Addressing his native city, Dante congratulates her on the fact that
hell is peopled with Florentines (the fifth element in the universe according
to Boniface VIII)—an apostrophe made all the more trenchant when we learn
that it was almost certainly based on the proud boast inscribed on the Palazzo
del Bargello in 1255: "Florence is full of wealth; she defeats her enemies in war
and civil strife . . . she owns the sea and the land and the whole earth . . . like
Rome, she is ever triumphant."[1] The inscription's *quae mare, quae terram, quae
totum possidet orbem* (which owns the sea, the earth, the whole world) is in fact a
barely modified line of verse from Lucan's *Pharsalia* (1.110: *quae mare, quae terras,
quae totum possidet orbem*), quoted by Dante (*Mon.* 2.8.12) in order to prove that
world dominion belonged exclusively to Rome. Unlike Rome, Florence's only

real triumph is the "empire" her citizens have set up among the damned souls in hell. In order to understand what led the poet to this impassioned condemnation of his native city, we must examine certain aspects of the complex web of Florentine history down to 1321, as well as Dante's reactions to this in his life and writings.[2]

Emergence of Florence as a republic

In 1115, on the death of Countess Matilda of Tuscany (the staunch ally of Pope Gregory VII in his struggles with the emperor), Florence seized an opportunity to declare itself a free commune. In 1125 Florence destroyed its hilltop neighbor, Fiesole, and began its expansion into the surrounding countryside or *contado*. Dante refers to the "beasts" from Fiesole who came down to settle in Florence, thereby contaminating the "holy seed" of the Romans who had founded the city (*Inf.* 15.61–78). Villani (2.1) also ascribes their constant strife to the fact that the Florentines were "born and descended from two peoples so opposite, hostile and of such different customs as were the virtuous Roman nobles and the uncouth, warlike Fiesolans." In 1138 we find a reference to four consuls chosen to govern the commune, although its dominion was not recognized by the emperor (Henry VI) until 1187. Evidence of the commune's development (aided by the growth of the textile industry in Western Europe) is the fact that the urban area based on the twenty hectares of the Roman site increased to fifty-five hectares in 1172 and was enclosed by a new set of walls. The town was now divided into six neighborhoods or *sestieri,* each with a militia responsible for its section of the walls and watchtowers.

Just before 1200, a supreme magistrate, known as the *podestà* and guided by the deliberations of two councils, replaced the collegiate system of the consular era. From the beginning of the thirteenth century, the *podestà* was chosen from other cities and regions in an attempt to find an impartial officer who should be above the fierce rival factions that plagued Florence. Ironically, this office was to be held by the bitterly partisan king of Naples, Charles of Anjou, from 1267 to 1282, when his loss of Sicily made it possible for Florence once again to assert her independence.[3]

Frederick II and the papacy

Unfortunately, deep internal divisions accompanied Florence's rise to economic supremacy in the thirteenth century, in part as a result of the struggle for supremacy between the empire and the papacy. The repeated placing of the emperor Frederick II (1194–1250) under the ban of the Holy See (in 1227, 1238, 1239, 1243) demonstrates all too clearly that "excommunication was an occupational hazard of medieval emperors" (Abulafia 1988, 167). After Gregory IX's attacks against him in 1227, Frederick began to accuse the Church of betraying its founder's principles, especially through its ostentatious display of wealth—a matter on which the pope was especially vulnerable as the patron of the newly formed Franciscan Order with its ideal of poverty. This civil war in the heart of Christendom was later chosen by Dante to signal the beginning of the corruption of virtually the whole of northern Italy. In *Purgatorio* 16.115–17 he makes Marco Lombardo claim that valor and the ideals of courtesy flourished in the land watered by the rivers Adige and Po "before Frederick encountered opposition." Coming at the center of the *Comedy,* immediately after the condemnation of papal interference in the temporal sphere, the denunciation of such corruption is an integral part of the poem's universal message, here offered as proof of the catastrophic results of the spiritual sun's eclipse of the temporal sun: "Cast your mind to the result, for every plant is known by its seed" (ll. 113–14; Matt. 7.16).

Guelfs and Ghibellines

The polarization arising from this conflict is usually indicated by the terms "Guelf" and "Ghibelline," which were imported into Italy from Germany to indicate propapal and proimperial supporters and their policies during the internecine political feud waged between empire and papacy.[4] According to both Dante (*Inf.* 28.106–8) and Villani (6.38), the murder of Buondelmonte dei Buondelmonti in Florence on Easter Sunday 1216 was the cause of a split that rent the city-state for some fifty tragic years of bitter rivalry, which erupted at times into civil war. Historians rightly stress the fact that in general the two factions were ruled by political and economic self-interest and that (despite the propaganda of the Guelfs, who were quick to accuse their opponents of heresy) for the most part the Ghibellines acknowledged the spiritual authority of the Church but not papal intrusions into the temporal realm or its claims to political hegemony.[5]

In February 1248 Guelfs who had castles in the *contado* left Florence, where the Ghibellines destroyed some thirty-six of their towers. However, just before Frederick II's death in December 1250, the Guelfs defeated their opponents at Figline. Upon their return, a new form of government was set up, known to historians as that of *il primo popolo.* It governed Florence for a decade, after which power reverted to the Ghibellines from 1260 to 1266. From the time Dante (b. 1265) was one year old, and as a consequence of the Ghibelline rout at

Benevento, Florence gradually asserted its power and influence as the leading Guelf commune, eventually proving to be the sinews of Italian resistance to the Emperor Henry VII (1310–13)—as Dante was to lament in his Latin epistle of March 1311, addressed to the most iniquitous Florentines "who transgress every law of God and man" by madly rebelling "against the glory of the Roman Emperor" (*Ep.* 6.2.5). One month later, Dante urged Henry to hasten to crush his beloved native city, now cast in the role of a "viper that turns against the vitals of her own mother" (*Ep.* 7.7.24).

Regime of the *primo popolo* (1250–60)

At first, the new government did its best to minimize party conflicts by excluding both Guelfs and Ghibellines from holding political office, although many Ghibellines were forced to flee in 1251 (*Inf.* 10.46–48). On the basis of new economic and social realities, the regime did everything to protect the interests of the Florentine guilds and their *popolo*—not the "people" as understood in modern democracies but what we tend to think of as the bourgeoisie or middle class.[6] Florence issued the first gold florin in 1252, "the first gold coin to be minted in large amounts in Western Europe since Carolingian times" (Brucker 1984, 77); it quickly took on a role similar to that of the modern dollar in international trade and commerce. A new office was created, that of *capitano del popolo*. Like the *podestà*, the *capitano del popolo* was chosen from a friendly town or province, usually from a noble family, and appointed for one year. For readers of the *Comedy*, it is fascinating to note that Francesca's brother-in-law and lover, Paolo Malatesta (*Inf.* 5.73–140), assumed this office in February 1282, when the sixteen-year-old Dante may well have met him. This, together with the fact that Dante at the end of his life found a patron in Francesca's nephew, the lord of Ravenna, helps to bring home the topical (at times, scandalous) nature of a number of the pilgrim's encounters in the *Comedy*. A new emblem came to symbolize political innovations in the city. Instead of a white lily on a red background, Florence's emblem became a red lily on a white field: a change given symbolic significance by our poet in *Paradiso* 16.154, when Dante's ancestor Cacciaguida evokes an earlier, idealized Florence, whose lily had not yet been "made scarlet by division."[7]

The rout at Montaperti (1260)

In 1258 a conspiracy organized by Cardinal Ottaviano degli Ubaldini (*Inf.* 10.120) led to the expulsion of the remaining Ghibelline leaders and the destruction of their property. Many took refuge in Siena, Florence's great banking rival and traditional foe. A Florentine-led Guelf army of about 70,000 men arrived at the castle of Montaperti on September 3, 1260. The Sienese could muster only a far smaller force, partly composed of Ghibelline exiles from Florence and mercenaries from Germany and southern Italy, sent by Frederick's illegitimate son, Manfred, who had accepted the lordship of Siena in May of the previous year. Wading across the river Arbia, the Sienese boldly attacked the Florentines, who were not yet ready to oppose them. The initial confusion turned into a rout, after the turncoat Bocca degli Abati cut off the hand of the Guelf standard-bearer, an act of treachery punished in the pit of Dante's hell (*Inf.* 32.77–82). Some 20,000 prisoners were taken by the Sienese, and the waters of the Arbia ran red with the blood of 10,000 dead Guelfs (*Inf.* 10.85–86). At the Council of Empoli, the victorious Ghibellines had decided to raze Florence to the ground, but they were dissuaded by Farinata degli Uberti (ll. 91–93). Nevertheless, in Florence, one hundred Guelf buildings *(palazzi)*, some six hundred houses, and nearly ninety towers were demolished, as were workshops, mills, and cloth-drying sheds belonging to the vanquished Guelfs. The Ghibellines soon asked the exiled Guelfs to return, but this move was thwarted by two French popes: Urban IV (1261–64), responsible for aligning "the Church with a faction" (Larner 1980, 42); and Clement IV (1265–68). Both these vicars of Christ were bent on annihilating the power of the Hohenstaufen dynasty and replacing it with a French kingdom in southern Italy and Sicily to be held as a papal fief.

The triumph of Guelf Florence

In June 1263, Urban IV (the first non-Italian pope since Adrian IV's death in 1159) chose the ambitious Charles of Anjou, brother of Louis IX of France, to be king of Sicily, after he had first excommunicated the occupant of the Sicilian throne, Frederick II's natural son, Manfred. His successor, Clement IV, was even more aggressively French in his political strategy. Charles reached Rome at about the time of Dante's birth in May 1265 and was crowned king in June. Despite huge loans from exiled Guelf Florentine bankers and others, Charles was desperately short of money to pursue his expedition. Clement raised necessary funds by pawning the plate from his personal chapel. On February 26, 1266, Charles destroyed Manfred and his army near Benevento (*Purg.* 3.112–45). With the subsequent defeat of Conradin in 1268 and the death of the last of the Hohenstaufen four years later, the whole of southern and central Italy, Sicily, and Tuscany (where Charles assumed the title of imperial vicar) were now under Guelf control.

Florence in Dante's time (1265-1302)

After Manfred's death, the Florentine commons began to agitate against the Ghibelline government of Guido Novello. In an attempt to placate the factions, it was decided that the office of *podestà* should be held jointly by a Ghibelline and a Guelf. Two founders of the Knights of Our Lady (popularly known as *Frati Gaudenti,* Jolly Friars), one a Guelf (Catalano dei Catalani) the other a Ghibelline (Loderingo degli Andalò), were invited to collaborate in establishing just, impartial rule. They established the ineffectual Council of Thirty-Six Good Men, but, as pawns of Clement IV, they connived at the return of the Guelf exiles and the expulsion of the Ghibelline leaders. Condemned as hypocrites by Dante (*Inf.* 23.76–109), they prepared the way for the popular Guelf uprising led by the Ghibelline "traitor" Gianni dei Soldanieri (*Inf.* 32.121–22). In 1266, as part of the process of reconciliation, a leading Guelf noble who was to become Dante's "first friend," Guido Cavalcanti, was betrothed by his father, Cavalcante (*Inf.* 10.52–72), to Beatrice, daughter of Farinata degli Uberti (d. 1264). However, the popular uprising of 1267 restored Guelf supremacy, exiled the remaining Ghibellines, and caused the destruction of the Uberti palace at what is now Piazza della Signoria (*Inf.* 23.108). Charles of Anjou now came to Florence, where he stayed until May 1268, assuming the title of *podestà* and acting as virtual ruler of the commune until the rebellion known as the Sicilian Vespers on Easter Monday of 1282 drove him out of Sicily, although he and his descendants continued to rule the kingdom of Naples (known as *Il regno*) until 1434. The result of the Vespers was a tragedy, for it led to a war between Angevin Naples and Aragonese Sicily that was to last for some ninety years and would exhaust the resources of a region already impoverished by its Norman rulers. Dante sees Charles among the negligent rulers in antepurgatory (*Purg.* 7.113, 124–26), during his encounter with the troubadour Sordello, who had been a staunch follower of Charles on his fateful Italian expedition.[8]

After Conradin's death in 1268, the *Parte Guelfa* was instituted in Florence to administer confiscated Ghibelline property. It soon became a state within a state, with its own palace, budget, two councils, captains and other officials, one of whom, the head of its secret police, rejoiced in the title of "Accuser of the Ghibellines." Its arms (those of Gregory IX) displayed a red eagle victorious over a green dragon. The imperial eagle was banned in Guelf Florence and replaced by the lion (its opposite in medieval heraldry), later chosen by the poet to act as one of the three beasts that barred the pilgrim's way toward salvation (*Inf.* 1.44–48).

Since the upper clergy belonged in the main to the nobility, the partisan bishop and partisan monk or friar (as in the case of the Cavalieri Gaudenti, Catalano and Loderingo) became a not uncommon feature in Tuscany and north-ern Italy. Two notorious examples belonged to the same family. Ottaviano degli Ubaldini (d. 1273), "the Cardinal"—mentioned above and condemned by Dante as a heretic who denied the soul's immortality (*Inf.* 10.120)—is reported to have cried out, "If the soul exists, I have lost it for the Ghibelline party"; and Villani (7.80) claims that he alone at the papal curia rejoiced at the news of the Guelf defeat at Montaperti. Ottaviano's nephew, Ruggieri della Pila Ubaldini, became archbishop of Pisa, Florence's fiercely Ghibelline rival, in 1278. As head of the Ghibellines, Archbishop Ruggieri conspired with his associates, the Gualandi, Sismondi, and Lanfranchi (*Inf.* 33.32), to trick, imprison, and starve to death Count Ugolino della Gherardesca and his progeny. In Dante's hell, this Church leader's head is eternally gnawed upon by his antagonist (who had betrayed his own Guelf party) in a bestial parody of the Eucharist (*Inf.* 32.133–34) that serves as a terrifying example of the way in which contemporary Italians are doomed to mutual destruction (*Purg.* 6.76–90).

In 1278 Cardinal Latino was sent by Pope Nicholas III to act as peacemaker between the Guelfs and Ghibellines in Florence. The pope, aware of the im-mense power acquired by Charles of Anjou, sought to establish some kind of po-litical equilibrium. This was achieved for a brief period with the appointment of eight Guelfs and six Ghibellines as *buonomini* or "good men" chosen to govern Florence. However, they were replaced by a new (Guelf) organ of government, the priorate, in June 1282. As for Pope Nicholas, this proto-Machiavellian was destined to be damned by Dante for simony (*Inf.* 19.31–120) rather than for his advice to his Orsini nephews that in political matters "you must make much use of dissimulation, keep many things hushed up, and feel your way cautiously" (Waley 1975, 40).

The priorate

In 1283 the office of *capitano del popolo* was suppressed and replaced by a "defender of the guilds," assisted by two councils. The supreme office of the commune now consisted of six priors (one from each of the Florentine *se-stieri*), elected by twelve guilds to serve for only two months (after two years—increased to three in 1293—a prior would be eligible for office again). Vigorous campaigns were mounted against neighboring Ghibelline cities. Arezzo was de-feated in 1289 at the battle of Campaldino, where the Ghibelline leader Bon-conte da Montefeltro was slain (*Purg.* 5.85–129). Among the Florentines were Vieri dei Cerchi and Corso Donati (later to become the heads of the White and Black parties in Florence); from a reading of *Inferno* 22.4–5 it seems likely that Dante, then twenty-four years old, also took part in the battle. However, the long drawn-out hostilities against Arezzo and Pisa precipitated a financial crisis in Florence, where Giano della Bella mobilized a popular reaction against the ruling classes, whose management of the war against Pisa had been marked by corruption and ineptitude.

The *Ordinamenti di giustizia* (1293)

Giano, a wealthy merchant from a noble family (*Par.* 16.127–32), dominated the commune for a brief but significant period (1293–95). He was the guiding spirit behind the *Ordinamenti di giustizia* (January 1293), which were clearly directed against the ruling elite of the previous decade. They excluded from the priorate anyone who did not practice a trade or profession within a guild, and set up a new office, that of *gonfaloniere di giustizia,* specially designed to control the behavior of the *magnati.* As Ottokar (1926) has shown, it is not possible to distinguish the *magnati* from the *popolani* by applying purely economic or social criteria. In fact, the term "magnate" came to be used and exploited in a way similar to that of "counterrevolutionary" and "communist" in recent times. A revolutionary step was taken in April 1293, when five provisions were added that effectively deprived all magnates of their political rights. A list was drawn up of over 150 families (including the Cavalcanti) whose members were ipso facto declared to be magnates, and thus some 3,000 Florentines were excluded from holding political office.[9] In evidence, the word of a *popolano* was to be preferred to that of a *magnate.*

Although Giano della Bella "did his utmost for the sake of justice against the guilty" (Compagni, 1.12) and Villani (13.44) includes him—with Farinata and Dante—among Florence's great benefactors treated with base ingratitude by their fellow-citizens, his actions brought about his downfall. Unjustly accused of supporting one of the nobles, the tyrannical Corso Donati (*Purg.* 24.79–90), Giano was forced to seek refuge in France.

Dante's political career

The *Ordinamenti di giustizia* were modified in July 1295 to allow magnates (except "knights") to enroll in a guild and thereby to enjoy full political rights. Dante, who belonged to the minor, impoverished nobility, became a member of the Guild of Physicians and Apothecaries (a pantechnicon which included saddlers, packers, hatters, painters and other craftsmen). Thus, although he had officially reached the age of political enfranchisement at twenty-five, before the *ordinamenti* were passed, Dante now—at the age of thirty—became active on the political stage of the Florentine commune, taking part at the end of the year in the procedural debate concerning the election of the priors. As a poet and an ardent student of philosophy,[10] he now became passionately interested in ethical problems such as the true nature of nobility. The study of Aristotle's *Ethics,* the influence of Guido Guinizzelli, and Giano della Bella's political reforms all led the poet to abandon the "sweet rhymes of love" for "harsh and subtle" verses (*Rime* LXXXII:69.14; *Convivio* 4) capable of expressing philosophical, moral, and social truths. The bitter experience of exile was to complete the transformation of the youthful love poet into the solitary voice of Italy's "singer of righteousness" (*DVE* 2.2.8).

Pope Celestine V (1294)

The previous year had seen the election to the papal see of Pietro da Morrone, eighty years old, "simple and unlettered" (Villani 9.5), as Celestine V. Celestine abdicated on December 13, 1294, and his acts were abrogated by his successor, Boniface VIII (1294–1303), who had him imprisoned. Celestine died in 1296. He was canonized by Clement V in 1313, partly as a political move against the memory of Boniface's anti-French policies. It is virtually certain that Dante, the "world-judge," condemned Celestine in *Inferno* 3.59–60 for abdicating and thus betraying the hopes of the faithful that he would purge the Church and the papacy of the desire for worldly power and riches. During his four months in office Celestine did not move to Rome but remained in Naples, where he was King Charles's puppet, creating no fewer than eight French and four Neapolitan cardinals. The hapax used by Dante to characterize Celestine's abdication, *rifiuto* (*Inf.* 3.60), expresses the poet's moral outrage at Celestine's "great refusal" to obey God's will, the divine command to feed Christ's sheep and to "lead mankind to eternal life" (*Mon.* 3.16.10). Already in 1294 Iacopone da Todi had forecast Celestine's damnation if he proved unequal to the task of leading the Church toward salvation.[11] Although for Dante (as for most Christians in the Middle Ages) the contemplative life was theoretically superior to the active life, the poet's conception of the human condition required that the man chosen to lead Christ's Church on earth must not retire from the world but must instead reform and guide the Church Militant on its path to salvation.

Pope Boniface VIII (1294–1303)

The drama that led to Dante's lifelong exile from Florence began with the election of Benedetto Caetani as Boniface VIII, eleven days after

Celestine's abdication. Boniface's political ambitions were immense, but ultimately, as a result of his machinations, both the papacy's political prestige and its spiritual authority were degraded. The *Comedy* shows us Boniface destined to be punished among the simoniacs in hell (*Inf.* 19.52–57) and disowned by St. Peter in heaven (*Par.* 27.22–27). Boniface is further accused of having turned the crusading ideal into a private vendetta against Christians (ll. 49–51). Such was the poet's judgment based on his experience of Boniface's pontificate.

Dante elected prior (1300)

The climax of Dante's political career came in the year he was later to choose for his vision of the other world, when he was elected one of the six priors on June 18, 1300, for the traditional two months' term of office. In March, Cardinal Matteo d'Acquasparta had excommunicated the Florentine priors on behalf of Pope Boniface, thus preparing the way for "the *coup d'état* carried out by Charles of Valois at the instigation of the pope in 1301" (Partner 1965, 81). In May the feud that split the ruling Guelf party came to a head, and its two factions acquired new names, *Bianchi* and *Neri* (from the White and Black factions of Pistoia, which the Florentine Guelfs had tried to reconcile). The Florentine Whites were led by the Cerchi, *nouveaux riches,* the Blacks by the Donati, "of more ancient lineage, but not so wealthy" (Compagni, 1.20). For the moment (and until 1304), Dante found himself aligned with the White Guelfs and their policy of defending Florentine autonomy, although he was later to condemn both Whites and Blacks (*Inf.* 15.70–72), the Cerchi (*Par.* 16.65, 94–98), and his White companions in exile as evil and vindictive men (*Par.* 17.61–66).

Dante's first act as prior was to reaffirm Florence's right to discipline her own citizens, even when, as papal bankers, they were under the pope's protection. On June 23, some magnates attacked the consuls of the guilds and leading members of the popular government. The priors acted resolutely, exiling fifteen leaders of both the Black and the White factions. Dante thus agreed to the exile of seven White Guelfs, including his friend and fellow poet Guido Cavalcanti. The Blacks refused to leave Florence. The government was able to save the situation *in extremis,* but it became embroiled in conflict with the papal legate, Cardinal Matteo d'Acquasparta, whose policies were so unpopular that an attempt was made on his life in the middle of July. On July 22 Pope Boniface reacted, attributing the cardinal's failure to the work of devils in league with the wicked priors of Florence. The cardinal left the city toward the end of September and excommunicated the new priors (Dante's successors), after they revoked the sentence of exile against the White leaders.

Boniface now sought a more radical solution in the person of Charles of Valois, brother of Philip IV of France, by calling upon Charles to come to Tuscany to act as peacemaker (offering the mirage of the Sicilian throne as a reward). In June 1301 Dante was of the minority in the Council of One Hundred that voted against the pope's request that Florence should continue to support Boniface's military operations in the Maremma against Margherita Aldobrandeschi.[12] On September 13 Dante reaffirmed his support for the popular regime. Charles of Valois's arrival in Italy (*Purg.* 20.70–78), and his meetings with Black envoys in Bologna and with the pope at Anagni, created a state of crisis. After September 28 the Florentine government sent a special mission (which may have included Dante) to Boniface to try to save the situation. The mission was a failure. On November 1 Charles entered Florence, Corso Donati returned from exile, and the priors were forced to resign. Their successors, elected on November 8, were all Black Guelfs. On March 10, 1302, Dante Alighieri and fourteen other Whites were condemned to death *in absentia:* should any fall into the power of the Florentine commune, he would be burned at the stake *(igne comburatur sic quod moriatur).* By June of that same year, no fewer than 559 death sentences had been decreed.

This summary account of events in Florence before and during the first thirty-seven years of Dante's lifetime will help readers to understand what led the poet of the *Comedy* to condemn the constant changes that plagued Florence's laws and constitution. With trenchant irony, in *Purgatorio* 6.136–51, her greatest son declares that Florence alone in the troubled Italian peninsula is at peace and wisely governed; then, the ugly reality leads him to compare his native city to a sick woman who cannot find rest but desperately tries to lessen her pain by tossing and turning on her bed. Florence, in her folly and discord, is merely the plaything of the whims of Fortune, which governs her as the moon does the tides of the sea (*Par.* 16.82–84). Blinded by pride, envy, and avarice (*Inf.* 6.74–75, 15.67–68), Florentines are, as we have seen, omnipresent in the poet's depiction of hell.

Exile (1302–21)

Dante's long years in exile (until his death in Ravenna in 1321) led him to denounce the corruption encountered or imagined in virtually every part of Italy. At the poem's center (*Purg.* 14.37–66), the heart of Tuscany and its "royal" river, the Arno, have been turned into a "ditch" of iniquity, its inhabitants transformed into beasts. Florence is now an "evil wood" (*trista selva*, l. 64) reminiscent of the "savage wood" *(selva selvaggia)* in which the pilgrim found himself near to perdition in the *Comedy*'s opening scene. Northern Italy is a moral wasteland, devoid of all love and courtesy (*Purg.* 16.115–20). The *Comedy*'s fiftieth canto—set at the poem's mathematical center—also analyzes the root cause of this moral and political decadence (*Purg.* 16.106–14):

> Soleva Roma, che 'l buon mondo feo,
> due soli aver, che l'una e l'altra strada
> facean vedere, e del mondo e di Deo.
>   L'un l'altro ha spento; ed è giunta la spada
> col pasturale, e l'un con l'altro insieme
> per viva forza mal convien che vada;
>   però che, giunti, l'un l'altro non teme:
> se non mi credi, pon mente a la spiga,
> ch'ogn' erba si conosce per lo seme.

―――――

Rome, which made the good world, used to have two suns, which lit up the two paths, of the world and of God. The one has extinguished the other; and the sword has been joined to the shepherd's crook; and it is wrong for them to be violently forced together; because, when joined, neither fears the other; if you do not believe me, examine the result, for every plant is known by its seed.

"By their fruits you shall know them" (Matt. 7.16). The same diagnosis is given by Beatrice in heaven. She tells Dante that the universal corruption of the "human family" is due to the fact that "no one governs on earth" (*Par.* 27.139–41), a direct consequence of the popes' meddling in the temporal sphere and their hostility to the empire.

P apal opposition to the empire

For Dante, in 1300, the villain was Boniface VIII. In a letter addressed to the imperial electors in Germany (May 13, 1300), Boniface stated that the Holy See had transferred the empire to the Germans through *translatio imperii,* indicating that the empire could be transferred from one people to another, a concept that was anathema to Dante, for whom the empire was intended by God to be Roman for all time (*Mon.* 2). The pope also declared that the Holy See intended to reassert its authority over the province of Tuscany. However, Boniface was now aware of the disastrous results of the papacy's manifold attempts to play off France against the empire, ever since Innocent III's statement (made in 1202) that the king of France acknowledged no superior in temporal matters. One hundred years later, the conflict between Boniface and the king of France reached its climax—ironically enough, after the notorious bull *Unam sanctam* (November 18, 1302), in which the pope asserted that "the temporal authority [must be] subject to the spiritual power."[13] Papal claims, however, bore little relationship to political reality. On the eve of the promulgation of the decree excommunicating Philip IV, the latter's henchmen imprisoned the pope in his residence at Anagni (*Purg.* 20.85–90), and although he was liberated by the townsfolk, Boniface died a few weeks later (October 11, 1303).

The Capetian dynasty continued to cast its poisonous shadow over the whole of Christendom (*Purg.* 20.43–45), depriving Christians of the beneficial effects of the "two suns." Its accomplices (according to the author of the *Comedy*) included the Gascon pope, Clement V (1305–14), guilty of initiating the Church's seventy years of Babylonish exile by moving the seat of the papacy from Rome to Avignon in 1309. Dante depicted him as the nameless villain (once even called "the new Pilate") in the three sections of his *Comedy* (e.g., *Inf.* 19.85–87; *Purg.* 20.85–93; *Par.* 30.142–48). In the nightmarish vision of *Purgatorio* 32.136–60, the king of France who refused to acknowledge the emperor's overlordship is depicted as a giant who first dallies with, then flays, the harlot symbolizing the corrupt papacy (Anagni), finally dragging her and the now-monstrous chariot into the depths of the forest (captivity at Avignon).[14] The medieval repugnance for everything monstrous and therefore unnatural underscores the poet's evident intention to shock his readers and arouse their moral outrage at this apocalyptic tragedy.

Emperor Henry VII (1308–13)

If there are relatively few direct references to events during the period 1301–21, this is of course due to the fact that the pilgrim's journey through the otherworld is supposed to take place at Eastertide in 1300. Nevertheless, the immense hopes and subsequent disappointments created by the election of Henry, count of Luxembourg, as Emperor Henry VII in November 1308 seared Dante's soul. When Henry decided to come to Italy to pacify the peninsula and to be crowned in Rome, he was at first encouraged by the pope, who ordered all Italians to accept him as their rightful emperor (*Exultet in gloria,* September 1, 1310). Dante now wrote the first of his three "political" letters, addressed to the rulers and peoples of Italy and comparing Henry's mission to that of Moses. Flushed by the prospect of an apparently ideal cooperation between the spiritual and temporal leaders of Christendom, Dante here accepted the idea that the empire was "the lesser luminary" with regard to the papacy, according to the political interpretation of the two "great lights" of Genesis 1.16—a concept which, as we have already noted, Dante was to abandon for the unscientific but potent image of the two suns, placed at the very center of his poem (*Purg.* 16.106–8; cf. *Mon.* 3.4.16). The epistle is clear evidence that the Florentine exile now saw himself as invested with a prophetic mission.[15] What came to pass, however, constituted a tragic denial of Dante's deepest hopes and aspirations. A spirit of rebellion spread throughout northern Italy and Tuscany. Florence refused to refer to Henry as "emperor" or "king of the Romans," choosing instead the alienating formula "king of the Germans." His native city's role at the heart of the resistance to the emperor moved Dante to write the two letters of March 31 and April 17, 1311. He urged Henry to leave northern Italy and hasten to crush "the viper," Florence (*Ep.* 7.7.24). More and more, the emperor was forced to act as leader of the Ghibellines (against his stated intention of acting as peacemaker above all parties) in a desperate attempt to countervail strong Guelf opposition. The pope commanded Henry to leave Rome on the very day of his coronation (June 29, 1312); and he went so far as to threaten the emperor with excommunication if he should invade the Angevin kingdom in southern Italy. While preparing to march against King Robert of Naples, Henry died of malarial fever on August 24, 1313. Clement died some six months later.

In the bull *Romani principes,* issued just before he died, Clement claimed that the late emperor had sworn fealty to the papacy, declaring himself to be a vassal of the Church. The bull *Pastoralis cura* (March 14, 1314) revoked all of Henry's pronouncements against King Robert on the grounds that the pope was superior to the emperor as a consequence of the "plenitude of power" Christ allegedly conferred on Peter and his successors. The bitter experiences of this power struggle would eventually lead the *Comedy*'s aging author to return to the political drama played out in these fateful years. At the very point where he summons all his poetic powers to describe the reality of heaven and the beatific vision, Dante makes Beatrice point to just one of the few vacant seats. This is reserved not for some holy person or contemplative soul but for "lofty Henry," who would be betrayed by Pope Clement, himself destined for hell (*Par.* 30.133–48).

The world deprived of both "suns"

In 1314 both Church and empire were without leaders. Dante wrote another Latin epistle, this time to the cardinals assembled in conclave, accusing them of espousing greed and leading the Church astray. The Italian cardinals (now in a minority) must realize that Rome is still "the country of the illustrious Scipios" (11.10.25)—a surprising enough reminder addressed to churchmen, but one reiterated in *Paradiso* 27.61–62, where the reference to Scipio as an instrument of Divine Providence is placed in the august mouth of St. Peter himself. Jeremiah's prophecy of the destruction of Jerusalem is here used to describe the contemporary situation. The letter is an attack of truly biblical intensity on the whole Church leadership, "without equal in any other writer of the Middle Ages" (Morghen 1983, 115). In August 1316 Jacques Duèse was elected pope as John XXII. From the Heaven of Justice (Jupiter), Dante launched one of his most scathing invectives, accusing the pope of leading the whole world astray and of destroying Christ's vineyard, owing to his obsession with the image of John the Baptist found on the Florentine florin, which makes him despise SS. Peter and Paul (*Par.* 18.115–36, "the fisherman and Old Paul," where the Pope's French pronunciation is sarcastically caught in the rhyme-word *Polo [Paolo]*). In *Paradiso* 27.58–60, St. Peter prophesies: "Cahorsines [John XXII] and Gascons [Clement V] make ready to drink of our blood. O good beginning, to what vile ending must you fall!"

In October 1314 there was a dual election to the imperial throne: Lewis of Bavaria and Frederick of Austria were both crowned in Germany, events which led to a long drawn-out struggle between the two contenders. In April 1317 the pope exploited their weaknesses in the bull *Si fratrum*. He thus inserted into canon law an act proclaiming that, whenever the throne was vacant, the empire's jurisdiction devolved upon the pope, since God had conferred on him the right to command both in heaven and on earth. He also acted against the imperial vicars created by Henry VII in northern Italy, including Dante's patron, Cangrande della Scala (*Par.* 17.76–93). It was at this time that Dante wrote his *Monarchia* in order to refute papal claims to supremacy over the emperor.[16] He then left Verona, the Ghibelline capital of northern Italy, and made his way to the moderately Guelf but peaceful town of Ravenna, where Guido da Polenta, nephew of Francesca da Rimini, was *podestà*. There, he was able to finish his *Comedy* just before his death, while reviving the Vergilian bucolic tradition in a poetic exchange with Giovanni del Virgilio (*Eclogues* 2 and 4). On his way back to Ravenna from Venice, where he had been sent as member of an embassy to the doge, Dante contracted malarial fever and died during the night of September 13–14, 1321.

The poet's condemnation of Florence

We have seen that Dante's *Inferno* is peopled with Florentines; in *Purgatorio* 6, he condemns Florence as a desperately sick woman; and, when he is about to be introduced into God's very presence among the blessed in heaven,

Dante speaks of his overpowering amazement at the contrast of what he now beholds with things on earth. This contrast is expressed through a crescendo of opposites:

> ïo, che al divino da l'umano,
> a l'etterno dal tempo era venuto,
> e di Fiorenza in popol giusto e sano.
> $(Par. 31.37–39)^{17}$

———

> I, who had come to the divine from the human, to eternity from time, and from Florence to a people just and whole.

A Florentine has finally found a people truly just, upright, and whole! Not even a barbarian gazing at the grandeur of Rome at her most magnificent could have experienced the wonder and ecstasy that overwhelm Dante the pilgrim as he gazes at God's *sicuro e gaudïoso regno* (l. 25, this safe and joyful kingdom). Not just in hell, but even in heaven, Florence remains a yardstick for the poet to measure corruption and its antithesis.

The most extensive analysis of Florence's degradation in 1300 is found at the center of Dante's *Paradiso* (15–16), when he meets his crusading ancestor Cacciaguida, Dante's great-great grandfather, who quickly delineates the peaceful, sober, and modest town where he was born. In four consecutive *terzine* (*Par.* 15.100–111), Cacciaguida hammers home with the forceful, initial *NON* the fact that in his day Florentines did not indulge in sumptuous dress and ornamentation;[18] they did not marry off daughters at the cost of crippling dowries;[19] they did not indulge in effeminate luxury and sexual corruption; they did not try to outdo Rome in the extravagance of their buildings. Men were sober in their habits, their women content to sit at the spinning wheel. Moreover, women were not abandoned by husbands desperate for commercial gain abroad;[20] they devoted themselves to the care of their children (ll. 112–26). Mutual trust was a feature of that *bello viver di cittadini* in a united Florence supremely at peace with herself (ll. 130–31). Such was the exiled poet's nostalgia for the city he both cherished as a mother and hated with equal intensity as a cruel and perfidious *noverca* or stepmother (*Par.* 17.46–48).

As Charles Davis has shown, Dante dated Florence's golden age earlier than other Florentine chroniclers. Moreover, "it was precisely in the period of the most remarkable growth of his city, celebrated by all the other Florentine writers, and even in the glorious decade 1250–60 of rule by the *Primo Popolo,* that he found the seeds of her moral downfall" (Davis 1984, 74). Everything that had contributed to Florence's greatness and economic supremacy was rejected by her exiled son. Particularly striking is Dante's denunciation of the very symbol of Florentine prestige: the gold florin, first minted in 1252 and a source of intense municipal pride.[21] Having become universal currency, the florin was praised even by the Dominican friar Remigio de' Girolami. Remigio told his Florentine audience that God had given Florence "seven singular gifts: abundance of money, a noble coinage, abundance of population, a civilized way of life, the wool industry, skill in the production of armaments, and a vigorous building activity in the *contado*." Remigio's eulogy of the florin "praised its 'nobility' for three reasons: it was made of the best gold, it was decorated on one side with the image of John the Baptist and on the other with the Florentine lily, and it was accepted throughout the world [even among the Saracens, *etiam inter Saracenos*]" (Davis 1984, 206). Dante, on the other hand, alludes to the lily as the "accursed flower," a metonymy in Dante for the greed that has corrupted both the head of Christ's Church and the body of the faithful (*Par.* 9.127–32). Although the Dominican sounded the usual warning that these gifts could be used either *in bono* to bring glory to Florence or *in malo* to blind the Florentines with false pride, it is a piquant touch to find a layman cursing—and a religious praising—the very symbol of Florence's immense wealth.

Another of what Remigio praises as God's gifts to Florence, her *multitudinem populi,* is also condemned by Dante. In *Paradiso* 16.46–48, Cacciaguida is made to rejoice in the fact that in his day the population of Florence was only one fifth of what it had reached in 1300.[22] He also (ll. 49–57) deprecates the immigration from the surrounding countryside or *contado*—which in fact produced the workforce necessary for Florence's massive industrial and economic expansion. Although it has been claimed that Florence did not surpass Pisa in population before 1250, her demographic explosion was spectacular, so that by 1300 it was one of the very few cities in Europe to have from 90,000 to 100,000 inhabitants.[23] However approximate the figures given by the contemporary chronicler, Villani's account builds up a fascinating picture of a great urban center, where in the fourteenth century "the population density was greater than in the twentieth century" (Anderson and Zinsser 1990, 1, 354). Villani's chronicle claims that, together with a population of some 90,000 "mouths," there were always about 1,500 foreigners in Florence. Boys and girls learning to read numbered from 8,000 to 10,000; from 550 to 600 boys studied grammar and logic "in four large schools"; the churches in Florence and its suburbs numbered 110; there were 30 hospitals totaling more than 1,000 beds. A major source of wealth was the wool worked in over 200 workshops under the control of the Arte della Lana, and up to a third of the population made its living by the wool trade.[24] Eighty "banks" or offices of money changers existed in Florence. Over 350,000 gold florins were coined each year. There were 60 physicians and surgeons, and some 600 notaries. Every year about 4,000 oxen and calves were consumed, as well as 60,000

sheep, 20,000 goats, and 30,000 pigs. Throughout, Villani's pride in his na-
tive city shines through—so much so that he claims that any foreigner arriv-
ing for the first time in Florence was bound to be overwhelmed by everything
he saw, including the magnificence of its buildings and monuments (Villani
12.94).

In this twelfth chapter, Villani compares Florence's greatness as a city to that
of Rome. Indeed, his ninth book (9.36) tells us that he was inspired to compose
his chronicle of Florentine history, because "our city of Florence, the daugh-
ter and creature of Rome, was on her way up and in pursuit of great things,"
similar to those achieved by Rome.[25] For the author of *Convivio*, Florence
was without doubt "the most beautiful and most famous daughter of Rome"
(*Conv.* 1.3.4); and, in 1311, Dante condemned his fellow Florentines for "sharp-
ening the horns of rebellion against Rome, which made her [Florence] in her
own image and after her own likeness" (*Ep.* 7.7.25), where the echo of God's
creation of humankind "in our image and likeness" (Gen. 1.26) resonates. Nev-
ertheless, Cacciaguida's words in *Paradiso* 15.109–11 (Rome's "Monte Mario was
not yet outdone by your Uccellatoio, which, even as it is outdone in its ascent
will likewise be outdone in its decline") deplore the fact that Florence's skyline
in 1300 is more impressive than Rome's. Instead, the exiled Florentine seizes
upon this source of Florentine pride as yet another example of hubris, which
will be punished as surely as was that of "proud Troy" (*Inf.* 1.75). Dante thus
resolutely sets his face against the building boom that had graced Florence with
the Palazzo del Bargello (1255), the Palazzo dei Priori (commissioned in 1298),
the enlargement of Santa Maria Novella (1294), extensions to Santa Croce (1295),
and the building of one of the largest cathedrals in Christendom (for which the
commission was entrusted to Arnolfo di Cambio in 1294). Florence's most fa-
mous hospital, Santa Maria Nuova, was founded by Beatrice's father, Folco Por-
tinari, in 1286. Large squares were created in front of Santa Maria Novella and
Santa Croce, in order to accommodate the crowds that flocked to hear Domini-
can and Franciscan preachers. Wooden houses were replaced by constructions in
brick and stone. Private mansions were enlarged and embellished, and new
palazzi built for the banking elite, such as the Spini and the Mozzi.[26] Villas were
built on the surrounding hills. Florence was not yet the Florence dear to world
tourism, which is of course largely the product of the Renaissance. Never-
theless, Florence could boast of being one of the very first cities in Europe
to pave its streets (1237), and by 1300 it had a municipal sewerage system. Im-
mense changes occurred during Dante's lifetime. All this is decried by the poet in
his oblique reference to the decision taken in 1284 to expand the city walls, yet
again. Cacciaguida begins his paean to the Florence of old by describing her
nestling within the "ancient circle" of city walls (*Par.* 15.97). Built in 1078, they
had enclosed the city's Roman core of 20 hectares, an area increased to 80

hectares with the second set of walls, in 1172. In 1284 the decision to wall in an area of 630 hectares (which proved ample for the next five hundred years) led to an expansionism that for Dante came to symbolize Florentine megalomania.[27]

Dante even condemns immigration from the surrounding countryside (*Par.* 16.52–69), where the local gentry had been under the protection and jurisdiction of the empire. With the treaty of San Genesio in 1197, however, Florence was able to seize control over the whole of the surrounding *contado;* otherwise, Cacciaguida points out, even the immensely wealthy Cerchi family would have remained in their rural Val di Sieve (l. 65). Whereas Cacciaguida's fellow citizens were all of pure Florentine stock, in Dante's time the city had been invaded by "non-Florentines" from Campi, Certaldo, Figline, and elsewhere (ll. 49–51). What one translator calls "the intermingling of persons" (l. 67, *la confusion de le persone*) is always a curse, a cause of discord in any city; and Florence's greatly increased population does not in fact make her stronger, for "one sword can often cut more and better than five" (ll. 71–72). While Dante's attitude is evidently reactionary, any anachronistic association of his ideas with "ethnic cleansing" and its atrocities in recent times must be avoided and his view equated with that fierce *campanilismo* or civic pride that has been a familiar feature of Italian history. Another influence was Aristotle, who declared that "a great city and a populous one are not the same . . . I know of no well-constituted city that does not restrict its numbers" (*Politics* 7.4).[28] Citizenship must be a right granted to good men, who form a "community of like persons whose end or aim is the best life possible" (*Politics* 7.8). Dante would have been struck by Aristotle's strictures against trade: "Citizens must not live a banausic or commercial life" (7.9). In medieval times, "commerce almost always figured on the lists drawn up by theologians of professions qualified as 'dishonest' and 'impure'" (Gurevich 1990, 246–47); and Dante decried the *nouveaux riches* and their *súbiti guadagni,* acquired through commerce (*Inf.* 16.73–75). Indeed, as Gurevich (1990, 262–63) points out, "In no other part of Europe . . . was there such a large segment of the population involved in commercial activities [as in the cities of Tuscany and northern Italy]."[29] Florentines had invented double-entry bookkeeping and the forerunner of the banking check; they were (with the Venetians and the Genoese) pioneers of international finance, regarded as the world's leading experts in international trade. Florence itself—*la gran villa* on the banks of the Arno (*Inf.* 23.95)—already attracted tourists, as Compagni (*Cronica* 1.1) boasts: "Many come to visit her from faraway lands, not of necessity, but on account of the goodness of her trades and guilds, and for the city's beauty and ornamentation." Yet, in his *Comedy,* Dante resolutely denounced virtually everything that made Florence great: her abundance of people, civic pride, immense wealth, and entrepreneurial spirit. The poet's dislike of usury was so great that he placed the usurers on a cliff-edge overhanging the circles of

Fraud (*Inf.* 17.43–78). In fact, it is hardly an exaggeration to say that, insofar as Florence's dynamic expansion was to be emblematic of the future course of European capitalism, the greatest poet of the Christian Middle Ages prophetically condemned many of capitalism's most salient features.[30]

Dante and the Church

Dante's attitude toward the contemporary Church combined obedience with the harshest possible strictures. This combination is particularly striking in the apparent contradiction between the claim (made by St. Peter in *Par.* 27.22–24) that the papacy is vacant in 1300, on the one hand, and the denunciation of the "scandal of Anagni," on the other (*Purg.* 20.85–90). Boniface is condemned as "the prince of the new Pharisees" (*Inf.* 27.85) for having purchased his election (*Inf.* 19.56–57) and for transforming St. Peter's sacred burial place into a sewer (*Par.* 27.25). Yet when the henchmen of Philip the Fair come to lay hands on Boniface and make him their prisoner at Anagni (in 1303), Dante "foresees" in this evil wretch Christ Himself captured, mocked, and once more put to death "among living thieves" (*Purg.* 20.85–90). Boniface's sacrilegious political ambitions had forced the emperor-elect, Albert of Austria (stigmatized as "Alberto tedesco" in *Purg.* 6.97), to accept unconditionally the pope's claim that he possessed a *plenitudo potestatis,* supreme authority in both the spiritual and the temporal spheres: "For the first and only time the terms *fidelis et obediens* are found in an imperial pledge . . . All imperial care about the subtlety of papal formulae had been completely abandoned" (Boase 1933, 330). But if in denouncing the pope's behavior as typical of the "new Pharisees" Dante resembled the Spiritual Franciscans, who wished to remain faithful to Francis's desire to espouse absolute poverty,[31] he differed from many of them in regarding Boniface as the rightful pope.

Evangelical poverty

The leading intellectuals among the Spirituals—Piero Olivi (Pierre de Jean Olieu) and Ubertino da Casale—both taught in Florence at Santa Croce from 1287 to 1289. In both, we find the ideal of a poor Church, an *Ecclesia spiritualis* utterly given up to things of the spirit.[32] Yet "Dante seems more radical even than the Spiritual Franciscans. He thought that the clergy as a whole should have remained poor, and should have shunned all temporal jurisdiction, from the time of Christ to the end of history" (Davis 1984, 53), whereas the Spirituals conceded that it was permissible for prelates and the Church (but not their own

order) to own property, at least until the full flowering of the new age inaugu-
rated by St. Francis. Dante's veneration for Francis and his marriage to Lady
Poverty forms the central idea in his eulogy of the *alter Christus* (*Par.* 11.58–117).
Poverty in the life of St. Dominic is also emphasized as "the first injunction that
Christ gave [to the world]" (*Par.* 12.75; Matt. 19.21), although Dante's spokesman
St. Bonaventure condemns Ubertino da Casale for his fundamentalist interpre-
tation of Francis's Rule (*Par.* 12.124–26). The need for Christ's Church to return
to its original state of poverty is an essential part of the *Comedy*'s message. Dante
goes so far as to claim that poverty had been widowed at Christ's death (when
she alone had remained with Jesus on the cross) and then neglected for well over
a thousand years, until Francis espoused her (*Par.* 11.64–72).[33] The scandal of
churchmen enjoying immense wealth and living off the fat of the land had
sparked a reaction that gained prominence in the second half of the twelfth cen-
tury. In 1173 Pierre Valdès, a merchant of Lyons, took to heart that same verse
(Matt. 19.21): "Go, sell all your possessions, give the proceeds to the poor . . .
Then come and follow me." He and his followers, the "Poor Men of Lyons,"
were sworn to apostolic poverty and spiritual reform. The ideal of evangelical
poverty spread. In 1318 Pope John XXII issued a decretal in which he con-
demned the Spiritual Franciscans' view that there were now two churches: the
one carnal, packed with riches and stained with crimes; the other, a spiritual
church, bound by poverty and cleansed by frugality, beautiful in virtue. Then,
two years after Dante's death, the same pope designated as "erroneous and hereti-
cal" the belief that Christ and his disciples "did not possess any goods or other
property, either privately or in common."[34]

It is against the background of this violent polemic that we must read *Para-
diso* 21 and 22, in which Dante describes his encounters with St. Peter Damian
and St. Benedict, who appear among those who had dedicated their lives above
all to contemplation. Peter Damian tells how he had reluctantly accepted a car-
dinal's hat, which now "passes down from bad to worse," contrasting the cor-
ruption of modern churchmen with the austerity of SS. Peter and Paul, who
had spread abroad Christ's message, "lean and barefoot, taking their food from
any source" (*Par.* 21.127–35). Now, the leaders of Christ's Church are so gross
that they need servants to get them up into the saddle, where their ample purple
capes cover two beasts: their mount and themselves. The crude language of
sì che due bestie van sott' una pelle (l. 134, so that two beasts go under one hide)
drives home the anger felt by the poet and expressed through the persona of an
ardent and celebrated ecclesiastical reformer.

In the following canto, St. Benedict (c. 480–c. 550), "the patriarch of West-
ern monks" (Lawrence 1984, 17), points to the presence of St. Macarius the
Younger (d. 404), who, with nearly five thousand monks under his charge, is
regarded as the founder of monasticism in the East. Benedict points to a golden

ladder whose summit reaches up to God's very presence in the Empyrean.[35]
Now, he tells Dante, no one climbs it, and Benedict's famous rule is a waste
of the paper it is written on; the monasteries have become dens of thieves; the
monks' habits are nothing but sacks of rotten flour. Once again, the vigorous
earthiness of Dante's vernacular "comic" style gives added impetus to the saint's
wrath at the spectacle of what has become of the monastic ideal:

> Ma, per salirla, mo nessun diparte
> da terra i piedi, e la regola mia
> rimasa è per danno de le carte.
>   Le mura che solieno esser badia
> fatte sono spelonche, e le cocolle
> sacca son piene di farina ria.
> *(Par.* 22.73–78)

———

But no one now lifts his feet from the earth to climb it, and my rule re-
mains to waste the paper it was written on. The walls that were once
abbeys have now become dens [of thieves], and the cowls are sacks full
of rotten flour.

Even the worst form of usury is not so displeasing to God as the abuse of
the income enjoyed by the monasteries, which now fills the monks' hearts with
mad pride and ambition: *quel frutto / che fa il cor de' monaci sí folle* (ll.
80–81)—
where *frutto* is opposed to the *frutti santi,* those "holy fruits" or good works in-
spired by charity. A leitmotif of *Paradiso* is here encapsulated in three words
(l. 93): *bianco fatto bruno,* the white of good intentions and piety turned into the
darkness of vice and corruption.[36] Benedict highlights the way in which Peter,
the first pope, began his work without any kind of wealth, silver, or gold; he
himself founded his great order with prayer and fasting; Francis set the example
of humility to his followers:

> Pier cominciò sanz' oro e sanz' argento,
> e io con orazione e con digiuno,
> e Francesco umilmente il suo convento.
> *(Par.* 22.88–90)

To live in poverty *(sanz' oro e sanz' argento),* with prayer and fasting *(con
orazione e con digiuno),* accompanied by humility in all things: such was the
monastic ideal in utter contrast to the reality perceived by Dante in 1300. For
centuries, monasteries had set themselves up as the gateway to heaven, the surest
path to salvation. A good example of monkish claims is provided by the abbot

of Saint-Benoît-sur-Loire at the end of the tenth century, who chose Christ's parable of the sower and the harvest (Matt. 13.1–23) to prove that the faithful will be rewarded in heaven according to their status in this world: in the precise ratio of 100 for monks, 60 for the clergy, and 30 for the laity (Miccoli 1990, 54). Judged by the claims they made for themselves, monks and friars were all too often found to be hypocritical and scandalously lacking in the virtues they purported to practice.[37] Although Dante does not hesitate to portray the hypocrites in hell as members of a cloistered community, the *collegio de l'ipocriti tristi* (*Inf.* 23.91–92) dressed in Cluniac pomp, it is in heaven that he thunders against the decadence of the monastic orders and the mendicants, whose good wine has turned sour and moldy (*Par.* 12.114).

Beatrice vs. theologians and unworthy preachers

Whereas the poet chooses various holy men as a mouthpiece for his denunciation of corruption—St. Bonaventure (the Franciscan Order), St. Thomas (the Dominicans), St. Peter Damian (those at the summit of the Church hierarchy), St. Benedict (the monastic orders in general)—his choice of Beatrice to attack the follies of preachers is truly astonishing for his age. St. Paul had forbidden women to teach (1 Tim. 2.12): they were to be subject to men, especially to priests and religious. Instead, as Joan Ferrante has brilliantly documented, "only Beatrice and God are infallible in the *Commedia* . . . Dante gives the office of major theologian in his heaven to someone whose sex would have shocked virtually all the doctors of the church . . . he does not hesitate to have her correct them" (1992, 11).[38] Beatrice contradicts St. Gregory the Great on the angelic orders, St. Jerome on the creation of the angels, and St. Thomas in his attribution of a kind of memory to angels (*Par.* 28.133–35, 29.37–45, 29.76–81). Beatrice berates the many theologians who claim to affirm the truth, both in good and in bad faith, whereas in fact they are a prey to error and illusion (*Par.* 29.82–83). Worst of all are those whose sermons consist solely of *motti e . . . iscede* (l. 115, jests and tomfoolery), anything that will make the audience laugh, instead of concentrating on the lance and shield provided by the truth of Christ's Gospel (ll. 109–14). They mislead and exploit people with false indulgences, betraying the pious intentions of St. Anthony the Great (born c. 250), the founder of Christian monastic institutions.[39]

Church corruption and renewal

In the apocalyptic spectacle played out at the end of *Purgatorio* 32, we see the Giant Antichrist kissing the Harlot before scourging her from head to foot and dragging the monstrous chariot of the Carnal Church into the forest. The kisses exchanged between the Harlot and the Giant are in fact a "perverse and sacrilegious parody" of the holy kiss celebrated in the Song of Songs and "of the kiss with which, through His sacrifice on the cross, Christ espouses the Church and redeems lost humanity."[40] The bride of the Song of Songs finds her antithesis in the Harlot, herself a reflection of the "great whore who is seated on many waters, with whom the kings of the earth have committed fornication . . . and on her forehead was written a name: a Mystery: 'Babylon the great, mother of whores and of earth's abominations'" (Apoc. 17.1–5). Dante follows the *Lectura super Apocalypsim* by Olivi, a Spiritual Franciscan, in equating (at least at one level) the Great Whore with the corrupt Church as a whole and, in particular, with the avaricious, simoniacal papacy (cf. *Inf.* 19.106–11).[41] Again, Beatrice's words "Know that the vessel [the Church] which the serpent broke was and is not" (*Purg.* 33.34–35) echo Apocalypse 17.8, while their import is reminiscent of such pronouncements as that made by a radical Beguine, who went so far as to claim "that the church is spiritually dead."[42]

Unlike Olivi, Dante does not make his Giant kill the Whore. Like Olivi—but unlike the more radical Ubertino da Casale—the poet of *Purgatorio* 20 accepted Boniface's legitimacy, much as he deplored his actions. Unlike both Franciscans, however, Dante placed his hopes in an emperor who should come and reform the whole Church by killing both the Whore and the Giant (*Purg.* 33.37–45), possibly that "Last World Emperor who is Christ's harbinger, sent to prepare the way for his second coming" (Davis 1984, 67). And, unlike the Spiritual Franciscans, Dante located the origins of papal corruption in the Donation of Constantine, with the appearance of "the first rich pope" (*Inf.* 19.115–17) and a cargo of temporal goods that has almost sunk the ship of the Church (*Purg.* 32.128–29).[43] Whereas the Spirituals believed that reformation would come from within the Church and especially their own order, Dante was convinced that the purity of primitive Christianity could be regained only "if the emperor were totally powerful and the clergy totally poor" (Davis 1984, 70).

Dante's orthodoxy

Any temptation to turn Dante into a proto-Protestant must be dismissed out of hand. Criticism of churchmen and Church leaders was a feature of medieval life and culture: the higher the regard for the office, the greater the condemnation of those who blatantly failed to live up to the ideals embodied in their office. Hence, we find that among the fifteen popes mentioned by Dante from Innocent III (1198–1216) to John XXII (1316–34) only one—John XXI (1276–77)—is "canonized" by the poet *(Par.* 12.134–35: *Pietro Spano)*. St. Bernard in the twelfth century and (an even more striking example) St. Catherine of Siena in the fourteenth century both admonished popes and chastised them for any perceived failure to nourish Christ's flock and guide his Church.[44] Although aware of the dangers inherent in his role as prophet upbraiding corrupt Church leaders, Dante "is Uzzah [2 Kings 6.2–8; *Purg.* 10.55–57; *Ep.* 11.5.9], but [he] does not attempt to straighten the itinerant and tipsy Church, but only to lash the lazy bishops who allow her to lumber astray" (Hollander 1998, 149). In *Inferno* 19.88, Dante shows his awareness of the dangers of overstepping the mark—highlighted by the word *folle* (used to indicate Ulysses' "mad flight" in *Inf.* 26.125, and again in *Par.* 27.82–83)—in his apostrophe to the damned simoniac popes: "I do not know whether now I was too rash [*folle*]." The poet's condemnation of heresy is evident in the sixth circle of his *Inferno,* while he praises St. Dominic for his zeal in combating heretics in *Paradiso* 12.97–102.[45] Indeed, in heaven, Dante's orthodoxy is guaranteed by a trinity of saints, when he passes *summa cum laude* his examinations in the theological virtues with the supreme authority in each: Faith (with St. Peter acting as examiner in *Par.* 24.52–147), Hope (St. James, *Par.* 25.40–99), and Love (St. John the Evangelist, *Par.* 26.7–69). Once more (but this time, it is the pilgrim's voice), present Church corruption is denounced when Dante tells St. Peter:

> ché tu intrasti povero e digiuno
> in campo, a seminar la buona pianta
> che fu già vite e ora è fatta pruno.
> (*Par.* 24.109–11)

---

for you were poor and hungry when you entered the field, in order to sow the good plant that was once a vine and is now a thornbush.

The Lord's vineyard is now overgrown with thorns (cf. *Par.* 12.86–87). Yet, despite the apparent pessimism of Dante's portrayal of the world in 1300 (especially prominent in the last section of the poem), Beatrice tells St. James that *no Christian on earth* possesses to a higher degree than Dante the virtue of Hope, which "is a sure expectation of future glory, the result of God's grace and preceding merit" (*Par.* 25.67–69). As previously noted, it is in fact the reason why Dante has been granted the extraordinary privilege of the beatific vision that will be granted him in the Heavenly Jerusalem:

> "La Chiesa militante alcun figliuolo
> non ha con piú speranza, com' è scritto
> nel Sol che raggia tutto nostro stuolo:

> però li è conceduto che d'Egitto
> vegna in Ierusalemme per vedere,
> anzi che 'l militar li sia prescritto."
>   (*Par.* 25.52–57)

———

"The Church Militant has no child with greater hope, as it is written in the Sun Who irradiates all our host: therefore, it is granted to him to come from Egypt to Jerusalem in order to see [the heavenly City], before the end of his preordained struggle [on earth]."

The pilgrim's indomitable hope is grounded in his unshakable faith (l. 75), while the greatest virtue—Love—has been instilled in him by God as a natural desire for the Supreme Good, nourished and augmented by philosophical proofs, Apocalypse, and God's creation (*Par.* 26.25ff.).[46]

Dante's political vision in the *Comedy* [47]

Again and again, in the *Comedy*, Dante denounces the political divisions and enmities endemic to the Italian peninsula, with a particularly trenchant attack on Italy, the "garden of the empire" but now a desert (*Purg.* 6.105), a "brothel" whose towns are "full of tyrants" and whose citizens are everywhere "at each other's throats *[l'un l'altro si rode]*" (ll. 76–87). Like so many others, Dante's Florentine "mentor," Brunetto Latini (d. 1294), longed for a truly united republican regime, with all the citizens pulling on the rope of peace and good works (*Il Tesoretto,* ll. 170–79: an idea later given visual reality at Siena, in Lorenzetti's fresco of Good Government), even as he echoed the biblical warning that a divided city is doomed *(che già non può scampare / terra rotta di parte)*.[48] Another of Dante's contemporaries, Dino Compagni (*Cronica* 1.2), decried the origins of "the accursed parties of the Guelfs and Ghibellines," and in his treatise *De bono communi* Remigio de' Girolami lamented the disorders of Italy and Florence, while in his *Speculum* he wrote, "There was never so much disjunction or clash of wills between Ghibellines and Guelfs or between peoples and nobles *[plebem et ingenuos]* as is now seen to exist between Whites and Blacks" (Davis 1984, 207). Henry VII did all he could to distance himself from both Guelfs and Ghibellines, proclaiming himself emperor and protector of all his subjects, and—at first—"he came down, moving from city to city, conferring peace as though he were an angel of God" (Compagni, *Cronica* 1.24: *mettendo pace come fusse uno agnolo di Dio*), until the reality of internal divisions and Guelf opposition overcame his good intentions.

Although brought up in a Guelf city-state, for which he fought and of which he became a prior, Dante likewise condemned both parties:[49]

> Faccian li Ghibellin, faccian lor arte
> sott' altro segno, ché mal segue quello
> sempre chi la giustizia e lui diparte;
>   e non l'abbatta esto Carlo novello
> coi Guelfi suoi, ma tema de li artigli
> ch'a piú alto leon trasser lo vello.
> (Par. 6.103–8)

—————

Let the Ghibellines, let them carry out their business under some other sign, for anyone who divorces this [the eagle] from justice betrays it; and let not this new Charles strike it down with his Guelfs, but let him fear the claws that flayed a greater lion.

The poet's indictment of both Guelfs *and* Ghibellines is placed in the mouth of Justinian, emperor from 527 to 565, whose name bespoke his divinely inspired task of creating the *Corpus iuris civilis,* the codex of Roman laws that formed the basis of government in most of continental Europe for well over a thousand years. To dispense justice to all is the emperor's God-given task, symbolized by the imperial eagle—identified as God's bird and the sign that "made the Romans revered throughout the world" (*Par.* 19.101–2)—which illuminates Jupiter, the Heaven of Justice. As we have seen, in both his *Monarchia* and *Comedy* Dante placed all his hopes in a reforming emperor who should be immune from greed and thus able to serve justice and chase the she-wolf of cupidity back to hell. Far from Ugo Foscolo's vision of Dante as the "exiled Ghibelline," the *Comedy* reveals the exiled poet as standing in towering isolation, truly "a party to yourself," as Cacciaguida "forecasts" in *Paradiso* 17.68–69. From this lofty vantage point, Dante condemned many of the features that characterized contemporary Italy—demographic, urban, and economic expansion, mercantile entrepreneurialism, internal divisions and factions—and Europe: the rise of the *regnum particulare* or nation state, ecclesiastical corruption and greed. In his *Comedy,* the "sacred" poem to which both heaven and earth have lent a hand (*Par.* 25.2), Dante sent a complex message to his world, a world that had gone terribly astray. In this task he was bolstered by the conviction that "the poetic imagination is the faculty empowered to resurrect and glue together the fragments of a broken world" (Mazzotta 1993, 14). In *Convivio* (1.10.12) poetry is judged to be inferior to prose as a medium for the transmission of knowledge, on account of the exigencies of rhyme and meter. In the *Comedy,* on the other hand, the poet rejoices in his ability to express in verse things that are difficult enough even to conceive or imagine: *forti cose a pensar mettere in versi (Purg.* 29.42). Dante's "reconversion" to poetry was perhaps due in part to new horizons opened up by a rereading of Vergil (Leo 1951); it was certainly inspired by the knowledge that poetry engages not only our rational faculty but every part of our complex being, and that it can cast light on all aspects of the human condition.[50]

The entire poem reveals the dynamic interplay of the opposing forces of good and evil in this world. Hell is clearly the realm of those who are eternally separated from God, "the good of the intellect" (*Inf.* 3.18), those who remain fixed for all eternity in their sin (*Inf.* 14.51). In the binary vision of the two cities that inspired humanity in the Middle Ages, hell is of course the Devil's City, utterly opposed in all things to heaven, God's City; but for Dante hell is also reflected in the Florence of 1300, eaten up by "pride, envy, and avarice" (*Inf.* 6.74, 15.68). *Purgatorio* shows Italy as rent by warring factions, and the whole of Europe as the prey of negligent rulers—or worse (*Purg.* 6–7). Christians have been led astray by the evil example of the one who should be their guide to heaven (*Purg.* 16.100–102). Lastly, one of the most remarkable features of Dante's *Paradiso* is the dialectic between the ideals glimpsed in heaven and the destructive reality found on earth, that "small patch of land that makes us so ferocious" (*Par.* 22.151). Yet, as we have seen, Dante's vision of the world in 1300 was tempered by an abundance of hope. Lucifer's bat (*Inf.* 34.46–50) cannot—*must not*—be allowed to overcome the divine eagle that gazes directly into the rays of God's Justice. Endowed with free will, humanity can return to a state of right order, peace, and unity, for "if the present world has gone astray, the cause lies in you, in you it must be sought" (*Purg.* 16.82–83). It is this belief in the possibility of a better order, in our ability to change the world about us, that sounds its challenge to readers of Dante's *Comedy.*

twelve

Latin epistles, *Questio de aqua et terra,* and eclogues

The Latin epistles

Dante's Latin epistles span virtually the entire period during which he was active as a writer. In *Vita Nova* 30.1, he tells us that he wrote a letter in Latin, beginning with a quotation from Jeremiah's Lamentations (1.1): *Quomodo sedet sola civitas.*[1] The letter mourning the effects of Beatrice's death (June 1290) was addressed to the leading citizens or rulers of Florence, *li principi de la terra.*[2] Dante does not give us the text of the letter, because in *Vita Nova* he wished to use only the vernacular (*VN* 30.2). In 1314 he was to have recourse to the same biblical text in his epistle addressed to the Italian cardinals about to elect a pope, again citing "How solitary dwells the city once so populous; the queen of all peoples is now virtually a widow" (*Ep.* 1.1)—but this time the city is Rome, abandoned by the transference of the papal see to Avignon. A letter was sent to a friend in Florence in 1315; and, in the last years of his exile and life, Dante probably wrote the now notorious *Epistle to Cangrande.* There is therefore evidence for some thirty years of epistolary activity. Although some precious elements are missing, the thirteen letters we have are valuable testimony to certain crucial moments and attitudes in the period Dante spent in exile from Florence.

Epistle 1

The first of Dante's epistles in modern editions is addressed to Cardinal Niccolò da Prato, who was appointed by Benedict XI "peace-maker in Tuscany, Romagna, the March of Treviso, and neighboring regions" at the end of January 1304, and who arrived in Florence on March 10. The letter is written by Dante on behalf of the White Guelfs exiled from Florence; in it, they welcome the cardinal's promise to restore peace to their city and declare that their only purpose in taking up arms in a civil war has always been—and always will be—to guarantee the peace and freedom of all Florentines (1.2.6: *quietem solam et libertatem populi Florentini*). The exiles declare their readiness to lay down their swords and submit to the cardinal's judgment. This is the only document in which Dante allies himself with his fellow exiles. On June 10 Cardinal Niccolò left Florence, placing the city under interdict. Less than a month later, Pope Benedict died, and with him disappeared the hope for a possible reconciliation between the exiles and the triumphant Black Guelfs. It was at this point that Dante seems to have decided to "make a party for himself," refusing to take part in what proved to be the Whites' final attempt to return to Florence by force (July 20, 1304). Eventually, he will make Cacciaguida "prophesy" the immense shame his great-great-grandson will be forced to endure in being associated with the exiles, evil and senseless *(Par.* 17.62: *la compagnia malvagia e scempia),* who will turn against him in their folly.

Epistle 2

The authenticity of *Epistle* 2 has been questioned, because of the praise it lavishes on Alessandro da Romena. In offering his condolences to Counts Oberto and Guido for their uncle's death (spring or early summer, 1304), the writer refers to Alessandro as his "lord" (2.1.1) and expresses the certainty that the dead man is now in glory as "a courtier in the eternal palace of the heavenly Jerusalem" (2.2.5), because his heroic actions on earth had been a scourge driving away all vice (2.1.2). All this is in utter contrast to the description of Alessandro's "wicked soul" in *Inferno* 30.77. However, this would not be the only instance of Dante's praising an individual in the first years of his exile whom he later condemned to nether hell.[3] The description of the writer as suffering an unjust exile (2.1.3: *exul inmeritus*) favors Dante's authorship, as this Ovidian phrase figures prominently in the titles of *Epistles* 3, 5, 6, and 7.

Epistle 3

This letter is addressed by the "Florentine unjustly exiled" to the "Pistoian in exile," Dante's friend Cino da Pistoia, the famous jurist and poet, who was exiled from 1301 to 1306. Probably written in 1305 or 1306, it answers the question posed in Cino's sonnet, *Dante, quando per caso s'abbandona:* whether the soul can pass "from passion to passion with the same intensity but directed toward different objects of the same species" (*Ep.* 3.1.2). To our amazement, we find that Beatrice's lover replies in the affirmative—and he even attaches a sonnet, *Io sono stato con Amore insieme* (CXI: 86), in which Dante denies that the human will is free to refuse a new beauty imposed by Love (for a discussion of Dante's *Io sono stato con Amore insieme,* see chapter 3, "Sonnets exchanged with Cino"). In the letter, the fact that love for one person can die and a similar love for another human being can take root in the soul is proved not only by experience but also by "reason and authority" (3.3.5). Reason takes the form of a syllogism that Cino is invited to work out for himself from the major and minor propositions. Dante next turns to the supreme authority on the subject of love and cites Apollo's amorous adventures as narrated in *Metamorphoses* 4 by Ovid, *Magister Amoris.*[4] The appeal to syllogistic reasoning and the recommendation to Cino to seek comfort against the vicissitudes of fortune by studying a sixth-century work, *Fortuitorum Remedia,* show that this letter is indeed written by the same pen that composed *Convivio* and *Monarchia.*

Epistle 4

Dante wrote his fourth epistle while staying in the Casentino, addressing it to Marquis Moroello Malaspina, the Guelf captain whose victories against the Whites (including the capture of Pistoia in 1306) are "prophesied" by Vanni Fucci in *Inferno* 24.145–50. In 1306–7/8 Dante was the guest of Moroello Malaspina (who had married the "good" Alagia, niece of Pope Adrian V: *Purg.* 19.142–45). The letter explains the reason for Dante's silence since moving away from Lunigiana: it had been caused by the sudden appearance (4.2.2: "like a flash of lightning from on high") of a woman's beauty that immediately enthralled him, despite his "praiseworthy resolve" that had until then kept him away "from women and from songs about them." Now, this imperious love has banished all other thoughts from his mind and made impossible "those assiduous meditations during which I pondered the things of both heaven and earth" (4.2.4). Love has once more enchained his free will: *liberum meum ligavit arbitrium. Epistle* 3, with its sonnet addressed to Cino (CXI: 86), and this letter, accompanied by the canzone *Amor, da che convien pur ch'io mi doglia* (CXVI: 89), clearly reinforce the hypothesis that Dante only began writing his *Comedy* around 1307/8, for in that work he recants his affirmation of Love's omnipotence by placing it in the mouth of the damned Francesca (*Inf.* 5.103), and then by utterly refuting it through a philosophical-theological discourse placed at the very center of the poem, which proclaims that human beings are essentially free to choose what is good and just.[5]

Epistle 5

We now make a leap forward of some four or five years to a time when Dante had already begun work on his *Comedy*. In November 1308 Henry, count of Luxembourg, was elected emperor. In June 1309 he promised the pope in Avignon that, as soon as he had been crowned "King of the Romans," he would set out on a crusade to liberate the Holy Land. After gaining Clement's official recognition, Henry announced his plans to be crowned in Rome and his intention of pacifying the warring factions in the Italian peninsula. His ambassadors had a mixed reception in the various states; they were acclaimed and welcomed in Pisa, but when they arrived in Florence with the request that the commune abandon its siege of Ghibelline Arezzo, Betto Brunelleschi expressed in a few words what was to become official Florentine policy: that "never had the Florentines lowered their horns for any lord" (Compagni, *Cronica* 3.35.24–26). It was clear that Henry needed unambiguous papal support—which he received with the encyclical *Exultet in gloria* of September 1, 1310, wherein all Italians were ordered to accept Henry as their rightful emperor. After Henry and his small army crossed the Alps and arrived at Susa (October 23), Dante penned his own circular "To all and singular Princes of Italy, and the Senators of the Sacred City, as also the Dukes, Marquises, Counts, and Peoples" of the peninsula.

The letter is an astonishing document. It is the result of surging enthusiasm for one who has come to release the Italians from slavery (who is therefore compared to Moses, who freed the Israelites from bondage and led them to the promised land: *Ep.* 5.1.4). Like the Israelites of old, Dante had waited many years to be allowed to return from exile. His enthusiasm overflows; biblical tropes abound. Henry is saluted with the messianic title "lion of the tribe of Judah" (*Ep.* 5.1.4; cf. Gen. 49.9–10; Apoc. 5.5). As the Good Shepherd, he will recognize and guard his entire flock (*Ep.* 5.5.17). The opening words set the tone of joyous expectation for the whole epistle by citing a Pauline text: "Behold now is the acceptable time" (2 Cor. 6.2). Dante calls upon all Italians to "lift up your hearts, for your salvation is near" (*Ep.* 5.5.15). In Luke's Gospel, a similar cry of exultation is preceded by a reference to Christ's Second Coming in "full power and majesty" (Luke 21.27–28). It is even possible to perceive an echo of the *Regina Coeli* (cf. *Par.* 23.127–29), with its triumphant call to rejoice at the Lord's resurrection, in the exhortation "Rejoice even now, woeful Italy!" (*Ep.* 5.2.5). The epistle ends on a note of exultation in the fact that Henry's mission has received the "light of the apostolic blessing" (5.10.30). In this letter, Dante still accepts the traditional interpretation of the two "great lights" (Gen. 1.16) that had been reiterated in Clement's *Divina sapientie* (addressed to Henry on July 26, 1309), according to which the greater light of the sun was understood as signifying papal authority, while the moon's lesser light indicated the temporal power. This symbolism was later to be supplanted by the potent image of the "two suns" in *Purgatorio* 16.106–8 and deconstructed on account of its hierarchical implications in *Monarchia* 3.4.12–20 (Scott 1995b). Already here, in *Epistle* 5.5.17, Dante asserts his cardinal belief in the independence of the two supreme powers, whose authority proceeds directly from God. He drives home the point by recalling Christ's decision to leave unto Caesar the things that are Caesar's "as if He were dividing two kingdoms" (5.9.27).

Two essential features emerge. For the first time, we have clear evidence of Dante's conception of the emperor's function in his role as the inheritor of Christ's kingship: most importantly, he envisages "the emperor's two natures, human and divine, or rather, in the language of that age, a ruler 'human by nature and divine by grace'" (Kantorowicz 1957, 65). The second point is that Dante now regards himself as invested with a prophetic mission.[6]

Epistle 6

Epistle 6, dated March 31, 1311, and addressed to "the most nefarious Florentines within the city" who had organized the opposition to Henry, opens with a declaration of God's entrustment of human affairs *(res humanas)* to the Holy Roman Empire. Proof of this is to be found in Scripture, but its truth is also attested by the fact that "when the imperial throne is vacant, the whole world goes astray, the helmsman and rowers of Peter's ship slumber, and unhappy Italy . . . is tossed by winds and waves that no words can describe" (6.1.3).[7] Like the builders of Babel, the Florentines "who transgress every law of God and man" are guilty of attempting to set up a Florentine—as opposed to a Roman—*civilitas* or polity (6.2.5–8). Dante's role as prophet denouncing corruption and predicting God's punishment on evildoers is most in evidence in the fourth paragraph, where he thunders against the wicked Florentines, foretelling the city's doom: "You will see your buildings . . . crash to the ground . . . You will see your populace united . . . crying out against you in their fury . . . your churches pillaged . . . and your children . . . destined to pay for their father's sins" (6.4.15–16). Here is a clear echo of the Old Testament prophets' warning that God's punishment shall be visited even unto the third and fourth generation (Exod. 20.5, 34.7; Jer. 32.18; Lam. 5.7)—an echo immediately followed by a reference to Dante's "prophetic soul" *(presaga mens mea),* instructed "by unmistakable omens as well as by irrefutable arguments" to foretell the doom-laden future to these barbaric slaves of greed. For good measure, Dante proclaims the emperor's Christological role, asserting that Henry shares "our pains of his own free will, as though to him—after Christ—the prophet Isaiah had pointed the finger of prophecy, when he foretold what God's Spirit revealed: 'Surely he hath himself borne our griefs, and carried our sorrows'" (*Ep.* 6.6.25; Isa. 53.4).

Epistle 7

Dante's native city refused to refer to Henry as "King of the Romans" or "Emperor"; instead, they used the alienating formula "King of the Germans" and rejected the imperial titles. On April 1, 1311, the Florentine commune declared that it and its Guelf allies would no longer allow Henry or his forces to enter the territories under their control. On April 17, as *exul inmeritus,* Dante addressed the emperor directly and on behalf of "Tuscans everywhere who desire peace." He describes Henry as "our sun" (7.2.7: *sol noster*)—a pointer to the "two suns" we shall find in *Purgatorio* 16.107, but also a clear indication of the emperor's messianic role as "God's minister, son of the Church and promoter of Rome's glory" (*Ep.* 7.2.8). The letter's second paragraph develops the Christological implications of Henry's office. John the Baptist is quoted twice: first, his question to Jesus, "Art thou he that should come or must we look for another?" (Matt. 11.3, Luke 7.19), then his pronouncement, "Behold the Lamb of God, behold him who taketh away the sins of the world" (John 1.29). These sacred words, Dante declares, sprang to his lips when he saw the emperor in person and his spirit rejoiced within (cf. the Magnificat, Luke 1.47). John the Baptist, Florence's patron, was judged by many to be the greatest of the prophets, the one "who preceded the true light" (*VN* 24.4). Indeed, by endowing Henry with a Christological mission, Dante himself becomes here a postfiguration of John. Yet, like the prophets of old who upbraided the kings of Israel for their sins, Dante does not hesitate to chide the emperor for his neglect of Tuscany, as if the imperial custodianship were limited to northern Italy. Instead, Henry must remember that the extent of his universal imperial rule is limited only "by the Ocean" (*Aen.* 1.287). The description of Henry's son as "a second Ascanius" (*Ep.* 7.5.18) implies moreover that the emperor must act like Aeneas, who was "chosen in the Empyrean heaven to be the father of glorious Rome and of her empire" (*Inf.* 2.20–21). So, too, rebellious Florence is likened to Amata, who committed suicide in despair over her daughter's marriage (willed by heaven) to Aeneas (*Aen.* 7.341–434, 12.593–607). Florence is also the "viper" of civil war, the multiheaded hydra, the Goliath that must be slain so that "the Philistines shall flee and Israel shall be liberated," while Henry, "new son of Jesse," is seen as the new David (*Ep.* 7.8.29), the most prominent *typus Christi* or forerunner of Christ. In the last section, Dante urges Henry to repeat David's deed so that "Israel"— Italy—may be free once more. The last biblical image is that of "the most holy Jerusalem," recalled by those Italians who are now mourning "as exiles in Babylon" (7.8.30). Dante's self-appointed task was clear to Villani, who recorded that Dante wrote this epistle to Henry during the siege of Brescia, "upbraiding him for his dilatoriness, virtually in the guise of a prophet" (10.136). No one has understood this aspect better than Bruno Nardi, who defined a prophet as one who passionately takes part in the sufferings, turmoil, and aspirations of his age, so that he is perforce led to "denounce and attack the wicked, and point to the goal set by God. His language is not the clever, circumspect speech used by politicians . . . the inner heat that consumes him brings to his lips fiery words of passion, commanding and threatening" (Nardi 1983, 295).

Epistles 8–10

These letters were addressed to Henry's wife, the empress Margaret (who died at Genoa on December 14, 1311), in the name of the countess of Battifolle. With their indirect Vergilian quotations, they appear to have been written by Dante when he was the guest of the countess's husband, Guido di Battifolle, who had recently declared his active support for the emperor. In all three epistles, the countess expresses her joy at the apparent success of Henry's imperial venture.

Epistle 11

Henry died of malarial fever on August 24, 1313. The following April saw the death of Pope Clement (the "lawless shepherd" of *Inf.* 19.83). Both the empire and the Church were now without leaders. Dante decided to write to the Italian cardinals participating in the conclave held at Carpentras. He laments the virtual destruction of the Church and the abandonment of Rome, "to which . . . Christ confirmed the empire of the world, that Rome which Peter and Paul, the apostle to the gentiles, consecrated as the apostolic see by the sprinkling of their blood" (*Ep.* 11.2.3). Dante does not hesitate to accuse the princes of the Church of leading her astray, by selling and bartering in the temple, espousing greed, and eclipsing the sun of Rome (cf. *Par.* 27.34–45). He bewails the fact that the writings of the Church Fathers are ignored while the decretals are studied only for "riches and benefices" (*Ep.* 11.7.16; *Par.* 9.133–35). He urges the Italian cardinals to take to heart his admonition that Rome (whose present condition would move "even Hannibal to pity") is still "the homeland of the illustrious Scipios"— a surprising reminder when addressed to churchmen, but one reiterated in *Paradiso* 27.61–62, where it is placed on the lips of St. Peter himself, the archetypal pope. And he exhorts them to unite in order to fight the good fight for "the Spouse of Christ, for the seat of the Spouse, which is Rome, for our Italy, and . . . for the entire community now in pilgrimage on earth" (*Ep.* 11.11.26).

The epistle's prophetic voice is heard at the outset in Dante's favorite quotation from Lamentations: "How solitary dwells the city once so populous; the queen of all peoples is now virtually a widow" (cf. *Purg.* 6.112–13:"Rome that weeps, a widow and alone"). Jeremiah's prophecy of the destruction of Jerusalem, brought about by the leaders of the Pharisees, is made to describe the contemporary scene, in which Christ's Bride, the Church, has been brought to such a pass that even the "Jews, Saracens, and Gentiles . . . cry out 'Where is their God?'" (*Ep.* 11.3.4; cf. Ps. 78.10). Though addressed to the Italian cardinals—in particular, to Napoleone Orsini, who had played a leading part in the disastrous election of Clement V at Perugia in 1305—the letter is a passionate attack on the entire Church leadership, which "has espoused avarice . . . ever the mother of impiety and iniquity" (11.7.14). Only Dante dares to proclaim what everyone is muttering. False prophets assert that everything is governed by necessity, whereas in truth the cause lies in the cardinals' misuse of their free will (11.3.4; cf. *Purg.* 16.67–83). Let no one think that Dante is guilty of Uzzah's sin (2 Kings 6.6–7; *Purg.* 10.55–57), for he does not concern himself with the Ark of the Church but "with the unruly oxen that are dragging it away into the wilderness" (*Ep.* 11.5.12). Indeed, like St. Paul, Dante declares himself to be one of the least of Christ's sheep: "By the grace, then, not of riches but of God, I am what I am, and the zeal of His house has devoured me" (11.5.9), adding the zeal of the Old Testament prophets (Ps. 68.10) to Paul's cry "by God's grace, I am what I am" (1 Cor. 15.9). The blind man has proclaimed the truth the Pharisees strove to conceal and pervert (John 9.1–41). Such are the precedents that justify Dante's missive. The result is of a truly biblical intensity, "without equal in any other writer of the Middle Ages" (Morghen 1983, 115).

Epistle 12

Henry was dead, and Dante's hopes for a reformation of the Church were dashed in 1316 with the election as Pope John XXII of the Frenchman Jacques Duèse of Cahors (*Par* 18.118–36; 27.58–60), who issued a bull (*Si fratrum,* April 1317) declaring that whenever the imperial throne was vacant, its jurisdiction devolved upon the pope. It also expressed astonishment that those (including Dante's patron, Cangrande della Scala) who had received vicariates from the late emperor had not sought ratification by the Holy See and threatened that if they did not resign forthwith they would be excommunicated. The previous year had seen the Florentine Guelfs slaughtered at the Battle of Montecatini (August 29, 1315). The Ghibelline victory led to the proclamation of a series of amnesties by Florence's Guelf rulers. On May 19, 1315, Dante and his sons were implicitly offered the possibility of return from exile. A fine would be levied, and all the exiles would have to suffer a humiliating public ceremony in the Florentine baptistery, Dante's "beautiful San Giovanni" (*Inf.* 19.17). In *Epistle* 12, the exile (now fifty years old) acknowledges receipt of a letter from a friend and expresses his gratitude for the attempt to make possible his return to Florence. However, he understands from other letters received that he will be allowed to go back only if he accepts certain humiliating conditions. Dante's proud spirit rebels: "Is this then the gracious recall of Dante Alighieri to his native city, after the sufferings of almost fifteen years of exile? Is this the reward of innocence which is obvious to all?" (*Ep.* 12.3.5). Such pusillanimity cannot be entertained by a man nurtured in philosophy. The thought of paying those who had wronged him is inconceivable for the man who preaches justice (12.3.6–7: *Absit a viro phylosophie domestico . . . Absit a viro predicante iustitiam . . .*). If some other way can be found that "does not lessen Dante's reputation and honor," he will accept the offer without delay. Otherwise, he "will never enter Florence . . . What! Can I not contemplate the most precious truths under any sky?" (12.4.8–9). Although there were further amnesties (at least three in 1316), Dante and his sons were never pardoned by the Florentine commune.

Epistle 13

This, by far the longest of the epistles—addressed to Cangrande della Scala, imperial vicar and lord of Verona—has caused endless controversy.[8] If the letter was written by Dante, the most likely date for its composition is during the years 1315–17 when Dante was Cangrande's guest at Verona (Petrocchi 1983, 190), although Padoan (1998, 115) would place it as late as 1320. The epistle falls into three broad sections. The first four paragraphs constitute a formal dedication to "the magnificent and victorious lord, Lord Cangrande della Scala, Vicar General of the most holy Caesar in Verona and Vicenza" by "his most devoted Dante Alighieri, a Florentine by birth but not by conduct." The writer then undertakes the role of commentator to the work offered (13.4.13). The second section, covering paragraphs five to sixteen, offers an introduction to the *Comedy* as a whole, dealing with six topics: the subject, its form, title, author, purpose, and the philosophical genre to which it belongs. From paragraph seventeen to the end (paragraph thirty-three), the epistle offers a literal commentary on *Paradiso,* dividing the third *cantica* into two parts, a prologue (*Par.* 1.1–36) and the rest.

The arguments against the epistle's authenticity cannot be lightly dismissed (see, e.g., Nardi [1960a]; Brugnoli's commentary in *Opere minori* [1979]; Dronke [1986, 103–11]; Barański [1991]).[9] Nevertheless, I agree with Étienne Gilson (1965, 220 n. 7) that what the letter has to say about Dante's poem is true to its author's ideas and purpose—so that, even if Dante did not write the epistle, "it is fortunate that another did so in his name." Furthermore, I am convinced by the argument formulated by Lino Pertile in 1991 which shows that the *Epistle to Cangrande* is the only text composed in the early fourteenth century that uses Dante's idiosyncratic terminology knowingly and correctly. In the letter's ninth and tenth paragraphs, we read that "the first division is the one by which the whole work is divided into three *cantiche [canticas]*. The second, the one by which each *cantica* is divided into *cantos [cantus]* . . . The book's title is: 'Here begins the *Comedy* of Dante Alighieri . . .'" (*Ep.* 13.9.26, 10.28; cf. 3.11: Comedie *sublimem* canticam *que decoratur titulo Paradisi* [my emphasis]). As Pertile remarks (1991b, 106), "Only Dante could decide the specific nomenclature relevant to the three parts of his poem and . . . he could only do so after finishing *Purgatorio* [cf. *Purg.* 33.140] . . . there is only one document that meets . . . all these requirements . . . [namely] the *accessus* to the *Comedy* in the Epistle to Cangrande."

What, then, does Dante tell us about his unique poem? Of paramount importance is the declaration (13.7.20) that it is "polysemous" in that, like Scripture, it contains various levels of meaning. The first sense is the literal, then come the three allegorical or "mystical" senses. Psalm 113 *In exitu Israel de Aegypto* (cf. *Purg.* 2.46–48) is chosen to illustrate these four senses or levels of meaning. The literal refers to the historical Exodus; the allegorical signifies "our redemption through Christ"; the moral (tropological) sense indicates "the soul's conversion from the sorrow and wretchedness of sin to a state of grace"; finally, the anagogical sense points to the sanctified soul's passage "from the bondage of this corruption to the freedom of eternal glory" (13.7.21). Much has been written about the phrase "literal or historical sense" in the same paragraph (13.7.22). Not a few scholars tend to emphasize the epithet "historical." They frequently muddy the waters by claiming that, when he came to compose his *Comedy,* Dante abandoned the "allegory of poets" (with its truth hidden beneath a beautiful lie: *Conv.* 2.1.3) in order to use the "allegory of theologians." This term ("allegory of theologians") does not in fact appear in Dante's writings. Instead, as we have seen in chapter 4, in *Convivio* 2.1.4, Dante tells his readers that *in his exposition* of his canzoni he will proceed according to the way allegory was understood by poets—whereas theologians used a different method in interpreting the Bible. Every theologian knew, however, that certain passages in Holy Scripture (such as the Song of Songs) were not be interpreted "literally" (Scott 2000b, 300).

The literal subject is declared to be "the state of souls after death without qualification, since on and about that the whole work is based," while its allegory is concerned with the way human beings use their free will and thus deserve reward or punishment (13.8.24–25). The form of the work is threefold (13.9.26), and, as Pertile notes, we find the term *canticas* employed to indicate the three *cantiche,* each subdivided into cantos *(cantus).* The manner of treatment *(Forma sive modus tractandi)* is "poetic, fictive, descriptive, digressive, and figurative" (*trasumptivus:* 13.9.27). The title of the work proclaims that it is "the Comedy of Dante Alighieri" (13.10.28). To understand what is meant by this title it is necessary to know that "comedy is a kind of poetic narration differing from all others" (13.10.29). In particular, comedy differs from tragedy, for tragedy begins in a wonderful and tranquil manner but its end is "foul and terrible." Comedy, instead, begins with a harsh situation, but it has a happy ending.[10] Moreover, tragedy employs "exalted and sublime" language, while comedy is characterized by the "lowly and humble" style *(remisse et humiliter).* Dante's *Comedy* begins with a tragic situation, but it has a happy ending in paradise. Its style is appropriately "lowly and humble, since it is cast in the vulgar tongue, in which even simple women *[muliercule]* communicate" (cf. *Ecl.* 2.52–54). The subject is said again to be "the state of souls after death," and its allegorical meaning to signify reward and punishment in the next world (13.11.33–34). To those (e.g., Nardi 1944, 60) who would object that the subject of the poem is Dante's journey through the other world at Eastertide 1300, Hollander points out (1969, 46 n. 34) that "the . . . subject of the poem includes what Dante does and what Dante sees," and again (ibid., 134), ". . . the state of the souls after death involves what he sees."

The purpose of the *Comedy* is "to remove those living in this life from a state of wretchedness." The poem therefore comes under the purview of ethics, the branch of philosophy concerned with morals, "because the whole and each part were conceived *not* for speculation but for action. For if in certain places or passages the subject is treated in a speculative manner, it is not for the sake of speculation, but for a practical purpose" (13.15.40–41). As Hollander notes (1993a, 91), "the meaning . . . is not, as Barański [1991] and others believe, to remove speculation as an end of the poem, but, in good Christian fashion, to use speculation as the basis for action" (cf. *Mon.* 1.4.1).

The *accessus* to the poem is now complete. The rest of the epistle offers a commentary on the first eighteen verses of *Paradiso,* in which we find clear evidence of the Neoplatonic element in Dante's thought—beginning with the references to the *Liber de causis* in 13.20.57 and 13.21.61 and Pseudo-Dionysius in 13.21.60. The latter's *The Celestial Hierarchy* is cited as proof of the basic conception that "the lower intelligences receive the rays of the higher intelligence that irradiates them and they reflect in the manner of mirrors these rays to the intelligence that is beneath them . . . Reason therefore demonstrates that the divine light . . . shines in every part" (13.21.60–61).

In the final section (13.32.88–90) the writer expresses the hope that Cangrande's liberality will make it possible for him to complete his exposition of "the Prologue" to his *Paradiso* and also deal with other matters "profitable to the common good." To round off his argument, he writes that the description of ascending from heaven to heaven will demonstrate that "true happiness consists in the knowledge of Him who is the beginning of truth" (13.33.89).

Questio de aqua et terra

Delivered as a formal lecture at Verona on January 20, 1320, Dante's *Questio de aqua et terra* is a final testimony to the passionate interest in philosophy nurtured by its author, who in its concluding paragraph describes himself as "the least among true philosophers" (24.87).[11] In the *Questio* Dante tackles the question raised by the fact that, according to Aristotelian physics and cosmology—which placed the earth at the center of the universe, in a sublunar world made up of four concentric circles (in ascending order: earth, water, air, and fire)—the sphere of water should cover the entire sphere of earth. The problem arose with the emergence of Aristotelian science in the first half of the thirteenth century, which appeared to contradict both human experience (the fact that the Eurasian landmass is higher than the seas and ocean) and the account of Creation found in Genesis—in particular, Genesis 1.9: "And God said: 'Let the waters, which are under the heavens, be gathered in one place, so that dry land may appear.'[12] And this was done." Albert the Great, Giles of Rome, and others had examined the problem (Mazzoni 1979, 704–10). One of Dante's contemporaries, Antonio Pelacani, who taught at Bologna and Verona (both cities where the exiled poet-philosopher had spent some time), not only maintained the quasi-heretical idea that the earth contained all lakes, rivers, and seas within its "valleys" (which he compared to the indentations on some fruit), but he also postulated the existence of other tracts of dry land in the Southern Hemisphere. Such an idea, then seen as contradicting the evidence of Genesis, was clearly anathema to the author of *Inferno* 26 who had condemned Ulysses' "mad flight" into "the world without people" (*Inf.* 26.125 and 117).

In this most Scholastic of Dante's writings, the author proceeds to examine the explanations to be demolished by rational argument and appeal to authority. The answer must be sought in nature's purpose: there must be an intermingling of water and earth on the globe in order to maximize its potential for supporting human life. Only thus, could the creation of terrestrial vegetation and living creatures ensue, with all things necessary for the sustenance and happiness of God's masterpiece, humankind. Some part of the earth had to rise above the waters, in order that "all the things [in the universe] capable of being mixed, namely, elements, might come into contact" (18.47). Nevertheless, "the concentricity of earth and water is preserved . . . provided we philosophize rightly" (19.50). The fact that the land in the Northern Hemisphere is a hump in the shape of a half-moon shows that it emerged in accordance with its regular or central circumference.

The Primary Cause is always God the Creator, but which instrument did he use to bring about this "hump"? The efficient cause is identified as the eighth heaven of the fixed stars, which has "unity of substance" and a multiplicity of virtue or powerful influences on the world below (21.70–71). Since "the land exposed stretches from the equinoctial line to the line which the pole of the zodiac describes round the pole of the universe . . . it is evident that the lifting power is in those stars that are in the region of heaven contained between those two circles" (21.73). If, however, someone wishes to know why the elevation occurred in the Northern Hemisphere rather than in the other, the answer must be curt, for as Aristotle writes (*De coelo* 2.5), "Such questions arise from great folly or great presumption, because *they are beyond our intellect.* That is why we must reply to this question that . . . God . . . made these things for the best" (21.75–76; my emphasis). An impassioned appeal follows for human beings to accept the limitations imposed on the human intellect (cf. *Conv.* 3.8.2):

> Let men desist, therefore, let them desist from searching out things that are above them . . . leaving aside whatsoever is too great for them . . . Let them listen to the friend of Job . . . Let them listen to the Psalmist . . . let them listen to Isaiah when he says, "As far as the heavens are above the earth, so far are my ways above your ways" . . . And let this suffice for the inquiry into the truth we have undertaken to examine. (22.77)

The penultimate section (23.79–86) lists Dante's answers to five major objections. In the concluding paragraph, we are told that this scientific lecture was given by Dante Alighieri in the illustrious city of Verona, in the Church of Sant'Elena, in the presence of the assembled clergy. Dante writes sarcastically that some did not attend: either because of an "excess of charity" or as a result of excessive humility that made them unwilling to appear to accept the excellence of others (*aliorum excellentiam*: 24.87). The date is recorded as Sunday, January 20, 1320.[13]

This scientific explanation is at variance with the theological solution put forward by "pagan" Virgil in *Inferno* 34.121–26, when he refers to Lucifer's rebellion and expulsion from heaven: "It was on this side [at the antipodes to Jerusalem, in the Southern Hemisphere] that he fell from Heaven; and the dry land that used to stand, above, through fear of him immersed itself under a veil of water, and came up into our hemisphere." The fact that Dante gives two widely divergent explanations at an interval of some ten years or so should hardly surprise us, since we have seen him change his views on many other matters (e.g., the themes permitted to vernacular poets; the angelic orders and their governance of the spheres; the fate of Guido da Montefeltro). However, the divergence is such that it provides ammunition for those who (like Nardi 1959) would deny the *Questio*'s authenticity. For those of us who accept it as one of Dante's last attempts to prove his philosophical expertise and scientific knowledge, the fact that the *Questio* ignores the theological account given at the end of *Inferno* is characteristic of the author's *mentalité*. Philosophy and theology must remain autonomous. What the poet-theologian had written in *Inferno* 34 could only be confirmed by divine revelation: its inclusion in a scientific treatise would have contravened Dante's belief that rational inquiry must proceed according to criteria and methodology that are necessarily different from those used by theologians dealing with matters of doctrine and religious belief; hence, Siger of Brabant is placed in Dante's heaven of the wise (*Par.* 10.133–38). There can be no contradiction between dogma and the teachings of philosophy: both Lucifer's fall and the landmass in the Northern Hemisphere are constants. Philosophical investigation shows that the fixed stars are the instrument through which God made the landmass emerge above the waters. Revelation places this in the overall context of Lucifer's expulsion from heaven and the "poetic" or "mythical" description of the earth's reaction to this.[14] Although we still await the definitive critical edition of the text, the *Questio de aqua et terra* was well defined many years ago as a work that is "thoroughly Dantesque in the whole texture of its style, language and forms of thought" (Moore 1899, 355).

The eclogues

Probably in 1319, while in Ravenna, Dante received an epistle in Latin hexameters by Giovanni del Virgilio, a professor at Bologna, in which Giovanni reproached him for casting pearls before swine by writing in the vernacular on such grave themes as the "regions of the threefold destiny" to which human beings are assigned according to their deserts (*Ecl.* 1.3–4). Why does Dante write nothing for scholars who are "pale" from long years of study, when his themes are "croaked forth" without understanding by buffoons on street corners (1.12–13)? He supposes that Dante may well reply that he is not writing for them but rather for those who have dedicated their lives to study (cf. *Par.* 2.1–15). But what he writes is couched in popular verse (15: *carmine laico*)! Scholars scorn vernacular tongues, of which there are a thousand idioms.[15] No classical poet "in whose band you are the sixth" (a clear reference to *Inf.* 4.102) ever wrote in the speech of the marketplace. Let Dante therefore turn his hand to writing poems in Latin on lofty contemporary themes, such as Henry VII's (26: *Iovis armiger*) ascent to the stars or the Guelfs slaughtered by Uguccione della Faggiola at Montecatini (1315), Cangrande's victories against the Paduans, or Robert of Anjou besieged in Genoa (from July 1318 to February 1319). Especially after Albertino Mussato's coronation as poet and historian in Padua (1315), any of these subjects treated in an elevated Latin would secure the poetic crown for Dante; moreover, if Dante's fame is dear to him, he cannot be satisfied to earn the admiration of the common people. And, if the exiled *poeta* does not write on lofty themes, they will surely remain unsung (45–46).

Dante's *First Eclogue*[16]

Giovanni del Virgilio's style recalls that of the pastoral eclogue. And it was his beloved Vergil's *Eclogues (Bucolica)* that provided Dante with a model for what is the first eclogue written since antiquity. Dante seizes another opportunity to display his originality by replying to Giovanni's epistle with a pastoral eclogue in sixty-eight hexameters. Vergil's *First Eclogue* contrasts the good fortune of Tityrus with the enforced exile of Meliboeus. Assuming the name of Tityrus (as Vergil had done), Dante converses with his friend Meliboeus (probably the Florentine Dino Perini, a fellow exile in Ravenna). On receiving the letter from Mopsus (Giovanni del Virgilio), Tityrus-Dante tells Meliboeus that Mopsus has invited him to receive the laurel wreath (*Ecl.* 2.33) but that he will wait until his *Paradiso* (and the whole poem) is complete; only then will he joyfully gird his brows with oak and laurel leaves (ll. 48–50; cf. *Par.* 1.22–33, 25.1–9). Tityrus then turns to the criticism of his use of the vernacular in his epic, for Meliboeus too "disapproves of the comic style *[comica . . . verba],* both because it sounds trite on women's lips and because the Castalian sisters [the Muses] scorn to accept it" (ll. 52–54). To counter this accusation, Tityrus decides to send ten pails of milk from his best-loved ewe *(ovis gratissima):* not ten eclogues, as Vergil had composed, but ten cantos of his *Paradiso.*

Del Virgilio's reply and Dante's *Second Eclogue*

In reply, Giovanni del Virgilio composes a poem of ninety-seven hexameters modeled on Vergil's *Second Eclogue.* He praises Dante (at fifty-five, *divine senex!*) as a second Vergil (*Ecl.* 3.33–34). He renews the invitation to come to Bologna, where they shall sing together: Giovanni with a light reed, Dante "gravely displaying greater mastery" (ll. 49–50). Dante is assured of a splendid welcome, where "no pleasure shall be lacking" (l. 66: *Nulla est cessura voluptas*). The eclogue ends with the warning that if Dante refuses to accept his invitation, Giovanni will slake his thirst in the waters of the Musone (a stream in Padua, thus indicating that Giovanni, the Latin scholar, will then pay court to that other prehumanist, Albertino Mussato—to whom he was in fact to send a true eclogue, with the essential dialogic structure, in 1327).[17]

A note (perhaps by Boccaccio) states that Dante's answer was penned one year after the arrival of Giovanni del Virgilio's eclogue, and that it was forwarded by one of Dante's sons just after the poet's death in September 1321. Dante is careful to reply with the same number of verses (ninety-seven), as was the custom in the *tenzone;* however, the architect of the *Comedy's* hundred cantos points out that if Giovanni had simply added another three hexameters he would have charmed his audience with the perfect number, "one hundred verses" *(Ecl.* 4.42–43: *centum carminibus).* Tityrus-Dante states that he would be happy to venture to rocky Etna (Bologna) to see Mopsus (Giovanni), but he cannot for fear of Polyphemus. A friend, Alphesiboeus (cf. Vergil's *Eighth Eclogue;* here, the doctor, Fiduccio de' Milotti), describes Polyphemus in all his cruelty, his jaws dripping with human gore (l. 77); he pleads with Tityrus not to venture to Bologna. Polyphemus may well signify Fulcieri da Calboli, who was elected *capitano del popolo* in Bologna late in 1320 or early in 1321, and whose bestial cruelty had already been denounced in *Purgatorio* 14.58–66. Another strong candidate is Ranieri di Zaccaria, Robert of Anjou's representative in the Guelf stronghold of Bologna in 1318–19, who had sentenced Dante and his sons to death in 1315. All in all, as John Took (2000, 335) observes, this second Latin eclogue by Dante, is composed "in an altogether novel register—the poem presents itself as an opportunity for technical self-assertion, for an outdoing of his correspondents in point of poetic procedure."

As well as providing further evidence of his innovative powers, Dante's eclogues constitute a final homage to Vergil, the poet he loved most and esteemed as the greatest he knew. His *First Eclogue* also pays a last tribute to his faith in the power of his Italian vernacular, which has made possible the existence of his *ovis gratissima* or beloved ewe, his sacred poem, now universally known as the *Divine Comedy.* It seems especially fitting that his correspondent Giovanni del Virgilio should have written his epitaph beginning with the lines "Dante, the theologian, expert in every branch of knowledge that philosophy cherishes in her illustrious bosom" *(Theologus Dantes, nullius dogmatis expers / quod foveat claro philosophia sinu).*

Glossary

a maiore   When a verse begins with a longer hemistich, it is termed *a maiore.*

Inf. 1.1	*Nel mezzo del cammin*	6 syllables
	di nostra vita	5 syllables

a minore   When a verse begins with a shorter hemistich, it is termed *a minore.*

Inf. 1.2	*mi ritrovai*	4 syllables
	per una selva oscura	7 syllables

Averroist   Also termed "radical Aristotelian." In their determination to remain faithful to the writings of Aristotle, Averroists tended to deny the immortality of the individual soul and asserted that the world is eternal.

ballata   The *ballata* consists of two *mutationes* (cf. the *pedes* of a canzone) and a *volta* or *sirma.* It opens with a *ripresa* (or *ritornello*) stating the poem's theme. The *ripresa* of the *ballata mezzana* has three verses, whereas the *ballata grande* has four.

canzone (sing.), canzoni (pl.)   Originating in the Provençal *cansó,* the Italian canzone first appeared at the court of Frederick II (Palermo, Sicily), but without a *tornada* or final *envoi.* For Dante's canzoni, see chapter 3 *(Rime).*

coblas capfinidas   Stanzas *(coblas)* in Provençal poetry that were linked through the repetition in the first line of a word or concept carried over from the last line of the preceding stanza.

cursus

> *cursus planus*   Found when a clause ends with a paroxytone word, followed by a trisyllabic paroxytone.
>
> | *DVE* 2.6.4 | *Marchiónis Esténsis* |
> |---|---|
>
> *cursus velox*   Found when a clause ends with a word with proparoxytone stress, followed by a four-syllable word with paroxytone stress.
>
> | *DVE* 2.6.4 | *magnificéntia preparáta* |
> |---|---|
>
> *cursus tardus*   Found when a clause ends with a proparoxytone tetrasyllable, preceded by a paroxytone.
>
> | *DVE* 2.6.4 | *túo, Floréntia* |
> |---|---|

The *cursus velox* was judged to be the most elegant.

frons   The first section of the stanza of a canzone, which may be divided into *pedes* (q.v.).

gematria   The interpretation of a name or text by computing the numerical value of words, based on their constituent letters (e.g., A = 1, B = 2, etc.).

pes **(sing.),** *pedes* **(pl.)**   Subdivision(s) of the first section of the stanza of a canzone (*frons).*

rimalmezzo   A rhyme found within the body of the line of verse, echoing the rhyme at the end of the preceding line. For example, ll. 2–3 of Dante's *Poscia ch'Amor del tutto m'ha lasciato:*
> *non per mio* grato,
> *ché* stato *non avea tanto gioioso*

Rimalmezzo is an outstanding feature of Guido Cavalcanti's canzone *Donna me prega, perch'eo voglio dire.*

rimas caras   Difficult, unusual rhymes, a characteristic feature of Provençal hermetic poetry or *trobar clus.*

rime composte   These are made up of two or three words.
> *Inf.* 30.87   *non ci ha − oncia − sconcia*

Non ci ha is pronounced *nòncia.* In medieval manuscripts *non ci ha* appears as *nonciha.*

rime derivative   Occur when the rhyming words have the same stem.
> *Inf.* 11.92−96   *solvi − rivolvi − solvi*

rime equivoche   Rhymes created by homographs.
> *Purg.* 26.65−67   *cerchi*   −   *cerchi*
>   circles (noun) − you search (verb)

rime identiche   A word is made to rhyme with itself.
> *Par.* 12.71−75   *Cristo − Cristo − Cristo*

rime piane   Rhyme-words accented on the penultimate syllable ("feminine" rhyme). This is the standard form in Italian.

rime ricche   The initial consonants of the stressed syllables are identical.
> *Inf.* 1.39−41   *cagione − stagione*

rime sdrucciole   These are accented on the antepenultimate syllable.
  Inf. 15.1–3   *màrgini – àrgini*

rime tronche   These are accented on the final syllable ("masculine" rhymes).
  Inf. 20.73–78   *può – co – Po*

settenario (**sing.**), *settenari* (**pl.**)   Italian verse with seven syllables.

sirma   The second section of the stanza of a canzone, which may be divided into *versus* (q.v.).

sonetto   A fourteen-line poem invented by a Sicilian poet. The sonnet uses only hendecasyllables. Traditionally, in Italian metrics, the *sonetto* is divided into two major sections (octave and sestet), often subdivided into two quatrains and two tercets. *Sonetto doppio* (double sonnet) is a misnomer, for it consists of twenty (or more) lines, with the insertion of *settenari*. See, e.g., *VN* 7.3–6.

tenor   The tenor of a simile or metaphor is the subject of the comparison. In Robert Burns's simile "O my love's like a red, red rose," the tenor is *My love,* as it is in the metaphor "My love is a red rose."

vehicle   The vehicle of a simile or metaphor consists of the "image" or whatever is comparable to the "tenor." In Robert Burns's simile "O my love's like a red, red rose," the vehicle is *a red rose,* as it is in the metaphor, "My love is a red rose."

versus   A term peculiar to Dante, which he uses in *DVE* to indicate the subdivisions of the *sirma* or second half of the stanza of a canzone.

Notes

one. Dante's *New Life: Vita Nova*

1. This work has traditionally been referred to as Dante's *Vita Nuova*. However, I accept Gorni's emendation to the Latin *Vita Nova,* as in *VN* 1.1 (Gorni 1996). For practical reasons, it is unfortunately impossible to quote Gorni's revised numbering of chapter and verse; however, Gorni's edition gives the standard references in the notes. My citations will follow the division of the text set up by Barbi in his critical edition (Barbi 1932).

2. Dante's title echoes Psalm 39.4: "He placed a new song in my mouth, a song to our God."

3. "Writing orders the past and thus keeps the sources of memory alive; it is a liturgy that sustains love, a cult of memory that constitutes and renews the writer's pained consciousness" (Braunstein 1988, 544).

4. For the connotations surrounding the Book of Memory, see Branca 1988, 123–24; Brugnoli 1997.

5. *VN* 31.8–17, l. 15, "Beatrice has gone to high heaven" *(Ita n'è Beatrice in l'alto cielo),* and l. 55, "I call Beatrice, and say: 'Are you now dead?'" *(chiamo Beatrice, e dico: 'Or se' tu morta?').* See also, less directly, *VN* 40.9–12, when (l. 12) pilgrims are told by the poet that Florence has lost her *beatrice (Ell'ha perduta la sua beatrice).*

6. See Picone 1983 and 1987; Botterill 1994b.

7. I follow Hollander (1974; 2001, 30), who points out that the perfect number ten is reached with Dante's final vision of Beatrice in glory (*VN* 42).

8. Whether or not Dante was influenced in this association of ideas by the assonance between *donna* (lady) and *dona* (gives, from *donare*), we find this association in a Provençal poem by William IX (1071–1127): *Si·m vol mi dons s'amor donar* (9.37), where the association between *dons (dominu, domina)* and *donar* illustrates the fact that the lady is a "giver."

9. The censors replaced the eleven occurrences of *beatitudine* in *Vita Nova* by *felicità* (happiness), at *VN* 3.2, 5.1, 9.2, 18.4, 18.6, 18.8; by *quiete* (peace, quietude), at *VN* 10.2, 11.4; by *chiarezza* (clarity) at *VN* 11.3; by *allegrezza* (joy, happiness) at *VN* 12.1; and by *fermezza* (resolve) at *VN* 18.4. For these and other changes imposed by the inquisitor general, Francesco da Pisa, see Russo 1994.

10. "We can thus date at least the idealized beginning of Dante's career as poet of Beatrice with great precision: ten o'clock of an evening in late May 1283" (Hollander 2001, 20). Baldelli (1973, 934) illustrates the conventional nature of the sonnet's rhyme structure, with its gerunds *(tenendo – dormendo – piangendo)* and quatrains based on a typical rhyme sequence: *Amore – core – ore – orrore* ("una delle costanti di tutta la rimeria stilnovistica e prestilnovistica").

11. Both poems can be found in Foster and Boyde 1967, 1:1, 14, 16.

12. Levers (2002, 12) suggests that "the narrative voice [in *Vita Nova*] is really a multiplicity of voices, . . . Dante, as a narrator, is divided into a group of narrative characters, each character having a different function." For a radically different interpretation of the phrase *lo verace giudicio del detto sogno . . . ora è manifestissimo a li più semplici* (*VN* 3.15), see Stone (1994, 146), who argues that its author implies "that *if* you say that *lo verace giudicio* is singular, obvious and clear, *then* you belong to the vulgar herd, you are one of the masses, one of *li più semplici*" (cf. Harrison [1988, 20], who refers to the dream's "hermeneutic provocation"). Indeed, Stone asserts (151) that "for Dante, who is not a simpleton, there is no such thing as *lo verace giudicio* ('*the* true meaning') but only *diverse sentenzie* ('various meanings')."

13. For the Book of Lamentations (*Threni,* in Latin) "as a model and intertext that illuminates the *Vita Nova* in depth, breadth, and detail commensurate with Dante's reliance on the Biblical book throughout his career," see Martinez 1998.

14. For the critical edition of this epistle (formerly attributed to Richard of St. Victor), see Gervais Dumeige, ed., *Épître à Séverin sur la charité [par] Ives: Les quatre degrés de la violente charité [par] Richard de Saint-Victor* (Paris: Vrin, 1955). For the vexed question of the *stilnovisti* and the *dolce stil novo,* see Barański 2000a; Calenda 1998; and Hollander 1992a.

15. For an extended analysis, see Durling and Martinez 1990, 53–70.

16. Cf. Moleta 1994, esp. 95: "the line *'voi le vedete Amor pinto nel viso'* can be read as a secular prefiguration of the beatific vision."

17. For Cicero's *De Amicitia* and the Christian tradition, see De Robertis 1961, 93 ff.

18. Ardizzone (2002, 42) highlights Dante's polemic with Cavalcanti and the younger poet's rejection of Guido's conception of love, based on Aristotle: "Here Dante seeks to erase a notion crucial to Aristotle's physics as applied to love: that of potentiality and act. . . . Dante's major concern in these poems is to eliminate every connection between love and necessity."

19. "It was in all likelihood the public conviviality of this period, when the Florentine elite felt compelled to celebrate civic harmony and its own wealth and social standing with displays of courtly sociability, that provided the opportunity for Dante to make intimate contact with an otherwise closely chaperoned girl" (Green 1994, 116).

20. The death of Dante's mother when he was a small child, his father's remarriage and probable activity as a moneylender: these elements may help to explain the poet's lifelong silence regarding his father, as well as his adoption of Virgil as his surrogate father and guide in the *Comedy* (cf. De Rosa 1990).

21. See Singleton 1958, 112–14; Branca 1988, 158 ("a 'speculum Christi,' as every man must be and as, in effect, every saint is"); Mazzoni 1997a.

22. Cf. Singleton 1958, 114: "The unique achievement of the *Vita Nova* as a theory of love is the seeing how love of woman may be kept all the way up to God."

23. See Barolini 1984, 94–135.

24. A useful distinction can be made between Vergil (the historical Roman poet, Publius Vergilius Maro) and Virgil (Dante's guide in *Inferno* and *Purgatorio*). The form

Virgil is "the medieval misspelling of his name, Virgilius the virginal" (Highet 1957, 74)—based on the legend about the poet's virginity—and is also associated with his powers as a magician "because *virga* means wand" (Highet 1957, 584 n. 13).

25. Cf. Gianfranco Contini's masterly study of this sonnet (reprinted in Contini 1976, 21–31), in which he points out that the meaning of no fewer than three of the six words in the first line *(gentile, onesta, pare)* has changed radically in current usage. *Gentile* = "noble"; *onesta* = "stately decorum"; and *pare* does not mean "seems" but rather "appears," with epiphanic connotations (25–26).

26. See the edition of *Vita Nova* by Domenico De Robertis 1984, 182, n.: "corretto da Dante su 'credo che' della tradizione ante *Vita Nuova* del sonetto, con eliminazione di ogni ipotesi di partecipazione e appropriazione personale." This early version of *Tanto gentile* is now published in De Robertis 2002, 398.

27. Bruno Sandkühler (1967) clearly established a parallel between the divisions found in *Vita Nova* and the methodology of Scholastic commentaries on scriptural and theological texts. Boccaccio "emarginated" them (literally, by confining them to the margins of the two copies he made of *Vita Nova* [Gorni 1996, xxviii]). Michele Barbi (1932, xvi–xvii, n. 1) quotes Boccaccio's reasons for removing them from the body of Dante's text, including the fact that various "trustworthy persons" had told him that, in his old age, Dante came to regret having written such a "childish" work for a number of reasons—including the fact that he had placed the "divisions" in the text of *Vita Nova.*

28. Afribo 2002, 23–24: "*forte* . . . è una parola ossessiva proprio in Cavalcanti, e iconica in generale di un amore dalla cui forza 'spesso segue morte' . . . Dante dunque cita il suo primo amico per citarlo in giudizio, per condannarlo con le sue stesse parole . . . con le sue stesse rime."

29. "The quotation of Threni 1.1 as the incipit to chapter 28 is the sole instance of such a Biblical incipit in *Vita Nova,* and one of the few incipits cited in the whole book. . . . [T]he voice of Threni disrupts all three modes of Dante's text: the prose, as the narrator excuses himself from discussing Beatrice's death . . . the poetry, as the canzone is left a fragment . . . and the divisions, not only shifted in place but on this occasion only omitted entirely for the fragmentary canzone" (Martinez 1998, 16–17). Gorni, in his edition of *Vita Nova* (Gorni 1996), highlights this, the only Latin sentence to open a chapter of Dante's *libello,* as the dividing line between the two major sections: the first comprises poems written during Beatrice's lifetime; the second, poems composed after her death.

30. As we shall have occasion to repeat, the fascination with numbers and number symbolism was encouraged by the biblical verse "You have set out everything in measure, number and weight" (Wisd. 11.21). As Curtius (1953, 504, n. 10) comments: "Every reader of medieval Latin texts knows that few Bible verses are so often quoted and alluded to. . . . Through this verse, number was sanctified as a form-bestowing factor in the divine work of creation. . . . This is the imposing background of numerical composition in literature."

31. Gorni 1990, 39. According to *gematria* (a cabbalistic method of interpreting texts by computing the numerical value of words), the value of both AMOR and BEATRIX

in the Latin alphabet may be calculated as 44 (AMOR) and 44 + IX; BEATR + IX = the sum of "Love" and "Miracle" (Gorni 1990, 41).

32. The divisions within *Vita Nova* also display possible number symbolism. Provided we accept Barbi's chapter numbering, we have a text with thirty-one poems and forty-two prose units, for a total of seventy-three portions: 73 = 7 + 3 = 10 = 1 + 0 = 1. In this pattern, the total number of poems plus prose units resolves itself into the number of creation (7) plus the number of the Trinity, which in turn equals the number of perfection (10); the perfect number 10 resolves itself into the primal number 1, a symbol of unity. With regard to the number of prose units, Hollander (2001, 31) finds that "the number forty-two is particularly significant in Christian exegesis … it is the number of the Exodus."

If we turn to Guglielmo Gorni's edition of *Vita Nova* (Gorni 1996), the division between the poems written before and after Beatrice's death produces the following results: the first section *(in vita)* contains 434 lines of verse, the second 242 lines, for a total of 676 verses. Numerical symmetry in each section is evident in the correspondence between the first and last number of each of the three sets of verses (4, 2, 6). The numbers of each set may be broken down as follows (see Gorni 1990, 102): 434 = 2 × 7 × 31; 242 = 2 × 11 × 11; 676 = 2 × 2 × 13 × 13, with each set yielding a series of multiplications of prime numbers. The drawback, of course, lies in the impossibility of discovering the author's intended symmetry. The 676 lines of verse can also be analyzed as 6 + 7 + 6 = 19 = 1 + 9 + 10, which brings us back to Beatrice's nine and the perfect number ten. Gorni (1996, xxv–xxvi) also reveals an intriguing pattern in the structure and positioning of the twenty-five sonnets included in *VN,* as well as their structural affinities with the four canzoni having stanzas of fourteen lines.

For a radically different approach, see Raffa 2000, 29: "the textual 'matter' of the *Vita nuova* can . . . be divided into three equal groups . . . chapters 1–14; chapters 15–28; and chapters 29–42. The ninth, tenth, and eleventh positions of the three groups produce a series of symmetries whose significance is enhanced rather than diminished by its 'symmetrical' incompleteness."

33. See Vecce 1994. See also Schimmel 1994, 137: "The number 9 can be variously interpreted. At times, the purely negative aspect is stressed, thus by Petrus Bungus, who equates 9 with pain and sadness and points out that the ninth psalm contains a prediction of the Antichrist. . . . Another type of exegesis, known from classical antiquity, emphasized the near-perfection of the 9. . . . This type of interpretation is typical of much medieval Christian exegesis." For number symbolism in the Middle Ages, see Meyer and Suntrup 1987.

34. De Robertis 1984, 214, n.: "Sta di fatto . . . che la tradizione estravagante . . . reca solo il 2° cominciamento." On the likely compositions written expressly for inclusion in *Vita Nova,* see Carrai 2002.

35. For the discrepancies with the assertion (in *Conv.* 2.12.5–9) that the *donna gentile* was none other than Lady Philosophy, see chapter 4. De Robertis (1950, 121) suggests that the sonnet that signals the return to Beatrice, *Lasso! per forza di molti sospiri* (39.8–10), was written especially for *Vita Nova.*

36. There are 177 occurrences of *tribulatio* in the Vulgate, beginning with Jacob's "There let us make an altar to God, who answered me in the day of my distress *[in die tribulationis meae]* and who accompanied me on my journey."

37. For this perspective, see Picone 1979, 129–92.

38. *Par.* 30.101–2: "that creature which finds peace only in seeing him" *(quella creatura / che solo in lui vedere ha la sua pace).* Cf. *S. Th.* 1.2.2.8: "it is impossible for man's happiness to be in any created good" *(Respondeo dicendum quod impossibile est beatitudinem hominis in aliquo bono creato).*

39. Cf. Reynolds 1969, 11–12: "The *Vita Nova* is a treatise by a poet, written for poets, on the art of poetry . . . this is a work on the art and technique of poetry."

t w o .   Language and the craft of literature: *De vulgari eloquentia*

1. A translation of Raimon Vidal's the *Razos de trobar,* under the title "The Rules of Sir Raimon Vidal," may be found in Shapiro 1990, 113–31.

2. Cf. Grayson 1965, 76: "On the particular question of nobility, Dante's thought in *Conv.* IV and *D. V. E.* I appears consistent and complementary. . . . [J]ust as natural human virtue can be fostered . . . so can the natural vernacular be trained and cultivated by art. The contradiction lies with *Conv.* I, which must have been written before he evolved such a theory about language." "Grammatical discipline on the one hand and the figure of the wet nurse on the other were vivid human realities in Dante's Florence" (Cestaro 2003, 50).

3. See Jan Pinborg, "Speculative Grammar," in *The Cambridge History of Later Medieval Philosophy,* ed. Norman Kretzmann, Anthony Kenny, Jan Pinborg, and Eleonore Stump, 254–69 (Cambridge: Cambridge University Press, 1988). See also Alfonso Maierú, "The Grammar of the *Modistae,*" in *History of Linguistics,* ed. Giulio Lepschy, 2:288–302 (London: Longman, 1994).

4. For a critique of Corti's thesis concerning the *Modistae* and Dante, see Pagani 1982, 253–73.

5. The phrase *formam locutionis* has been interpreted in widely differing ways. For the debate, see Corti 1992, 193–94, with bibliography.

6. Hence, Cacciaguida speaks to Dante in the Florentine vernacular of his time and "not in this modern tongue" (*Par.* 16.33), although no trace of it is found in his speech as recorded by the poet in *Par.* 15–17. For a different interpretation, see Pézard 1967.

7. See Faral 1924; Murphy 1974.

8. "In the etymological and historical sense, *convenientia* (conformity, or the quality of that which is suitable) is synonymous with beauty" (Bruyne 1969, 110). John Took (1984, 68–69) makes the point that "what Dante has in mind is not so much the impersonal *convenientia* of the *poetrie,* the discreet matching of beauty and goodness *ex parte operis,* as the value of form as the coefficient, and indeed principle, of humanity in the poet himself."

9. Gorni describes as "scandalous" this choice of Cino as the Italian poet of love. It is yet another wrong inflicted on Guido Cavalcanti, whose *Donna me prega* was "il testo per antonomasia sull'amore, paradigma assoluto della speculazione poetica in materia" (Gorni 2001, 33–34).

10. Even as the poet of love and Beatrice, in *VN* 27.2, Dante tells us that he decided that it was not possible to describe the effects of her power over him "in the brevity of a sonnet. I therefore began a canzone."

11. See Pazzaglia 1967, 100–106; see also Mengaldo's note in his edition of *DVE* (Mengaldo 1979, 161–63).

12. Cf. Jakobson 1960, 358: "Only in poetry with its regular reiteration of equivalent units is the time of the speech flow experienced, as it is—to cite another semiotic pattern—with musical time."

13. For the difficulties raised by the insertion of elegy in Dante's tripartite stylistic scale, see Mengaldo 1978, 200–222.

14. Cino's *I' no spero che mai per mia salute* is cited (as *Non spero che giamai per mia salute* 2.5.4) in order to illustrate the use of the supreme (hendecasyllabic) line by Italian poets, although it contains many pentasyllabic verses (ll. 3, 7, 12, 17 in each stanza, with others created by *rimalmezzo* in ll. 4, 8, 10, and 15).

15. The first example given (2.6.4), *Petrus amat multum dominam Bertam* (Peter loves greatly Dame Berta), is the only Latin sentence devoid of ornamentation and without any kind of rhythmic clause or *cursus* (see Glossary). The other three examples consist of sentences with more than one clause, each clause ending with a rhythmical *cursus*. In the first two, a clause ending with a *cursus planus (sompniándo revísunt . . . ésse diléctum)* also contains a *cursus velox (exílio tabescéntes . . . magnificéntia preparáta)*. The last example, which belongs to "the most excellent degree of construction" (2.6.5), contains not only a *cursus tardus (túo, Floréntia)* and a *cursus planus (secúndus adívit)* but is further elevated by the use of *transumptio* (here, metaphor and personification: the "flowers" are the virtuous citizens who have been expelled from the personified city's bosom, *eiecta maxima parte florum de sinu tuo, Florentia*).

16. As Barolini (1984, 93) points out: "The nationalities [of the eleven poets selected] are represented according to Dante's estimation of their importance: five Provençals, one Old French, and five Italians."

17. The first part *(frons)* is longer than the *sirma* in another five of Dante's canzoni, including his favorite *Donne ch'avete* (8 + 6). For a basic structural outline of Dante's twenty-three canzoni (as well as those by Cavalcanti, Cino, and others), see Marigo 1968, 282–98.

18. It was only in Dante's times that the hendecasyllabic line came to be associated with the canzone (whereas sonnets were composed exclusively of hendecasyllables). Many early examples do not include any: e.g., Giacomo da Lentini's *Madonna mia, a voi mando* and his *S'io doglio no è meraviglia* (composed entirely of *settenari* and *ottonari*, respectively).

19. Gorni (1981, 195) offers a table displaying the number of heptasyllabic lines *(settenari)* in Dante's lyrics, which range from their exclusion in two poems (*Donne ch'avete intelletto d'amore* [LXXIX: 59] and *Voi che 'ntendendo il terzo ciel movete* [XIV: 33]) to

as many as nine in the canzone already cited (*Doglia mi reca ne lo core ardire* [CVI: 83]). Baldelli gives an excellent analysis of Dante's use of the *settenario* in *Enciclopedia Dantesca* 5:200–202.

20. See T. S. Eliot's judgment that "of the very few poets of similar stature there is none, not even Virgil, who has been a more attentive student of the *art* of poetry, or a more scrupulous, painstaking and *conscious* practitioner of *craft*" (cited in Hawkins and Jacoff 2001, 36).

t h r e e.   Dante's lyric poetry: *Rime*

1. Scholars continue to debate the authenticity of the tenson between Dante and Forese Donati (LXXIII, LXXV, LXXVII: 73–75). See, for example, Cursietti 1995, Cursietti 2000, and Esposito 1997, but also the strong case made by Alfie (1998) for the traditional ascription. As this book went to press, the long-awaited edition of Dante's *Rime* by Domenico De Robertis (De Robertis 2002) was published, which agrees with the traditional attribution of the tenson to Dante and Forese.

De Robertis also attributes to Dante the following poems: the canzone "in lingua trina" (French, Latin, literary Tuscan) *Aï faus ris, pour quoi traï aves;* the "double sonnet" *Quando 'l consiglio degli ucce' si tenne;* and the five sonnets *Se 'l viso mio a la terra si china, Questa donna ch'andar mi fa pensoso, Non v'accorgete voi d'un che·ssi more, Degli occhi di quella gentil mia dama,* and *Io sento pianger l'anima nel core.*

In this chapter, quotations of the Italian text are taken from Contini's edition (1984, 251–552). For information about the poems' numbering, see below, note 2.

2. In all references to Dante's lyric poems, the roman numerals refer to the order as found in Barbi's edition of the *Rime,* sponsored by the Società Dantesca Italiana (Barbi 1960). The arabic numerals following the colon after the roman numerals refer to the order used in the outstanding contribution, *Dante's Lyric Poetry* (Foster and Boyde 1967). For the exchange with Dante da Maiano, Foster and Boyde (1967, 2:6–9) follow Santangelo and others in inverting the traditional attributions of the five sonnets; I follow this ordering.

3. For Guittone's influence on the mature Dante, see Gorni 2001, 15–42, and Giunta 1998.

4. Pointing to Cavalcanti's sonnet *Voi che per li occhi mi passaste 'l core,* with its characteristic emphasis on the destructive force of Love, Afribo (2002, 21–24) shows that in both *Io mi senti' svegliar dentro a lo core* (*VN* 24.7–9) and *Sí lungiamente m'ha tenuto Amore* (*VN* 27.3–5), the younger poet employs the same essential rhyme words *core, amore, segnore, segnoria* as in Cavalcanti's lamentation, so that "Dante . . . cites his first friend . . . in order to condemn him with his own words, with his own rhyme-words, with his own rhymes." Afribo's study should be consulted for its detailed (and complex) analysis of rhymes and rhyme sequences in the Italian lyric of the thirteenth and fourteenth centuries.

5. The "Sicilian" rhymes found in Petrocchi's edition of the *Comedy* (Petrocchi 1994) have been eliminated in Sanguineti's critical edition of the work (Sanguineti 2001).

6. De Robertis (2002, 331) gives a version, *No me poriano zamai far emenda,* that has a pronounced "veste [linguistica] emiliana" and may well be the first of Dante's linguistic experiments with non-Tuscan forms not sanctioned by tradition.

7. The *ballata* may consist of one stanza or of several identical stanzas, which are governed by rules similar to those of the canzone (for the latter, see chapter 2). The distinguishing feature of the *ballata* is the *ripresa,* which announces the main theme and whose last line rhymes with the last line in each *sirma* of the stanza(s). The term *ripresa* indicates the refrain that was repeated when the *ballata* was set to music and accompanied by dancing (as in the conclusion to the First and subsequent Days in Boccaccio's *Decameron*). Dante uses this feature as an indication of the *ballata's* inferior status, given the canzone's artistic autarchy (*DVE* 2.3.5).

8. In Dante's lyrics, rhyme words with the stress on the antepenultimate syllable *(rime sdrucciole)* are found only in lines 33 and 34 of *Poscia ch'Amor del tutto m'ha lasciato* (LXXXIII: 70: *intèndere – vèndere*). There are sixteen occurrences (with forty-eight proparoxytones) in the *Comedy,* with only three instances of *rime sdrucciole* in *Paradiso (Par.* 19.14–18, 26.125–29, 29.65–69).

9. Regarding Dante's use of *pargoletta,* as in *I' mi son pargoletta bella e nova,* cf. LXXXIX: 66.2 *(esta bella pargoletta)* and C: 77.72 *(se in pargoletta fia per core un marmo).* This second quotation, from the canzone *Io sono venuto al punto de la rota,* is the one exception to the rule that the diminutive suffix *-etta (pargoletta, giovinetta)* is not found in Dante's elevated style, the only style suited to the canzone form.

10. For what Dante means by harsh sounds *(asprezza)* in verse, see chapter 2, "Structure of the Canzone," discussion of *DVE* 2.13.13.

11. As noted in chapter 2, *Donne ch'avete intelletto d'amore* remained a favorite, quoted twice in *De vulgari eloquentia* as an example of the canzone, the noblest form of poetry in the vernacular (*DVE* 2.8.8), and of the elevated style based entirely on hendecasyllables (*DVE* 2.12.3).

12. For conceptual and verbal links between Bonagiunta and Dante, see Giunta 1998, 332–43.

13. The *pedes* are longer than the *sirma* in the following lyric poems: *Amor, che movi tua virtú dal cielo* (XC: 67 [8 lines to 7 lines]), *Poscia ch'Amor del tutto m'ha lasciato* (LXXXIII: 70 [12:7]), *Cosí nel mio palar voglio esser aspro* (CIII: 80 [8:5]), *Sí lungiamente m'ha tenuto Amore* (XXIV: 46 [8:6]), and *Lo meo servente core* (XLIX: 9 [8:6]). *Lo meo servente core* is unique in Dante's oeuvre for its opening line, which is a heptasyllable, or *settenario.*

14. Took (1984, 70–73) gives an excellent analysis of the first stanza of *Donne ch'avete* and of the sonnet *Tanto gentile.*

15. For an illuminating analysis of the "major poetic breakthrough" achieved by Dante in *Donne ch'avete,* see Durling and Martinez 1990, 55–70.

16. For a detailed analysis, see Boyde 1971, 90 ff.

17. *Settenario* refers to a line with seven syllables, i.e., a heptasyllable *(septenarius).* Dante introduced the pentasyllabic line *(quinario)* only once, in the structurally eccentric canzone *Poscia ch'Amor del tutto m'ha lasciato* (LXXXIII: 70).

18. Although in *DVE* 2.10.4, Dante states that *frons* signifies an undivided first section (i.e., one without *pedes*), and *sirma* a unitary second section (without *versus*), I shall

follow modern usage and use *frons* and *sirma* to indicate the two major sections in the canzone, whether those sections are unitary or divided.

19. See Durling and Martinez 1990. It is impossible for me to do justice to this innovative, full-length study of the *petrose* (and of *Donne ch'avete intelletto d'amore*). For the significance of astronomical references in the *Comedy,* see Cornish 2000.

20. Amidei (2002, 103) points out that Dante found in Arnaut's poems a truly "rich thematic and stylistic palette . . . capable of ranging . . . from the 'comic' [style] to the 'tragic.'" An important study appeared (Allegretti 2002) as this book was going to press; it documents the way in which Dante's *petrose* combine key elements of Vergil's bucolic poetry with the technical virtuosity of Arnaut Daniel and the troubadour tradition.

21. Scholars make many references to troubadour poetry (written in *langue d'oc* or Provençal, although the most famous troubadours came from the Limousin or Périgord regions of southwest France), yet few readers realize how much was produced: we have some 2,542 poems by 460 poets, as well as 251 anonymous compositions.

22. This structure is in fact found in another poem by Arnaut Daniel, *Lo ferm voler q'el cor m'intra.*

23. All six key words in *Al poco giorno e al gran cerchio d'ombra* (CI: 78) have very few rhyming possibilities in Italian verse. *Donna* can only rhyme with *gonna, colonna,* and *assonna.* The word *petra* (designating an antitype of Beatrice?) never appears in the *Comedy;* the form *pietra* occurs fifteen times there, but only once in the rhyming position, necessitating the *rimas caras* formed by *cetra* and *penètra* (*Par.* 20.20–24). Three of the key words have the tonic accent on *o (donna, ombra, colli),* while the other three have an accented *e (petra, erba, verde).* All six key words are nouns, although *verde* is also used adjectivally.

24. Significantly, in the *Comedy*—a poem in which Dante wishes to impart an urgent moral message to the widest possible audience—Arnaut Daniel's words are uncharacteristically straightforward and heralded by his intention not to "cover" or hide his identity *(Purg.* 26.141: *ieu no me puesc ni voill a vos cobrire).*

25. Cf. Boyde 1971; Masini 1990; and Rossi 1995.

26. The rhyme pattern of *Così nel mio parlar,* with five rhyming couplets in thirteen verses (ABbC / ABbC // CDdEE), was destined to be the most popular in the Italian lyric tradition (Gorni 1993, 45), surpassing even the success enjoyed by Petrarch's celebrated *Chiare, fresche et dolci acque* (abC / abC // cdeeDff). It is noteworthy that Cino da Pistoia used the structure of the stanzas of *Così nel mio parlar* in his canzone lamenting Dante's death *(Su per la costa, Amor, de l'alto monte).*

27. In *Donne ch'avete intelletto d'amore* (*VN* 19; XIV: 33), no fewer than fifty of the seventy rhyme words end with this combination of vowel-consonant-vowel.

28. The exceptional rhyme *squatra – latra* is already found in a canzone by Monte Andrea (a Florentine disciple of Guittone), *Tanto m'abondai* (ll. 81–82: *Ché tal colpo sí 'l cor de l'ommo squatra, / dir non si puote bene co' tal latra!).* The rhyme *s'arretra – petra* was first used by Guittone in *De coralmente amar* (ll. 2–4).

29. Martinez (1993, 219) illustrates more fully than any other scholar the relevance of the image of the bear in *Così nel mio parlar voglio esser aspro* (CIII: 80), l. 71 *(anzi farei com'orso quando scherza):* "Bear-lore is surely relevant to the emphasis on the speaker's lust

and violence, but also to his status as a battered figure struggling with powerful impulses . . . to the presentation of the sexual embrace as a struggle. . . . [I]t is relevant, finally, to the ambiguous status of the speaker-lover, both angelic and bestial. . . . Dante's playful bear offers an indispensable facet of Dante's conception of the full range of the human."

30. Baldelli (1976b, 201) points to lines such as *e 'n su la man si posa / come succisa rosa* (ll. 20–21) to bolster his claim that *Tre donne* contains perhaps the most beautiful *settenari* ever penned by Dante.

31. Gorni (2001, 18–19) emphasizes the "natura trina" of the *envoi,* which is then divided into the first *congedo* of ten lines (ll. 91–100), a second of five lines (101–5), and the third composed of the rhyming couplet with its aphoristic *"camera di perdon savio uom non serra, / ché 'l perdonare è bel vincer di guerra."* As Gorni points out, no fewer than four of Guittone d'Arezzo's canzoni have three *envois,* while two *envois* are found in twelve canzoni.

32. For an excellent account of the development of the sonnet form, see Kleinhenz 1986b.

33. For Cino's *Avegna ched el m'aggia più per tempo* and its metrical model, Dante's *Donna pietosa e di novella etate,* see *VN* 23.17–28. See also above, chapter 1, "Premonition of Beatrice's Death."

34. As Contini observes (1976, 7), rhymes such as those in XCV: 84, the first of Dante's sonnets in the exchange with Cino of Pistoia, already point to the "magnanimità lessicale" (lexical magnanimity) of the *Comedy.*

35. Gorni (1995a, 141) suggests that the body of *Amor, da che convien pur ch'io mi doglia* (CXVI: 89) was conceived early in Dante's poetic career but refashioned during his exile, with an *envoi* (ll. 76–84) added and addressed to "Florence, my city" (l. 77). An edition and detailed analysis of this canzone appears in Allegretti 2001 (with a preface by Guglielmo Gorni).

36. For a parallel between the persona's loss of his rational powers in *Amor, da che convien pur ch'io mi doglia* (CXVI: 89) and the metamorphosis of Vanni Fucci in *Inf.* 24, see Ginsberg 1999, 153–57.

37. On average, the *canso* (the Provençal equivalent of the canzone) contained about 50 lines of verse (often, set out in five to seven stanzas). With 158 verses, *Doglia mi reca* follows the example set by Guittone in his moral or political canzoni (Guittone's canzoni on love average some 72 lines): *Gente noiosa e villana* (146 verses); *Magni baroni certo e regi quasi* (140 verses); *O dolce terra aretina* (132 verses). Guido Guinizzelli's *Al cor gentil rempaira sempre amore* is composed of 60 lines; Guido Cavalcanti's famous *Donna me prega, per ch'eo voglio dire* has 75 lines.

38. For Guittone's lasting influence on Dante's canzoni, see Gorni (2001, 17 ff.), who points out that every canzone with stanzas of more than fourteen lines ("misura aurea del Dante stilnovista") is "di respiro 'guittoniano'"; Gorni also reveals Guittonian elements in Dante's sonnet in praise of Guinizzelli's conception of love *(VN* 20.3–5: *Amore e 'l cor gentil sono una cosa).*

39. Gorni 1981, 159: "La sacralità dell'incipit è una cosa nuova rispetto alla trattatistica precedente."

40. Gorni gives the following statistics: Dante composed three canzoni with one stanza; two with two; three with three; four with four; eight with five; four with six; and three with seven. As Gorni notes, the range from one to seven stanzas is large, whereas in Petrarch's *Rerum vulgarium fragmenta* (with twenty-five canzoni), no canzone has fewer than five stanzas, while two have eight and the last two (CCLX and CCCLXVI) have ten— "la codificazione del genere col Petrarca si chiude" (Gorni 1993, 49).

41. The fact that the three major canzoni included in *Vita Nova* all have fourteen-line stanzas is pointed out by Kleinhenz (1986b, 211).

f o u r.   Dante's Banquet of knowledge: *Convivio*

1. Cf. Barański 2000a, 26: "When we speak of Aristotelianism or Neo-Platonism or mysticism, we speak of 'high' intellectual movements . . . of great complexity. Instead, if we truly want to understand Dante's mind and chart his ideological formation . . . we must begin with far 'lower' areas *[partire da zone molto piú basse]*."

2. Although salaried university teachers gradually gained acceptance, Dante and his contemporaries were still influenced by "an archaic state of mind . . . [that] held that knowledge was a gift from God and consequently could not be sold, under the threat of simony . . . In a famous text St. Bernard had denounced the earnings of masters as shameful profit *(turpis questus)*" (Le Goff 1993, 95).

3. "Anyone born between the years 1000 and 1400 would . . . not have understood the meaning of the word 'intellectual' *(intellectualis)* attributed to a person" (Brocchieri 1990, 181).

4. For Orpheus as *figura Christi,* see Dronke 1997a, 272–75.

5. Pietrobono (1936, 1–137) and Nardi (1944, 1–20; 1992 [1960], 127) were the principal champions of the idea that, after interrupting work on his *Convivio,* Dante went back to *Vita Nova* and changed the message of its final chapters, by reworking chapter 31 and adding chapter 39, thus transforming *Vita Nova* into a "prelude . . . of the *Comedy*" (Nardi 1944, 18). The lack of any concrete evidence of two contradictory versions is one of the chief weapons in the demolition of this hypothesis, carried out by Marti (1965); cf. Sarteschi 1996 [1990]. Pietrobono's and Nardi's hypothesis has been more cautiously reformulated by Corti (1983, 146–55).

6. See Davis 1957, 80–86; 1984, 198–223.

7. Cf. Lagarde 1958.

8. Cf. Foster (1965, 68), who suggests that "a risk of heresy" accompanied Dante's tendency, in *Convivio,* "to resolve the theologian's distinction between nature and grace into a philosopher's distinction between time and eternity."

9. See Newman's essential study (2003, 191): "The matriarch of medieval goddesses . . . called Hagia Sophia in Byzantium, Sapientia and Philosophia in Latin Christendom, Dame Sapience or Lady Wisdom or die ewige Weisheit in the vernaculars, this figure was far better known to medieval clerics than she is today" (chap. 5: "Sapientia: The Goddess Incarnate," 190–244); "Dante . . . was unique in granting the

language of poetic hyperbole its full theological seriousness" (182), eventually making (in *Paradiso*) "his Beatrice a doctor of the Church" (300).

10. Although Corti has frequently stressed certain intellectual affinities between Dante and such radical Aristotelians as Boethius of Dacia (Denmark), she rightly judges that the author of *Convivio* "never left . . . the grounds of orthodoxy and when he reached its extreme boundary . . . he always kept Albert the Great as a beloved model" (Corti 1983, vii). For an overview of the problem, see Scott 1990.

11. See Nardi 1983 [1942], 197–208; Foster 1976, 636–37; Dronke 1997a, 55–56.

12. See, e.g., Freccero 1973 (1986, 186–94); Hollander 1975.

13. Vasoli (1988, lxxx) mentions certain "traces" of *Convivio* found in the so-called Ottimo Commento, Pietro Alighieri, Giovanni Villani, and Boccaccio.

14. "The opposition set by *Purgatorio* II is not between theology (the Bible) and philosophy (the *Convivio*), but . . . between two different poetic genres: one religious . . . which leads to 'gaudium', and the other secular . . . leading to 'planctum'" (Pertile 1993a, 60). Pertile (1995a) also illustrates the biblical connotations of the *scoglio* (*Purg.* 2.122) that prevents the soul from enjoying the beatific vision in paradise.

15. As Cogan (1999, 252) points out, "Not only is the philosophy of the *Convivio* thoroughly Christian, so is the Christian doctrine of the *Commedia* thoroughly philosophical."

16. See Leo 1951; cf. Hollander 2001, 193 n. 107.

17. As Mazzotta (1993, 215) points out, Dante "is also a peace poet." Western writers "almost never, if one excepts Tolstoy, Isaiah, and the Gospels," write "of peace as a scandalous reproach to the ways of the world. Dante belongs to this tradition of scandal."

18. The paradox evident in Dante's selection of heroes and episodes taken from the history of republican Rome in order to celebrate the providential establishment of the Roman Empire is highlighted by Scott (1977, 315–18) and especially Hollander and Rossi (1986).

19. "This reference to the city itself as a physical fact . . . is especially interesting in view of the total absence in Dante of the cult of 'ruin-worship,' that adoration of the tangible remains of the past which would later find in Petrarch so indefatigable an exponent" (Davis 1957, 45).

20. Nardi 1960b, 9–68.

21. See Russo 1971, 103–58; Boyde 1981, 270–95.

22. Corti 1983, 123–45. Dronke (1997a, 56–71), however, rejects Corti's radical approach; instead, Dronke emphasizes the parallels between "the love-language celebrating the Donna Gentile . . . [and] his language of seed and fruit, celebrating Nobility," while pointing to the final chapter of *Convivio*, "which brings Nobility and Philosophy together, and closes exultantly. . . . [T]he unity of intention of the third and fourth treatises also emerges decisively."

23. See Dronke's elaboration of the "symphony of images of organic fertility [found in *Conv.* 4]: the seed, shoot and bud, leaves and fronds, flowers and fruit" (Dronke 1997a, 57).

24. For a comprehensive treatment of justice in Dante, see Boyde 2000, 198–224.

25. See Segre 1963, 227–70. See also Grayson 1972, 56–60: "The *Comedy* may be regarded as the formal solution to a problem that Dante had resolved or attempted to resolve by grafting prose onto poetry. . . . [I]n order to reach his full stature as a poet he was indebted no less to vernacular prose than to poetry."

26. For all that this expression signifies, see Hollander 2000.

five.   Dante's vision of world empire and peace: *Monarchia*

1. For a critical analysis of the manuscript tradition, Ficino's translation, and the *editio princeps* of 1559, see Shaw's edition (Shaw 1995, xxxviii–xxxix, with bibliography).

2. An excellent case is made by Kay (1998, xxviii–xxx) for attributing the composition of *Monarchia* to the period immediately following the publication of the decretal *Si fratrum* (March 31, 1317) and the papal challenge to Dante's patron, Cangrande della Scala.

3. Throughout this chapter, quotations of *Monarchia* follow Shaw's edition (Shaw 1995), and I use the numbering of *Monarchia*'s chapters in that edition as well.

4. See K. Kuksewicz, "The Potential and the Agent Intellect," in Kretzmann, Kenny, and Pinborg 1988, 595–601. See also Boyde 1981, 276–78 and 374–77.

5. "Quod in omnibus hominibus est unus solus intellectus, quod quidem . . . est error pessimus cuius auctor et inventor fuit ille Averroes quem allegat" (Guido Vernani's refutation of *Monarchia,* cited in Matteini 1958, 97).

6. For a dissenting voice, see Marenbon (2001, esp. 371), who rejects the judgments of both Étienne Gilson (1948, 166–71) and Nardi (1979, 298–302): "It seems very probable that Dante held the Averroist position on the single possible intellect *as the right position within philosophical discussion.* It would be quite wrong, however, to conclude that he held this position to be the right one to take in theological argument, where revealed truths are taken into account; or that he held it to be true without qualification."

7. Davis 1957; 1984, 198–223. Remigio went as far as to assert that "peace ought to be established and preserved whether or not this means disobeying the laws and prohibitions of the pope himself" (Davis 1984, 201); this reflects a frequent dilemma in an age when political excommunications were current and whole cities might be placed under ecclesiastical interdict. Remigio "even remarked that a citizen should be willing to go to hell, if he could do so without offending God, rather than see his commune there, and . . . spoke admiringly of Marcus Curtius, who [chose] to go to hell to save his city" (Davis 1992, 92).

8. Ricci 1965. Ricci rejected the traditional separation of chapter 10 into two chapters (10.1–17 and 11.1–2, coalesced in some manuscripts and in Ricci's edition as 10.1–20). Ricci's chapter divisions were maintained in both Nardi (1979) and Kay (1998).

9. See the chapter on justice in Boyde 2000, 198–224.

10. Fabricated probably in the eighth century, this forgery was produced in order to prove that the Emperor Constantine (288–337) had donated the city of Rome and the

western half of the empire to Pope Sylvester in recompense for the pope's having converted him to Christianity and for having cured him of leprosy in the year 314. In the twelfth century, the document was incorporated into the text of Gratian's *Decretum*. It was invoked by Boniface VIII (1294–1303) to affirm the temporal (as well as the spiritual) supremacy of the papacy. For Dante's denunciation of this supposed act, see *Inf.* 19.115–17 and *Purg.* 32.124–29. Ironically, Constantine was placed by the poet and seen by the pilgrim in the Heaven of Justice, in spite of the consequences of his "good intention that produced evil fruit . . . whereby the world is destroyed" (*Par.* 20.55–60).

11. Davis (1957, 140–41) cites a text in which Frederick I is made to refer to himself as *christus eius* (his Christ [God's Anointed One]), while Cino da Pistoia wrote in his commentary that "the laws consider the emperor to be God, or a divine person, and rightly so, because the empire is from God."

12. Barański offers a comprehensive study of "un Dante fedele dei *vestigia divini*" (Barański 2000a, 39).

13. As Ferrante observes: "Dante's identification with the female is underscored by a small but significant fact: he has Cacciaguida say that Dante's *sopranome* comes from a woman, Cacciaguida's wife (*Par.* XV, 138)" (Ferrante 1993b, 18, n. 12).

14. For Vernani's scathing attack on Dante's *Monarchia,* see Matteini 1958.

15. Davis 1957, 84: "It is . . . likely that Remigio was the teacher who began to change Dante's idea of Rome" and to discard the Guelf-Augustinian view.

16. For a full discussion of Dante's attitude toward Cato and the poet's choice of this pagan Roman suicide to "guard" Christian purgatory, see Scott 1996b, 69–84.

17. Ullmann 1975, 104: "The development in the twelfth century leading to the concept of the pope as the vicar of Christ" resulted in the fact that "a number of biblical passages which referred to Christ were now directly applied to the pope, so, for instance, the Matthean passage: 'All power is given unto me.'" The idea of the pope as the vicar of Christ was "a rare concept in law before 1198" (Morris 1991, 569). Cf. Maccarone 1952.

18. See Davis 1984, 42–70. "In one important way . . . Dante seems more radical even than the Spiritual Franciscans. He thought that the clergy as a whole should have remained poor" (Davis 1984, 53). Cf. Pasquini 2001, 155: "egli rifugge dagli estremismi faziosi degli Spirituali piú intransigenti . . . ma è forse piú di loro intransigente nell'estendere il mito francescano dell'*usus pauper* ad àmbiti e personaggi di ogni epoca."

19. Readers are reminded that chapter 11 has been restored by Shaw in her edition (Shaw 1995). References in brackets will include the numbering found in Ricci's and Nardi's editions.

20. Whereas I have indicated the locations for 3.10/11 in both the Ricci/Nardi/Kay editions and those by Vinay/Shaw, henceforth I shall follow the numbering of chapters in Vinay/Shaw (e.g., 3.12 in Vinay/Shaw = 3.11 in Ricci/Nardi/Kay).

21. Nardi (1960b, 92–96, 292–93) argues that Dante agreed with Aristotle that human beings could be fully happy in this life (hence, the symbol of the terrestrial paradise in *Mon.* 3.16.7).

22. The phrase *in aerola ista mortalium* (in this little abode of mortals) throws light on the word *aiuola* found in *Par.* 22.151 (*l'aiuola che ci fa tanto feroci*) and *Par.* 27.86, which is all too often translated as "threshing-floor." In fact, *aiuola / areola* describes the re-

stricted inhabitable area of our tiny terrestrial globe: "the compass of the whole earth compared to the scope of heaven is no bigger than a pinpoint . . . only the fourth part is known to be inhabited by living creatures known to us" (Boethius, *De consolatione philosophiae* 2.7).

23. Reeves (1965, 102) goes so far as to claim that *Monarchia*'s final paragraph brings about the collapse of Dante's "whole case for the independence of the secular ruler." Nardi seizes upon the term *quodammodo* to buttress his hypothesis that Dante wrote *Monarchia* c. 1308 (before embarking on the *Comedy*) and that, at the end of the Latin treatise, he became aware of the difficulties inherent in the position he had adopted in book 3: "The *quodammodo*, which Aquinas would never have tolerated, still displays a degree of uncertainty. But this uncertainty is about to be erased by the strong light of the prophetic 'vision'" (Nardi 1992 [1960], 310). Nardi (ibid., 300–313) rightly insists that the phrase does not imply any kind of subordination of the empire to the papacy. An anonymous tract, the *Quaestio in utramque partem* (c. 1302), specifies that the pope's right to intervene in the temporal domain is limited to special cases that pertain "in some way" *(quodammodo)* to spiritual matters. An exhaustive survey is to be found in Martinelli 1983; cf. Di Scipio 1988, esp. 276; and Trovato 1988. As Martinelli (1983, 210) remarks, it is significant that Dante's concluding statements in *Monarchia* were not even mentioned in Vernani's fierce attack (cf. n. 14).

six.   The *Comedy*, prolegomena: The prologue scene (*Inferno* 1–2)

Inferno 1–2, though not separated from the beginning of *Inferno* 3, have the rhetorical function of a prologue. As Singleton (1977, 9) remarks, "In a sense it might be regretted that somehow a curtain does not fall to mark off the first two cantos of the poem for the prologue which they are." For detailed analyses of each line in the first two cantos, see Mazzoni 1967, 14–313. See also Armour 1981; Barański 2000a, 103–26; Cassell 1989; Gorni 1995b; Hollander 1990a; Jacoff and Stephany 1989.

1. For a brilliant overview of the significance of this choice, see Cornish 2000, 26–42, "The Date of the Journey." Although astronomical descriptions in the poem are inconsistent with the "real" situation of the heavens in 1300, their "truth-value is far greater than any observed or retrospectively calculated astronomical data. This fiction, if we may call it that, is the calendar date of Easter" (35).

2. Dante offers his readers a spectacular exception to the chronological limit that all souls encountered by the pilgrim must have died before March 1300. The souls of certain traitors, as soon as they murdered their guests, plunged down into the depths of hell while a devil took over their bodies for the rest of their time on earth (*Inf.* 33.124–33). For example, the pilgrim meets the soul of a certain Frate Alberigo (*Inf.* 33.109–50), who was still alive in 1300; the poet condemns him to hell for having had his relatives assassinated at a meal that was supposed to mark their reconciliation. Branca Doria and an unnamed relative are also prematurely condemned for a similar crime (Branca in fact outlived Dante by several years).

3. For the prophecies that can be divided into two groups (those made after and those made before the events predicted), see the detailed analysis in Palma di Cesnola 1995, 37–52.

4. Padoan (1993, 90) suggests that *Inferno* was completed only by April– November 1314, a possibility that would have allowed Dante to insert the prophecy *post factum* in that year.

5. The "modern scholar" is Giovanni Ferretti (1935, esp. 335–76); see also Boc- caccio 1965, 446–50. Recently, Padoan (1993, 33) has argued that the papers received by the exiled poet probably contained not the first seven cantos of *Inferno* but the beginning of a poem in the vernacular in honor of "blessed Beatrice," composed c. 1294.

6. Petrocchi 1969, 85. Cf. Renucci's hypothesis that, begun in the spring of 1304, *Inferno* was interrupted at the end of canto 7 in 1306. This would mean that during the years 1304–6 Dante was working not only on his *De vulgari eloquentia* and *Convivio* but also on the first seven cantos of the poem (Renucci 1954, 88–127).

7. See *DVE* 2.8.8; 2.2.7; see also the present volume, chapter 2, "Who May Use the Illustrious Vernacular, and for Which Subjects?"

8. See Giovanni del Virgilio, *Ecl.* 1.6–7. Cf. the statement in Dante's *Ep.* 13.31 that the *Comedy* is written in a style that is "modest and humble, since it is in the vulgar tongue, which is used even by simple women."

9. *Conv.* 1.13.12. Cf. the well-argued claim that, for the author of the *Comedy,* "not the philosopher or the theologian but the poet . . . plays a crucial role in determin- ing the shape of knowledge" (Mazzotta 1993, 135).

10. Capitani (1999, 62–63) argues that the epithet *invidïosi* signifies "unseen" in the sense of "not understood" (from the Latin *invideo,* "I do not see"); the truths taught by Siger concern the "autonomy of human reason with all the consequences that follow on the political plane." On the supposed incompatibility between Dante's passionate love of philosophy as expressed in *Convivio* and his standpoint in the *Comedy,* see Hollander 1980, esp. 104–5; Hollander 1990b, 28–45; and Cassell 1976, 33–58. My own conclusions are argued in Scott 1990. *Par.* 26.23–48 is crucial evidence in this debate: when asked by St. John what had led him to the love of God, the pilgrim answers that this love was "imprinted" in him by *both* philosophy and the authority of revelation (*Par.* 26.25–27; cf. *Par.* 26.46–48). See also above, chapter 4, "Dante's Orthodoxy."

11. For the idea that Dante discovered the riches offered by Vergil's *Aeneid* by a new, direct familiarity with Vergil's text (and masterpieces by Ovid, Lucan, and Statius) while composing book 4 of *Convivio,* see Leo 1951. See also Hollander 2001, 193 n. 107.

12. See *Conv.* 4.28.15: "And what earthly man was more worthy to signify God than Cato? None, surely" (cf. *Purg.* 1.37–39). See also the images of the false forest and the true way in *Conv.* 4.24.12 (cf. *Inf.* 1.1–12), the rose in *Conv.* 4.27.4 (cf. *Par.* 22.56–57), and the simile comparing the return to God in old age to the return to port after a long sea voyage in *Conv.* 4.28.1–7. The basic image of the *Comedy* as a pilgrimage (as well as an essential part of Marco Lombardo's discourse at the poem's center, *Purg.* 16.85–92) is already to be found in *Conv.* 4.12.15–18. For the relationship between *Con- vivio* and the *Comedy,* see Simonelli 1970, 200–201; Scott 1995a.

13. See above, chapter 4.

14. See Hollander's classic essay, Hollander 2000.

15. Petrocchi (1994, 3:383, at *Purg.* 22.113) and Lanza (1996, 447) discuss several suggested emendations of *Purg.* 22.113: Padoan (*ED* 3.811) not only shares in the general reluctance to admit the possibility of a momentary lapse of the poet's memory, but also he advocates the reading *èvvi la figlia di Chirone, Teti* (there is Chiron's daughter, Thetis)— instead of the normative *èvvi la figlia di Tiresia, e Teti.* But cf. Torraca and Parodi, who suggest *èvvi la figlia di Nereo, Teti.* Hollander (1991, 92), however, proposes an alternative solution: "The Manto of the Malebolge is Virgil's creature; she of limbo, the virgin daughter of the fourth *Thebaid.*"

16. Whereas Boccaccio's claim (1974, 484: 183) that *Paradiso* was composed in batches of "six or eight or more or fewer cantos" is generally accepted by scholars, the possibility that the poet "published" any section of *Inferno* and *Purgatorio* before 1313–14 is usually denied. The possibility, however, remains that Dante did make known (perhaps orally) at least parts of the first two *cantiche* before the first known written reference to the *Comedy* (viz., to *Inf.*), found in a note by Francesco da Barberino written in 1313/1314.

17. Nevertheless, it must be noted that, in the *Proemio* to his *Chiose,* Dante's son Jacopo Alighieri asserts that of four styles, comedy is the one that may be used for any and every subject: "Il secondo, commedia, sotto il quale generalmente, e universalmente si tratta di tutte le cose, e quindi il titol del presente volume procede" (Dartmouth Dante Project: Jacopo Alighieri's commentary on the *Comedy*).

18. In the ongoing debate about the authenticity of the *Epistle to Cangrande,* weighty evidence has been put forward by Pertile (1991b), who demonstrates that the *accessus* section of the epistle is the only fourteenth-century text to use the three terms "canto," "cantica," and "comedía" correctly. See also Hollander 1993a.

19. See, for example, Hollander 1983, 131: "Tutti questi aspetti tragici di Virgilio, il suo stile sublime, la sua epica tragica, il fallimento della sua vita, fanno da sfondo al momento virgiliano piú palpabilmente tragico dell'intero poema, quello in cui Dante perde il padre poetico nel XXX del *Purgatorio* (40–54)."

20. Agamben 1978, 14. Cf. Frye's use of the terms in "It is true that Oedipus belongs to tragedy and Christ to a divine comedy" (Frye 1982, 156).

21. *DVE* 2.4.6: *Si vero comice [canenda videntur], tunc quandoque mediocre quandoque humile vulgare sumatur.* For the definitions of the tragic, comic, and elegiac styles as given in *DVE* 2.4, see above, chapter 2, "The Noblest Style." Macrobius had in fact defined Vergil's *Aeneid* as *sacrum poema* (Schiaffini 1965, 53); as we have seen, however, it was a *tragedía* for Dante—yet one more element in the complex relationship between the two poets.

22. Barański 1991, 38; cf. Barański 1995a. For the relationship between the style of the *Comedy* and the Bible's *sermo humilis,* see the classic study by Auerbach (1965). Augustine (*Confessions* 3.5) admits that he was alienated when he "first read the Scriptures. To me they seemed quite unworthy of comparison with the stately prose of Cicero, because I had too much conceit to accept their simplicity and not enough insight to penetrate their depths." The *Comedy*'s polyphony led Osip Mandelstam to claim that "Long before Bach . . . Alighieri constructed in verbal space an infinitely powerful organ

and already delighted in all its conceivable stops, inflated its bellows, and roared and cooed through all its pipes" (Hawkins and Jacoff 2001, 51).

23. Villa (2001, 204 and 209) makes the interesting observation that Servius describes book 4 of Vergil's *Aeneid* as virtually written in the comic style *(nam pene comicus stilus est),* noting: "It is the only case in which a great tragedy, like the *Aeneid,* includes a comic book; it therefore seems possible to say that it is from this [work] that Dante took the idea that dominates the entire *Comedy,* namely, the possibility of constructing a sacred poem within the area of 'comedy.' . . . [T]he fourth book of the *Aeneid* is a comic book . . . the whole of love pertains to the comic genre."

24. Russo (1984, 48) develops Györg Lukács's insight that, as a protonovel, the *Comedy* constitutes a new genre in the European literary tradition:"il precedente piú arcaico della forma letteraria del romanzo . . . Il romanzo inteso come storia della ricerca di valori etici condotta da parte di un eroe problematico in una società degradata."

25. For a recent informative account in English of Dante's life, see Bemrose 2000.

26. Bruni 1917, 211: "Tutti gli mali e l'inconvenienti miei dalli infausti comizi del mio Priorato ebbono cagione e principio."

27. See Gorni (1990, 126–29), who also highlights a passage in the Bible (Dan. 12.11–12) where two numbers—1,290 and 1,335—may well have struck Dante as bearing great significance for his own life: the first, the year of Beatrice's death; the second, indicating the end of his own lifespan of seventy years on earth. Daniel 12.12—"Blessed is the one who waits and attains the thousand three hundred and thirty-five days" (with the common transposition of days to years)—contains an initial *beatus,* which could have been taken to imply Dante's own elevation to heaven, after Beatrice's "assumption" in 1290. Charity (1987, 93 and 260): "Typology of that kind which we called 'subfulfilment' . . . is involved in the New Testament's conceptions of the *imitatio Christi,* the believer's 'incorporation,' and the 'dying and rising' of the Christian with Christ. . . . We return, then, to the Christian view of Christ's history as the *absolute* norm of divine action and human existence." For Christ's *descensus ad inferos,* see Hawkins 1999, 99–110.

28. See Armour 1983, 145 ff; Esposito 2000; Frugoni 2000, 173–258. Cf. *Inf.* 18.28–33; *Purg.* 2.98–102.

29. The year 1300 was, of course, the last year of the thirteenth century. However, as recent confusion over the beginning of the third millennium shows yet again, 1300 "was the year naturally and popularly associated with a new century, as we have lately discovered by experience, since the nineteenth-century public needed a good deal of educating out of this notion" (Moore 1903, 175). *Vox populi!* The German writer Heinrich Heine, born on the night between December 31, 1799, and January 1, 1800, claimed to be "one of the first men of the nineteenth century," and Victor Hugo's famous opening proclaiming "Ce siècle avait deux ans!" at the time of his birth in 1802 would also seem to have been inspired by this popular misconception. We may add that the Jubilee (originally intended to take place every hundred years) helped to introduce the concept of the century into Christian chronology.

30. The commencement of the year differed in various places, according to the three methods in vogue in the Middle Ages. The first—the one we now take for granted—began on January 1 *(anni a circumcisione);* the second, called the "Roman" use,

began on December 25 *(anni a nativitate);* the third, the "Florentine" or "Pisan" use, began on March 25 *(anni ab incarnatione).*

31. Canto 1 has 136 lines of verse. The length of individual cantos in the poem varies from 115 *(Inf.* 6) to 160 *(Purg.* 32). For the overall scheme, see Ferrante 1993a, 154–55. The average number of *terzinas* in a canto is 47 (Boyde 2000, 72).

32. Cf. St. Augustine's claim *(De Trinitate* 6.10.12) that all things bear the stamp of the Trinity *(vesitigia Trinitatis)* by virtue of their possessing unity, kind, and order.

33. Curtius (1953, 505) points out that "Villon names the name of Christ in stanzas 3 and 33 of his *Testament.*" Near the end of his life, Dante received a second Latin eclogue from Giovanni del Virgilio. He answered it in the same number of verses (97), but pointed out that with the addition of three lines it would have truly gladdened the hearts of its audience. This brief remark *(Ecl.* 4.42–43) illustrates Dante's awareness of the significance given in his day to numbers in general (few modern readers would think of counting the number of verses in a poem sent to them!). For a comprehensive guide to medieval number symbolism, see Meyer and Suntrup 1987.

34. For numerical symmetries perceived in Dante's works, see Sarolli 1976; Hardt 1988, 1989, 1995; Curtius 1953, 501–9; Hart 1988. According to Hardt (1988, 83), before the poet began work on the *Comedy,* "the *abacus* must have belonged to Dante's daily working tools, he must have constructed many systematic charts, diagrams and word concordances. Without the help of these . . . the *oeuvre* which he envisaged could not have been realized." Hardt's calculations and interpretations are based on the following symbolic relationships:

1	=	the Creator
3	=	the Trinity
4, 40	=	the cross
5	=	human sensuality
7	=	grace and the gifts of the Holy Spirit
17	=	the Law and Grace
39	=	Beatrice's number
61	=	Cacciaguida and Beatrice (by *gematria*)
116	=	Justice (by *gematria*)
118	=	Dante Alighieri (by *gematria*)
153	=	God's elect (cf. John 21.11)

Readers may test their reactions to the striking analysis of the occurrences of the word for "love" in *Inf.* 5: in lines 66, 69, and 78, we find three occurrences *(amore, amor, amor)* in the third line of the tercets; in lines 119, 125, and 128 there are also three occurrences, but in the second line of the tercets; in the central group (as has long been recognized), three tercets begin with the word *Amor* (ll. 100, 103, 106). These make a total of nine quotations in the fifth canto of *Inferno* (born out of "his love of Beatrice and . . . his feelings of guilt towards her" [Hardt 1988, 91]), which are flanked by two groups of five quotations in the rest of this *cantica* (from 1.39 to 3.6, and from 11.56 to 30.39): "One cannot overlook that the first appearance of the word is in a 39th verse . . . and the last appearance of the word 'amor' in the *Inferno* is again in the 39th verse of the 30th Canto in which wrongly directed love is once more described. . . . The interval consists of 3993 verses, i.e. of a four figure number which only has the numbers three and nine as factors apart from the 'corner numbers' of the decimal system" (Hardt 1988, 91). Hardt (1995, 77) also sets out to prove that "il Veltro è Dante, il 515 è Dante e il Novenne [*Par.* 17.80–81] è Dante." The author claims that Dante Alighieri's "gemiatric" number (118) is evident in *Inferno*'s structure; in *Purgatorio,* 118 is linked with Beatrice's number (9); and "il *Paradiso* infine si basa esclusivamente sui numeri di Beatrice . . . l'*Inferno* comprende in tutto 4.720 versi, numero che risale al prodotto di 40 x 118. . . . Il *Purgatorio* comprende 4.755 versi in tutto: sono (39 x 118) + 153 righe. Il *Paradiso* invece comprende 4.758 versi, numero che è il prodotto di 2 x 39 x 61" (Hardt 1989, 20–21). As Hardt himself points out, "Naturalmente si può analizzare il numero totale dei versi del *Purgatorio* anche in modo diverso, per esempio in (40 x 118) + 35 = 4755. *Tuttavia questi numeri sono poco plausibili, cioè difficilmente interpretabili. Secondo me, l'interpretazione data sopra . . . .è la più probabile*" (Hardt 1989, 21 n. 33, my emphasis).

35. Dante is reported by a contemporary source to have claimed that the exigencies of rhyme had always remained subservient to his purpose. A lord of language, he bent words to his poetic will: "Io scrittore udii dire a Dante, che mai rima nol trasse a dire altro che quello ch'avea in suo proponimento; ma ch'elli molte e spesse volte facea li vocaboli dire nelle sue rime altro che quello, ch'erano appo gli altri dicitori usati di sprimere" (Ottimo 1827, 183).

36. As Augustine wrote (*In Iohannem* 4, tr. 16.6), the world prepared for humankind by God was transformed into a hostile forest as a result of original sin: "Amara silva mundus hic fuit."

37. For a stimulating approach to the ontological status of the three beasts, see Barański 1987, esp. 90: "È ovvio che, alla luce delle glosse fatte ai primi 63 versi nella prospettiva della *historia* dell'incontro tra Virgilio e Dante-personaggio, anche la 'selva,' il 'monte,' e le tre fiere non sono delle invenzioni poetiche . . . ma delle entità fisicamente reali." Barański rightly insists on "la storicità di stampo biblico di cui [Dante] volesse che godesse la 'lettera' della *Commedia*" (94). Gorni (1995b, 31–32) points out that each of the words *lonza, leone, lupa* begins with an "l" (*El,* God's name in *Par.* 26.136), so that they form an antitrinity: "un segno negato della divinità." They also prefigure the antitrinitarian *Lucifero,* with his three faces on one head.

38. No one has illustrated this more clearly than Barański in his essay "La presenza esegetica di *Inferno* I" (2000a, 106–26).

39. Gilson 1948, 267–68; Auerbach 1959; Hollander 1969; Armour 1981; Charity 1987; Picone 1987; Mazzoni 1997a. For what is often referred to as the "Allegory of the theologians," see above.

40. 1 Tim. 6.10. The Vulgate reads *Radix enim omnium malorum est cupiditas,* where the word *cupiditas,* "greed," is the one used by Dante in affirming (*Mon.* 1.11.11) its total opposition to justice: when all greed has been extinguished, nothing remains contrary to justice. St. Bernard could claim that "the furnace of avarice" was responsible for forging the instruments of Christ's Passion (*Sermones in cantica canticorum,* 39.8), while he insisted that greed and avarice are sisters, both born of pride. It must be remembered that the

connotations of *avaritia* were not restricted to the love of money: indeed, for Aquinas and Vincent of Beauvais (*Speculum doctrinalis* 4.144) avarice was "the insatiable and sinful desire for any [earthly] thing" (cf. *S. Th.* 2.2.118.2).

41. Cassell 1989, 65. For a recent examination of the various hypotheses concerning the three beasts, see Gorni 1995b, 23–55; Hollander and Hollander 2000, 15–16. The early commentators all interpret them to signify lust, pride, and avarice.

42. Pietro Alighieri 2002, 199: "Que fictio corde supradicte potuit allegorice trahi per ipsum auctorem ex verbis illis Phylosophi, dicentis in vii° *Ethicorum: Concupisencis quedam Venerem aiunt, dolose enim, Cyprigene et variam corigiam.*"

43. Barański (2000a, 116) claims that Virgil's arrival on the scene and his speech to Dante mark the moment of transition from *fabula* to "the world of *historia,* and, in particular, of profane *historia.*"

44. Cf. Statius's tribute to Virgil (which underscores the latter's tragic destiny in limbo) in *Purg.* 22.73: "Through you I became a poet, through you a Christian."

45. Readers are reminded that "Vergil" is used to designate the Latin poet, whereas "Virgil" indicates the character in Dante's poem. See above, chapter 1, note 24.

46. Comparetti 1966; Ronconi 1976; Hollander 1983. Servius's commentary on the *Aeneid* first promoted the concept of Vergil's boundless wisdom and knowledge.

47. Macrobius (c. 400) had described Vergil's epic as *sacrum poema* (Schiaffini 1965, 53).

48. For a fuller discussion of the various possibilities inherent in *Inf.* 1.63, see Hollander (1983, 23–79)—who concludes that Virgil was silent "in quanto non ha portato testimonianza alla Verità" (77)—and Cassell 1989, 84–93. Recently, Hollander (2000, 17 n. 63) has accepted the view put forward by Casagrande (1997, 246–48) that *lungo* signifies "vast, extensive" (with a spatial reference); hence, the translation "faint, in the wide silence."

49. Cf. Highet 1957, 59: "The spirit of Vergil, with its solemnity, its devotion to duty, its otherworldliness, and its profound sense of the divine, is reincarnated in the Roman Catholic church and its greatest literary monument, the *Comedy* of Dante."

50. Ferrante (1995, 373) makes the trenchant observation: "Dante's guides on the journey to God are not churchmen, but a pagan poet and a woman."

51. For a fuller treatment of this interpretation of Beatrice as a mirror reflecting God's image *(speculum Dei),* see Mazzoni 1997a; for Beatrice's role as teacher, see Ferrante 1992.

52. Culler 1981, 103: "'Intertextuality' thus has a double focus. On the one hand, it calls our attention to the importance of prior texts, insisting that the autonomy of texts is a misleading notion and that a work has the meaning it does only because certain things have previously been written. Yet in so far as it focuses on intelligibility, on meaning, 'intertextuality' leads us to consider prior texts as contributions to a code which makes possible the various effects of signification. . . . The study of intertextuality is thus not the investigation of sources and influences as traditionally conceived." Chapter 9 expands on Dante's relationship with Vergil; chapter 10 appendix will explore more of the biblical allusions in the *Comedy.*

53. 1 Tim. 6.10 and Aquinas, *S. Th.* 1–2.84.1, resp.

54. Frugoni 1991, 10.

55. Le Goff 1992, 177, who examines "the fundamental dualism" found in the medieval West "between nature and culture, expressed more in terms of an opposition between what was built, cultivated and inhabited (city, castle, village) and what was essentially wild (the sea and the forest, western equivalents of the eastern desert)" (169).

56. For what he terms the reader's retrospective "vistas in memory, dimensions of meaning, that could not lie closer to the heart of Dante's poetry," see Singleton 1965d.

57. See Freccero 1986, 29–54.

58. Letter to William, Patriarch of Jerusalem (quoted in Freccero 1986, 10).

59. Hugh of St. Victor, *Miscellanea* 1.111 (quoted in Mazzoni 1967, 89).

60. See Singleton's classic essay, "In Exitu Israel de Aegypto" (Singleton 1965a, 102–21). The term *figura* was brought back into circulation by Auerbach: "*[Figura]* differs from most of the allegorical forms known to us by the historicity both of the sign and [of] what it signifies . . . in the figural interpretation the fact is subordinated to an interpretation which is fully secured to begin with: the event is enacted according to an ideal model which is a prototype *situated in the future* and thus far only promised" (Auerbach 1959, 54 and 59; my emphasis). Thus, the Old Testament was generically a *figura* of Christ's coming and redemption of humanity. Dante scholars now tend to use the term to signify a *retrospective parallel.* Mazzoni (1997a) has rightly criticized this (at times, useful) misusage. For the centrality of the Exodus story, see Frye 1982, 171–72: "Exodus is the definitive deliverance and the type of all the rest; we may say that mythically the Exodus is the only thing that really happens in the Old Testament."

61. Cf. the angel, who "needs no oars nor any sail but his wings, between shores so distant" (*Purg.* 2.32–33), and Ulysses and his companions, who attempt to turn their oars into wings: "Of our oars we made wings for the mad flight" (*Inf.* 26.125). The whirlwind that destroys Ulysses' craft is also contrasted with the pilgrim's reed of humility by the rhymes of *Inf.* 26.137–41 *(nacque – acque – [com' altrui] – piacque)* and *Purg.* 1.131–35 *(acque – [com' altrui] piacque – rinacque).*

62. Readers are reminded that all biblical quotations are taken from the Latin Vulgate Bible (see above, preface).

63. For the nine invocations in the *Comedy* (*Inf.* 2.7–9, 32.10–12; *Purg.* 1.7–12, 29.37–42; *Par.* 1.13–36, 18.83–88, 22.112–23, 30.97–99, 33.67–75), see Hollander (1980, 31–38), who observes that "the Muses, rising steadily in veiled significance, remain objects of invocation only so long as Dante's intellect is not perfected" (37). See also Ledda 2002, 30–55.

64. Mazzoni (1967, 294–303), quoting Augustine, stresses the river's metaphorical character, highlighted by the phrase *onde 'l mar non ha vanto* (l. 108, rather than Petrocchi's reading *ove 'l mar non ha vanto*); the river represents all the mortal dangers that surround us in life. Freccero (1986, 55–69) identifies the river with Jordan (p. 68: "Bonaventure tells us that Jordan signifies death"); Armour (1983, 176–82) nominates the River Tiber; Ryan (1994) identifies it as the river of cupidity (cf. *Mon.* 3.16.11: "the waves of seductive greed"). The polysemic possibilities of medieval allegory are well illustrated in a work by Richard de Saint Laurent (formerly ascribed to Albert the Great): "And note that Christ is a rose, Mary is a rose, the Church is a rose, the soul of the faithful is a rose" (*De laudibus beatae Mariae Virginis* 12.4.33).

65. For the whole question of the linking of the *fiumana* of *Inf.* 2 with both Edenic rivers, as well as with the *fiumana* of *Paradiso* 30, see Jacoff and Stephany 1989, 51–55. I would add that the chanting of the penitential psalm *Miserere mei, Deus* (Psalm 50, "Have mercy on me, O God"), as indicated by its ninth verse ("Sprinkle me with hyssop and I shall be made clean; wash me, and I shall be whiter than snow"), indicates an essential stage in the pilgrim's progress: first arrested by a river in *Inf.* 2, it is accelerated by a river in *Purg.* 31 (and 32), and finally reaches its goal in the river of light, the *(f)lumen gloriae* of *Par.* 30. Psalm 50 is even more appropriate to Dante's condition, if we accept the argument (Sarolli 1971, 233–46) that the poet discovered in his very name *(Dante, not Durante)* "the *providentiality* of his mission," parallel to that of the prophet Nathan *(Nathan dedit, sive Dantis). Miserere* is in fact the first word uttered by the protagonist *(Inf.* 1.65). Gorni (1995b, 83) points out that there are three occurrences of this Latin word, with its biblical and liturgical connotations, in the poem: *Inf.* 1.65, *Purg.* 5.24, and *Par.* 32.12.

66. Pietro Alighieri 2002, 108–9: "duplex dicitur gratia in nobis hominibus a Deo collata: prima [operans] dicitur motiva et gratuita, a Deo venians . . . Et pro hac prima gratia anagogice, idest spiritualiter loquendo, auctor accipit primam predictam dominam gentilem [Mary] . . . Est et alia Gratia secundaria . . . vocatur hec secunda Gratia cohoperans . . . Et pro ista secundaria accipit auctor hanc secundam dominam sub nominee Lucie, hic et infra in Purgatorio in capitulo viiii° . . ."

67. For the overall structural pattern in *Inf.* 1–2, see Hollander 1990a; 2001, 32. The first section in both cantos describes the pilgrim's mortal danger *(Inf.* 1) and his uncertainty *(Inf.* 2), followed by a simile (1.22–27; 2.37–40); three beasts threaten him *(Inf.* 1) and three ladies intervene on his behalf *(Inf.* 2), followed by a simile (1.55–58; 2.127–30); Virgil outlines the divine plan for his pilgrimage *(Inf.* 1), and the pilgrim's will is firmed *(Inf.* 2). "Dante thus succeeds in giving his two proemial cantos distinct purposes while combining them into an introductory unit" (Hollander 1990a, 97).

68. For an exhaustive structural analysis of the simile contained in *Inf.* 2.127–32— "che . . . ha, come la similitudine del naufrago, un significato complessivo che è centrale alla concezione stessa di tutta l'opera . . . il rapporto salvifico Beatrice-Dante vi si articola nei suoi momenti cruciali, ponendosi insieme come significante del rapporto Cristo-Umanità"—see Ferretti Cuomo 1994 (quote is from p. 141).

69. Cursietti (1997, 216) argues that Guido Cavalcanti was the author of *Il Fiore*. Hence, "Il *Fiore* costituirebbe a questo punto—se abbiamo ragione di scorgere nella deflorazione finale la piú spregiudicata delle parodie del culto mariano, confermato dal sonetto *Una figura della Donna mia*—il documento poetico del 'disdegno'; il passato remoto *ebbe* coinciderebbe con il tempo della composizione del poemetto blasfemo." For Guido's (heretical) denial of the immortality of the individual soul, see Nardi 1983, esp. 106–7. Ardizzone (2002, 46) discusses the combination of Beatrice and Virgil as the object of Guido's disdain: "the 'cui' . . . indicates . . . Beatrice because she embodies not only transcendent love but also the possibility for a new kind of poetry, and the medieval Virgil because he was seen as the poet who implied the survival of the individual soul."

70. The power and concision of this phrase are highlighted by Auerbach (1957, 159): "Is it conceivable that so short and yet incomplete a formulation of such a thought in particular, that so incisive a semantic organization in general, and a *da* used in this

sense, should occur in the work of an earlier vernacular author?" The pilgrim's words are in fact echoed by Virgil, when he tells Cato in *Purg.* 1.52–54: "I have not come on my own *(Da me non venni):* a lady came down from heaven, because of whose entreaties I came to aid this man with my company."

seven.   Dante's other world: Moral order

1. *Inf.* 11.79–84 refers to *three* "dispositions" condemned by God's justice: incontinence, malice, and "mad bestiality." Although some understand the latter term to refer to the sins of violence (with the bestial Minotaur as their guardian), Mazzoni (1972, 219–20) identifies it with those of the treachery or fraud complex. More recently, Cogan (1999, 12) has argued that Dante has taken the term *malizia,* "which in Aristotle refers to vice generally," and restricted it "to one specific sort of vice, injustice." As Hollander (2001, 114) observes, "What was intended by Dante as a clear representation of the moral order of the sins of *Inferno* has become the cause for an endless squabble among those who deal with the question." Instead, Barański (2000a, 137) claims that Virgil is incapable of reconciling the differing definitions of *malitia* given by Aristotle and Cicero, thus displaying the limitations of his pagan intellect; indeed, "Piuttosto che chirarire l'organizzazione dell'*Inferno,* Virgilio mette in evidenza la propria limitatezza intellettuale, culturale e religiosa" (140).

2. Barolini (2000, 86) highlights this coupling as an "anomalous feature of Dante's eschatological scheme that reflects his commitment to contaminating theological culture with classical culture . . . [B]oth the fourth circle of hell and the fifth terrace of purgatory are devoted to avarice *and* prodigality, despite there being no official or for that matter unofficial Church doctrine in support of such an idea." Moreover, Barolini suggests that "the golden mean is captivating to Dante because it signifies for him the ethical ground where Aristotle and Augustine meet. . . . At the foundation of Dante's theology of hell is a theory of human desire that is laid out by Aristotle, parsed by Aquinas, but arguably for Dante most spiritually attuned to Augustine" (102). On a lighter note, Gorni (1995b, 109) speaks of Dante's hell, with its orderly, rational circles and subdivisions as "a kind of Warburg Institute of mortal sin."

3. Cogan (1999, 62) points out that Dante's two categories of heresy—Epicureanism (denial of the soul's immortality) and Photinism (denial of Christ's divine nature)—do not include contemporary heretical movements, such as Catharism; in fact, Dante's selection is "extraordinarily narrow."

4. For an extensive examination of this opposition, see Ferrante 1995.

5. This essential truth is most convincingly illustrated by Ferrante (1984). Cogan (1999) claims that the same ethical criteria are observed throughout the *Comedy:* sins of the will are the worst (fraud, in *Inf.;* in *Purg.,* pride and envy), followed by sins of the irascible appetite (violence, in *Inf.;* in *Purg.,* anger and sloth); sins of the concupiscible appetite are lowest in the scale, because of the sway of passion (incontinence, in *Inf.;* in *Purg.,* avarice, gluttony, and lust). Cogan applies the same moral grid to *Paradiso:* the first three groups of souls that appear to Dante in *Paradiso,* who enjoy the lowest degrees

of beatitude, all suffered from some defect of the will; the irascible appetite governed the actions of those souls who appear in the fourth, fifth, and sixth spheres; the concupiscible appetite (love) ruled the actions of souls appearing in the seventh and eighth spheres; the ninth sphere reveals "a simple and immediate love of God . . . of which only angels are truly capable" (217).

6. This same image was taken up by Machiavelli in a famous section (chap. 18) of *The Prince.*

7. As Barolini (1990b, 337) points out, "Dante is here troping his master fiction: instead of 'living' dead people, we now must contend with the idea of dead living people."

8. The "theologically perverse" idea (that a human creature can be condemned to hell *before* death, thus negating the hope or possibility of conversion) may well have been suggested by John's dramatic account of the Last Supper: "After he [Judas] received the piece of bread, Satan entered into him" (John 13.27; cf. Luke 22.3).

9. The fact that Guido da Montefeltro's spectacular conversion is praised in *Conv.* 4.28.8 and nullified in *Inf.* 27.79–129 may be due to Dante's having acquired some new information (possibly from Riccobaldo da Ferrara's *Historiae*) regarding Guido's last years on earth. However, it is just as likely that Dante, the world judge of the *Comedy,* decided to offer his readers a spectacular example of the corruption of souls and their eventual damnation for which Boniface was responsible. The pope should have acted as Guido's spiritual father and encouraged him in his quest for salvation. Guido's initial reluctance to advise Boniface concerning the use of fraud in the pope's fratricidal "crusade" against the Colonna is finally overcome by the supreme pontiff's reminder (*Inf.* 27.103–4): "I can open and shut heaven, as you know; hence, there are two keys which my predecessor did not value." The two keys are of course a traditional symbol of papal supremacy, harking back to Matthew 16.19, while the claim that the pope is able to open and shut the gates of heaven is based on Christ's words to Peter: "And I will give you the keys of the kingdom of heaven, and whatever you bind on earth shall be bound in heaven, and whatever you loose on earth shall also be loosed in heaven." As we have seen in chapter 5, Dante attacks the all-embracing interpretation of "whatever" *(quodcumque)* in *Mon.* 3.8.7 (see above, chap. 5, "Biblical Precedents"). Guido da Montefeltro's tragedy is an ironic example of this authority abused, as in the closing phrase of Boniface's bull, *Unam Sanctam:* "We declare, define and pronounce that it is altogether necessary to salvation for every human creature to be subject to the Roman pontiff." By submitting to Boniface's wiles, Guido damned himself for all eternity, since he could not repent of the sin before committing it, and therefore could not receive valid absolution, as a diabolical logician gleefully points out in *Inf.* 27.119–20 (thus contradicting Dante's assertion in *Conv.* 3.13.2 that devils cannot philosophize!). Too many critics assert, without proof, that Guido's *first* conversion (when he made his peace with the Church and became a Franciscan) was insincere. On the other hand, the tragic irony in his damnation—the trickster tricked himself—is far greater if, as Dante stated (*Conv.* 4.28.8), Guido had honestly attempted to make his peace with God when he joined the Order of Friars Minor in 1296.

10. As I pointed out many years ago (Scott 1970, 470–71; cf. Scott 1977, 94–95), the *attacco* or opening of *Inf.* 19 signals a radical departure in the poet's narrative strategy.

Whereas in previous cantos the poet-narrator had concentrated on diegetic elements (e.g., *Inf.* 10.1–3: *Ora sen va . . . ;* 18.1–9: *Luogo è in inferno detto Malebolge . . .*), here—for the first time—the nature of the sin is revealed and condemned in the opening *terzine:* "O Simon Magus! o wretched followers who prostitute for gold and silver the things of God, which should be brides of goodness; now, let the trump sound for you who are in the third pouch." See also Blasucci 2000, 380: "un caso a sé è rappresentato dall'esordio al canto XIX."

11. *Folle* is used by Dante to indicate an attitude or an emotion that oversteps certain essential limits imposed on humankind. Its emblematic use is found in the description by Ulysses of his fateful voyage as a *folle volo* or "mad flight," in *Inf.* 26.125 (cf. *Par.* 27.82–83). At the outset, Dante the pilgrim is fearful that his own journey may turn out to be *folle* (*Inf.* 2.35) and thus lead to disaster. For a comparable emotional charge, reminiscent of the prophets of the Old Testament, see, e.g., *Par.* 18.115–36 and *Par.* 27.19–66 (St. Peter's denunciation of his unworthy successors).

12. Quoted in Le Goff 1984, 285, from an appendix to the Second Council of Lyons's constitution *Cum sacrosancta,* promulgated in November 1274. The "birth certificate of Purgatory as a doctrinally defined place" is a letter from Innocent IV to his legate to the Greeks, written just before the pontiff's death and sent on March 6, 1254 (Le Goff 1984, 283–84). As Le Goff notes, "To move from binary [hell/paradise] to tertiary [hell/purgatory/paradise] schemes was to cross a dividing line in the organization of social thought, a step the importance of which Claude Lévi-Strauss has pointed out" (7).

13. Although by definition the souls in purgatory must have confessed their sorrow for having committed any capital sin, there remains "a theological distinction between the meritorious satisfaction enjoined in confession and the type of satisfaction required by divine justice in Purgatory. . . . As acts of justice they [the pains of Purgatory] pay off a debt to God, and as acts of virtue they uproot the causes of sin" (Armour 1983, 68–69).

14. Morgan 1990, 110. The seven capital ("deadly") sins or vices were first formulated from Cassian's list of eight by St. Gregory the Great (c. 540–604). See Gregory's *Moralia in Job* 31.45 (*PL* 76:620 ff.), where *tristitia* takes the place of *accidia.* For a history of the seven capital vices in medieval thought, see Casagrande and Vecchio 2000.

15. See the section in Cogan 1999, 104–19, "The Seven Capital Vices and the Three Appetites: The Underlying Symmetry of Hell and Purgatory." Cogan stresses the fact that "Dante's overall distribution of the vices to the appetites—his association of pride and envy to the will, of anger and sloth to the irascible appetite, and of avarice, gluttony, and lust to the concupiscible appetite—are [*sic*] essentially unique to him" (104).

16. Cogan (1999, 106–7) points out that St. Thomas's definition of pride does "not involve others at all. . . . It is distinctly unconventional to conceive of pride, as related to injustice, but by making this relation, Dante can link pride to the will."

17. Le Goff 1984, 244. Cf. Aquinas, *S. Th.* 3. Suppl. 97.1, ad, 2: "The punishment of purgatory is not intended principally to torment but to purify: hence, it must be inflicted by fire alone which is above all possessed of the power to purify." Paul's remark

that "the fire will test what sort of work each has done" (1 Cor. 3.13) was cited "throughout the Middle Ages, as the biblical basis for Purgatory" (Le Goff 1984, 8).

18. See, e.g., Gautier de Metz's poem *Le miroir du monde,* written c. 1247, in which Eden is described as "enclosed by flaming fire that rises up to heaven" ("il est cloz de feu ardant / qui jusqu'aux nues va flammant" [cited in Delumeau 1994, 68]). It is surprising that Le Goff (1984, 345) should write, "Dante frequently alludes to the one feature that before his time was more or less identified with Purgatory: fire," when Dante's economical use of fire is in fact one of the truly original elements in his description of purgatory.

19. Claire Honess (1998, 39) points out that Bertrand's *contrapasso* "is more perfect than has been generally recognized, for his sin is not simply that of dividing father and son, king and prince, but more particularly of *using his poetry* in order to effect this division. . . . The character of Bertran thus offers Dante-*personaggio* an object lesson which he must bear in mind when he returns to write the *Commedia*."

20. As Cogan (1999, 38) observes, "If Dante has waited until encountering these sowers of discord before making the notion of a *contrapasso* explicit, it is, I believe, so we can hear the echo of Paul in Galatians: 'Quae enim seminaverit homo, haec et metet' (Gal. 6:7). Whatever a man sows, so shall he reap. And this is precisely what Bertram is undergoing."

21. Barański (2000a, 166) contrasts the salvific role of the baptismal font (*Inf.* 19.16–21) and the hole in the rock of hell: "l'opposizione tra una pietra con fessure che salva e un'altra che danna per l'eternità."

22. Cf. the juxtaposition found in Brunetto Latini, *Tresor* (1:71; 62): "Il [St. Peter] fist cheir a la terre Simon Magues ki s'en aloit au ciel contremont . . . Noiron le fist crucefiier le chief desous et les piés contremont .xxxviii. ans aprés la passion Jhesucrist .ii. iors a l'issue du mois de jung . . . "

23. Cf. Cogan 1999, 40: "While it would be proper to say that the souls in Purgatory are being purged by the opposite of their sins, the sinners in Hell are not tormented by a sin's opposites, but by the sin itself."

24. For further analysis, see Ferrante 1993a, 155–56. Moore (1899, 194–95) shows that Dante followed St. Bonaventure rather than Aquinas in his ordering of the seven deadly vices, which was most likely inspired by "the very chapter of that treatise *[Speculum Beatae Mariae Virginis]* from which Dante seems to have derived the idea of making the Blessed Virgin his first example of each successive virtue . . . held up as the antidote to each of the Seven Deadly Sins on the several *Cornici* of Purgatory."

25. "The presence of desire in the pilgrim allows the poet to describe his ascent as a dynamic progression; likewise, the preservation of desire in the blessed allows him to portray them as individual characters" (Pertile 1993b, 155). Psaki (2000, 56) rightly takes Dante scholars to task for the way in which they have desexualized the pilgrim / poet's descriptions of his reactions to Beatrice's celestial beauty: "The language Dante uses to describe the love that we cannot begin to understand, the underlying machine which powers the pilgrim's ascent . . . is the language of bodily, sexual love."

26. For the complex interplay between the properties of the planets, as understood in medieval astrology, and the souls portrayed in each, see Kay 1994. However, Cornish

(2000, 9) does well to point out that the planets and constellations displayed in the *Comedy* "usually have more to do with their being models of beauty, order, and justice. Rather than determining human behavior . . . [they] would seem to serve as standards for moral conduct."

27. The idea that the spots on the moon were caused by variations in the density of the planet's substance is found in a number of medieval texts, including Averroës's *De substantia orbis* and the *Roman de la Rose* (ll. 16840–85). For Dante's metaphysics of light, see Mazzeo 1960, 56–132. The concept that God is light is at the core of the treatise *Of the Celestial Hierarchy,* falsely attributed to Dionysius the Areopagite, which inspired not only Dante (*Par.* 10.115–17) but also Suger at St. Denis and the designers of Gothic cathedrals. The whole of creation stems from and reflects uncreated, divine light, which links together all creatures with love. Robert Grosseteste asserted: "Light is what constitutes the perfection and the beauty of bodily forms" (cited in Duby 1981, 148).

28. For a good analysis of Dante's angelology, see Bemrose 1983, including the important observation that "this precise one-to-one correspondence between heavens and angelic orders seems to be peculiar to Dante. . . . I have not found it in any other Christian writer" (85, n. 20).

29. Franciscan hagiography made use of this concept, e.g., in praise of St. Clare: "Her angelic face was clearer and more beautiful after each prayer, so radiant it was with joy. Truly the gracious Lord . . . so filled his humble spouse with his rays that she gave off the divine light all about her" (cited in Duby 1981, 148).

30. See above, chap. 4, "Astronomy and Angels." In the *Comedy* Dante used the sequence of angelic orders given by Pseudo-Dionysius and most strikingly illustrated in the mosaics of the Florentine Baptistery, his *bel San Giovanni* (cf. *Par.* 28.130–35, where Gregory is described as laughing at his own—and Dante's former—mistake, on his arrival in the Crystalline Heaven).

31. Cf. Auerbach 1946, 483–84, where Joshua (aided by Rahab at Jericho) is recorded as a *figura* of Christ, with the essential proviso that "both terms of a figurative relation are equally true, equally real, equally present: the figurative sense does not destroy the literal, and the literal does not deprive the figurative of its quality of *a real historical event*" (my emphasis).

32. See Aquinas, *S. Th.* 1.2.3.4.5: "human beatitude consists in the knowledge of God, which is an act of the intellect [quae est actus intellectus]." Aquinas quotes (1.2.3.4.5, ad quartum) Augustine, who asserted that only what is known can be loved (*De Trinitate* 10.1–2: "Non enim diligitur nisi cognitum").

33. For the problems surrounding the presence of Siger in Dante's paradise, see the differing conclusions by Gilson (1948, 257–76) and Mazzotta (1993, 112–15). For a good introduction to Joachim and Dante, see Reeves 1980.

34. For Albert's influence on Dante, see Nardi 1944, 1960b, 1983.

35. Just as God gave Solomon more than he had requested (3 Kings 3.13), so—for Dante and his contemporaries—Solomon had been granted the extraordinary privilege of writing the Book of Proverbs (*Conv.* 3.11.12) and Ecclesiastes (*Conv.* 2.10.10) and, above all, of composing the Song of Songs (*Conv.* 2.5.5), which set forth under an alle-

gorical veil of erotic language and imagery the ideal relationship between Christ and his Church, as well as that between Christ and the individual human soul.

36. Those who delight in numerology will be interested to note that twenty-four was the number indicating the twelve prophets plus the twelve apostles; twenty-four elders appear in Revelation 44—these could be interpreted as signifying the universal body of saints or *universitas sanctorum* (Meyer and Suntrup 1987, 680–81).

37. See Scott 1996b, 82–84. The other pagan, Trajan, was saved through the intercession of St. Gregory the Great on account of his act of mercy and justice to a poor widow (*Purg.* 10.73–93).

38. Lawrence (1984, 25–26) makes the point that in fact Benedict "did not envisage anything that could be called a monastic order. . . . But the essence of Benedict's ideas impressed itself upon the Western ascetical tradition. Men came to think of monks as people whose religious life was governed by a written code . . . the 'regular life'—life according to a rule."

39. Southern 1990, 214. The hegemony of monks is well illustrated in the following anecdote: "Abbon of Fleury, the abbot of Saint-Benoît-sur-Loire at the end of the tenth century, went on to refer to Jesus' parable of the sower and the different yields from seed to express the idea of different and precisely defined rewards awaiting Christians in the other world according to their status in this life—in the ratio of 100 for monks, 60 for the clergy, and 30 for the laity" (Miccoli 1990, 54).

40. *The Rule of St. Benedict,* ed. and trans. J. McCann (Westminster, Md.: Newman, 1952), 39.

41. As already noted, astral determinism (the belief that human beings were entirely conditioned by the stars) is specifically rejected in the central (fiftieth) canto of the poem, because it eliminated free will. Nevertheless, it was a part of medieval belief that the stars influenced things, events, and people on earth. Indeed, as Scaglione (1967, 154) has written, "Deep in the medieval man there lay an instinct that compelled him to attribute life and soul to every part of the universe . . . and the astrological view of astral influences on our destinies tended not to dehumanize man . . . but rather to make the whole world anthropomorphic." See *Par.* 2.127–41 and 8.97–148.

42. The striking omission of St. Dominic from the list (cf. *Par.* 12) may be explained not only by the poet's penchant for the number three but also by the fact that the Dominicans followed what was known as the Rule of St. Augustine (Lawrence 1984, 204–5).

43. The significance of the harrowing of hell has been well illustrated by Iannucci in various essays (e.g., Iannucci 1997).

44. For Dante's limbo, see Mazzoni 1965, esp. 69–84; Padoan 1977, 103–24; Pertile 1980; Iannucci 1979–80. Iannucci states: "The structure of medieval depictions of Limbo is comic. . . . Only a man like Dante, who possessed a sense of tragedy as well as comedy, a humanistic sympathy for pagan culture . . . , could overturn this structure" (104–5). For "The Pagans and Grace" in Dante, see Foster (1977, 220–53), who remarks, "A strange isolation from God seems then to be the lot of pagan man, as Dante represents him. . . . [H]e can only expect, after death, an eternity of unsatisfied longing. And the grace that

would save him from this unhappy destiny is not *normally* available to him. The gap between nature and grace has been enlarged to the widest extent consistent with Christian belief" (249).

45. Aquinas, *S. Th.* 3.15.9, resp and ad 1: "then the action undertaken for justice is not to be attributed to anger but to reason" (cf. Matt. 21.12–13). Cf. Hollander 2001, 107: "the protagonist's at times harsh reaction to various sinners . . . is not . . . a sign of his falling into sinful attitudes himself, but proof of his righteous indignation as he learns to hate sin."

46. Cf. Barbi 1941, 318–27; Padoan 1975, 12; Petrocchi 1983, 8.

47. For "the heterogeneity of the ethical values which have been homogenised by means of the apparently rigorous classification" of sins in *Inferno*, see Boyde 2000, 67–69.

e i g h t.   Dante's other world: Topography and demography

1. For a comprehensive list of this visionary literature, see Morgan (1990, 201–33).

2. This change in emphasis is reflected in the various versions of the *Apocalypse of Paul,* which range from the third to the fourteenth centuries: "the twelfth- and thirteenth-century redactions omit to discuss Paradise altogether in favour of an increased concentration on Hell" (Morgan 1990, 172). Cf. Ariès (1981, 97–104): "The people of the early Middle Ages awaited the return of Christ without fear of the Last Judgment. Their conception of the end of time was inspired by the Book of Revelation, and passed silently over the dramatic scene of the Resurrection and the Last Judgment recorded in Saint Matthew . . . The Vulgate used the word *sancti* to refer to those whom modern translators designate by the name of *believers* or *faithful* . . . The saints had nothing to fear from the severity of the Last Judgment . . . The relationship between baptism and resurrection without judgment is clear. Those who have been baptized were assured of resurrection and the eternal salvation it implied . . . In the thirteenth century the apocalyptic inspiration disappeared . . . The idea of judgment was now predominant . . . There is a relationship between this judicial conception of the world and the new idea of life as a biography . . . what had originally been the book of the elect became the book of the damned."

3. It is important to note that in his commentary on Aristotle's *Ethics* (*Expositio* 3, lect. 14), Aquinas declared that it is in fact impossible for the living to "see" or know anything regarding the souls' condition after death ("Ea enim quae pertinent ad *statum animarum post mortem* non sunt visibilia nobis"—the words highlighted are also found in the *Epistle to Cangrande* [8.24], which asserts that the subject of the whole *Comedy,* if taken literally, is precisely "the state of souls after death" *[status animarum post mortem]*). See Mazzoni (1997b, 224–25), who points out that, for Dante, "The veto pronounced by Thomas, the rational Aristotelian, yielded to the visionary experience of contemplatives belonging to the generation of Bernard and the Victorines." Simonelli (2000, 312–13) quotes a passage from Bernard Gui's *Practica officii Inquisitionis heretice pravitatis,* in which those who claim to have knowledge of the state of the souls of the dead *(de statu animarum defunctorum)* are declared guilty of heresy.

4. Corti (1995), while pointing out correspondences between the *Liber scalae* and aspects of Dante's *Paradiso* and Earthly Paradise, claims that it is especially the violence and realism of the infernal punishments in the Islamic text that worked upon the Christian poet's imagination, especially with regard to Dante's *Malebolge*. An English version is now available (Hyatte 1997). Muhammad's vision of the eight heavens is narrated in chapters 12–19; hell is described in chapters 54–60 and 71–72. Segre (1984, 13) points out that the *Liber scalae* offers "the fullest and most organic description of the other world before the *Comedy*." For a useful overview, see Tardiola (2000, 59–67).

5. Hawkins (1999, 269) rightly emphasizes Dante's originality in creating this "blend of topography, sacred history, and belief—a treatment of geography as a kind of scriptural exegesis . . . theology generates landscape, and faith has the power to invent mountains as well as to cast them into the midst of the sea."

6. Le Goff (1984, 454). Nardi (1967, 311–40) demonstrated that some writers linked Eden with purgatory, with the angel's flaming sword (Gen. 3.24) interpreted as a prefiguration of purgatorial fire.

7. The earliest translations of the Bible seemed to give credence to the idea that the Earthly Paradise was situated in the Far East, while many claimed that it was found on the earth's surface just below the moon, so that it remained untouched by the Flood (Delumeau 1994, 57–96).

8. As we saw in chapter 3, in a sonnet composed c. 1304–6 (only a few years or months before the poet began work on the *Comedy*), Dante expressed the view that human will is never free when it comes under love's sway (*Io sono stato con Amore insieme,* ll. 9–11)—a view that he would condemn by placing it in the mouth of the adulterous Francesca da Rimini (*Inf.* 5.103).

9. Hell's vestibule was most likely suggested to the poet by the vestibule to Vergil's Avernus (*Aen.* 6.273) and by the tradition of the "neutral angels" (Nardi 1992, 331–50; Freccero 1986, 110–18).

10. A good analysis of the dreams is found in Cervigni (1986) and in Barański (1989a, 220), who stresses the dreams' function as "mental maps . . . Rather than glimpses of the future, they are sophisticated signs of the pilgrim's emotional, intellectual, and spiritual condition at the moments when they occur . . . They can thus be taken as yardsticks with which to measure his progress." For the thread linking the three dreams to the Earthly Paradise, see Scott (1996b, 129–37).

11. For the way in which Dante inverts the medieval view of Jerusalem in his depiction of hell, see Rose (1991).

12. For further reading, see Lewis (1964), Boyde (1981), and E. Grant (1996).

13. For an analysis of Beatrice's discourse—"one of the marvels of *Paradiso* and one of the most remarkable passages ever written of poetry inspired by ideas"—see Boyde (1981, 138–41).

14. Eco (1986, 49–50) closes these quotations with the judgment "Light was thus the principle of all beauty." See also Took (1984).

15. For the function of light in the *Comedy,* see Mazzeo (1960, 56–132), Brandeis (1960), and Di Pino (1962).

16. About half of the six hundred "are mentioned in simile only, and are not said to be resident in the other world," while of the three hundred souls (excluding "staff" and symbolic figures), "only five classical characters occupy more than fifty lines, compared with twenty-two contemporaries" (Morgan 1990, 55).

17. In *Conv.* 2.14.13, Dante states the common belief that humanity had entered the final stage of history and that the end of the world was to be expected. This must be weighed against the pilgrim's words to Cacciaguida in *Par.* 17.118–20, when he expresses the fear that, if he does not reveal the whole truth of what he has witnessed, he will lose all credit with "those who will call these times ancient."

18. The great nineteenth-century critic Francesco De Sanctis was the first to indicate (in 1870) the link between the *Comedy* and the *Decameron:* "Here you find, in such proximity, the comedy and the anti-comedy, the 'divine comedy' and its parody, the 'human comedy'!" (De Sanctis 1964, 1, 315).

19. "The discovery of the individual was one of the most important cultural developments in the years between 1050 and 1200," at a time when there developed "a new self-consciousness, a capacity for individual evaluation and criticism" (Morris 1991, 158 and 160), which prepared the way for a poetic masterpiece in which the souls of the dead speak to us as individuals.

20. Celestine V (who is not named in *Inf.* 3) is a controversial candidate for this position, as he was canonized in 1313 *(after* Dante had written *Inferno).* However, most scholars agree that the soul mentioned in *Inf.* 3.59–60 must be that of a contemporary (the pilgrim "sees" and "recognizes" him: this would seem to exclude candidates such as Esau, Pontius Pilate, and Diocletian). The best study of the question remains that by Padoan (1977, 64–102). See also Simonelli (1993, 39–58).

21. Cf. Morgan (1990, 79–82), who places Sordello among the commoners, although he was in fact a nobleman, described by Charles of Anjou as a faithful knight of the royal household *(miles dilectus familiaris et fidelis noster)* in a deed of March 1269 that assigned several castles in the Abruzzi to Sordello and his heirs.

22. In the early Church, "it was agreed that only the holy martyrs and confessors had the privilege of enjoying the beatific vision immediately after their death" (Ariès 1981, 147). St. Bernard was one of the theologians who insisted that souls could not enjoy the beatific vision until they were reunited with their bodies at the end of time. The controversy continued until some years after Dante's death, when it became particularly intense as a result of John XXII's assertion (in 1331) that the elect will be granted full vision of the divine essence only after the resurrection of the body. These ideas were formally refuted by Benedict XII in *Benedictus Deus* in 1336 (Bynum 1995, 164 and 283–85).

23. Morgan (1990, 78) lists eighty-four "true classical characters," but I include Minos and Phlegyas, both discounted by Morgan "as being to some extent symbolic."

24. On the paradoxical salvation of Cato and Ripheus, the reader may wish to consult Scott (1996b, 69–84).

25. All the blessed in heaven are saints. A canonized saint is one who has been declared by the pope as sharing in eternal glory and for whom a public cult has been instituted throughout the Church. A number of future saints had not been canonized

when the poem was written: Thomas Aquinas was canonized in 1323, two years after the poet's death; his master, Albert the Great, only in 1931; despite a centuries-old controversy regarding his status as a Christian, Boethius was finally canonized in 1884; Peter Damian—never formally canonized—was venerated as a saint from the time of his death in 1072 and declared a Doctor of the Church by Leo XII in 1828.

26. For "The Birth of the Intellectuals," see Le Goff (1993, 5–64).

nine.   Dante and classical antiquity

1. Comprehensive studies of this essential aspect of Dante's literary work and personality include those by Moore (1896), Renucci (1954), Paratore (1968, 25–126), Jacoff and Schnapp (1991), and Brownlee (1993). See also Pasquini (2001, 73–121).

2. Cogan has shown that "despite Nardi's efforts to convince us that Albert the Great was Dante's preferred philosophical source, it is Aquinas whom Dante chooses as the principal spokesman for theology in the *Paradiso* . . ." (1999, xxiii, and cf., e.g., 321 n. 48: "the association of justice with the will is not part of the earlier medieval Aristotelian tradition . . . Aquinas [is] the first commentator definitively to assign justice as the virtue of the will . . .").

3. A good selection of the 219 errors condemned is to be found in Peters (1980, 223–30).

4. For Remigio de' Girolami, a student of Aquinas and a leading intellectual figure and preacher at Santa Maria Novella during Dante's formative years, see Davis (1984, 198–223).

5. See Boyde (1993) for the influence of Aristotelian epistemology, ethics, and physics on Dante's writings.

6. Readers are reminded that Vergil refers to the Roman poet, while Virgil signifies Dante's guide in *Inferno* and *Purgatorio*.

7. Despite the obvious differences, the following description may make us aware of the stylistic affinities between Italy's two greatest poets: "The style of the poem [the *Aeneid*] is the supreme triumph of the Latin language: richly melodious, supple, and suggestive in a way less characteristic of ancient than of modern poetry" (Griffin 1992, 126).

8. See, e.g., Hollander (1983, 1988, 1989), who illustrates "a series of devaluations of Virgil," while warning of the pitfall of underestimating the "enormous debt of gratitude and affection" felt by Dante for his poetic master and guide (1988, 25).

9. Dante's fiction that, shortly after his death, Virgil had been summoned by the Thessalian sorceress Erichtho (who, in Lucan's *Pharsalia*, 6.507–830, conjured up the spirit of a dead soldier in order to discover the outcome of the impending battle) has proved to be a double-edged qualification, for at times it has been taken to indicate that Dante subscribed to the legend that Vergil was a magician (*solennissimo astrolago*, as Boccaccio terms him in his gloss to *Inf.* 1.70). Nevertheless, as Domenico Consoli points out (*ED* 5.1031), Dante's Virgil is merely the passive victim in that episode: "And that is not sufficient to turn him into a magician." The *Comedy*'s attempt to clear Vergil of such charges has similarly backfired, since—as Robert Hollander has conclusively

demonstrated—in *Inf.* 20, Dante's Virgil contradicts Vergil's history of the foundation of Mantua related by "prophetic Manto" (*Aen.* 10.198–203), in a critical revision of Vergil's text "which relegates the author of the greatest pagan epic to the role of censor of his own lies" (Hollander 1991, 81). As Barolini (1984, 219) points out, if Dante had wanted to distance his Virgil "from the necromancer of medieval legend, the best course would surely have been . . . not to feed [such legends] by inventing a posthumous connection between the sage and so infamous a practitioner of the black arts as Erichtho." For those legends, see Comparetti (1966) and Spargo (1934).

10. Dante would surely have agreed with Tertullian that Vergil was *anima natu-raliter Christiana* (Kennedy 1997, 39).

11. For an excellent analysis of the "*veltro*" prophecy and its reverberations in Dante scholarship, see Davis (1976b).

12. Cf. *Mon.* 3.4.14: "If man had remained in the state of innocence in which he was made by God, he would have had no need for such guidance, for these directive powers are remedies for the infirmity of sin."

13. Vergil's *Eclogue* 4.6 is also quoted in *Mon.* 1.11.1, where its sole purpose is to demonstrate that Justice is most necessary to humanity's well-being. In the Latin treatise, no mention is made of Christ's coming, while the Vergilian line is correctly glossed: "Justice was called 'the Virgin' and also 'Astraea'; and the best of times were called 'Saturn's realms,' also known as 'the Golden Age.'" This supports Dante's main point that "for the best ordering of the world there needs to be a Monarchy or Empire" (1.11.2). The very same reference to the Virgin and Saturn's realms was used by Dante to greet the coming of the emperor Henry VII in April 1311, when "many, anticipating what they longed for in their rejoicing, chanted with Vergil of the Golden Age and the Virgin's return" (*Ep.* 7.1.6).

14. Francesco da Buti's gloss to this passage in *Purg.* 22 reads: "li Autori usano l'altrui autorità arrecarle a loro sentenzia quando commodamente vi si possano arrecare, non ostante che colui che l'ha ditta l'abbia posta in altra sentenzia" (Dartmouth Dante Database). Pompeo Venturi, in 1732, would seem to be the first commentator to assert that Dante had misunderstood Vergil's meaning, possibly by mistaking the meaning of *sacra* and thus taking *sacra fames* to indicate a virtue.

15. Most recent commentators (e.g., Sapegno, Giacalone, Bosco-Reggio, Chiavacci Leonardi) interpret *intesi* as meaning "I meditated on" (e.g., Sapegno, Bosco-Reggio) or "I turned my attention to" (e.g., Giacalone, Chiavacci Leonardi). However, I believe that the context of *Purg.* 22.38 suggests that Statius *understood* the relevance of Vergil's words to his own condition. In other words, Statius carried out a personal operation like that mentioned in *Conv.* 2.12.10, whereby the "fictitious word" *(parola fittizia)* has been transformed from its apparent or superficial meaning *(quello ch'ella suona)* into its deeper meaning *(in quello ch'ella 'ntende)*. Cf. *Conv.* 2.7.3: "So, when you say that a man 'lives,' you must understand that he makes use of his reason" *(Onde, quando si dice l'uomo vivere, si dee* intendere *l'uomo usare la ragione* [my emphasis]). Statius's *io intesi* therefore refers to his own, personal interpretation of Vergil's text. Benvenuto da Imola refers to Statius's *amplification* of Vergil's words condemning *intemperantiam divitiarum* to include both spending and hoarding *(Statius largius interpretatur istud dictum . . . tam in*

dando quam in retinendo). We may also note that, in *Par.* 4.43–45, Holy Scripture is said to attribute hands and feet to God, but to understand something else by these physical attributes, which point to a deeper, spiritual/allegorical meaning: *e altro intende.* Dante's son Pietro states that Statius's conversion from prodigality was due especially to the way in which he *understood* Vergil's words (*maxime* intellectis *illis verbis, quae dicit Virgilius* [my emphasis]).

16. For example, the aptly named chapter on "Travisamenti danteschi dell'*Eneide*" in Hollander (1983, 81–115; also 1985, 1989, 1991). Cf. Schnapp 1986 and 1991c. As Hawkins (1999, 124) concludes, "We can say that the poet of the *Commedia* insists on harrowing the *Aeneid,* drawing it up into the biblical realm of his own imagination . . ."

17. See Teodolinda Barolini's vigorous debate (1990a) with Allan Mowbray, as well as her incisive observation that "it is an essential condition of his [Virgil's] existence in the poem that he shall also cease to exist: his presence is predicated on his talent for absence" (1984, 200). Cf. Schnapp (1991c, 156): "It is evident that Dante's epic is in a very real sense founded on the damnation of his literary forefather."

18. For Vergil the *vates* of the empire, see Davis (1957, 100 ff.). For Vergil as representing the summit as well as the limitations of ancient humanism, see Ryan (1982) and Armour (1986).

19. Toynbee (1968, 483) extends the list to include the *Ars amatoria* and the *Heroides;* Paratore (1976a, 225–36) includes the *Fasti* and—possibly—the *Tristia* (for which, see n. 20).

20. See Picone (1999, 10): "Nella *Commedia* Dante combina questa visione cristiana dell'esilio . . . con la concezione elaborata da Ovidio nei *Tristia* . . . egli proietta la *fictio* ovidiana, pur cosí intrisa di verità psicologica, nella prospettiva della *veritas* religiosa attestata nella Bibbia . . ." In the same study, Picone argues convincingly that Dante "sul modello (oseremmo dire) esclusivamente dei *Tristia,* ha 'inventato' il luogo per antonomasia dell'esilio cristiano: il lago gelato di Cocito . . . Dante, creatore del Cocito infernale, ha superato Ovidio descrittore del Danubio e del Mar Nero gelati" (18–19).

21. I take my cue from the "hypothesis" mentioned in Michelangelo Picone's "L'Ovidio di Dante": "Se . . . Dante, invece di un titolo 'generico' come *commedia,* avesse scelto per il suo *magnum opus* un titolo giustificativo della sua *fabula* diegetica, avrebbe verosimilmente preferito quello di 'metamorfosi cristiane' . . . " (Picone 1993, 134).

22. "Having fallen asleep under the enchantment of Ovid, Dante wakes to the sound of Scripture calling him from death to life" (Hawkins 1985, 132).

23. The semantic range of the epithet *novo/nuovo* extends from the positive connotations of Dante's *Vita Nova* (cf. St. Paul's "New Man," reborn to love in Justice and Truth, Eph. 4.24) to these terrifyingly unnatural "new roots" of Pier della Vigna's bush and the monstrously corrupt "new beast" *(nova belva)* of *Purg.* 32.160.

24. See also Curtius (1953, 162–65) on the topos "Outdoing." Among many examples in classical and medieval verse, he cites Claudian's *Taceat superata vetustas* (Let antiquity, now surpassed, be silent). Cf. *Inf.* 25.94–102 *(Taccia Lucano . . . Taccia di Cadmo e d'Aretusa Ovidio),* preceded by *Inf.* 24.85 *(Piú non si vanti Libia con sua rena).* "Dante shows why Ovid's style was too thin to hide truly substantive transformations like the Incarnation or Eucharist within its folds" (Ginsberg 1999, 18).

25. *Purg.* 28.139–44: "*Quelli ch'anticamente poetaro / l'età de l'oro e suo stato felice, / forse in Parnaso esto loco sognaro. / Qui fu innocente l'umana radice; / qui primavera sempre e ogne frutto; / nettare è questo di che ciascun dice.*"

26. Ovid, *Metamorphoses,* with an English translation by Frank Justus Miller, 3rd ed., revised by G. P. Goold (Cambridge, Mass.: Harvard University Press; London: Heinemann, 1977), 3.

27. Dante's hope that he will one day return to Florence *as a poet,* "with a different voice, with a different fleece *[con altro vello]*" (*Par.* 25.7), uses two crucial terms: *poeta* and *vello* (fleece), indicative of the Christian poet's new prophetic role (Sarolli 1971, 393–405) and possibly alluding to John the Baptist, the greatest of the prophets and Florence's patron saint, whose garment of camel hair is mentioned in both Matt. 3.4 and Mark 1.6.

28. A recent study stresses the fact that, while Ovid was "a curator of the fallen world in all its hideous permutations . . . the Ovidian persona, the writer as Ovid, becomes a kind of model for Dante—the poet of the new and unprecedented, of *trasumanare*" (Hawkins 1999, 148 and 155).

29. For the most compelling analysis of the exchange between the pilgrim and Bonagiunta (*Purg.* 24.49–92), see Calenda (1998).

30. In a fascinating essay, Schnapp (1991b, 219–20) suggests that "in Ovid's spirituality, with its opening towards woman and the world of love, Dante may have perceived a pre-Christian model for his own insistence upon the decisive importance of feminine and, especially, *maternal* mediation in overcoming the central threats of the epic world."

31. The words cited are taken from Hollander and Rossi (1986, 79 n. 22), who illustrate "Dante's consciously subversive reading of the major Roman martial epic which delineates republican themes, the *Pharsalia* . . . It is indeed precisely Dante's vision of a divine providence operant in history which he sees as filling the void he finds where God should be in Lucan . . ."

32. For a more comprehensive discussion of the reasons why Dante placed Cato in purgatory, with detailed references, see Scott (1996b, 69–84).

33. *Phars.* 2.439–46. All quotations are taken from Lucan, *The Civil War,* with an English translation by J. D. Duff (London: Heinemann; Cambridge, Mass.: Harvard University Press, 1962).

34. The griffin pulling the chariot in the Earthly Paradise has traditionally been seen as a symbol representing Christ. For the present interpretation, based on the emperor's dual nature (Kantorowicz 1957), see Armour (1989) and Scott (1996b, 187–89; 1999, 100–103).

35. See: Lucain, *La Guerre civile,* texte établi et traduit par A. Bourgery, vol. 1 (Paris, 1926), 45. The parallel with Christ is reinforced by the description of "the inflexible rule of austere Cato . . . to give his life for his country, to believe that he was born to serve the whole world and not himself" (*Phars.* 2.380–83; cf. *Conv.* 4.27.3).

36. Wilson (1997) points out that none of the prophets (Nathan, David, Joachim of Fiore) utters a prophecy in the *Comedy,* while knowledge of the future is granted to a damned soul (e.g., Vanni Fucci, *Inf.* 24.140–51): "Clearly knowledge of the future is not

granted as any special favour [in Dante's poem], but is instead an attendant feature of the afterlife state" (21).

37. For Dante's rejection of the traditional genres in his *Comedy,* see Barański (1995a; 1995b; 1996, 15–77).

38. "Statius, rising from his purgation to ascend to heaven (*Purg.* XXI, 7–10) has long been understood to play the role of a 'postfigured' resurrected Christ" (Hollander 2001, 102–3). For the Christological significance of the mountainquake (*Purg.* 20.127–41, indicating that Statius, having fulfilled the necessary period of purgation, is free to ascend to paradise), see Scott (1996a).

39. The *Thebaid* is quoted according to: *Statius,* with an English translation by J. H. Mozley, 2 vols. (Cambridge, Mass.: Harvard University Press; London: Heinemann, 1982). For the parallel between the altar to Clementia and the one before which St. Paul converted many pagans, see Padoan (1977, 126–27).

40. Lewis (1957, 139). *Thebaid* 10.628–30: "Now, tell who fired the youth with joy in a noble death *(pulchrae mortis)*—for never without heaven's aid is this mind given to men."

41. For explications of Statius's "lecture," see: Nardi (1960a, 9–68), Gilson (1967), Russo (1971, 103–8), and Barański (2001).

42. Passages that may have suggested this perilous voyage to Dante include Ovid, *Met.* 14.435–40 (where Ulysses and his companions are described as *tardi* [cf. *Inf.* 26.106], and l. 439 might well indicate the dangers of a hostile element *[saevi . . . pericula ponti];* Cicero, *De officiis* 3.26.99 ("for him it was better to battle not only with the enemy but also with the waves, as he did . . ."); Servius's commentary to Vergil; Seneca, *Epistulae morales* 88, *De brevitate vitae* 13.2–3. A medieval legend ascribed the foundation of Lisbon *(Ulixbona)* to Ulysses. For a fuller discussion of the whole episode, see Scott (1971), Hollander and Stull (1997), and Boyde (2000, 231–72).

43. Readers will note the diegetic rarity of the combination of past and present in *Allor mi* dolsi *e ora mi* ridoglio / *quando drizzo la mente a ciò ch'io vidi, e più lo 'ngegno affreno ch'i' non soglio (Inf.* 26. 19–21: "Then I *grieved,* and now I *grieve* once more, when I turn my mind to what I saw, and I rein in my intellect more than is my custom; my emphasis). Cf. *Inf.* 4.119–20.

44. Freccero (1986, 15–24) connects the "wingèd oarage" of Ulysses' craft with Neoplatonic imagery symbolizing "the flight of the soul to the absolute" and its inevitable failure when inspired by "philosophical pride." Shankland (1977) points to Dante's family name, Alighieri/Alaghieri, and its significance as "wing-bearer" in this context.

45. Roman writers delighted in contrasting Roman forthrightness in word and deed to the subtlety and wiliness of the Greeks. Cato's great-grandfather, Marcus Porcius Cato (234–149 B.C.E.), tried to combat social and political corruption in Rome "by removing what seemed to him the root of the evil, that is, the influence of Greece" (Rostovtzeff 1960, 95).

46. Dante's profound conviction is highlighted by the fact that, for once, he immediately agrees with the view implied in Charles Martel's leading question: " 'Now, tell me: would it be worse for man on earth, if he were not a citizen?' 'Yes,' I replied; 'and

here I do not ask for any explanation'" (*Par.* 8.115–17). Cf. *Conv.* 4.4.1: "The Philosopher [Aristotle] says that man is by nature a social animal *(compagnevole animale),*" requiring a family, a city, a state, and an empire to satisfy all his needs.

47. For legends about Alexander current in the Middle Ages, see Cary (1956). Already in antiquity, Seneca (*Epistulae morales* 94.62–63) denounced Alexander's hubris in going "beyond the ocean and the sun" *(it tamen ultra oceanum solemque).*

48. *S. Th.* 2.2.55.4, ad 2 (translation by the Fathers of the English Dominican Province; hypertext version).

49. Barolini (1992, 130), and "Ulysses, Geryon, and the Aeronautics of Narrative Transition" (ibid., 48–73).

50. For Dante's attitude toward his children, Umberto Bosco points out that, in June 1302, the Florentine authorities decided to appoint an official whose task it was to expel from the city "the male children and grandchildren and male descendants on the male side . . . and even . . . wives" of exiles; so that "from the very first moment, Dante knew that his behavior would have repercussions on his family" (Bosco 1966, 177).

51. Bolgar (1964, 191–92).

52. Nardi (1992, 137–39). The allusion is to *Purg.* 29.37–42: "O sacrosanct Virgins . . . Now . . . Urania must help me with her choir to put in verses things hard to conceive" *(forti cose a pensar mettere in versi).*

t e n.   The poet of the *Comedy*

1. Hence, Dante points out, Homer was not translated into Latin and the verses of the Psalms in Greek and Latin translations are now "without sweetness of music and harmony" (*Conv.* 1.7.14–15; cf. Jerome, *Interpretatio Chronicorum Eusebi, PL* 27, 223). The importance of a poem's overall harmony, its *dulcedo* or *dolcezza* (sweetness), is attested in *DVE* 2.13.4 and implied in the definition of poetry as an artifact composed of both rhetoric and music *(DVE* 2.4.2: *fictio rhetorica musicaque poita).* A poem's "music" is inevitably lost in any translation. Seriani (2001) provides a useful guide to specific characteristics and anomalies of the language used by Italian poets.

2. On the poet's belief in the worth of poetic and sacred eloquence, see Botterill (1994a, 242–53, and 1996b). In my discussion of the phonic effects of Dante's verse, I am aware that some critics have exaggerated the significance or emotive qualities of certain sounds. This tendency has been sharply corrected by, e.g., Beccaria (1975) and Robey (2000b, 161: "There is little evidence of vowel sounds being used systematically by Dante for expressive purposes," although Robey also finds that "the slightly higher incidence of accented odd syllables at the end of *Inferno* is like the higher incidence of assonances in *o* in the same *cantica:* it shows a slight, but only a slight tendency for the feature to be connected with a particular kind of situation or feeling" [160]). It should be obvious that no sound has any significance *per se.* However, poetry achieves its effect by a combination of sounds, connotations, and rhythm (including repetition): that effect has been described above as "synergetic," since the whole is not only greater than its parts but it is in fact

impossible to isolate any of these parts, except for purposes of critical or theoretical analysis, such as the one attempted in the present chapter.

3. "Intellectual light, full of love; Love of true good, full of joy; Joy that transcends all sweetness." Although, as noted, the text of the *Comedy* is quoted as given by Petrocchi, anyone concerned with the *sound* as well as the linguistic forms of Dante's language must now be ready to take into account the results of the fundamental textual research carried out by Federico Sanguineti for his edition of the *Comedy* (Sanguineti 2001; for a critical analysis of this edition, see Mengaldo 2001 and Segre 2002). For obvious reasons, quotes in this chapter will be in Italian; some translations are provided where they have been thought useful.

4. Dante's example remains unique. Petrarch's overwhelming influence (not only on Italian poets but on European poets in general) narrowed the lexical range of lyric and epic poetry to exclude all but the "noblest" or "purest" words and forms. In his *Prose della volgar lingua* of 1525 (2.20), the highly influential Renaissance poet and linguistic legislator Pietro Bembo deplored Dante's use of coarse language and compared the *Comedy* to a beautiful cornfield full of weeds and chaff.

5. For the phenomenon of syntactic doubling of consonants in spoken Italian, see Lepschy and Lepschy (1988, 67–69).

6. Fasani (1992, 20–21) gives the following "rules" for the *Comedy* (where Dante's practice differs from that displayed in his *Rime*): "Se i vocaboli *e, è, a, ha, o, ho,* costituiti da un'unica vocale, s'incontrano con una vocale seguente, vengono a formare: a) di regola una sillaba sola, se questa vocale è *i;* b) sempre due sillabe, se questa vocale è diversa da *i.* 2) Se una parola che finisce col dittongo discendente, o accentato sulla prima vocale, s'incontra con una vocale seguente, ne risultano due sillabe. Questo dittongo, però, è di due specie: a) con la seconda vocale più aperta, e allora abbiamo due soluzioni . . . *Io / era* (*Inf.* 2.52) e separazione sillabica in mezzo al dittongo . . . se la prossima vocale è atona: *io avea = i /oa / vea* (*Par.* 27.79); b) con la seconda vocale più chiusa, dove il dittongo . . . dovrebbe sempre formare una sillaba per sé: *alzai / al sole* (*Purg.* 4.56) come *guardai / in alto* (*Inf.* 1.16). 3) Se la vocale tonica e finale di una parola s'incontra con una vocale sia tonica sia atona, fa con essa due sillabe." For no. 3 (ibid., 24): "Per dare un esempio, *miei* non si fonde mai, nella *Commedia,* con la vocale seguente," whereas it does in Petrarch. Cf. Dante's *Or t'ammonisco, perch'io t'ho allevata* (where the eighth syllable is formed by *t'hoal-* [*Donne ch'avete,* l. 59]) and his usual practice in the *Comedy* (e.g., *Inf.* 28.55; *Par.* 26.49: *Ma dí / ancor se tu senti altre corde.* See also Robey (2000a).

7. Readers will be aware that the phonetic outcome in Italian verbs of the first person of the imperfect is *-a (era),* which was gradually replaced by the distinctive *-o* ending *(ero),* although the latter did not win the day completely until the appearance of Manzoni's masterpiece, *I promessi sposi,* in the nineteenth century. For Fasani (1992, 55–56) there are only three cases of diaeresis with *io* in the *Comedy,* since he rejects Casella's and Petrocchi's reading *cosí vid'io la gloriosa rota* (*Par.* 10.145). Instead, he claims that *ri* followed by a stressed vowel always scans as two syllables, and the line should be read thus: *cosí vid'io la glorïosa rota.* It is interesting to note that the adjective *pio* (with seven occurrences) always counts as two syllables (most probably because it recalls Vergil's

hero, *pius Aeneas*). Cf. *Purg.* 19.106, with its diaeresis *(La mia conversïone, omè!, fu tarda)*, and *Inf.* 19.116 *(non la tua conversion, ma quella dote),* where the tardiness of Bonconte da Montefeltro's conversion is "echoed" in the stretching of the word into five syllables *(conversïone)* instead of the usual four (or even three, as in the second example).

   8. In this canto, there are three examples of various effects created by a syntactical pause after the seventh syllable, creating a *quaternario* or subsidiary unit of four syllables (preceded by a stress on the sixth syllable): *"S'egli han quell'arte,"* disse, *"male appresa,"* (*Inf.* 10.77), *El par che voi veggiate, se ben odo,* (l. 97), *poeta volsi i passi, ripensando* (l. 122).

   9. As we have seen, caesura (a marked pause between words within the line of verse) is used to break up the metrical pattern and thus achieve variety. It is especially prevalent in dialogue: *e disse:—Or ha bisogno il tuo fedele* (*Inf.* 2.98); *Di subito drizzato gridò: "Come? / dicesti 'elli ebbe'? non viv' elli ancora? . . ."* (*Inf.* 10.67–68); with a double caesura in *Par.* 31.95: *"perfettamente," disse, "il tuo cammino."*

   10. De Mauro (2000) demonstrates that 86 percent of Dante's lexis is composed of words still used by Italians in everyday life.

   11. *DVE* 2.7.4–5 (and see chapter 2).

   12. Russo (1995, 184–85): "Un simile intarsio di suoni in rima non è riscontrabile in nessun altro punto della *Commedia.* L'espressività tonale punta qui chiaramente sui gruppi fonematici *-nt(nd)* e *ett(et)*; ad essa si aggiungono 'allitterazioni' e 'ripetizioni' ('tanto-tanto,' 'già-già-già,' 'organar-Or-or-cor-ancor-organo,' 'Ma-animal,' 'fé-fé,' ecc.); l''antinomia concettuale' di v. 63 ('che piú savio di te fé già errante'), la 'figura etimologica' ai vv. 71–72 ('. . . e spira / spirito novo'), le rime 'ricche' tra i vv. 59 e 63 ('generante-errante'), l' 'apostrofe' ai vv. 67 ss. ('Apri a la verità che viene il petto'), che include la formula 'Sappi che' dal latino filosofico *Scias quod,* ecc." See also Russo 1971, esp. 141–58.

   13. Not surprisingly, Virgil introduces himself with a Latin phrase in the very first canto of the poem (Nacqui *sub Iulio, Inf.* 1.70); Ser Brunetto Latini speaks of those who left Fiesole for Florence "ab *antico*" (*Inf.* 15.62); St. Thomas describes St. Francis's marriage to Lady Poverty (*et coram patre* le si fece unito, *Par.* 11.62); and *Beatrix loquax* displays her knowledge of the Gospels (John 16.16) in *Purg.* 33.10–12 *(Modicum, et non videbitis me; / et iterum,* sorelle mie dilette, */ modicum, et vos videbitis me).* Ulysses' highly rhetorical speech to Virgil is preceded by *in questa forma lui parlare* audivi (*Inf.* 26.78); the chariot symbolizing the Church Militant is *un carro . . .* trïunfale *(Purg.* 29.107 and 32.119: *trïunfal veiculo).* The heavenly "feast" is "quelle *dape*" *(Par.* 23.43).

   14. The ineffability topos is repeated in *Par.* 1.5–9, 10.43–48, 18.7–12, 23.55–63, 30.16–33, 31.133–38, 33.106–8, and 121–23.

   15. In this linguistic eclecticism, Dante follows a poetic usage established by his Provençal predecessors, who drew upon "doppie forme provinciali e dialettali, come p. es. *tener* e *tenir, luenh* e *lonh*" (Rohlfs 1990, 135).

   16. In Dante's prose works, *lo* is the dominant form: see Ambrosini (1978, 135), "*Lo*, dominatore incontrastato nella tradizione lirica, appare, cosí, tipico della prosa, per modesta che ne fosse la levatura culturale; assente in libri di conti [toscani] . . . *lo* suonava piú solenne di *il* . . ."

17. Brunetto Latini judged the French language to be "the most delightful" (*Tresor* 1.1.7). As already mentioned in chapter 2, in *DVE* 1.10.2, Dante recognized the supremacy of French prose and the sweetness and perfection of poetry written in Provençal *(langue d'oc, cella de Lemosin)*.

18. The manuscript tradition of Dante's text offers a wide variety of readings. However, as P. V. Mengaldo points out (*ED* 4.116), the rhyme-words offer a guarantee of authenticity, apparently with two morphological errors: *cobrire* (l. 141) and *deman* (l. 144). Moreover, a number of scholars have pointed out that *escalina* (l. 146) does not exist in Provençal: Fasani (1992, 65) and Chiavacci Leonardi (1994, 788) both prefer the reading *ses dol e ses calina* (without pain and without heat), found in three authoritative manuscripts. Folena (1977, 507) puts forward the version *que us guida al som ses freg e ses calina* (that it [God] may guide you to the summit without cold and without heat).

19. *Mei si noma, francescamente, il semplice Lombardo* may well be a verbal sidewinder at the French custom of referring to moneylenders or usurers as *Lombarts* (cf. Boccaccio, *Decameron* 1.1, where the Burgundians refer to Ser Ciapelletto and his Tuscan associates as "these Lombard dogs"). *Alluminare . . . in Parisi* (Fr. *enluminer*, often rendered as *illuminare* in Italian), together with the reference to the *Vico de li Strami (Par.* 10.137; the Rue du Fouarre in Paris, with its celebrated schools of philosophy), has been offered as evidence that Dante visited Paris (as was claimed, e.g., by Villani, Boccaccio, Buti, and Benvenuto: cf. Petrocchi 1983, 103).

20. In notes for a lecture, Gerard Manley Hopkins highlighted two elements "in the beauty rhyme has to the mind, the likeness or sameness of sound and the unlikeness or difference of meaning" (cited by Steele 1999, 301).

21. "A large proportion of the forms used in rhyme position in the *Commedia* do not appear at all in other positions in the line—substantially more . . . than the comparable figures for later poets such as Pulci, Ariosto, and Tasso, as well as for Dante's own lyric poetry" (Robey 2000c, 809; cf. Robey 2000b, 64: "a total of 5320 tokens, or well over a third of the rhyme-words in the poem"). Equally striking is the fact that this feature is spread more or less evenly across the three *cantiche*, with 2420 tokens *(Inf.);* 2376 *(Purg.);* 2428 *(Par.).* The neologism mentioned above *(s'inzaffira)* points to the two occurrences of *zaffiro* in the poem: in both cases *(Purg.* 1.13; *Par.* 23.101) it appears in the rhyming position. In Petrarch, it occurs only once, indicating the color and beauty of Laura's eyes *(RVF* 325.17: *d'avorio uscio, et fenestre di zaffiro).* As Afribo (2002) points out, in both this context (poems written after Laura's death) and in *Par.* 23.97–102 one finds a sequence of rhymes marked by strong alliteration and the description of a woman in heaven—further evidence of Dante's influence on Petrarch, despite the latter's reluctance to reveal the role played by the author of the *Comedy* and the *rime petrose* in his own vernacular poetry.

22. Of the 202 words that occur only once in the *Comedy*, no fewer than 173 are found in the rhyming position (Rohlfs 1990, 134). As we noted in chapter 6, Andrea Lancia tells us (regarding the use of *tempio* in *Inf.* 10.87) that he heard Dante claim that no rhyme had ever obliged him to write anything but what he intended; moreover, he had frequently made words signify things beyond the semantic range they held in the

writings of other poets (Ottimo 1827, 1, 183). Dante's innovations in the multiplicity and polyphony of rhymes introduced into his *rime petrose* and the *Comedy* are analyzed and tabulated by Afribo (2002). A striking difference is found in the rhymes ending in vowel + consonant + vowel *(rime vocaliche),* which were favored by Duecento poets: these make up 63 percent of the total rhymes in Guittone's verse and 75 percent of those found in the *Vita Nova* poems (where they contribute to the "sweet" harmonies of the *dolci rime d'amore*). In Dante's *rime petrose,* however, such rhymes make up only 34 percent of the total; and, in the *Comedy,* just 48 percent (Afribo, 2002, 7–8). With regard to *rime consonantiche,* we find a veritable "explosion" in the *Comedy* of as many as ninety-nine rhyme-forms based on a combination rarely found in Duecento poetry (vowel + *r* + consonant + vowel): e.g., *-arba, -erchi, -irci, -orbi, -orto* (ibid., 11).

23.   The reading *per ammenda* in *Purg.* 20.67 is controversial. Recently, Lanza (1996, 427–28) has revived the alternative *per vicenda,* which was preferred as the *lectio difficilior* by both Vandelli and Barbi. Petrocchi admits that both readings are "equally satisfying," although he (after Casella and most modern editors) opts for *per ammenda*. Ferrante (1983, 125) points out that, in *Par.* 19.104–8, the name *Cristo* "occurs four times in the pattern of a cross."

24.   Robey (2000c, 809): "The total number of different rhymes in the *Commedia* is 753; of these, 240 occur only once: 214 [*sic,* corrected to 213: Robey 2000b, 61] in tercets and 27 in couplets at the beginning or end of the canto . . . what is most striking . . . is the way in which substantial numbers of new rhymes are introduced as the poem progresses." Robey also claims that Dante's rhymes "never have a final syllable ending in a consonant" (Robey 2000c, 809), whereas in the *Comedy* we find three lines of Italian verse ending with a consonant: *Purg.* 4.68–72: *Sïòn – orizzòn – Fetòn;* see, moreover, Arnaut Daniel's speech in *langue d'oc, Purg.* 26.140–47 (with the following rhyme-words: *deman, cantan, folor, denan, valor, dolor*), as well as the Latin sequence in *Purg.* 30.17–21, *senis – venis – plenis,* and the Hebraic *malacòth – sabaòth, Par.* 7.1–3 *(malacòth* is in fact a corruption of the Hebrew *mamlacoth).*

25.   A parallel development is found in the use of consonants in rhyming syllables. The number of consonants in the rhymes drops markedly from *Inferno* to *Purgatorio* and remains at this lower level in *Paradiso*. At the same time, the proportion of liquids and nasals increases while the proportion of alveolar, plosive, and sibilant consonants decreases, in conformity with "the association that Dante himself makes *(Inf.* 32.1) of *rime aspre* with the bottom of *Inferno"* (Robey 2000, 809).

26.   Pézard (1965, 1711–12) claims that *pareglio* signifies "parhelion," which the *OED* defines as a fainter image or reflection, citing *inter alia* "Only the parhelius or reflection of the visible glory of him [Christ]" in a work by a certain J. Scott, published in 1699.

27.   "Et est istud *lici* vocabulum Florentinorum, quod tantum sonat quantum 'ibi'" (Guido da Pisa 1974, 272).

28.   Robey (1997, 113) makes an interesting comparison between the *Fiore* (attributed to Dante by Contini and others) and *Inferno:* "All the most frequent rhymes in the *Fiore* are also either verbal inflections or common substantival endings; it is very clear, in contrast, how far these are avoided by the author of *Inferno*." The figures given for

rhymes in -*are* are 164 occurrences in the *Fiore,* with only 12 in the comparable sample from *Inferno.*

29. Boyde (1971, 95): "21.6 per cent of the total [in the *Comedy*], as opposed to 2.6 per cent [*Vita Nova* poems]. Few of the stylistic differences between the *Comedy* and the early poems can be represented more economically than this, and few are more important."

30. How far Dante's practice here diverges from the rhymes used by Guinizzelli, Cavalcanti, Lapo Gianni, Gianni Alfani, Dino Frescobaldi, and Cino da Pistoia may be quickly discovered by consulting the *rimari* in Marti (1969, 973–1076).

31. A foretaste of such rhymes is found in *Inf.* 6.50–54 and 7.1–27. In *Inf.* 6 the sequence *sacco – Ciacco – fiacco* constitutes a "rimema-segnale ben preciso" (Afribo 2002, 20) that recurs in Petrarch's sonnet *L'avara Babilonia à colmo il sacco* (*RVF* 137), with *sacco* and *fiacco* in lines 1 and 5, and a proper name (*Bacco* and *Baldacco* in Petrarch; *Ciacco* in Dante). Both sequences are an integral part of the condemnation of a corrupt city (Avignon [Petrarch]; Florence [Dante]).

32. Baldelli (1973) is a gold mine of information. To his inventory, I would add that there are six groups of *rime sdrucciole* in the poem (*Inf.* 15.1–3, 23.32–36, 24.62–66, 28.80–84, *Par.* 26.125–29, 28.125–29); four groups that include one *rima composta* (*Inf.* 7.26–30, 28.119–23, 30.83–87, *Purg.* 20.2–6); and eight groups of *rima tronca* (four ending in -*í: Inf.* 23.143–47, 28.32–36, *Purg.* 23.74–78, *Par.* 25.98–102; two ending in -*ò: Inf.* 20.74–78, 31.143–45; one ending in -*ú: Inf.* 32.62–66; and one ending in -*òn: Purg.* 4.68–72).

33. As Beccaria points out (1975, 39): "Inconsueti alla tradizione i latinismi in rima, di cui Dante fa largo uso (Petrarca oserà una sola volta far rimare *bibo:describo:delibo* CXCIII 4–5, 8)."

34. Gorni (2000, 58) indicates the repetition of rhymes with the collocations *tutta quanta/tutte quante* in *Inf.* 20.114, *Purg.* 10.58, 32.63, *Par.* 14.45; *Inf.* 6.37, 20.42, *Purg.* 2.74, 6.25, 7.36, *Par.* 22.133. Another interesting variation is found near the end of the poem, in the description of the celestial rose, where two expressions are made to rhyme: *di soglia in soglia* with *di foglia in foglia* (*Par.* 32.13–15).

35. This total does not include *vedute* signifying "stars" (*Par.* 2.115), but it does include the substantive *viso,* when this means "sight" (e.g., *Par.* 27.6, 73, 78). In the poem, the word *vidi* appears no fewer than 170 times, while *occhi* with 213 occurrences is by far the most frequent noun (followed by *mondo* [143], *terra* [136], and *dio* [128]). The poet's intention of revealing the truth concerning God's justice as it is revealed in the other world is discernible in the fact that the Latinism *manifesto* and its derivatives are found no fewer than 22 times in the emphatic, rhyming position (cf. Cacciaguida's exhortation in *Par.* 17.128: *tutta tua visïon fa manifesta,* and the poet's bold claim in *Par.* 30.95–96: *io vidi / ambo le corti del ciel manifeste*).

36. I wish to acknowledge the debt I owe to Ignazio Baldelli's study of the *terzina* (Baldelli 1976a).

37. The crescendo is achieved with the threefold repetition of the verb *crescere* (to grow, to increase). For a list of such "trinitarian" effects, see Gorni (1988, 327–35).

38. As already noted, Dante accepts the Thomistic view that beatitude consists in an act of the intellect (*S. Th.* 1.2.3.4), as opposed to the mystical and Franciscan traditions, which emphasized the primacy of love.

39. *Par.* 28.109–11: "Hence you can see how beatitude depends on the act of vision, not on the act of love, which follows on from it"; *Par.* 9.70–72: "On high, joy is expressed through brightness, as through a smile here on earth; but down below the soul is darkened . . ." That light makes possible the beatific vision is stated in line 48 of Solomon's reply. The belief in the resurrection of the body and its reunion with the soul is obviously basic to Dante's Christian epic (and its denial is the hallmark of the heretics encountered by the pilgrim on his entry into the Devil's City: *Inf.* 10.13–15). Concerning the poet's choice of Solomon at this juncture, see Dronke (1976, 9–10).

40. For this and most of the statistical information, I follow Robey (1997, 2000b).

41. Scaglione (1967, 18) points to eighteen occurrences of enjambment in *Par.* 11: in eleven cases a strong caesura in the next line rounds it out.

42. Beccaria (1975, 64–65) goes so far as to claim that enjambment "not only modifies the meter but it also modifies the meaning."

43. In the rest of the poem the following judgment holds good: "studiandiosi nell'esordio e nel verso di chiusa di segnarne nettamente e vigorosamente i confini" (Fubini 1966, 82). A table of the opening lines of the *Comedy*'s one hundred cantos may be found in Gorni (1981, 183–86), whose analysis of their first and last verses shows, *inter alia*, that the idea of movement is predominant especially in the opening verse (178). Only one such line (that of *Inf.* 15) ends with a proparoxytone. A comprehensive analysis of canto openings is offered by Luigi Blasucci (2000). He divides them into two groups: *esordi retorici* and *esordi narrativi*. According to this taxonomy, there are eleven *esordi retorici* (with twenty-three *esordi narrativi*) in *Inferno,* ten in *Purgatorio* (twenty-three *esordi narrativi*), and eighteen (fifteen *esordi narrativi*) in *Paradiso.* The *esordio* of *Par.* 6 (Justinian's speech) continues throughout the canto (ll. 1–142), and the last canto of the poem opens with Bernard's prayer to the Virgin, which extends over thirteen *terzine* (*Par.* 33.1–39): "un vertice dello sperimentalismo dantesco" (Blasucci 2000, 31). See also Bertoletti (2000).

44. Whereas the etymology of "alliteration" indicates the repetition of the same *litera* or letter, what may be termed effects of "concealed alliteration" are also created by phonic affinities between such consonants as *m, b, p; n, d, t.*

45. Freccero (1986, 98–99): "For the first and only time in this poem, perhaps in any poem, we directly share the protagonist's experience . . . we read a text and imagine a gate on which we *see* the text we have read." The use of direct "speech" at the beginning of a canto is one of the most original elements in Dante's narrative technique.

46. Eco (1981, 68) claims that metonymy and metaphor are germane concepts and that "each metaphor can be traced back to a subjacent chain of metonymic connections which constitute the framework of the code and upon which is based the constitution of any semantic field . . ."

47. The section entitled "Il dominio metaforico" repays careful study (Pasquini 2001, 179–217; see 191–92 for the analysis of *Purg.* 20.73–75).

48. Brunetto Latini, *Il Tesoretto,* ll. 186–96, in *Poeti del Duecento,* tomo 2, ed. Gianfranco Contini (Milan-Naples: Ricciardi, 1960), 182–83.

49. Cf. the frescos *The Effects of Good Government* and *The Effects of Bad Government,* painted by Ambrogio Lorenzetti (c. 1338–39) in the Palazzo Pubblico at Siena.

50. "Universus enim mundus iste sensibilis quasi quidam liber est scriptus digito Dei" (*Eruditio didascalica,* PL 176.813).

51. For the significance of binding the book (as opposed to the Sibyl's leaves: *Par.* 33.65–66), see Ahern 1982.

52. For this dependence on images, see Boyde (1981, 350–51 n. 3).

53. As Maria Corti points out: "The conception of the world as a single text created by God . . . [means that] there can only exist a unitary reading, where everything is correlated to everything else" (1987, 12).

54. See chapter 3 for this characteristic and for the "explosion" of imagery in the *petrose* and later poems (especially *Doglia mi reca ne lo core ardire*), as well as chapter 4 for this same phenomenon in the final sections of *Convivio.* As Mazzeo (1958, 151) remarks, "The number of similes in the final section is one-third more than is found in either of the other parts, for it is the imagery of the *Paradiso* which substitutes for the drama of the rest of the poem and makes it, in one sense, a prolonged lyrical pageant."

55. The third chapter of St. James's letter is devoted to the need to curb the tongue. In 3.4–5, the tongue is compared to a ship "guided by a small rudder," "so also the tongue is a small member, yet it boasts of great exploits *[et magna exaltat]*." And see James 3.6: "And the tongue is a fire, a universe of iniquity." It is interesting to note that the epistle tells us (3.3) that the tongue must be curbed by the bit of reason, just as horses are guided by the bridle; so, too, the poet tells us that even in the act of writing he now reins in his intellect more than ever (*Inf.* 26.21–22: *e piú lo 'ngegno affreno ch'i' non soglio, / perché non corra che virtú nol guidi;* my emphasis).

56. See Lansing (1977, 11), who also writes of the Dantean simile's effect in heightening "the reader's awareness of the process of discovery of meaning. Similes obligate the reader to look for similarity in the nature of things . . . to extrapolate from likenesses the true nature of reality" (Lansing 2000b, 779).

57. See, e.g., . . . *e stetti come l'uom che teme* (*Inf.* 13.45), . . . *com' om che sale* (*Inf.* 34.80), followed in line 83 by *ansando com' uom lasso; Purg.* 1.119, *com' om che torna a la perduta strada; Par.* 13.113, *per farti mover lento com' uom lasso.* For these and other images in the poems of Dante's predecessors at the court of Frederick II, see Walter Pagani (1968, 429–74).

58. Commentaries usually offer variations on Attilio Momigliano's "cosí Dante vuol dire che il diletto dei vani pensieri macchia il candore della mente"; Casini-Barbi points to the "carattere enimmistico di questa terzina," possibly due to the "tirannia della rima rara: la rima *-elsa* è unica nel poema" (Mazzoni 1973, 773). The need to find another rhyme-word after *eccelsa* and *Elsa* (ll. 65, 67) would explain the synecdoche *gelsa* (the fruit) indicating *gelso,* the tree.

59. See, e.g., Tibor Wlassics (1975, 22): "'Interpretare' non vorrà dire escludere una delle accezioni a favore arbitrario dell'altra, bensí accogliere ambedue e rilevare l'effetto della multipla coloratura."

60. See esp. Hollander (1969, 226–32), Picone (1998); also Hawkins (1999).

61. As Kay (1989, 246) points out, according to the Julian calendar of Dante's times, the sun was in the constellation of the Gemini from May 15 to June 14 (*not* May 21–June 21, as so many scholars reiterate).

62. Cf. Eliot (1965, 50): "And I do not know anywhere in poetry a more authentic sign of greatness than the power of association which could . . . when the poet is speaking of the Divine vision, yet introduce the Argo passing over the head of wondering Neptune."

63. See Hollander (1969, 231–32): "Here he [Dante] gives us a kind of Alpha and Omega of human history, not in terms of Adam and Judgment Day, but in terms of . . . the voyage of 1223 B.C. and that of 1300 A.D. . . . The midpoint . . . thirteen centuries from either terminus, is the Incarnation, the *terminus ad quem* and *a quo* for the poem and for all human life."

64. *Amor mi spira . . . e' ditta dentro:* the highly suggestive image of Love as dictating to the poet is traditionally applied to those who wrote the books of the Bible (with God as their *unicus . . . dictator* in *Mon.* 3.4.11). It is noteworthy that the hapax *dictator* in Dante's Latin writings is also found only once in Dante's Italian works *(Purg.* 24.59: *dittator).* *Spira/spirare* likewise brings to mind the inspiration afforded by the Holy Spirit, *l'etterno spiro* of *Par.* 4.36, 11.98, and 14.76 *(Santo Spiro).* Cf. another hapax in the *Comedy: quella materia ond' io son fatto* scriba *(Par.* 10.27; my emphasis).

65. Dante may well have been the recipient of Cino da Pistoia's sonnet *O voi che siete voce nel diserto* (Marti 1969, 818–19).

66. It is now assumed by many scholars that Dante was influenced by Giotto's *Last Judgment* fresco in the Arena Chapel at Padua (consecrated on March 25, 1305). I would point to the depiction of Christ's baptism to illustrate the importance of John the Baptist's camel-hair garment, clearly visible underneath his pink mantle.

67. Bonaventure, *Sermones de B. Virg. Maria, De assumptione BVM,* Sermo 1: ". . . in Patriarchis fides, *in Prophetis spes,* in Apostolis charitas; et omnia tamen haec in his omnibus" (cited by Mineo 1968, 269; my emphasis). For the poet of the *Comedy's* prophetic role, Mineo's comprehensive monograph should be consulted together with the essays by Nardi (1983, 265–326), Gorni (1984, 49–68), and Iannucci (2001).

68. Gimpel 1988, 154. Cf. Dronke (1986, 101–2): "It is possible, as Gmelin noted, that Dante could have seen a clock that chimed the hours: the earliest attested in Italy was built in Milan in 1306, and Dante might have observed it at the coronation of Henry VII."

69. The image of a mill fed by water channeled through a canal or sluice, chosen by the poet to indicate the rapidity of Virgil's flight from the devils in hot pursuit *(Inf.* 23.46–51), is yet another instance of the poetic inspiration drawn by Dante from the "astonishing" fact that "medieval man was surrounded by machines" (Gimpel 1988, 1).

70. John Freccero (1986, 255) claims that the word *disio* in *Par.* 33.143 refers to intellectual desire. He rightly argues that "the word *velle* here denotes, as it does for Thomas Aquinas, the unshakable adherence of the will to its natural end, which it loves in itself" (256). This surely sends us back to Virgil's explanation of the essential bond between natural, instinctive love (which gives rise to all forms of *disio*) and the will or

reason that must curb and direct this instinct (*Purg.* 18.19–75). "On both levels, then, the full realization of the journey and of the poem is conditioned by the existence of desire" (Pertile 1993b, 153).

71. Cf. *Mon.* 1.15.5: "It is clear that a unity of wills *[unitatem voluntatum],* which is what is signified by their uniform motion *[que per uniformem motum datur intelligi],* is the root of concord or simply concord itself."

72. As Marguerite Chiarenza has written: "There are . . . stages in the development of Dante's imagery in the *Paradiso* . . . We find, first, concrete shapes which can barely be perceived, then shapes in which symbolic meaning overshadows concrete form, and at last purely conceptual shapes not found in the material universe. These stages lead the poet to the point where he can go no further but must end his poem in order that it become fully imageless" (Chiarenza 1972, 85–86).

73. For a detailed analysis of the way *Inf.* 19 is "appropriately circumscribed and defined by Holy Scripture," see Barański (2000a, 147–72: "I segni della Bibbia: II. La lezione profetica di *Inferno* XIX").

74. Barański (2000a, 154) suggests that Dante here wished to "imitate the figural relationship that united the episodes and persons of the Old Testament with those of the New," and reveals a complex web of "interconnections" set up by the poet between Christ's baptism and the *bolgia dei simoniaci* (155). In this important study, Barański also demonstrates the way in which Mount Sinai and God's pact with his chosen people prefigures the Rock on which Christ founded his Church (170).

75. For a discussion of the possible reasons why Dante referred to his poem as his "comedy," see chapter 6.

eleven.   Dante and his contemporary world

1. Rubinstein (1942, 213). The inscription was first pointed out by A. Chiappelli in *Il Marzocco,* November 23, 1930. Vergil's claim that the Romans were destined to hold dominion over the sea and every land *(Aen.* 1.234–36, cited approvingly by Dante in *Mon.* 2.8.11: *qui mare, qui terras omnis ditione tenerent)* must surely have helped to inspire the poet's denunciation of Florentine hubris.

2. For a detailed analysis of this interaction, see Scott (1996b, 3–59) and Bemrose (2000). For aspects of daily life in Dante's Florence: Antonetti (1983). For contemporary education and libraries: Davis (1984, 137–65; 1988). See also Najemy (1993).

3. The term *podestà* is made to refer to Christ as the Universal Judge in *Inf.* 6.96.

4. "Ghibelline" is derived from *Waiblingen,* a fief of the Hohenstaufen, whose name was used as a war cry by supporters of Conrad III at the battle of Weinsberg in 1140. "Guelf" indicated the followers of his Welf opponent, Henry the Proud, duke of Bavaria and Saxony.

5. Just one example of self-interest: the Pulci and the Rimbertini, both Guelf families, were bankers to the Emperor Frederick II. Cf. Partner (1965, 77–79): "The Roman noble Napoleon Orsini remarked . . . 'you will never find a true Roman who is either guelf or ghibelline' . . . Both early and late it could be true for Florence as for the

other guelf communes, that 'guelf" policy was often scarcely or not at all concerned with the papacy."

6. "A Milanese chronicler saw the city's *Popolo* as composed of 'those who live by buying and selling and not by manual labour, such as merchants and men halfway between wealth and poverty'" (Waley 1998, 131).

7. The lily, as a symbol both of purity and of royalty, is the flower of the Virgin Mary, Queen of Heaven. This association inspired the decision, in 1294, to consecrate Florence's new cathedral (formerly Santa Reparata) to Santa Maria del Fiore (cf. Villani, *Cronica* 9.9).

8. Sordello received fiefs in Piedmont and the Abruzzi from Charles, who referred to him as "our beloved companion and faithful follower." For the Sordello episode (*Purg.* 6–8), see Scott (1996b, 96–127).

9. The list of *magnati* "is about evenly divided between Guelf families and families that had traditionally been Ghibelline" (Najemy 1993, 90).

10. Dante tells us that he turned to the study of philosophy in order to seek consolation after Beatrice's death, first through a reading of Boethius and Cicero, then by attending the "schools of the religious and the disputations of the philosophers" (*Conv.* 2.12.7). Through the Franciscans at Santa Croce in Florence he no doubt "discovered" Plato and Augustine (especially through the writings of St. Bonaventure), together with the cult of St. Francis, a humble, popular style of preaching, and an emphasis on the virtue of poverty. With the Dominicans at Santa Maria Novella, he would have become acquainted with Aristotle, "the master of those who know" (*Inf.* 4.131), and Aquinas (*Par.* 10–13), intellectual rigor and subtle disputation, accompanied by a respect for the classical legacy of pagan Rome. For this crucial stage in Dante's development, see Davis (1976a, and 1984, 137–65).

11. See the poem *Che farai, Pier da Morrone?* in Jacopone da Todi, *Laude,* ed. F. Mancini (Bari: Laterza, 1974), 218–20.

12. On June 19, 1301, Dante was the only one to speak out against the request that Florence should provide one hundred horsemen for the papal force. Forty-nine voted in favor of sending this contingent (with thirty-two against) later that same day. On May 13, 1300, Boniface had written to the imperial electors stating that the Apostolic See intended to reassert its authority over Tuscany as part of its imperial inheritance (Holmes 1980, 21).

13. For the text of *Unam sanctam,* see, e.g., Tierney (1980, 188–89).

14. For the sacrilegious parody of the Song of Songs, see Pertile (1998).

15. For Dante as prophet, see Nardi (1983, 265–326) and Mineo (1968).

16. See especially Kay (1998, xxvi–xxix).

17. Antonio Lanza gives the reading "e di Fiorenz'a ppopol giusto e sano." The manuscript reading *fiorençapopol,* with a *titulus* over the *a,* indicating "raddoppiamento della *p* per fonosintassi," indicates that the poet wishes to stress the fact that he has at last found *the* just and upright people "per eccellenza: quello dei beati." This also follows the pattern set by *al divino, all'etterno* in lines 37–38 (Lanza 2002, 79; 1996, 757).

18. Villani (*Cronica* 13.4) accuses the French of having corrupted Florentine attire in the 1340s, which, similar to the Roman toga, had until then been "the finest, the most

noble and virtuous." Each Italian city had its own distinctive fashion, and his dress makes Dante recognizable as a Florentine even in the gloom of hell (*Inf.* 16.7–8).

19. In 1312 Giotto Peruzzi, a Florentine, "noted in his *Libro segreto* the amounts to be paid by each male member of his lineage as contributions to the enormous dowry his daughter was to bring to the Adimari family" (Klapisch-Zuber 1990, 288).

20. "It was common practice for Florentine merchants to remain in one foreign city or region for several years, taking advantage of their special knowledge of local conditions, and of their ties with the political establishment. 'I have been in Venice for more than forty-five years,' Bernardo Davanzati wrote to his son (1393)" (Brucker 1984, 85). The trend was already firmly established by Dante's times. Florentine merchants and bankers "had branches in all the great centers, among them Milan, Avignon, Lyons, Paris, Bruges and London" (Bernard 1972, 296).

21. The florin's stability and strength over its first 150 years were outstanding. Already, by the time of Dante's death in 1321, it was worth more than three times its original value (one *lira,* indicating one *libra* or "pound" of silver).

22. Cacciaguida's words refer to those who could be called upon to do military service (about six thousand, over 150 years before Dante's times).

23. A salutary warning is given by N. J. G. Pounds (1974, 123): "Medieval man, like classical man before him, was little interested in figures. Neither showed any desire to formulate a precise estimate of population . . ." Pampaloni (1973, xvii) gives the following figures for Florence: 50,000 inhabitants in 1200; 75,000 in 1260; 95,000 in 1300. Antonetti (1996, 28): 15,000 at the end of the twelfth century; 50,000 "half-way through the thirteenth century"; 110,000 "at the beginning of the fourteenth." After the transfer of the nation's capital from Florence to Rome in 1871, Florence counted some 167,000 inhabitants. If the population of the *contado* under Florentine control is included, an estimate of about 250,000 inhabitants has been made, with an overall density of about 65 persons to the square kilometer.

24. "A Firenze, all'inizio del secolo XIV, la produzione annua di panni avrebbe toccato le 100.000 pezze, vendute da 300 botteghe e rappresentanti un valore di 600.000 fiorini" (Le Goff 1997, 207).

25. Rubinstein (1942, 207): "At Florence 'nationalism' is intimately connected with another idea which occurs more than once in the *Chronica:* that of the Roman origins of Florence." Villani hails Charlemagne as the second founder of Florence: "The town was rebuilt and, as in ancient times, again populated by the most noble Roman families" (217).

26. Built on the Oltrarno, the Palazzo Mozzi had a garden, even an orchard. When Pope Gregory X visited Florence in 1273, he stayed in this, the finest of the city's new private mansions.

27. Davis (1984, 89–93) points to "the closest parallel to Dante's description of the *buon tempo antico* . . . in a contemporary author, Riccobaldo of Ferrara." Dante's view of Florence's decline from Cacciaguida's day, hastened by the struggle between papacy and empire, "was alien to the spirit of most early Florentine historical writing. Partially inspired by Riccobaldo and perhaps to some extent by classical Roman authors, it was created by a poet, adapted by a chronicler [Villani]."

28. Quotations are taken from: Aristotle, *The Politics,* translated and with an introduction by T. A. Sinclair (Harmondsworth: Penguin Books, 1972). Although some have denied that Dante knew *The Politics,* the general consensus now is that he was most probably acquainted with that work (as always, in Latin translation and through commentaries).

29. Readers will recall Dante's diatribe against riches in *Conv.* 4, where he denies that nobility has anything to do with wealth (cf., however, *Mon.* 2.3.4). Nobility in Tuscany and northern Italy was partly the result of a social mobility unique in medieval Europe: "Certain families were described or described themselves as 'noble.' The term had no clear meaning. It . . . was used of a wide variety of men among whom there were great disparities of wealth, status, and manner of life" (Larner 1980, 83).

30. Cf. Cipolla (1972, 16): "The roots of all subsequent developments including the Industrial Revolution and its products can be traced to the urban development of the Middle Ages." Florence was clearly in the forefront of this development.

31. For a detailed account of the Spiritual Franciscans, see Lambert (1961). For a briefer account: Lambert (1992, 189–214). For the broad legalistic concepts of poverty versus property, see Coleman (1991, esp. 607–44). It is one of the trenchant ironies of history that St. Francis, who had disowned his merchant father in public, was proclaimed the patron saint of merchants by the archbishop of Pisa in 1261 (Rossiaud 1990, 168).

32. Olivi's defense of evangelical poverty, as preached and practiced by St. Francis, is expounded in his *De usu paupere* (Olivi 1992).

33. Cf. Ubertino da Casale, *Arbor Vitae Crucifixae Jesu,* 5.3: "Even Thine own Mother . . . even she, I say, and such a Mother, could not reach up to Thee; Lady Poverty, with all her penury . . . held Thee more than ever closely embraced" (cited by Gardner 1968, 235). For St. Francis, poverty was "the essential element in the imitation of Christ, which was all he wanted" (Southern 1990, 282).

34. For the text of the two decretals (*Gloriosam ecclesiam,* 1318, and *Cum inter nonnullos,* 1323), see Peters (1980, 245–47).

35. For a thorough analysis of the ladder's role, see Di Fonzo (1991).

36. The same binary opposition, where *bruno* is equivalent to black, is found in *Par.* 15.51 *(du' non si muta mai bianco né bruno),* while the dark spots on the moon, indicating moral failings, are described as *quel bruno* in *Par.* 2.73.

37. On the flyleaf of a thirteenth-century Florentine manuscript, "we read that 'The devil has nine daughters whom he has married off: simony to the secular clerks; hypocrisy to the monks . . .'" (Le Goff 1988, 263).

38. Ferrante (1992, 11). In 1304, in Florence (at Santa Maria Novella), Giordano da Pisa fulminated: "The office of preaching is not granted to just any man; and, more especially, it is everywhere and always forbidden for women to preach . . ." (Hawkins 1999, 29). Ferrante also points to major exceptions to the general rule that women should be silent and submissive, such as Jerome's Marcella, Héloïse, and Hildegard of Bingen "who traveled and preached" (19). Dante's representation of Beatrice in Eden (*Purg.* 30–33) prefigures Christ's role as judge at his Second Coming. Women in general appear in the *Comedy* essentially as: pagan figures taken from Trojan-Roman history (*Inf.* 4); lustful sinners (from Semiramis to Myrrha, *Inf.* 5 and 30); penitents (Pia and Sapia, *Purg.* 5 and

13); and saints (Piccarda, Cunizza, Rahab, *Par.* 3 and 9). However, in the "allegory" of heaven presented to him during his ascent through the spheres, no feminine figure is found among the "active spirits" (Mercury), the "wise" (Sun), the "warriors" (Mars), the "just" (Jupiter), the "contemplatives" (Saturn). Forese Donati upbraids Florentine women for their immodest behavior and dress (*Purg.* 23.94–111), and Cacciaguida does the same, while reminding us that a woman's supreme role is to spin and look after the children (*Par.* 15.113–29). See Ferrante (1985), Anderson and Zinsser (1990, vol. 1), Duby and Perrot (1990, vol. 2), Amt (1993).

39. In Boccaccio's *Decameron* (6.10), a knavish Augustinian friar opens his chaotic, nonsensical sermon to the folk of Certaldo with a reference to "baron messer santo Antonio" and the latter's reputation as a guardian of animals. Fra Cipolla's speech, which mesmerizes his audience, is an extreme (and comic) example of the kind of ecclesiastical legerdemain castigated by Dante in *Par.* 29.

40. Pertile (1998, 214). Cf. Perella (1969, 12–73).

41. The historical parallel with the "Babylonian" exile of the papacy in Avignon is indicated in all standard commentaries on the *Comedy*. Of particular interest are Olivi's words, written years before the papacy's removal from Rome "*from the soles of her feet to the top of her head* [cf. *Purg.* 32.156: *dal capo infin le piante*] almost the whole church is infected and . . . is become virtually a new Babylon" (Manselli 1965, 133 n. 42 [emphasis mine]; cf. 125: "Il poeta si distacca dalla esegesi scritturale corrente, per aderire invece a quella di Gioacchino da Fiore, dello Olivi, degli Spirituali").

42. Manselli (1965, 133 n. 47): "Una beghina delle piú radicali, na Prous Bonete, non esita a dire . . . 'quod ecclesia mortua est spiritualiter.'"

43. In his *Contra falsos Ecclesie professores* (written before 1304), the Dominican Remigio de' Girolami refers to the legend that when the Western empire was given to the Church, a voice from heaven declared: "'Today, poison has been injected into God's Church.' And therefore Christ, the founder of the Church, chose to be a pauper in temporal things, and when the Jews wanted to make him king he fled . . ." (Remigio 1981, 58–59). Cf. *Purg.* 32.124–29.

44. Commenting on Western Christendom in and after 1300, Southern (1990, 301) notes that "the spiritual warrior was out; the critic and contemplative came in . . . In the place of the warrior [and crusader], the new hope of Christendom lay in the individual prophet."

45. In Tuscany and northern Italy, "after the Guelf triumph in the 1260s, communes became more willing to admit the inquisitors . . . From the 1280s 'heresy' was clandestine, eccentric, and of little importance" (Larner 1980, 233)—perhaps as a result of the activities of such inquisitors as the Franciscan Salomone da Lucca, who in 1283 posthumously condemned both Farinata and Adaleta, his wife, and had their bones disinterred and burned. As for the descendants of the Chosen People, theologians, "repudiating the Bernardine tolerance of the twelfth century now taught that all Jews were to be seen as participating in the guilt of Christ's death" (ibid., 207); cf. *Inf.* 23.115–23, *Par.* 6.82–93, and the terrible line *ch'a Dio e a' Giudei piacque una morte* (*Par.* 7.47).

46. Controversy will continue over the question whether Dante was a "real" mystic or whether he imagined the experiences described in the *Comedy*—a question that lies

outside our present discussion. For the nonce, I would point to the following statement, taken from the *Epistle to Cangrande:* "The form or manner of treatment is poetic, fictive, descriptive, digressive, and figurative . . . the whole [poem] . . . was conceived . . . not for the sake of speculation, but for a practical purpose [to remove those living in this life from a state of misery, and to bring them to a state of happiness]" (*Ep.* 13.9.27–16.41). The judgment of an expert in medieval theology may be cited: namely, that Dante is "the greatest religious poet the world has ever known without a doubt, but neither a holy contemplative nor a mystic raised up by grace to extraordinary experiences; it is not easy to write the *Divine Comedy* if one sets out to be at one and same time a Saint Paul and a Saint Bernard of Clairvaux" (Gilson 1974, 116). Another authority on medieval spirituality, the Dominican G. G. Meerseman, refused to accept that Dante was in any real sense a mystic (Meerseman 1965, 192), while his colleague Kenelm Foster, O.P., took Charles Williams to task for not seeing "clearly enough that Dante was not a mystic" (Foster 1957, 50). The opinion of expert scholars in the field of medieval theology and mysticism is in striking contrast with claims made by some Dante scholars. This is not to deny the influence of mystical writings on Dante's writings (for which, see, e.g., Mazzoni 1997b, Masseron 1953, Gardner 1968, Pertile 1998). As Pertile has demonstrated, the driving force in *Paradiso* is the protagonist's desire for the vision of God, a desire so overwhelming that it "drives the pilgrim upwards and at the same time [serves as] the artistic device that enables the poet to accomplish his creative task" (1993b, 147).

47. For a comprehensive treatment of this theme, see Ferrante (1984) and Scott (1996b).

48. In his *Tresor* (1.37) Brunetto recounts that the place where Florence stands was formerly called "chiés Mars, c'est a dire maisons de batailles," for Mars "is called the god of battles"; hence, it is no surprise that the Florentines are always at war and full of discord ("li florentin sont tozjors en guerre et en descort, car celui planete regne sor aus"). Cf. *Inf.* 13.143–50.

49. As mentioned above, the poet also condemned his fellow White-exiles as "evil and senseless . . . utterly ungrateful and utterly mad" (*Par.* 17.61–65). For the various stages in Dante's political thought, see Scott (1975 and 1996b, 3–59).

50. For Dante's definition of poetry as an artistic construct based on rhetoric and music *(fictio rhetorica musicaque poita),* see *DVE* 2.4.2 and cf. *Conv.* 2.11.9. Music's power over human emotions and its ability to enchant us is well illustrated in antepurgatory, when Dante encounters Casella, the musician who in life had calmed the poet's soul with his *amoroso canto* (*Purg.* 2.107–8) and who now chants one of the poet's canzoni *(Amor che ne la mente mi ragiona)* with such sweetness that it makes its audience forget the need to "run to the mountain" of purification, while it still resounds in Dante's memory (ll. 112–17). Cf. *Conv.* 2.13.23–24. Dante, an amateur artist (*VN* 34.1), mentions Giotto's supremacy in painting (*Purg.* 11.94–96). Contemporary sculpture (especially the art of Giovanni Pisano) clearly made an indelible impression on the poet, whose eyes— he tells us in *Purg.* 10.103–4—were always on the lookout for something new, *novitadi;* such sculpture inspired the vision of a divine synesthetic art, a *visibile parlare* (*Purg.* 10.95), that aids the purification of the proud on the first terrace of purgatory (Scott 2000b, 186–92).

twelve.   Latin epistles, *Questio de aqua et terra,* and eclogues

1. "How solitary dwells the city." The first verse reads: "How solitary dwells the city once so populous; the queen of all peoples is now virtually a widow; she who had once commanded provinces is now a tributary." In *Ep.* II.1.1, we read *Quomodo sola sedet civitas . . .* , with added emphasis placed on *sola* in that it is made to precede the verb.

2. The phrase *li principi de la terra* may be translated literally as "the princes [rulers] of the earth" (Cervigni and Vasta 1995, 117). I would, however, agree with Gorni that Dante frequently uses *terra* to indicate a city (specifically Florence, in *Rime* XCI: 68.97–98 and CXVI: 89.77); moreover, "*Vita Nova* is a consistently municipal work . . ." (Gorni 1996, 172 n.).

3. Dante's praise of Guido da Montefeltro (*Conv.* 4.28.8) is of course in total opposition with his damnation (dramatically portrayed in *Inf.* 27).

4. Cf. the emblematic title of the study by Alastair Minnis, *"Magister amoris." The "Roman de la Rose" and Vernacular Hermeneutics* (Oxford: Oxford University Press, 2001).

5. For Marco Lombardo's discourse, see *Purg.* 16.67–114. For the canzone *Amor, da che convien pur ch'io mi doglia,* see chapter 3.

6. See Sarolli (1971, 64–74), Mineo (1968, 143–60), Nardi (1983, 265–326), and Palma di Cesnola (1995).

7. The same message is delivered by Beatrice some years later, in *Par.* 27.139–41: "In order not to be amazed, you must realize that on earth there is no one who governs; therefore the human family goes astray."

8. An extensive bibliography is found in Hollander (1993a); see also Ascoli (2000) and "The Cangrande Dispute" (exchanges between Henry Ansgar Kelly and Robert Hollander), *Lectura Dantis* 14–15 (1994): 61–115.

9. Dronke uses a sophisticated method (developed by Tore Janson in 1975), which demonstrates that "the Cangrande expositor shows rhythmic habits significantly different from those of Dante the expositor in the Latin didactic prose that is undoubtedly his" (1986, 110). More recently, Dronke agrees with the argument that, with regard to the expository part of the epistle, "one should not expect any systematic presence of *cursus* in a commentary . . . yet that one and the same author should, just this once, show no trace whatever of his lifelong rhythmic habits would still seem to me surprising" (Dronke 1997a, 14 n. 29). See also the detailed analysis of the *cursus* in *Epistles* 1–13 provided by Laura Rossetto (1993), which strengthens the case for Dante's authorship of the *Epistle to Cangrande.*

10. Scholars have objected to the definitions (and etymologies) given of the comic and tragic genres. In his *DVE* Dante uses the terms exclusively as indicators of stylistic levels (the tragic being the noble, supreme style, for which, see chapter 2). The reference to Seneca's tragedies (here opposed to Terence's comedies) has been judged to be an anachronism, as they were scarcely known in the Middle Ages. For a rebuttal of this criticism, see esp. Mezzadroli (1990, 10–14), who points out that references to Seneca the tragedian begin to reappear "at the end of the twelfth century" (13). It is also possible that Dante knew Albertino Mussato's tragedy, *Ecerinis,* which earned him the laurel wreath at Padua in 1315.

11. Francesco Mazzoni, a persuasive champion of the authenticity of the *Epistle to Cangrande* (Mazzoni 1966, 7–37), has also established the *Questio* as the work of Dante, through his discovery of a passage in the third redaction of Pietro Alighieri's commentary and through his magisterial edition, published in the second volume of Dante Alighieri, *Opere minori* (Milan-Naples: Ricciardi, 1979) 693–880. The passage gives a brief account of Dante's disputation "whether the earth was higher than the water or vice versa."

12. Barański (1997, 153) points out that the hermeneutic tradition on Gen. 1.9 "focused on those who accepted God's will and those who challenged it; more specifically, it addressed the sinful dangers of intellectual arrogance . . ." Barański argues forcefully that in the *Questio* Dante based his arguments on "the methods of Scripturally-based *sapientia* rather than . . . philosophical *scientia*" (154). He also argues that the Book of Job (cited in *Questio* 22.77) is the most likely biblical authority for Virgil's account in *Inf.* 34 of the emergence of the landmass in the Northern Hemisphere: "In the *Inferno,* great syncretist that he was, Dante brought together Gregory's 'spiritual' and Thomas' 'literal' explanations of Job 38, 29–30 into a new synthesis which reconciled the exegete and the philosopher" (157).

13. Kay (1998, xxix n. 47) cites the observation by Mollat (1963, 81 n. 2; my emphasis) that "at Verona the secular and regular clergy *except for the cathedral canons* contravened the [papal] interdict against the town" (December 16, 1317), adding, "This split may explain why Dante's presentation of the *Questio* . . . took place in a small church near the cathedral and was boycotted by some of the Veronese clergy."

14. As Mazzoni (1979, 714 ff.) notes, a poetic account is banished from the *Questio,* as in this philosophical work he did not wish to speak *fictive et transumptive.* Cf. Freccero (1961), who has shown that, in his *Questio,* Dante "reconfirmed the divine 'authority' for Virgil's elucidation in *Inferno* XXXIV, as well as the fundamental truthfulness of the *sacrato poema,* that 'modern' *vestigium Dei."*

15. This is precisely the reason Dante adduces in *DVE* for the "creation" of artificial languages, such as Latin (see chapter 2).

16. Readers should be aware of the fact that Dante's *First Eclogue* is number two in editions of the correspondence between Giovanni and Dante.

17. Giovanni del Virgilio's eclogue to Albertino Mussato is found, with an English translation, in Wicksteed and Gardner (1902, 170–95).

Works Cited

Abardo, Rudy. 2001. Review of Federico Sanguineti, critical edition of Dante's *Comedy*. *Rivista di Studi Danteschi* 1(1):153–62.

Abulafia, David. 1988. *Frederick II: A Medieval Emperor.* London: Pimlico.

Afribo, Andrea. 2002. "Sequenze e sistemi di rime nella lirica del secondo Duecento e del Trecento." *Stilistica e metrica italiana* 2:3–46.

Agamben, Giorgio. 1978. "Comedía: La svolta comica di Dante e la concezione della colpa." *Paragone* 29:3–27.

Ageno, Franca Brambilla, ed. 1995. Dante Alighieri, *Convivio.* 3 vols. Florence: Le Lettere.

Ahern, John. 1982. "Binding the Book: Hermeneutics and Manuscript Production in *Paradiso* 33." *Proceedings of the Modern Language Association* 97:800–809.

Alfie, Fabian. 1998. "For Want of a Nail: The Guerri-Lanza-Cursietti Argument Regarding the *Tenzone.*" *Dante Studies* 116:141–59.

Alighieri, Pietro. 1978. *Il "Commentarium" di Pietro Alighieri nelle redazioni ashburnhamiana e ottoboniana.* Edited by Roberto Della Vedova and Maria Teresa Silvotti. Florence: Leo S. Olschki.

———. 2002. *Comentum super poema Comedie Dantis. A Critical Edition of Pietro Alighieri's "Commentary" on Dante's "Divine Comedy."* Edited by Massimiliano Chiamenti. Medieval & Renaissance Texts & Studies, vol. 247. Tempe: Arizona Center for Medieval & Renaissance Studies.

Allegretti, Paola, ed. 2001. Dante Alighieri, *La canzone "montanina."* Preface by Guglielmo Gorni. Verbania: Tararà.

———. 2002. "Il maestro de 'lo bello stilo che m'ha fatto onore' (*Inf.* I, 87), ovvero la matrice figurativa della sestina, da Arnaut Daniel a Virgilio." *Studi Danteschi* 67:11–55.

Ambrosini, Riccardo. 1978. "Articolo. Morfologia.—1." *Enciclopedia Dantesca* 5:135–36. Rome: Istituto della Enciclopedia Italiana.

Amt, Emilie, ed. 1993. *Women's Lives in Medieval Europe: A Sourcebook.* London: Routledge.

Anderson, Bonnie S., and Judith P. Zinsser. 1990. *A History of Their Own: Women in Europe from Prehistory to the Present.* Vol. 1. Harmondsworth: Penguin Books.

Anderson, W. B., and P. R. Hardie. 1998. "Lucan." In *The Oxford Companion to Classical Civilization*, edited by S. Hornblower and A. Spawforth, 424–28. Oxford: Oxford University Press.

Antonelli, Roberto. 2001. "Cavalcanti e Dante: Al di qua del Paradiso." In *Dante: Da Firenze all'aldilà. Atti del terzo Seminario Dantesco Internazionale (Firenze, 9–11 giugno 2000),* edited by Michelangelo Picone, 289–302. Florence: Cesati.

Antonetti, Pierre. 1983. *La vita quotidiana ai tempi di Dante.* Milan: Rizzoli.

———. 1996. *Histoire de Florence.* 3d ed. Paris: Presses Universitaires de France.

Ardizzone, Maria Luisa. 2002. *Guido Cavalcanti: The Other Middle Ages.* Toronto: University of Toronto Press.

Ariès, Philippe. 1981. *The Hour of Our Death.* Translated by H. Weaver. Harmondsworth: Penguin Books.

Armour, Peter. 1981. "The Theme of Exodus in the First Two Cantos of the *Purgatorio.*" In *Dante Soundings,* edited by David Nolan, 59–99. Dublin: Irish Academic Press.

———. 1983. *The Door of Purgatory.* Oxford: Clarendon Press.

———. 1986. "Dante's Virgil." In *Virgil in a Cultural Tradition: Essays to Celebrate the Bimillenium,* edited by Richard A. Cardwell and Janet Hamilton, 65–76. Nottingham: University of Nottingham Press.

———. 1989. *Dante's Griffin and the History of the World: A Study of the Earthly Paradise ("Purgatorio," Cantos xxix–xxxiii).* Oxford: Clarendon Press.

———. 2000. "Dante's *Contrapasso:* Context and Texts." *Italian Studies* 55:1–20.

Ascoli, Albert Russell. 1990. *"Neminem ante nos:* History and Authority in the *De vulgari eloquentia." Annali d'italianistica* 8:186–231.

———. 1993. "The Unfinished Author: Dante's Rhetoric of Authority in *Convivio* and *De vulgari eloquentia."* In *The Cambridge Companion to Dante,* edited by Rachel Jacoff, 45–66. Cambridge: Cambridge University Press.

———. 2000. "Epistle to Cangrande." In *The Dante Encyclopedia,* edited by Richard Lansing, 348–52. New York: Garland.

Auerbach, Erich. 1946. "Figurative Texts Illustrating Certain Passages of Dante." *Speculum* 21(4):474–89.

———. 1949. "Dante's Prayer to the Virgin (*Par.* XXXIII) and Earlier Eulogies." *Romance Philology* 3:268–78.

———. 1957. *Mimesis: The Representation of Reality in Western Literature.* Translated by W. Task. New York: Doubleday Anchor.

———. 1959. "Figura." In E. Auerbach, *Scenes from the Drama of European Literature,* translated by R. Manheim, 11–76. New York: Meridian.

———. 1965. *Literary Language and Its Public in Late Antiquity and the Middle Ages.* Translated by R. Manheim. Princeton: Princeton University Press.

Baldelli, Ignazio. 1973. "Rima." In *Enciclopedia Dantesca* 4:930–49. Rome: Istituto della Enciclopedia Italiana.

———. 1976a. "Terzina." In *Enciclopedia Dantesca* 5:583–94. Rome: Istituto della Enciclopedia Italiana.

———. 1976b. "Settenario." In *Enciclopedia Dantesca* 5:200–202. Rome: Istituto della Enciclopedia Italiana.

———. 1978. "Lingua e stile della *Commedia.*" In *Enciclopedia Dantesca,* Appendix, 93–112. Rome: Istituto della Enciclopedia Italiana.

———. 1997. "Le *fiche* di Vanni Fucci." *Giornale storico della letteratura italiana* 114:1–38.

Barański, Zygmunt G. 1987. "La lezione esegetica di *Inferno* I: Allegoria, storia e letteratura nella *Commedia.*" In *Dante e le forme dell'allegoresi,* edited by Michelangelo Picone, 79–97. Ravenna: Longo.

———. 1989a. "Dante's Three Reflective Dreams." *Quaderni d'Italianistica* 10:213–36.

———. 1989b. "Dante's Biblical Linguistics." *Lectura Dantis [Virginiana]* 5:105–43.

———. 1991. "*Comedía:* Notes on Dante, the Epistle to Cangrande, and Medieval Comedy." *Lectura Dantis* 8:26–55.

———. 1995a. "*'Libri poetarum in quattuor species dividuntur': Essays on Dante and 'Genre.'*" *The Italianist* 15 (Special Supplement).

———. 1995b. "The Poetics of Meter: *Terza rima, canto, canzon, cantica.*" In *Dante Now: Current Trends in Dante Studies,* edited by Theodore J. Cachey, Jr., 3–41. The William and Katherine Devers Series in Dante Studies, vol. 1. Notre Dame, Ind.: University of Notre Dame Press.

———. 1996. *"Sole nuovo, luce nuova": Saggi sul rinnovamento culturale in Dante.* Turin: Scriptorium.

———. 1997. "The Mystery of Dante's *Questio de aqua et terra.*" In *In Amicizia: Essays in Honour of Giulio Lepschy*, edited by Zygmunt G. Barański and Lino Pertile, 146–64. *The Italianist* 17 (Special Supplement).

———. 2000a. *Dante e i segni: Saggi per una storia intellettuale di Dante Alighieri.* Naples: Liguori.

———. 2000b. "Dolce stil novo." In *The Dante Encyclopedia,* edited by Richard Lansing, 308–11. New York: Garland.

———. 2001. "Canto XXV." In *Lectura Dantis Turicensis: "Purgatorio,"* edited by G. Güntert and M. Picone, 389–406. Florence: Cesati.

Barański, Zygmunt G., and Patrick Boyde, eds. 1997. *The "Fiore" in Context: Dante, France, Tuscany.* The William and Katherine Devers Series in Dante Studies, vol. 2. Notre Dame, Ind.: University of Notre Dame Press.

Barbellini, Beatrice Amidei. 2002. "Dante, Arnaut e le metamorfosi del cuore." *La parola del testo* 6 (1):91–108.

Barbi, Michele, ed. 1932. *La "Vita Nuova" di Dante Alighieri.* Florence: Bemporad.

———. 1941. *Problemi di critica dantesca: Seconda serie.* Florence: Sansoni.

———, ed. 1960. *Rime.* Società Dantesca Italiana. Florence: Le Monnier, 1960.

Barblan, Giovanni, ed. 1988. *Dante e la Bibbia.* Florence: Leo S. Olschki.

Barolini, Teodolinda. 1984. *Dante's Poets: Textuality and Truth in the "Comedy."* Princeton: Princeton University Press.

———. 1990a. "Critical Exchange [with Allan Mowbray]." *Modern Language Notes* 105:138–49.

———. 1990b. "Narrative and Style in Lower Hell." *Annali d'Italianistica* 8:314–44.

———. 1992. *The Undivine "Comedy."* Princeton: Princeton University Press.

———. 1993. "Dante and the Lyric Past." In *The Cambridge Companion to Dante,* edited by Rachel Jacoff, 14–33. Cambridge: Cambridge University Press.

———. 2000. "Medieval Multiculturalism and Dante's Theology of Hell." In *The Craft and the Fury: Essays in Memory of Glauco Cambon,* edited by Joseph Francese, 82–102. Italiana 9. West Lafayette, Ind.: Bordighera.

Beccaria, Gian Luigi. 1975. *L'autonomia del significante. Figure del ritmo e della sintassi: Dante, Pascoli, D'Annunzio.* Turin: Einaudi.

Bemrose, Stephen. 1983. *Dante's Angelic Intelligences: Their Importance in the Cosmos and in Pre-Christian Religion.* Rome: Edizioni di Storia e Letteratura.

———. 2000. *A New Life of Dante.* Exeter: University of Exeter Press.

Benvenuto. 1887. Benvenuti de Rambaldis de Imola, *Comentum super Dantis Aldigherij "Comoediam."* Edited by G. F. Lacaita. 3 vols. Florence: Barbèra.

Beonio Brocchieri, Mariateresa Fumagalli. 1990. "The Intellectual." In *The Medieval World,* edited by Jacques Le Goff, translated by Lydia G. Cochrane, 181–209. London: Collins and Brown.

Bergin, Thomas G. 1970. *Perspectives on the "Divine Comedy."* Bloomington: Indiana University Press.

Bernard, Jacques. 1972. "Trade and Finance in the Middle Ages, 900–1500." In *The Fontana Economic History of Europe: The Middle Ages,* edited by Carlo M. Cipolla, 274–338. London: Collins.

Bertoletti, Nello. 2000. "Alcune note sugli esordi temporali del *Purgatorio.*" *La parola del testo* 4(2):233–51.

Blasucci, Luigi. 2000. "Per una tipologia degli esordi nei canti danteschi." *La parola del testo* 4(1):17–46.

Boase, T. S. R. 1933. *Boniface VIII.* London: Constable.

Boccaccio, Giovanni. 1965. *Esposizioni sopra la "Comedia" di Dante.* Edited by G. Padoan. Milan: Mondadori.

———. 1974. *Trattatello in laude di Dante.* Edited by P. G. Ricci. Milan: Mondadori.

Bolgar, R. R. 1964. *The Classical Heritage and Its Beneficiaries: From the Carolingian Age to the End of the Renaissance.* New York: Harper and Row.

Bosco, Umberto. 1966. *Dante vicino: Contributi e letture.* Caltanissetta: Sciascia.

Bosco, Umberto, and Giovanni Reggio, eds. 1979. Dante Alighieri, *La Divina Commedia.* 3 vols. Florence: Le Monnier.

Botterill, Steven. 1994a. *Dante and the Mystical Tradition: Bernard of Clairvaux in the "Commedia."* Cambridge: Cambridge University Press.

———. 1994b. *"Però che la divisione non si fa se non per aprire la sentenzia de la cosa divisa (V.N., XIV, 13):* The *Vita Nuova* as Commentary." In *La gloriosa donna de la mente: A Commentary on the "Vita Nuova,"* edited by V. Moleta, 61–76. Florence: Leo S. Olschki; Perth: University of Western Australia Press.

———, ed. and trans. 1996a. Dante Alighieri, *De vulgari eloquentia.* Cambridge: Cambridge University Press.

———. 1996b. "Dante's Poetics of the Sacred Word." *Philosophy and Literature* 20(1): 154–62.

———. 2001. "Ideals of the Institutional Church in Dante and Bernard of Clairvaux." *Italica* 78(3):297–313.

Bowsky, William M. 1960. *Henry VII in Italy: The Conflict of Empire and City-State, 1310–1313.* Lincoln: University of Nebraska Press.

Boyde, Patrick. 1971. *Dante's Style in His Lyric Poetry.* Cambridge: Cambridge University Press.

———. 1981. *Dante Philomythes and Philosopher: Man in the Cosmos.* Cambridge: Cambridge University Press.

———. 1993. *Perception and Passion in Dante's "Comedy."* Cambridge: Cambridge University Press.

———. 2000. *Human Vices and Human Worth in Dante's "Comedy."* Cambridge: Cambridge University Press.

Branca, Vittore. 1988. "Poetics of Renewal and Hagiographic Tradition in the *Vita nuova*." In *Lectura Dantis Newberryana,* edited by P. Cherchi and A. C. Mastrobuono, 1:123–52. Evanston, Ill.: Northwestern University Press.

Brandeis, Irma. 1960. *The Ladder of Vision: A Study of Dante's "Comedy."* London: Chatto and Windus.

Braunstein, Philippe. 1988. "Toward Intimacy: The Fourteenth and Fifteenth Centuries." In *A History of Private Life.* Vol. 2, *Revelations of the Medieval World,* edited by Georges Duby, translated by A. Goldhammer, 535–630. Cambridge: Harvard University Press.

Brownlee, Kevin. 1993. "Dante and the Classical Poets." In *The Cambridge Companion to Dante,* edited by Rachel Jacoff, 100–119. Cambridge: Cambridge University Press.

Brucker, Gene A. 1984. *Florence 1138–1737.* London: Sidgwick and Jackson.

Brugnoli, Giorgio. 1997. "Un libello della memoria asemplato per rubriche." *La parola del testo* 1(1):55–65.

Bruni, Leonardo. 1917. *Della vita, studi e costumi di Dante.* In *Le vite di Dante,* edited by G. L. Passerini. Florence: Sansoni.

Bruyne, Edgar de. 1969. *The Esthetics of the Middle Ages.* Translated by Eileen B. Hennessy. New York: Frederick Ungar.

Bynum, Caroline Walker. 1995. *The Resurrection of the Body in Western Christianity, 200–1336.* New York: Columbia University Press.

Calenda, Corrado. 1998. "Ancora su Cino, la *Commedia* e lo stilnovo (*Purg.* XXIV e XXVI)." In *Sotto il segno di Dante: Scritti in onore di Francesco Mazzoni,* edited by L. Coglievina and D. De Robertis, 75–83. Florence: Le Lettere.

Capitani, Ovidio. 1999. "Dante politico." In *"Per correr miglior acque …": Bilanci e prospettive degli studi danteschi alle soglie del nuovo millennio. Atti del Convegno di Verona-Ravenna, 25–29 ottobre 1999,* 1:57–69. Rome: Salerno Editrice.

Carrai, Stefano. 2002. "Critica genetica in assenza di autografo: Per una protostoria della *Vita Nova.*" *Rassegna europea di letteratura italiana* 19:9–17.

Cary, George. 1956. *The Medieval Alexander.* Cambridge: Cambridge University Press.

Casagrande, Gino. 1997. "Parole di Dante: Il *lungo silenzio* di *Inferno* I, 63." *Giornale storico della letteratura italiana* 174:221–54.

Casagrande, Gino, and Silvana Vecchio. 2000. *I sette vizi capitali: Storia dei peccati nel medioevo.* Turin: Einaudi.

Casciani, Santa, and Christopher Kleinhenz, trans. 2000. *The "Fiore" and the "Detto d'amore": A Late 13th-Century Translation of the "Roman de la Rose" Attributable to Dante.* The William and Katherine Devers Series in Dante Studies, vol. 4. Notre Dame, Ind.: University of Notre Dame Press.

Cassell, Anthony K. 1976. "Failure, Pride, and Conversion in *Inferno* I." *Dante Studies* 94:33–58.

———. 1989. *Lectura Dantis Americana: "Inferno" I.* Philadelphia: University of Pennsylvania Press.

Cecchini, Enzo, ed. 1979. *Egloghe.* In Dante Alighieri, *Opere minori* 2:647–89. Milan and Naples: Ricciardi.

Cecco d'Ascoli [Francesco Stabili]. 1927. *L'acerba.* Edited by Achille Crespi. Ascoli Piceno: Giuseppe Cesari.

Cervigni, Dino S. 1986. *Dante's Poetry of Dreams.* Florence: Leo S. Olschki.

Cervigni, Dino S., and Edward Vasta, trans. 1995. *Dante Alighieri: Vita Nuova.* Italian text with facing English translation. Notre Dame, Ind.: University of Notre Dame Press.

Cestaro, Gary. 2003. *Dante and the Grammar of the Nursing Body.* The William and Katherine Devers Series in Dante Studies, edited by Theodore J. Cachey, Jr., and Christian Moevs, vol. 5. Notre Dame, Ind.: University of Notre Dame Press.

Charity, Alan C. 1987. *Events and Their Afterlife: The Dialectics of Christian Typology in the Bible and Dante.* Cambridge: Cambridge University Press.

Chiamenti, Massimiliano. 1995. *Dante Alighieri traduttore.* Florence: Le Lettere.

Chiarenza, Marguerite Mills. 1972. "The Imageless Vision and Dante's *Paradiso.*" *Dante Studies* 90:77–92.

———. 1975. "Pagan Images in the Prologue of the *Paradiso.*" *Proceedings of the Pacific Northwest Conference on Foreign Languages* 26(1):133–36.

———. 1983. "Time and Eternity in the Myths of *Paradiso* XVII." In *Dante, Petrarch, Boccaccio: Studies in the Italian Trecento in Honor of Charles S. Singleton,* edited by Aldo S. Bernardo and Anthony L. Pellegrini, 133–50. Medieval & Renaissance Texts & Studies, vol. 22. Binghamton, N.Y.: Medieval & Renaissance Texts & Studies.

Chiavacci Leonardi, Anna Maria, ed. 1994. Dante Alighieri, *Commedia.* Vol. 2, *Purgatorio.* Milan: Mondadori.

———, ed. 1997. Dante Alighieri, *Commedia.* Vol. 3, *Paradiso.* Milan: Mondadori

Cipolla, Carlo M. 1972. "The Origins." In *The Fontana Economic History of Europe.* Vol. 1, *The Middle Ages,* edited by Carlo M. Cipolla, 11–23. London: Collins.

Cogan, Mark. 1999. *The Design in the Wax: The Structure of the "Divine Comedy" and Its Meaning.* The William and Katherine Devers Series in Dante Studies, vol. 3. Notre Dame, Ind.: University of Notre Dame Press.

Coleman, Janet. 1991. "Property and Poverty." In *The Cambridge History of Medieval Political Thought, c. 350–c. 1450,* edited by J. H. Burns, 607–48. Cambridge: Cambridge University Press.

Comparetti, Domenico. 1966. *Vergil in the Middle Ages.* Translated by E. F. M. Benecke, with an introduction by R. Ellis. Hamden, Conn.: Archon Books.

Contini, Gianfranco, ed. 1946. Dante Alighieri, *Rime.* 2d ed. Turin: Einaudi.

———. 1976. *Un'idea di Dante: Saggi danteschi.* Turin: Einaudi.

———, ed. 1984. Dante Alighieri, *Rime.* In Dante Alighieri, *Opere minori,* vol. 1, part 1, 251–552. Milan and Naples: Ricciardi.

Cornish, Alison. 2000. *Reading Dante's Stars.* New Haven: Yale University Press.

Corti, Maria. 1983. *La felicità mentale: Nuove prospettive per Cavalcanti e Dante.* Turin: Einaudi.

———. 1987. "Il modello analogico nel pensiero medievale e dantesco." In *Dante e le forme dell'allegoresi,* edited by Michelangelo Picone, 11–20. Ravenna: Longo.

———. 1992. "*De vulgari eloquentia* di Dante Alighieri." In *Letteratura italiana: Le Opere,* edited by Alberto Asor Rosa, 1:187–209. Turin: Einaudi.

———. 1995. "La *Commedia* di Dante e l'oltretomba islamico." *Belfagor* 50(3):301–14.

———. 2001. "Dante e la cultura islamica." In *"Per correr miglior acque . . .": Bilanci e prospettive degli studi danteschi alle soglie del nuovo millennio. Atti del Convegno di Verona-Ravenna, 25–29 ottobre 1999*, 1:183–202. Rome: Salerno Editrice.

Culler, Jonathan. 1981. *The Pursuit of Signs: Semiotics, Literature, Deconstruction*. London: Routledge and Kegan Paul.

Cursietti, Mauro. 1995. *La falsa tenzone di Dante con Forese Donati*. Anzio: De Rubeis.

———. 1997. "Ancora per il *Fiore*: Indizi cavalcantiani." *La parola del testo* 1:197–218.

———. 2000. "Dante e Forese alla taverna del Paníco: Le prove documentarie della falsità della tenzone." *L'Alighieri* 16 (n.s.):7–22.

Curtius, Ernst R. 1953. *European Literature and the Latin Middle Ages*. Translated by W. R. Trask. New York: Pantheon.

Davis, Charles Till. 1957. *Dante and the Idea of Rome*. Oxford: Clarendon Press.

———. 1976a. "Scuola: La scuola al tempo di Dante." *Enciclopedia Dantesca* 5:106–9. Rome: Istituto della Enciclopedia Italiana.

———. 1976b. "Veltro." *Enciclopedia Dantesca* 5:908–12. Rome: Istituto della Enciclopedia Italiana.

———. 1984. *Dante's Italy and Other Essays*. Philadelphia: University of Pennsylvania Press.

———. 1988. "The Florentine *Studia* and Dante's 'Library.'" In *The "Divine Comedy" and the Encyclopedia of Arts and Sciences,* edited by Giuseppe Di Scipio and Aldo Scaglione, 339–66. Amsterdam: John Benjamins.

———. 1992. "The Middle Ages." In *The Legacy of Rome: A New Appraisal,* edited by Richard Jenkyns, 61–96. Oxford: Oxford University Press.

De Angelis, Violetta. 1997. "Il testo di Lucano, Dante e Petrarca." In *Seminario dantesco internazionale/International Dante Seminar 1: Atti del primo convegno tenutosi al Chauncey Conference Center, Princeton, 21–23 ottobre 1994,* edited by Zygmunt G. Barański, 67–109. Florence: Le Lettere.

Delmay, Bernard. 1986. *I personaggi della Divina Commedia. Classificazione e registro*. Florence: Leo S. Olschki.

Delumeau, Jean. 1994. *Storia del paradiso: Il giardino delle delizie*. Translated by L. Grasso. Bologna: Il Mulino.

De Mauro, Tullio, ed. 1963. *Storia linguistica dell'Italia unita*. Bari: Laterza.

———. 2000. *Grande Dizionario Italiano dell'Uso*. 6 vols., with CD-Rom. Turin: UTET.

De' Negri, Enrico. 1958. "Tema e iconografia del *Purgatorio*." *Romanic Review* 49:81–104.

De Robertis, Domenico. 1950. "Cino e le 'imitazioni' dalle rime di Dante." *Studi Danteschi* 29:103–77.

———. 1961. *Il libro della "Vita Nuova."* Florence: Sansoni.

———, ed. 1984. Dante Alighieri, *Vita Nuova*. In Dante Alighieri, *Opere minori,* vol. 1, part 1, 3–247. Milan and Naples: Ricciardi, 1984.

———, ed. 2002. Dante Alighieri, *Rime*. Vol. 3, *Testi*. Florence: Le Lettere.

De Rosa, Mario. 1990. *Dante e il padre ideale*. Naples: Federico & Ardia.

De Sanctis, Francesco. 1964 [1870–71]. *Storia della letteratura italiana*. Edited by Benedetto Croce. 2 vols. Bari: Laterza.

Di Fonzo, Claudia. 1991. "*La dolce donna dietro a lor mi pinse/con un sol cenno su per quella scala (Par.* XXII, 100–101)." *Studi Danteschi* 63:141–75.

Dionisotti, Carlo. 1967. *Geografia e storia della letteratura italiana.* Turin: Einaudi.

Di Pino, Guido. 1962. *La figurazione della luce nella "Divina Commedia."* Messina and Florence: D'Anna.

Di Scipio, Giuseppe. 1988. "Dante and Politics." In *The "Divine Comedy" and the Encyclopedia of Arts and Sciences,* edited by G. Di Scipio and A. Scaglione, 267–84. Amsterdam: John Benjamins.

Di Scipio, Giuseppe, and A. Scaglione, eds. 1988. *The "Divine Comedy" and the Encyclopedia of Arts and Sciences.* Amsterdam: John Benjamins.

Dronke, Peter. 1976. "*Orizzonte che rischiari.*" *Romance Philology* 29:1–19.

———. 1986. *Dante and Medieval Latin Traditions.* Cambridge: Cambridge University Press.

———. 1994. *Verse with Prose from Petronius to Dante: The Art and Scope of Mixed Form.* Cambridge: Harvard University Press.

———. 1997a. *Dante's Second Love: The Originality and the Contexts of the "Convivio."* Leeds: Maney and Sons.

———. 1997b. *Source of Inspiration: Studies in Literary Transformations, 400–1500.* Rome: Edizioni di Storia e Letteratura.

Duby, Georges. 1981. *The Age of the Cathedrals: Art and Society 980–1420.* London: Croom Helm.

Duby, Georges, and Michelle Perrot. 1990. *Histoire des femmes en Occident.* Vol. 2, *Le Moyen Âge,* edited by Christiane Klapisch-Zuber. Paris: Plon.

Durling, Robert M., and Ronald L. Martinez. 1990. *Time and the Crystal: Studies in Dante's "Rime Petrose."* Berkeley: University of California Press.

———, trans. 1996. *The "Divine Comedy" of Dante Alighieri.* Vol. 1, *Inferno.* Edited and translated by Robert M. Durling, with introduction and notes by Ronald L. Martinez and Robert M. Durling. Oxford: Oxford University Press.

———, trans. 2003. *The "Divine Comedy" of Dante Alighieri.* Vol. 2, *Purgatorio.* Edited and translated by Robert M. Durling, with introduction and notes by Ronald L. Martinez and Robert M. Durling. Oxford: Oxford University Press.

Eco, Umberto. 1981. *The Role of the Reader: Explorations in Semiotic Texts.* London: Hutchinson.

———. 1986. *Art and Beauty in the Middle Ages.* Translated by H. Bredin. New Haven: Yale University Press.

———. 1997. *The Search for a Perfect Language.* London: Fontana.

Eliot, Thomas Stearns. 1965. *Dante.* London: Faber and Faber.

Esposito, Enzo. 1997. "Tenzone *no.*" *La parola del testo* 1(2):268–71.

———, ed. 2000. *Dante e il Giubileo.* Florence: Leo S. Olschki.

Esposito, Enzo, R. Manica, N. Longo, and R. Scrivano. 1996. *Memoria biblica nell'opera di Dante.* Rome: Bulzoni.

Faral, Edmond. 1924. *Les Arts poétiques du XIIe et du XIIIe siècle.* Paris: Champion.

Fasani, Remo. 1992. *La metrica della "Divina Commedia" e altri saggi di metrica italiana.* Ravenna: Longo.

Fenzi, Enrico. 1997. *"Sollazzo* e *leggiadria:* Un'interpretazione della canzone dantesca *Poscia ch'amor." Studi Danteschi* 63:191–280.

Ferguson, George. 1961. *Signs and Symbols in Christian Art.* New York: Oxford University Press.

Ferrante, Joan M. 1983. "Words and Images in the *Paradiso:* Reflections of the Divine." In *Dante, Petrarch, Boccaccio: Studies in the Italian Trecento in Honor of Charles S. Singleton,* edited by Aldo S. Bernardo and Anthony L. Pellegrini, 115–32. Medieval & Renaissance Texts & Studies, vol. 22. Binghamton, N.Y.: Medieval & Renaissance Texts & Studies.

———. 1984. *The Political Vision of the "Divine Comedy."* Princeton: Princeton University Press.

———. 1985 [1975]. *Woman as Image in Medieval Literature from the Twelfth Century to Dante.* Durham, N.C.: Labyrinth.

———. 1992. *Dante's Beatrice: Priest of an Androgynous God.* Center for Medieval & Early Renaissance Studies, Occasional Papers, no. 2. Binghamton, N.Y.: Medieval & Renaissance Texts & Studies.

———. 1993a. "A Poetics of Chaos and Harmony." In *The Cambridge Companion to Dante,* edited by Rachel Jacoff, 153–71. Cambridge: Cambridge University Press.

———. 1993b. "Why Did Dante Write the *Comedy?" Dante Studies* 111:9–18.

———. 1995. "Hell as the Mirror Image of Paradise." In *Dante's "Inferno": The Indiana Critical Edition,* edited by Mark Musa, 367–80. Bloomington: Indiana University Press.

Ferretti, Giovanni. 1935. *I due tempi di composizione della "Divina Commedia."* Bari: Laterza.

Ferretti Cuomo, Luisa. 1994. *Anatomia di un'immagine ("Inferno" 2.127–132): Saggio di lessicologia e di semantica strutturale.* New York: Lang.

Fido, Franco. 1986. "'Writing Like God'—or Better? Symmetries in Dante's 26th and 27th Cantos." *Italica* 43:250–64.

Folena, Gianfranco. 1977. "Il canto di Guido Guinizzelli." *Giornale storico della letteratura italiana* 154:481–508.

Forti, Fiorenzo. 1977. *Magnanimitade: Studi su un tema dantesco.* Bologna: Pàtron.

Foster, Kenelm. 1957. *God's Tree.* London: Blackfriars.

———. 1965. "Religion and Philosophy in Dante." In *The Mind of Dante,* edited by U. Limentani, 47–78. Cambridge: Cambridge University Press.

———. 1976. "Tommaso d'Aquino." In *Enciclopedia dantesca* 5:626–49. Rome: Istituto della Enciclopedia Italiana.

———. 1977. *The Two Dantes and Other Studies.* London: Darton, Longman & Todd.

Foster, Kenelm, and Patrick Boyde, ed. and trans. 1967. *Dante's Lyric Poetry.* 2 vols. Oxford: Clarendon Press.

Freccero, John. 1961. "Satan's Fall and the *Quaestio de Aqua et Terra." Italica* 38(2): 99–115.

———. 1973. "Casella's Song." *Dante Studies* 91:73–80.

———. 1986. *Dante: The Poetics of Conversion.* Edited by Rachel Jacoff. Cambridge: Harvard University Press.

Frugoni, Arsenio, and Giorgio Brugnoli, eds. 1979. Dante Alighieri, *Epistole.* In Dante Alighieri, *Opere minori,* vol. 2, 506–643. Milan and Naples: Ricciardi.

Frugoni, Chiara. 1991. *A Distant City: Images of Urban Experience in the Medieval World.* Translated by W. McCuaig. Princeton: Princeton University Press.

———. 2000. *Celestino V, Bonifacio VIII e il primo Anno Santo.* Milan: Rizzoli.

Frye, Northrop. 1982. *The Great Code: The Bible and Literature.* London: Routledge and Kegan Paul.

Fubini, Mario. 1966. *Il peccato di Ulisse e altri scritti danteschi.* Milan and Naples: Ricciardi.

Gardiner, Eileen, ed. 1989. *Visions of Heaven and Hell before Dante.* New York: Italica Press.

Gardner, Edmund. 1968 [1913]. *Dante and the Mystics: A Study of the Mystical Aspects of the "Divina Commedia" and Its Relations with Some of Its Mediaeval Sources.* New York: Haskell House.

———. 1972 [1900]. *Dante's Ten Heavens: A Study of the "Paradiso."* Freeport N.Y.: Books for Libraries Press.

Giacalone, Giuseppe, ed. 1968–69. Dante Alighieri, *La Divina Commedia. Commento e postille critiche di G. Giacalone.* 3 vols. Rome: Signorelli.

Gibbons, David. 2002. *Metaphor in Dante.* Oxford: Legenda.

Gilson, Étienne. 1948. *Dante the Philosopher.* Translated by D. Moore. London: Sheed and Ward.

———. 1965. "Poésie et théologie dans la Divine Comédie." In *Atti del Congresso Internazionale di Studi Danteschi* 1:197–223.

———. 1967. "Dante's Notion of a Shade: *Purgatorio* XXV." *Mediaeval Studies* 24:124–42.

———. 1974. *Dante et Béatrice: Etudes dantesques.* Paris: Vrin.

Gilson, Simon A. 2000. *Medieval Optics and Theories of Light in the Works of Dante.* Lewiston, N.Y.: Edwin Mellen Press.

Gimpel, Jean. 1988. *The Medieval Machine: The Industrial Revolution of the Middle Ages.* Aldershot: Wildwood House.

Ginsberg, Warren. 1999. *Dante's Aesthetics of Being.* Ann Arbor: University of Michigan Press.

Giunta, Claudio. 1998. *La poesia italiana nell'età di Dante: La linea Bonagiunta-Guinizzelli.* Bologna: Il Mulino.

Gorni, Guglielmo. 1981. *Il nodo della lingua e il verbo d'Amore: Studi su Dante e altri duecentisti.* Florence: Leo S. Olschki.

———. 1984. "Spirito profetistico duecentesco e Dante." *Letture Classensi* 13:49–68.

———. 1988. "Parodia e scrittura in Dante." In *Dante e la Bibbia,* edited by Giovanni Barblan, 323–40. Florence: Leo S. Olschki.

———. 1990. *Lettera nome numero: L'ordine delle cose in Dante.* Bologna: Il Mulino.

———. 1993. *Metrica e analisi letteraria.* Bologna: Il Mulino.

———. 1995a. "La canzone *montanina.*" *Letture Classensi* 24:129–50.

———. 1995b. *Dante nella selva: Il primo canto della Commedia.* Parma: Nuova Pratiche Editrice.

———, ed. 1996. Dante Alighieri, *Vita Nova.* Turin: Einaudi.

———. 2000. "I «riguardi» di Ercole e l'«arto passo» di Ulisse." *Letteratura italiana antica* 1:43–58.

———. 2001. *Dante prima della "Commedia."* Fiesole: Cadmo.

Grant, Edward. 1996. *The Foundations of Modern Science in the Middle Ages: Their Religious, Institutional, and Intellectual Contexts.* Cambridge: Cambridge University Press.

Grant, Michael. 1998. *Myths of the Greeks and Romans.* London: Phoenix.

Grayson, Cecil. 1965. "*Nobilior est vulgaris*: Latin and Vernacular in Dante's Thought." In *Centenary Essays on Dante by Members of the Oxford Dante Society,* 54–76. Oxford: Clarendon Press.

———. 1972. *Cinque saggi su Dante.* Bologna: Pàtron.

Green, Louis. 1994. "*Bono in alto grado* (*V.N.*, XXII, 2): Beatrice's Father, Nobility, and the Nobility in Dante's Florence." In *"La gloriosa donna de la mente": A Commentary on the "Vita Nuova,"* edited by V. Moleta, 97–117. Florence: Leo S. Olschki; Perth: University of Western Australia Press.

Griffin, Jasper. 1992. "Virgil." In *The Legacy of Rome: A New Appraisal,* edited by Richard Jenkins, 125–50. Oxford: Oxford University Press.

Guido da Pisa. 1974. *Guido da Pisa's "Expositiones et Glose super Comediam Dantis," or "Commentary on Dante's 'Inferno.'"* Edited, with an introduction and notes, by Vincenzo Cioffari. Albany: State University of New York Press.

Gurevich, Aron Ja. 1990. "The Merchant." In *The Medieval World,* edited by Jacques Le Goff, translated by Lydia G. Cochrane, 243–83. London: Collins and Brown.

Hardt, Manfred. 1988. "Dante and Arithmetic." In *The "Divine Comedy" and the Encyclopedia of Arts and Sciences,* edited by G. Di Scipio and A. Scaglione, 81–94. Amsterdam: John Benjamins.

———. 1989. "I numeri nella poetica di Dante." *Studi danteschi* 61:1–23.

———. 1995. "I numeri e le scritture crittografiche nella *Divina Commedia.*" In *Dante e la scienza,* edited by Patrick Boyde and Vittorio Russo, 71–90. Ravenna: Longo.

Harrison, Robert Pogue. 1988. *The Body of Beatrice.* Baltimore: Johns Hopkins University Press.

———. 1993. "Approaching the *Vita nuova.*" In *The Cambridge Companion to Dante,* edited by Rachel Jacoff, 34–44. Cambridge: Cambridge University Press.

Hart, Thomas Elwood. 1988. "Geometric Metaphor and Proportional Design in Dante's *Commedia.*" In *The "Divine Comedy" and the Encyclopedia of Arts and Sciences,* edited by G. Di Scipio and A. Scaglione, 95–146. Amsterdam: John Benjamins.

Hawkins, Peter S. 1985. "Transfiguring the Text: Ovid, Scripture and the Dynamics of Allusion." *Stanford Italian Review* 5(2):115–39.

———. 1999. *Dante's Testaments: Essays in Scriptural Imagination.* Stanford: Stanford University Press.

———. 2000. "Bible." In *The Dante Encyclopedia,* edited by Richard Lansing, 100–103. New York: Garland.

Hawkins, Peter S., and Rachel Jacoff, eds. 2001. *The Poets' Dante.* New York: Farrar, Straus and Giroux.

Hazelton, Richard. 1957. "The Christianization of 'Cato': The *Disticha Catonis* in the Light of Late Mediaeval Commentaries." *Mediaeval Studies* 19:157–73.

Herzman, Ronald B. 1992. "Dante and the Apocalypse." In *The Apocalypse in the Middle Ages,* edited by R. K. Emmerson and B. McGinn, 398–413. Ithaca, N.Y.: Cornell University Press.

Highet, Gilbert. 1957. *The Classical Tradition: Greek and Roman Influences on Western Literature.* New York: Oxford University Press.

Hinds, Stephen E. 1998. "Ovid." In *The Oxford Companion to Classical Civilization,* edited by S. Hornblower and A. Spawforth, 508–12. Oxford: Oxford University Press.

Hollander, Robert. 1969. *Allegory in Dante's "Commedia."* Princeton: Princeton University Press.

———. 1974. "*Vita Nuova:* Dante's Perceptions of Beatrice." *Dante Studies* 92:1–18.

———. 1975. "Cato's Rebuke and Dante's *scoglio*." *Italica* 52:348–63.

———. 1980. *Studies in Dante.* Ravenna: Longo.

———. 1983. *Il Virgilio dantesco: Tragedia nella "Commedia."* Florence: Leo S. Olschki.

———. 1985. "Dante's Pagan Past: Notes on *Inferno* XIV and XVIII." *Stanford Italian Review* 5(1):23–36.

———. 1988. "Dante's *Commedia* and the Classical Tradition: The Case of Virgil." In *The "Divine Comedy" and the Encyclopedia of Arts and Sciences,* edited by Giuseppe Di Scipio and Aldo Scaglione, 15–26. Amsterdam: John Benjamins.

———. 1989. "Dante's Virgil: A Light That Failed." *Lectura Dantis Virginiana* 4:3–9.

———. 1990a. "The 'Canto of the Word' (*Inferno* 2)." In *Lectura Dantis Newberryana,* edited by P. Cherchi and A. C. Mastrobuono, 2:95–119. Evanston, Ill.: Northwestern University Press.

———. 1990b. "*Purgatorio* II: The New Song and the Old." *Lectura Dantis* 6:28–45.

———. 1991. "Dante's Misreading of the *Aeneid* in *Inferno* 20." In *The Poetry of Allusion: Virgil and Ovid in Dante's "Commedia,"* edited by Rachel Jacoff and Jeffrey T. Schnapp, 77–93. Stanford: Stanford University Press.

———. 1992a. "Dante and Cino da Pistoia." *Dante Studies* 110:201–31.

———. 1992b. *Dante and Paul's Five Words with Understanding.* Center for Medieval & Early Renaissance Studies, Occasional Papers, no. 1. Binghamton, N.Y.: Medieval & Renaissance Texts & Studies.

———. 1993a. *Dante's Epistle to Cangrande.* Ann Arbor: University of Michigan Press.

———. 1993b. "Le opere di Virgilio nella *Commedia* di Dante." In *Dante e la "bella scola" della poesia: Autorità e sfida poetica,* edited by Amilcare A. Iannucci, 247–343. Ravenna: Longo.

———. 1997. *Boccaccio's Dante and the Shaping Force of Satire.* Ann Arbor: University of Michigan Press.

———. 1998. "Dante as Uzzah? (*Purg.* X 57 and *Ep.* 11.9–12)." In *Sotto il segno di Dante,* edited by Leonella Coglievina and Domenico De Robertis, 143–51. Florence: Le Lettere.

———. 2000 [1976]. "Dante *Theologus-Poeta.*" *Dante Studies* 118:261–302.

———. 2001. *Dante: A Life in Works.* New Haven: Yale University Press.

Hollander, Robert, and Jean Hollander, trans. 2000. Dante Alighieri, *Inferno.* New York: Doubleday.

———. 2003. Dante Alighieri, *Purgatorio.* New York: Doubleday.

Hollander, Robert, and A. L. Rossi. 1986. "Dante's Republican Treasury." *Dante Studies* 104:59–82.

Hollander, Robert, and W. Stull. 1997. "The Lucanian Source of Dante's Ulysses." *Studi Danteschi* 63:249–88.

Holmes, George. 1980. "Dante and the Popes." In *The World of Dante: Essays on Dante and His Times,* edited by Cecil Grayson, 18–43. Oxford: Clarendon Press.

Honess, Claire. 1998. "Dante and Political Poetry in the Vernacular." *Journal of the Institute of Romance Studies* 6:21–42.

Howard, Lloyd H. 2001. *Formulas of Repetition in Dante's "Comedia": Suggested Journeys across Textual Space.* Montreal: McGill–Queen's University Press.

Howatson, M. C., ed. 1991. *The Oxford Companion to Classical Literature.* 2d ed. Oxford: Oxford University Press.

Hyatte, Reginald, trans. 1997. *The Prophet of Islam in Old French: "The Romance of Muhammad" (1258) and "The Book of Muhammad's Ladder" (1264).* Leiden: Brill.

Iannucci, Amilcare A. 1979–80. "Limbo: The Emptiness of Time." *Studi Danteschi* 52:69–128.

———. 1997. "The Mountainquake of *Purgatorio* and Virgil's Story." *Lectura Dantis* 20–21:48–58.

———. 2001. "Dante: Poeta o profeta?" In *"Per correr miglior acque . . .": Bilanci e prospettive degli studi danteschi alle soglie del nuovo millennio. Atti del Convegno di Verona-Ravenna, 25–29 ottobre 1999,* 1:93–114. Rome: Salerno Editrice.

Jacoff, Rachel. 1991a. "Intertextualities in Arcadia: *Purgatorio* 30.49–51." In *The Poetry of Allusion: Virgil and Ovid in Dante's "Commedia,"* edited by Rachel Jacoff and Jeffrey T. Schnapp, 131–44. Stanford: Stanford University Press.

———. 1991b. "The Rape/Rapture of Europa: *Paradiso* 27." In *The Poetry of Allusion: Virgil and Ovid in Dante's "Commedia,"* edited by Rachel Jacoff and Jeffrey T. Schnapp, 233–46. Stanford: Stanford University Press.

———. 2000. "'Our Bodies, Our Selves': The Body in the *Commedia.*" In *Sparks and Seeds: Medieval Literature and Its Afterlife. Essays in Honor of John Freccero,* edited by Dana E. Stewart and Alison Cornish, 119–37. Turnhout: Brepols.

Jacoff, Rachel, and Jeffrey T. Schnapp. 1991. "Introduction." In *The Poetry of Allusion: Virgil and Ovid in Dante's "Commedia,"* edited by Rachel Jacoff and Jeffrey T. Schnapp, 1–15. Stanford: Stanford University Press.

Jacoff, Rachel, and William A. Stephany. 1989. *Lectura Dantis Americana: "Inferno" II.* Philadelphia: University of Pennsylvania Press.

Jager, Eric. 2000. *The Book of the Heart.* Chicago: University of Chicago Press.

Jakobson, Roman. 1960. "Linguistics and Poetics." In *Style in Language,* edited by Thomas A. Sebeok, 350–77. New York: Massachusetts Institute of Technology and J. Wiley and Sons.

Jakobson, Roman, and Paolo Valesio. 1966. *"Vocabulorum constructio* in *Se vedi li occhi miei." Studi Danteschi* 43:7–33.

Kantorowicz, Ernst H. 1957. *The King's Two Bodies: A Study in Medieval Political Theology.* Princeton: Princeton University Press.

Kay, Richard. 1989. "Il giorno della nascita di Dante e la dipartita di Beatrice." In *Studi americani su Dante,* edited by Gian Carlo Alessio and Robert Hollander, 243–65. Milan: Franco Angeli.

———. 1994. *Dante's Christian Astrology.* Philadelphia: University of Pennsylvania Press.

———, trans. 1998. *Dante's "Monarchia."* Toronto: Pontifical Institute of Mediaeval Studies.

Kelly, Henry Ansgar. 1989. *Tragedy and Comedy from Dante to Pseudo-Dante*. Berkeley: University of California Press.

Kennedy, Duncan F. 1997. "Modern Receptions and Their Interpretative Implications." In *The Cambridge Companion to Virgil*, edited by Charles Martindale, 38–53. Cambridge: Cambridge University Press.

Klapisch-Zuber, Christiane. 1990. "Women and the Family." In *The Medieval World*, edited by Jacques Le Goff, translated by Lydia G. Cochrane, 285–311. London: Collins and Brown.

Kleiner, John. 1994. *Mismapping the Underworld: Daring and Error in Dante's "Comedy."* Stanford: Stanford University Press.

Kleinhenz, Christopher. 1986a. "Dante and the Bible: Intertextual Approaches to the *Divine Comedy*." *Italica* 63:225–36.

———. 1986b. *The Early Italian Sonnet: The First Century (1220–1321)*. Lecce: Milella.

———. 1988. "Virgil, Statius, and Dante: An Unusual Trinity." In *Lectura Dantis Newberryana*, edited by P. Cherchi and A. Mastrobuono, 1:37–55. Evanston, Ill.: Northwestern University Press.

———. 1997. "Dante and the Bible: Biblical Citation in the *Divine Comedy*." In *Dante: Contemporary Perspectives*, edited by Amilcare A. Iannucci, 74–93. Toronto: University of Toronto Press.

Kretzmann, Norman, Anthony Kenny, and Jan Pinborg. 1988. *The Cambridge History of Later Medieval Philosophy: From the Rediscovery of Aristotle to the Disintegration of Scholasticism, 1100–1600*. Cambridge: Cambridge University Press.

Lagarde, Georges de. 1958. *La Naissance de l'esprit laïque au déclin du Moyen Âge*. 2 vols. Louvain: Nauwelaerts.

Lambert, M. D. 1961. *Franciscan Poverty: The Doctrine of the Absolute Poverty of Christ and the Apostles in the Franciscan Order, 1210–1323*. London: SPCK.

———. 1992. *Medieval Heresy: Popular Movements from the Gregorian Reform to the Reformation*. Oxford: Blackwell.

Lansing, Richard H. 1977. *From Image to Idea: A Study of the Simile in Dante's "Commedia."* Ravenna: Longo.

———, ed. 2000a. *The Dante Encyclopedia*. New York: Garland.

———. 2000b. "Simile." In *The Dante Encyclopedia*, edited by Richard Lansing, 778–81. New York: Garland.

Lanza, Antonio, ed. 1996. Dante Alighieri, *La Commedia: Testo critico secondo i più antichi manoscritti fiorentini (nuova edizione)*. Anzio: De Rubeis.

———. 2002. *Freschi e Minii del Due, Tre e Quattrocento: Saggi di letteratura italiana antica*. Fiesole: Cadmo.

Larner, John. 1980. *Italy in the Age of Dante and Petrarch 1216–1380*. London: Longman.

Lawrence, C. H. 1984. *Medieval Monasticism: Forms of Religious Life in the Middle Ages*. London: Longman.

Ledda, Giuseppe. 2002. *La guerra della lingua: Ineffabilità, retorica e narrativa nella "Commedia" di Dante*. Ravenna: Longo.

Le Goff, Jacques. 1982. *Time, Work, and Culture in the Middle Ages*. Translated by A. Goldhammer. Chicago: University of Chicago Press.

———. 1984. *The Birth of Purgatory*. Translated by A. Goldhammer. London: Scolar Press.

———. 1988. *Medieval Civilization 400–1500*. Translated by Julia Barrow. Oxford: Blackwell.

———, ed. 1990. *The Medieval World*. Translated by Lydia G. Cochrane. London: Collins and Brown.

———. 1992. *The Medieval Imagination*. Translated by A. Goldhammer. Chicago: University of Chicago Press.

———. 1993. *Intellectuals in the Middle Ages*. Translated by T. Lavender Fagan. Oxford: Blackwell.

———. 1997. *Il Basso Medioevo*. Translated by Elena Vaccari Spagnol. Milan: Feltrinelli.

Leo, Ulrich. 1951. "The Unfinished *Convivio* and Dante's Rereading of the *Aeneid*." *Mediaeval Studies* 13:41–64.

Leonardi, Lino. "Cavalcanti, Dante e il nuovo stile." In *Dante: Da Firenze all'aldilà. Atti del terzo Seminario Dantesco Internazionale, Firenze 9–11 giugno 2000,* edited by Michelangelo Picone, 331–54. Florence: Cesati.

Lepschy, Anna Laura, and Giulio Lepschy. 1988. *The Italian Language Today*. London: Routledge.

Levers, Toby. 2002. "The Image of Authorship in the Final Chapter of the *Vita Nuova*." *Italian Studies* 57:5–19.

Lewis, C. S. 1957. "Dante's Statius." *Medium Aevum* 25(3):133–39.

———. 1964. *The Discarded Image: An Introduction to Medieval and Renaissance Literature*. Cambridge: Cambridge University Press.

Lisio, Giuseppe. 1902. *L'arte del periodo nelle opere volgari di Dante Alighieri e del secolo XIII*. Bologna: Zanichelli.

Maccarrone, Michele. 1952. *Vicarius Christi: Storia del titolo papale*. Rome: Facultas Theologica Pontificii Athenei Lateranensis.

Manselli, Raoul. 1965. "Dante e l'*Ecclesia Spiritualis*." In *Dante e Roma*, 115–35. Florence: Le Monnier.

Marenbon, John. 2001. "Dante's Averroism." In *Poetry and Philosophy in the Middle Ages: A Festschrift for Peter Dronke,* edited by John Marenbon, 349–74. Leiden: Brill.

Marigo, Aristide, ed. 1968. Dante Alighieri, *De vulgari eloquentia*. In *Opere di Dante*, vol. 6, 3d ed., edited by Pier Giorgio Ricci. Florence: Le Monnier.

Marti, Mario. 1965. "Vita e morte della presunta doppia redazione della *Vita nuova*." In *Studi in onore di Alfredo Schiaffini*, 657–69. Rome: Edizioni dell'Ateneo.

———. 1969. *Poeti del dolce stil nuovo*. Edited by Mario Marti. Florence: Le Monnier.

Martinelli, Bortolo. 1983. "Sul *Quodammodo* di *Monarchia*, III. xv. 17." In *Miscellanea di studi in onore di Vittore Branca*, 2:193–214. Florence: Leo S. Olschki.

Martinez, Ronald L. 1993. "Dante's Bear": A Note on *Cosí nel mio parlar*." *Dante Studies* 111:213–22.

———. 1998. "Mourning Beatrice: The Rhetoric of Threnody in the *Vita nova*." *Modern Language Notes* 113:1–29.

Masini, Andrea. 1990. "Lettura linguistica di *Cosí nel mio parlar voglio esser aspro*." *Studi Danteschi* 62:289–322.

Masseron, Alexandre. 1953. *Dante et saint Bernard*. Paris: Albin Michel.

Mastrobuono, Antonio C. 1990. *Dante's Journey of Sanctification*. Washington, D.C.: Regnery Gateway.

Matteini, Nevio. 1958. *Il piú antico oppositore di Dante: Guido Vernani da Rimini. Testo critico del "De reprobatione Monarchiae."* Padua: CEDAM.

Matthew of Vendôme. 1981. *Ars versificatoria (The Art of the Versemaker)*. Translated, with an introduction, by Roger P. Parr. Milwaukee: Marquette University Press.

Mazzeo, Joseph A. 1958. *Structure and Thought in the "Paradiso."* Ithaca, N.Y.: Cornell University Press.

———. 1960. *Mediaeval Cultural Tradition in Dante's "Comedy."* Ithaca, N.Y.: Cornell University Press.

Mazzoni, Francesco. 1965. "Saggio di un nuovo commento alla *Commedia:* Il canto IV dell'*Inferno*." *Studi Danteschi* 42:29–206.

———. 1966. *Contributi di filologia dantesca*. Florence: Sansoni.

———. 1967. *Saggio di un nuovo commento alla "Divina Commedia": "Inferno," Canti I–III*. Florence: Sansoni.

———, ed. 1972. Dante Alighieri, *La Divina Commedia: Inferno*. With a commentary by T. Casini, S. A. Barbi, and A. Momigliano. Florence: Sansoni.

———, ed. 1973. Dante Alighieri, *La Divina Commedia: Purgatorio*. With a commentary by T. Casini, S. A. Barbi, and A. Momigliano. Florence: Sansoni.

———, ed. 1979. Dante Alighieri, *Questio de aqua et terra*. In Dante Alighieri, *Opere minori*, vol. 2, 693–880. Milan and Naples: Ricciardi.

———. 1989. "Il canto VI del *Paradiso*." In *"Paradiso": Letture degli anni 1979–1981*, 167–82. Rome: Bonacci.

———. 1997a. "Il 'trascendentale' dimenticato." In *Omaggio a Beatrice (1290–1990)*, edited by Rudy Abardo, 93–132. Florence: Le Lettere.

———. 1997b. "San Bernardo e la visione poetica della *Divina Commedia*." In *Seminario dantesco internazionale/International Dante Seminar 1: Atti del primo convegno tenutosi al Chauncey Conference Center, Princeton 21–23 ottobre 1994*, edited by Zygmunt G. Barański, 171–241. Florence: Le Lettere.

Mazzotta, Giuseppe. 1979. *Dante, Poet of the Desert: History and Allegory in the "Divine Comedy."* Princeton: Princeton University Press.

———. 1993. *Dante's Vision and the Circle of Knowledge*. Princeton: Princeton University Press.

McDannell, Colleen, and Bernard Lang. 1988. *Heaven: A History*. New Haven: Yale University Press.

Meerseman, Gilles G. 1965. "Dante come teologo." In *Atti del Congresso Internazionale di Studi Danteschi*, 1:177–93. Florence: Sansoni.

Mengaldo, Pier Vincenzo. 1978. *Linguistica e retorica di Dante*. Pisa: Nistri-Lischi.

———, ed. 1979. Dante Alighieri, *De vulgari eloquentia*. In Dante Alighieri, *Opere minori*, vol. 2, 3–237. Milan and Naples: Ricciardi.

———. 1997. "Dante come critico." *La parola del testo* 1(1):36–54.

———. 2001. "Una nuova edizione della *Commedia*." *La parola del testo* 5(2):279–89.

Menichetti, Aldo. 1993. *Metrica italiana: Fondamenti metrici, prosodia, rima*. Padova: Antenore.

Meyer, Heinz, and Rudolf Suntrup. 1987. *Lexikon der mittelalterlichen Zahlenbedeutungen*. Munich: Wilhelm Fink.

Mezzadroli, Giuseppina. 1990. *Seneca in Dante: Dalla tradizione medievale all'officina dell'autore*. Florence: Le Lettere.

Miccoli, Giovanni. 1990. "Monks." In *The Medieval World,* edited by Jacques Le Goff, translated by Lydia G. Cochrane, 37–73. London: Collins and Brown.

Mineo, Niccolò. 1968. *Profetismo e apocalittica in Dante: Strutture e temi profetico-apocalittici in Dante (dalla "Vita Nuova" alla "Commedia")*. Catania: Università di Catania.

Moevs, Christian. 2000. "Pyramus at the Mulberry Tree: De-petrifying Dante's Tinted Mind." In *Imagining Heaven in the Middle Ages: A Book of Essays,* edited by Jan Swango Emerson and Hugh Feiss, O.S.B., 211–44. New York: Garland.

Moleta, Vincent. 1994 [1992]. "*Voi le vedete Amor pinto nel viso (V.N.,* XIX, 12): Prehistory of a Metaphor." In *La gloriosa donna de la mente: A Commentary on the "Vita Nuova,"* edited by Vincent Moleta, 77–95. Florence: Leo S. Olschki; Perth: University of Western Australia Press.

———. 1997. "Virgil in Cocytus." *Lectura Dantis* 20–21:33–47.

Mollat, Guillaume. 1963. *The Popes at Avignon, 1305–1378*. Translated by Jane Love. London: Nelson.

Moore, Edward. 1896. *Studies in Dante*. 1st series. Oxford: Clarendon Press.

———. 1899. *Studies in Dante*. 2d series. Oxford: Clarendon Press.

———. 1903. *Studies in Dante*. 3d series. Oxford: Clarendon Press.

Morgan, Alison. 1990. *Dante and the Medieval Other World*. Cambridge: Cambridge University Press.

Morghen, Raffaello. 1951. *Medievo cristiano*. Bari: Laterza.

———. 1983. *Dante profeta: Tra la storia e l'eterno*. Milan: Jaca.

Morris, Colin. 1991. *The Papal Monarchy: The Western Church from 1050 to 1250*. Oxford: Clarendon Press.

———. 1995. *The Discovery of the Individual: 1050–1200*. Reprint, Toronto: University of Toronto Press.

Murphy, James J. 1974. *Rhetoric in the Middle Ages: A History of Rhetorical Theory from Saint Augustine to the Renaissance*. Berkeley: University of California Press.

Musa, Mark, trans. 1962. *Dante's "Vita Nuova."* Bloomington: Indiana University Press.

Najemy, John M. 1993. "Dante and Florence." In *The Cambridge Companion to Dante,* edited by Rachel Jacoff, 80–99. Cambridge: Cambridge University Press.

Nardi, Bruno. 1944. *Nel mondo di Dante*. Rome: Istituto Grafico Tiberino.

———. 1959. *La caduta di Lucifero e l'autenticità della "Quaestio de aqua et terra."* Turin: SEI.

———. 1960a. "Il punto sull'Epistola a Cangrande." *Lectura Dantis Scaligera*. Florence: Le Monnier. Reprinted in B. Nardi, *"Lecturae" e altri studi danteschi,* edited by Rudy Abardo, 205–25. Florence: Le Lettere.

———. 1960b. *Studi di filosofia medievale*. Rome: Edizioni di Storia e Letteratura.

———. 1967 [1930]. *Saggi di filosofia dantesca*. Florence: La Nuova Italia.

———, ed. 1979. Dante Alighieri, *Monarchia*. In Dante Alighieri, *Opere minori*, vol. 2, 241–503. Milan and Naples: Ricciardi.

———. 1983 [1942]. *Dante e la cultura medievale.* Introduction by Tullio Gregory. Rome and Bari: Laterza.

———. 1992 [1960]. *Dal "Convivio" alla "Commedia": Sei saggi danteschi.* Introduction by Ovidio Capitani. Rome: Istituto Storico Italiano per il Medio Evo.

Newman, Barbara. 2003. *God and the Goddesses. Vision, Poetry, and Belief in the Middle Ages.* Philadelphia: University of Pennsylvania Press.

Olivi, Petrus Ioannis. 1992. *De usu paupere: The "Quaestio" and the "Tractatus."* Edited by D. Burr. Florence: Leo S. Olschki; Perth: University of Western Australia Press.

Ottimo. 1827. *L'ottimo commento della "Divina Commedia."* Vol. 1. Pisa: Capurro.

Ottokar, Nicola. 1926. *Il Comune di Firenze alle fine del Dugento.* Florence: Vallecchi.

Padoan, Giorgio. 1968. *Dante: De situ et forma aque et terre.* Edited by G. Padoan. Florence: Le Monnier.

———. 1975. *Introduzione a Dante.* Florence: Sansoni.

———. 1977. *Il pio Enea, l'empio Ulisse. Tradizione classica e intendimento medievale in Dante.* Ravenna: Longo.

———. 1993. *Il lungo cammino del "poema sacro": Studi danteschi.* Florence: Leo S. Olschki.

———. 1998. "Il vicariato cesareo dello Scaligero: Per la datazione dell'Epistola a Cangrande." *Lettere italiane* 50(2):161–75.

Pagani, Ileana. 1982. *La teoria linguistica di Dante.* Naples: Liguori.

Pagani, Walter. 1968. *Repertorio tematico della scuola poetica siciliana.* Bari: Adriatica.

Pagliaro, Antonino. 1976. "Similitudine." In *Enciclopedia dantesca* 5:253–59. Rome: Istituto della Enciclopedia Italiana.

Palma di Cesnola, Matteo. 1995. *Semiotica dantesca: Profetismo e diacronia.* Ravenna: Longo.

Pampaloni, Guido. 1973. *Firenze al tempo di Dante: Documenti sull'urbanistica fiorentina.* Pubblicazioni degli Archivi di Stato, Fonti e Sussidi, vol. 4. Rome: Ministero dell'Interno.

Paratore, Ettore. 1968. *Tradizione e struttura in Dante.* Florence: Sansoni.

———. 1976a. "Ovidio." In *Enciclopedia dantesca* 4:225–36. Rome: Istituto della Enciclopedia Italiana.

———. 1976b. "Stazio." In *Enciclopedia dantesca* 5:419–25. Rome: Istituto della Enciclopedia Italiana.

Partner, Peter. 1965. "Florence and the Papacy 1300–1375." In *Europe in the Late Middle Ages,* edited by John Hale, Roger Highfield, and Beryl Smalley, 76–121. London: Faber and Faber.

Pasquini, Emilio. 1987. "Le metafore della visione nella *Commedia.*" *Letture Classensi* 15:129–51.

———. 2001. *Dante e le figure del vero: La fabbrica della "Commedia."* Milan: Bruno Mondadori.

Pasquini, Emilio, and Antonio Quaglio, eds. 1987. Dante Alighieri, *Commedia.* Milan: Garzanti.

Pazzaglia, Mario. 1967. *Il verso e l'arte della canzone nel "De vulgari eloquentia."* Florence: La Nuova Italia.

Perella, Nicolas J. 1969. *The Kiss Sacred and Profane: An Interpretative History of Kiss Symbolism and Related Religio-Erotic Themes.* Berkeley: University of California Press.

Pertile, Lino. 1980. "Il nobile castello, il paradiso terrestre e l'umanesimo dantesco." *Filologia e critica* 5(1):1–29.

———. 1991a. "L'antica fiamma: La metamorfosi del fuoco nella *Commedia* di Dante." *The Italianist* 11:29–60.

———. 1991b. "*Canto–cantica–Comedía* e l'Epistola a Cangrande." *Lectura Dantis [Virginiana]* 9:105–23.

———. 1993a. "Dante's *Comedy* beyond the *Stilnovo*." *Lectura Dantis [Virginiana]* 13:47–77.

———. 1993b. "*Paradiso:* A Drama of Desire." In *Word and Drama in Dante*, edited by John C. Barnes and Jennifer Petrie, 143–80. Dublin: Irish Academic Press.

———. 1995a. "Dante, lo scoglio e la vesta." In *Da una riva all'altra: Studi in onore di Antonio Andrea,* edited by D. Della Terza, 85–101. Fiesole: Cadmo.

———. 1995b. "Poesia e scienza nell'ultima immagine del *Paradiso*." In *Dante e la scienza,* edited by Patrick Boyde and Vittorio Russo, 133–48. Ravenna: Longo.

———. 1996. "Bonconte e l'anafonesi (*Purg.* V 109–18)." *Filologia e critica* 21(1):118–26.

———. 1998. *La puttana e il gigante: Dal Cantico dei Cantici al Paradiso Terrestre di Dante.* Ravenna: Longo.

Peters, Edward, ed. and trans. 1980. *Heresy and Authority in Medieval Europe: Documents in Translation.* London: Scolar Press.

Petrocchi, Giorgio. 1969. *Itinerari danteschi.* Bari: Adriatica.

———. 1978. "Biografia: Attività politica e letteraria." In *Enciclopedia dantesca* 6 (Appendix):3–53. Rome: Istituto della Enciclopedia Italiana.

———. 1983. *Vita di Dante.* Rome and Bari: Laterza.

———. 1988. *La selva del protonotario: Nuovi studi danteschi.* Naples: Morano.

———, ed. 1994. Dante Alighieri, *La Commedia secondo l'antica vulgata.* 2d, rev. ed. 4 vols. Florence: Le Lettere.

Pézard, André, ed. 1965. *Dante: Oeuvres complètes.* Paris: Gallimard.

———. 1967. "Les trois langues de Cacciaguida." *Revue des Études italiennes* 13(3):217–38.

Piattoli, R. 1950. *Codice diplomatico dantesco.* Florence: Gonnelli.

Picone, Michelangelo. 1979. *"Vita Nuova" e tradizione romanza.* Padua: Liviana.

———. 1983. "Rito e *Narratio* nella *Vita Nuova*." In *Miscellanea di studi in onore di Vittore Branca,* 1:141–57. Florence: Leo S. Olschki.

———. 1987. "La *Vita Nuova* fra autobiografia e tipologia." In *Dante e le forme dell'allegoresi,* edited by M. Picone, 59–69. Ravenna: Longo.

———. 1993. "L'Ovidio di Dante." In *Dante e la "bella scola" della poesia,* edited by Amilcare A. Iannucci, 107–44. Ravenna: Longo.

———. 1995. "All'ombra della fanciulla in fiore: Lettura semantica della sestina dantesca." *Letture Classensi* 24:91–108.

———. 1998. "Dante e il mito degli Argonauti." *Rassegna europea di letteratura italiana* 11:9–28.

———. 1999. "Dante, Ovidio e la poesia dell'esilio." *Rassegna europea di letteratura italiana* 14:7–23.

———. 2000. "Il corpo della/nella luna: Sul canto II del *Paradiso*." *L'Alighieri* 15 (n.s.):7–25.

Pietrobono, Luigi. 1936. *Saggi danteschi.* Rome: Signorelli.

Pounds, N. J. G. 1974. *An Economic History of Medieval Europe.* London: Longman.

Psaki, F. Regina. 2000. "The Sexual Body in Dante's Celestial Paradise." In *Imagining Heaven in the Middle Ages,* edited by Jan S. Emerson and Hugh Feiss, O.S.B., 47–61. New York: Garland.

Raffa, Guy P. 2000. *Divine Dialectic: Dante's Incarnational Poetry.* Toronto: University of Toronto Press.

Reade, W. H. V. 1909. *The Moral System of Dante's "Inferno."* Oxford: Clarendon Press.

Reeves, Marjorie. 1965. "Marsiglio of Padua and Dante Alighieri." In *Trends in Medieval Political Thought,* edited by Beryl Smalley, 86–104. Oxford: Blackwell.

———. 1980. "Dante and the Prophetic Vision of History." In *The World of Dante: Essays on Dante and His Times,* edited by Cecil Grayson, 44–60. Oxford: Clarendon Press.

Remigio. 1981. Fra Remigio dei Girolami, O.P. *Contra falsos Ecclesie professores.* Edited by F. Tamburini, with a preface by Charles T. Davis. Rome: Libreria Editrice della Pontificia Università Lateranense.

Renucci, Paul. 1954. *Dante disciple et juge du monde gréco-latin.* Paris: Les Belles Lettres.

———. 1958. *Dante.* Paris: Hatier.

Reynolds, Barbara, ed. and trans. 1969. Dante Alighieri, *La Vita Nuova (Poems of Youth).* Harmondsworth: Penguin Books.

Ricci, D., ed. 1967. *Il processo di Dante.* Florence: Arnaud.

Ricci, Pier Giorgio, ed. 1965. Dante Alighieri, *Monarchia.* Milan: Mondadori.

Robey, David. 1997. "The *Fiore* and the *Comedy:* Some Computerized Comparisons." In *The "Fiore" in Context: Dante, France, Tuscany,* edited by Zygmunt G. Barański and Patrick Boyde, 109–34. The William and Katherine Devers Series in Dante Studies, vol. 2. Notre Dame, Ind.: University of Notre Dame Press.

———. 2000a. "Hendecasyllable." In *The Dante Encyclopedia,* edited by Richard Lansing, 477–78. New York: Garland.

———. 2000b. *Sound and Structure in the "Divine Comedy."* Oxford: Oxford University Press.

———. 2000c. "Terza rima." In *The Dante Encyclopedia,* edited by Richard Lansing, 808–10. New York: Garland.

Rohlfs, Gerhard. 1990. *Studi e ricerche su lingua e dialetti d'Italia.* Florence: Sansoni.

Ronconi, Alessandro. 1976. "Virgilio Marone, Publio: La tradizione medievale e il problema della 'magia' virgiliana." In *Enciclopedia dantesca* 5:1030–32. Rome: Istituto della Enciclopedia Italiana.

Rose, Claire. 1991. "Dante's Hell and the Medieval Idea of Jerusalem." *The Italianist* 11:7–28.

Rossetto, Laura. 1993. "L'uso del *cursus* nelle epistole dantesche." In M. Bordin, P. Fusco, and L. Rossetto, *Tre studi danteschi,* 61–131. Rome: Jouvence.

Rossi, Luciano. 1983. "Il cuore, mistico pasto d'amore: Dal *Lai Guirun* al *Decameron.*" In *Studi provenzali e francesi* 82:28–128 [*Romanica vulgaria: Quaderni* 6]. L'Aquila: Japadre.

———. 1995. "*Così nel mio parlar voglio esser aspro* (CIII)." *Letture Classensi* 24:69–89.

Rossiaud, Jacques. 1990. "The City-Dweller and Life in Cities and Towns." In *The Medieval World,* edited by Jacques Le Goff, 139–79. Translated by Lydia G. Cochrane. London: Collins and Brown.

Rostovtzeff, M. 1960 [1927]. *Rome*. Translated by J. D. Duff. Oxford: Oxford University Press.

Rubinstein, Nicolai. 1942. "The Beginnings of Political Thought in Florence." *Journal of the Warburg and Courtauld Institutes* 5:198–227.

Russo, Vittorio. 1970. "Appello al lettore." In *Enciclopedia Dantesca* 1:324–26. Rome: Istituto della Enciclopedia Italiana.

———. 1971. *Esperienze e/di letture dantesche*. Naples: Liguori.

———. 1984. *Il romanzo teologico: Sondaggi sulla "Commedia" di Dante*. Naples: Liguori.

———. 1994. "Beatrice *beatitudinis non artifex* nella *Princeps* (1576) della *Vita Nuova*." In *Beatrice nell'opera di Dante e nella memoria europea 1290–1990,* edited by M. Picchio Simonelli, 77–86. Fiesole: Cadmo.

———. 1995. "Tecniche e forme della poesia dottrinale di Dante." In *Dante e la scienza,* edited by Patrick Boyde and Vittorio Russo, 173–89. Ravenna: Longo.

———. 2002. *Il romanzo teologico*. 2d ed. Naples: Liguori.

Ryan, Christopher J. 1982. "Virgil's Wisdom in the *Divine Comedy*." *Classica et Medievalia* 11:1–38.

———. 1994. "'Su la fiumana onde 'l mar non ha vanto' (*Inf.* II.108): A Continuing Crux." *Italian Studies* 49:1–20.

Sandkühler, Bruno. 1967. *Die frühen Dantekommentare und ihr Verhältnis zur mittelalterlichen Kommentartradition*. Munich: Max Hueber.

Sanguineti, Federico. 1998. "Prolegomeni all'edizione critica della *Comedía*." In *Sotto il segno di Dante: Scritti in onore di Francesco Mazzoni,* edited by L. Coglievina and D. De Robertis, 261–82. Florence: Le Lettere.

———, ed. 2001. Dante Alighieri, *Comedia*. Florence: Edizioni del Galluzzo.

Sapegno, Natalino, ed. 1957. Dante Alighieri, *La Divina Commedia*. Milan and Naples: Ricciardi.

Sarolli, Gian Roberto. 1971. *Prolegomena alla "Divina Commedia."* Florence: Leo S. Olschki.

———. 1976. "Numero." In *Enciclopedia Dantesca* 4:88–96. Rome: Istituto della Enciclopedia Italiana.

Sarteschi, Selene. 1996 [1990]. "Ancora a proposito della presunta doppia redazione della *Vita Nuova*." *Studi Danteschi* 62:249–88.

Scaglione, Aldo. 1967. "Periodic Syntax and Flexible Meter in the *Divina Commedia*." *Romance Philology* 21:1–22.

Schiaffini, Alfredo. 1965. *Momenti di storia della lingua italiana*. Rome: Studium.

Schimmel, Annemarie. 1994. *The Mystery of Numbers*. New York: Oxford University Press.

Schnapp, Jeffrey T. 1986. *The Transfiguration of History at the Center of Dante's "Paradise."* Princeton: Princeton University Press.

———. 1991a. "Dante's Ovidian Self-Correction in *Paradiso* 17." In *The Poetry of Allusion: Virgil and Ovid in Dante's "Commedia,"* edited by Rachel Jacoff and Jeffrey T. Schnapp, 214–23. Stanford: Stanford University Press.

———. 1991b. "Dante's Sexual Solecisms: Gender and Genre in the *Commedia*." In *The New Medievalism,* edited by Marina S. Brownlee, Kevin Brownlee, and Stephen G. Nichols, 201–25. Baltimore: Johns Hopkins University Press.

————. 1991c. "'Sí pïa l'ombra d'Anchise si porse': *Paradiso* 15.25." In *The Poetry of Allusion: Virgil and Ovid in Dante's "Commedia,"* edited by Rachel Jacoff and Jeffrey T. Schnapp, 145–56. Stanford: Stanford University Press.

————. 1997. "Lucanian Estimations." In *Seminario dantesco internazionale / International Dante Seminar 1: Atti del primo convegno tenutosi al Chauncey Conference Center, Princeton, 21–23 ottobre 1994,* edited by Zygmunt G. Barański, 111–34. Florence: Le Lettere.

Scott, John A. 1970. "The Rock of Peter and *Inferno,* XIX." *Romance Philology* 23(4): 462–79.

————. 1971. "*Inferno* XXVI: Dante's Ulysses." *Lettere Italiane* 23(2):145–86.

————. 1972. "Dante's Admiral." *Italian Studies* 27:28–40.

————. 1975. "An Uncharted Phase in Dante's Political Thought." In *Essays in Honour of John Humphreys Whitfield,* edited by H. C. Davis et al. London: St. George's Press.

————. 1977. *Dante magnanimo: Studi sulla "Commedia."* Florence: Leo S. Olschki.

————. 1989 [1995]. "Dante, Boezio e l'enigma di Rifeo." *Studi Danteschi* 61:187–92.

————. 1990. "Dante and Philosophy." *Annali d'Italianistica* 8:258–77.

————. 1995a. "The Unfinished *Convivio* as a Pathway to the *Comedy.*" *Dante Studies* 113:31–56.

————. 1995b. "Una contraddizione scientifica nell'opera dantesca: I *due soli* di *Purg.* XVI 107." In *Dante e la scienza,* edited by Patrick Boyde and Vittorio Russo, 149–55. Ravenna: Longo.

————. 1996a. "Dante's Miraculous Mountainquake (*Purgatorio* 20.128)." In *Electronic Bulletin of the Dante Society of America,* October 23, 1996.

————. 1996b. *Dante's Political Purgatory.* Philadelphia: University of Pennsylvania Press.

————. 1999. "Il mito dell'imperatore negli scritti danteschi." In *Dante: Mito e Poesia,* edited by M. Picone and T. Crivelli, 89–114. Florence: Cesati.

————. 2000a. "*Purgatorio* XII." In *Lectura Dantis Turicensis,* edited by G. Güntert and M. Picone, 2:173–97. Florence: Cesati.

————. 2000b. "'Veramente li teologi questo senso prendono altrimenti che li poeti' (*Conv.* II i 5)." In *Sotto il segno di Dante: Scritti in onore di Francesco Mazzoni,* edited by L. Coglievina and D. De Robertis, 299–309. Florence: Le Lettere.

Segre, Cesare. 1963. *Lingua, stile e società.* Milan: Feltrinelli.

————. 1984. "*L'itinerarium animae* nel Duecento e Dante." *Letture Classensi* 13:9–32.

————. 2002. "Postilla sull'edizione Sanguineti della *Commedia* di Dante." *Strumenti critici* 17:2(n.s.):312–14.

Seriani, Luca. 2001. *Introduzione alla lingua poetica italiana.* Rome: Carocci.

Shankland, Hugh. 1975. "Dante 'Aliger.'" *Modern Language Review* 70:764–85.

————. 1977. "Dante's 'Aliger' and Ulysses." *Italian Studies* 32:21–40.

Shapiro, Marianne, trans. 1990. Dante Alighieri, *"De Vulgari Eloquentia": Dante's Book of Exile.* Lincoln: University of Nebraska Press.

Shaw, Prue, ed. and trans. 1995. Dante Alighieri, *Monarchia.* Cambridge: Cambridge University Press.

Shoaf, R. A. 1978. "*Auri sacra fames* and the Age of Gold (*Purg.* XXII, 40–41 and 148–50)." *Dante Studies* 96:195–99.

Simonelli, Maria Picchio. 1970. "*Convivio.*" In *Enciclopedia Dantesca* 2:193–204. Rome: Istituto della Enciclopedia Italiana.

———. 1993. *Lectura Dantis Americana: Inferno III.* With a new translation of the canto by Patrick Creagh and Robert Hollander. Philadelphia: University of Pennsylvania Press.

———. 2000 [1979]. "L'Inquisizione e Dante: Alcune osservazioni." *Dante Studies* 118:303–21.

Singleton, Charles S. 1958 [1949]. *An Essay on the "Vita Nuova."* Cambridge: Harvard University Press.

———. 1965a [1960]. "In Exitu Israel de Aegypto." In *Dante: A Collection of Critical Essays,* edited by J. Freccero, 102–21. Englewood Cliffs, N.J.: Prentice-Hall.

———. 1965b. "*Inferno* XIX: O Simon mago!" *Modern Language Notes* 80:92–99.

———. 1965c. "The Poet's Number at the Center." *Modern Language Notes* 80:1–10.

———. 1965d. "The Vistas in Retrospect." In *Atti del congresso internazionale di studi danteschi* 1:279–303. Florence: Sansoni.

———. 1967. *Journey to Beatrice.* Cambridge: Harvard University Press.

———. 1977. *Dante's "Commedia": Elements of Structure.* Baltimore: Johns Hopkins University Press.

Southern, Richard. 1990. *Western Society and the Church in the Middle Ages.* Harmondsworth: Penguin.

Spargo, John Webster. 1934. *Virgil the Necromancer.* Cambridge: Harvard University Press.

Steele, Timothy. 1999. *All the Fun's in How You Say a Thing.* Athens, Ohio: University of Ohio Press.

Stefanini, Ruggero. 1997. "Fra *Commèdia* e *Com(m)edìa*: Risalendo il testo del poema." *Lectura Dantis* 20–21:3–32.

Stone, Gregory B. 1994. "Dante's Averroistic Hermeneutics (On 'Meaning' in the *Vita Nuova*)." *Dante Studies* 112:133–59.

Stull, William, and Robert Hollander. 1997 [1991]. "The Lucanian Source of Dante's Ulysses." *Studi Danteschi* 63:1–52.

Tardiola, Giuseppe. 2000. "'Ancor nel libro suo che *Scala* ha nome . . .': Fazio degli Uberti, *Dittamondo* V xii 94." *Letteratura italiana antica* 1:59–67.

Tarrant, Richard J. 1997. "Poetry and Power: Virgil's Poetry in Contemporary Context." In *The Cambridge Companion to Virgil,* edited by Charles Martindale, 169–87. Cambridge: Cambridge University Press.

Tierney, Brian. 1980. *The Crisis of Church and State, 1050–1300.* Englewood Cliffs, N.J.: Prentice-Hall.

Took, John F. 1984. *"L'etterno piacer": Aesthetic Ideas in Dante.* Oxford: Clarendon Press.

———. 1990. *Dante, Lyric Poet and Philosopher: An Introduction to the Minor Works.* Oxford: Clarendon Press.

———. 2000. "Eclogues." In *The Dante Encyclopedia,* edited by Richard Lansing, 334–35. New York: Garland.

Toynbee, Paget. 1968. *A Dictionary of Proper Names and Notable Matters in the Works of Dante.* Revised by Charles S. Singleton. Oxford: Clarendon Press.

Trovato, Mario. 1988. "Dante and the Tradition of the 'Two Beatitudes.'" In *Lectura Dantis Newberryana,* edited by P. Cherchi and A. Mastrobuono, 1:19–36. Evanston, Ill.: Northwestern University Press.

Ullmann, Walter. 1975. *Medieval Political Thought.* Harmondsworth: Penguin Books.

Valency, Maurice. 1961. *In Praise of Love*. New York: Macmillan.

Vasoli, Cesare. 1982. "Filosofia e politica in Dante fra *Convivio* e *Monarchia*." *Letture Classensi* 9–10:11–37.

———, ed. 1988. *Convivio*. In Dante Alighieri, *Opere minori*, vol. 1, part 2. Milan and Naples: Ricciardi.

———. 1995. *Otto saggi per Dante*. Florence: Le Lettere.

———. 2001. "Dante scienziato e filosofo." In *"Per correr miglior acque . . ." Bilanci e prospettive degli studi danteschi alle soglie del nuovo millennio. Atti del Convegno di Verona-Ravenna, 25–29 ottobre 1999,* vol. 1, 71–91. Rome: Salerno Editrice.

Vecce, Carlo. 1994. "*Ella era uno nove, cioè uno miracolo (V.N. XXIX, 3)*: Il numero di Beatrice." In *La gloriosa donna de la mente: A Commentary on the "Vita Nuova,"* edited by V. Moleta, 161–79. Florence: Leo S. Olschki.

Villa, Claudia. 2001. "Discussione: Prospettive filologiche." In *Dante: Da Firenze all'aldilà. Atti del terzo Seminario Dantesco Internazionale, Firenze, 9–11 giugno 2000,* edited by Michelangelo Picone, 203–4 and 209. Florence: Cesati.

Vinay, Gustavo. 1962. *Interpretazione della "Monarchia" di Dante*. Florence: Le Monnier.

Waley, Daniel. 1975. *Later Medieval Europe: From St. Louis to Luther*. London: Longman.

———. 1998. *The Italian City-Republics*. London: Longman.

Wetherbee, Winthrop. 1988. "Dante and the *Thebaid* of Statius." In *Lectura Dantis Newberryana,* edited by P. Cherchi and A. Mastrobuono, 1:71–92. Evanston, Ill.: Northwestern University Press.

Whitfield, J. H. 1989. *Dante and Ovid*. Donald Dudley Memorial Lecture. Birmingham: University of Birmingham.

Wicksteed, Philip H., and Edmund G. Gardner. 1902. *Dante and Giovanni del Virgilio*. Westminster: Archibald Constable.

Wilkins, Ernest Hatch. 1983 [1927]. "Dante and the Mosaics of His *Bel San Giovanni*." In *Dante in America: The First Two Centuries,* edited by A. Bartlett Giamatti, 144–59. Medieval & Renaissance Texts & Studies, vol. 23. Binghamton, N.Y.: Medieval & Renaissance Texts & Studies.

Wilson, Robert. 1997. "Prophecy by the Dead in Dante and Lucan." *Italian Studies* 52:16–37.

Wlassics, Tibor. 1975. *Dante narratore: Saggi sullo stile della "Commedia."* Florence: Leo S. Olschki.

Index of Names and Notable Matters

Index of Passages from Dante's Works

Comedy

Paradiso

Convivio

Book 1

Book 2

Book 3

Book 4

De vulgari eloquentia

Eclogues, xxix, 350–52

Epistole

Monarchia

Questio de aqua et terra

Rime

Vita Nova

JOHN A. SCOTT

is a senior research fellow in the department of European Languages

and Studies at the University of Western Australia.